CW00953385

British Tax Guide:
Value Added Tax 2012–13

British Tax Guide:
Value Added Tax 2012–13

CCH
a Wolters Kluwer business

© 2012 Wolters Kluwer (UK) Limited

Wolters Kluwer
145 London Road
Kingston upon Thames
KT2 6SR
Telephone: (0) 844 561 8166
Facsimile: (0) 208 247 2638
E-mail: cch@wolterskluwer.co.uk
Website: www.cch.co.uk

ISBN 978-1-84798-510-1

British Library Cataloguing-in-Publication Data

A catalogue record for this book is available from the British Library.

Typeset by Innodata
Printed by Gutenberg Press Ltd, Malta

About the authors

About the general editor

Roger Barnard LLB LLM FCA CTA (Fellow)

Roger Barnard has worked for over 30 years as a tax practitioner, and is a tax director at RSM Tenon. He is on the council of the Chartered Institute of Taxation and was, for many years, involved in the setting of the institute's examination papers.

About the authors

Shelagh Pearce LLB (Hons) and **Stephen Taylor CTA (Fellow) ATT** are partners in Pearce Taylor Taxation, an independent firm based in Devon providing VAT consultancy services to accountants, lawyers and other businesses. Stephen and Shelagh are also contributors to CCH's Tax Workflow and VAT Reporter. Previous CCH publications which they wholly or partly wrote include VAT in Practice, VAT Planning and Tax on Property.

Stephen is currently a member of the technical committee of the Association of Taxation Technicians and a representative on the joint VAT Consultative Committee. He is a former chairman of the South West of England branch of the Chartered Institute of Taxation and was awarded a Certificate of Merit by the Chartered Institute of Taxation in 2012.

Pearce Taylor Taxation may be contacted at:

2 Primley House
Sidford Road
Sidmouth
Devon
EX10 9LN
Tel: 01395 577202
Fax: 01395 515620
email: pearcetaylortaxation@btinternet.com

Preface

This edition of *British Tax Guide: Value Added Tax* provides clear, practical and accessible commentary on the tax issues likely to be of widespread interest to tax advisers dealing with their clients' 2012–13 Value Added Tax affairs. To achieve this aim, it has been necessary either to omit, or to cover in summary form, some less mainstream topics. The authors welcome comments from readers about the scope and depth of the coverage.

This new VAT Guide provides a compact overview of Value Added Tax and includes the main rules and procedures that will help with most VAT problems. This help and guidance is supported by cross-references to:

- Current legislation.

- HMRC source materials.

- The British Value Added Tax Reporter.

- Key Court and Tribunal cases.

The special feature of this Guide is the informative, easy-to-use flowcharts that aid the user in putting the legislation into practice.

The *British Tax Guide: Value Added Tax* will be of use and benefit to both those who only occasionally deal with VAT issues as well as those who encounter VAT matters daily. It provides straightforward guidance to resolving practical issues. This Guide is fully up to date in accordance with the *Finance Act* 2012 and case law to August 2012. For more information, see the 'What's New' section.

The other books in the British Tax Guide series provide straightforward but authoritative commentary on the UK's other main taxes. In each book, extensive cross-referencing is provided to relevant legislation, cases and HMRC guidance as well as to CCH's in-depth commentary in the British Tax Reporter and VAT Reporter, making them an ideal desktop companion to CCH's comprehensive online services.

What's new?

- The book has been updated to cover *Finance Act* 2012 including the relevant changes in thresholds and also includes cases decided until August 2012. HMRC policy changes to the end of July 2012 are also covered.

- Changes coming into effect on 1 October 2012 include measures affecting the liabilty of the following:

- Alterations to listed buildings: information is also given about the transitional arrangements that allow ongoing zero-rated relief for certain projects.

- Self-storage – including information about the relief for certain capital expenditure prior to 2012.

- Clarity about the treatment of hairdressing chair rental agreements.

- The definition of sports drinks.

- Hot take-away food – the final version of the 'pasty tax'.

- The changes affecting certain caravans that come into effect in April 2013 (postponed fron October 2012) are discussed.

- There is information available about the cost-sharing exemption.

- Cases include the decisions released in July 2012 affecting interest payable on repayments and the liability of charges for portfolio management by financial advisers and similar.

- The material in the book has been reviewed and amended to enable the user to access information easily and it continues to be improved to provide practical relevant help.

Contents

Key Data

KEY DATA

BUDGET 2012

1-000 Budget 2012 amendments and proposals

The following is an outline of the Budget changes announced on 1 March 2012.

Borderline anomalies

The following 'borderline anomalies' are to be addressed and a consultation on the relevant legislation announced.

Supplies of catering and hot food

The proposals will standard rate all food sold 'above the ambient temperature' other than hot bread. The draft legislation proposes that the measure will be implemented on 1 October 2012.

In addition the sale of all food for consumption in areas adjacent to a retailer or areas shared with other retailers will become standard rated from 1 October 2012 (see 12-800).

Supplies of sports drinks

From 1 October 2012 the sale of all 'sports nutrition drinks' will be standard rated. Currently certain drinks are not regarded as beverages and hence benefit from zero-rating.

This measure will include all sports drinks that are sold to enhance physical performance, accelerate recovery after exercise, or build bulk. It will include syrups, concentrates, powders, crystals, etc.

Self-storage

Self-storage facilities will be excluded from exemption and standard rated from 1 October 2012. Anti-forestalling legislation comes into effect from 21 March 2012 (see 11-640).

Hairdressers' chair rentals

From 1 October 2012 the rental of a chair by self-employed hairdressers in hairdressing salons is to be standard rated (see 15-060).

Holiday caravans

From 1 October 2012 caravans not designed for year-round occupation will be standard rated. This will mean that all holiday caravans – not merely mobile caravans – will be standard rated (see 13-450).

Alterations to listed buildings

From 1 October 2012 all alterations to listed buildings will cease to be zero-rated (see 15-380).

Anti-forestalling arrangements will be put in place for contracts signed after 21 March 2012 although there will be some benefit remaining to those with contracts in place prior to Budget Day and where 10 per cent of the work is completed prior to that date (see 11-640).

Registration and de-registration thresholds

With effect from 1 April 2012 these will be raised to £77,000 and £75,000 respectively (see 1-140 and 1-280).

Removal of threshold for non-UK businesses

From 1 December 2012 all non-UK established businesses making any taxable supplies will be required to register for UK VAT without the benefit of a VAT registration threshold (see 8-550).

Fuel scale charges

The values to be used are amended for VAT accounting periods beginning on or after 1 May 2012 (see 1-700).

In addition there is to be consultation on changes to be introduced by Finance Bill 2013 which will give the force of law to an annual public notice, rather than the announcement of these values via statutory instrument and will also give the force of law to certain extra statutory concessions.

Relief for European Research Infrastructure Consortia (ERICs)

Secondary legislation is to be introduced in the autumn to give VAT relief to ERICs.

Low value consignment relief

From 1 April 2012 the low value consignment relief for mail order goods imported into the UK from the Channel Islands is to be removed (see 5-260(1)).

Cost sharing exemption

The cost sharing exemption is intended to benefit charities and also businesses making exempt supplies. It will facilitate a supply chain through which these persons may gain by joining together and buying services in bulk without incurring additional VAT liabilities. The facility is not available for buying goods in bulk.

Subject to quite stringent conditions, charities and/or relevant businesses may form a separate independent legal entity ('a cost sharing group') to buy services. The 'cost sharing group' buys in the relevant services and in turn supplies them to its members.

The supply of the relevant services by the cost sharing group to its members will not be liable to VAT. It will be an exempt supply.

By forming a cost sharing group participating members will be able to benefit from economies of scale when buying relevant services. They will not incur more VAT on the supply of the services by the cost sharing group to its members.

Tackling VAT fraud on imported vehicles

From 15 April 2013, persons bringing a road vehicle into the UK for permanent use on UK roads will have to inform HMRC within 14 days. These vehicles will not be able to be taxed or licensed until VAT due has been paid or secured.

Online registration

From October 2012 businesses will be able to register and deregister for VAT and to amend their VAT registration details electronically (8-220).

Grouping – extra statutory concession

Legislation is to be introduced with effect from Royal Assent to replace the current ESC allowing a reverse charge to be based on the cost of services purchased by group members established overseas rather than the actual charge made to UK members.

Supplies of goods or services by public bodies

From Royal Assent 2012 the definition of 'public body' will be clarified. Supplies by such bodies are treated as not being in the course or furtherance of business except where this treatment would lead to distortion of competition or in specific designated cases (see 17-730).

Reduced rate for energy saving material in charity buildings

Legislation is to be brought in by Finance Bill 2013 to prevent non-residential relevant charitable buildings benefiting from the reduced rate on the supply and installation of energy saving materials.

Zero-rate for adapted vehicles and boats for wheelchair users

A voluntary disclosure scheme is to be introduced in an effort to gather information about a scheme said to be open to abuse.

Refunds for NHS bodies

Legislation will be included in Finance Bill 2013 to enable certain NHS bodies to claim refunds of VAT under VATA 1994, s. 41.

Invoicing rules

Certain invoicing rules are to be simplified from 1 January 2013 following the EU Invoicing Directive (see 9-280).

Universal credit

The introduction of the new universal credit necessitates amendments to VAT legislation. The amendments will ensure that VAT reliefs linked to a person receiving a welfare benefit will be available to persons claiming the new universal credit.

Education providers

A consultation on the VAT treatment of education is to be carried out especially for university level provision, to ensure that commercial universities are treated fairly.

Freight transport services

By concession the place of supply of freight transport supplied to charities is varied when the freight transport takes place wholly outside the EU. This relief will be made statutory later this year.

Small cable-based transport

The rate of VAT applied to the carriage of passengers on small cable-based transport will be reduced from 20 per cent to 5 per cent from 2013. This will apply when vehicles carry less than 10 passengers – transport in larger vehicles is zero-rated. The situation will be evaluated after three years.

Gaming machines

Changes to the definition of gaming machine takings for VAT purposes will change somewhat with effect from 1 February 2013. The definition in VATA 1994, s. 23 of takings and how they are calculated is changing due to the introduction of a machine games duty. This replaces the amusement games duty (see 14-350).

RATES AND REGISTRATION

1-050   Rates

Period of application	Standard rate %	Higher rate %	Lower rate %	VAT fractions		
From 4/1/11	20	N/A	5	$\frac{1}{6}$	N/A	$\frac{1}{21}$
1/1/10–3/1/11	17½	N/A	5	$\frac{7}{47}$	N/A	$\frac{1}{21}$
1/12/08–31/12/09	15	N/A	5	$\frac{3}{23}$	N/A	$\frac{1}{21}$
1/9/97–30/11/08	17½	N/A	5	$\frac{7}{47}$	N/A	$\frac{1}{21}$
1/4/94–31/8/97	17½	N/A	8	$\frac{7}{47}$	N/A	$\frac{2}{27}$
1/4/91–31/3/94	17½	N/A	N/A	$\frac{7}{47}$	N/A	N/A
18/6/79–31/3/91	15	N/A	N/A	$\frac{3}{23}$	N/A	N/A
12/4/76–17/6/79	8	12½	N/A	$\frac{2}{27}$	$\frac{1}{9}$	N/A
1/5/75–11/4/76	8	25[1]	N/A	$\frac{2}{27}$	$\frac{1}{5}$	N/A
18/11/74–30/4/75	8	25[2]	N/A	$\frac{2}{27}$	$\frac{1}{5}$	N/A
29/7/74–17/11/74	8	N/A	N/A	$\frac{2}{27}$	N/A	N/A
1/4/73–28/7/74	10	N/A	N/A	$\frac{1}{11}$	N/A	N/A

Notes
[1] Re petrol, electrical appliances and luxury goods.
[2] Re petrol.

The lower rate originally applied to supplies of fuel and power for domestic, residential and charity non-business use, but has been extended to other supplies now specified in VATA 1994, Sch. 7A.

Imports of certain works of art, antiques and collectors' items are charged at an effective rate of five per cent from 27 July 1999.

The zero rate has been in force from 1 April 1973 to date.

1-100   Flat rate scheme

The following are the rates to be used after 3 January 2011:

Category of business	Appropriate percentage
Accountancy or book-keeping	14.5
Advertising	11
Agricultural services	11
Any other activity not listed elsewhere	12
Architect, civil and structural engineer or surveyor	14.5
Boarding or care of animals	12
Business services that are not listed elsewhere	12
Catering services including restaurants and takeaways	12.5
Computer and IT consultancy or data processing	14.5
Computer repair services	10.5
Dealing in waste or scrap	10.5
Entertainment or journalism	12.5
Estate agency or property management services	12
Farming or agriculture that is not listed elsewhere	6.5
Film, radio, television or video production	13
Financial services	13.5
Forestry or fishing	10.5
General building or construction services*	9.5
Hairdressing or other beauty treatment services	13
Hiring or renting goods	9.5
Hotel or accommodation	10.5
Investigation or security	12
Labour-only building or construction services*	14.5
Laundry or dry-cleaning services	12
Lawyer or legal services	14.5
Library, archive, museum or other cultural activity	9.5
Management consultancy	14
Manufacturing fabricated metal products	10.5
Manufacturing food	9
Manufacturing that is not listed elsewhere	9.5
Manufacturing yarn, textiles or clothing	9
Membership organisation	8
Mining or quarrying	10
Packaging	9
Photography	11

Category of business	Appropriate percentage
Post offices	5
Printing	8.5
Publishing	11
Pubs	6.5
Real estate activity not listed elsewhere	14
Repairing personal or household goods	10
Repairing vehicles	8.5
Retailing food, confectionery, tobacco, newspapers or children's clothing	4
Retailing pharmaceuticals, medical goods, cosmetics or toiletries	8
Retailing that is not listed elsewhere	7.5
Retailing vehicles or fuel	6.5
Secretarial services	13
Social work	11
Sport or recreation	8.5
Transport or storage, including couriers, freight, removals and taxis	10
Travel agency	10.5
Veterinary medicine	11
Wholesaling agricultural products	8
Wholesaling food	7.5
Wholesaling that is not listed elsewhere	8.5

* 'Labour-only building or construction services' means building or construction services where the value of materials supplied is less than 10 per cent of relevant turnover from such services; any other building or construction services are 'general building or construction services'.

The following were the rates in use from 1 January 2010 to 3 January 2011:

Category of business	Appropriate percentage
Accountancy or book-keeping	13
Advertising	10
Agricultural services	10
Any other activity not listed elsewhere	10.5
Architect, civil and structural engineer or surveyor	13
Boarding or care of animals	10.5
Business services that are not listed elsewhere	10.5
Catering services including restaurants and takeaways	11

Category of business	Appropriate percentage
Computer and IT consultancy or data processing	13
Computer repair services	9.5
Dealing in waste or scrap	9.5
Entertainment or journalism	11
Estate agency or property management services	10.5
Farming or agriculture that is not listed elsewhere	6
Film, radio, television or video production	11.5
Financial services	12
Forestry or fishing	9.5
General building or construction services*	8.5
Hairdressing or other beauty treatment services	11.5
Hiring or renting goods	8.5
Hotel or accommodation	9.5
Investigation or security	10.5
Labour-only building or construction services*	13
Laundry or dry-cleaning services	10.5
Lawyer or legal services	13
Library, archive, museum or other cultural activity	8.5
Management consultancy	12.5
Manufacturing fabricated metal products	9.5
Manufacturing food	8
Manufacturing that is not listed elsewhere	8.5
Manufacturing yarn, textiles or clothing	8
Membership organisation	7
Mining or quarrying	9
Packaging	8
Photography	10
Post offices	4.5
Printing	7.5
Publishing	10
Pubs	6
Real estate activity not listed elsewhere	12.5
Repairing personal or household goods	9
Repairing vehicles	7.5
Retailing food, confectionery, tobacco, newspapers or children's clothing	3.5
Retailing pharmaceuticals, medical goods, cosmetics or toiletries	7
Retailing that is not listed elsewhere	6.5
Retailing vehicles or fuel	6
Secretarial services	11.5

Category of business	Appropriate percentage
Social work	10
Sport or recreation	7.5
Transport or storage, including couriers, freight, removals and taxis	9
Travel agency	9.5
Veterinary medicine	10
Wholesaling agricultural products	7
Wholesaling food	6.5
Wholesaling that is not listed elsewhere	7.5

* 'Labour-only building or construction services' means building or construction services where the value of materials supplied is less than 10 per cent of relevant turnover from such services; any other building or construction services are 'general building or construction services'.

The following were the rates applicable to the flat rate scheme for small businesses from 1 December 2008 to 31 December 2009:

Category of business	Appropriate percentage
Accountancy or book-keeping	11.5
Advertising	8.5
Agricultural services	7
Any other activity not listed elsewhere	9
Architect, civil and structural engineer or surveyor	11
Boarding or care of animals	9.5
Business services that are not listed elsewhere	9.5
Catering services including restaurants and takeaways	10.5
Computer and IT consultancy or data processing	11.5
Computer repair services	10
Dealing in waste or scrap	8.5
Entertainment or journalism	9.5
Estate agency or property management services	9.5
Farming or agriculture that is not listed elsewhere	5.5
Film, radio, television or video production	9.5
Financial services	10.5
Forestry or fishing	8
General building or construction services*	7.5
Hairdressing or other beauty treatment services	10.5
Hiring or renting goods	7.5
Hotel or accommodation	8.5
Investigation or security	9

Category of business	Appropriate percentage
Labour-only building or construction services*	11.5
Laundry or dry-cleaning services	9.5
Lawyer or legal services	12
Library, archive, museum or other cultural activity	7.5
Management consultancy	11
Manufacturing that is not listed elsewhere	7.5
Manufacturing fabricated metal products	8.5
Manufacturing food	7
Manufacturing yarn, textiles or clothing	7.5
Membership organisation	5.5
Mining or quarrying	8
Packaging	7.5
Photography	8.5
Post offices	2
Printing	6.5
Publishing	8.5
Pubs	5.5
Real estate activity not listed elsewhere	11
Repairing personal or household goods	7.5
Repairing vehicles	6.5
Retailing food, confectionery, tobacco, newspapers or children's clothing	2
Retailing pharmaceuticals, medical goods, cosmetics or toiletries	6
Retailing that is not listed elsewhere	5.5
Retailing vehicles or fuel	5.5
Secretarial services	9.5
Social work	8
Sport or recreation	6
Transport or storage, including couriers, freight, removals and taxis	8
Travel agency	8
Veterinary medicine	8
Wholesaling agricultural products	5.5
Wholesaling food	5
Wholesaling that is not listed elsewhere	6

* 'Labour-only building or construction services' means building or construction services where the value of materials supplied is less than 10 per cent of relevant turnover from such services; any other building or construction services are 'general building or construction services'.

The following were the rates applicable to the flat rate scheme for small businesses from 1 January 2004 to 30 November 2008:

Trade Sector (from 1 January 2004)	Flat Rate Percentage
Retailing food, confectionery, tobacco, newspapers or children's clothing	2
Membership organisation	5.5
Postal and courier services	
Pubs	
Wholesaling food	
Farming or agriculture that is not listed elsewhere	6
Retailing that is not listed elsewhere	
Wholesaling agricultural products	
Retailing pharmaceuticals, medical goods, cosmetics or toiletries	7
Retailing vehicles or fuel	
Sport or recreation	
Wholesaling that is not listed elsewhere	
Agricultural services	7.5
Library, archive, museum or other cultural activity	
Manufacturing food	
Printing	
Repairing vehicles	
General building or construction services*	8.5
Hiring or renting goods	
Manufacturing that is not listed elsewhere	
Manufacturing yarn, textiles or clothing	
Packaging	
Repairing personal or household goods	
Social work	
Forestry or fishing	9
Mining or quarrying	
Transport or storage, including couriers, freight, removals and taxis	
Travel agency	

Trade Sector (from 1 January 2004)	Flat Rate Percentage
Advertising	9.5
Dealing in waste or scrap	
Hotel or accommodation	
Photography	
Publishing	
Veterinary medicine	
Any other activity not listed elsewhere	10
Investigation or security	
Manufacturing fabricated metal products	
Boarding or care of animals	10.5
Film, radio, television or video production	
Business services that are not listed elsewhere	11
Computer repair services	
Entertainment or journalism	
Estate agency or property management services	
Laundry or dry-cleaning services	
Secretarial services	
Financial services	11.5
Catering services, including restaurants and takeaways	12
Hairdressing or other beauty treatment services	
Real estate activity not listed elsewhere	
Architect, civil and structural engineer or surveyor	12.5
Management consultancy	
Accountancy or book-keeping	13
Computer and IT consultancy or data processing	
Lawyer or legal services	
Labour-only building or construction services*	13.5

*'Labour-only building or construction services' means services where the value of the materials supplied is under 10 per cent of turnover of such services. Other building or construction services are 'General building or construction services'.

1-140   Registration limits

(1) Taxable supplies

Introduction

Taxable supplies at *both* the zero rate and the positive rates (standard, higher or lower) are included in the limits. All of a *person's* taxable supplies are considered, because it is 'persons' not 'businesses' who can or must register.

These limits are *exclusive* of VAT as VAT is not chargeable unless a person is registered or liable to be registered. The limit which applies for a particular past period is that which is in force at the *end* of the period.

There are now two *alternative* tests of the liability to notify Customs of a person's liability to register as a result of making taxable supplies:

● past 12 months turnover limit; and
● future 30 days turnover limit.

The value of capital supplies (other than of land) is *excluded* from the supplies for the purpose of applying the registration limits.

Any supplies made at a previous time when the person was registered are *disregarded* if all necessary information was given to Customs when the earlier registration was cancelled.

If a person took over a business as a 'going concern' from a taxable person (i.e. someone who was, or should have been, registered for VAT), he is *deemed* to have made the vendor's supplies for the purposes of registration. This does not apply if a business is taken over as a going concern from a non-taxable person.

	Past turnover (£)		Future turnover (£)
Period of application	**1 year** £	**Unless turnover for next year will not exceed** £	**30 days** £
From 01/04/12	77,000	75,000	77,000
01/04/11–31/03/12	73,000	71,000	73,000
01/04/10–31/03/11	70,000	68,000	70,000
01/05/09–31/03/10	68,000	66,000	68,000
01/04/08–30/04/09	67,000	65,000	67,000
01/04/07–31/03/08	64,000	62,000	64,000
01/04/06–31/03/07	61,000	59,000	61,000
01/04/05–31/03/06	60,000	58,000	60,000

(2) Supplies from other Member States (Distance Selling)

Period of application	Cumulative relevant supplies from 1 January in year to any day in same year £
From 1/1/93	70,000

(VATA 1994, Sch. 2; Notice 700/1.)

If goods subject to excise duty are removed to the UK from another Member State and the person acquiring the goods is not a taxable person then registration is mandatory and the turnover limit does not apply.

(3) Acquisitions from other Member States

Period of application	Cumulative relevant supplies from 1 January in year to any day in same year £
From 01/04/12	77,000
01/04/11–31/03/12	73,000
01/04/10–31/03/11	70,000
01/05/09–31/03/10	68,000
01/04/08–30/04/09	67,000
01/04/07–31/03/08	64,000
01/04/06–31/03/07	61,000
01/04/05–31/03/06	60,000

Future prospects rule: a person is also liable to register at any time if there are reasonable grounds for believing that the value of his relevant acquisitions in the period of 30 days then beginning will exceed the given limit. This limit is the same as that for the period starting on 1 January above.

1-280 De-registration limits

(1) Taxable supplies

Introduction

For the purposes of de-registration taxable supplies at zero, reduced and standard rates must be aggregated when considering the limits below. The amounts concerned are VAT exclusive and the value of supplies of capital assets may be excluded when determining the turnover for de-registration purposes.

De-registration at any time

A registered person ceases to be liable to be registered if at *any* time the commissioners are satisfied that the value of his taxable supplies in the period of one year then beginning will not exceed a certain limit. If the person actually wishes to be de-registered, it is necessary to make an application to the commissioners and satisfy them that the conditions are met. The limits and periods of application are set out below:

Period of application	Future turnover £
From 01/04/12	75,000
01/04/11–31/03/12	71,000
01/04/10–31/03/11	68,000
01/05/09–31/03/10	66,000
01/04/08–30/04/09	65,000
01/04/07–31/03/08	62,000
01/04/06–31/03/07	59,000
01/04/05–31/03/06	58,000
01/04/04–31/03/05	56,000
10/04/03–31/03/04	54,000

(2) Supplies from other Member States

A person who registered because their sales to the UK exceeded the distance selling threshold (see earlier) may de-register when both the following apply:

- the turnover in the year ending on previous 31 December was below the threshold; and
- the turnover in the year beginning 1 January will not exceed the relevant registration threshold.

Traders who opted to register in order to have their sales taxed in the UK must remain registered for two years unless it so happens that they made no taxable supplies.

(3) Acquisitions from other Member States

Period of application	Past relevant acquisitions in last year to 31 December £	Future relevant acquisitions in immediately following year £
From 01/04/11	73,000	73,000
01/04/10–31/03/11	70,000	70,000
01/05/09–31/03/10	68,000	68,000
01/04/08–30/04/09	67,000	67,000
01/04/07–31/03/08	64,000	64,000
01/04/06–31/03/07	61,000	61,000
01/04/05–31/03/06	60,000	60,000

1-320 Special Accounting Limits

Cash Accounting Scheme – admission to the scheme

Period of application	Annual turnover limit (includes zero-rated supplies, but excludes any capital assets previously used in the business. Exempt supplies are also excluded) £
From 1/4/07	1,350,000
1/4/04–31/3/07	660,000
1/4/01–31/3/04	600,000
1/4/93–31/3/01	350,000
1/10/90–31/3/93	300,000

A person must stop using the cash accounting scheme at the end of the prescribed accounting period if the value of his taxable supplies in the one year ending at the end of the prescribed accounting period has exceeded (from 1 April 2007) £1,600,000 (*Value Added Tax Regulations* 1995 (SI 1995/2518), Pt. VIII; Notice 731).

Annual accounting – admission to the scheme

Period of application	Annual turnover limit (positive and zero-rated supplies excluding any supplies of capital assets and any exempt supplies) £
From 1/4/06	1,350,000
1/4/04–31/3/06	600,000
1/4/01–31/3/04	600,000
9/4/91–31/3/01	300,000

A person must stop using the annual accounting scheme at the end of a prescribed accounting period if the value of his taxable supplies in the one year ending at the end of the prescribed accounting period has exceeded (from 1 April 2006) £1,600,000 (*Value Added Tax Regulations* 1995 (SI 1995/2518), Pt. VII; Notice 732).

INTEREST

1-420 Default interest

Interest on VAT, which was recovered or recoverable by assessment, applies to prescribed accounting periods which began after 31 March 1990 (VATA 1994, s. 74).

Period of application	Days in period	Interest rate %
From 29/09/09	–	3.0
24/3/09–29/09/09	189	2.5
27/1/09–23/3/09	56	3.5
6/1/09–26/1/09	21	4.5

Period of application	Days in period	Interest rate %
6/12/08–5/1/09	31	5.5
6/11/08–5/12/08	30	6.5
6/1/08–5/11/08	305	7.5
6/8/07–5/1/08	153	8.5
6/9/06–5/8/07	365	7.5
6/9/05–5/9/06	365	6.5
6/09/04–5/09/05	365	7.5
6/12/03–5/9/04	274	6.5
6/09/03–5/12/03	91	5.5
6/11/01–5/09/03	669	6.5
6/5/01–5/11/01	184	7.5
6/2/00–5/5/01	455	8.5
6/3/99–5/2/00	337	7.5
6/1/99–5/3/99	59	8.5
6/7/98–5/1/99	184	9.5
6/2/96–5/7/98	881	6.25
6/3/95–5/2/96	337	7
6/10/94–5/3/95	151	6.25
6/1/94–5/10/94	273	5.5
6/3/93–5/1/94	306	6.25
6/12/92–5/3/93	90	7
6/11/92–5/12/92	30	7.75
6/10/91–5/11/92	397	9.25
6/7/91–5/10/91	92	10
6/5/91–5/7/91	61	10.75
6/3/91–5/5/91	61	11.5
6/11/90–5/3/91	120	12.25
1/4/90–5/11/90	219	13

From 7 January 2009, the rate of interest awarded will be amended 13 working days after the meeting of the Monetary Policy Committee of the Bank of England.

1-560   Interest on overpaid VAT

Interest on overpaid VAT arises under VATA 1994, s. 78 in certain cases of official error. Such interest is not free of income or corporation tax:

Period of application	Interest rate %
From 12/8/09	0.50
27/1/09–11/8/09	0
6/1/09–26/1/09	1
6/12/08–5/1/09	2
6/11/08–5/12/08	3
6/1/08–5/11/08	4
6/8/07–5/1/08	5
6/9/06–5/8/07	4
6/9/05–5/9/06	3

Period of application	Interest rate %
6/9/04–5/9/05	4
6/12/03–5/9/04	3
6/09/03–5/12/03	2
6/11/01–5/9/03	3
6/5/01–5/11/01	4
6/2/00–5/5/01	5
6/3/99–5/2/00	4
6/1/99–5/3/99	5
1/4/97–5/1/99	6
6/2/93–31/3/97	8
16/10/91–5/2/93	10.25
1/4/91–15/10/91	12
1/11/89–31/3/91	14.25
1/1/89–31/10/89	13
1/11/88–31/12/88	12.25
1/8/88–31/10/88	11
1/5/88–31/7/88	9.5
1/12/87–30/4/88	11
1/11/87–30/11/87	11.25
1/4/87–31/10/87	11.75
1/1/87–31/3/87	12.25
1/8/86–31/12/86	11.5
1/4/84–31/7/86	12
1/4/83–31/3/84	12.5
1/7/82–31/3/83	13
1/3/82–30/6/82	14
1/12/81–28/2/82	15
1/1/81–30/11/81	12.5
1/1/80–31/12/80	15
1/3/79–31/12/79	12.5
1/2/77–28/2/79	10
1/3/74–31/1/77	9
1/4/73–28/2/74	8

From 7 January 2009, the rate of interest awarded will be amended thirteen working days after the meeting of the Monetary Policy Committee of the Bank of England.

ROAD FUEL

1-700 VAT on private petrol

The fuel scale charges only apply to cars. However, if the business funds private motoring in a van or commercial vehicle, output tax is due on the private use.

From May 2012

Fuel scale charges for 12-month period

CO$_2$ band	VAT fuel scale charge, 12-month period, £	VAT on 12-month charge, £	VAT exclusive 12-month charge, £
120 or less	665	110.83	554.17
125	1,000	166.67	833.33
130	1,065	177.50	887.50
135	1,135	189.17	945.83
140	1,200	200.00	1,000.00
145	1,270	211.67	1,058.33
150	1,335	222.50	1,112.50
155	1,400	233.33	1,166.67
160	1,470	245.00	1,225.00
165	1,535	255.83	1,279.17
170	1,600	266.67	1,333.33
175	1,670	278.33	1,391.67
180	1,735	289.17	1,445.83
185	1,800	300.00	1,500.00
190	1,870	311.67	1,558.33
195	1,935	322.50	1,612.50
200	2,000	333.33	1,666.67
205	2,070	345.00	1,725.00
210	2,135	355.83	1,779.17
215	2,200	366.67	1,833.33
220	2,270	378.33	1,891.67
225 or more	2,335	389.17	1,945.83

Fuel scale charges for 3-month period

CO$_2$ band	VAT fuel scale charge, 3-month period, £	VAT on 3-month charge, £	VAT exclusive 3-month charge, £
120 or less	166	27.67	138.33
125	250	41.67	208.33
130	266	44.33	221.67
135	283	47.17	235.83
140	300	50.00	250.00
145	316	52.67	263.33
150	333	55.50	277.50
155	350	58.33	291.67
160	366	61.00	305.00
165	383	63.83	319.17
170	400	66.67	333.33
175	416	69.33	346.67
180	433	72.17	360.83
185	450	75.00	375.00

CO_2 band	VAT fuel scale charge, 3-month period, £	VAT on 3-month charge, £	VAT exclusive 3-month charge, £
190	467	77.83	389.17
195	483	80.50	402.50
200	500	83.33	416.67
205	517	86.17	430.83
210	533	88.83	444.17
215	550	91.67	458.33
220	567	94.50	472.50
225 or more	583	97.17	485.83

Fuel scale charges for 1-month period

CO_2 band	VAT fuel scale charge, 1-month period, £	VAT on 1-month charge, £	VAT exclusive 1-month charge, £
120 or less	55	9.17	45.83
125	83	13.83	69.17
130	88	14.67	73.33
135	94	15.67	78.33
140	100	16.67	83.33
145	105	17.50	87.50
150	111	18.50	92.50
155	116	19.33	96.67
160	122	20.33	101.67
165	127	21.17	105.83
170	133	22.17	110.83
175	138	23.00	115.00
180	144	24.00	120.00
185	150	25.00	125.00
190	155	25.83	129.17
195	161	26.83	134.17
200	166	27.67	138.33
205	172	28.67	143.33
210	177	29.50	147.50
215	183	30.50	152.50
220	189	31.50	157.50
225 or more	194	32.33	161.67

From 1 May 2011 to 30 April 2012

Fuel scale charges for 12-month period

CO_2 band	VAT fuel scale charge, 12-month period, £	VAT on 12-month charge, £	VAT exclusive 12-month charge, £
120 or less	630	105.00	525.00
125	945	157.50	787.50

CO$_2$ band	VAT fuel scale charge, 12-month period, £	VAT on 12-month charge, £	VAT exclusive 12-month charge, £
130	1,010	168.33	841.67
135	1,070	178.33	891.67
140	1,135	189.17	945.83
145	1,200	200.00	1,000.00
150	1,260	210.00	1,050.00
155	1,325	220.83	1,104.17
160	1,385	230.83	1,154.17
165	1,450	241.67	1,208.33
170	1,515	252.50	1,262.50
175	1,575	262.50	1,312.50
180	1,640	273.33	1,366.67
185	1,705	284.17	1,420.83
190	1,765	294.17	1,470.83
195	1,830	305.00	1,525.00
200	1,890	315.00	1,575.00
205	1,955	325.83	1,629.17
210	2,020	336.67	1,683.33
215	2,080	346.67	1,733.33
220	2,145	357.50	1,787.50
225 or more	2,205	367.50	1,837.50

Fuel scale charges for 3-month period

CO$_2$ band	VAT fuel scale charge, 3-month period, £	VAT on 3-month charge, £	VAT exclusive 3-month charge, £
120 or less	157	26.17	130.83
125	236	39.33	196.67
130	252	42.00	210.00
135	268	44.67	223.33
140	283	47.17	235.83
145	299	49.83	249.17
150	315	52.50	262.50
155	331	55.17	275.83
160	346	57.67	288.33
165	362	60.33	301.67
170	378	63.00	315.00
175	394	65.67	328.33
180	409	68.17	340.83
185	425	70.83	354.17
190	441	73.50	367.50
195	457	76.17	380.83
200	472	78.67	393.33
205	488	81.33	406.67
210	504	84.00	420.00
215	520	86.67	433.33
220	536	89.33	446.67
225 or more	551	91.83	459.17

Fuel scale charges for 1-month period

CO$_2$ band	VAT fuel scale charge, 1-month period, £	VAT on 1-month charge, £	VAT exclusive 1-month charge, £
120 or less	52	8.67	43.33
125	78	13.00	65.00
130	84	14.00	70.00
135	89	14.83	74.17
140	94	15.67	78.33
145	99	16.50	82.50
150	105	17.50	87.50
155	110	18.33	91.67
160	115	19.17	95.83
165	120	20.00	100.00
170	126	21.00	105.00
175	131	21.83	109.17
180	136	22.67	113.33
185	141	23.50	117.50
190	147	24.50	122.50
195	152	25.33	126.67
200	157	26.17	130.83
205	162	27.00	135.00
210	168	28.00	140.00
215	173	28.83	144.17
220	178	29.67	148.33
225 or more	183	30.50	152.50

For journeys carried out between 4 January 2011 (20 per cent VAT rate) and 30 April 2011

Fuel scale charges for 12-month period

CO$_2$ band	VAT fuel scale charge, 12 month period, £	VAT on 12 month charge, £	VAT exclusive 12 month charge, £
120 or less	570.00	95.00	475.00
125	850.00	141.67	708.33
130	850.00	141.67	708.33
135	910.00	151.67	758.33
140	965.00	160.83	804.17
145	1,020.00	170.00	850.00
150	1,080.00	180.00	900.00
155	1,135.00	189.17	945.83
160	1,190.00	198.33	991.67
165	1,250.00	208.33	1,041.67
170	1,305.00	217.50	1,087.50
175	1,360.00	226.67	1,133.33
180	1,420.00	236.67	1,183.33
185	1,475.00	245.83	1,229.17
190	1,530.00	255.00	1,275.00

CO_2 band	VAT fuel scale charge, 12 month period, £	VAT on 12 month charge, £	VAT exclusive 12 month charge, £
195	1,590.00	265.00	1,325.00
200	1,645.00	274.17	1,370.83
205	1,705.00	284.17	1,420.83
210	1,760.00	293.33	1,466.67
215	1,815.00	302.50	1,512.50
220	1,875.00	312.50	1,562.50
225	1,930.00	321.67	1,608.33
230 or more	1,985.00	330.83	1,654.17

Fuel scale charges for 3-month period

CO_2 band	VAT fuel scale charge, 3 month period, £	VAT on 3 month charge, £	VAT exclusive 3 month charge, £
120 or less	141.00	23.50	117.50
125	212.00	35.33	176.67
130	212.00	35.33	176.67
135	227.00	37.83	189.17
140	241.00	40.17	200.83
145	255.00	42.50	212.50
150	269.00	44.83	224.17
155	283.00	47.17	235.83
160	297.00	49.50	247.50
165	312.00	52.00	260.00
170	326.00	54.33	271.67
175	340.00	56.67	283.33
180	354.00	59.00	295.00
185	368.00	61.33	306.67
190	383.00	63.83	319.17
195	397.00	66.17	330.83
200	411.00	68.50	342.50
205	425.00	70.83	354.17
210	439.00	73.17	365.83
215	454.00	75.67	378.33
220	468.00	78.00	390.00
225	482.00	80.33	401.67
230 or more	496.00	82.67	413.33

Fuel scale charges for 1-month period

CO_2 band	VAT fuel scale charge, 1 month period, £	VAT on 1 month charge, £	VAT exclusive 1 month charge, £
120 or less	47.00	7.83	39.17
125	70.00	11.67	58.33
130	70.00	11.67	58.33

CO$_2$ band	VAT fuel scale charge, 1 month period, £	VAT on 1 month charge, £	VAT exclusive 1 month charge, £
135	75.00	12.50	62.50
140	80.00	13.33	66.67
145	85.00	14.17	70.83
150	89.00	14.83	74.17
155	94.00	15.67	78.33
160	99.00	16.50	82.50
165	104.00	17.33	86.67
170	108.00	18.00	90.00
175	113.00	18.83	94.17
180	118.00	19.67	98.33
185	122.00	20.33	101.67
190	127.00	21.17	105.83
195	132.00	22.00	110.00
200	137.00	22.83	114.17
205	141.00	23.50	117.50
210	146.00	24.33	121.67
215	151.00	25.17	125.83
220	156.00	26.00	130.00
225	160.00	26.67	133.33
230 or more	165.00	27.50	137.50

From 1 May 2010 to 3 January 2011

Annual charges (figures are inclusive of VAT)

CO$_2$ band	VAT fuel scale charge, 12 month period, £
120 or less	570.00
125	850.00
130	850.00
135	910.00
140	965.00
145	1,020.00
150	1,080.00
155	1,135.00
160	1,190.00
165	1,250.00
170	1,305.00
175	1,360.00
180	1,420.00
185	1,475.00
190	1,530.00
195	1,590.00
200	1,645.00
205	1,705.00
210	1,760.00
215	1,815.00

CO$_2$ band	VAT fuel scale charge, 12 month period, £
220	1,875.00
225	1,930.00
230 or more	1,985.00

Quarterly charges (figures are inclusive of VAT)

CO$_2$ band	VAT fuel scale charge, 3 month period, £
120 or less	141.00
125	212.00
130	212.00
135	227.00
140	241.00
145	255.00
150	269.00
155	283.00
160	297.00
165	312.00
170	326.00
175	340.00
180	354.00
185	368.00
190	383.00
195	397.00
200	411.00
205	425.00
210	439.00
215	454.00
220	468.00
225	482.00
230 or more	496.00

Monthly charges (figures are inclusive of VAT)

CO$_2$ band	VAT fuel scale charge, 1 month period, £
120 or less	47.00
125	70.00
130	70.00
135	75.00
140	80.00
145	85.00
150	89.00
155	94.00
160	99.00
165	104.00
170	108.00
175	113.00

CO$_2$ band	VAT fuel scale charge, 1 month period, £
180	118.00
185	122.00
190	127.00
195	132.00
200	137.00
205	141.00
210	146.00
215	151.00
220	156.00
225	160.00
230 or more	165.00

From 1 May 2009 to 31 April 2010

CO$_2$ band	VAT fuel scale charge, 12 month period, £	VAT on 12 month charge, £	VAT exclusive 12 month charge, £
120 or below	505.00	75.21	429.79
125	755.00	112.45	642.55
130	755.00	112.45	642.55
135	755.00	112.45	642.55
140	805.00	119.89	685.11
145	855.00	127.34	727.66
150	905.00	134.79	770.21
155	960.00	142.98	817.02
160	1,010.00	150.43	859.57
165	1,060.00	157.87	902.13
170	1,110.00	165.32	944.68
175	1,160.00	172.77	987.23
180	1,210.00	180.21	1,029.79
185	1,260.00	187.66	1,072.34
190	1,310.00	195.11	1,114.89
195	1,360.00	202.55	1,157.45
200	1,410.00	210.00	1,200.00
205	1,465.00	218.19	1,246.81
210	1,515.00	225.64	1,289.36
215	1,565.00	233.09	1,331.91
220	1,615.00	240.53	1,374.47
225	1,665.00	247.98	1,417.02
230	1,715.00	255.73	1,459.57
235 or more	1,765.00	262.87	1,502.13

CO$_2$ band	VAT fuel scale charge, 3 month period, £	VAT on 3 month charge, £	VAT exclusive 3 month charge, £
120 or below	126.00	18.77	107.23
125	189.00	28.15	160.85
130	189.00	28.15	160.85

CO$_2$ band	VAT fuel scale charge, 3 month period, £	VAT on 3 month charge, £	VAT exclusive 3 month charge, £
135	189.00	28.15	160.85
140	201.00	29.94	171.06
145	214.00	31.87	182.13
150	226.00	33.66	192.34
155	239.00	35.60	203.40
160	251.00	37.38	213.62
165	264.00	39.32	224.68
170	276.00	41.11	234.89
175	289.00	43.04	245.96
180	302.00	44.98	257.02
185	314.00	46.77	267.23
190	327.00	48.70	278.30
195	339.00	50.49	288.51
200	352.00	52.43	299.57
205	365.00	54.36	310.64
210	378.00	56.30	321.70
215	390.00	58.09	331.91
220	403.00	60.02	342.98
225	416.00	61.96	354.04
230	428.00	63.74	364.26
235 or above	441.00	65.68	375.32

CO$_2$ band	VAT fuel scale charge, 1 month period, £	VAT on 1 month charge, £	VAT exclusive 1 month charge, £
120 or below	42.00	6.26	35.74
125	63.00	9.38	53.62
130	63.00	9.38	53.62
135	63.00	9.38	53.62
140	67.00	9.98	57.02
145	71.00	10.57	60.43
150	75.00	11.17	63.83
155	79.00	11.77	67.23
160	83.00	12.36	70.64
165	88.00	13.11	74.89
170	92.00	13.70	78.30
175	96.00	14.30	81.70
180	100.00	14.89	85.11
185	104.00	15.49	88.51
190	109.00	16.23	92.77
195	113.00	16.83	96.17
200	117.00	17.43	99.57
205	121.00	18.02	102.98
210	126.00	18.77	107.23
215	130.00	19.36	110.64
220	134.00	19.96	114.04
225	138.00	17.55	117.45
230	142.00	21.15	120.85
235 or above	147.00	21.89	125.11

From 1 May 2008 to 30 April 2009

CO$_2$ band	VAT fuel scale charge, 12 month period, £	VAT on 12 month charge, £	VAT exclusive 12 month charge, £
120 or below	555.00	82.66	472.34
125	830.00	123.62	706.38
130	830.00	123.62	706.38
135	830.00	123.62	706.38
140	885.00	131.81	753.19
145	940.00	140.00	800.00
150	995.00	148.19	846.81
155	1,050.00	156.38	893.62
160	1,105.00	164.57	940.43
165	1,160.00	172.77	987.23
170	1,215.00	180.96	1,034.04
175	1,270.00	189.15	1,080.85
180	1,325.00	197.34	1,127.66
185	1,380.00	205.53	1,174.47
190	1,435.00	213.72	1,221.28
195	1,490.00	221.91	1,268.09
200	1,545.00	230.11	1,314.89
205	1,605.00	239.04	1,365.96
210	1,660.00	247.23	1,412.77
215	1,715.00	255.43	1,459.57
220	1,770.00	263.62	1,506.38
225	1,825.00	271.81	1,553.19
230	1,880.00	280.00	1,600.00
235 or more	1,935.00	288.19	1,646.81

CO$_2$ band	VAT fuel scale charge, 3 month period, £	VAT on 3 month charge, £	VAT exclusive 3 month charge, £
120 or below	138.00	20.55	117.45
125	207.00	30.83	176.17
130	207.00	30.83	176.17
135	207.00	30.83	176.17
140	221.00	32.91	188.09
145	234.00	34.85	199.15
150	248.00	36.94	211.06
155	262.00	39.02	222.98
160	276.00	41.11	234.89
165	290.00	43.19	246.81
170	303.00	45.13	257.87
175	317.00	47.21	269.79
180	331.00	49.30	281.70
185	345.00	51.38	293.62
190	359.00	53.47	305.53
195	373.00	55.55	317.45
200	386.00	57.49	328.51

CO$_2$ band	VAT fuel scale charge, 3 month period, £	VAT on 3 month charge, £	VAT exclusive 3 month charge, £
205	400.00	59.57	340.43
210	414.00	61.66	352.34
215	428.00	63.74	364.26
220	442.00	65.83	376.17
225	455.00	67.77	387.23
230	469.00	69.85	399.15
235 or above	483.00	71.94	411.06

CO$_2$ band	VAT fuel scale charge, 1 month period, £	VAT on 1 month charge, £	VAT exclusive 1 month charge, £
120 or below	46.00	6.85	39.15
125	69.00	10.28	58.72
130	69.00	10.28	58.72
135	69.00	10.28	58.72
140	73.00	10.87	62.13
145	78.00	11.62	66.38
150	82.00	12.21	69.79
155	87.00	12.96	74.04
160	92.00	13.70	78.30
165	96.00	14.30	81.70
170	101.00	15.04	85.96
175	105.00	15.64	89.36
180	110.00	16.38	93.62
185	115.00	17.13	97.87
190	119.00	17.72	101.28
195	124.00	18.47	105.53
200	128.00	19.06	108.94
205	133.00	19.81	113.19
210	138.00	20.55	117.45
215	142.00	21.15	120.85
220	147.00	21.89	125.11
225	151.00	22.49	128.51
230	156.00	23.23	132.77
235 or above	161.00	23.98	137.02

From 1 May 2007 to 30 April 2008

The basis of the existing VAT private use charge is changed from being based upon engine size to being based upon carbon dioxide emissions.

CO$_2$ band	VAT fuel scale charge, 12 month period, £	VAT on 12 month charge, £	VAT exclusive 12 month charge, £
140 or below	730.00	108.72	621.28
145	780.00	116.17	663.83
150	830.00	123.62	706.38
155	880.00	131.06	748.94
160	925.00	137.77	787.23

CO$_2$ band	VAT fuel scale charge, 12 month period, £	VAT on 12 month charge, £	VAT exclusive 12 month charge, £
165	975.00	145.21	829.79
170	1,025.00	152.66	872.34
175	1,075.00	160.11	914.89
180	1,120.00	166.81	953.19
185	1,170.00	174.26	995.74
190	1,220.00	181.70	1,038.30
195	1,270.00	189.15	1,080.85
200	1,315.00	195.85	1,119.15
205	1,365.00	203.30	1,161.70
210	1,415.00	210.74	1,204.26
215	1,465.00	218.19	1,246.81
220	1,510.00	224.89	1,285.11
225	1,560.00	232.34	1,327.66
230	1,610.00	239.79	1,370.21
235	1,660.00	247.23	1,412.77
240 or above	1,705.00	253.94	1,451.06

CO$_2$ band	VAT fuel scale charge, 3 month period, £	VAT on 3 month charge, £	VAT exclusive 3 month charge, £
140 or below	182.00	27.11	154.89
145	195.00	29.04	165.96
150	207.00	30.83	176.17
155	219.00	32.62	186.38
160	231.00	34.40	196.60
165	243.00	36.19	206.81
170	256.00	38.13	217.87
175	268.00	39.91	228.09
180	280.00	41.70	238.30
185	292.00	43.49	248.51
190	304.00	45.28	258.72
195	317.00	47.21	269.79
200	329.00	49.00	280.00
205	341.00	50.79	290.21
210	353.00	52.57	300.43
215	365.00	54.36	310.64
220	378.00	56.30	321.70
225	390.00	58.09	331.91
230	402.00	59.87	342.13
235	414.00	61.66	352.34
240 or above	426.00	63.45	362.55

CO$_2$ band	VAT fuel scale charge, 1 month period, £	VAT on 1 month charge, £	VAT exclusive 1 month charge, £
140 or below	60.00	8.94	51.06
145	65.00	9.68	55.32
150	69.00	10.28	58.72
155	73.00	10.87	62.13
160	77.00	11.47	65.53

CO$_2$ band	VAT fuel scale charge, 1 month period, £	VAT on 1 month charge, £	VAT exclusive 1 month charge, £
165	81.00	12.06	68.94
170	85.00	12.66	72.34
175	89.00	13.26	75.74
180	93.00	13.85	79.15
185	97.00	14.45	82.55
190	101.00	15.04	85.96
195	105.00	15.64	89.36
200	109.00	16.23	92.77
205	113.00	16.83	96.17
210	117.00	17.43	99.57
215	121.00	18.02	102.98
220	126.00	18.77	107.23
225	130.00	19.36	110.64
230	134.00	19.96	114.04
235	138.00	20.55	117.45
240 or above	142.00	21.15	120.85

Where the carbon dioxide emissions figure for a vehicle is not a multiple of 5, the figure is rounded down to the next multiple of 5 to calculate the charge.

For a bi-fuel vehicle that has two emissions figures, the lower one should be used.

The fuel scale charge for vehicles that are too old to have CO$_2$ emissions figures will have to pay the fuel scale charge based upon a level of emissions as prescribed by HMRC. These are:

- Emissions level of 140 or less for cars with engine size of cc 1,400 or less;
- Emissions level of 175 for cars with engine size exceeding 1,400cc but less than 2,000cc;
- Emissions level of 240 for cars with engines exceeding 2,000cc.

1-703   Road fuel purchased by employees

HMRC have agreed the following to be the average fuel element of any motor allowance that is paid to employees.

For journeys from 1 September 2012

Engine size	Petrol	LPG
1400cc or less	15p	10p
1401cc to 2000cc	18p	12p
Over 2000cc	26p	17p

Engine size	Diesel
1600cc or less	12p
1601cc to 2000cc	15p
Over 2000cc	18p

Petrol hybrid cars are treated as petrol cars for this purpose. These rates are calculated from the fuel prices in the tables below:

Petrol

Engine Size (cc)	Mean MPG	Applied MPG	Fuel price (per litre)	Fuel price (per gallon)	Pence per mile	AFR
up to 1400	48.1	40.9	135.7	617.0	15.1	15
1401 to 2000	40.7	34.6	135.7	617.0	17.8	18
over 2000	27.8	23.7	135.7	617.0	26.1	26

Diesel

Engine Size (cc)	Mean MPG	Applied MPG	Fuel price (per litre)	Fuel price (per gallon)	Pence per mile	AFR
up to 1600	61.1	51.9	140.8	640.0	12.3	12
1601 to 2000	50.6	43.1	140.8	640.0	14.9	15
Over 2000	41.2	35.0	140.8	640.0	18.3	18

LPG

Engine Size (cc)	Mean MPG	Applied MPG	Fuel price (per litre)	Fuel price (per gallon)	Pence per mile	AFR
up to 1400	38.5	32.7	71.0	322.8	9.9	10
1401 to 2000	32.6	27.7	71.0	322.8	11.7	12
over 2000	22.3	18.9	71.0	322.8	17.0	17

For journeys from 1 June 2012 to 31 August 2012

Engine size	Petrol	LPG
1400cc or less	15p	11p
1401cc to 2000cc	18p	13p
Over 2000cc	26p	19p

Engine size	Diesel
1600cc or less	12p
1601cc to 2000cc	15p
Over 2000cc	18p

Petrol hybrid cars are treated as petrol cars for this purpose. These rates are calculated from the fuel prices in the tables below:

Petrol

Engine Size (cc)	Mean MPG	Applied MPG	Fuel price (per litre)	Fuel price (per gallon)	Pence per mile	AFR
up to 1400	48.1	40.9	135.2	614.7	15.0	15
1401 to 2000	40.7	34.6	135.2	614.7	17.8	18
over 2000	27.8	23.7	135.2	614.7	26.0	26

Diesel

Engine Size (cc)	Mean MPG	Applied MPG	Fuel price (per litre)	Fuel price (per gallon)	Pence per mile	AFR
up to 1600	61.1	51.9	143.2	650.8	12.5	13
1601 to 2000	50.6	43.1	143.2	650.8	15.1	15
Over 2000	41.2	35.0	143.2	650.8	18.6	19

LPG

Engine Size (cc)	Mean MPG	Applied MPG	Fuel price (per litre)	Fuel price (per gallon)	Pence per mile	AFR
up to 1400	38.5	32.7	74.1	336.9	10.3	10
1401 to 2000	32.6	27.7	74.1	336.9	12.2	12
over 2000	22.3	18.9	74.1	336.9	17.8	18

For journeys from 1 March to 31 May 2012:

Engine size	Petrol	LPG
1400cc or less	15p	10p
1401cc to 2000cc	18p	12p
Over 2000cc	26p	18p

Engine size	Diesel
1600cc or less	13p
1601cc to 2000cc	15p
Over 2000cc	18p

Petrol hybrid cars are treated as petrol cars for this purpose. These rates are calculated from the fuel prices in the tables below:

Petrol

Engine Size (cc)	Mean MPG	Applied MPG	Fuel price (per litre)	Fuel price (per gallon)	Pence per mile	AFR
up to 1400	48.1	40.9	135.2	614.7	15.0	15
1401 to 2000	40.7	34.6	135.2	614.7	17.8	18
over 2000	27.8	23.7	135.2	614.7	26.0	26

Diesel

Engine Size (cc)	Mean MPG	Applied MPG	Fuel price (per litre)	Fuel price (per gallon)	Pence per mile	AFR
up to 1600	61.1	51.9	143.2	650.8	12.5	13
1601 to 2000	50.6	43.1	143.2	650.8	15.1	15
Over 2000	41.2	35.0	143.2	650.8	18.6	19

LPG

Engine Size (cc)	Mean MPG	Applied MPG	Fuel price (per litre)	Fuel price (per gallon)	Pence per mile	AFR
up to 1400	38.5	32.7	74.1	336.9	10.3	10
1401 to 2000	32.6	27.7	74.1	336.9	12.2	12
over 2000	22.3	18.9	74.1	336.9	17.8	18

For journeys from 1 December 2011 to 29 February 2012:

Engine size	Petrol	LPG
1400cc or less	15p	10p
1401cc to 2000cc	18p	12p
Over 2000cc	26p	18p

Engine size	Diesel
1600cc or less	12p
1601cc to 2000cc	15p
Over 2000cc	18p

Petrol hybrid cars are treated as petrol cars for this purpose. These rates are calculated from the fuel prices in the tables below:

Petrol

Engine Size (cc)	Mean MPG	Applied MPG	Fuel price (per litre)	Fuel price (per gallon)	Pence per mile	AFR
up to 1400	48.1	40.9	133.4	606.3	14.8	15
1401 to 2000	40.7	34.6	133.4	606.3	17.5	18
over 2000	27.8	23.7	133.4	606.3	25.6	26

Diesel

Engine Size (cc)	Mean MPG	Applied MPG	Fuel price (per litre)	Fuel price (per gallon)	Pence per mile	AFR
up to 1600	61.1	51.9	141.1	641.3	12.4	12
1601 to 2000	50.6	43.1	141.1	641.3	14.9	15
Over 2000	41.2	35	141.1	641.3	18.3	18

LPG

Engine Size (cc)	Mean MPG	Applied MPG	Fuel price (per litre)	Fuel price (per gallon)	Pence per mile	AFR
up to 1400	38.5	32.7	73.9	336	10.3	10
1401 to 2000	32.6	27.7	73.9	336	12.1	12
over 2000	22.3	18.9	73.9	336	18.7	18

For journeys from 1 September 2011 to 1 December 2011:

Engine size	Petrol	LPG
1400cc or less	15p	11p
1401cc to 2000cc	18p	12p
Over 2000cc	26p	18p

Engine size	Diesel
1600cc or less	12p
1601cc to 2000cc	15p
Over 2000cc	18p

Petrol hybrid cars are treated as petrol cars for this purpose. These rates are calculated from the fuel prices in the tables below:

Petrol

Engine Size (cc)	Mean MPG	Applied MPG	Fuel price (per litre)	Fuel price (per gallon)	Pence per mile	AFR
up to 1400	48.1	40.9	134.6	611.7	15	15
1401 to 2000	40.7	34.6	134.6	611.7	17.7	18
over 2000	27.8	23.7	134.6	611.7	25.8	26

Diesel

Engine Size (cc)	Mean MPG	Applied MPG	Fuel price (per litre)	Fuel price (per gallon)	Pence per mile	AFR
up to 1600	61.1	51.9	139	632.1	12.2	12
1601 to 2000	50.6	43.1	139	632.1	14.7	15
Over 2000	41.2	35	139	632.1	18.1	18

LPG

Engine Size (cc)	Mean MPG	Applied MPG	Fuel price (per litre)	Fuel price (per gallon)	Pence per mile	AFR
up to 1400	38.5	32.7	75.8	344.6	10.5	11
1401 to 2000	32.6	27.7	75.8	344.6	12.5	12
over 2000	22.3	18.9	75.8	344.6	18.2	18

For journeys from 1 June 2011 to 31 August 2011:

Engine size	Petrol	LPG
1400cc or less	15p	11p
1401cc to 2000cc	18p	13p
Over 2000cc	26p	18p

Engine size	Diesel
1600cc or less	12p
1601cc to 2000cc	15p
Over 2000cc	18p

Petrol hybrid cars are treated as petrol cars for this purpose. These rates are calculated from the fuel prices in the tables below:

Petrol

Engine Size (cc)	Mean MPG	Applied MPG	Fuel price (per litre)	Fuel price (per gallon)	Pence per mile	AFR
up to 1400	47.36	40.3	136.1	618.8	15.4	15
1401 to 2000	40.21	34.2	136.1	618.8	18.1	18
over 2000	28.22	24.0	136.1	618.8	25.8	26

Diesel

Engine Size (cc)	Mean MPG	Applied MPG	Fuel price (per litre)	Fuel price (per gallon)	Pence per mile	AFR
up to 1600	60.48	51.4	140.8	639.9	12.4	12
1601 to 2000	50.24	42.7	140.8	639.9	15.0	15
Over 2000	41.45	35.2	140.8	639.9	18.2	18

LPG

Engine Size (cc)	Mean MPG	Applied MPG	Fuel price (per litre)	Fuel price (per gallon)	Pence per mile	AFR
up to 1400	37.9	32.2	77.3	351.4	10.9	11
1401 to 2000	32.2	27.3	77.3	351.4	12.9	13
over 2000	22.6	19.2	77.3	351.4	18.3	18

For journeys from 1 March 2011 to 31 May 2011:

Engine size	Petrol	Diesel	LPG
1400cc or less	14p	13p	10p
1401cc to 2000cc	16p	13p	12p
Over 2000cc	23p	16p	17p

Petrol hybrid cars are treated as petrol cars for this purpose. These rates are calculated from the fuel prices in the tables below:

Petrol

Engine Size (cc)	Mean MPG	Applied MPG	Fuel price (per litre)	Fuel price (per gallon)	Pence per mile	AFR
up to 1400	47.36	42.6	128.9	586.1	13.7	14
1400 to 2000	40.21	36.2	128.9	586.1	16.2	16
over 2000	28.22	25.4	128.9	586.1	23.1	23

Diesel

Engine Size (cc)	Mean MPG	Applied MPG	Fuel price (per litre)	Fuel price (per gallon)	Pence per mile	AFR
up to 2000	53.85	48.5	134.0	609.4	12.6	13
over 2000	41.45	37.3	134.0	609.4	16.3	16

LPG

Engine Size (cc)	Mean MPG	Applied MPG	Fuel price (per litre)	Fuel price (per gallon)	Pence per mile	AFR
up to 1400	37.9	32.2	77.3	351.4	10.9	11
1401 to 2000	32.2	27.3	77.3	351.4	12.9	13
over 2000	22.6	19.2	77.3	351.4	18.3	18

For journeys from 1 December 2010 but before 28 February 2011:

Engine size	Petrol	Diesel	LPG
1400cc or less	13p	12p	9p
1401cc to 2000cc	15p	12p	10p
Over 2000cc	21p	15p	15p

Petrol hybrid cars are treated as petrol cars for this purpose. These rates are calculated from the fuel prices in the tables below:

Petrol

Engine Size (cc)	Mean MPG	Applied MPG	Fuel price (per litre)	Fuel price (per gallon)	Pence per mile	AFR
up to 1400	47.4	42.6	119.0	540.9	12.7	13
1400 to 2000	40.2	36.2	119.0	540.9	14.9	15
over 2000	28.2	25.4	119.0	540.9	21.3	21

Diesel

Engine Size (cc)	Mean MPG	Applied MPG	Fuel price (per litre)	Fuel price (per gallon)	Pence per mile	AFR
up to 2000	53.9	48.5	122.7	558.0	11.5	12
over 2000	41.5	37.3	122.7	558.0	15.0	15

LPG

Engine Size (cc)	Mean MPG	Applied MPG	Fuel price (per litre)	Fuel price (per gallon)	Pence per mile	AFR
up to 1400	37.9	34.1	66.4	301.9	8.9	9
1400 to 2000	32.2	29.0	66.4	301.9	10.4	10
over 2000	22.6	20.3	66.4	301.9	14.9	15

For journeys after 31 May 2010 until 1 December 2010, rate per mile

Engine size	Petrol	Diesel	LPG
1400cc or less	12p	11p	8p
1401cc to 2000cc	15p	11p	10p
Over 2000cc	21p	16p	14p

For journeys from 1 December 2009 but before 1 June 2010, rate per mile

Engine size	Petrol	Diesel	LPG
1400cc or less	11p	11p	7p
1401cc to 2000cc	14p	11p	8p
Over 2000cc	20p	14p	12p

For journeys from 1 July 2009 but before 1 December 2009, rate per mile

Engine size	Petrol	Diesel	LPG
1400cc or less	10p	10p	7p
1401cc to 2000cc	12p	10p	8p
Over 2000cc	18p	13p	12p

Petrol hybrid cars are treated as petrol cars for this purpose. These rates are calculated from the fuel prices in the tables below:

Petrol

Engine Size (cc)	Mean MPG	Applied MPG	Fuel price (per litre)	Fuel price (per gallon)	Pence per mile	AFR
up to 1400	48.8	43.9	108.7	494.3	11.3	11
1400 to 2000	40.0	36.0	108.7	494.3	13.7	14
over 2000	28.1	25.3	108.7	494.3	19.5	20

Diesel

Engine Size (cc)	Mean MPG	Applied MPG	Fuel price (per litre)	Fuel price (per gallon)	Pence per mile	AFR
up to 2000	50.9	45.8	109.9	499.5	10.9	11
over 2000	38.7	34.8	109.9	499.5	14.3	14

LPG

Engine Size (cc)	Mean MPG	Applied MPG	Fuel price (per litre)	Fuel price (per gallon)	Pence per mile	AFR
up to 1400	39.0	35.1	53.3	242.3	6.9	7
1400 to 2000	32.0	28.8	53.3	242.3	8.4	8
over 2000	22.5	20.3	53.3	242.3	12.0	12

For journeys from 1 January 2009 until 30 June 2009, rate per mile

Engine size	Petrol	Diesel	LPG
1400cc or less	10p	11p	7p
1401cc to 2000cc	12p	11p	9p
Over 2000cc	17p	14p	12p

Petrol hybrid cars are treated as petrol cars for this purpose. These rates are calculated from the fuel prices in the tables below:

Petrol

Engine Size (cc)	Mean MPG	Applied MPG	Fuel price (per litre)	Fuel price (per gallon)	Pence per mile	AFR
up to 1400	48.8	43.9	93.1	423.3	9.6	10
1400 to 2000	40.0	36.0	93.1	423.3	11.8	12
over 2000	28.1	25.3	93.1	423.3	16.7	17

Diesel

Engine Size (cc)	Mean MPG	Applied MPG	Fuel price (per litre)	Fuel price (per gallon)	Pence per mile	AFR
up to 2000	50.9	45.8	107.8	490.0	10.7	11
over 2000	38.7	34.8	107.8	490.0	14.1	14

LPG

Engine Size (cc)	Mean MPG	Applied MPG	Fuel price (per litre)	Fuel price (per gallon)	Pence per mile	AFR
up to 1400	39.0	35.1	55.0	249.8	7.1	7
1400 to 2000	32.0	28.8	55.0	249.8	8.7	9
over 2000	22.5	20.3	55.0	249.8	12.3	12

For journeys from 30 June 2008 until 31 December 2008, rate per mile

In May 2008, HMRC gave notice that the rates are revised for journeys after 30 June 2008.

Engine size	Petrol	Diesel	LPG
1400cc or less	12p	13p	7p
1401cc to 2000cc	15p	13p	9p
Over 2000cc	21p	17p	13p

The rates from 1 January 2008 until 29 June 2008 were:

Engine Size	Petrol	Diesel	LPG
1400cc or less	11p	11p	7p
1401cc to 2000cc	13p	11p	8p
Over 2000cc	19p	14p	11p

Petrol hybrid cars are treated as petrol cars for this purpose. These rates are calculated from the fuel prices in the tables below:

Petrol

Engine Size (cc)	Mean MPG	Applied MPG	Fuel price (per litre)	Fuel price (per gallon)	Pence per mile	AFR
up to 1400	46.7	42.0	102.1	464.3	11.0	11
1400 to 2000	38.5	34.7	102.1	464.3	13.4	13
over 2000	27.9	25.1	102.1	464.3	18.5	19

Diesel

Engine Size (cc)	Mean MPG	Applied MPG	Fuel price (per litre)	Fuel price (per gallon)	Pence per mile	AFR
up to 2000	50.3	45.3	106.3	483.0	10.7	11
over 2000	37.5	33.7	106.3	483.0	14.3	14

LPG

Engine Size (cc)	Mean MPG	Applied MPG	Fuel price (per litre)	Fuel price (per gallon)	Pence per mile	AFR
up to 1400	37.4	33.6	50.2	228.2	6.8	7
1400 to 2000	30.8	27.7	50.2	228.2	8.2	8
over 2000	22.3	20.1	50.2	228.2	11.4	11

The rates from 1 August 2007 to 31 December 2007 were:

Engine Size	Petrol	Diesel	LPG
1400cc or less	10p	10p	6p
1401cc to 2000cc	13p	10p	8p
Over 2000cc	18p	13p	10p

Petrol hybrid cars are treated as petrol cars for this purpose. These rates are calculated from the fuel prices in the tables below:

Petrol

Engine Size (cc)	Mean MPG	Applied MPG	Fuel price (per litre)	Fuel price (per gallon)	Pence per mile	AFR
up to 1400	46.7	42.0	96.6	439.2	10.4	10
1400 to 2000	38.5	34.7	96.6	439.2	12.7	13
over 2000	27.9	25.1	96.6	439.2	17.5	18

Diesel

Engine Size (cc)	Mean MPG	Applied MPG	Fuel price (per litre)	Fuel price (per gallon)	Pence per mile	AFR
up to 2000	50.3	45.3	97.2	441.9	9.8	10
over 2000	37.5	33.7	97.2	441.9	13.1	13

LPG

Engine Size (cc)	Mean MPG	Applied MPG	Fuel price (per litre)	Fuel price (per gallon)	Pence per mile	AFR
up to 1400	37.4	33.6	46.2	210.0	6.2	6
1400 to 2000	30.8	27.7	46.2	210.0	7.6	8
over 2000	22.3	20.1	46.2	210.0	10.5	10

The rates from 1 February 2007 to 31 July 2007 were:

Engine Size	Petrol	Diesel	LPG
1400cc or less	9p	9p	7p
1401cc to 2000cc	11p	9p	7p
Over 2000cc	16p	12p	10p

Petrol hybrid cars are treated as petrol cars for this purpose.

The rates from 1 July 2006 to 31 January 2007 were:

Engine Size	Petrol	Diesel	LPG
1400cc or less	11p	10p	7p
1401cc to 2000cc	13p	10p	8p
Over 2000cc	18p	14p	10p

ADDRESSES AND CONTACTS

1-704   Information and initial contact

Telephone contact

HMRC National Advice Service is generally available from 8am to 8pm Monday to Friday on 0845 010 9000. International enquiries are dealt with on +44 2920 501 261.

The NAS are usually able to supply contact numbers for individual HMRC offices or are able to transfer calls to the local office.

Charities

The dedicated line for Charities is 0845 302 02 03.

Textphone

People with hearing difficulties may contact HMRC via the textphone service on 0845000 0200.

Website address

The internet address for HMRC is *www.hmrc.gov.uk*.

Head Office

100 Parliament Street
London SW1A 2BQ
Tel (020) 7620 1313

1-705 Where to register, de-register or send amendments of details

Online VAT Registration Applications

Online applications for VAT registration will be directed to one of the four National Registration Units at Carmarthen, Grimsby, Newry and Wolverhampton.

Telephone contact

The general telephone number for the National VAT Registration Service is 0845 039 0129.

Postal applications

All postal applications should be sent to Wolverhampton.

De-registration

Applications for deregistraton should be sent to Grimsby.

Changes in details

Notifications of changes in details should be sent to Grimsby.

Overseas traders

Registration and de-registration of *overseas traders* is generally dealt with by the Non-Established Taxable Persons Unit ('NETPU') at the Aberdeen office (see 1-715).

Where a VAT representative is appointed by an overseas trader, registration and de-registration is dealt with by the local VAT office or specialist unit that would normally deal with the principal place of business of the VAT representative.

Overseas traders that own a UK property business are required to register through Aberdeen if they have no UK establishment other than a 'care of' address. This reflects a change of policy and means that some existing registrations may be moved to Aberdeen.

Group registrations

Applications for group registrations should be sent to the Grimsby registration office.

1-706 VAT Returns

The address to which VAT returns should be submitted is:

VAT Controller
VAT Central Unit
BX5 5AT

This is in Shipley. Prior to August 2008, all returns were dealt with in Southend.

If exceptionally you need to use a courier service to deliver your return the following address should be used:

HMRC
Alexander House
Southend SS99 1AA

1-710 VAT 68 Applications

Applications under the VAT 68 procedure – to retain the VAT number of the previous owner of a business – should be submitted to:

HMRC
Imperial House
Grimsby DN31 1DB

1-715 Office addresses and telephone numbers: registration and de-registration units

Name of Office	Address & Telephone Number
Non-Established Taxable Person Unit	HMRC Ruby House 8 Ruby Place Aberdeen AB10 1ZP
Carmarthen Registration & de-registration Unit	HMRC Ty-Myrddin Old Station Road Carmarthen SA31 1BT 0845 7 585831
Grimsby Registration Unit	HMR CImperial House 77 Victoria Street Grimsby DN31 1DB 0845 039 0279
Newry Registration & de-registration Unit	HMRC PO Box 40 Carnbane Way Damolly Newry Co Down BT35 6PJ 0845 7 112114

Name of Office	Address & Telephone Number
Wolverhampton Registration & de-registration Unit	HMRC Deansgate 62–70 Tettenhall Road Wolverhampton WV1 4TZ 0845 039 0129

1-717   Annual Accounting Scheme applications

Applications to use the annual accounting scheme should be sent to:

HMRC
Imperial House
77 Victoria Street
Grimsby DN31 1DB
Tel 0845 039 0279

1-720   Addresses for written and email enquiries

All written enquiries on VAT should be sent to:

HMRC
National Advice Service
Written Enquiries Section
Alexander House
Victoria Avenue
Southend
Essex SS99 1BD

There is an exception for any VAT matter connected with Charities in which case the dedicated charity team should be contacted at:

HMRC Charities
St John's House
Merton Road
Bootle
Merseyside L69 9BB
Tel: 0845 302 02 03

All written enquiries concerning aspects of international trade should be sent to:

HMRC
International Trade
Written Enquiries Team
Crownhill Court
Plymouth PL6 5BZ

HMRC have stated that they will, where necessary, forward the enquiry to a specialist team and therefore the reply may come from a different office.

Email enquiries

- General enquiries by email should be sent to Enquiries.estn@hmrc.gsi.gov.uk.
- Charity enquiries should be sent to the dedicated charity team at charities@hmrc.gsi.gov.uk.
- Specific enquiries about International Trade should be submitted to intenquiries@hmrc.gsi.gov.uk.
- International enquirers may use voes@hmrc.gsi.gov.uk.

HMRC state that they generally try to respond to emails within 15 working days.

1-721 Clearances

Large businesses should send their applications to their Client Relationship Manager. Other applications should be submitted to HMRC Clearances Team, Alexander House, 21 Victoria Avenue, Southend on Sea, Essex SS99 1BD.

HMRC say that applications will be dealt with more efficiently if submitted by email to hmrc.southendteam@hmrc.gsi.gov.uk.

Advance notification of any particularly sensitive issues may be discussed prior to submission with John Woodham on 01733 355208.

1-723 Addresses to which to submit form VAT 652

Use the following postcode table to match your business postcode to the correct office. All correspondence addresses and telephone numbers for HM Revenue and Customs offices dealing with voluntary disclosures for each region follow, after the postcode table.

NB: For information about specific voluntary disclosures submitted, contact the appropriate regional office. For general enquiries about voluntary disclosure procedures, contact the National Advice Service on 0845 010 9000.

Postcode	Region
AB	Northern Ireland
AL	South
B	South
BA	South
BB	North
BD	North
BH	South
BL	North
BN	South
BR1–7	London

Postcode	Region
BR8	South
BS	South
BT	Northern Ireland
CA	North
CB	South
CF	Northern Ireland
CH1–3, 41–49, 60–66	North
CH4–8, 88, 89, 99	Northern Ireland
CM	South
CO	South
CR0, 2, 4, 5, 7, 9	London
CR3, 6	South
CT	South
CV	North
CW	North
DA1–4, 9–13	South
DA5–8, 14–18	London
DD	Northern Ireland
DE	North
DG	Northern Ireland
DH	North
DL	North
DN	North
DT	South
DY	London
E	London
EC	London
EH	Northern Ireland
EN1–5	London
EN6–11	South
EX	South
FK	South
FY	North
G	Northern Ireland
GL	South
GU	South
HA	London
HD	North
HG	North
HP	South
HR	South
HS	Northern Ireland
HU	North
HX	North
IG	London
IP	North
IV	Northern Ireland
KA	Northern Ireland

Postcode	Region
KT1–6, 9	London
KT7, 8, 10–24	South
KW	Northern Ireland
KY	Northern Ireland
L	North
LA	North
LD	Northern Ireland
LE	North
LL	Northern Ireland
LN	North
LS	North
LU	South
M	North
ME	South
MK	South
ML	Northern Ireland
NE	North
N	London
NG	North
NN	South
NP	Northern Ireland
NR	North
NW	London
OL	North
OX	South
PA	Northern Ireland
PE1-21, 26-30, 33-34, 38	South
PE22-25, 31-32, 35-37	North
PH	Northern Ireland
PL	South
PO	South
PR	North
RG	South
RH	South
RM1–3, 5–14	London
RM4, 15–20	South
S	North
SA	Northern Ireland
SE	London
SG	South
SK	North
SL	South
SM1–6	London
SM7	South
SN	South
SO	South
SP	South
SR	North

Postcode	Region
SS	South
ST1-15	North
ST16-21	South
SW	London
SY1–9, 11–14	North
SY10, 15–25	Northern Ireland
TA	South
TD1–11, 13, 14	North
TF1-10, 12, 13	North
TF11	South
TN	South
TQ	South
TR	South
TS	North
TW1–14	London
TW15–20	South
UB	London
W	London
WA	North
WC	London
WD	South
WF	North
WR	South
WS	South
WV	South
YO	North
ZE	Northern Ireland

Regional Office addresses and telephone numbers

Note: When making contact please quote your VAT registration number.

London Office
VAT Error Correction Team
HM Revenue & Customs
Valiant House
365 High Road
Wembley HA9 6AY

North Office
VAT Error Correction Team
HM Revenue & Customs
Queen's Dock
22 Kings Parade
Liverpool L74 4AA
Tel 0113 389 4432

Northern Ireland Office
VAT Error Correction Team
HM Revenue & Customs
Custom House
Custom House Square
Belfast BT1 3ET
Tel 028 9056 2687

South Office
VAT Error Correction Team
HM Revenue & Customs
Merrywalks House
2 The Hill
Stroud GL5 1QD
Tel 01453 847785

1-724 Complaints

Complaints direct to HMRC should be sent to the Complaints Manager for the office with which the dispute has arisen.

Details may be found on the factsheet 'Complaints and putting things right' issued in May 2007 and found on HMRC's website or obtained via the National Advice Service.

Complaints to the adjudicator

Complaints about HMRC may ultimately be made to the adjudicator. The adjudicator's office is at:

8th Floor
Euston Tower
286 Euston Road
London NW1 3US
Tel 0300 057 1111
Fax 0300 057 1212 or 020 7667 1830
Email adjudicators@gtnet.gov.uk
www.adjudicatorsoffice.gov.uk

1-725 Notification and queries relating to 'option to tax'

All notifications and queries relating to the 'option to tax' should be addressed to:

Option to Tax National Unit
Cotton House, 7 Cochrane Street,
Glasgow G1 1GY
Fax 0141 285 4454
Tel 0141 285 4174/4175 (Monday to Thursday 09.00 to 17.00; Friday 09.00 to 16.30)
Email optiontotaxnationalunit@hmrc.gsi.gov.uk

Businesses that become liable to register for VAT as a result of an 'option to tax' – election to waive the exemption – should send the notification of the option to tax together with the application to register for VAT to the relevant VAT Registration Unit.

1-727   D-I-Y builders claims

All claims for DIY builders and converters repayments should be submitted to: HM Revenue and Customs, 2 Broadway, Broad Street, Five Ways, Birmingham, West Midlands, B15 1BG. *Tel* 0121 697 4000; *Fax* 0121 697 4002.

1-730   Verification of validity of VAT numbers

Customs offer a facility whereby the validity of another trader's VAT number may be checked.

For the computer, mobile phone, alcohol and road fuel trade sectors the contact number in 01737 734 then 516, 577, 612 or 761.

For other trade sectors, the contact number is the National Advice Service 0845 010 9000.

The validity of VAT numbers in other Member States may be checked through the Europa website. A link is found on HMRC homepage.

In addition, the National Advice Service will check the validity and the address of a trader in another Member State. They will not give you the address, only check if the address which you have for a supplier or customer is correct.

1-733   Authority to act for a client

Form 64-8 has been redesigned so that a client can select to give an agent authority to act in specific areas, including VAT.

The form can be accessed through HMRC's website at *www.hmrc.gov.uk/forms/64-8.pdf.*

Usually, the form should be returned to:

HMRC
CAA Team
Longbenton
Newcastle upon Tyne NE98 1ZZ

However, when it accompanies an application for registration it should be sent with the application form to the relevant VAT registration unit. If it is in connection with a specific matter it should be included with the correspondence to whichever HMRC office is involved.

1-734   Payment support and help

Business Payment Support Service

Businesses that are having difficulty in meeting their VAT payments should contact HMRC on 0845 302 1435.

HMRC will require the VAT number of the business, details of the debt with which there is difficulty and some indication of the income and expenditure of the business.

National Insolvency Helpdesk

Call 0151 703 8450 (08.30 to 17.00 hrs Monday to Thursday, 08.30 to 16.00 hrs Friday).

1-735   Disclosure of VAT Avoidance Schemes

Disclosures of VAT avoidance schemes should be sent to:

VAT Avoidance Disclosures Unit
Anti Avoidance Group (Intelligence)
HMRC
1st Floor
22 Kingsway
London WC2B 6NR

Details may also be emailed to vat.avoidance.disclosures.bst@hmrc.gsi.gov.uk

1-737   Appeals to the First Tier Tribunal (Tax)

Appeals to the First Tier Tribunal (Tax) should be submitted to:

Tribunals Service (Tax)
2nd Floor
54 Hagley Road
Birmingham B16 8PE
Tel 0845 223 8080
Textphone via Typetalk 1800108452238080
Website www.tribunals.gov.uk/Tribunals/About/about.htm.
Email taxappeals@tribunals.gsi.gov.uk

TERRITORY OF THE EUROPEAN COMMUNITY

1-740   Territory of the European Community

Member states

The territory of the European Community for VAT purposes consists of the following member states (Directive 2006/112, art. 5; Notice 725, para. 1.3 (2002 edn)):

(1)   Austria;

(2) Belgium;

(3) Denmark;

(4) Finland;

(5) France (including Monaco);

(6) Germany;

(7) Greece;

(8) The Republic of Ireland;

(9) Italy;

(10) Luxembourg;

(11) Netherlands;

(12) Portugal (including the Azores and Madeira);

(13) Spain (including the Balearic Islands);

(14) Sweden; and

(15) UK (including the Isle of Man).

New Member States

The following countries joined the EU on 1 May 2004:

(1) Cyprus;

(2) the Czech Republic;

(3) Estonia;

(4) Hungary;

(5) Latvia;

(6) Lithuania;

(7) Malta;

(8) Poland;

(9) Slovakia; and

(10) Slovenia.

The following countries joined the EU on 1 January 2007.

(1) Bulgaria;

(2) Romania.

This enlarged the total number of EU States to 27.

Excluded territories

The following territories of member states are excluded from the 'territory of the country':

(1)   re Finland: the Aland Islands;

(2)   re France: the overseas departments (Martinique, French Guiana, Guadeloupe, Reunion and St Pierre and Miquelon); and

(3)   re Germany:

    (a)   the Island of Heligoland; and
    (b)   the territory of Büsingen;

(4)   re Greece: Mount Athos (also known as Agion Poros);

(5)   re Italy:

    (a)   Livigno;
    (b)   Campione d'Italia; and
    (c)   the Italian waters of Lake Lugano;

(6)   re Spain:

    (a)   the Canary Islands;
    (b)   Ceuta; and
    (c)   Melilla; and

(7)   re UK:

    (a)   the Channel Islands; and
    (b)   Gibraltar;

(8)   re Cyprus: the United Nations buffer zone and the part of Cyprus to the north of the buffer zone where the Republic of Cyprus does not have control;

(9)   re Denmark: the Faroe Islands and Greenland.

(10) re Netherlands: Antilles.

Monaco and the Isle of Man

Monaco and the Isle of Man are not treated as 'third territories'. They are part of France and the UK respectively. Thus transactions originating in or intended for:

(1)   Monaco are treated as transactions originating in or intended for France; and

(2)   the Isle of Man are treated as transactions originating in or intended for the UK.

Areas not within the EC

Andorra, San Marino, the Vatican City and Liechtenstein are not within the EC for VAT purposes.

Introduction

OVERVIEW

2-000   Overview

Value added tax (VAT) was introduced in the United Kingdom on 1 April 1973 shortly after the UK joined the European Economic Community (EEC). VAT is the common tax of the Community, and is intended (eventually) to apply in the same manner in each Member State.

Although VAT has now been with us for over 30 years, it is rarely understood properly and causes problems to large and small businesses alike.

The aim of this publication is to provide people in the business world and their advisers with a general understanding of the operation of the tax, and to help them to deal with it in the context of the businesses within which they work. It is intended to provide a basic reference work on VAT, and to assist in grasping its principles and in applying them to the circumstances which arise in practice. It also seeks to identify some of the common danger areas and to suggest ways of dealing with these.

VAT is a complex tax far short of the simple book-keeping tax that it was said to be in 1972. Throughout the publication are flowcharts designed to assist in understanding the concepts and identifying critical decision points.

OUTLINE OF VALUE ADDED TAX

2-050   Application

VAT is charged on taxable supplies of goods and services made in the UK, where these are made in the course of business. It is also charged on imports of goods into the UK from outside the European Community (EC), on the acquisition of goods from elsewhere in the EC and on some imports of services.

Businesses which make taxable supplies are obliged to register with Her Majesty's Revenue and Customs (HMRC), the Government department which controls the tax. Registered businesses are often referred to as traders, although the term includes businesses which would not generally be regarded as trades (e.g. a practising solicitor is normally regarded as being engaged in a profession rather than a trade, but in VAT terms would be called a trader).

VAT Reporter: ¶1-100

2-080 Records and returns

Each registered trader is obliged to keep a record of the supplies which he makes in the course of any business carried on by him, and of the VAT due on them. He must also keep a record of VAT incurred on supplies to him, and on his imports and acquisitions. There are special rules for traders using the 'Flat Rate scheme'.

He must then complete a periodical VAT return, and submit this to HMRC with a remittance for any tax due for the period. Returns are normally due quarterly, although some traders complete monthly or annual returns.

The trader must enter on his VAT return the totals of supplies made by him and of supplies (and imports and acquisitions) which he has obtained for the purposes of his business. He must also enter on it the total VAT due on the supplies and acquisitions which he has made, and the amount incurred on supplies to him and on imports and acquisitions. He may set the VAT incurred by him against the VAT due on his own supplies. The VAT which he is due to pay to HMRC is the difference between the two. If the VAT due on his own supplies is less than the VAT which he has incurred, he receives a repayment from HMRC.

Example: periodical VAT return

Henrietta is a consultant and makes quarterly VAT returns. Her records for the last three months show that she has made supplies with a value of £8,000, plus VAT (at 20 per cent) of £1,600. She has incurred VAT of £175 on various expenses, and has also purchased a computer for £2,500 plus £500 VAT.

Her VAT return for the quarter will show:

	£
VAT due on supplies made	1,600.00
Less: VAT incurred on supplies obtained (£175 + £500)	(675.00)
Net amount due to HMRC	925.00

It will be noted from the above example that VAT can be reclaimed in respect of capital equipment purchased, as well as on day-to-day running expenses.

VAT Reporter: ¶101(4)

2-110 Outputs and inputs

The supplies which a trader makes are referred to as his outputs, and the VAT due on them is called output tax. The supplies which the trader uses are referred to as inputs, and the VAT on them (and on imports and acquisitions which the trader receives) is called input tax.

This nomenclature sometimes causes confusion, because the associated money flows seem to go the wrong way. When a trader makes a sale, there is an output, as goods or services flow out of the business, and this leads to money flowing into the business. The best way to think about this is to remember that VAT is technically a tax on the supply, which flows out, not on the income which results from it. Indeed, it will be seen at 3-160 that a supply can arise without any associated flow of money.

When a trader makes an acquisition of goods from elsewhere in the EC he becomes liable to pay output tax on it, but simultaneously obtains the right to treat that tax as input tax. Thus, an acquisition is both an output and an input.

VAT Reporter: ¶1-750

2-140   Evidence for input tax deduction

As might be imagined, HMRC are unwilling to allow credit for input tax based on the unsupported word of the trader. Consequently, the law provides for evidence to be generated in respect of each supply which takes place.

Taxable supplies

A trader who makes a taxable supply to another trader is obliged to prepare and issue a VAT invoice in respect of the transaction. This is a document (usually in the form of an invoice) which provides details of the transaction, the parties involved and the amount of VAT accountable on the supply. If the customer wishes to reclaim the VAT on the transaction, he must retain the VAT invoice as evidence of the VAT and be able to produce it to HMRC if requested.

As the details on the invoice provide HMRC with details of the supplier, they are in a position to verify that the VAT shown has been accounted for by him. This introduces an element of self-policing into the system.

Importations from outside the EC

A trader who pays VAT on the importation of goods from outside the EC must obtain the relevant HMRC document, which acts as the supporting evidence for his subsequent claim for its deduction as input tax. If a trader claims input tax without holding the related HMRC import certificate (Form C79), the claim will almost certainly be denied when discovered by HMRC. It follows that staff engaged on the purchase side of the business need to be able to identify the relevant documentation and to withhold payment for supplies received until it has been provided.

Acquisitions from other Member States

A trader who becomes liable to account for VAT on goods bought from elsewhere in the EC (such purchases are called *acquisitions*) must hold a VAT invoice issued by his supplier, citing the UK trader's VAT registration number and providing other details, such as the value of the supply. This, combined with returns of intra-EC trade, enables the revenue authorities to carry out cross-checking exercises to satisfy themselves that VAT is being properly accounted for.

VAT Reporter: ¶19-000

2-170 VAT chargeable

VAT is charged on taxable supplies. It is worth considering the types of supply which may be made in the course of business, and also whether it is possible to receive money without making a supply.

The UK has one main positive rate of VAT, the standard rate.

From 4 January 2011	20%
1 January 2010 to 3 January 2011	17.5%
1 December 2008 to 31 December 2010	15%
Prior to 30 November 2008	17.5%

There is also a lower rate of five per cent. If a UK trader makes a supply, then VAT is due at the standard rate unless the supply is specifically relieved from VAT (or subjected to the five per cent lower rate). In very broad terms, this means that VAT is due on sales made, and on the gift of business assets or free use of business assets for non-business purposes.

Although the default position is that supplies are standard-rated, they may be zero-rated, liable at the reduced rate or exempt from VAT if they fall into certain closely defined categories.

Supplies which are zero-rated attract VAT, but at a rate of zero per cent, so no tax is actually due. However, they remain taxable supplies. The importance of this is that a person who makes zero-rated supplies must register for VAT (since the supplies made are taxable, albeit at a rate of zero per cent) and so can reclaim input tax on expenses incurred. In some countries, this kind of supply is referred to as 'exempt with credit'. This is a fair description, as no VAT is due in respect of the supplies made, but VAT charged by others on the costs associated with making the supplies can be reclaimed in full. The effect is that supplies of this sort reach the final consumer without the imposition of any VAT burden.

The other kind of supply on which VAT is not chargeable is an exempt supply. Again, there is a closely defined set of supplies which qualify for exemption from VAT.

The difference between exempt supplies and zero-rated supplies is that a person who makes only exempt supplies cannot register for VAT and so cannot recover VAT incurred on expenses. Consequently, such trader's costs are increased to the extent that his expenses bear VAT.

Of course, it is possible for a trader to make both taxable supplies (whether taxable at the standard rate, reduced rate or zero-rated) and also to make exempt supplies. Such a trader will need to register for VAT, but can only recover tax on expenses to the extent that they relate to taxable supplies made. How this actually operates is covered later.

A supply can take place (and VAT become due) without any money being received by the trader. By the same token, the receipt of money does not necessarily mean that a supply has taken place. However, it is a good general rule to play safe and assume that any receipt of money indicates that a supply has occurred until it is proven otherwise.

The introduction of capital into a non-corporate business does not indicate that a supply has been made. Likewise a company is not making supply when it issues shares to raise capital. There may be a supply when capital is raised by issuing other types of financial instruments or securities.

VAT Reporter: ¶140

2-200   Input tax credit

A VAT-registered trader must account for output tax on the taxable supplies which he makes, but is entitled to deduct from this liability the input tax paid in respect of the goods and services which he consumes in making his taxable supplies. In other words, the trader receives credit for input tax incurred, and this is set against his liability. If the input tax for a period exceeds the output tax liability, the difference is repaid to the trader by HMRC. There are special rules for traders using certain schemes.

Input tax credit is available in respect of:

- tax paid on supplies of goods or of services made to the trader;
- tax paid on imports of goods by the trader; and
- tax paid on acquisitions of goods by the trader from elsewhere in the EC.

The goods or services concerned must be used by the trader for the purposes of his business activities. Tax incurred on private or business expenditure is not normally recoverable.

There is some leeway to reclaim input tax when goods are purchased and used for both business and non-business purposes. Details of the options may be found at 6-820.

There are some categories of input tax which can never be reclaimed. The most common of these are:

(1)   VAT paid on purchases of new cars for use in the business, but which are available for some (even very minimal) private use;

(2)   VAT paid on supplies used for the purposes of business entertainment; and

(3)   VAT included in the costs of goods sold to the trader under a second-hand goods margin scheme (there will not normally be a VAT invoice supplied with such purchases).

Input tax incurred in respect of exempt supplies is not normally reclaimable. Businesses that make taxable and exempt supplies are known as partially exempt. These businesses must comply with particular regulations when dealing with input tax recovery.

The trader is not entitled to input tax credit unless he holds proper evidence to support his claim. In the case of supplies received by the trader (including acquisitions of goods from elsewhere in the EC), the evidence required is a VAT invoice issued by the supplier. In the case of an importation of goods, the evidence is the VAT certificate, Form C79.

VAT Reporter: ¶150

2-230 Partial exemption

A trader who makes only exempt supplies cannot register for VAT, and so cannot obtain credit for input tax paid on his business expenses. A trader who makes only taxable supplies can reclaim all of his input tax (except that incurred on business entertaining, etc.).

Special rules are needed in the case of a trader who makes both taxable supplies and exempt supplies (referred to as a partially exempt trader), in order to prevent distortion of competition between him and a trader who makes similar exempt supplies but no taxable supplies.

In principle, a partially exempt trader can reclaim in full any input tax incurred in relation to the making of taxable supplies, and cannot reclaim any input tax incurred in relation to the making of his exempt supplies. Input tax paid on supplies used both for the purposes of his taxable supplies and for the purposes of his exempt supplies must be apportioned between the two activities, and only the part relating to the taxable supplies made can be reclaimed.

The initial input tax deduction for certain expenditure on land and buildings and on computer equipment must be reviewed by reference to the use of the assets over a review period of five or ten years (see 7-760).

The detailed application of these general rules, and the different ways of apportioning input tax between the types of activity, is a complex area covered in the 'Input Tax Recovery' division at 6-000ff.

2-260 Retail schemes

In principle, the VAT system relies upon traders issuing tax invoices for the supplies which they make. Copies of these are used as the prime accounting document in calculating the liability of a trader to account for output tax. The originals, when supplies are made to other registered traders, constitute the evidence required to substantiate a claim to deduct input tax.

Clearly it would be ridiculous to expect all retailers to issue tax invoices for all supplies made, however small. Because this would be impossible, special schemes are available to enable retailers to account for VAT without keeping a detailed record of each individual transaction.

Each retail scheme is based on a daily record of gross sales. The gross sales are recorded VAT inclusive. The gross sales at each rate of VAT are multiplied by the relevant VAT fraction to calculate the tax due.

Example: the VAT fraction

Harry only sells standard rated goods. His gross sales which include VAT at 20 per cent are £1,000. The VAT fraction when the standard rate is 20 per cent is $\frac{1}{6}$ or $\frac{20}{120}$ The tax included in Harry's sales of £1,000 is £166.66 (i.e. £1,000 multiplied by $\frac{1}{6}$).

Things become more complex where a retailer sells goods liable to tax at a number of different rates. The retailer must select one or other of the retail schemes which are available to him to work out his VAT liability. These schemes provide various ways of estimating how much of his takings represents supplies taxable at the standard rate. Some schemes work from a detailed record of purchases for resale, with or without adjustment for expected mark-ups. Another depends upon an analysis of takings at the point of sale, usually by the use of a multi-total till.

Detailed rules for each of the retail schemes are published by HMRC. Whichever scheme is in use, these rules must be followed accurately.

Retail schemes are covered in more detail at 16-000.

VAT Reporter: ¶1-100

2-290   Second-hand goods scheme

A special scheme is available for most goods traded between the business and private sectors, other than certain precious metals and gem stones. A dealer who has bought goods from a private individual (so cannot recover input tax on the purchase) can charge VAT, when he re-sells them, on the difference between the purchase price and the selling price.

The second-hand goods scheme is covered at 16-430ff.

VAT Reporter: ¶48-625

2-360   Review of the system for control and enforcement

VAT is administered by Her Majesty's Revenue and Customs.

The system of VAT registration is online. Businesses registering for VAT must complete and submit the relevant registration forms online.

Following registration, the trader is issued with a VAT Registration Certificate which states the VAT Registration number and indicates when the first VAT return is to be submitted. The VAT Central Unit will periodically issue VAT returns to the trader.

VAT returns with the related payment must be submitted online to HMRC by the end of the month following the accounting period concerned. Failure to submit returns – or related payments – on time makes the trader liable to incur a penalty. The trader is responsible for completing the returns correctly. See 9-370.

HMRC periodically check that a trader is dealing with VAT correctly. The checks are usually made by officers from a VAT office who may ask that a questionnaire be completed, inspect the books and records and may visit the business. See 9-660.

These officers visit the trader's premises to inspect the VAT records to satisfy themselves that VAT is being accounted for correctly. Such visits are referred to as assurance visits and may be combined with a visit to inspect other taxes. The intervals between assurance visits vary considerably, depending upon the size and type of business and the trader's own record of compliance (or non-compliance) with the VAT accounting requirements. Very large businesses are likely to have frequent visits, while smaller businesses may be visited only at intervals of several years. Visits can also be triggered by changes of pattern becoming apparent from the VAT returns submitted by the trader.

If an assurance visit reveals that the trader has under-declared his VAT liabilities, an assessment will normally be issued to collect the tax. The trader may also become liable to pay interest and penalties in respect of the under-declaration. Where under-declarations arise because of dishonesty on the part of the trader, rather than because of errors, penalties may be due either under the civil law or under criminal law. In the latter case, a dishonest trader may also be imprisoned.

VAT Reporter: ¶3-500

WHY VAT CAUSES PROBLEMS

2-430   General

Some of the main reasons why businesses find themselves with VAT problems – and often with large unexpected tax bills – are as follows:

- misunderstanding of concepts (2-460);
- disregard by decision makers (2-490);
- disregard by administrators (2-520);
- cumulative effect (2-550); and
- enforcement techniques (2-580).

It is worth giving brief consideration to each of these factors. The first is one which this publication specifically addresses; the next two illustrate the usefulness and importance of acquiring some understanding of VAT; and the last two give an indication of the growing importance of dealing correctly with VAT from the outset.

2-460   Misunderstanding of concepts

The concepts used in VAT are different from those of commerce and accounting, and from those of other taxes such as income tax and corporation tax (which at least bear some passing resemblance to commercial concepts). If VAT is thought of as a sales tax then it will be difficult to understand its concepts and will lead to risk in business dealings.

VAT is not a tax on profits or on income. It rarely distinguishes between transactions of a capital nature and those of a revenue nature. And it is not, in principle, a tax on sales. It affects organisations which seek to make a profit (such as trading companies), and those which do not (such as charities), without distinction.

The basic concept of VAT is that of 'supply', and this concept is unique to VAT.

VAT Reporter: ¶5-650

2-490   Disregard by decision makers

There is a tendency to regard VAT as a fact of life about which nothing can be done. As a result, the men and women who make the decisions affecting the operation of a business frequently ignore VAT in reaching their decisions. It is assumed that any VAT aspects will automatically work their way through, and that commercial decisions are 'VAT-neutral'. In fact, this is often not the case, and the cost of ignoring VAT can be very large.

Many decision makers are accustomed to considering or taking advice on the direct tax consequences of their decisions, but do not treat VAT in the same way. This is a pity, since the VAT at stake can often be much greater than any income tax or corporation tax involved.

Decision makers who ignore direct taxes are often rescued from the tax consequences by the ability of their tax advisers to neutralise any damage by the judicious use of various claims and elections which can be made after the event. For VAT, this is rarely possible, and the VAT aspects need to be considered in advance. This means that VAT, much more than other taxes, needs to be brought into the ordinary business planning process.

Another unusual aspect of VAT is that it directly affects the relationships between the parties to commercial contracts. For most taxes, it is only relations between each party and the revenue authorities which are affected by the tax legislation.

> **Example:**
>
> Harry contracts to sell goods to Agnes for £8,000. The contract does not mention VAT. The VAT law provides that, where a supply is made for a consideration in money, the price includes VAT. Thus, Harry must account for VAT at 20 per cent out of the £8,000 which he receives from Agnes. This will cost him £1,333.33 (being $\frac{1}{6}$ of £8,000).
>
> If Harry had thought about VAT, he might have contracted to supply the goods for £8,000 plus VAT. Then, he would have received £9,600 from Agnes and would have had £8,000 left after paying £1,600 of VAT (VAT at 20 per cent).

2-520 Disregard by administrators

Because VAT is a tax levied on individual transactions, compliance with the VAT legislation requires that the accounting and bookkeeping systems of each business cope correctly with VAT from the level of individual transactions. This has an interesting, but harmful, effect on the way in which VAT is perceived.

Book-keeping functions are traditionally carried out by relatively low grade staff. It is the matters resulting from the assembly of the detailed information, such as appraising the performance of the business or ascertaining the residual profits liable to direct taxes, which tend to be dealt with by highly trained staff. The nature of VAT is such that much of the administration relating to it must be carried out by the junior staff who do the routine bookkeeping. This often results in the tax itself being regarded as a simple and straightforward matter, of no concern to senior administrative staff. Consequences which flow from this are:

(1) this perception of VAT transmits itself to the people making the decisions for the business;

(2) because the tax is thought to be straightforward, the book-keeping staff may not receive adequate training, either in dealing with routine compliance matters or in identifying occasions when special attention is needed;

(3) no senior member of staff takes specific responsibility for monitoring the overall VAT position of the business, or for advising the decision makers on the VAT aspects of proposed actions; and

(4) because there is no real monitoring of the VAT position by senior administrators, mistreatments of routine transactions may continue for years and build up into substantial unexpected liabilities.

Although these matters are couched in terms of a large business, with several levels of staff, they apply in much the same way to small businesses. In these cases, much of the accounting function may be carried out by an outside firm of accountants, but again it is common for much of the VAT work to be carried out by junior staff.

VAT Reporter: ¶101

2-550 Cumulative effect

Most businesses make large numbers of similar transactions. If a quantity of article X is sold today, a further quantity of article X will be sold tomorrow. Usually, the VAT treatment will not be reconsidered on each sale. Whatever treatment was adopted for the first one is likely to be followed for all the subsequent sales.

The effect of this is that, if the first sale was treated wrongly, this initial mistake will automatically be carried through to all of the future sales. Eventually, it will be discovered (usually by HMRC). When this happens, the initial mistake on what was probably a minor transaction may have accumulated into a major liability.

There are many occasions when the VAT treatment of a transaction is far from clear. Carrying on business without checking and confirming the VAT treatment is as absurd as ordering components without first finding out the price of them. But it is often done.

VAT Reporter: ¶101

2-580 Enforcement techniques

The differences between the nature of VAT and of other taxes lead inevitably to differences in the way it is enforced.

VAT is levied at the level of individual transactions. It is self-assessed. Reliefs from VAT are to some extent based on documentation received from other businesses. It is also structured in such a way that there are opportunities for individuals to extract money from the tax authorities, and the criminal fraternity have shown no reluctance to avail themselves of these opportunities. Because of these factors, the tax authorities take a far keener interest in the detailed documentation relating to transactions (such as invoices) than is traditional for direct taxes.

VAT officers visit the premises of the business from time to time, or ask for the books and records of the business to be sent to them, in order that they may examine the detailed records of the business to verify the liability as shown on the returns. The frequency of such assurance visits varies depending on the nature and size of the business. A very small business may not have a visit for several years, while very large businesses can have VAT officers on the premises for most of the time. Long intervals between visits can pose a problem for small businesses. Such businesses generally have fewer resources to cope with the complexities of VAT, so there can be several years' worth of errors to be corrected following a visit (subject to the four year cap on errors). There is also a natural tendency to take the benefit of the doubt when preparing VAT returns. When the VAT officer finds that there is no doubt, and that tax is due, a hefty liability has often accumulated as a result of a succession of small errors.

This does not mean that large businesses obtain any special protection from the frequency of visits made to them. An assurance visit does not in itself give rise to any agreement of liability. So, errors missed at one visit may be picked up at a subsequent one.

As with all taxes, there are a series of penalties in place for businesses that fail to register at the correct time, make errors on returns, fail to pay tax which is due or similar. Failure to comply with the VAT legislation is very costly.

VAT Reporter: ¶57-800

SOURCES OF LAW AND PRACTICE

2-650   Legislation: statutes and directives

The main VAT legislation is contained in VATA 1994. In addition, there is a large body of statutory instruments made under powers contained in the Value Added Tax Act and other statutes. In some areas, and particularly concerning imports of goods, customs and excise legislation (such as the *Customs and Excise Management Act* 1979) has effect for VAT purposes.

The UK law on VAT derives from EC law, notably the sixth directive on VAT. Under the Treaty of Rome, the Government is obliged to enact the UK law in such a way as to implement the provisions contained in the European directives and regulations. Consequently, it is sometimes possible to refer to the EC legislation for guidance on the interpretation of the UK law. Furthermore, if the UK law fails to implement the EC law, the citizen is entitled to rely on the EC law where it has direct effect in the UK.

January 2007

The First and the Sixth VAT Directives have been replaced by a new revised EC VAT Directive which came into effect on 1 January 2007. It does not change current EC or UK law.

The Sixth VAT Directive was amended 31 times and this new Directive is a re-write taking into account the amendments made. It is claimed that the new form is clearer and set out in a more logical and coherent way in order to make the law more accessible to businesses, tax professionals and officials.

All UK law that refers to either the First or the Sixth VAT Directive will be construed as references to the new Directive. In order to help with this, a table has been annexed to the new Directive which correlates the old and new references.

The new Directive can be found at *http://eur-lex.europa.eu* following the directions for access to European law.

Legislation: Directive 77/388 of 17 May 1977 (OJ 1977 L145/1); Directive 2006/112 was adopted on 28 November 2006 and came into force on 1 January 2007

Other material: Business Brief 22/06, 11 December 2006

VAT Reporter: ¶2-000

2-680   Finance and Tax Tribunal

When a dispute arises between a trader and HMRC, the trader may appeal to a tribunal. The decisions are on the public record. These provide important guidance as to the effects of the legislation. Some of these cases have been the subject of appeal to the higher courts in the UK, and also of referrals to the European Court of Justice, providing further guidance. In addition, decisions of the European Court of Justice on matters referred to it from other Member States can be of relevance.

The contact details are at 1-737.

www.financeandtaxtribunals.gov.uk

VAT Reporter: ¶61-300

Adjudicator investigates complaints

HMRC appointed an external adjudicator to investigate complaints made against them. The adjudicator is not part of HMRC's management structure. Certain complaints can be referred to the adjudicator's office without charge. The office can investigate complaints about the way HMRC deal with cases, including where HMRC have exercised their discretionary power, for example, requests for time to pay. The adjudicator also considers complaints about attitude, incompetence, errors and delays.

Excluded matters

The adjudicator does not usually consider:

(1)   appeals about matters of VAT law and liability, and thus cases which are appealable to a tribunal are outside the adjudicator's remit;

(2)   cases once they are before the criminal courts, although the adjudicator can consider any matters raised subsequently which could not have been considered by the courts; and

(3)   complaints which have been investigated by the Parliamentary Ombudsman.

Official publication

The publication AO1 'The Adjudicator' concerns the adjudicator's role and how complaints are dealt with.

VAT Reporter: ¶61-105

2-710   HMRC publications

HMRC have issued numerous notices on matters relating to VAT. In general, these notices and leaflets provide a useful explanation of the views of HMRC. In some parts, they go further than this and actually have the effect of law. Particular examples of this are the parts of Notice

700 ('The VAT guide') which relate to the records to be retained by traders, and the booklets concerning retail schemes and second-hand goods schemes.

As well as describing the views of HMRC, these publications sometimes describe concessions which are available to traders.

The notices published by HMRC are available to traders free of charge. As new and revised versions are issued, these are listed in a leaflet called 'VAT notes' which is generally published about twice a year and issued to all registered traders with their VAT returns. It is a good idea for traders to obtain copies of those publications which are, or may be, relevant to their businesses and of updated copies when these are issued.

Other useful sources of information are the news releases and business briefs published by HMRC, and notes published by professional bodies on matters agreed with HMRC.

HMRC's publications may be obtained from the National Advice Service or by accessing the website at *www.hmrc.gov.uk*.

VAT Reporter: ¶4-200

2-720   Set-off across other taxes

HMRC are formally empowered to set off repayments against outstanding debts within tax systems.

This procedure does not need the permission of the taxpayer but HMRC will inform the taxpayer in writing what has been done.

HMRC admit that the main impact of this is felt in the setting-off of some indirect tax repayments against direct tax debts.

Although there is no formal appeal against this procedure, HMRC state that they consider the situation where a taxpayer has specific concerns.

Other information: *www.hmrc.gov.uk/finance-bill/set-off-taxes.htm*

Supplies by Business

VAT ON SUPPLIES BY THE BUSINESS

3-000   Liability to VAT: general

This section is mainly concerned with the rules for determining whether you are liable to pay value added tax (VAT) to HMRC. As VAT is in principle a tax on supplies, this generally means that a person has to account for VAT when he makes supplies. There are other occasions when VAT becomes due, and these are also covered in the following two sections.

The main technical areas covered in this section are:

*   when VAT is chargeable on supplies (and what is a supply);
*   who is a taxable person;
*   the rules on registration;
*   the meaning of 'business' for VAT purposes;
*   goods and services;
*   place of supply;
*   time of supply; and
*   value of supply.

Most of the matters covered here are also of importance in other areas of VAT (such as whether tax can be reclaimed from HMRC), so it is important to study this section carefully.

VAT Reporter: ¶10-000

3-040   When VAT is chargeable

United Kingdom VAT is intended to be charged on the consumption of goods or of services within the UK, but is generally levied on the supplier of those goods or services rather than directly on the consumer. Because the tax is generally accounted for by suppliers, rather than the consumers who are ultimately intended to bear it, there are several occasions of charge. This is to prevent consumers from avoiding the tax by, for instance, obtaining taxable supplies from overseas suppliers.

The main occasions on which VAT is chargeable are illustrated in the flowchart at 4-880. The charge on supplies of goods or of services made within the UK (including certain imports of services) is covered in this section. The charge on imports of goods into the UK from outside the EC is covered at 5-040ff., and the charge on acquisitions of goods from elsewhere in the EC is dealt with at 5-320ff.

Some businesses may become liable to account for VAT on supplies which they are deemed to make to themselves (see 3-200). Some businesses may become liable to account for VAT in other EC States.

VAT Reporter: ¶10-001

3-080   VAT on UK supplies

The main charge to VAT in the UK is on supplies made in the UK. As far as the law is concerned, this charging of VAT arises from a single sentence of law, and all of the other complexities of VAT flow from this one sentence. Although this publication is mainly concerned with explaining the law, rather than quoting it, this particular provision is so important that it is well worth looking at the words used in the law. The charging provision in VATA 1994, s. 4(1) reads as follows:

> 'VAT shall be charged on any supply of goods or services made in the United Kingdom, where it is a taxable supply made by a taxable person in the course or furtherance of any business carried on by him.'

Five tests for chargeability

Close examination of this provision reveals that there are five tests, all of which must be met before VAT becomes due. These are:

(1)   there must be a supply (either of goods or of services);

(2)   the supply must be made in the UK rather than elsewhere;

(3)   the supply must be a taxable supply;

(4)   the supply must be made by a taxable person, rather than by some other kind of person; and

(5)   the supply must be made in the course or furtherance of a business carried on by the taxable person who makes the supply.

Zero-rating

It is convenient to consider the question of zero-rating at the same time, although it is not strictly concerned with whether tax is chargeable or not. Tax is chargeable on a zero-rated supply (if the other tests are met) but the rate is zero per cent, so the amount of the tax is nil.

Terminology

This charging provision contained in VATA 1994, s. 4(1) gives some interesting insight into the way law is constructed, and into the way in which this publication (which seeks to explain the law) has to be constructed. The sentence in itself is fairly easy to read and, in a sense, to understand. However, it is unlikely that anyone who has merely read and understood that sentence in isolation will be able to look at transactions which occur and say with confidence which of them give rise to VAT liability and which do not. This is because the sentence

16

uses a number of specialised terms, and the full meaning of it is not clear without a proper understanding of these terms. The terms are:

(1)   supply;

(2)   goods;

(3)   services;

(4)   United Kingdom (and, by implication, a means of telling whether things take place inside or outside the UK for VAT purposes is needed);

(5)   taxable (supply);

(6)   taxable person; and

(7)   business.

This section is largely devoted to explaining these terms, and how they fit into the framework of VAT. It also addresses some additional matters, such as when tax becomes chargeable, the amount of tax, and the rates of VAT which can apply.

It is necessary to deal with each piece of terminology separately, but if the main charging provision quoted above is borne in mind, it should be possible to keep the terms sufficiently in context to understand the implications of the matters discussed. If things do not slot into place easily, it is a good idea to skim the section, then re-read it in more detail.

Second-hand goods

Commentary on the second-hand goods scheme, e.g. for certain second-hand motor cars, is at 16-430.

VAT Reporter: ¶10-001

Legislation: VATA 1994, s. 4(1)

SUPPLY

3-120   The meaning of supply

As indicated above, VAT is primarily a tax on supplies.

The UK law does not give a precise definition of the term 'supply', but states that it includes all forms of supply. Things done for no consideration are not supplies, unless there is specific provision within the law to class them as supplies. Anything done for consideration constitutes a supply.

It is apparent from this that:

(1)   anything which is done for a consideration is a supply for VAT purposes; and

17

(2)   anything which is not done for a consideration is not a supply unless the law specifically states that it is a supply.

In fact, the law does specify that a transfer of the property in goods, or of their possession, constitutes a supply. It follows that, where goods are provided, a supply arises whether or not there is consideration; only services can be provided for no consideration without a supply arising.

There are other occasions when a supply is deemed to arise (e.g. de-registration, certain self-supplies). The outline for the meaning of supply is given in the flowchart at 4-890, and the detailed points are discussed below.

Legislation: VATA 1994, s. 5(2)(a), (b); and Sch. 4, para. 1

VAT Reporter: ¶10-010

3-140   Consideration

(1) Meaning of consideration

The term 'consideration' has long been used in UK law, particularly with reference to contract law. However, the UK law on VAT derives from EC law, and particularly the EC directive 2006/112 on VAT. The UK courts are, therefore, obliged to construe the UK legislation so as to give effect to the directive, if that is possible.

Although 'consideration' is not defined in this directive, a definition was given in the second directive (67/228) as follows:

> 'The expression "consideration" means everything received in return for the supply of goods or the provision of services, including incidental expenses (packing, transport, insurance, etc.) that is to say not only the cash amount charged, but also, for example, the value of the goods received in exchange or, in the case of goods or services supplied by order of a public authority, the amount of the compensation received.'

In *C & E Commrs v Apple & Pear Development Council*, the House of Lords considered that the intended scope of VAT was set by the Sixth Directive but that there was no clear authority in European law on the meaning of consideration, and reference was made to the European Court of Justice for guidance on this point. The House of Lords noted the definition of consideration given in the second directive, and presumed that the term had the same meaning when used in the Sixth Directive. The Advocate General also made reference to the second directive in analysing the meaning of consideration for VAT purposes. The European Court considered that there must be a direct link between the supply made and the consideration received if there is to be consideration in the VAT sense. It has also been held that consideration for VAT purposes must be capable of being expressed in money.

A good rule of thumb is to regard consideration as meaning anything (not only money) provided in exchange for something else, where the one is conditional on the other.

Example: consideration

Jack is a window cleaner. He cleans Edna's windows for £5. He cleans George's windows on condition that George (who is a carpenter) repairs his ladder. He cleans Lucy's windows free of charge, because Lucy is unwell and Jack wants to help out. Lucy is grateful for Jack's help and gives him a new sponge.

Clearly Jack cleaned Edna's windows for consideration, being the fee of £5.

He cleaned George's windows for consideration too, the consideration being George's work on Jack's ladder. By the same token, George mended Jack's ladder for consideration in the form of Jack cleaning George's windows. Thus, there are two supplies for consideration in this instance, one by Jack and one by George.

Jack did not receive any consideration for cleaning Lucy's windows. Although Lucy gave him a sponge (and presumably regarded it as a quid pro quo for the cleaning of the windows), she was under no obligation to do this. The cleaning of the windows in this case was done freely, as was the giving of the sponge. Since Jack was providing services, rather than goods, and there was no consideration, his action did not amount to a supply for VAT purposes.

It should be noted that in practice, where something is done freely but a quid pro quo is received, it may often be difficult to prove that the one is not consideration for the other.

It is also interesting to note that, while Jack has not made a supply to Lucy, Lucy has made a supply to Jack in giving him the sponge, since the transfer of the property in goods (in this case, the sponge) is a supply. In practice, it is likely that no VAT will be due, either because her supply is not made in the course of a business or because it falls into the exclusion for small business gifts. Both of these aspects are covered later in this section.

While the 'anything in exchange' concept gives a good rule of thumb, it cannot be regarded as a complete expression of the law. The exact meaning of consideration is not entirely clear, and continues to be a matter of debate.

HMRC have emphasised that, where services are supplied in consideration for other services, this gives rise to supplies in each direction.

Cases: *C & E Commrs v Apple & Pear Development Council* (1986) 2 BVC 200,198; *Staatssecretaris van Financiën v Coöperatieve Aardappelenbewaarplaats GA* [1981] ECR 445; *Edinburgh Leisure, South Lanarkshire Leisure and Renfrewshire Leisure* [2005] BVC 2,146

Other material: Notice 700, para. 8.7, Barter and part-exchange

VAT Reporter: ¶10-985

Legislation: Directive 2006/112, art. 72 et seq

Supplies by Business

(2) Cases on concept of 'anything in exchange'

Apple & Pear Development Council

The most important cases on the point have been dealt with by the European Court of Justice. In one, the *Apple & Pear Development Council* case referred to above, the question was whether levies made on fruit growers by a body empowered by statute to make such levies amounted to consideration for the activities which it carries on. The court held that there was insufficient link between the levies and benefits accruing directly to particular growers for the levies to be regarded as consideration for supplies. It should be noted, however, that various levies in the agricultural sector, such as Meat and Livestock Commission levies, are now regarded by HMRC as representing consideration for taxable supplies.

Naturally Yours Cosmetics Ltd

Another case, that of *Naturally Yours Cosmetics Ltd v C & E Commrs*, concerned supplies of cosmetics under a party plan arrangement. The company made its supplies via self-employed beauty consultants, to whom it sold its wares. The consultants arranged for members of the public to hold parties at their homes, at which the cosmetics were sold. In order to induce people to hold parties, the consultants offered them a commission on sales made plus a 'gift' of a jar of cosmetic cream. The cream was normally sold to consultants for about £10, but the price was reduced to about £2 where it was required as a gift to a hostess.

The point at issue in this case was whether the consultant's promise, to use a jar of cream bought as a 'hostess gift' as an inducement to a member of the public to hold a party, amounted to further consideration for the supply on top of the £2 cash consideration paid by the consultant. The tribunal considered that, under UK law alone, it would be additional consideration. However, the tribunal was not convinced that it would be consideration in the sense meant by the EC law, and referred the matter to the European Court for guidance.

The European Court held that there was a direct link between the jar of cream and the consultant's procurement of a hostess to hold a party, and that this consideration could be expressed in money.

This decision was essentially followed in *Rosgill Group Ltd v C & E Commrs*.

Boots Co Plc

A later reference to the European Court was that in *Boots Co Plc v C & E Commrs*. The court held that certain items specified in art. 11A, para. 2 of the Sixth Directive are to be treated as part of the consideration for a supply, while others specified in para. 3 of the same article are to be excluded from the consideration. These inclusions and exclusions are specified in the law, and apply whether or not the items concerned would fall to be treated as consideration according to the natural meaning of the term. In the *Boots* case, certain vouchers were seen by the court as merely evidencing entitlement to discounts. Since price discounts accounted for at the time of supply are specifically excluded from the definition of consideration by para. 3, the handing over of the vouchers was not to be included in the consideration for supplies made by the appellant company.

An important point to bear in mind concerning consideration is that it will not necessarily be received from the person to whom the supply is made. Thus, if something is provided to party A, and payment is received from party B, there is still a supply for VAT purposes even though no consideration is received from the person to whom the supply is made.

> **Example: consideration from third party**
>
> Phoebe is a solicitor. She agrees to carry out certain legal work for Thomas, and this is to be paid for by Peter. Carrying out the work for Thomas amounts to a supply for VAT purposes, even though Phoebe receives no consideration from Thomas. Under the terms of the agreement, she is to be paid by Peter, and this amounts to consideration, even though Phoebe provides no service to Peter.

Empire Stores Ltd

Another case which has been referred to the European Court of Justice is *Empire Stores Ltd v C & E Commrs*. The circumstances in this case were similar to those of the *GUS Merchandise Corporation Ltd* case referred to at (3) below. The appellant argued, on the basis of the EC law, that 'gifts' provided to customers placing their first orders were not made for consideration in the form of the placing of the order, but that the price of the goods ordered was consideration both for the goods ordered and for the 'gift' goods.

The court ruled that the 'gifts' were supplied for consideration, and that the value of the supply was the cost to the company of buying the goods, this being the amount which it was prepared to lay out to obtain the new customers. Where it was necessary to attribute a value to the consideration received, this should be a subjective value in the eyes of the person receiving the consideration.

Tolsma v Inspecteur der Omzetbelasting, Leeuwarden

Tolsma v Inspecteur der Omzetbelasting, Leeuwarden concerns street musicians, and the question referred was whether they are to be regarded as supplying services for consideration. There was a supplementary question, asking whether this was affected by the fact that the payments received by such musicians from the public were not required to be made, but were solicited and could be expected to be made, although the amount of them could not be quantified in advance.

The court found that the payments were not consideration for supplies. Although they might indicate that the members of the public making them had enjoyed the music, they had not requested it nor were they under any obligation to make the payments. This decision will provide comfort for those who seek donations in the course of fund-raising events (e.g. admission £2, donation of a further £8 requested but not compulsory).

Supplies by Business

21

Tron Theatre Ltd

In *C & E Commrs v Tron Theatre Ltd*, the Court of Session overturned a tribunal decision on the treatment of payments which included a significant donation element. A theatre seeking funds to refurbish its seating invited subscriptions from the public, offering in return certain benefits (such as a brass plaque on a seat) which were acknowledged to be of minimal value. The tribunal had held that, given that the benefits were of such low value, the payments could be apportioned under what is now VATA 1994, s. 19(4), so that tax was only payable on the amount referable to the supplies.

The court found that the whole of the amount paid was consideration for the supplies. Accordingly, the whole amount was subject to tax. The key point was that the theatre was not prepared to accept any lesser payment, so the whole payment must be regarded as consideration in money, and the VAT treatment then followed. This should be distinguished from the position when payments are voluntary, as in *Tolsma* (above).

Thorn Plc

In *Thorn Plc ('Mobile Phones')*, the appellant (via its Radio Rentals subsidiary) supplied mobile phones to existing customers under a special business promotion scheme. Under the terms of the scheme, a customer in possession of a voucher relating to the scheme could obtain a 'free' mobile phone by signing a 12-month airtime agreement with Vodafone. Each voucher issued had a stated value of 0.0001p, so that no monetary value could be attributed to the vouchers. The phones cost Thorn £190 (plus VAT) each. Under a separate agreement with a Vodafone company, Thorn was entitled to a bonus of £190 for each Thorn customer connected (reduced for disconnections within three months due to fraud or deception). Thorn was also entitled to additional payments relating to call charges for handsets supplied by it, plus an extra £700,000 if it effected more than 100,000 connections under the scheme by a specified date.

HMRC took the view that Thorn supplied the handsets to customers for no consideration, and assessed for output tax of £495,125 based on the cost of the phones to Thorn. Thorn appealed.

The tribunal found that Thorn did not supply the phones otherwise than for consideration (mentioning that it could safely conclude that this was not a case of Thorn distributing Christmas presents to its customers). It received consideration from the customer, in the form of the customer's signing up to an airtime agreement with Vodafone, and from Vodafone in the form of its payments of money. Because of the agreement between Thorn and Vodafone, and the related agreement between Thorn and the customer (entered into when the customer took up Thorn's offer) there was a contractual link between Thorn's supply of the phone and Vodafone's payment to Thorn. The tribunal concluded that the assessment, based as it was on the notion that Thorn supplied the phones otherwise than for consideration, was bad and, therefore, allowed the appeal.

Legislation: VATA 1994, s. 19(2), (4); Sch. 4, para. 5(1); Sch. 6, para. 6(2)

Cases: *C & E Commrs v Apple & Pear Development Council* (1986) 2 BVC 200,198; *Naturally Yours Cosmetics Ltd v C & E Commrs* (1988) 3 BVC 428; *Rosgill Group Ltd v C & E Commrs* [1997] BVC 388; *Boots Co Plc v C & E Commrs* (1990) 5 BVC 21; *Empire Stores Ltd v C & E Commrs* (Case C-33/93) [1994] BVC 253; *Tolsma v Inspecteur der Omzetbelasting, Leeuwarden* (Case C-16/93) [1994] BVC 117; *C & E Commrs v Tron Theatre Ltd* [1994] BVC 14; *Thorn Plc ('Mobile Phones')* [1998] BVC 2,090

VAT Reporter: ¶10-780

(3) Caveat

The main thing which the business manager who is not a VAT specialist needs to bear in mind is the potentially wide meaning of 'consideration'. It is often assumed that any VAT liability will be picked up by the ordinary accounting systems of the business. This may often be the case; however, it can be seen that transactions which might not ordinarily enter the accounting systems (as no invoice would be generated) can readily give rise to VAT liability. Managers need to be aware of 'hidden' consideration, and preferably to take account of it when projects are being planned.

Particular care needs to be taken where commercial terminology is used which conceals the true nature of what is happening. This applies particularly where marketing activities are carried on which involve offers of 'gifts' or 'prizes' which are not really free, but have to be earned in some way. Frequently, there is consideration for the provision of the 'gift' or 'prize', and this can affect the VAT position.

An example of this arose in *GUS Merchandise Corporation Ltd v C & E Commrs*. The appellant promised a 'free gift' to anyone who was appointed as one of its agents on the occasion of the first order placed. It was held that the placing of the order (without which the gift would not be made) amounted to 'consideration' for the gift. This view is supported by the decision in *Empire Stores* (see above), although the value placed on the consideration was lower than in *GUS* (which is now superseded on the question of value).

The 'anything in exchange' concept referred to above will provide a useful way of spotting potential supplies. As indicated, it should not be relied upon to produce an infallible answer in all cases. The best plan is to use it to spot transactions which might give problems, and to seek expert advice on borderline cases.

Another point worthy of note is that, while the receipt of money will often indicate that consideration is being received for a supply made, there are a number of occasions when money may be received without being consideration, and without there being a supply. A number of these are considered at 3-280 below.

Cases: *GUS Merchandise Corporation Ltd v C & E Commrs* (1981) 1 BVC 432

VAT Reporter: ¶10-987

3-160 Specified supplies

The law specifically states that some transactions are to be treated as supplies for VAT purposes, whether or not there is consideration present, and these are indicated in the flowchart at 4-890.

These are:

(1) the transfer or disposal of goods which are business assets (made under the directions of the person carrying on that business) so that they are no longer assets of the business, unless they are excepted from this as being small gifts or gifts of industrial samples (see below). This includes, in the case of a sole trader business, the transfer of the goods to the sole proprietor in his personal capacity;

(2) the use for non-business purposes of goods which are business assets and in respect of which input tax has previously been recovered. In the case of a sole trader business, this includes use for the personal purposes of the sole proprietor. For more details, see 6-820. This charge covers a change of use of services on which there has been full recovery of input tax; and

(3) when a person ceases to be registered for VAT, any goods remaining on hand are deemed to be supplied at that point unless it can be shown that tax has not been reclaimed on their acquisition, or that the total tax involved is below £1,000.

It should be noted that, in applying these rules, land is specifically treated as being goods. This becomes especially important when the option for taxation has been exercised (see 15-300).

The legislation deems the gift or private use of goods to be a supply only where VAT on the goods concerned (or their component parts) was wholly or partly deductible by the supplier (or, in the case of goods obtained VAT-free under a transfer of a going concern, by a predecessor of the supplier).

Legislation: VATA 1994, Sch. 4, para. 8 and 9; *Value Added Tax (Supply of Services) Order 1993 (SI 1993/1507)*

(1) Small gifts

Although there is normally a supply if goods which are business assets are transferred so as no longer to form part of the assets of the business, this does not apply if a gift is made in the course of the business and the cost of the goods to the business was less than £50. If the gift forms part of a series, there is a supply even if the cost of the gift was less than £50. A gift forming part of a series is not treated as a supply, provided that the total cost of gifts to the same person does not exceed £50 in any 12-month period.

The ECJ have ruled that gifts are not given to the same person when given to different employees of the same firm.

It should be noted that this relief only applies to genuine gifts. As indicated earlier, there are many occasions where items are described as gifts but, in fact, they are provided in return for consideration. Where goods have been obtained following a transfer of a going concern (or a series of such transfers), the cost for this purpose is taken as being the cost to the predecessor who originally bought or produced the goods.

Legislation: VATA 1994, Sch. 4, para. 5

(2) Gifts of samples

A gift of a sample is not treated as a supply. The UK operated a restriction that, if more than one identical item was given to the same recipient, the relief was restricted to the first item. In 2010 the ECJ ruled that this was not allowable. Following the ruling HMRC announced that they would accept claims for tax that had been wrongly accounted for. The legislation changes were included in the Finance Bill 2011.

Legislation: Directive 2006/112 art. 16; VATA 1994, Sch. 4, para. 5(2)(b)

Cases: *EMI Group v HMRC* (Case C-581/08)

Other material: Revenue and Customs Brief 51/10 VAT – change in treatment of business samples

VAT Reporter: ¶13-855

3-180 Supply by another

There is another occasion when a person can be treated as making a supply, without actually making a supply. If a receiver is appointed over assets of a business, then any supplies of goods made by the receiver are treated as if they had been made by the person carrying on the business. In this case, the receiver is liable to account directly to HMRC for the tax due, although the VAT continues to be shown on the trader's return.

This is in contrast to the position where a receiver is appointed over the whole of a company's assets. In this case, the company is regarded as having become incapacitated, and it is for the receiver to make returns and payments of tax currently due on behalf of the company.

Legislation: VATA 1994, s. 46(4); VATA 1994, Sch. 4, para. 7; *Value Added Tax Regulations 1995* (SI 1995/2518), reg. 27, 9 and 30

VAT Reporter: ¶13-935

3-200 Self-supplies

In some circumstances, a business can be treated as making supplies to itself. This arises in certain cases specified in statutory instruments, in certain cases relating to land, and in other instances shown in the flowchart at 4-890. In these cases, the business must account for tax on the self-supply, but can then treat it as input tax as if the supply had been obtained from another trader. This might seem self-defeating, in that the tax would simply appear on both sides of the VAT return and cancel out. In fact, the occasions when self-supplies arise are such that the trader will generally be unable to recover some, or all, of the tax arising.

(1) Self-supply of motor car

In the normal course of events, a business cannot recover VAT charged to it on the purchase of a motor car for business use. However, tax charged on the purchase of a vehicle which is not a motor car is deductible, as is tax on the purchase of car parts. A way of avoiding the incidence of non-deductible input tax would therefore be to buy, say, a van and convert it into a motor car, or to buy parts for a motor car and assemble them.

In order to prevent this, the law provides that a self-supply arises if:

(1) a business produces a car for its own use otherwise than by converting some other vehicle into a car;

(2) a business converts an existing vehicle into a car, having been charged tax on the acquisition of the vehicle and been able to recover that tax; or

(3) a business has recovered tax on the acquisition of a car because it is to be put to a qualifying use (as a taxi, driving instruction car or self-drive hire car, or for letting for such use; see 4-380) and it ceases to be put to such use.

The effect is that the business must account for output tax on the self-supply, but will generally be unable to recover it as input tax.

If a person (such as a garage) purchases a new motor car for resale, the tax on the purchase is deductible as input tax. In many cases, cars will be bought for resale, but then appropriated for use in the business (e.g. as a demonstrator, or as a staff car). When this happens, a self-supply arises.

Legislation: *Value Added Tax (Cars) Order* 1992 (SI 1992/3122), art. 5

VAT Reporter: ¶13-040

(2) Self-supply of residential or charitable building

A self-supply occurs when zero-rating under VATA 1994, Sch. 8, Grp. 5 has been obtained on the purchase or construction of a building for relevant residential or charitable use and, within 10 years, the building is put to non-qualifying use. This is covered in the flowchart at 4-900.

With effect from 21 March 2007, HMRC will not always enforce this self-supply charge. It will not be enforced when a charity relied on extra statutory concession 3.29 to obtain zero-rating AND the change of use which otherwise would trigger the self-supply charge was not anticipated at the time the building was zero-rated.

Interestingly, this self-supply charge does not apply when zero-rating has been obtained for a listed residential or charitable building under the similar zero-rating provisions of the VATA 1994, Sch. 8, Grp. 6.

There is no self-supply on the sale of a residential or charitable building within 10 years for non-qualifying use. Instead, the actual supply is standard-rated.

Legislation: VATA 1994, Sch. 10, Part 2

VAT Reporter: ¶36-025

Other material: HM Revenue and Customs Brief 29/07; VAT Information Sheet 04/11; Notice 708, Section 19

(3) Self-supply of construction services

Another occasion when a self-supply can arise concerns construction services. This is covered in the flowchart at 4-910.

The self-supply arises if works of construction of a new building or civil engineering work, or extension, etc. work such that the floor area is increased by 10 per cent or more, are carried out by a business without using outside contractors. If the value of the works is £100,000 or more, and they would have been positive-rated if bought in, a self-supply arises.

Legislation: *Value Added Tax (Self-supply of Construction Services) Order* 1989 (SI 1989/472)

VAT Reporter: ¶36-052

(4) Self-supply on acquisition of business by group

The next head of self-supply is outlined in the flowchart at 4-920.

The self-supply arises where a business is transferred, as a going concern, to a VAT group of companies, and is intended to counter certain planning techniques which were previously available.

If the group is partially exempt either during the prescribed accounting period (i.e. VAT return period) in which the supply takes place, or in the 'longer period' (see 6-950ff.) which includes it, then a self-supply takes place. However, there is no self-supply if it can be shown that all of the assets transferred were acquired by the transferor more than three years before the transfer.

Legislation: VATA 1994, s. 44

VAT Reporter: ¶13-150

Supplies by Business

3-210　Movement of own goods to another EC State

If goods are transferred within the same legal entity to another Member State for business purposes, there is a deemed supply of goods for VAT purposes. There is no such supply if the goods are temporarily removed for repair and return, for temporary use to provide a service, or for temporary use qualifying for a temporary importation relief.

For information regarding the time of supply and conditions applying to removal of goods from the UK, see 4-480.

There may be a requirement to register for VAT in the Member State of destination of the goods in order to account for VAT on the acquisition of the goods and, if necessary, to account for VAT on any onward supply. Registering for VAT will also enable a business to use its VAT-registration number in the other Member State to secure zero-rating of the goods when they leave the UK.

Example

A VAT-registered business in the UK transferring goods to its Italian branch is deemed to be making a supply of goods. The UK business may be required to register for VAT in Italy to account for acquisition tax on receipt of the goods.

If the business registers for VAT in Italy, the Italian VAT number may be used to transfer subsequent goods from the UK to the Italian branch at the zero-rate. The Italian branch will account for acquisition tax on receipt of the goods. Any onward supplies of the goods within Italy will be subject to Italian VAT.

Legislation: VATA 1994, Sch. 4, para. 6; *Value Added Tax (Removal of Goods) Order* 1992 (SI 1992/3111)

VAT Reporter: ¶63-220

Other material: *www.hmrc.gov.uk/vat/int-exports.htm*

3-220　Reverse charge supplies

In some instances where a supply of services is made, it is treated as if it had been made by the customer rather than by the person who really made the supply (the 'reverse charge'). The effect is that the customer (if registrable for VAT) must account for output tax on the supply and can treat the same amount as input tax. The input tax may, or may not, be deductible in full depending on the use to which the supplies are put.

Reverse charge supplies also count when considering whether the taxable turnover of the person carrying on the business exceeds the VAT turnover limits, making registration necessary (see 8-070).

The occasions when reverse charge supplies arise are the acquisition of certain services from an overseas business and the anti-avoidance measure applying to certain supplies of mobile phones and computer chips (see 11-620).

The ECJ ruled that *Kollektivavtalsstiftelsen* (a Swedish firm) must apply the 'reverse charge' to consultancy services bought from Denmark. The Court concluded that 'the fact that the customer uses those services for activities which fall outside the scope of ... (VAT) ... does not preclude the application of' the 'reverse charge'.

Application of the reverse charge

The reverse charge applies:

- Transfer of a business as a going concern to a group registration – 18-460;
- Imported services – 5-986;
- Certain supplies of mobile phones and computer items – 11-620, and
- Investment gold – 14-850.

Importing services

Until 1 January 2010 UK businesses/organisations had only to apply the 'reverse charge' to the intangible services listed in Schedule 5 to the VAT Act. Now it is necessary to apply it to nearly all services imported into the UK

There remains a group of services for which the overseas supplier may have to account for UK VAT. The services concerned are taxable in the UK but, from 1 January 2010, who accounts for UK varies as follows:

- when the UK customer is not VAT registered; the foreign supplier (who may have to register for UK VAT) accounts for UK VAT, or
- when the UK customer is VAT registered, the customer accounts for VAT using the 'reverse charge' procedure (VATA 1994, section 8(2)).

The group of services to which this applies are as follows:

(1)   Services relating to UK land or buildings.

(2)   Passenger transport.

(3)   Short-term hire of a means of transport.

(4)   Cultural, educational and entertainment services.

(5)   Restaurant and catering services (including those served on a ship or aircraft during an intra-EU passenger transport operation).

(6)   Short-term hire of a means of transport.

(7)   Telecommunication and broadcasting services.

(8)   Electronically supplied services.

Supplies by Business

These are services listed in Parts 1 & 2 of Schedule 4A of VATA 1994. They are the services which are taxed where the land is situated, they are performed and, with 6, 7 and 8, where they are 'effectively used and enjoyed' in the UK. This is regardless of where the supplier is located.

Transitional provisions apply to ensure the reverse charge does not apply if VAT was accounted for in another EU State under the legislation in force before 1 January 2010.

For further information about who accounts for VAT on services imported into the UK see paragraph 5-986.

Example 1

Subs UK Ltd is the subsidiary of a USA firm. Subs UK sells sports gear and insurance products in the UK and is VAT registered. It is a partially exempt business and normally reclaims approximately 55% of its input tax.

Subs UK buys advertising costing £10,000 from a TVA registered business in France. It also receives administration service values at £8,000 from its parent company in the USA.

Subs UK applies the 'reverse charge' to both the advertising and administration services.

The reverse charge affects Subs UK as follows:

Output tax due	advertising	at 20%	£2,000
	administration	at 20%	£1,600
			£3,600
Input tax claim	residual tax	say 55%	£1,980
Payable to HMRC			£1,620

Example 2

Aussie UK Ltd is the subsidiary of an Australian firm. Aussie UK sells boomerangs in the UK. Its turnover is £55,000; it is not VAT registered.

Aussie UK buys advertising costing £10,000 from a TVA registered business in France. It also receives administration service values at £8,000 from its parent company in Australia.

The implications of the 'reverse charge' for Aussie UK is as follows:

Until 31 December 2010

Sales	boomerangs	£55,000
Reverse charge supplies	advertising	£10,000
Turnover for registration purposes		£65,000

From 1 January 2010

Sales	boomerangs	£55,000
Reverse charge supplies	advertising	£10,000
	administration	£8,000
Turnover for registration purposes		£73,000

Legislation: VATA 1994, s. 8

Cases: *Kollektivavtalsstiftelsen TRR Trygghetsradet v Skatteverket* [2008] (Case C-291/07)

Other material: Notice 741 Place of Supply of Services; *www.hmrc.gov.uk/vat/managing/ international/exports/services.htm*

VAT Reporter: ¶65-620

3-240   Imports and acquisitions

Value added tax arises not only on supplies, but also on the importation of goods from outside the EC, and on their acquisition from elsewhere in the EC. These chargeable events are covered at 5-100ff. and 5-180ff.

VAT Reporter: ¶64-200

NON-SUPPLIES

3-280   Receipt of money which is not consideration

As indicated earlier, when something is done for consideration, there is a supply for VAT purposes. It is therefore wise to suspect that, whenever a business receives money, it is likely to be consideration for something, so it is likely that there is a supply. However, it is possible to receive money without that money being consideration for anything. A number of examples of this follow, but please note:

(1)   this is not a comprehensive list of occasions when the receipt of money does not indicate the existence of a supply;

(2)   a little care is needed, in that there may be receipts which seem very similar to the examples given, but where a supply does in fact arise. It would be necessary to go into much more detail to provide a fully authoritative list. Furthermore, it is perfectly possible that an officer of HMRC will take the view that there is a supply when, in law, there is not. This gives rise to particular difficulty when the amounts involved are too small to warrant litigation; and

(3)   in some cases, there may be further difficulty in that, if the facts could be established, there would be no supply, but there is insufficient evidence available to substantiate the true relationships between the parties.

VAT Reporter: ¶10-985

3-300   Dividends received

A dividend paid to a shareholder is generally not consideration for a supply made by the shareholder to the company paying the dividend.

VAT Reporter: ¶10-602

3-320   Theft of goods

If goods are stolen, this does not represent a supply by the business. Although business assets have ceased to be such, it did not occur (one hopes) under the directions of the person carrying on the business. If cash is stolen this also does not represent a supply, but the business is not relieved from liability to account for tax on supplies which led to the receipt of the cash.

> ### Example: theft of goods
>
> Doreen runs a shop which is raided by burglars. They take the previous day's takings of £500 and goods to the value of £1,150. Doreen does not have to account for any VAT in respect of the theft of the goods, as it does not involve any supply by her. However, she remains liable to account for tax on the previous day's sales. The supplies have been made, even though the proceeds of them have disappeared.

HM Revenue and Customs also accept, in principle, that there is no supply where goods are obtained from a trader by fraud (e.g. where a person purports to buy goods, and makes off with them without paying). This is in accordance with *Harry B Litherland & Co Ltd*. If a part payment is received from the fraudster, this is outside the scope of VAT as no supply is considered to have taken place.

In practical terms, HMRC are unwilling to accept that goods have been lost due to theft or fraud without some supporting evidence of this. They will expect, for instance, that the person running the business will have reported the matter to the police. Their internal instructions contain the following passage concerning evidence:

> 'You should see:
>
> - evidence that the trader has been victim of the fraud proved in the courts or, where the fraudster goes missing, you should check with the police that they are satisfied that a fraud has actually taken place;
> - evidence that the trader has made a statement to the police for use in the prosecution; and
> - a verifiable description of the goods involved.
>
> Suitable evidence might take the form of police letters and press reports describing the injured party and the goods.'

However, they have announced a relaxation in the case of goods obtained by fraud (which presumably applies also to stolen goods). They no longer require that a conviction be obtained (in the case of a fraudster who has not gone missing) provided that they are satisfied that a fraud has taken place and that the matter has been reported to the police.

Cases: *Harry B Litherland & Co Ltd* (1978) 1 BVC 1,102

Other material: Notice 700, para. 8.10, Loss of goods

VAT Reporter: ¶10-985

3-340 Supplies in bonded warehouse

When goods are bought and sold while in bonded warehouse, the 'supply' which takes place is generally ignored for VAT purposes. However, if the goods concerned include any manufactured or produced in the UK, or acquired from another EC Member State, this non-supply treatment does not extend to the last supply made while in bond. The tax on the supply is payable to HMRC not by the supplier, but by the person who removes the goods from bond.

Example: supplies in bond

A quantity of UK-produced whisky is placed in bond by A Ltd. While the whisky is in bond, A Ltd sells it to B Ltd, which sells it to C Ltd, which sells it to D Ltd. D Ltd removes it from bond.

The supplies by A Ltd and B Ltd are not regarded as supplies for UK VAT purposes. The supply by C Ltd is regarded as a supply, this being the last supply made while the whisky is in bond. The tax is not payable to HMRC by C Ltd (which will not have charged tax to D Ltd, as it had no way of knowing whether there might be further supplies in bond). Instead, it is payable directly by D Ltd at the time when it removes the goods from bond.

Legislation: VATA 1994, s. 18

Anti-avoidance measure

There is an anti-avoidance measure that allows HMRC to disapply the tax-free trading of goods in circumstances where they suspect cases of abuse.

HMRC have the power to disallow VAT free trading where retail goods are sold to or are to be sold by persons who are not VAT-registered or are not required to be. This anti-avoidance measure was designed to counter schemes where the value for VAT could be manipulated by businesses selling goods for retail or to buyers for onward retail sale.

Legislation: *Value Added Tax Regulations* 1995 (SI 1995/2518), reg. 145K

VAT Reporter: ¶63-840

3-350 Supplies in fiscal warehouse

A fiscal warehousing regime is available for:

(1)   imported goods on which import duties have been either paid or deferred;

(2)   imported goods on which import VAT has been either paid or deferred;

(3)   goods subject to a duty of excise which has been either paid or deferred.

In each case, the goods must be of a description specified in the legislation, such as various metals, cereals, tea and coffee, bulk chemicals, etc.

HMRC can approve registered persons who apply to act as fiscal warehouse keepers. A non-retail supply of eligible goods which are within a fiscal warehouse, or which are placed within a fiscal warehouse before any resupply takes place, is generally treated as being a supply outside the UK. However, when the goods are removed from warehouse, the last supply within the warehouse (or, if they have not been supplied in the warehouse, the supply under which they entered the warehouse) is treated as made at the time of removal by the person removing them. If the goods are not already in the warehouse, the customer must provide the supplier with a certificate to the effect that they are being placed in warehouse before any resupply, for outside of scope treatment to apply.

A similar relief applies to goods acquired from another Member State which are already within a fiscal warehousing regime, or are placed in a fiscal warehouse before being supplied. In this case, the person making the acquisition must make a certificate showing that the goods are being placed in the warehouse.

The supply of services of a fiscal warehousekeeper in respect of goods in warehouse, or a supply of operations on goods in warehouse, is zero-rated. However, if the goods are then removed from warehouse without having been supplied within the warehouse after the performance of the zero-rated services, the value of the services is added to the taxable amount on the removal of the goods from the warehouse.

Legislation: VATA 1994, s. 18A–18F, Sch. 5A

Other material: Notice 702/8

VAT Reporter: ¶63-845

3-360 Compensation

Payments of compensation often do not represent consideration for supplies. Thus, if a business receives compensation for, for instance, loss of profits caused by work carried on at a neighbouring property (e.g. because of lack of access for potential customers), this will not normally be regarded as consideration for a supply.

The position might be different if the payment were in return for permission to carry out the work (assuming that this was needed), when it could be regarded as consideration for the granting of the right to proceed with the work.

Also, if the recipient business had a legal right to sue for compensation, but the matter was settled out of court, there is a possibility that HMRC might consider that a supply had taken place, particularly if the recipient entered into a formal agreement not to take court proceedings. In this instance, the payment might be seen as consideration for surrendering the right to sue for compensation.

The court held that a compensation payment on the termination of a contract to manage a hotel was outside the scope of VAT.

However, in another case a tribunal held that compensation on the termination of a lease, under a variation agreed immediately before notice of termination was given, was consideration for a supply. It is clear that caution is needed before deciding that any 'compensation' payment is outside the scope of VAT.

A reference was made to the European Court of Justice in *Mohr v Finanzamt Bad Segeberg (Case C-215/94)*. This case concerned the treatment of a compensation payment made by the EC to compensate a farmer who undertook to discontinue milk production in return for the payment. The German tax authorities sought to treat the payment as being subject to VAT.

Both the German and the Italian governments argued that there was a direct link between the payment of the compensation and the undertaking to cease milk production, and that the acceptance of the obligation to refrain from an act is a supply within art. 6(1) of Directive 77/388, the sixth VAT directive (now Directive 2006/112 art. 24(1), 25 (a), (b) and (c)). Thus, there was a taxable supply for consideration and VAT was due on it.

The court referred to art. 2(1) of Directive 67/227, which provides that VAT is a tax on consumption. It held that, in the circumstances of this case, the Community did not acquire goods or services for its own use, but merely acted in the common interest. There was no benefit either to the EC or to the national authorities such as would enable them to be regarded as consumers of a service. As there was no consumption, there could be no liability to tax.

This decision implies that most government grants fall outside the scope of VAT.

Cases: *Holiday Inns (UK) Ltd* [1994] BVC 543; *Lloyds Bank Plc* [1996] BVC 2,875; *Mohr v Finanzamt Bad Segeberg (Case C-215/94)* [1996] BVC 293

Other material: VATSC34000 – Consideration: Compensation Payments

VAT Reporter: ¶10-000

3-380 Disbursements

If a business meets an expense on behalf of the customer, then the recharging of that expense to the customer does not represent consideration for a supply by the business.

For this treatment to apply, it must be clear from the outset that the expense was the legal responsibility of the customer, not of the business. An example would be where a solicitor pays stamp duty on behalf of a client, and recovers it from the client when billing. If the expense is really the expense of the business, but is disclosed as a separate item when billing, this does not qualify it for treatment as a disbursement even if it is described as such.

This can be a difficult area in practice, and it is well worth studying s. 25.1 of Notice 700 ('The VAT guide'), which sets out the position in some detail.

'25.1 Disbursements for VAT purposes

25.1.1 Introduction and conditions for VAT disbursements

It is the practice in some trades and professions for some or all of the costs incidental to a supply, such as travelling expenses, to be described as disbursements and shown or charged separately on the invoice issued to the client. In many cases, these items do not qualify to be treated as disbursements for VAT purposes.

If....	Then...
these costs have been incurred by suppliers in the course of making their own supply to their clients	they must be included in the value of those supplies when VAT is calculated.

However,

If....	Then....
you merely pay amounts to third parties as the agent of your client and debit your client with the precise amounts paid out	you may be able to treat them as disbursements for VAT purposes and exclude these amounts when you calculate any VAT due on your main supply to your client.

You may treat a payment to a third party as a disbursement for VAT purposes if all the following conditions are met:

- you acted as the agent of your client when you paid the third party;
- your client actually received and used the goods or services provided by the third party (this condition usually prevents the agent's own travelling and subsistence expenses, telephone bills, postage, and other costs being treated as disbursements for VAT purposes);
- your client was responsible for paying the third party (examples include estate duty and stamp duty payable by your client on a contract to be made by the client);
- your client authorised you to make the payment on their behalf;
- your client knew that the goods or services you paid for would be provided by a third party;
- your outlay will be separately itemised when you invoice your client;
- you recover only the exact amount which you paid to the third party; and
- the goods or services, which you paid for, are clearly additional to the supplies which you make to your client on your own account.

All these conditions must be satisfied before you can treat a payment as a disbursement for VAT purposes.

Generally, it is only advantageous to treat a payment as a disbursement for VAT purposes where no VAT is chargeable on the supply by the third party, or where your client is not entitled to reclaim it as input tax.

If you treat a payment for a standard-rated supply as a disbursement for VAT purposes, you may not reclaim input tax on the supply because it has not been made to you. Your client may also be prevented from doing so because the client does not hold a valid VAT invoice.

25.1.2 Evidence for VAT disbursements

If....	Then....
you treat a payment as a disbursement for VAT purposes	you must keep evidence (such as an order form or a copy invoice) to enable you to show that you were entitled to exclude the payment from the value of your own supply to your principal. You must also be able to show that you did not reclaim input tax on the supply by the third party.

This example illustrates the invoicing procedure:

A registered person supplies standard-rated services to a client for a basic fee of £80. In addition, the supplier incurs £20 expenses which are passed on to the client, but which do not qualify for treatment as disbursements for VAT purposes. The supplier also pays £50 on behalf of the client in circumstances which qualify that payment to be treated as a disbursement.

The supplier must issue a VAT invoice to the client, showing:

	£
Services	80.00
Expenses	20.00
Value for VAT	100.00
17.5% VAT	17.50
Disbursements	50.00
Total	167.50

25.1.3 Examples of supplies which cannot be treated as VAT disbursements

The following are examples of supplies which might, for accounting purposes, be charged or itemised separately, but which cannot be treated as disbursements for VAT purposes:

Example 1: A solicitor pays a fee to a bank for the transfer of funds telegraphically or electronically to, or from, the solicitor's own business or client account.

VAT treatment: The solicitor cannot treat the bank's fee as a disbursement for VAT purposes. The service for which the charge is made is supplied by the bank to the solicitor rather than to the client. Although the bank's supply may be exempt from VAT, the fee when re-charged, even though at cost, is part of the value of the solicitor's own supply of legal services to the client and VAT is due on the full amount.

Example 2: A solicitor pays a fee for a **personal** search of official records such as a Land Registry, in order to extract information needed to advise a client.

VAT treatment:	The solicitor cannot treat the search fee as a disbursement for VAT purposes. The fee is charged for the supply of access to the official record and it is the solicitor, rather than the client, who receives that supply. The solicitor uses the information in order to give advice to the client and the recovery of this outlay represents part of the overall value of the solicitor's supply. The solicitor must account for output tax on the full value of the supply. **Note:** Where a solicitor pays a fee for a **postal search**, this may be treated as a disbursement since the solicitor merely obtains a document on behalf of the client. The client will normally need to use the document for their own purposes, such as to obtain a loan.
Example 3:	A consultant is instructed by the client to fly to Scotland to perform some work.
VAT treatment:	The consultant cannot treat the air fare as a disbursement for VAT purposes. The supply by the airline is a supply to the consultant, not to the client. The recovery of outlay by the consultant represents part of the overall value of the consultant's supply of services to the client. The consultant must account for output tax on the full value of this supply.
Example 4:	A private function is held at a restaurant. The customer pays for the food, drink and other facilities provided, and also agrees to meet the costs of any overtime payments to the staff.
VAT treatment:	The restaurant cannot treat the overtime payments as disbursements for VAT purposes. The supply by the staff is made to the restaurant, not to the customer. The staff costs are part of the value of the supply by the restaurant and VAT is due on the full amount.
Example 5:	A manufacturer makes a separate charge to a customer for royalty or licence fees, which were incurred in making a supply to the customer.
VAT treatment:	The manufacturer cannot treat the royalty or licence fees as disbursements for VAT purposes. The recovery of these fees is part of the manufacturer's costs in making the supply to the customer. The manufacturer must account for output tax on the full value of the supply, including the royalty or licence fees.'

VAT Reporter: ¶11-245

MOT test charges

Special difficulties have arisen concerning charges for MOT tests, where the test is performed by an approved test centre on behalf of an unapproved garage, which passes on the charge to the customer. Where the approved centre allowed a discount to the unapproved garage, HMRC sought to see the discount as representing consideration for a supply by the unapproved garage to the approved one of introducing the customer or, if the unapproved centre charged the full price to the customer, a supply to the customer of arranging the test. Their policy is as follows:

(1) the charge by an approved centre to a customer remains outside the scope of VAT, provided that it does not exceed the statutory maximum;

(2) where an approved centre charges a discounted fee to an unapproved garage, this will be treated as an ordinary trade discount so will have no VAT effect;

(3) if the unapproved garage shows on its invoice the exact amount actually charged by the approved centre, and meets the conditions for agency disbursements in s. 25.4 of Notice 700, this amount can be treated as a disbursement and outside the scope of VAT; and

(4) any additional amount charged by the unapproved garage, over and above the recharged amount, will be seen as consideration for a taxable supply of arranging for the test.

In *K Lower and S Lower (20567)*, a garage that was not approved for MOT testing took cars to another garage for the test. The Tribunal gave a summary of the law and practice affecting these unapproved garages. It is common for an unapproved garage to take cars to and from a testing station and to obtain a discounted price. It is also common for the customer to pay the full MOT fee. It is the treatment of the difference between the exempt fee and the taxable top-up that frequently gives rise to problems. It is the way in which the garage copes with the charging of what is in effect a disbursement that causes problems. It is whether the garage is acting as an agent for the customer or for the testing station that colours the situation. The Tribunal suggested that an unapproved garage should display a notice to inform customers of the arrangements for MOT testing vehicles.

Other material: Notice 700, s. 25.4

VAT Reporter: ¶18-590

Cases: *K Lower and S Lower* (2008) BVC 4,058

Postal and delivery charges

The general rule is that a separate postal and/or delivery charge is consideration for a standard-rated supply, even if the goods supplied are zero-rated. The delivery element cannot be exempted, in the case of delivery via the postal service, since the exemption for postal delivery supplies applies only to the Post Office.

When there is a contract for a single supply of delivered goods, the delivery charge is additional consideration for the goods and attracts the same VAT liability as the goods. Thus the delivery charge for books would be zero-rated whereas the delivery charge for chocolates would be standard-rated.

While it may be possible to obtain exemption for postal delivery charges where the supplier pays the Post Office on the customer's behalf, and reclaims the cost from the customer as a disbursement, this is unlikely to succeed in practice unless arrangements are in place for the customer to contract directly with the Post Office for delivery.

Cases: *C & E Commrs v Plantiflor Ltd* [2002] BVC 572; *C & E Commrs v British Telecommunications Plc* [1999] BVC 306

Other material: Notice 700, s. 25.1 and Notice 700/24 Postage and Delivery Charges

VAT Reporter: ¶27-225

3-400   Internal payments

It is not uncommon for an entity which amounts to one 'person' for VAT purposes to be organised in such a way that different parts of the entity act independently and payments flow between those separate parts. These 'internal' payments do not represent consideration for supplies as a person is, for VAT purposes, incapable of making supplies to itself (the self-supply rules mentioned above are the exception to this general rule).

Examples of such internal payments include the following.

(1)   A retail business operates a number of branches. Goods are transferred from one branch to another, and payment is passed between the branches in respect of the goods.

(2)   Two separate partnerships each have the same partners. Because of the special VAT rules for partnerships (see 3-720), the two partnerships are treated as one 'person' for VAT purposes. Consequently, payments between them for supplies made to one partnership by the other do not, for VAT purposes, represent consideration for supplies.

(3)   There are two separate companies, and one makes supplies to the other and receives payment for these supplies. If the two companies are included in the same group for VAT purposes (see 17-080), they are effectively regarded as one person for most VAT purposes. Thus, the payments are on a par with those between two branches of a single legal entity, and do not represent consideration for supplies. It should be noted that the precise effect of the VAT grouping rules has become a matter of debate, and the latest position should be confirmed with specialist advisers.

3-420   Capital introduced

When capital is introduced into a partnership or a sole trader business by a partner or sole proprietor, this does not represent consideration for a supply by the business.

Cases: *KapHag Renditefonds 35 Spreecenter Berlin-Hellesdorf 3. Tranche GbR v Finanzamt Charlottenburg*, European Court of Justice. Case C-442/01

Other material: VATSC68000 – Consideration Partnership Contributions

VAT Reporter: ¶5-650

3-425   New Share Issues

The issuing of new shares is outside the scope of VAT. This was decided in *Kretztechnik AG v Finanzamt Linz*.

The UK always maintained that issuing new shares was a supply for VAT purposes. HMRC considered that such a supply was an exempt transaction within the scope of VATA 1994, Sch. 9, Grp. 5. This reasoning was wrong. The ECJ concluded that 'a new share issue ... was not a supply for a consideration ... and did not fall within the scope ...' of VAT.

The ECJ decision is contrary to the Court of Appeal decision in *Trinity Mirror Plc v C & E Commrs*. In this case, the Court of Appeal decided that the issue of shares was an exempt supply. However, the UK is bound by the ECJ decision in *Kretztechnik AG*.

Kretztechnic AG also has implications for input tax recovery because the decision has effect retrospectively. Input tax that was not recovered previously may now be reclaimable. For more information, see 7-110.

Cases: *Kretztechnik AG v Finanzamt Linz* (C-465/03), [2006] BVC 66; *Trinity Mirror Plc v C & E Commrs* (2001) BVC 167

VAT Reporter: ¶10-602

3-430 Partnership 'shares' – purchase and disposal

When a new partner is admitted for a consideration, there is no supply by the existing partners to the new partner.

If, or when, the new partner disposes of the acquired interest, there may or may not be a supply. There is no supply when the 'share' is disposed of for no consideration or the new partner was an investor who had 'no involvement in the running of a partnership'. There may be other circumstances when the disposal of such a 'share' is not a supply.

Cases: *Kaphag Rendifonds 35 Spreecenter Berlin-hellesdorf3. Tranche GbR v Finanzamt Charlottenburg* (C-442/01) [2003] ECR I-6851

Other material: VATSC68000 – Consideration Partnership Contributions; VATSC564000 – Direction of Supplies: Companies Issuing Their Own Shares

VAT Reporter: ¶18-640

3-440 Loan repayments

When a loan is made, the lender is regarded as making a supply of credit. The consideration for this is usually the payment of interest by the borrower. Thus, when the borrower pays interest, this is regarded as consideration for the supply of credit. When the borrower repays the loan, this capital repayment is not consideration for anything, and merely represents the termination of the original supply of credit.

3-460 Gifts and donations

The receipt of a genuine gift does not represent consideration for any supply. The gift must be freely given with nothing done or due to be done in return for it.

Supplies by Business

Difficulties frequently arise in connection with fund-raising events, where people are admitted to some function (such as a dinner or a rock concert) in return for an admission charge. The organisers often regard the admission charge as including a 'donation' element. It can only be treated as such if there is a basic charge for admission, and the extra amount is truly optional and clearly held out as such in all advertising, etc. If people are admitted to the event on payment of the basic charge, whether or not they pay the donation element as well, then the donation element does not represent consideration for a supply and is not subject to VAT. If admission is conditional on payment of the donation element as well, then it is not a true donation and is subject to VAT.

Where a charity solicits donations and gives some small emblem, such as a flag, to donors, HMRC do not regard the amounts given as consideration for the supply of the emblems.

In some cases, these difficulties may be overcome by the exemption for one-off fund-raising events by charities (see 14-750).

VAT Reporter: ¶50-110

Other material: *www.hmrc.gov.uk/charities/vat/income*

Gift Aid – admission charges

An admission charge which is a donation for Gift Aid is normally a payment for a standard or exempt supply of services. One way in which a relevant admission charge may qualify for Gift Aid is for the visitor to make a donation that is at least 10 per cent more than the admission charge. As long as the 10 per cent addition is voluntary and a visitor receives no more, then the right of admission the 10 per cent can be a donation for VAT purposes. For further information, see *www.hmrc.gov.uk/charities/gift_aid/rules/admissions.htm.*

VAT Reporter: ¶50-160

Gratuities, tips and service charges

A common form of gift is a voluntary tip or service charge. Provided that these are genuinely freely given, they are not seen as consideration for supplies. HMRC internal guidance on this topic is as follows:

'8.6 Gratuities, tips & service charges

These are voluntary extra payments made by customers for services, given, for example, by hairdressers, waiters, hotel staff and taxi-drivers. If these are genuinely freely given then they are outside the scope of VAT as they are not for any supply. This is so even if a customer expressly asks for a gratuity or tip to be shown on the bill in order to support an expenses claim or where payment is made by cheque or credit card, and the amount shown includes the tip. But where the element of choice has been removed the payment is part of the consideration for a supply.

Service charges made by a hotel or restaurant are part of the consideration for the underlying supply if there is no option on whether they are paid. This applies even if these are passed on in full as bonuses to the staff.

Optional service charges were at one time treated as part of the consideration for the supply of food or hotel accommodation, and standard-rated. Since May 1982, if the customer has a genuine option on whether to pay these, it has been accepted that they are not consideration, whether or not the amount appears on the invoice. The Tribunal case of *NDP Co Ltd* refers.'

Cases: *NDP Co Ltd* (1988) 3 BVC 711

Other material: Internal Guidance Vol. V1.3, Ch. 2B, para. 8.6; Notice 701/1; VATSC 564000 – Consideration: payments that are not consideration: gratuities, tips and other service charges

VAT Reporter: ¶10-165

3-480   Grants

As a general rule, grants do not represent consideration for supplies made by the recipient, but are merely a form of deficit-funding. It should be noted, however, that non-supply treatment cannot be obtained merely by describing a payment as a grant. It is not the label attached to the payment which determines the VAT treatment, but the underlying position.

It is necessary to determine whether the person paying the grant receives anything in return. For instance, if a person makes a payment to a team of scientists carrying out research work, there will be no supply if the payer obtains no rights over the fruits of the research, or privileged access to information. There is probably no supply if the payer receives a copy of a report which goes into the public domain. However, if the payer obtains intellectual property rights in any inventions arising, or a confidential report on the area of research, there will probably be a supply.

The decision in *Mohr v Finanzamt Bad Segeberg* implies that most forms of government grant fall outside the scope of VAT (see 3-360).

Additional guidance is provided by the judgments of the European Court of Justice in *Keeping Newcastle Warm Ltd v C & E Commrs* and *Office des produits wallons ASBL v Belgian State.*

Keeping Newcastle Warm Ltd (KNW)

KNW was involved in the promotion of energy efficiency and was a network installer for Newcastle and surrounding areas under a grant scheme backed by a government agency. Under the scheme, where KNW carried out works for householders meeting certain criteria, the agency might award grants in respect of the work.

The dispute concerned the treatment of grants relating to KNW's provision of energy advice to householders. It appears that KNW made no charges to householders for this advice but that, in suitable cases, the agency was prepared to pay to KNW a grant covering the cost of it, up to a maximum of £10. It was agreed that, in practice, the advice could not be provided for a cost less than £10 so that, in practice, the full £10 was paid in each qualifying case where advice was provided.

Supplies by Business

Initially, KNW accounted for output tax on the energy advice grants. Considering this to be incorrect, it subsequently made a claim for repayment of around £1 million output tax overpaid in the period 1991 to 1996. HMRC refused the claim, saying that the grants amounted to consideration for supplies made to householders.

The argument for HMRC was that the grants either were consideration for supplies by KNW to householders as a question of fact, or amounted to subsidies directly linked to the price of such supplies and so were to be treated as consideration by virtue of art. 11(A)(1)(a) of Directive 77/388, the sixth VAT directive (now Directive 2006/112 art. 73). KNW argued that the grants, being a form of subsidy, could only form part of the consideration if they were linked to the price of the services supplied to householders. Since in practice the advice could never be provided at a cost below £10 and no charge was made to the householder, they could not be regarded as so linked.

The court decided that, whether or not the grants amounted to subsidies, they were paid in return for the provision of specific services to specific categories of recipient. As such, they formed part of the consideration for these supplies.

Office des produits wallons (OPW)

OPW was a private non-profit making association. Its function was to advertise and sell agricultural products from the Walloon Region, and it received an annual subsidy from the Region to contribute towards its running costs. Under its agreement with the Region, OPW was responsible for:

(1)   publication of a catalogue;

(2)   publication of a magazine;

(3)   running local offices;

(4)   participating in local events.

The Belgian authorities took the view that the subsidy formed part of the consideration for OPW's supplies to its customers, by virtue of art. 11(A)(1)(a) of Directive 77/388, the sixth VAT directive (now Directive 2006/112 73), which provides that the taxable amount includes 'everything which constitutes the consideration which has been or is to be obtained by the supplier from the purchaser, the customer or a third part for such supplies including subsidies directly linked to the price of such supplies'.

The Belgian court referred a question to the ECJ for guidance on the principles to be applied in deciding whether the subsidies in this case did indeed constitute 'subsidies directly linked with the price' so as to form part of the consideration for the supplies.

The substantive part of the judgment is as follows:

'10. It should first be noted that, as has been pointed out both by the Commission in the observations which it has submitted to the Court and by the Advocate General in point 40 of his Opinion, in circumstances such as those in the main proceedings it is immaterial whether or not there is a distinct service by a taxpayer such as OPW to the body paying the subsidy. Article 73 of the Directive deals with situations where three parties are involved: the authority which grants the subsidy, the body which benefits from it and the purchaser of the goods or services delivered or supplied by the subsidised body. Thus, transactions covered by Article 73 Directive 2006/112 are not those carried out for the benefit of the authority granting the subsidy.

11. It should also be noted that subsidies such as those identified in the first question referred – namely operating subsidies covering a part of running costs – nearly always affect the cost price of the goods and services supplied by the subsidised body. In so far as it offers specific goods or services, that body can normally do so at prices which it would be unable to offer if were obliged at the same time both to pass on its costs and make a profit.

12. However, the mere fact that a subsidy may affect the price of the goods or services supplied by the subsidised body is not enough to make that subsidy taxable. For the subsidy to be directly linked to the price of such supplies, within the meaning of Article 73 Directive 2006/112 , it is also necessary, as the Commission has rightly pointed out, that it be paid specifically to the subsidised body to enable it to provide particular goods or services. Only in that case can the subsidy be regarded as consideration for the supply of goods or services, and therefore be taxable.

13. In order to establish whether the subsidy constitutes such consideration, it should be noted that the price of the goods or services must, in principle, be determined not later than the time of the triggering event. It should also be noted that the undertaking to pay the subsidy made by the person who grants it has as its corollary the right of the beneficiary to receive it, since a taxable supply has been made by the latter. That link between the subsidy and the price must appear unequivocally following a case by case analysis of the circumstances underlying the payment of that consideration. On the other hand, it is not necessary for the price of the goods or services – or a part of the price – to be ascertained. It is sufficient for it to be ascertainable.

14. It is therefore for the referring court to establish the existence of a direct link between the subsidy and the goods or services at issue. That makes it necessary to verify at an early stage that the purchasers of the goods or services benefit from the subsidy granted to the beneficiary. The price payable by the purchaser must be fixed in such a way that it diminishes in proportion to the subsidy granted to the seller or supplier of the goods or services, which therefore constitutes an element in determining the price demanded by the latter. The court must examine, objectively, whether the fact that a subsidy is paid to the seller or supplier allows the latter to sell the goods or supply the services at a price lower than he would have to demand in the absence of subsidy.'

The court went on to suggest that the referring court needed to verify whether each activity gave rise to a specific and identifiable payment, or whether the subsidy was paid globally to cover the whole of OPW's running costs. It was only the part (if any) which could be identified with specific supplies which might be subject to VAT. The court would then need to establish whether there was any link between the subsidy and the price at which the products were sold, such as to indicate that the price was significantly reduced due to receipt of the subsidy (although the price reduction, if any, need not correspond exactly with the amount of the subsidy).

Its formal judgment was that the subsidies referred to in art. 11(A)(1)(a) (now Directive 2006/112, art. 73) were 'only subsidies which constitute the whole or part of the consideration for a supply of goods or services and which are paid by a third party to the seller or supplier. It is for the national court to determine, on the basis of the facts before it, whether or not a subsidy constitutes such consideration'.

45

Grants for government-funded research

The majority of wholly government-grant-funded research is likely to be outside the scope of VAT even when intellectual property rights are transferred because such a measure is not taken as a means of securing a consumable benefit but rather as a means of the government recouping the grant in the event of the research producing income-generating supplies.

There is, however, a potential problem where the research grant is part of the funding and there is also an element of matched funding from commercial participators. Another problem area is where any part of the research is subcontracted to a third party when it is likely that there will be a supply for VAT purposes. Each case must be considered on its merits and HMRC urge suppliers to contact the National Advice Service for clarification of any situation.

Legislation: Directive 2006/112, art. 73

Cases: *Mohr v Finanzamt Bad Segeberg* (Case C-215/94) [1996] BVC 293; *Keeping Newcastle Warm Ltd v C & E Commrs* (Case C-353/00) [2003] BVC 283; *Office des produits wallons ASBL v Belgian State* (Case C-184/00) [2001] ECR I-9115

Other material: VAT Information Sheet 04/08 Supplies of Government funded research

VAT Reporter: ¶10-990

3-500 Payments for group relief

Where companies are in the same group for corporation tax purposes, certain losses, etc. arising in one company can be surrendered to another and set against profits arising in that other company. Frequently, the claimant company makes a payment to the surrendering company in respect of the losses. If the payment is solely in respect of the surrender of the losses, and does not exceed the amount surrendered, it is not regarded as consideration for a supply.

Care must be taken with any formal arrangements made in such circumstances. In one case, a legal agreement was drawn up whereby such a payment was expressed as being in return for management services provided by the surrendering company. HMRC successfully contended that the payment represented consideration for a supply of management services and levied VAT on it.

Cases: *C & E Commrs v Tilling Management Services Ltd* (1978) 1 BVC 185

VAT Reporter: ¶11-016

3-520 Indemnity payments

Payments under a contract of indemnity do not represent consideration for supplies. The most common example of this is in the case of insurance policies. When a policy is taken out, the payment of the premium by the insured is a payment for the supply of insurance by the insurer, whereby the parties enter into the contract of indemnity. No VAT is charged as the supply of insurance happens to be exempt from VAT. When a claim is made by the insured, the payment made by the insurer in settlement of the claim is a payment under the contract of indemnity, and does not represent consideration for a supply by the insured to the insurer.

Indemnity payments sometimes arise under property lease agreements. It is not uncommon for such agreements to permit the tenant to carry out improvements to the property or sublet the property, with permission of the landlord, and to provide that the tenant will meet any legal costs, etc. incurred by the landlord. In such a case, the tenant's payment in respect of the landlord's costs is not regarded as payment for an onward supply by the landlord of the legal services, etc. However the payment to the landlord may be consideration for the variation of the lease and only exempt if the landlord has not opted to tax the property.

Other material: Notice 742, para. 10.8

VAT Reporter: ¶11-018

3-540 Sale of a business as a going concern

If a business is sold as a going concern, and certain conditions are met, the transaction is treated as not being a supply (although a 'reverse charge' supply may arise for a purchaser which is a member of a VAT group). The transfer of a business as a going concern is covered in more detail at 18-120ff.

VAT Reporter: ¶11-007

3-560 Supplies made outside the UK

UK VAT is charged only on supplies made within the UK. It is perfectly possible for a business which is established in the UK to make a supply which, although taxed in the UK for other purposes, is regarded as made outside the UK for VAT purposes and so does not attract UK VAT.

The rules for determining whether a supply is made in the UK are quite technical, and are covered at 3-900–3-940.

VAT Reporter: ¶13-350

3-580 Repossessed goods

Certain disposals of goods repossessed by insurance and finance companies, etc. are treated as not being supplies, if their supply by the previous owner would not have attracted VAT, or attracted it on some amount less than the total proceeds.

The transactions affected are:

(1) the disposal of goods falling within a second-hand goods scheme, or of a used motor car, by a person who repossessed them under a finance agreement, or an insurer who acquired them as part of the settlement of an insurance claim;

(2) the disposal of a boat by a mortgagee who has taken possession of it under a marine mortgage; and

(3) the disposal of an aircraft by a mortgagee who has taken possession of it under an aircraft mortgage.

In each case, the relief is denied if the goods have previously been relieved of VAT, as being exported, and have been reimported, or to goods which have been imported into the UK free of VAT. Also, the goods must be resold in the same condition as that in which the person making the disposal acquired them.

In *C & E Commrs v General Motors Acceptance Corporation (UK) Plc* [2004] BVC 611 (GMAC), the High Court considered the meaning of 'repossessed' in this context. It decided that '… wherever GMAC resells a car after it has regained possession … the resale is within art 4(1)(a) even if the hirer has voluntarily returned the car'.

Until 12 April 2006, goods repossessed under the terms of a finance agreement were not liable to tax when resold by the finance company. The resale was not a taxable supply.

The purpose of these provisions was to avoid double taxation. Goods subject to tax when sold should not be taxed again when repossessed and sold for a second time.

As well as not having to pay tax when selling the repossessed goods, the finance company is entitled to bad debt relief – *C & E Commrs v General Motors Acceptance Corporation (UK) Plc.* [2004] BVC 611. Bad debt relief is due because usually some instalments are unpaid when goods are re-possessed. Output tax accounted for on the sale may then be adjusted because the full consideration was not received – see 9-520.

This double relief is ended with effect from 13 April 2006. From then, tax is due when the repossessed goods are resold. It will be due 'where VAT on the first sale can be adjusted' (i.e. when the finance company may claim bad debt relief). The new measures affect finance agreements 'entered into on or after 13 April 2006 where the goods concerned are delivered on or after 1 September 2006').

Legislation: *Value Added Tax (Special Provisions) Order* 1995 (SI 1995/1268), art. 4(1); *Value Added Tax (Cars) Order* 1992 (SI 1992/3122), art. 4

Cases: *C & E Commrs v General Motors Acceptance Corporation (UK) Plc* [2004] BVC 611

Other material: VAT Information Sheet 05/06 (VAT: Supplies of goods under finance agreements)

VAT Reporter: ¶18-660

3-600   Gift of motor car

The gift of a motor car is treated as not being a supply if the tax on its acquisition or importation was non-deductible.

Legislation: *Value Added Tax (Cars) Order* 1992 (SI 1992/3122), art. 4(1)(c)

3-610   Sale of assets used for business and private purposes

A taxpayer may choose to assign only part of an asset used for both business and private purposes to the business. This decision is made when the asset is acquired. VAT incurred on the part assigned to private use is not recoverable.

Later when the asset is sold or the business de-registers, output tax is not due on the part of the asset assigned to private use.

The European Court considered a case in which a taxable person sold a building used partly as a guesthouse and restaurant and partly as his private residence. In his VAT return, the taxpayer included only the sale of the part of the building used for business purposes as VATable and treated the price received in respect of the private dwelling as exempt. He accordingly invoiced the purchaser for VAT only in respect of the part used for business purposes. The court upheld this treatment.

Cases: *Finanzamt Uelzen v Armbrecht* (Case C-291/92) [1996] BVC 50

Other material: VAT Information Sheet 14/07

VAT Reporter: ¶19-040

TAXABLE AND EXEMPT SUPPLIES

3-640   General

As seen above, VAT is primarily a tax on supplies, and so it is necessary to decide whether a transaction amounts to a supply in order to establish whether liability to VAT arises. Once it is known that there is a supply, further analysis is needed to determine its status for VAT purposes, since the tax applies only to taxable supplies.

The legislation does not define a taxable supply directly. Instead, it states that any supply made in the UK is a taxable supply unless it is an exempt supply, and goes on to provide a means of identifying exempt supplies. The legislation provides a list of supplies which are exempt from VAT. The supplies falling within this list are considered at 14-100ff.

49

Taxable supplies can be further subdivided by reference to the rate of tax which applies to them. In principle, there is a standard rate of VAT (from 1 April 1991 to 30 November 2008 it was 17.5 per cent, then 15 per cent from 1 December 2008, followed by 17.5 per cent until 4 January 2011 when it was raised to 20 per cent) which applies to all taxable supplies not specifically allocated to a different rate band.

Legislation: VATA 1994, s. 4(2); Sch. 9

VAT Reporter: ¶1-100

3-660 Exempt and zero-rated supplies

Supplies which are zero-rated attract VAT at the rate of zero per cent. The distinction between zero-rated supplies and exempt supplies is that the makers of zero-rated supplies can (indeed, must) register for VAT and can recover tax on their expenses. As with exempt supplies, the legislation provides a list of supplies qualifying for zero-rating, and there is also a general zero-rating which applies to exports of goods from the EC and to certain deliveries of goods to other EC Member States. The types of supply which qualify for zero-rating are considered at 12-000ff.

The general rule is that exempt and zero-rated supplies are identified by inspecting the lists of exempt and zero-rated supplies to see whether the supplies under review are listed. Any supply which falls into neither of the lists is liable to VAT at the standard rate, or as applicable, the reduced rate.

Zero-rating overrides exemption

It is possible for a supply to fall within the list of exempt supplies, and also within the list of zero-rated supplies. In this case, the zero-rating takes priority, so the supply is treated as zero-rated.

Legislation: VATA 1994, s. 30; VATA 1994, Sch. 8; *Value Added Tax Regulations* 1995 (SI 1995/2518), reg. 134

VAT Reporter: ¶20-150

3-670 Illegal supplies

The ECJ considered that to produce and sell drugs or counterfeit currency was illegal and therefore not taxable. The counterfeit supplies were not in the furtherance of a (legal) business (the court added 'legal'). Supplies of such goods are absolutely prohibited and VAT is not chargeable where the activity is inherently unlawful and no lawful competition is allowed. When there is a legal trade in the goods or services but where the particular business merely is not licensed for that trade (for example, the selling of alcohol), the activity is taxable because it would be unfair on the legal business for this not to be so.

Cases: *Einberger v Hauptzollamt Freiburg (Case C-294/82)* (1988) 3 BVC 78; *Mol v Inspecteur der Invoerrechten en Accijnzen (Case C-269/86)* (1989) 4 BVC 205; *Vereniging Happy Family Rustenburgerstraat v Inspecteur der Omzetbelasting (Case 289/86)* (1989) 2

BVC 216 re narcotics and *Witzemann v Hauptzollamt München-Mitte (Case C-343/89)* [1993] BVC 108 re counterfeit currency; *C & E Commrs v Polok & Anor* [2002] BVC 327

VAT Reporter: ¶18-070

TAXABLE PERSONS AND REGISTRATION

3-700 General

Tax will be due on a supply only if it is made by a taxable person in the course or furtherance of a business carried on by him.

A taxable person is defined as one who makes (or intends to make) taxable supplies and is (or is required to be) registered for VAT (see flowchart at 4-930). In broad terms, a person is liable to be registered for VAT if taxable supplies made exceed an annual threshold (see Hardman's Tax Rates and Tables 19-080 or Key Data 1-140). Persons with turnover below this limit can also register for VAT, but are not obliged to do so. A person can also become liable to register for VAT because of the level of acquisitions from other EC Member States or because of the level of 'distance sales' to the UK. The question of determining liability to register, and of establishing the proper time and manner of registration, can become quite complex. It is dealt with separately at 8-000ff.

Legislation: VATA 1994, ss. 3(1) and 4(1)

VAT Reporter: ¶3-130

3-720 Person

Although VAT applies to supplies made in the course of a business, the taxable unit is not the business as such but the person who carries it on. This concept becomes of particular significance in the context of the VAT registration limits which apply in the UK. In considering these, all of the taxable supplies made by a particular person must be aggregated, even though they may be made in the course of different businesses. Once a person becomes liable to register for VAT, the tax will apply to all of his business activities. However, it does not necessarily apply to a business activity carried on by a different person with which he is involved. Thus, the fact that a sole trader is registered for VAT does not affect the position of a partnership in which he is a partner.

For instance, suppose that a scientist employed by a company receives a small additional income in the form of royalties from books which he has written, the amount of royalties falling below the VAT registration limits. At this point, he is not obliged to register for VAT. But, if he then leaves his employment and sets up as a self-employed consultant, with fees in excess of the registration limits, he will have to account for VAT, not only on his consultancy fees, but also on the royalties which he receives. This is because both activities are carried on by the same person.

The term 'person' is not defined in UK VAT law, but is taken to include any body having separate legal personality (such as a company, a trust, a trade union, etc.). A partnership is also regarded as a person for VAT although it does not have separate legal personality (except in Scotland). An unincorporated association (such as a club) is also regarded as a person in practice.

Two partnerships, formed under different agreements but having identical sets of partners, are regarded as being the same person for VAT purposes, even though the profit-sharing arrangements may be different in each partnership. However, if one of the partnerships had a partner who was not in the other partnership, they would be regarded as separate persons.

A limited partner does not count as a partner for these purposes. In one case, two individuals carried on two businesses. Each was a general partner in one of the businesses and a limited partner in the other. HMRC sought to register the two partnerships under a single registration, considering that they amounted to a single person under the rule in *Glassborow*. A tribunal held that there were two separate businesses carried on by two separate persons for VAT purposes.

A limited liability partnership is regarded as having its own legal personality, and so treated as a separate person. It is also regarded as a corporate body, with the consequences which follow for group treatment (see 17-110).

The position where an activity is carried on as a joint venture is far from clear. Often, an arrangement intended to be a joint venture will in fact amount to a partnership (despite protestations to the contrary by the venturers). Where it falls short of this, the interesting position arises that there is an identifiable business being carried on, but it is difficult to identify a single person who is carrying it on. In practice, it will often be best to avoid uncertainty by using a recognised vehicle for the enterprise, such as a partnership or a jointly owned company, or to structure the activity such that one party carries it on and the other acts as contractor to him. However, this may not be possible. In this case, it will be a good idea to agree a treatment with HMRC at an early stage.

Joint ventures are considered further at 17-050.

Cases: *C & E Commrs v Glassborow* (1974) 1 BVC 4; *Harris* (CAR/76/220) No. 373; *Saunders and Sorrell* (1980) 1 BVC 1,133

3-740 Sideline activities

As indicated above, the taxable person is the accounting unit for VAT purposes. So it is necessary when looking at a new business carried on by a person to have regard to other activities which may be regarded as businesses. This is relevant in determining whether registration limits have been reached, and in determining whether VAT has to be accounted for in respect of those other activities.

It also has implications when there are other business activities which give rise to exempt supplies. This can result in unfavourable consequences, of which the businessman needs to be warned, if the exempt supplies cause him to be treated as partially exempt for VAT purposes. In this instance, he will be prevented from recovering part of the VAT input tax arising on his expenses. Unless proper steps are taken, the input tax lost can exceed that relating strictly to the exempt activity. If the main business giving rise to VAT registration includes some exempt supplies, but not enough to lead to partial exemption, an exempt sideline activity can tip the balance and cause partial exemption to apply.

There can also be favourable implications, which may not be immediately obvious. If there is an exempt sideline activity, but the scale of it is too small for the partial exemption rules to apply, then the businessman may find himself with an unexpected bonus. In this case, he will be able to reclaim tax on expenses relating to the exempt sideline business, which he could not have done before.

> ### Example: exempt sideline activity
>
> An individual sets up a new business, and his accountant advises him that he is obliged to register for VAT. The annual taxable turnover of the business is likely to be in the region of £110,000 per annum.
>
> The accountant notices from his client's tax return that he owns three houses, which are rented out and produce gross rentals totalling £8,500 per annum.
>
> The property-letting activity is a business for VAT purposes. It seems likely that the input tax relating to the exempt activity will be sufficiently low compared with the scale of the new business that the businessman can recover the tax on expenses incurred in relation to the property business. This would include VAT on estate agents' fees for managing the properties as well as on repairs, refurbishment expenses, etc.
>
> Note that the VAT position could alter significantly in a year in which input tax relating to the exempt activity exceeded the partial exemption de minimis limits (see 6-950ff.).

This interaction of different activities for VAT purposes affects partnerships and companies just as much as individuals. In these cases, it is usually more obvious that there may be an interaction, since the accounts of a company or partnership are more likely to include all business activities.

3-760 Business

VAT affects supplies only when they are made in the course or furtherance of a business. So when a parent sells a child's old bicycle, no VAT is due since the transaction is a personal one, not done in the course of a business.

Supplies by Business

53

The meaning of 'business' in UK VAT law is outlined in the flowchart at 4-940 and the meaning of supplies made 'in the course of furtherance of a business' is outlined at 4-950.

(1) Whether a business carried on

It is easy to assume that the term 'business' for VAT is synonymous with the term 'trade' used in income tax law. Indeed, the term 'business' does include a trade, profession or vocation. But the VAT term goes far wider than this, and covers many activities which would be regarded for income tax purposes as generating investment income. For instance, the letting of property is regarded as a business for VAT purposes.

Specific activities treated as business

The following activities are regarded as done in the course of a business by definition:

(1)   the carrying on of a trade, profession or vocation;

(2)   the admission of persons to premises for consideration; and

(3)   the provision by a club, association or organisation (for subscription or other consideration) of the facilities or advantages available to its Members.

General meaning of business

The list of activities treated as business activities which is given in the VATA 1994 is not complete. The Act merely states that the term includes these activities. Each case has to be looked at on the basis of its facts, to see whether the activities carried on should be regarded as business activities within the ordinary meaning of that term. Furthermore, because VAT stems from European law, it is necessary to bear in mind the terms of Directive 2006/112 when construing the UK law. The directive does not use the term business, but refers to a taxable person as one who 'independently' carries on certain economic activities. The economic activities concerned are those of:

> 'producers, traders and persons supplying services including mining and agricultural activities and the activities of the professions. The exploitation of tangible or intangible property for the purpose of obtaining income therefrom on a continuing basis shall also be considered an economic activity.'

It has been held that the mere fact that an activity is carried out in pursuance of a statutory duty does not prevent it from being considered an economic activity, or a business.

However, where a person carries out functions which are regarded as being primarily within the sphere of the state, and not having the character of an economic activity, then this will not be regarded as amounting to a business for VAT purposes. There are no clear guidelines on what is, and is not, to be regarded as an activity having the characteristics of an economic activity and, in particular, the House of Lords in the *Institute of Chartered Accountants* gave weight to EC competition law cases, which took no account of the special definition of an economic activity contained in the sixth VAT directive (now directive 2006/112).

The European Court of Justice has held that a purely passive intermediate holding company, which did no more than receive dividends from subsidiaries and pass them on to its parent, was not carrying on an economic activity.

A UK tribunal has held that the holding of shares and securities by a charity, receiving interest and dividends thereon, and buying and selling shares and securities in maintaining the portfolio, did not amount to the carrying on of a business.

In *Wellcome Trust Ltd v C & E Commrs*, the court held that the purchase and sale of shares and other securities by a trustee in the course of the management of the assets of a charitable trust did not amount to an economic activity.

There have been fears that bodies such as pension funds might be regarded as not carrying on a business, and lose input tax on share dealings with non-EC counter-parties. However, HMRC have announced that they regard the outcome of *Wellcome* as only affecting the position of charitable trusts. The treatment of other bodies is unaffected, at least for the time being.

Without probing the depths of the directive too deeply, it is possible to arrive at a rule of thumb that, where an activity is carried on which involves the making of supplies, and the receipt of consideration thereon, there is almost a presumption that a business activity is carried on. It is wise to be cautious in these circumstances unless it can clearly be demonstrated that the activity does not have the characteristics of a business.

It is clear in both European and UK law that, for a business to exist, there is no requirement that the person carrying on an activity should be seeking to make a profit. The quest for profit is generally an indication that a business is carried on, but its absence provides no indication to the contrary.

The UK courts and tribunals have consistently declined to propound any definitive test to tell whether a business is carried on. But a number of factors to be considered have been put forward. These include the following:

(1)   if the activity amounts to a 'serious undertaking earnestly pursued' or 'a serious occupation not necessarily confined to commercial or profit making undertakings', then this is a pointer to its being a business;

(2)   if it is an occupation or function which is actively pursued with reasonable or recognisable continuity, then this is a pointer to its being a business;

(3)   if it has a certain measure of substance as measured by the quarterly or annual value of taxable supplies made, this points towards a business;

(4)   if it is properly organised in a regular manner and on sound and recognised business principles, this points to a business;

(5)   if it is mainly concerned with the making of supplies to consumers for consideration, this points to a business; or

Supplies by Business

55

(6)   if it involves the making of taxable supplies which are commonly made by others with a view to profit, then it is likely to be a business.

Although these factors must be considered, they are not in themselves decisive as to the existence of a business. The whole of the activity concerned must be looked at, not just some isolated aspect of it, and its nature considered. The presence of an intention to make a profit is very likely to lead to an activity being considered to be a business. But the lack of such an intention does not of itself give any indication that it is not a business.

In the High Court case of *C & E Commrs v St Paul's Community Project Ltd*, these tests were considered and it was decided that the answers to five indicated that there was a business, one did not. The charity was not carrying out an activity predominately concerned with making taxable supplies for a consideration. The same rationale was reached in *C & E Commrs v Yarburgh Childrens Trust*. Both organisations provided nursery and creche facilities as part of their charitable objectives. They charged fees for their services. In each instance, it was found that there was a lack of commercial reasoning in setting the fees; the overall intention was merely to cover costs and there was social concern for disadvantaged children.

HMRC have grudgingly accepted that charities making the same type of supplies as these two may be able to show that the supplies are not those of a business. This may help charities that make other supplies albeit not on all fours with Yarburgh or St Paul's.

The overall message is that any entity which makes taxable supplies needs to consider carefully whether it may be liable to register for VAT, even if it would not normally regard itself as being in business, and even though it may have exemption (e.g. as a charity) from other taxes.

Legislation: Directive 2006/112, art. 9(1); VATA 1994, s. 94

Cases: *C & E Commrs v Apple & Pear Development Council* (1986) 2 BVC 200,198; *Institute of Chartered Accountants in England and Wales v C & E Commrs* [1999] BVC 215; *Polysar Investments Netherlands BV v Inspecteur der Invoerrechten en Accijnzen, Arnhem* (Case C-60/90) [1993] BVC 88; *National Society for the Prevention of Cruelty to Children* [1993] BVC 701; *Wellcome Trust Ltd v C & E Commrs* (Case C-155/94) [1996] BVC 377; *C & E Commrs v Morrison's Academy Boarding Houses Association* (1977) 1 BVC 108; *C & E Commrs v Lord Fisher* (1981) 1 BVC 392; *C & E Commrs v St Paul's Community Project Ltd* [2005] BVC 12; *C & E Commrs v Yarburgh Childrens Trust* [2002] BVC 141

Other material: HM Manuals Vol V1-6 Section 2

VAT Reporter: ¶10-635

(2) Whether supply made in the course or furtherance of business

Once it is established that a business is being carried on, it is necessary in order to establish whether a particular supply may be liable to VAT, to establish whether it is done in the course or furtherance of the business.

It will be seen from the flowchart at 4-950 that the legislation provides that a number of things which might not be seen as done in the course of a business or in its furtherance, such as closing it down, are brought within the meaning of the term by statute. Things which will be seen as done in the course or furtherance of a business are as follows:

(1) the supply of a business asset or a supply made for business purposes – this is not a specific statutory addition, but a general inference from the legislation and cases;

(2) things done in connection with closing a business down, such as selling the remaining business assets;

(3) transferring a business as a going concern; and

(4) supplies made as the holder of an office by a person carrying on a trade, profession or vocation if he accepted that office in the course of his trade, profession or vocation. An example of this would be a lawyer who accepts office as a director of a company in the course of carrying on his profession.

Legislation: VATA 1994, s. 94(4)–(6)

VAT Reporter: ¶140

GOODS AND SERVICES

3-800 Introduction to goods and services

VAT is charged on supplies of goods and supplies of services. There are many detailed rules covering such matters as whether a supply is regarded as made in the UK or elsewhere, the time when the supply is regarded as taking place (and so when the tax on it falls due), and even the amount taxable and the rate of tax applicable, which vary depending on whether the supply is of goods or of services. It is therefore important to distinguish between the two.

The legislation specifies a number of supplies which are to be treated either as supplies of goods or as supplies of services. Any supply which is not specified as one or the other will have been made for consideration and is deemed to be a supply of services. The rules for distinguishing between supplies of goods and supplies of services are set out schematically in the flowchart at 4-960.

Legislation: VATA 1994, s. 5(2)(b); Sch. 4

3-820 Single and multiple supplies

As is apparent from the flowchart at 4-960, before the supply can be classified as being of goods or of services, its real nature must be established. Often, this is straightforward. For instance, if a person sells a van for a sum of money, there is clearly a supply of the van, and there is an end of it. However, if the van which is sold contains a load of carrots, and these

Supplies by Business

pass to the purchaser as well, there may well be two supplies, one of the van and the other of the carrots. This would be a multiple supply, where what appears to be a single transaction involves more than one supply.

Difficulty often arises with any transaction that may be a multiple supply, with a number of different elements making up a single supply. For instance, the sale of a calculator with an instruction manual might be looked at as two supplies, one of the calculator (standard-rated) and the other of the manual (zero-rated). In all probability though, it would be regarded as a single supply of a calculator. However, consider the position if the manual went beyond the operation of that particular calculator, and covered, for instance, mathematical techniques and number games. If the manual was of utility in its own right, the transaction might be regarded as a multiple supply. This would be even more likely if the manual were also available separately to people who did not wish to buy a calculator.

As can be seen, this is an area where questions of fact and degree abound, and great care needs to be exercised. The managers of the business need to be wary of transactions which might be seen in different ways, and take advice on them. See the flowchart at 4-970 for guidance on deciding whether a transaction is a single or multiple supply.

The principles to be used in situations such as this were formulated in the ECJ in *Card Protection Plan Ltd v C & E Commrs* (see below for more details of this case). A summary of the way in which it may be decided whether there is a single or multiple supply is as follows:

(1) Ascertain the essential feature or features

To determine the essential feature or features it is necessary to take account of:

(1)   all the essential features of the transaction;

(2)   what the typical customer is seeking from the transaction;

(3)   for what the typical customer pays.

The price structure is not decisive when determining if there are one or more supplies. There may be a single price for a number of supplies or vice versa. The price structure should be taken into account but one must not assume that a single price indicates a single supply.

The aim of this analysis is to dissect the transaction into the principle supply and any ancillary supplies.

(2) Apply the 'artificial to split' test

It is case law that something which from an economic point of view is in reality a single service should not be 'artificially split'.

It is necessary to form a judgment on whether the principal and ancillary supplies are so closely linked 'that they form, objectively, a single indivisible economic supply, which it would be artificial to split'. If they do, there is single supply and it is unnecessary to proceed to the principal/ancillary test.

For example, The Court of Appeal decided that it would be artificial to segregate a physician's services from the medicines administered by him or her. As a matter of common sense, breaking down a visit to a doctor into smaller units – the examination and the drugs applied – would 'artificially split' the transaction.

(3) Apply the principal/ancillary test

The second test – the 'principal/ancillary test' – requires making a judgment about the ancillary elements. To be a separate supply, an ancillary element must be considered from the customer's perspective. For a typical customer, which (if any) of the ancillary elements is 'an aim in itself' rather than merely 'a means of better enjoying the principal service'? (para. 24). Only the ancillary elements or features which are aims in themselves for the typical customer are separate supplies.

See also flowchart at 4-970.

Cases: *Card Protection Plan Ltd v C & E Commrs*[1999] BVC 155; [1992] BVC 54; *C & E Commrs v Madgett (t/a Howden Court Hotel)*(Joined Cases C-308/96 and C-94/97) [1998] BVC 458; *Levob Verzekeringen BV and OV Bank NV v Staatssecretaris van Financien* [2005] Case C-41/04 (2007) BVC 155; *Benyon & Partners v HMRC*[2005] BVC 3

Other material: HM Manuals Supply and consideration manual

VAT Reporter: ¶140; ¶14-800

Cases – packaging and delivery

A common area of difficulty concerns packaging and delivery.

Kimberley-Clark Ltd case

Kimberley-Clark launched 'Huggies' disposable nappies. As an initial campaign they sold one months supply of nappies in a toy box that was described as being free and could be used for any storage purpose. At the same time, they sold the same number of nappies packaged in an ordinary cardboard box at the same price. The firm treated the supply as being one single supply, nappies, that was zero-rated. HMRC disagreed and demanded that the supply be treated as a multiple supply of the zero-rated nappies and the standard-rated toy box and assessed accordingly. Kimberley-Clark appealed to the VAT and Duties Tribunal that decided in favour of HMRC.

The company then appealed to the High Court.

Lloyd J looked at the two main principles laid down in *Card Protection Plan*:

(1)   There was a single supply in cases where one or more elements were to be regarded as being the principal supply whilst one or more elements were ancillary to that supply and followed the liability of the principal supply.

(2)   A service must be regarded as ancillary to the principal service if it did not provide an aim in itself for the customers, but was more a means to better enjoying the principal service supplied.

The sale of the nappies in the box was a single supply because the provision of the toy box was ancillary to the main supply, that of the nappies. The supply of the nappies was the dominant element in the supply and therefore the box took on the same VAT liability as the nappies. It was not correct to divide up or dissect the transaction.

British Telecom Plc case

In *C & E Commrs v British Telecommunications Plc*, the House of Lords had to decide if there was one or two supplies when British Telecommunications Plc ('BT') purchased cars direct from manufacturers. The contracts and/or invoices with the manufacturers were structured so that delivering the cars to BT was charged as a separate amount. Nevertheless, the House of Lords ruled that there was a single supply. Its decision included the following comments:'In the present case the essential feature … is the purchase …of a delivered motor car … BT could have gone to the factory to take delivery of the motor car, but it was more convenient to get the manufacturer to deliver the car to BT. This seems to me to be a good example of the kind of case, in the context of a transaction which involves the supply of both goods and services, which the court had in mind when it referred in *Card Protection Plan Ltd v C & E Commrs*, para. 30, to a service which did not constitute for customers 'an aim in itself, but a means of better enjoying the principal service supplied'.

Cases: *Kimberley-Clark Ltd* [2003] BVC 4,050; *C & E Commrs v British Telecommunications Plc* [1999] BVC 306

Other material: VAT Notice 700/24 – Postage & Delivery Charges; VAT Notice 700/7 – Business Promotion Schemes

VAT Reporter: ¶15-215

Cases – general approach

Wellington Private Hospital case

C & E Commrs v Wellington Private Hospital Ltd also concerned the fundamental question whether there is a single, compound, supply embracing a number of elements, or a number of separate supplies.

Patients were admitted to the hospital on the recommendation of consultants who had admitting rights but who otherwise had no contractual connection with the hospital. The consultants invoiced the patients direct for their services, and the hospital invoiced them direct for its supplies.

The hospital made a daily charge to cover the provision of a room with bathroom, nursing services, table top meals and television. Separate additional charges were made for intensive care, progressive care, use of operating theatres, post-operative recovery facilities, telephone calls, etc. It also charged separately for various medical services and for drugs.

The case concerned the VAT liability of the charges made for drugs. HMRC contended that, even if they were supplied separately, they were not 'dispensed' by a pharmacist within the meaning of VATA 1983, Sch. 5, Grp. 14, item 1 (now VATA 1994, Sch. 8, Grp. 12, item 1). The arguments on this point were somewhat specialised and not very convincing, and the tribunal found in favour of the appellant on this point.

HMRC's main argument was that there was a single supply of care in a hospital, and this was exempt from VAT under former VATA 1983, Sch. 6, Grp. 7, item 1 or 4 or both (now VATA 1994, Sch. 9, Grp. 7, items 1 and 4).

In formulating its approach to this question, the tribunal quoted with approval remarks by Judge Medd in *Rayner & Keeler Ltd* to the effect that 'where it is practical and realistic to consider that the one supply is not an integral part of another overall supply, that course should be taken'. In other words, there should be a presumption in favour of multiple, rather than compound, supplies.

In the present case, it was both practical and realistic to see various separate supplies, for two main reasons:

(1)   there was a clear distinction between the 'core' supply of the room, meals, etc. at a daily rate and the various other goods and services available at a separate charge, the cost of the latter depending on the patient's requirements (e.g. for specially cooked meals) and the course of treatment (e.g. drugs, medical facilities, etc.); and

(2)   unlike the leading composite supply cases, there was not a single agreed charge for an overall supply, which would then need to be apportioned. Instead, the hospital itemised separately its charges for the various elements outside the core package.

Accordingly, the tribunal found that the supplies of drugs were separate supplies falling within the zero-rating, and allowed the appeal.

The High Court overturned this decision on appeal. It considered that the relevant EC legislation was framed in such terms that the supply of goods ancillary to the supply of medical services was subsumed into that supply of services and that the UK legislation must be construed accordingly. The transactions should therefore be regarded as involving a single exempt supply of medical services. The Court of Appeal reversed the High Court, and reinstated the tribunal's decision (Court of Appeal, Civil Division, judgment delivered 23 January 1997). Interestingly, the court noted that all previous cases which had reached this level had concerned a package provided for a single price, and the question was whether it should be split into its component parts. In this case, the taxpayer had charged separately for the different components, and HMRC sought to treat them as representing a single supply. The court commented that what the contracting parties had joined together, HMRC could seek to put asunder; however, where the contracting parties had separated the elements, HMRC could not join them together.

Leightons Ltd case: opticians

In *C & E Commrs v Leightons Ltd*, the tribunal held that, when an optician dispenses glasses there are, in reality, two supplies: one is a taxable supply of the glasses and the other is an exempt supply of medical services (former VATA 1983, Sch. 6, Grp. 7, item 1(b), now VATA 1994, Sch. 9, Grp. 7, item 1(b)).

The High Court upheld the tribunal's decision. If the optician was regarded as making a single supply of services, the exemption would only be available in exceptional cases, and this could not have been the intention of Parliament. The tribunal was right to attach weight to the general scheme of the tax, and it had reached the correct conclusion.

Subsequent to *Card Protection Plan*, HMRC attempted to reverse the effect of the above decision. They failed. *Leightons Ltd: Eye-Tech Opticians* rejected HMRC's contention that VAT was due on the full selling price of spectacles and contact lenses. The Tribunal found that customers buying these goods under prescription intended to purchase two supplies: the goods and the services of the dispensing optician. *Southport Visionplus Ltd* reiterated these findings and also went on to say that the Card Protection Plan ruling was not exhaustive. The division of the supply into the services of the dispensing optician and the supply of goods was not artificial.

Following this defeat, HMRC issued a Business Brief accepting the situation and clarifying their position.

Card Protection Plan Ltd case

Card Protection Plan Ltd provided a credit card registration service with a package of benefits. The issue was whether this was a single or multiple supply.

The package included elements of convenience and peace of mind (such as confidential registration of cards held, notification of loss of cards to banks, etc. ordering replacement cards, car hire discounts, emergency loans of cash worldwide) and elements of insurance (cover against fraudulent use of cards, emergency medical cover, etc.).

The card registration service was the first service mentioned, many of the services had no insurance element and in several others the insurance element was merely ancillary. The company's advertising material stressed the convenience and peace of mind aspects rather than the insurance aspect.

In *Card Protection Plan Ltd v C & E Commrs*, the ECJ provided the principles which the national court should apply in reaching its decision, although it observed at para. 27 that

'... having regard to the diversity of commercial operations, it is not possible to give exhaustive guidance on how to approach the problem correctly in all cases'.

The main pointers given by the court were:

(1) where the transaction involves a bundle of features, regard must be had to all of the circumstances in which the supply takes place;

(2) every supply of a service must normally be regarded as distinct and independent, but a supply which comprises a single service from an economic point of view should not be artificially split, as this would be distortive;

(3) there is a single supply if one or more elements are to be regarded as constituting the principle service, while other elements are merely ancillary and so share the same tax treatment as the principal service. A service is ancillary to the principal service if it does not constitute, for customers, an aim in itself, but provides a means of better enjoying the principal service supplied; and

(4) the fact that a single price is charged suggests that there is a single service, but is not decisive. If the circumstances suggested that customers intended to purchase two or more separate services liable at different rates, then the consideration must be apportioned. The simplest possible method of calculation or assessment should be used for this.

Applying the approach suggested by the ECJ, the House of Lords decided that there was a single supply by CPP.

Following this judgment, HMRC issued a VAT Information Sheet accepting the approach taken and summarising their view of the basic principles for determining what is supplied, which may be summarised as follows:

- regard must be had to all of the circumstances in which the transaction takes place;
- each supply must be regarded as separate and distinct, but a transaction which comprises a single supply from an economic point of view should not be artificially split. The essential features of the transaction must be ascertained in order to determine whether a typical customer is being provided with several distinct principal supplies or with a single supply;
- there is a single supply where one element is the principal service and other elements do not constitute an aim in themselves but a means of better enjoying the principal service; and
- the charging of a single price may suggest that there is a single supply, but it is not decisive. If the circumstances of the transaction indicate that customers are intending to purchase two or more distinct services, then the price may need to be apportioned.

HMRC consider, reasonably enough, that applying the ECJ tests as a package is likely to be the route to discovering the correct treatment in the majority of cases.

Lloyds TSB Group Ltd case

C & E Commrs v Lloyds TSB Group Ltd concerned the exemption in VATA 1994, Sch. 9, Grp. 5, item 5 for the making of arrangements for the granting of credit, but it is of wider interest for its treatment of the approach to be taken in characterising composite supplies.

Lloyds Bowmaker Ltd (LB), a company in Lloyds TSB's VAT group, had a business of financing and arranging the hire purchase and leasing of cars. Volkswagen Financial Services (UK) Ltd (VFS) carried on a similar business. In 1994, LB and VFS entered into an agreement whereby LB would provide VFS with a package of services. On the facts found by the tribunal, these fell into two main categories:

(1) 'new business', consisting of processing financing applications, running credit checks, accepting or rejecting applications, varying interest terms, etc.; and

(2) 'post-acceptance functions', such as receiving and passing on instalment payments, administering the agreements, etc.

There was a single, undivided, consideration for the whole package of services.

It was common ground between the parties that LB made a single supply to VFS, and the court agreed with this view. Citing *Card Protection Plan Ltd v C & E Commrs* [1994] BVC 20, the court noted that it is rarely appropriate to divide up a package of services where payment for that package takes the form of a single undivided sum. This should be contrasted with the view taken by the Court of Appeal in *C & E Commrs v Wellington Private Hospital Ltd* that, when the contracting parties have separated the different elements of a package, and allocated separate consideration to each, it is not open to HMRC to seek to treat them as a single supply.

The court then found that, where there was a single supply, it must be characterised by reference to its predominant nature. It agreed with the court in *Card Protection Plan* that this involved taking a broad view of what was supplied, while agreeing that this was a matter of impression on which different minds might reach different conclusions and noting that 'that may not, of course, necessarily provide much comfort to clients or to their legal advisers'. The taking of a broad view did not provide an immediate or precise test. It was necessary to look at the package as a whole and take account of all the relevant circumstances including, in the present case, the individual elements in the package and any evidence as to their relative importance.

The court found that the 'new business' elements of the package amounted to the making of arrangements by LB for the granting of credit by VFS, while the 'post-acceptance functions' fell more naturally within HMRC's description of the supplies as a whole, of services involved in the management of credit (as opposed to its arrangement or negotiation). It also took account of costings which showed that, both in terms of staff time and in terms of overall cost, the 'new business elements' accounted for around two-thirds of the resources used in making the supplies.

The court concluded that the predominant nature of the supply was concerned with the 'new business' elements, and the remaining services were ancillary to these. This view was supported by the costings as an indicator of what VFS was principally paying for and principally receiving.

Accordingly, the court upheld the tribunal's decision that the supplies were exempt, and dismissed HMRC's appeal.

It follows from this judgment that there are two stages to the analysis where there is a supply of a package of services:

(1) decide whether there is one supply or several. If there is a single, undivided consideration, there is probably only one supply. If the consideration is specifically allocated between the parts, there are almost certainly several; and

(2) if there is a single supply, determine its predominant character, taking account of all of the circumstances.

When structuring transactions, note that it may be possible to affect the liability of all or part of a package depending on the calculation and allocation (if any) of the consideration, and the overall terms of the agreement as written and as applied in practice.

Credit card fees and retailers

The following case was taken to the Tribunal and to the High Court as an example of the schemes that have been set up by retailers in order to stop accounting for VAT on the fees paid to credit card companies.

Debenhams Plc set up a system whereby the 2.5 per cent paid to a financial services company on each credit card transaction was treated as being exempt from VAT. Thus, the company accounted for VAT on 97.5 per cent of each credit card transaction. HMRC assessed for the VAT due on the 'exempt' amount. Debenhams appealed to the VAT and Duties Tribunal, who decided in favour of HMRC, and thence to the High Court who found in favour of Debenhams.

Simplistically, the scheme was that a company, Debenhams Card Handling Services Ltd (DCHS) was set up to process all credit or debit card transactions made by customers. The customers were informed that 2.5 per cent of the purchase price would be paid to DCHS and the remaining 97.5 per cent would go to Debenhams Retail Plc (DR). Amex, Diners and Style cards were evidently not included in the scheme. The total price paid by the customer was unaffected. DR subsequently accounted for VAT on the 97.5 per cent purchase price. This represented a reduction in VAT of about 37p per £100 transaction.

The Court of Appeal ruled that there was only one contract, that being between DR and the customer. The scheme failed. This was in line with European authorities that showed where the price paid by a Member and a non-Member of a scheme (in this instance, a credit card customer and a cash customer) is the same, that militates against any argument that the price to a Member includes an element attributable to vouchers or the like.

Supplies by Business

65

Distance learning

The House of Lords has supported the decision of the VAT and Duties Tribunal in agreeing with HMRC that the supply of distance learning is one supply of education rather than a multiple supply of printed material and education (*College of Estate Management v C & E Commrs*).

Other cases

There have been many cases concerned with the fundamental question of what it is which is being supplied. The small sample above provides a fair illustration of the difficulties which arise, and makes the point that this is not a trivial question. This is ultimately an area for subjective judgment, and cannot readily be codified. It is important to consider the possible different views which might be taken of a particular transaction and, where different tax results might otherwise arise, to take all possible steps to document the true nature of the transaction (e.g. by means of formal contracts).

Cases: *C & E Commrs v Wellington Private Hospital Ltd* [1997] BVC 251; *C & E Commrs v Leightons Ltd* [1995] BVC 192; *Leightons Ltd: Eye-Tech Opticians* [2002] BVC 2,027; *Southport Visionplus Ltd* [2002] BVC 2,047; *Card Protection Plan Ltd v C & E Commrs* (Case C-349/96) [1999] BVC 155; *Card Protection Plan Ltd v C & E Commrs* [2001] BVC 158; *C & E Commrs v Lloyds TSB Group Ltd* [1998] BVC 173; *R & C Commrs v Debenhams Retail Plc* [2005] EWCA Civ 892; [2005] BVC 554; *College of Estate Management v C & E Commrs* [2005] BVC 704 (HL)

Other material: HM Manuals Supply and consideration

VAT Reporter: ¶15-670

3-840 Supplies of goods

As indicated in the flowchart at 4-960, the following are specified as being supplies of goods:

(1) the transfer of the whole property in goods;

(2) the transfer of possession of goods under an agreement for the sale of the goods, or under an agreement which expressly contemplates that the property in the goods will also pass at some ascertainable future date;

(3) the supply of power, heat, refrigeration or ventilation;

(4) the granting, assignment or surrender of a 'major interest' in land. A major interest in land is the freehold or a leasehold interest having a term certain greater than 21 years. It also includes a lease for a period of 20 years or more in respect of land in Scotland; and

(5) the transfer or disposal of goods which are business assets so that they no longer form part of the business assets is treated as a supply of goods, even if no consideration passes. In view of the provisions at (1) and (2) above, this provision seems redundant in the context of distinguishing between supplies of goods and of services. It is presumably

included to put it beyond doubt that a gift of goods constitutes a supply, rather than to indicate the classification of the supply.

Legislation: VATA 1994, s. 96(1); Sch. 4, paras. 1(1) and (2), 3, 4 and 5

VAT Reporter: ¶10-455

3-860   Supplies of services

The following are specified as being supplies of services:

(1)   the transfer of an undivided share of the property in goods, or a transfer of the possession of goods except under a contract for their sale, etc. An example of the former would be the sale of a half-share in goods; and

(2)   the use of goods which are business assets, under the directions of the person carrying on the business, for a private or non-business purpose, whether or not there is any consideration.

Anything else which is a supply, but is not specifically stated to be a supply of goods, will be a supply of services.

There is deemed to be a supply of services where input tax is reclaimed on the obtaining of services and these are subsequently put to non-business use for no consideration.

However, this deemed supply does not apply:

(1)   if any part of the tax charged on the original supply of the services was disallowed as not being input tax (i.e. was apportioned as not being used for business purposes); or

(2)   to services used for the provision of catering or accommodation for employees falling within VATA 1994, Sch. 6, para. 10 (see 4-830); or

(3)   on the non-business use of a hired or leased car, where there is a 50 per cent disallowance of input tax (6-300).

HMRC have given some indication of the kinds of circumstances in which they expect this tax charge to apply. They see it as affecting major changes of use continuing over time (minor or occasional non-business use will be ignored) in respect of services such as computer software or services of constructing or refurbishing buildings. The main example they cite is of a domestic extension initially intended solely for business use, and so used, but subsequently put to non-business use.

In most cases of domestic extensions for, say, use as an office, there will generally be some element of private use. The trader will normally be wise to acknowledge this by making at least some disallowance of input tax from the outset, so that the main residence exemption for capital gains tax is not prejudiced. If this is done, then there is no question of a further charge arising under the *Value Added Tax (Supply of Services) Order* 1993 (SI 1993/1507), even if the whole extension is subsequently put to entirely private use. See 6-830 for details of the

Lennartz mechanism for reclaiming input tax in full and accounting for output tax on the non-business/personal use of an asset.

Legislation: VATA 1994, Sch. 4, paras. 1(1) and 5(4); *Value Added Tax (Supply of Services) Order* 1993 (SI 1993/1507)

Other material: Notice 700, para. 4.5

VAT Reporter: ¶10-455

PLACE OF SUPPLY

3-900 Determining where supplies are made

VAT is charged on supplies which are deemed to occur in the UK, but not on supplies made outside of the UK. It is essential, therefore, that those running the business should be able to tell where supplies are made. Any business with international connections of any sort needs to take care, as the 'place of supply' is a common problem area. It is obvious that this applies to a business which makes supplies to an overseas customer. As can be seen at 6-000ff. and 5-550ff., it is equally important for a business which has overseas suppliers. If an overseas supplier charges UK VAT which is not properly chargeable on the transaction, the UK customer will have no legal right to recover that VAT from HMRC.

The determination of the place of supply is done separately for each supply made. This is in contrast with other taxes where the determination of tax jurisdiction is generally carried out for the person concerned, rather than for individual transactions. The rules for determining the place of supply fall into two quite distinct sets:

- the rules for determining where goods are supplied; and
- the rules for determining where services are supplied.

It follows that, before the place where a particular supply is made can be determined, it is first necessary to decide whether the supply is of goods or of services. This is covered at 3-800–3-860.

VAT Reporter: ¶140; ¶13-350

3-920 Place of supply of goods

The rules governing the place of supply of goods are markedly different from the rules for liability to other taxes, in that they entirely ignore the locations of the parties to the transactions. It is perfectly possible for a supply between two businesses, neither of which has any presence in the UK, to be treated as made in the UK for VAT purposes. By the same token, a transaction between two UK businesses having no establishments overseas may be treated as taking place outside of the UK.

(1) Basic rule

The basic rule is that goods are treated as supplied at the place where they are when their dispatch or transport to the customer begins, or the place where they are when the supply takes place if they are not to be dispatched or transported.

Example: place of supply of goods

Terry sells a lathe and a computer to Bill. The lathe is in the USA and the computer is in Huddersfield. Both are shipped to Bill's premises in Australia.

The lathe is treated as supplied outside of the UK, since the transport to Australia started when it was outside the UK.

The computer, on the other hand, is shipped from the UK and so is treated as supplied in the UK (this does not necessarily mean that VAT will be charged on the supply – in all probability, it will be zero-rated as an export of goods).

The rules are varied for trade between EC States. This is covered at 5-320.

Legislation: VATA 1994, s. 7

Other material: Notice 700, para 4.8

VAT Reporter: ¶140; ¶13-400

(2) Installed goods

There is a special rule if the goods are to be installed or assembled by the supplier, or by some other person acting on his behalf (e.g. a subcontractor). In this case, the goods are treated as supplied at the place where installation or assembly takes place.

Example: place of supply of installed goods

Wilbur Inc is a US supplier of computer hardware. It agrees to supply a mainframe computer to Retail Ltd, a company based in Billericay. The contract specifies that the computer is to be installed at Retail Ltd's Billericay head office.

The computer is shipped from Wilbur Inc's Seattle factory to Billericay, and installation of it is carried out by Wilbur (UK) Ltd, a subsidiary of Wilbur Inc, acting as subcontractor to Wilbur Inc.

The computer is regarded as supplied in the UK, since that is where it is installed on behalf of the supplier.

This special provision regarding the supply of installed goods gives rise to great difficulties in practice, since overseas suppliers (and their UK customers) are often unaware of the rules. Contracts are then made which set up responsibilities and procedures which are difficult to implement when the VAT law is taken into account, and which can give rise to loss of tax and to delays in completing the contract.

Supplies by Business

69

There is a special arrangement when installed goods are supplied by a supplier registered for VAT in another Member State but not in the UK. Instead of the supplier being required to register for VAT in the UK, his supply is ignored and the customer is treated as making an acquisition in the UK. In order to make use of this simplification, the supplier must notify HMRC (in Aberdeen) in advance, in respect of each customer affected, and must endorse his invoice 'Section 14(2) Value Added Tax Act invoice'.

Legislation: Directive 2006/112, art. 32, 36, and 73; VATA 1994, s. 7(3) and 14(2)

Other material: Notice 725, section 11

VAT Reporter: ¶63-235

(3) Imports

Where goods are imported into the UK from outside the EC, the supply of the goods by the importer, and any subsequent supplies, are treated as made in the UK (VATA 1994, s. 7(6)). This can shift the place of supply, as compared with the place fixed under the basic rules, depending upon who acts as the importer.

> ### Example: place of supply of imported goods
>
> Charleen is an Australian wine factor, based in Brisbane. She sells wine to Pat and to Harry, both based in London, and ships the wine to London. The consignment of wine for Pat is imported into the UK in Pat's name. The consignment for Harry is imported in the name of Charleen.
>
> Under the basic rules, both of these supplies are treated as made outside of the UK, since the goods are allocated to the contracts in Australia and this is where transportation commences. However, the consignment for Harry having been imported in Charleen's name, the place of the supply by Charleen is deemed (under EC law) to be the UK.

For further information see 5-060.

Legislation: VATA 1994, s. 7(6)

VAT Reporter: ¶13-400

(4) Intra EC supplies

There are special place of supply rules for intra EC supplies of goods. These are dealt with at 5-320.

3-940 Place of supply of services

The place of supply of a service is determined by the following factors:

(1)   the status of the recipient;

(2)   the location of the recipient;

(3)   the exceptions to the basic rule.

It is necessary to distinguish between business and non-business customers. For business customers the place of supply is where the customer belongs. For non-business customers the place of supply is where the supplier of the service belongs. How to determine where the supplier or customer belongs is dealt with at 5-670.

The basis rule does not apply to the following (see 5-710):

- services relating to land;
- passenger transport;
- hiring means of transport;
- restaurant and catering services;
- EC on-board restaurant and catering services;
- hiring goods;
- telecommunication and broadcasting services.

Business customers also have variations applied to the following:

- electronically supplied services;
- admissions to cultural, educational and entertainment activities, etc.

When supplying non-business customers, there are further variations for the following services (see 5-710):

- intermediaries;
- transport of goods;
- intra-EC transport of goods;
- ancillary transport services;
- valuation services;
- cultural, educational and entertainment activities, etc.;
- electronic services;
- customers who belong outside the EU.

All variations to the basic rule are explained at 5-710.

Services supplied before 1 January 2010

The basic place of supply changed significantly on 1 January 2010. A summary of the pre-January 2010 rules is available at 5-770.

Legislation: VATA 1994, s. 7A, Sch. 4A

Other material: *www.hmrc.gov.uk/vat/managing/international/exports/services.htm*;   and Notice 741 Place of Supply of Services (before 1 January 2010); Notice 741A (January 2010)

VAT Reporter: ¶13-466

3-950   Place of 'belonging'

The place where a person belongs is determined separately for each supply made. It is not unusual for a person to belong in one country in respect of one supply, and in another country in respect of a different supply.

(1) *Place where supplier belongs*

The basic rule is that a person belongs where he has his business establishment, or other fixed establishment. This is distinct from an owner's private residence.

When a German business relocated to Austria but the owner continued to live in Germany, the CEJ ruled that the business was located in Austria. It was not necessary to take into account where the owner of the business lived.

A person with more than one such establishment belongs at the location of the establishment most directly concerned with the particular supply – see flowchart 4-980. The equivalent provision of the EC directive uses slightly different terminology, and refers to the establishment from which the service is supplied.

An establishment for this purpose includes a branch or agency. It will not normally include a subsidiary or associated company acting independently (although such a company acting as agent might constitute an establishment).

Where there are several establishments, it will often be perfectly clear which is the one most directly concerned with any particular supply, or which is the one from which it is made. However, difficulties can arise, and HMRC have not issued any general guidance as to their views on the manner of determining which is the relevant establishment.

Example

A UK car-leasing company, CheerfulCrocks, had its base in Bristol. It decided to open and staff a depot in Utrecht. This depot secured a lucrative contract to supply vehicles to users in Frankfurt. The negotiations for this deal, including drawing up and administering the contract, were carried out by the staff in Utrecht. The arrangements were submitted for vetting to the CheerfulCrocks Bristol headquarters. The place of supply was Utrecht, not Bristol, because the Utrecht office was the one most directly concerned with making the supply.

In the unusual case where no business establishment, or other fixed establishment exists, a person is regarded as belonging at his usual place of residence. A company's usual place of residence is regarded as being the place where it is legally constituted.

The importance of the place of establishment in determining the place of supply was reinforced by *ARO Lease BV v Inspecteur der Belastingdienst Grote Ondermingen, Amsterdam*. This concerned a car leasing company established in the Netherlands, leasing a large number of cars to persons in Belgium. The Belgian authorities argued that the mere presence in Belgium of the fleet of leased cars constituted a business establishment. The European Court of Justice

(ECJ) considered that the place where the business was established (i.e. the main place of establishment) was a primary point in considering the place of supply. In the case of the leasing of means of transport, there was also a requirement for simplicity, bearing in mind the difficulty of determining where such assets were used. The place of supply was the place where the business was established.

However, the ECJ confined its decision to the facts of the particular case, and made specific reference to such factual points as ARO's lack of any offices, storage space, etc. in Belgium. The outcome in a case where there is some fixed establishment in the other State concerned may be different, and is likely to depend as much upon the ECJ's view of the desirable policy outcome as on the words of the law taken on their own.

An example of such an approach is *C & E Commrs v DFDS A/S*. This concerned a tour operator established in Denmark, marketing tours in the UK through the agency of a wholly owned subsidiary. The ECJ considered that, in such circumstances, it could be more appropriate to see supplies as made from a fixed establishment rather than the place where the company was established. The ECJ also considered that the subsidiary, although legally separate from its parent, acted as a mere auxiliary organ of the parent company and should properly be considered as a fixed establishment.

Thus, it is difficult to give a firm answer to the question of the place of supply where the general rule is in point, rather than one of the special rules considered below. Businesses, which may be affected by this uncertainty, often confirm the position with both tax authorities potentially involved at an early stage.

HMRC have published guidance on their views following *C & E Commrs v DFDS A/S* and *C & E Commrs v Chinese Channel (HK) Ltd*. HMRC consider that the two cases support their view that a UK agency can amount to a UK establishment of the principal supplier, even where that principal supplier is a separate legal entity. However, they also recognise that there are limitations on this approach, and not just any old subsidiary or agency amounts to an establishment. They consider that a UK subsidiary or associate of an overseas business, or even an unrelated UK business, constitutes a UK establishment of the overseas business for determining the place of supply of services if the following criteria are met:

(1)   it is of a certain minimum size with the permanent human and technical resources necessary for providing (or receiving) the services;

(2)   it is not, in function and substance, operating independently of the overseas business; and

(3)   it actually supplies (or receives) the services.

Legislation: VATA 1994, s. 9

Cases: *ARO Lease BV v Inspecteur der Belastingdienst Grote Ondermingen, Amsterdam* (Case C-190/95) [1997] BVC 547; *C & E Commrs v DFDS A/S* (Case C-260/95) [1997] BVC 279; *C & E Commrs v Chinese Channel (HK) Ltd* [1998] BVC 91; *Finanzamt Deggendor v Markus Stoppelkamp* (Case C-421/10) 6 October 2011

VAT Reporter: ¶13-471

(2) *Place where customer belongs*

Certain supplies of services are treated as made at the place where the customer belongs.

It is necessary to be able to tell where the customer belongs in respect of these sorts of services. The rules are as much as for the place where the supplier belongs. However, a business customer having more than one business establishment is regarded as belonging at the location of the one which most directly uses the supply in question.

A customer who is a private individual belongs at his usual place of residence.

Legislation: VATA 1994, s. 9

VAT Reporter: ¶65-560

(3) *Place of residence of transient workers*

The usual place of residence of transient workers has been considered by a number of tribunals.

American service personnel and their families posted to the UK for up to three years often have a home in America and the UK. In these circumstances a Tribunal found that the 'usual place of residence ' is the UK. The Tribunal commented as follows:

'I do not think it can fairly be said that an officer as described with his three year residence here has "a usual place of residence" in the USA ... I think the question is one of fact and degree ...'

Another Tribunal considered persons coming to the UK for a 'working holiday'. Although usually staying in UK for no more than 18 months, the UK was the 'usual place of residence' of these persons. The Tribunal said:

'... that they would be in the United Kingdom only temporarily and would return to their home countries at the end of a working holiday does not mean that they could not be ordinarily resident in the United Kingdom in the meantime.

... it is implicit in the wording of section 9(3) VATA and ... the 2006 Directive that the test of residence relates to the country of usual residence, rather than a particular street address.'

About ordinary tourists to the UK the Tribunal has commented as follows:

'an ordinary tourist in the United Kingdom for a period of days or weeks clearly could not be said to have their ordinary residence here ... Nevertheless, if the person had no home or employment in their country of origin, and if they rented a home in the United Kingdom for the year as a base from which to conduct travels and sightseeing, the conclusion might be reached that the person is ordinarily resident in the United Kingdom for the year in question.'

Evidently there must be some degree of permanence in order to satisfy the conditions for a 'usual place of residence'.

Cases: *USAA Ltd v C & E Commrs* [1993] BVC 1,612; *1st Contact Ltd* [2012] UKFTT 84 (TC); [2012] TC 07180

3-960   Supplies of natural gas and electricity

The place of supply depends on whether the supply is made to a customer who is offering it for resale (a wholesaler) or one who is going to use the gas or electricity (a consumer). When the supply is to a wholesaler, the place of supply is where the wholesaler is established. When the supply is to a consumer, it is where the consumption will take place.

Where supplies of gas or electricity are made in the UK to a VAT-registered customer by suppliers who are outside the UK, VAT must be accounted for by the customer under the reverse charges procedure. The amount upon which VAT should be accounted for is the consideration payable to the supplier.

Services involving access to and use of natural gas and electricity distribution systems are treated as taking place where the customer belongs.

Budget 2 2010 extends the scope so as to cover all supplies of natural gas pipeline; limits scope to such pipelines located in the EU or linked to such pipelines; and extends relief to importation of all natural gas imported via a network from 1 January 2011. The rules are amended to include supplies of heating and cooling through networks.

Legislation: VATA 1994, Sch. 5, para. 5A; *Value Added Tax (Place of Supply of Goods) Order* 2004 (SI 2004/3148), Pt. 3; *Value Added Tax (Removal of Gas and Electricity) Order* 2004 (SI 2004/3150)

Other material: VAT Information Sheet 21/10

VAT Reporter: ¶65-560

3-970   Greenhouse gas emissions

The place of supply for supplies of emissions allowances within a Member State is where the supplier is based.

The place of supply of emissions allowances when traded across borders is where the customer belongs so the reverse charge applies.

Legislation: VATA 1994, Sch. 5, para. 5A; Directive 2006/112 Article 56 (1)

Other material: Notice 741A, para. 15.13

TIME OF SUPPLY

4-020   Importance of time of supply

The time when a supply is deemed to occur for VAT purposes is important for a number of reasons. First and foremost, it determines the period for which the supplier must account for the tax, and so the date by which it must be paid over to HMRC. It also determines the period for which a VAT-registered customer can reclaim the tax. The correct identification of the time of supply for these purposes is especially important, because a civil penalty may arise if tax is entered on the wrong return.

When there are changes in the rate of tax, or in the classification of supplies which are exempt or zero-rated, the precise time of supply can be of crucial importance in determining the rate which attaches to supplies made around the time of the change. The time of supply is also important in ascertaining the amounts to be included in various calculations carried out by reference to set periods, such as calculations of turnover for registration purposes, and partial exemption calculations.

In principle, the time of supply (or 'tax point') is the earlier of:

(1)   the date when the supply is 'really' made (referred to by HMRC as the 'basic tax point' (4-040));

(2)   the date when a tax invoice is issued in respect of the supply (4-060); and

(3)   the date when payment is received for the supply (4-080).

In order to establish the tax point for a particular supply, it is necessary to identify each of these three dates and select the earliest. In practice, of course, it is necessary to be on the watch for all three, and account for VAT by reference to the first which occurs. See flowchart 4-990.

There are a number of refinements to be borne in mind in applying this basic rule (see below), and there are also special rules for certain kinds of supply. These are covered at 4-120 through to 4-520.

VAT Reporter: ¶11-700

4-040   The basic tax point

Identification of the basic tax point (or the time when the supply actually takes place) is based on different rules depending on whether the supply is of goods or of services (see flowchart 4-995). This is yet another area where the VAT law distinguishes between goods and services, and treats them differently.

(1) Basic tax point: goods

In the case of goods which are to be delivered to the customer, or collected by the customer, the basic tax point is the date when delivery commences. If the supply does not involve movement of the goods (e.g. a supply of land, or of goods which are erected on the customer's premises), the basic tax point is the date when the goods are made available to the customer. In the case of supplies of land, it appears that the basic tax point is normally the date of completion rather than the date when contracts are exchanged.

It is possible for goods to be delivered to a potential customer without a supply yet having taken place. This would happen, for instance, if they were sent on approval or on sale or return terms. If goods are delivered on such terms, so that it is uncertain whether there will in fact be a supply of them, the basic tax point does not arise until the supply becomes certain (e.g. by the customer adopting the goods, or the expiry of an agreed period within which they may be returned). However, the basic tax point will in any case arise if the customer holds the goods for 12 months without returning them, even if he still has the right to return them.

Example: goods on sale or return

Tilt Ltd delivers 200 bags of fertiliser to Giles Farms Ltd, on sale or return terms, on 1 January 2010.

On 1 July 2010, Giles Farms Ltd appropriates 100 bags of fertiliser, and returns 50 bags to Tilt Ltd. No decision is taken whether to appropriate the remaining 50 bags until some time in 2011.

The basic tax point for 100 bags of fertiliser arises on 1 July 2010. The 50 bags returned will clearly never be supplied. The basic tax point for the 50 bags still held by Giles Farms Ltd arises on 1 January 2011, and Tilt Ltd must account for the tax on this supply by including it on its VAT return for the period in which that date falls.

It will be seen from the above example that it is usually a bad idea, from a VAT point of view, to send goods on sale or return terms for a period greater than a year. If it is considered commercially desirable to allow such a long period, a special system needs to be developed to keep track of the goods in order to account for the tax correctly. It may also be desirable to require the customer to pay at least the VAT part of the price of goods held for more than a year, this being refundable if the goods are returned.

(2) Basic tax point: services

The basic tax point for a supply of services arises when the services are performed. HMRC generally take this to be the date when the service is completed except for invoicing.

There are many services where it is difficult to identify when the service is performed, or which extend over a considerable period. For instance, if a piece of plant is leased for a two-year period, the service is provided (or performed) throughout the two-year period, but completion of the service does not take place until the end of the two years. This type of supply is generally covered by the special rules for determining the time of supply, enabling the basic tax point to be left out of account.

Legislation: VATA 1994, s. 6(2) and (3)

Other material: Notice 700, section 14

VAT Reporter: ¶11-700

4-060   Issue of a tax invoice

The tax invoice is the formal document to be issued, in certain circumstances, to another trader. It is mandatory to issue a tax invoice to the customer when:

Supplies by Business

(a) The customer is registered or liable to be registered, in the UK and the goods or services are liable to UK VAT.

(b) Goods or services are supplied to business in another EU State except when the supply is exempt from VAT and the recipient does not require a VAT invoice.

The tax invoice provides the evidence which enables another taxable trader to claim input tax on the supply.

The characteristics of a tax invoice are discussed at 9-280ff. It should be noted that, according to HMRC, an invoice for a zero-rated supply is not a tax invoice, except in the case of an invoice to an overseas customer acquiring the goods in another Member State. Consequently, it cannot trigger a tax point. The comments and flow charts on time of supply need to be read with this in mind.

The date when a tax invoice is issued is the date when it is sent to the customer. If it is produced but simply kept in a drawer, or even shown to the customer but then retained by the supplier, it has not yet been issued.

If it is desired to request money from a customer in advance of a supply being made, care should be taken as to the form which the request takes. If the request is made by issuing what amounts to a tax invoice, then the tax will be accountable by reference to the date when the invoice is issued, even though the money may not be received, or the supply made, for some time afterwards. Indeed, if the customer never responds, and the supply is never made, the amount shown on the invoice as tax can still be collected by HMRC. This is intended to prevent loss to the revenue in the event that the customer fraudulently uses the tax invoice to reclaim the tax shown.

(1) Pro-forma invoices

Often payment is requested by issuing a document similar in appearance to a tax invoice, but which does not have the characteristics of one (e.g. a pro forma invoice). In such cases, great care should be exercised to ensure that the document cannot be treated as a tax invoice.

No VAT registration number should be quoted, and ideally no separate amount should be shown in respect of VAT. The document should be clearly marked to the effect that it is not a tax invoice. If such documents are to be used with any frequency, or for large amounts, it is wise to agree the exact form of them with HMRC.

(2) The 14-day rule

If a tax invoice is issued within 14 days after the basic tax point, then the basic tax point can be ignored in fixing the time of supply and the date when the invoice is issued is used instead. This can simplify VAT accounting in practice, as it is often easier to set up systems which operate by reference to the date of the invoice than it is to use the basic tax point. The 14-day rule was extended for supplies with a basic tax point between the 18–30 November 2008 – see also paragraph 4-520.

There is no obligation to use the 14-day rule, and accounting can be done by reference to the basic tax point if this is more convenient. However, a trader who does not wish to use the 14-day rule must notify HMRC of this in writing. This notification will then effectively cancel the 14-day rule for all supplies made by that trader. It is possible to use the 14-day rule for some supplies, but not for others, but in practice this should be agreed with HMRC.

If required, the 14-day rule can be used as if some longer period were mentioned instead of 14 days. Many businesses with monthly invoicing runs find it convenient to use a 31-day rule. If a longer period is required, the trader must ask HMRC to make a direction to that effect. Often, a longer period is used without the issuing of a formal direction. This is unwise, because it will expose the trader to possible penalties and interest for incorrect returns and late payments of tax (10-000ff.).

It should also be noted that the 14-day rule only overrides the basic tax point. The issue of an invoice cannot override an earlier tax point triggered by the receipt of payment for a supply (see below).

(3) On-account invoicing

If a tax invoice is issued for only a part of the total price of the supply, this will trigger the tax point only for that part of the supply. The tax point for the remainder of the supply, and the date when the tax on it becomes accountable to HMRC, will be determined separately.

> ### Example: account invoicing
>
> Alf agrees to sell goods to Selina for £100 plus VAT. Alf issues an invoice for £30 plus VAT on 1 March, and delivers the goods on 1 April. He issues an invoice for the remaining £70 plus VAT on 10 April. Selina pays for the supply on 30 April.
>
> The tax point is 1 March for the £30 plus £6.00 VAT invoiced on that date. The basic tax point for the remainder of the supply is 1 April, when Alf delivers the goods. However, a tax invoice for the remainder is issued within 14 days thereafter, so 10 April (the invoice date) becomes the tax point for the remainder of the supply, unless Alf has written to HMRC opting not to use the 14-day rule. The date when payment is received does not influence the tax point, as the other events which can trigger the tax point take place earlier.

Legislation: VATA 1994, s. 6(4) and (5)

Cases: *C & E Commrs v Woolfold Motor Co Ltd* (1983) 1 BVC 564

Other material: Notice 700/63 Electronic Invoicing; Notice 700, sections 16 & 17; VAT information sheet 10/07

VAT Reporter: ¶11-765

4-080   Date payment received, prepayments and deposits

The date when a payment is received by the supplier triggers the tax point to the extent of the payment, if the tax point not already arisen by reference to the basic tax point or the issue of a tax invoice.

Supplies by Business

79

This rule has led to a good deal of dispute when there were major changes in the VAT liability of certain types of construction work. Many suppliers took orders which could not be fulfilled until after increased VAT liability came into effect, and sought to avoid the increase by having customers pay for the supplies before the change, thus triggering the time of supply and bringing the supply concerned under the old rules.

The main points established in these cases are:

(1) if payment is by cheque, it is not actually received by the supplier until the cheque has been passed through the banking system and honoured by the payer's bank; and

(2) receipt of payment for a supply can fix the tax point, even if the payment is financed by a loan from the supplier, or by some other mechanism involving the supplier.

If a deposit is received from the customer, the precise terms on which it is held need to be considered to decide whether it amounts to payment. Usually, a deposit will amount to advance payment for a supply, in which case it gives rise to a tax point. However, a deposit which is merely security for, say, the return of goods which are let on hire, is not payment for a supply (even if forfeited) and so does not give rise to a tax point.

Most advance payments in respect of a supply will bring about a tax point, even if the money is refundable should the supply not proceed.

If a deposit is received for a supply, and represents payment for the supply, then it will be necessary to account for VAT on the amount of the deposit. If the supply is then cancelled by the customer, and the terms are such that the deposit is forfeited, it no longer represents consideration for a supply of any sort. The tax already accounted for can be claimed back on the next VAT return. However, care is needed if the deposit might be seen as consideration for some supply other than the one originally contemplated.

Amounts received by a supplier and, by specific agreement, held on trust for the customer pending performance of the intended supply, were held by the tribunal not to give rise to a tax point until the supply was made. However, this decision was overturned on appeal. Although the company held the money in trust, it was permitted to mix it with its own funds. The beneficiary under the trust (the customer) had no proprietorial interest in the ticket money and, in a liquidation, would rank equally with the supplier's other unsecured creditors.

Overpayments by customers, retained by the supplier and set against subsequent bills, were held not to give rise to a tax point until applied against those later bills. This decision was upheld by the High Court on appeal.

ECJ case on non-refundable hotel deposits

In *Société thermale d'Eugénie-les-Bains v Ministère de l'Économie, des Finances et de l'Industrie*, the question in essence was 'whether a sum paid as a deposit by a client to a hotelier is, where the client exercises the cancellation option available to him and that sum is retained by the hotelier, to be regarded as consideration for the supply of a reservation service, which is subject to VAT, or as fixed compensation for cancellation, which is not subject to VAT'.

When the contract for accommodation is performed, the deposit is applied towards the price of the services supplied and is therefore subject to VAT. If either party cancels, the deposit is retained by the hotelier or the client is paid compensation. This is not a fee for a service and is no part of the taxable amount for VAT. This must be distinguished from the situation where a hotel reserves a room and if it not cancelled before, say, 4 pm on the day of the reservation the fee for the room is charged. In these instances, the room is available and the hotel does not re-let the accommodation. In the ECJ case, there were reservation fees that were forfeit if the accommodation was cancelled even when the room was re-let to another client.

Cases: *Rampling* (1986) 2 BVC 205,438; *C & E Commrs v Faith Construction Ltd; Dormers Builders (London) Ltd v C & E Commrs; C & E Commrs v West Yorkshire Independent Hospital (Contract Services) Ltd; Nevisbrook Ltd v C & E Commrs* (1989) 4 BVC 111; *Clowance Plc* (1988) 3 BVC 1,344; *Richmond Theatre Management Ltd* [1993] BVC 872; [1995] BVC 47; *British Telecom Plc* [1993] BVC 972; *British Telecom Plc* [1995] BVC 37; *Société thermale d'Eugénie-les-Bains v Ministère de l'Économie, des Finances et de l'Industrie* (C-277/05)

Other material: Notice 700, section 14

VAT Reporter: ¶11-900

SPECIAL TIME OF SUPPLY RULES

4-120   General

There are a number of instances in which the normal time of supply rules would be inappropriate, and special rules are used instead. These generally operate by ignoring the basic tax point, and using the earlier of the date when an invoice is issued and the date when payment is received as the tax point.

It has been considered that, in the absence of a performance tax point, difficulties could arise in the case of supplies performed before registration and for which payment is received after registration. On the face of it, these supplies would be subject to VAT, as the tax point arises when the supplier is registered for VAT. However, the Court of Appeal held in *BJ Rice & Associates v C & E Commrs* that the time of supply provisions operated to determine when tax became chargeable, not whether there was a chargeable supply at all. The question whether there was a chargeable supply was to be determined under VATA 1994, s. 4, without reference to the time of supply provisions. If the supplier was not a taxable person when the supply was actually carried out, no tax was due even though payment was received after registration.

Legislation: *Value Added Tax Regulations* 1995 (SI 1995/2518), reg. 81–95

Cases: *BJ Rice & Associates v C & E Commrs* [1996] BVC 211

VAT Reporter: ¶12-305

4-140 Goods put to private use and free supplies of services

If there is a deemed supply because goods forming part of the assets of a business are put to non-business use, a tax point is deemed to arise at the end of each accounting period in which the goods are so used. Similarly, if services are provided for no consideration but are still treated as supplied because of an order under VATA 1994, s. 5(4), they are treated as supplied on the last day of each accounting period in which they are performed.

Legislation: *Value Added Tax Regulations* 1995 (SI 1995/2518), reg. 81

VAT Reporter: ¶13-870

4-160 Imported services

A deemed supply of imported services, under the reverse charge mechanism, is normally treated as arising when the services are performed. It is normally taken that services are performed 'when all the work except invoicing is completed'. Payments received prior to this create a tax point.

With continuous services, a deemed supply occurs whenever a payment is made or invoice issued. If in any calendar year there is not any payment or invoice, a charge is automatically triggered on 31 December.

Before 1 January 2010, a deemed supply of imported services, under the reverse charge mechanism, was normally treated as arising when the services were paid for. However, if the consideration was non-monetary, the supply was treated as taking place on the last day of the accounting period in which the services were performed.

Other material: Notice 741A, para. 18.6

Legislation: *Value Added Tax Regulations* 1995 (SI 1995/2518), reg. 82

VAT Reporter: ¶12-615

4-180 Land – compulsory purchase and undetermined consideration

A special rule applies where any interest in, or right over, land is compulsorily purchased and, at the time when possession is taken, the person from whom it is purchased does not know the amount of the consideration. In such a case, the 'vendor' is treated as making successive supplies of goods (or services) each time a payment is received.

There is also a special rule to deal with the supply of freehold land in a case where the total consideration cannot be ascertained at the ordinary time of supply. In such a case, the time of supply for that part of the consideration which can be ascertained is dealt with under the ordinary rules. The balance is treated as representing successive supplies of goods at the earlier of the issuing of a tax invoice or the receipt of payment for each part of the unascertained consideration.

There are two further considerations when dealing with standard-rated supplies of new commercial buildings or civil engineering works. These are as follows:

- payments received more than three years after the initial supply are also standard-rated;
- an anti-avoidance measure may apply.

An anti-avoidance measure revokes the second special rule in the following circumstances:

- the land is to be occupied either by the person granting the freehold, or those financing the grantor's development or anybody connected with them; and
- within 10 years of completion of the building work, the building will be used for the purposes of making exempt supplies or for non-business purposes.

Legislation: *Value Added Tax Regulations* 1995 (SI 1995/2518), reg. 84(1) and (2); VATA 1994, s. 96(10A)

Other material: Notice 700, s. 15.9

VAT Reporter: ¶12-329

4-200   Supply of land under major interest lease

The supply of land under a major interest lease is treated as being a supply of goods. Where rent under such a lease is due periodically or from time to time, the time of supply occurs on the earlier of the receipt of payment by the supplier or the issuing of a tax invoice.

Where the supply is exempt or zero-rated, the time of supply will arise when payment is received, since a tax invoice cannot be issued for such a supply.

It appears that the grant of a major interest in land for a single payment, as opposed to continuing rentals, will follow the normal rules for supplies of goods. The supply therefore arises at the earlier of the time when the land is made available to the purchaser, the date when payment is received or (in some cases), the date when a tax invoice is issued in respect of the supply.

It can sometimes be difficult to decide when the land supplied is 'made available' for these purposes. In *Cumbernauld Development Corporation v C & E Commrs*, the appellant supplied the interest of the proprietor of the *dominium utile* in land (which appears to be the Scottish equivalent of the freehold). However, the purchaser was allowed to go on the land and occupy it some months before this transaction was completed. The court held that the major interest in the land was not made available to the purchaser until completion. In the meantime, the purchaser had occupation of the land under a 'mere licence to occupy' and the personal right to call for the conveyance of the property. Neither of these rights constituted the major interest which was the subject of the supply.

There are additional special rules which, in effect, force a tax point to occur once a year even if there is no tax invoice or receipt of payment.

The special rules apply only where the parties to the transaction are connected persons within ICTA 1988, s. 839 or are grouped (without being in a VAT group) for the purposes of *Companies Act* 1985, s. 259. In the case of leases of assets, where there is a chain of leases, a connection between the end user and any one of the lessors in the chain will be sufficient to trigger the provisions.

Legislation: *Value Added Tax Regulations* 1995 (SI 1995/2518), reg. 85, reg. 94B

Other material: Notice 700, para. 15

VAT Reporter: ¶12-620

Cases: *Cumbernauld Development Corporation v C & E Commrs* [2002] BVC 384

4-220 Power, heat, etc.

Supplies of power, heat, refrigeration and ventilation are treated as occurring at the earlier of the date when payment is received or the date when a tax invoice is issued. To the extent that such supplies are zero-rated, a tax invoice cannot be issued for them, so the date when payment is received constitutes the tax point.

Special rules apply where the parties to the transaction are connected persons within ICTA 1988, s. 839 or are grouped (without being in a VAT group) for the purposes of *Companies Act* 1985, s. 259.

There are additional special rules which, in effect, force a tax point to occur once a year even if there is no tax invoice or receipt of payment.

VAT Reporter: ¶12-325

Gas and electricity supplied by persons belonging outside the UK

Where UK business has to account for supplies of natural gas or electricity under the reverse charge procedure, the time of supply is normally when the fuel is paid for. If the consideration is not in money, the tax point is the last day of the relevant prescribed accounting period.

Legislation: *Value Added Tax Regulations* 1995 (SI 1995/2518), reg. 82A

Other material: HMRC Manuals Vol V1-18 (Imports), para. 3.25

VAT Reporter: ¶13-560

4-240 Goods stored at customer's premises

There is a slight variation to the ordinary rules where goods are stored at the customer's premises and:

(1)   the supplier retains title to the goods until such time as the customer appropriates them to his own use; and

(2)   the price is determined at the time when the goods are appropriated.

In this instance, the basic tax point is the earlier of when the goods are appropriated, the date when a VAT invoice is issued or payment.

Legislation: *Value Added Tax Regulations* 1995 (SI 1995/2518), reg. 88

VAT Reporter: ¶12-645

4-260   Retention payments

The ordinary time of supply rules are suspended in any instance where the contract for a supply of goods or services allows the customer to retain any part of the consideration for the supply until full and satisfactory performance of the supply has taken place. In such a case, the basic tax point is ignored as regards that part of the value of the supply represented by the retention payment, and the supply is treated as taking place on the earlier of payment being received and a tax invoice being issued.

The tax point as regards the unretained part of the consideration is dealt with under the ordinary tax point rules.

Legislation: *Value Added Tax Regulations* 1995 (SI 1995/2518), reg. 89

VAT Reporter: ¶12-625

4-280   Supplies of services for a period

The basic tax point is ignored in respect of supplies of services if:

(1)   the services are supplied 'for any period'; and

(2)   the consideration for the supply is either determined or payable periodically or from time to time.

The tax point is therefore the earlier of the date when payment is received or the date when a tax invoice is issued. This rule can often apply to supplies of professional services by persons who act for their clients on a continuing basis, such as accountants. It also covers such transactions as the hiring of goods.

There are additional special rules which, in effect, force a tax point to occur once a year even if there is no tax invoice or receipt of payment.

The special rules apply only where the parties to the transaction are connected persons within ICTA 1988, s. 839 or are grouped (without being in a VAT group) for the purposes of

Supplies by Business

Companies Act 1985, s. 259. In the case of leases of assets, where there is a chain of leases, a connection between the end user and any one of the lessors in the chain will be sufficient to trigger the provisions. The provisions do not apply if the supplier is able to demonstrate that the recipient is able to recover in full any tax charged on the relevant supply.

If the supplier issues a tax invoice, or receives payment, within six months after the tax point created above, the date of the invoice or payment becomes the tax point. This is to recognise that time may be required to determine the value of the supplies based on the preparation of accounts, etc. HMRC can also allow a period longer than six months for these purposes.

If a supply of services meets the above conditions, and the agreement provides for a succession of payments, the supplier may issue a tax invoice which covers a period of up to one year, and which gives the following additional information:

(1) the date when each payment in the period falls due;

(2) the net of VAT amount of each payment; and

(3) the rate of tax in force when the invoice is issued, and the amount of tax chargeable on each payment.

The supply is treated, in respect of each payment, as taking place on the earlier of the date when payment is received and the due date for payment.

If such an invoice is issued, but the tax rate changes, it ceases to be regarded as a tax invoice for payments falling due after the change of rate. The supplier must therefore issue a revised invoice to cover the remaining payments.

Legislation: *Value Added Tax Regulations* 1995 (SI 1995/2518), reg. 90(1)–(3); *Value Added Tax Regulations* 1995 (SI 1995/2518), reg. 94B

Other material: Notice 700, para. 14.3

VAT Reporter: ¶12-505

4-300 Royalties, etc.

There are special rules for supplies of services not covered above where:

(1) the whole of the consideration could not be determined at the time when the services were performed; and

(2) further consideration subsequently becomes due by reference to the use made of the benefit of the services by a person other than the supplier.

This would cover, for instance, the case where an actor is paid a fee for taking part in the recording of a play, and then receives additional payments for that performance each time the recording is broadcast. It would also cover the case of an author who receives an advance royalty in respect of a book, and further royalties based on sales.

In these instances, the tax point for any initial supply is determined under whatever rules are applicable to the circumstances, and further supplies are treated as taking place each time a payment is received, or a tax invoice is issued.

Legislation: *Value Added Tax Regulations* 1995 (SI 1995/2518), reg. 91

Other material: Notice 700, para. 15.8

VAT Reporter: ¶12-590

4-320 Services of barristers and advocates

The tax point for services of barristers and advocates (in Scotland) is the earlier of the date when a tax invoice is issued and the date on which a fee is received.

If a barrister ceases to practise as such, the time of supply for all work carried out, but not yet invoiced or paid for, arises on the day when practice ceases.

There is a concessionary treatment whereby the barrister can defer payment of the tax due until payment is received, if certain conditions are met. However, the tax point still remains the last day of practice, and this determines the rate of tax which applies.

Legislation: *Value Added Tax Regulations* 1995 (SI 1995/2518), reg. 92

Other material: Notice 700/44

VAT Reporter: ¶12-595

4-340 Supplies in the construction industry

There are special time of supply rules where supplies of services, or of services with goods, are made in the course of the construction, alteration, demolition, repair or maintenance of any building or civil engineering work, if the contract for the work provides for payment to be made periodically or from time to time. The supply is treated as occurring at the earlier of the date when payment is received and the date when a tax invoice is issued.

There is a special rule if the works are intended to be used for non-taxable purposes by the contractor, a person financing the works (e.g. by loan, etc. and including various roundabout means of providing finance), or by a person connected with either of these. In such cases, a tax point arises on completion of the works, regardless of payments or invoices.

Legislation: *Value Added Tax Regulations* 1995 (SI 1995/2518), reg. 93

Other material: Notice 700, para. 15.3

VAT Reporter: ¶12-600

4-380   Self-supplies of cars

For self-supplies of cars, the tax point is the date when, 'by any positive and recorded action', the car concerned is transferred from the new car sales stock. The time of supply is fixed as being the date when the goods are appropriated for the use concerned.

Legislation: VATA 1994, s. 6(11)

Other material: Notice 700, para. 15.2

VAT Reporter: ¶13-040

4-400   Self-supply of residential or charitable building

A self-supply of a residential or charitable building (see 3-200) is treated as made when the building is first put to non-qualifying use. See the flowchart at 4-900. See also 15-280.

Legislation: VATA 1994, Sch. 10, para. 1(5)

VAT Reporter: ¶36-025

4-440   Self-supply of construction services

It is unclear what tax point applies to these services (see 3-200). In the absence of special provisions, the general rules presumably apply. Since there is no question of there being a payment or a tax invoice, the time of supply presumably arises on completion of the works. See the flowchart at 4-910.

VAT Reporter: ¶36-025

Legislation: *Value Added Tax Regulations Self Supply of Construction Services Order)* 1989 (SI 1989/472)

4-460   Self-supply on acquisition of a business by a VAT group

A self-supply on the acquisition of a business as a going concern by a VAT group (see 3-200) is deemed to take place on the day when the assets are transferred. See the flowchart at 5-940.

Legislation: VATA 1994, s. 44(5)

VAT Reporter: ¶13-150

4-480 Time of supply – movement of own goods to another EC State

In the absence of a specific provision covering the deemed supply on a movement of own goods (see 3-210), it will be covered by the normal rules for supplies of goods. Assuming that the trader is registered for VAT in the other Member State, and so zero-rates the supply by invoicing his overseas establishment, the supply will take place on the earlier of the date when the invoice is issued or the fifteenth of the month following removal. In other cases, it will be the date of removal.

Other material: Notice 725, para. 9

VAT Reporter: ¶63-220

4-490 Gold Supplies

The basic tax point applies to supplies of gold. Other tax points are disapplied.

Legislation: VATA 1994, s. 55(4) and (5)

4-520 Change in rate of tax: consequences

There is an option written in the VAT Act which is only relevant when there is a change in the rate. To know whether this option is beneficial it is necessary to know the following:

- the basic tax point (4-040); and
- actual tax points – date of invoice (4-060) or payment (4-080).

A transaction with a basic tax point on or after the date the rate changes may have been proceeded by one or actual tax points. For example, a payment or tax invoice may have been issued in advance of the completion of the service or the delivery of the goods.

Section 88 of the VAT Act allows the person making the supply to account for tax be reference to the basic tax point only. Any actual tax points may be ignored. This provision may only be invoked when there is a change in the rate applicable to the goods or services concerned.

> ### *Example*
>
> PJ provides consultancy services to a charity. PJ is VAT-registered and his services are taxable. The charity is unable to recover the tax charged.
>
> This particularly consultancy project commenced in August 2008 and is schedule to finish in by the end of November 2008. Due to delays the work finished on 7 December 2008.
>
> The terms of the engagement were that PJ would invoice work-in-progress monthly in arrears with a final invoice when the work was completed. Thus, invoices were raised on

Supplies by Business

31 August, 30 September, 31 October, 30 November and 10 December 2008. These were all actual tax points and 17.5 per cent VAT charged on all but the invoice dated 8 December 2008.

PJ may make a Section 88 election to account for VAT by reference to the basic tax point only. As this was 7 December 2008, 15 per cent VAT applies to the whole job rather than to only the work in progress invoiced on 10 December 2008.

The necessary adjustment to the VAT charged to the charity must be made by issuing a credit note headed 'Credit note – change of VAT rate'.

This provision requires the supplier to make an election for it to apply. However it may be adopted without notifying HMRC.

When Section 88 is applied a credit note must be issued within 45 days of the change of rate. Prior to 1 December 2008 this time limit was 15 days.

Limitations on the use of Section 88

Regulations are in place to determine the time of supply for specified supplies. Normally, these supplies are not be within the scope of Section 88. The specified supplies and relevant regulations are mostly in Part XI of VAT Regulations 1995 (SI 1995/2518).

Forestalling measures

Forestalling measures to counter manipulation of tax point rules when there is a change in the rate of VAT are discussed at 11-640.

Legislation: VATA 1994, s. 88(1) and (2); *VAT Regulations* 1995 (SI 1995/2518), reg. 15

Other material: VAT Notice 700, Section 30

VAT Reporter: ¶12-605

VALUE OF SUPPLY

4-560 Introduction to value of supply

The value of a supply, as determined for VAT purposes, is the amount on which VAT is charged. Clearly, it is important to understand the rules for determining the value of a supply (or the 'taxable amount', as it is called in the EC legislation), since this directly affects the amount of tax chargeable.

As is the case with the law governing the time of supply, there are some basic rules which cover most transactions, and then a set of special rules which apply in specified circumstances.

Legislation: VATA 1994, s. 19(1)

VAT Reporter: ¶14-200

4-580   Consideration in money

If a supply is made for consideration, and the consideration is wholly in money, the value of the supply (or taxable amount) is taken to be the amount which, with the addition of the tax chargeable, is equal to the consideration. In other words, if a supply is made for money, the price charged includes the VAT due.

This is a point which is crucially important when framing contracts. If a contract is entered into whereby a supply is to be made in return for a stated price, and no mention is made of VAT, then the stated price is taken to include VAT. The supplier has no contractual right to charge some higher amount to take account of any VAT which may be due.

It is wise, therefore, when contracting to make supplies, to frame the terms of the contract such that prices are expressed along the lines '£X plus VAT if applicable'. A supplier who incorrectly fails to add VAT in the first instance then has the opportunity to seek further consideration from the customer if it transpires that VAT was due on the supply. The customer, of course, will wish to think carefully before signing a contract which includes such a term.

Where payment is made using a credit card, the consideration is the amount paid by the customer, not the net amount (after deducting commission) passed on to the supplier by the credit card company.

In a case where a supplier of goods claimed to supply them on 'interest free' credit terms, the credit financed by a third party and (in effect) paid for by the supplier of the goods, the European Court of Justice held that the supplier was liable to account for VAT on the full price paid by the customer. It was not possible to regard some part of the price as consideration for a separate (exempt) supply of credit, either by the supplier of the goods or by the third party.

Amounts paid gratuitously, even though paid at the same time as the consideration for the supply, may well be outside the scope of VAT (see 3-460). However, there are instances where payments such as grants and subsidies may be considered not to be paid gratuitously, but to form part of the consideration (see 3-480).

In some cases involving certain gaming transactions and certain currency exchange transactions, the consideration for supplies may be regarded as equivalent to the supplier's gross margin over a period of time rather than the gross payments received.

The ECJ has ruled that where customers paying by certain methods (direct debit etc) paid a lower amount than customers paying by other means, the extra amounts collected were not separate payment handling charges and thus exempt from VAT as financial services but was extra consideration for the supply and therefore VAT was due.

Legislation: VATA 1994, s. 19(2)

Cases: *Chaussures Bally SA v Belgian State* (Case C-18/92) [1993] ECR I-2871; *C & E Commrs v Lloyds TSB Group Ltd* [1998] BVC 173; *HJ Glawe Spiel-und Unterhaltungsgeräte Aufstellungsgesellschaft mbH & Co KG v Finanzamt Hamburg-Barmbek-Uhlenhorst* (Case C-38/93) [1994] BVC 242; *Fischer v Finanzamt Donaueschingen* (Case C-283/95) [1998] BVC 431; *First National Bank of Chicago v C & E Commrs* (Case C-172/96) [1998] BVC 389; *Primback Ltd v C & E Commrs* (Case C-34/99) [2001] BVC 315; *Everything Everywhere (formerly T-Mobile UK Ltd) v HMRC* (Case C-276/09)

Other material: Notice 700, para. 7.3

4-590   Change in value of supply

Directive 2006/112 provides for the value of supply (or taxable amount) to be changed in certain circumstances. Its terms are as follows:

> 'In the case of cancellation, refusal or total or partial non-payment, or where the price is reduced after the supply takes place, the taxable amount shall be reduced accordingly under conditions which shall be determined by the member states.
>
> However, in the case of total or partial non-payment, member states may derogate from this rule.'

This is implemented in the UK by VAT Regulations 1995 (SI 1995/2518). For situations involving bad debt relief see 9-520.

Legislation: Directive 2006/112, art. 90; *Value Added Tax Regulations* 1995 (SI 1995/2518), reg. 24

Adjusting the VAT account

Adjustments to the VAT account may be made when there is an increase or decrease in the consideration evidenced by documentation. The documentation should be 'a credit or debit note or any other documentation having the same effect'.

The question of 'other documentation having the same effect' was considered by the High Court in *C & E Commrs v General Motors Acceptance Corporation (UK) Plc* (GMAC). When taking back a car, GMAC did not issue a credit note or debit note. However, the reduction in the consideration was recorded in its records in other ways. HMRC maintained that this was insufficient.

The High Court concluded that the purpose of the legislation was as follows:

(i)   to ensure that increases in the consideration are recorded by those parties to the supply who are taxable persons;

(ii) to guard against fictitious claims for adjustment; and

(iii) to enable the commissioners to verify adjustment … by inspecting the persons' nooks and records.

The records maintained by GMAC met these criteria. In addition, their records were sufficient to 'evidence the split in between capital and interest in the reduced consideration'. This could be obtained from their computer system.

Lesser amount received in full and final settlement

During the foot and mouth outbreak in 2001/02, Cumbria County Council invoiced DEFRA for in excess of £4.2m (excluding VAT) for services rendered. DEFRA refused to pay the full amount. They paid only £2.75m. This led to protracted litigation that was not settled until 2009. In 2009 there was a High Court settlement. Cumbria CC accepted 'in full and final settlement £200,000 ... inclusive of VAT'.

After the settlement Cumbria CC took steps to adjust their VAT account. They issued a credit note to DEFRA with VAT of £192,316. The credit note was included in the 02/10 return and reduced the amount due for the period by this amount.

HMRC rejected the credit note. In their view the amount unpaid by DEFRA was a bad debt. Cumbria CC could not claim bad debt relief because the time limits for making a such a claim had elapsed

Cumbria CC appealed to the First Tier Tax Tribunal. The First Tier Tribunal allowed the appeal on the following grounds:

(1) the consideration for CCC's supplies was reduced by the High Court settlement by which Cumbria CC accepted £200,000 in full and final settlement;

(2) as this was a reduction in the consideration, Cumbria CC were correct to adjust their VAT account by issuing a credit note rather than claiming bad debt relief;

(3) necessary adjustments when the consideration for the supply changes are not subject to any time limit.

In its decision the First Tier Tribunal said 'In our judgment, reg. 38 is the means whereby any claim settled similarly to that of CCC is to be adjusted as a reduction in consideration'.

At the time of writing it is not known if HMRC will appeal this decision.

Cases: *Cumbria County Council* [2011] UKFTT 621 (TC)

Legislation: *Value Added Tax Regulations* 1995 (SI 1995/2518), reg. 38

4-600 More than one supply

If a consideration in money relates to several items, then it must be split between those so that each supply is treated as made for a monetary consideration equal to the amount of the total consideration which is properly attributable to it.

Legislation: VATA 1994, s. 19(4)

VAT Reporter: ¶14-200

4-620   Change in rate of tax

If there is a change in the rate of tax attaching to a supply (including a change in classification of the supply as between standard-rated, zero-rated or exempt), then the consideration due under a pre-existing contract for the supply is automatically adjusted to take account of the change, unless the contract provides to the contrary. The value of the supply remains the same, but the total consideration alters.

> ### *Example: adjustment of contract*
>
> Borner contracts to sell goods to Bell for £5,750. Before the tax point arises, the standard rate of VAT changes from 15 per cent to 17.5 per cent.
>
> The value of the supply, or taxable amount, is £5,000 (£5,750 × 100115). This amount, with the addition of tax at 15 per cent, comes to £5,750.
>
> On the change in rate, the taxable amount remains the same. The tax chargeable becomes £875 (£5,000 × 17.5 per cent), so the consideration under the contract is increased to £5,875 (possibly to the annoyance of Bell).

The exercising of the option for taxation by a supplier of land, etc. is treated as a change of rate for this purpose.

However, a term under a lease or tenancy disapplying this rule is ineffective (so that s. 89 applies to vary the consideration) unless the term specifically refers either to VAT or to s. 89.

Legislation: VATA 1994, s. 89

Other material: Notice 700, para. 30; *www.hmrc.gov.uk/pbr/2008/vat-guide-det.pdf*

VAT Reporter: ¶14-200

4-640   Non-monetary consideration

If a supply is made for a consideration which is not in money, or is not wholly in money, then under UK law the value of the supply is taken as being the amount of money which, with the addition of the VAT due, is equal to the value of the consideration.

The value to be attributed to non-monetary consideration is to be a subjective value determined from the standpoint of the person receiving the consideration (see 3-140).

The Court of Appeal heard together four cases concerned with the valuation of non-monetary consideration. Before proceeding to give judgment in the individual cases, it carried out a review of a number of decisions of the European Court of Justice, and of UK cases providing examples of the application of the principles set out by the ECJ.

The following is a potted summary of some of the main principles which the court identified (the numbers in brackets refer to the paragraphs in the judgment where it makes these comments):

- there must be a direct link between the supply of goods or services and the consideration which is said to have been received for that supply [14];
- the consideration must be capable of being expressed in money, or a monetary equivalent [14];
- the basis of the assessment is the consideration actually received [14];
- developing the principle above, where the consideration is not entirely monetary and the parties themselves have, as between themselves, put a value on the non-monetary element, that is the value of the non-monetary element for VAT purposes [23];
- however, if the parties have not put a value on the non-monetary element, its value must be determined in some other way *(my comment: assuming, that is, that it is capable of valuation as mentioned in the second principle, this being an assumption which the courts now seem prone to make).* One common approach, which may not always be available, is to ascertain how much the supplier is prepared to pay to obtain the non-monetary consideration, and take that as the value;
- where the non-monetary consideration consists of a voucher which the supplier has agreed to accept in return for goods and services, the consideration is, in principle, the voucher itself, and it is necessary to seek a monetary equivalent for the voucher. This is generally the amount of money which the supplier has received (or will receive) as a result of agreeing to accept the voucher. In the case of a voucher issued by the supplier against payment, that is the amount of the payment received. In the case of a voucher issued by the supplier free of charge, that value is nil. In neither case does the face value of the voucher determine its monetary equivalent to the supplier.

The court then gave judgment on the cases before it, of which there follows the barest summary.

Littlewoods

Littlewoods sells goods by mail order through a network of agents. Agents can place orders for themselves or for others. They receive commission based on the payments made, whether by themselves or by others. The commission can be taken in one of two ways:

- cash, in which case the commission is at a rate of 10 per cent; or
- reduction in price of goods ordered from the catalogue, in which case it is at a rate of 12.5 per cent.

Littlewoods contended that, where the agent took the commission in goods, the proper treatment was to account for VAT on the catalogue price of the goods less 12.5 per cent. HMRC wanted them to account for VAT on the catalogue price less 10 per cent, on the basis that the agent had provided non-monetary consideration to Littlewoods in the form of services of procuring sales, etc. and that the 10 per cent cash commission was the proper measure of the cost which Littlewoods was prepared to pay to obtain this service.

The court held that, in using the commission to purchase goods, the agent was not providing non-monetary consideration. The commission was earned under separate transactions, and could then be taken in one of two pre-agreed ways. The commission was the same whether it arose from the agent's own purchases or from third party purchases. There was, therefore, no direct link between the supply of the fresh goods and any particular service performed by the agent. The commission taken in goods must be treated as a discount or rebate on the sale of the goods concerned, and the catalogue price must therefore be reduced by the full amount of that discount.

Littlewoods' appeal was allowed.

Lex Services Plc

Lex Services Plc sold cars, and often a customer's existing car would be taken in part exchange. In arranging a part exchange deal, Lex would produce documentation showing the price of the car sold and the part exchange allowance for the customer's car. However, it also had further conditions stating that, if the customer cancelled the purchase of the new car within a 30 day cancellation period, Lex would only pay a lesser amount (referred to as the 'true value') for the part exchange car.

Lex argued that it was only the true value of the part exchange car which should be seen as its value as non-monetary consideration for the supply of the new car.

The court held that the parties had, by consensus, put a value on the part exchange car for the purposes of the transaction involving the sale of the new car. The true value was not a value for the purposes of this transaction, but for an entirely separate transaction which might arise if the sale of the new car was cancelled.

Accordingly, the Lex appeal was dismissed.

Lex appealed to the House of Lords and the appeal was again dismissed.

Bugeja

Essentially, Mr Bugeja ran a video shop where he sold videos for £20. Each video had a security tag. He undertook, if a customer wished, to sell a fresh video for £10 plus the return of one previously purchased.

The tribunal had held that the only consideration on the sale of a video was the cash consideration, being £10 where the customer handed over one previously purchased. The High Court held that the video handed in was non-monetary consideration, albeit its maximum value was of the order of £2 to £3 (being the amount which it would cost Mr Bugeja to buy a replacement).

The court found that, for the purposes of the transactions under review, there was an agreement between Mr Bugeja and the customers as to the value to be placed on the returned videos, and that this amount was £10. This was, therefore, the value attributed to the non-monetary consideration by the parties (and, in particular, by the supplier) and therefore gave the measure of value for VAT purposes.

HMRC's appeal was allowed.

Kuwait Petroleum (GB) Ltd

Kuwait Petroleum (GB) Ltd (KPGB) operated a business promotion scheme under which purchasers of petrol also obtained vouchers which could subsequently be exchanged for reward goods from a catalogue published by KPGB. KPGB recovered input tax on the purchase of the reward goods, but accounted for no output tax on the supply of them, considering that the price paid by customers for petrol was consideration both for the supply of petrol and the ultimate supply of the reward goods. HMRC took the view that the amounts paid by motorists were not consideration for the reward goods (or for the vouchers issued), and that the handing over of the reward goods gave rise to a supply as a free gift of goods.

It was held, following the earlier proceedings (which included a reference to the ECJ), that the reward goods were business gifts, supplied for no consideration, so that VAT was due on the supply (where the cost of them exceeded the relevant limit).

Between the tribunal referring the case to the ECJ and the answer coming back, the ECJ judgment in *Elida Gibbs Ltd v C & E Commrs* was issued. As a result, at the resumed hearing the appellant raised a fresh point, that the provision of the redemption goods free of charge amounted to a retrospective price reduction or discount in respect of the original sales of petrol. The tribunal heard this argument and commented on it (disagreeing with it, as it happens) but raised no procedural points.

The court held that, since this point did not strictly relate to the originally appealed decision by HMRC, and the tribunal had made no order that it should be added to the proceedings, it was not something which could be considered by the court. Accordingly, the appeal was struck out.

In relation to all of the cases, the court stated that it did not feel it appropriate to refer any question to the ECJ. The ECJ had already issued ample guidance on the areas concerned, which the court felt able to apply without further assistance, and it was conscious of the need to exercise self-restraint in such matters to avoid overwhelming the ECJ.

Importance of contract terms

The incidence of VAT on non-monetary consideration gives rise to an important planning point when framing contracts which is frequently overlooked. As indicated at 4-580 above, it is important (from the supplier's point of view) to state that amounts of monetary consideration mentioned in the agreement do not include any VAT which may be due. However, this is not sufficient if there is also non-monetary consideration. Unless there is specific provision in the contract requiring the customer to pay over any VAT arising on supplies made wholly or partly for non-monetary consideration, the supplier will be left to bear the VAT (although the customer may still be able to recover it as input tax).

Legislation: VATA 1994, s. 19(3)

Other material: Notice 700, para. 7.4

Cases: *Empire Stores Ltd v C & E Commrs* (Case C-33/93) [1994] BVC 253; *C & E Commrs v Littlewoods Organisation Plc; Lex Services Plc v C & E Commrs; C & E Commrs v Bugeja; Kuwait Petroleum (GB) Ltd v C & E Commrs* [2002] BVC 71; *Elida Gibbs Ltd v C & E Commrs* [1997] BVC 80

VAT Reporter: ¶11-310

4-660 Prompt payment discounts

If a trader offers a discount for prompt payment, and assuming that the terms of supply do not allow payment by instalments, the value of supply is determined as if the supply were made for the sale price as reduced by the discount. This applies whether or not the discount is, in fact, taken.

Example: Prompt payment discount

Jane sells goods to Percy for £1,000 including VAT, subject to a five per cent discount for payment within 30 days. The value of the supply is determined as if she sold the goods for £950 (£1,000 − 5 per cent). The taxable amount is therefore £791.66 (£950 × 56) and the tax due is £158.34. This is so whether Percy pays £950 within the 30-day period, or £1,000 thereafter.

Legislation: VATA 1994, Sch. 6, para. 4

VAT Reporter: ¶14-400

4-680 Consideration in foreign currency

If a supply is made for a consideration expressed in a foreign currency, it must be converted into sterling by reference to the market rate at the time of supply, unless the trader opts to use an exchange rate published by HMRC.

Legislation: VATA 1994, Sch. 6, para. 11

VAT Reporter: ¶14-750

4-690 Vehicle scrappage scheme

The vehicle scrappage scheme was introduced by the 2009 Budget. It ran until March 2010. It was a voluntary scheme run by participating motor manufacturers and dealers, along with the Department for Business, Enterprise and Regulatory Reform (BERR).

Customers buying a new vehicle under the scheme paid £2,000 less for the vehicle, since BERR contributed £1,000 and the vehicle manufacturer contributed £1,000 towards the cost of the purchase. The contributions were settled between the manufacturer, dealer and BERR, so the customer did not receive these amounts.

Manufacturers could treat the VAT on their contribution as a reduction to the output tax due to HMRC on the sale of the car. Manufacturers were not able to reduce their output tax in respect of BERR's £1,000 contribution.

The cost of the new vehicle received by a dealer was unaffected because the manufacturer was not contributing £1,000 to the dealer but to the dealer's customer. The dealer did not adjust the VAT paid to the manufacturer, or claimed from HMRC as input tax. Further, the dealer's selling price for the vehicle had not changed and so the dealer could not reduce the output tax declared on his VAT return.

If the buyer was entitled to reclaim input tax on the purchase of the vehicle, the input tax available for credit was less. It was smaller by the amount of the VAT content in the manufacturer's discount (i.e. £1,000 × the appropriate VAT fraction). The buyer did not receive an amended invoice or credit note advising of this. However, the input tax correction should be done.

Other material: Revenue and Customs Brief 31/09 *Tax Implications of the Vehicle Scrappage Scheme*

VAT Reporter: ¶ 11-022

SPECIAL VALUE OF SUPPLY RULES

4-720 Modifications to basic rules

There are a number of modifications to these basic rules as to the value of supply, covering transactions between connected persons, sales under 'party-plan' arrangements, the treatment of supplies where there is no consideration, the treatment of tokens and vouchers, and special rules for long-stay hotel accommodation and for certain supplies to employees.

4-740 Supplies between connected parties

Power is given to HMRC to direct that the value of certain supplies between connected persons be taken as being the open market value, rather than the value determined in accordance with the normal rules. This power is available where:

(1) the supply is made for a consideration in money;

(2) the consideration is less than the market value of the supply;

(3) the supplier and the customer are connected within the meaning given in ICTA 1988, s. 839; and

(4) if the supply is a taxable supply, the customer is unable to recover some or all of the tax chargeable as input tax (e.g. if the customer is not registered for VAT, or is partially exempt).

Where these conditions are met, HMRC may issue a direction that the supply should be treated as made for an amount equal to its open market value. Such a direction must be made in writing, within three years after the time of supply. A direction may also specify that similar supplies in the future should be treated as taking place at open market value.

As indicated at (3) above, this power applies in respect of supplies between persons which are connected within the meaning of ICTA 1988, s. 839. This covers spouses, brothers, sisters, ancestors and lineal descendants, etc. Trustees of a settlement are connected with the settlor and with persons connected with the settlor. Partners are connected with one another, and with each other's relatives, except in relation to commercial dealings with partnership assets. Companies are connected with one another if they are under common control, and are also connected with persons who control them.

Legislation: VATA 1994, Sch. 6, para. 1

VAT Reporter: ¶19-465

4-760 Party plan arrangements

HMRC may also make a direction that supplies should be treated as made at retail value where part of a person's business consists of the sale of goods to non-taxable persons, the goods subsequently being sold by retail (whether by the customers of the taxable person, or by their customers).

This covers the position where, for instance, cosmetics are sold to individuals who hold parties to promote sales of the cosmetics. Typically, such individuals have turnover below the registration thresholds. In the absence of a direction, VAT is accounted for on the 'wholesale' price charged to the individuals running the parties, not on the retail value which they charge to their customers. The purpose of the power to make such directions is to enable HMRC to levy tax on the ultimate retail price.

The legality of such directions, under European law, has been called into question a number of times. Initially, the appellants were successful, as the UK provisions were outside the terms of the derogation which had been obtained. However, a further derogation was obtained and, in subsequent proceedings, the power of HMRC to make such directions was upheld.

Such a direction has been held to be valid, notwithstanding the facts that supplies were made both to registered and unregistered persons, that some purchases were for the customers' own use rather than for resale (the appellant would not know, in relation to any particular supply, whether the goods were for resale or not), and that in some instances agents might resell at prices below the recommended retail price. In practice, HMRC will normally accept survey evidence to take account of agents' own purchases and discounted sales, if the exact information is not readily available.

Legislation: VATA 1994, Sch. 6, para. 2

Cases: *Direct Cosmetics Ltd v C & E Commrs* (Case 5/84) (1985) 2 BVC 200,069; *Direct Cosmetics Ltd and Laughtons Photographs Ltd* (1989) 4 BVC 673; *Fine Art Developments v C & E Commrs (No. 2)* [1996] BVC 191

VAT Reporter: ¶14-350

4-770   Tokens, stamps and vouchers

A face value voucher is a token, stamp or voucher (in physical or electronic form) which represents a right to receive goods or services to the value of an amount stated or recorded in it.

VAT is accountable on single purpose face value vouchers when the voucher is issued. This change came about in May 2012 following a European Court case.

No VAT is due on the issue of a 'credit voucher' or a 'retailer voucher', nor on subsequent supplies of a 'credit voucher', except to the extent that the consideration exceeds the face value. Subsequent supplies of a 'retailer voucher' are subject to VAT. Supplies of postage stamps are ignored (unless the consideration exceeds face value). . Where vouchers are supplied with other goods or services, and the price is the same even if the customer declines to accept the vouchers, they are treated as supplied for no consideration.

Single purpose face value vouchers

HMRC describe a singe purpose face value voucher as 'one that carries the right to receive only one type of goods or services which are subject to a single rate of VAT'. The formal definition is in FA 2012 which amends the VAT Act accordingly.

The change of practice for accounting for VAT on single purpose face value is effective from 10 May 2012. From then single purpose vouchers are liable to tax when they are issued.

A single purpose voucher may also be a credit or retailer voucher. If it is, it is still from 10 May 2012 taxable when it is issued.

Credit vouchers

A credit voucher is one issued by a person who:

(1)   is not the person who will accept the voucher in payment for goods or services; but who

(2)   undertakes to give complete or partial reimbursement to a person accepting them in return for goods or services.

The consideration on any supply of a credit voucher is disregarded except to the extent that it exceeds the face value of the voucher.

The consequence of this is that no VAT is due until the vouchers are redeemed, at which point the reimbursement money will be subject to tax in the hands of the redeemer who receives the reimbursement, as part of the consideration for the supply of the goods or services. It also follows that the VAT liability will be determined by the nature of the supply in respect of which the voucher is redeemed.

However, the consideration on the supply of the voucher cannot be ignored if the person accepting the voucher fails to account for any of the VAT due on the supply to the person who uses the voucher in settlement. This appears to involve a retrospective adjustment if the redeemer fails to account properly for VAT on the redemption money.

Retailer vouchers

A retailer voucher is one issued by a person who:

(1)   is a person who will accept the voucher in payment for goods or services; and who,

(2)   if there are also other persons who may accept the voucher in return for goods or services, undertakes to give full or partial reimbursement to those other persons.

The consideration for the issue of a retailer voucher is ignored except to the extent that it exceeds face value. However, it cannot be ignored if the voucher is used to obtain goods or services from someone other than the issuer, and that person fails to account in full for the VAT due on the supply of the goods or services.

Where the voucher is redeemed by the issuer, the consideration received on the issue of it will form the measure for the value of the supply made on redemption.

Any supply of a retailer voucher subsequent to its issue is treated in the same way as a supply of an 'ordinary' voucher (above).

Postage stamps

The consideration for the supply of a postage stamp is ignored except to the extent that it exceeds face value. The effect of this is to prevent traders becoming involved with partial exemption calculations merely because they supply postage stamps.

Vouchers supplied free with other goods or services

Where a face value voucher is supplied with other goods or services, and the price of the package is no different (or not significantly different) from what it would be if the voucher were not supplied, the supply of the voucher is treated as being made for no consideration. See also 18-830.

Other vouchers before May 2012

Before May 2012 the default treatment of vouchers other than credit vouchers, retailer vouchers, or postage stamps was that the whole of the consideration was subject to VAT at the standard rate.

However, if the voucher could only be used to obtain goods or services in one particular non-standard rate category (i.e. zero-rated, exempt or subject to the reduced rate), the supply of the voucher also fell into that category.

If the voucher was used to obtain goods or services subject to different VAT treatments, the supply of the voucher was treated as several separate supplies at the different rates concerned, the value of each determined on a just and reasonable basis.

Cases: *Argos Distributors Ltd v C & E Commrs* [1996] BVC 64; *Lebara Ltd v R & C Commrs* (Case C-520/10)[2012] BVC 219

Other material: Information Sheet 12/03; Notice 700/7; HMRC Brief 12/12

Legislation: VATA 1994, s. 51B, Sch. 10A (as amended by FA 2012)

VAT Reporter: ¶49-160

4-800   Deemed supply on de-registration

The value of a supply, when a person ceases to be registered for VAT, is deemed to be equivalent to the current value of the goods, taking into account their current age and condition of the goods concerned. If this cannot be ascertained, then the value is taken to be equal to that of similar goods or, failing that, the current cost of production of such goods.

Legislation: VATA 1994, Sch. 6, para. 6

Other material: Notice 700/11, para. 6.7

VAT Reporter: ¶44-000

4-810   Non-business use of business assets and services

A deemed supply arises when goods which are business assets are put to non-business use for no consideration. The VAT value of such a deemed supply is the full cost to the trader of making the goods available.

This type of deemed supply frequently arises in respect of assets such as company boats which may have three classifications of use:

(1)   use for business purposes;

(2)   use for non-business purposes; and

(3)   idle time, where no use occurs.

HMRC take the view that the measure of the cost to the trader is the total cost of having, and running, the asset, pro-rated by reference to the periods of business and non-business use. This view has been disapproved of by a tribunal in *Teknequip Ltd*. It was held that the cost of the non-business use should be calculated, in the case of time based costs such as depreciation, by pro-rating by reference to the period of non-business use in the whole period under consideration, not merely the proportion in relation to time of business use. However, this decision was overturned on appeal, so that the view of HMRC has been vindicated.

Example: cost of making asset available

Perks Ltd owns a company plane, which is used for business purposes. It is also used for non-business purposes by the owners of the company. Standing costs which accrue by reference to time rather than use, such as depreciation, licensing fees, etc. amount to £4,000 per annum. The usage of the plane (per annum) is as follows:

Business use	30 days
Non-business use	35 days
Not in use	300 days
	365 days

On the formula preferred by HMRC, the amount of the standing costs attributable to non-business use would be £2,154 per annum (£4,000 × 3565). However, following the *Teknequip* tribunal decision, the cost would be spread by reference to the proportion of non-business use compared with the total period. This gives a cost for non-business use of £384 (£4,000 × 35/365). The *Teknequip* High Court decision switches the cost back to £2,154 per annum.

As can be seen from the above example, the difference between the two methods of calculation can be substantial.

The inclusion of standing costs on which no VAT has been reclaimed (as in the above example) has now been held to be incorrect by the European Court of Justice.

The decision in *Enkler v Finanzamt Homburg* reinforces this point, and also confirms both that costs on which no VAT recovery is available do not form part of the tax base for this purpose and that the costs included should be apportioned by reference to relative business and non-business use, ignoring periods of non-use.

The non-business use of supplies of services on which input tax has been reclaimed gives rise to a supply with a value based on the cost of the non-business use. However, that value is reduced as necessary to ensure that the output tax charge does not exceed the amount of input tax recovered.

Legislation: VATA 1994, Sch. 6, para. 7; *Value Added Tax (Supply of Services) Order* 1993 (SI 1993/1507), art. 5

Cases: *Teknequip Ltd v C & E Commrs QB* (1987) 3 BVC 107; *Lennartz v Finanzamt München III* (Case C-97/90) [1993] BVC 202; *Enkler v Finanzamt Homburg* (Case C-230/94) [1997] BVC 24

VAT Reporter: ¶13-870

Motor cars

No supply arises in respect of a leased car where a 50 per cent disallowance of input tax has been made because there is non-business use.

HMRC have the right to determine the value of supplies of stock-in-trade cars made by a motor dealer to an employee or other connected person (e.g. relative) for a consideration less than the market value. The value of such supplies may be directed by HMRC to be taken to be the open market value.

There is an agreed scale for the private use charge that must be accounted for when a manufacturer or dealer allows private use to employees of demonstrator or rental cars.

Legislation: VATA 1994, Sch. 6, para. 1A; *Value Added Tax (Supply of Services) Order* 1993 (SI 1993/1507), art. 6A and art. 7

Cases: *Teknequip Ltd v C & E Commrs* (1985) 2 BVC 205,288; (1987) 3 BVC 107; *Lennartz v Finanzamt München III* (Case C-97/90) [1993] BVC 202; *Enkler v Finanzamt Homburg* (Case C-230/94) [1997] BVC 24

Other material: VAT Information Sheet 07/09; Notice 700/57, para. 24

VAT Reporter: ¶13-870

4-820 Long-stay hotel accommodation

The provision of accommodation in a hotel, boarding house, etc. is subject to VAT at the standard rate. However, there are people who stay in hotels for long periods of time, at which point the nature of the supply becomes quite close to that which occurs when property is let to someone as their home. There is special provision to avoid imposing an undue amount of tax on what is, in essence, the provision of living accommodation.

If hotel accommodation is provided to an individual, or an individual and dependants, for a period in excess of four weeks, the value of the supply for the period in excess of four weeks is deemed to be reduced.

The value is reduced to that part of the total charge which relates to facilities other than the mere provision of accommodation, but cannot be reduced to a sum below 20 per cent of the total charge. The aim of this is to avoid charging VAT on the provision of accommodation, but to ensure that other components of the supply (e.g. meals, cleaning, laundry) continue to be taxed in the ordinary way.

Contract with local authority and the like

Prior to 2006, HMRC took the view that the reduced value rule only applies where the supply is to the individual who occupies the accommodation.

It has been agreed following the Tribunal decision in *Afro Caribbean Housing Association* that local authority contracts and the like will qualify for the reduced value rule. It is still a rule that the accommodation is occupied by the same person for a continuous period and the first 28 days are still subject to VAT. It will not apply where companies block book accommodation and it is used by different individuals for periods of less than 28 days, neither will it apply to any holiday accommodation.

Legislation: VATA 1994, Sch. 6, para. 9

Cases: *Afro Caribbean Housing Association* [2006] BVC 4,061

Other material: Business Brief 15/06; Notice 709/3, section 3

VAT Reporter: ¶3-190

4-830   Benefits for employees

Salary sacrifices

Astra Zeneca had a remuneration scheme that allowed employees to take goods and/or services instead of part of their salary. The goods/services included high street shopping vouchers. The CJEU decided that this was a supply of services effected for a consideration. Hence Astra Zeneca could recover input tax incurred on the purchase of the vouchers but output tax was due on the consideration received from its employees.

HMRC distinguish between deduction from salary schemes and salary sacrifice schemes. In the former, where salary is deducted for a supply of goods or services by the employer, output tax has always been due on the amount deducted from the salary and input tax recoverable according to the normal rules. Until this case however the salary sacrifice scheme has not constituted consideration for the benefits and output tax was not due. The case has altered the situation and the change in treatment is effective for supplies from 1 January 2012. After this date employers must account for output tax on the supplies.

HMRC's policy with regard to salary sacrifice agreements which span 1 January 2012 is explained in Revenue and Customs Brief 36/11

Catering

A reduction in value applies to the supply to employees of food or beverages (supplied in the course of catering) or of accommodation in a hotel, inn, boarding house, or similar establishment. The value of the supply for VAT purposes is limited to the amount of any cash consideration paid by the employee.

The effect of this provision is to encourage the provision of free or subsidised canteens for employees, and to avoid the necessity for a charge to VAT when employees' accommodation expenses are met while they are travelling on behalf of the business.

From 1 January 2012 if meals or catering are paid for by a salary sacrifice scheme then the above rules should be applied.

Legislation: VATA 1994, Sch. 6, para. 10

Cases: *Astra Zeneca UK Ltd v R & C Commrs (Case C-40/09)* [2011] BVC 101

Other material: Notice 709/1, para. 5.8; Revenue and Customs Brief 28/11; Revenue and Customs Brief 36/11

VAT Reporter: ¶14-700

4-840 Gaming machines

There is special provision covering the value of supplies made via gaming machines. In principle, the total amount paid into the machine would appear to be the consideration paid to the supplier. This value is reduced by the amount paid out by the machine to successful players (other than the supplier and his representatives). Thus, the taxable amount is equivalent to the net 'take' from the machine.

Tokens used in such machines are treated, in essence, as being equivalent to cash.

Legislation: VATA 1994, s. 23

Other material: Notice 701/13, para. 4.2

VAT Reporter: ¶18-560

4-850 Second-hand goods

Where goods are sold under a second-hand goods scheme (see 16-430ff.), the consideration for which they are sold is regarded as limited to any excess of the actual consideration over the cost of the goods to the supplier. Thus, the value of the supply is effectively reduced to that excess or to nil.

The same applies to car dealers who use the second-hand goods scheme for motor cars.

Legislation: *Value Added Tax (Special Provisions) Order* 1995 (SI 1995/1268), art. 4; *Value Added Tax (Cars) Order* 1992 (SI 1992/3122), art. 8

Other material: Notice 718

VAT Reporter: ¶48-625

4-860 Fuel for non-business use

If a business provides car fuel (or fuel for other vehicles) to an employee, partner, proprietor or director for use for non-business purposes (including home-to-work travelling) free or for less than cost, the supply is treated as being made for a consideration calculated by reference to the cylinder capacity of the vehicle. However, no scale charge arises if the business chooses not to reclaim any input tax on fuel.

The value is to be found in a table contained in VATA 1994, s. 57, as amended from time to time, and Hardman's Tax Rates and Tables 19-280 or Key Data 1-700.

If contributions are made by the employees concerned this also represents consideration for taxable supplies. In order to avoid double taxation, the amount of these contributions subjected to tax should be abated to take account of the scale charges (or vice versa – the result should be that tax is due on the higher of the contributions made and the scale charge).

Retrospective claims for tax wrongly paid

In April 2012 HMRC admitted that their interpretation of European law has been incorrect. The road fuel scale charge need not have been applied where fuel was supplied to employees for private use at less than cost. Businesses should have had the option of accounting for VAT on the charge actually made.

As a result of this retrospective claims for overpaid VAT may be made.

Legislation: VATA 1994, s. 56 and s. 57

Other material: Notice 700/64, section 9; Revenue and Customs Brief 11/12

Cases: *Allied Lyons Plc* [1995] BVC 665

VAT Reporter: ¶18-320

4-870 Conclusion

This section has covered the main rules which govern the incidence of VAT on supplies, including the amount of the tax and the time when it arises. Matters have been raised concerning the identification of taxable persons (and of businesses), and the identification of the national jurisdiction within which transactions fall to be taxed.

Some of these issues will need to be covered further in subsequent sections. In the meantime, the matters covered in this section should give a fair understanding of the circumstances in which a charge to VAT arises.

[This page is intentionally blank]

FLOWCHARTS

4-880   When VAT is chargeable

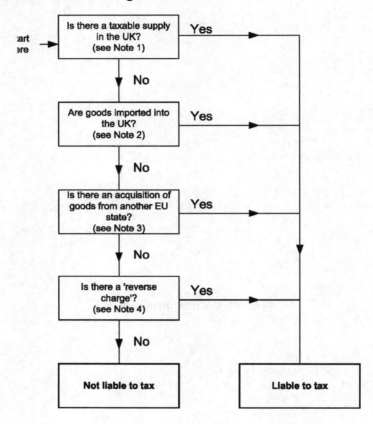

Notes

(1) Taxable supplies

A taxable supply is a supply of goods or services made in the UK but this does not include supplies which are exempt from tax (VATA 1994, s. 4(2)).

(2) Imported goods

These are goods which are imported into the UK from outside the EU. For further information, see 5-040.

(3) Acquisitions

Acquisitions are goods brought to the UK from another EU State. For further information, see 5-360.

(4) Reverse charges

A UK business must account for VAT on certain services supplied to it by business belonging outside the UK (VATA 1994, s. 8). This is known as the 'reverse charge' procedure.

Supplies by Business

4-890   Is there a supply?

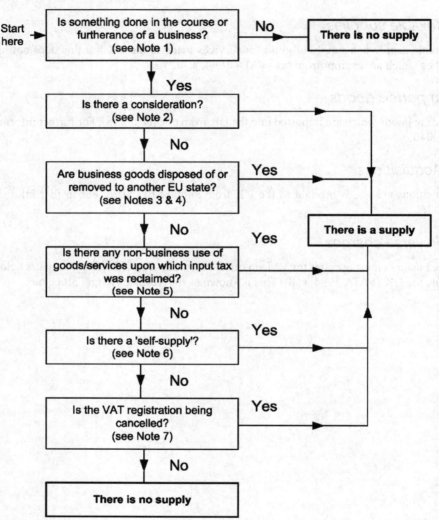

Notes

(1) Carried out in the course or furtherance of a business

To be liable to UK VAT a supply must be carried out in the course or furtherance of any business (VATA 1994, s. 4(1)).

(2) Consideration

A consideration is any form of payment in money or in kind, including anything which is itself a supply (Notice 700, para. 7.2). For further information, see 3-140.

(3) Disposing of goods for no consideration

There is a deemed supply when goods which are business assets are transferred or disposed so that they no longer form part of those assets (VATA 1994, Sch. 4, para. 5(1)). Some business gifts are not liable to this charge. Land may be liable to it.

(4) Moving own goods to another EU State

A deemed acquisition takes place when a UK business transfers its own goods to another EU State. This does not apply in the following circumstances:

- goods sent to another EU State for process/repair; or
- temporary transfer to another EU State in connection with services supplied by the transferee.

For further information, see 3-210.

(5) Non-business use of goods or services

A deemed supply may be triggered when business goods or services are used for non-business purposes. It does not normally apply if the business was unable to recover input tax on the goods or services concerned or apportioned the relevant input tax between business/non-business use. For further information, see 3-160.

(6) Self-supplies

In certain circumstances, a business is treated as making a supply to itself. This is known as a self-supply. A self-supply occurs in the following situations:

- using cars for which VAT has been recovered in a way which would 'block' input tax recovery;
- changing the use of a communal residential building or charity building that was zero-rated when new;
- certain developments using 'in-house' construction services; or
- the transfer of a business as a going concern to a VAT group.

(7) De-registration

Business assets on hand at de-registration are deemed to be supplied (VATA 1994, Sch. 4, para. 8). This gives rise to a tax liability subject to certain concessions.

Supplies by Business

4-900   Self supply of residential/charity buildings

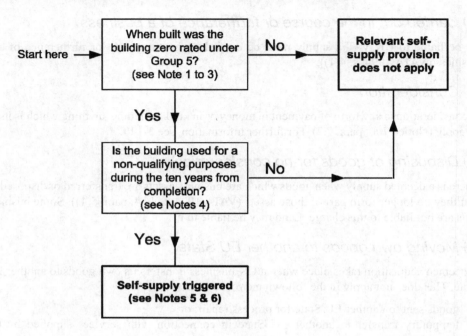

Notes

(1) Zero-rating of certain residential/charity buildings

Only certain relevant residential buildings and charity buildings may be zero-rated. The zero-rating is limited to the construction and/or the first grant of a major interest in such buildings. For more information, see 13-050.

(2) Relevant residential buildings

Relevant residential buildings are defined as follow (VATA 1994, Sch. 8, Grp. 5, Note (4)):

(a) a home or other institution providing residential accommodation for children;
(b) a home or other institution providing residential accommodation with personal care for persons in need of personal care by reason of old age, disablement, past or present dependence on alcohol or drugs or past or present mental disorder;
(c) a hospice;
(d) residential accommodation for students or school pupils;
(e) residential accommodation for members of any of the armed forces;
(f) a monastery, nunnery or similar establishment; or
(g) an institution which is the sole or main residence of at least 90 per cent of its residents.

A hospital, prison or similar institution or an hotel, inn or similar establishment is not a relevant residential building.

(3) Charity buildings

Charity buildings are defined as buildings used solely in the following ways: (VATA 1994, Sch. 8, Grp. 5, Note (6)):

(a) otherwise than in the course or furtherance of a business; or
(b) as a village hall or similarly in providing social or recreational facilities for a local community.

(4) Non-qualifying use

A building is used for a non-qualifying purpose in the following circumstances:

(a) changing the use so that building is no longer a 'communal residential building'; or
(b) ceasing to use the building solely for charitable purposes.

(5) Self-supply charge

The self-supply charge varies according to the number of years the building has been used for a qualifying purpose prior to the offending change of use (VATA 1994, Sch. 10, para. 1(5)).

(6) Certain charity buildings

With effect from 21 March 2007, HMRC will not always enforce this self-supply charge. It will not be enforced when a charity relied on extra statutory concession 3.29 to obtain zero-rating AND the change of use which otherwise would trigger the self supply charge was not anticipated at the time the building was zero-rated. HM Revenue and Customs Brief 29/07.

4-910 Self supply of construction services

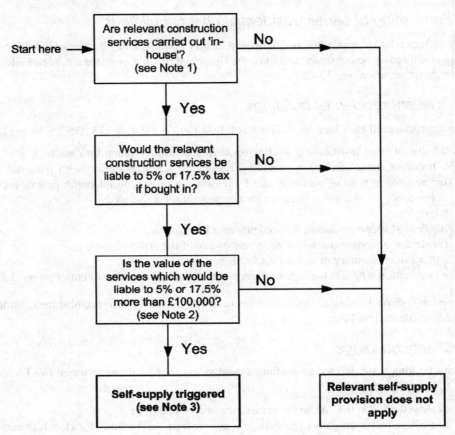

Start here → **Are relevant construction services carried out 'in-house'?** (see Note 1) — **No** →

↓ **Yes**

Would the relevant construction services be liable to 5% or 17.5% tax if bought in? — **No** →

↓ **Yes**

Is the value of the services which would be liable to 5% or 17.5% more than £100,000? (see Note 2) — **No** →

↓ **Yes**

Self-supply triggered (see Note 3)

Relevant self-supply provision does not apply

Notes

(1) 'In-house' construction services

'In-house' construction services occur when a business uses its 'own labour' labour to construct any of the following:

(a)   a building;
(b)   a civil engineering work; or
(c)   extend, alter or construct an annexe to a building such that the works increase the floor area by 10 per cent or more.

(2) Value

The relevant services are ones which if bought in would not be liable to zero per cent VAT or exempt from tax (*VAT (Self-supply of Construction Services) Order* 1989 (SI 1989/472), art. 3(2)).

(3) Further information

For further information, see Notice 708.

Supplies by Business

4-920   Self supply on acquisition of a business by a group

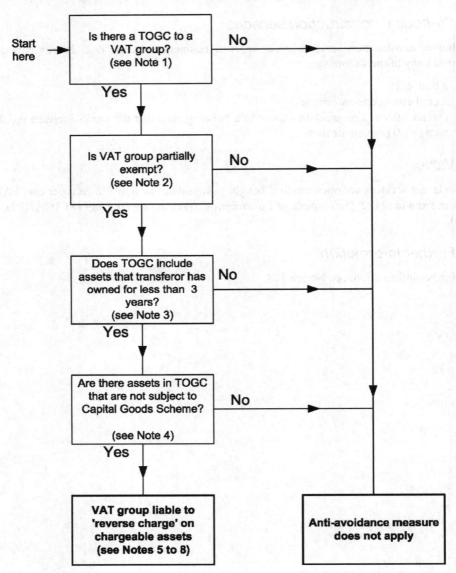

Start here → **Is there a TOGC to a VAT group? (see Note 1)**

No →

Yes ↓

Is VAT group partially exempt? (see Note 2)

No →

Yes ↓

Does TOGC include assets that transferor has owned for less than 3 years? (see Note 3)

No →

Yes ↓

Are there assets in TOGC that are not subject to Capital Goods Scheme? (see Note 4)

No →

Yes ↓

VAT group liable to 'reverse charge' on chargeable assets (see Notes 5 to 8)

Anti-avoidance measure does not apply

Notes

(1) Transfer of a going concern

Subject to certain conditions, the transfer of a business, or part of a business, as a going concern is not liable to VAT. It is deemed to be neither a supply of goods or services. For further information, see 18-120ff. However, a transfer of a going concern that, in normal circumstances, is neither a supply of goods or services may be subject to a VAT charge when the transferee is a VAT group.

(2) Partially exempt groups

The anti-avoidance measure is targeted at partially exempt VAT groups. It does not apply when the VAT group may recover all its input tax (subject to the normal exceptions) in:

(a)   the prescribed accounting period in which the assets are transferred; or
(b)   any partial exemption annual adjustment period in which the assets are transferred.

The annual adjustment period is normally 12 months ending on 30 March, 30 April or 31 May to coincide with the VAT periods. However, it may be shorter. For further information, see 6-950ff.

(3) Assets owned for more than three years

Assets owned by the transferor for more than three years prior to the transfer are excluded from the anti-avoidance measure. However, HMRC must be satisfied that the transferor owned the relevant assets for more than three years.

(4) Capital goods scheme items

The anti-avoidance measure does not apply to assets which are subject to capital goods scheme adjustments at the time of transfer. Responsibility for the adjustments passes to the representative member. The adjustments apply for five or 10 intervals/years according to whether the asset is a relevant computer item or land/building. For more information, see 7-760ff.

(5) Chargeable assets

For these purposes, chargeable assets are assets which, when supplied 'in the United Kingdom by a taxable person in the course or furtherance of his business', are normally liable to tax. However, this does not include ones which would be liable to the zero-rate.

(6) Reverse charge

When the anti-avoidance measure applies, the relevant assets trigger a reverse charge on the day of the transfer. The usual reverse charges principles apply. These are that:

(a)   the representative Member accounts for output tax on the chargeable assets concerned;

Supplies by Business

(b) the tax accounted for is deemed to be input tax and, as appropriate, included in the partial exemption computations; and

(c) the value of the chargeable assets are omitted from the partial exemption computations.

(7) Value of chargeable assets

It is necessary to use the 'open market value' when calculating the reverse charge. This is defined as 'the price that would be paid on a sale (on which no VAT is payable) between a buyer and a seller who are not in such a relationship as to affect the price.'

Comment: HMRC operate a policy of reducing the liability triggered by the reverse charge when the transferor did not fully recover the input tax incurred on assets concerned. As explained in HMRC's Manuals, 'the extra we want' is the difference between that recovered by the transferor and that to which the transferee is entitled.

(8) Further information

For further information see HMRC's Manuals Volume 1–10 (VAT-Transfer of a Going Concern), Ch. 2, s. 4.

[This page is intentionally blank]

4-930 Identifying a taxable person

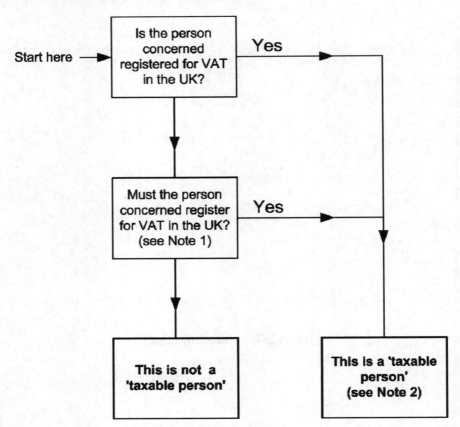

Notes

(1) Liability to register for VAT in UK

All the usual registration criteria must be considered to determine if the person concerned should be registered.

(2) 'Taxable person'

A person is a 'taxable person' whilst registered for VAT in the UK or throughout a period when they are, or were liable to register, for VAT in the UK (VATA 1994, s. 3).

Supplies by Business

4-940 Is a business carried on?

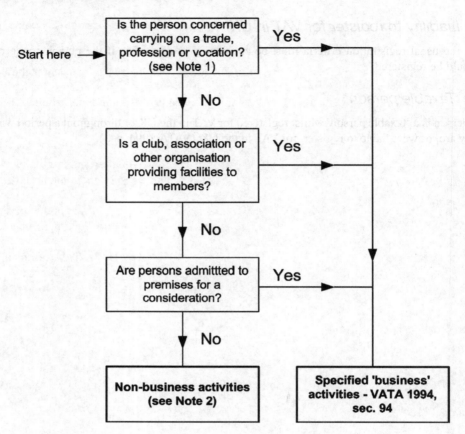

Notes

(1) Income from property

A property rental business or the like is a trade for VAT purposes.

(2) Goods or services provided for a consideration

Any goods or services provided in the UK for a consideration (even a nominal consideration) are potentially within the scope of VAT. It should not be assumed that an activity is not within the scope of VAT because it is not liable to Income or Corporation Tax.

Supplies by Business

4-950 Supplies in course or furtherance of a business

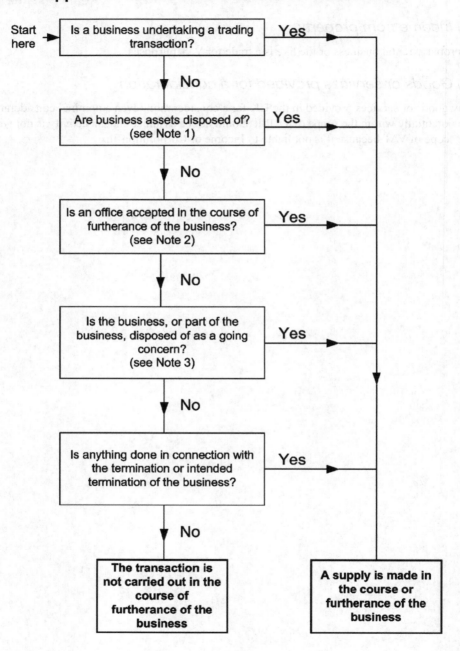

Notes

(1) Disposal of business assets

The disposal of an asset is carried out in the course of furtherance of a business even when given away (VATA 1994, Sch. 4, para. 5). See 3-160 for information about small gifts.

(2) Office holders

This provision only applies to persons such as solicitors, accountants and other practising consultants who were already in business to provide professional services and who continued to supply their services and skills in the course of their duties as office holders (HMRC VAT Guidance Manuals, V1-6, Section 6.3).

Office holders are not defined in the legislation. HM Revenue and Customs take this to mean '… any appointment of a responsible nature with a title, which gives an immediate idea of the duties, involved. For example, the director of a company, secretary to a tribunal or a clerk to a charity would be regarded as 'offices' in this context'. (HMRC VAT Guidance Manuals, V1-6, Section 6.2).

(3) Transfer of a business, or part of a business, as a going concern

Subject to complying with the necessary conditions, some TOGCs are not liable to VAT. For further information, see 18-120ff.

(4) Authority

This flowchart is based upon the transactions specified as 'business' transaction by VATA 1994, s. 94.

Supplies by Business

4-960 Supply of goods or services?

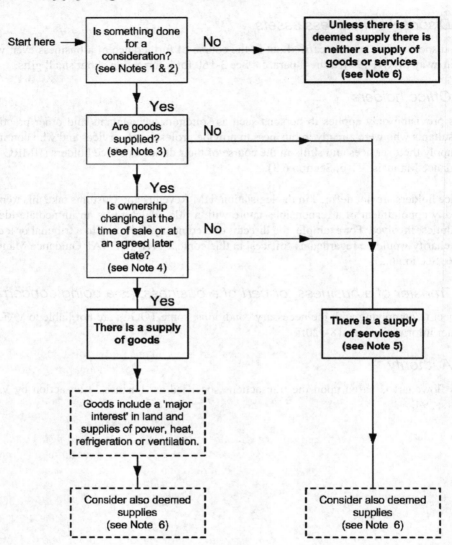

Notes

(1) Why the question is important

It is important to know whether a supply is of goods or of services because different tax point rules and place of supply rules apply to each.

(2) Need for a consideration

Except when the legislation deems there to be a supply, a supply does not arise without payment of a consideration (VATA1994, s. 5(2)(a)).

(3) Goods

Primarily goods are any form of tangible moveable property. If you can see it, it is probably goods.

(4) Change in ownership

This is when ownership of the whole will transfer at the time of sale. It includes arrangements where it is agreed that ownership will transfer 'at some time in the future ... but ... not later than when the goods are fully paid for' (e.g HP and lease purchase) (VATA 1994, Sch. 4, para. 1(2)).

(5) Services

Apart from transactions that clearly amount to a supply of services, any supply for VAT purposes that is not a supply of goods is a supply of services. In particular:

(a)   a lease or any other form of hire of movable goods;
(b)   the supply of an interest in land for consideration, other than a supply of a 'major interest'.

(6) Deemed supplies

When there is a deemed supply, the legislation specifies whether or not the supply is to be dealt with as goods or services.

Supplies by Business

4-970 Single or multiple supply?

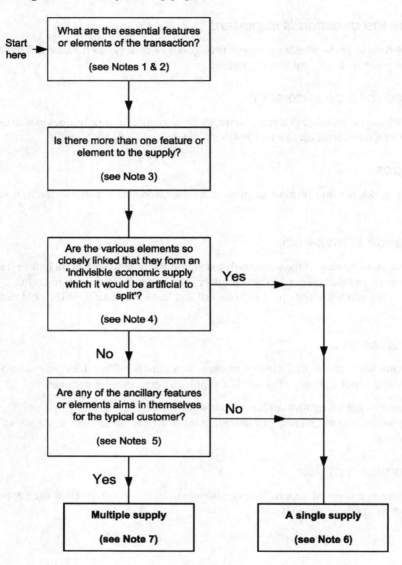

Notes

(1) Essential features or elements

To determine the essential features or elements of a transaction, it is necessary to take account of:

(a)   all the essential features of the transaction;
(b)   what the typical customer is seeking from the transaction; and
(c)   what the typical customer pays for.

(2) The price structure

The price structure is not decisive when determining if there are one or more supplies. The price structure should be taken into account but one must not assume that a single price indicates a single supply.

(3) Principal and ancillary features and elements

The various features or elements must be categorised into the principal supply and the ancillary features or elements.

(4) Artificial separation

'... a supply which comprises a single service from an economic point of view should not be artificially split so as to distort the functioning of the VAT system.'

Card protection Plan Ltd v C & E Commrs (Case C-349/96) [1999] BVC 155.

'... two or more elements or acts supplied ... to ... a typical customer ... (may be) ... so closely linked that that they form , objectively, a single , indivisible economic supply, which it would be artificial to split. '

Levob Verzekeringen BV & OV Bank NV v Staatssecretaris van Financiën [2005] (Case C-41/04)

(5) The aims of a typical customer

An ancillary element or feature is a separate supply when it is an aim in itself for a typical customer (*C & E Commrs v Madgett (t/a Howden Court Hotel)* (Joined Cases C-308/96 and C-94/97) [1998] BVC 458).

(6) When ancillary features are not separate supplies

The single supply is taxed according to the nature and characteristics of the principal supply.

(7) Multiple supply

A multiple supply is when both the principal supply and the ancillary supplies are aims in themselves for a typical customer. These supplies are taxed separately. It is usual to apportion the price between these features or elements. For information about this, see Notice 700 Section 32.

(8) Further information

For further information, see 3-820.

131

4-980 Where a business belongs

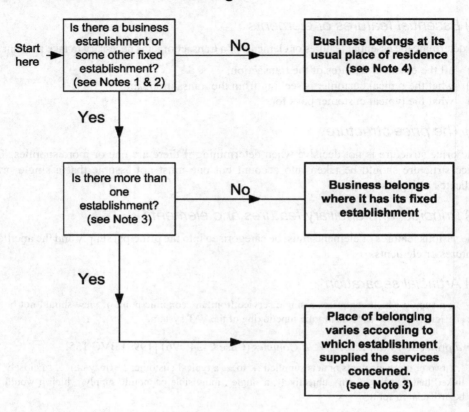

Start here → **Is there a business establishment or some other fixed establishment? (see Notes 1 & 2)**

→ **No** → **Business belongs at its usual place of residence (see Note 4)**

Yes ↓

Is there more than one establishment? (see Note 3)

→ **No** → **Business belongs where it has its fixed establishment**

Yes ↓

Place of belonging varies according to which establishment supplied the services concerned. (see Note 3)

Notes

(1) Business establishment

'The business establishment is the principal place of business and is usually the head office, headquarters or "seat" from which the business is run. There can be only one such place which may be an office, showroom or factory' – Notice 741, para. 3.3.

(2) Other fixed establishment

'A fixed establishment is an establishment other than the business establishment, which has both the technical and human resources necessary for providing or receiving services permanently present' – Notice 741, para. 3.4.

(3) More than one fixed establishment

'A business may have several fixed establishments, including a branch of a business or an agency' – Notice 741, para. 3.4.

'If … the supplier or the recipient of services, have establishments in more than one country, the supplies … have to be looked at separately. For each supply of services, you are regarded as belonging in the country where the establishment most directly connected with that particular supply is located' – Notice 741, para. 3.6.

(4) Usual place of residence

'If … your business is a limited company or other corporate body, it belongs where it is legally constituted' – Notice 741, para. 3.5.

'Individuals … are treated as belonging in the country where they have their usual place of residence' – Notice 741, para. 3.5.

(5) Legislation

The relevant legislation is VATA 1994, s. 9 and EU Directive 2006/112, article 56.

Supplies by Business

4-990   Time of Supply

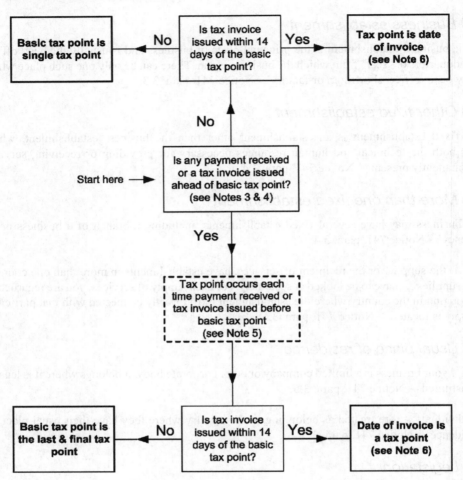

Notes

(1) Goods - imports and intra-EU trade

The basic tax point varies for imports from outside the EU and intra-EU trade in goods (see 5-040 and 5-810).

(2) Special time of supply rules

Special tax points apply to certain supplies (see 4-120 et seq).

(3) Basic tax point

The basic tax is different for goods or services (see 4-020).

(4) Tax invoice/payment

For details of tax invoices and payments, see 4-060 and 4-080 respectively.

(5) Multiple tax points

There is often a series of tax points due to issuing tax invoices and/or receiving payment (in part or in full) ahead of the basic tax point.

(6) Tax invoices issued within 14 days of basic tax point

The last possible tax point is the date of a tax invoice issued during the 14 days following the basic tax point.

(7) Legislation

The relevant legislation is VATA 1994, s. 6.

Supplies by Business

4-995 Basic tax point

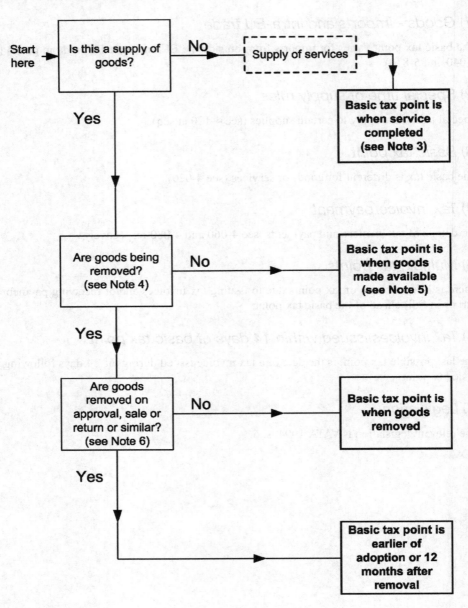

Notes

(3) Goods – imports and intra-EU trade

The basic tax point varies for imports from out side the EU and intra-EU trade in goods (see 5-040).

(4) Special time of supply rules

Special tax points apply to certain supplies (see 4-120 et seq).

(5) When service is completed

The date of completion '... is normally taken as the date when all the work except invoicing is completed' (VAT Notice 700, para. 14.2.1).

(6) Meaning of 'removed'

Removed is '... when you send them (the goods) to your customer or the customer takes them away' (VAT Notice 700, para. 14.2.1).

(7) When 'made available'

Made available is '... the date you make them available for your customer to use' (VAT Notice 700, para. 14.2.1).

(8) Goods supplied on sale or return, approval or similar terms

VAT Notice 700, para. 14.4 describes these goods as follows:

> '... you still own them (the goods) until such time as they are adopted by your customer. Adoption means that the customer indicates a wish to keep them. Until your customer does so, your customer has an unqualified right to return them at any time, unless you have agreed a time limit.'

(9) Legislation

The relevant legislation is VATA 1994, s. 6.

Supplies by Business

International Trade

VAT ON IMPORTS FROM OUTSIDE THE EC

5-040   Introduction to VAT on imports

The general rule is that the importation of goods from outside the EC is a chargeable event, and VAT is due on it, regardless of whether the person importing the goods does so in the course of a business. Only imports from 'third countries' (i.e. non-EC countries) are covered by this charge – imports from elsewhere in the EC are covered by the 'acquisition' rules reviewed at 5-320ff. The tax is chargeable as if it were a duty of HMRC, and is payable at the same time as any Customs duty arising.

There are a number of reliefs, and suspensions of liability, available, including some which also apply for customs duty purposes and some which are peculiar to VAT.

As a general rule, VAT on importation is payable when the goods enter the country (or during the month following, under duty deferment arrangements), although in some limited circumstances involving low value goods a registered trader may account for the tax via his VAT return.

This section provides a general outline of the system for applying VAT to imports of goods from countries outside the EC, and of the main reliefs and suspensions available.

VAT Reporter: ¶63-710

5-060   Place of supply of imports

Where goods are imported into the UK from outside the EC, the supply of the goods by the importer, and any subsequent supplies, are treated as made in the UK (VATA 1994, s. 7(6)). This can shift the place of supply, as compared with the place fixed under the basic rules, depending upon who acts as the importer.

Example: place of supply of imported goods

Charleen is an Australian wine factor, based in Brisbane. She sells wine to Pat and to Harry, both based in London, and ships the wine to London. The consignment of wine for Pat is imported into the UK in Pat's name. The consignment for Harry is imported in the name of Charleen.

Under the basic rules, both of these supplies are treated as made outside of the UK, since the goods are allocated to the contracts in Australia and this is where transportation commences. However, the consignment for Harry having been imported in Charleen's name, the place of the supply by Charleen is deemed (under EC law) to be the UK.

The position can become difficult if goods are imported in the name of an overseas business which does not have a business establishment in the UK. This can arise where, for instance, an overseas business agrees to supply goods and deliver them to the customer's premises, rather than to the dockside. The overseas business should register for UK VAT.

In the absence of such a registration, it may be impossible for anyone to obtain repayment of the VAT suffered on the importation of the goods. The problem is best avoided by carrying out the importation in these circumstances in the name of the UK customer.

United Kingdom businesses supplying customers elsewhere in the EC should note that other EC States are bound by the same directive as the UK. Thus, the place of allocation of goods, the question of installation, and the mechanics selected for importation into the other State must all be considered to determine whether the UK business has an obligation to register for VAT in the other Member State.

Legislation: VATA 1994, s. 7(6)

Other material: Place of supply – Goods manual, para. 3,600

VAT Reporter: ¶13-400

5-080   The charge to VAT on imports – general

Time of import

Tax is due when goods are imported into the UK from a place outside the EC. This is deemed to arise where:

(1)   the goods are removed from a place outside the EC and enter the territory of the EC;

(2)   they either enter the UK directly or enter it via another Member State; and

(3)   the circumstances are such that it is on entry into the UK that any liability to customs duty arises (or would arise if the goods were dutiable).

Legislation: VATA 1994, s. 15 and 16

VAT Reporter: ¶63-730

VAT charge

Usually, the charge will arise in the ordinary way on a direct importation into the UK at the time when the goods are entered. However, if on arrival in the UK, the goods are entered for some suspension regime (e.g. warehousing, etc.), the liability arises when they are removed into free circulation.

If goods first arrive in some other EC Member State and are entered into a duty suspension arrangement, and are in the UK when removed from this and entered for home use, the VAT charge on importation arises in the UK.

(1) Import by a business

Most imports are carried out by businesses. Any VAT due on importation will also rank as input tax in the hands of the importer, so is usually recoverable from HMRC via the importer's VAT returns (subject to the usual conditions concerning use in making taxable supplies, evidence, etc. – see ¶6-000ff. and ¶6-950ff.).

(2) Import by a private individual, etc.

As indicated earlier, VAT is due on importation regardless of the identity of the importer. If the importation is done by a private individual, or some other entity not carrying on a business, VAT continues to be due in the ordinary way. In this case, there is, of course, no question of recovering a similar amount as input tax. Thus, a non-taxable person who buys goods from outside the EC, and imports them, is put in the same VAT position as a person who buys from a taxable business.

(3) Zero-rated goods

The rate of VAT chargeable on imports is the same as that applicable when the same goods are bought in the UK.

Many goods bought in the UK are only zero rated or reduced rated if supplied with services or because of the status of the recipient. These conditions are not normally met in relation to imported goods making imports liable to the standard rate VAT.

Legislation: VATA 1994, s. 30(3)

Other material: Notice 700, para. 5.2

VAT Reporter: ¶63-750

(4) Exempt goods

There is no equivalent provision excluding from the charge on importation of goods which would be exempt from VAT if supplied in the UK. This is presumably because, to the extent that the UK exemptions apply to goods, they only apply when the goods are supplied in particular circumstances or by particular persons.

However, the importation of investment gold is specifically exempt (14-850).

Legislation: VATA 1994, s. 30(3); *Value Added Tax (Importation of Investment Gold) Relief Order* 1999 (SI 1999/3115)

VAT Reporter: ¶63-810

International Trade

(5) Specified reliefs

There are many specified and targeted reliefs to relieve certain goods from import VAT. Each of these has its own conditions.

Other material: Notice 702, para. 5.1

5-100   Procedure on importation – general

Goods entering the UK may only be landed at a HMRC control area, such as a Customs port or airport, and a vehicle arriving at such an area is obliged to report to HMRC. The importer of goods must enter them by presenting form C88 (the Single Administrative Document, or SAD).

The SAD gives details of the goods being imported, their value for customs and VAT purposes, the name of the importer, etc. Unless the goods are entered for a special regime, such as warehousing (see below), VAT (and any duty) payable on the importation is due at the time of importation (but see 5-220), and the goods will not normally be released by HMRC until payment has been made.

The SAD may be submitted either as a completed form or, at some ports, electronically by direct trader input (i.e. relevant information is transmitted from the trader's or shipping agent's computer to the HMRC computer).

Details of the various entry procedures are contained in vol. 3 of the Customs Tariff.

Legislation: CEMA 1979, Pt. III and IV

VAT Reporter: ¶63-760

5-120   Postal imports

Where the value of the goods is less than £2,000 and appropriate procedures are followed, the VAT-registered importer can account for the VAT on importation via his VAT return. However, for Datapost packets, the Post Office will collect the VAT at the time of delivery. For consignments whose value exceeds £2,000, a declaration must be made and returned to HMRC with payment of the VAT on importation.

VAT Reporter: ¶63-735

Other material: Notice 702, para. 4.3

5-140   Payment of VAT

As indicated above, VAT on importation is, in principle, due for payment at the time of importation.

It is also possible to enter into an arrangement whereby VAT on importation is collected by HMRC, by direct debit, on the fifteenth day of the month following importation. This involves providing HMRC with suitable security to cover deferrable charges (VAT, customs duty, etc.) each month and obtaining their approval. The amount of the guarantee can be topped up occasionally to cover unusually high levels of imports.

Certain importers are subject to a lesser security requirement. Importers have to apply for approval from HMRC in order to use this scheme. Details are accessed via HMRC's website and the specific SIVA (Simplified Import VAT Accounting) section.

Other material: Notice 101

VAT Reporter: ¶63-780

5-160   Identity of importer

The 'importer' of goods from the time of importation to the time when they are delivered out of charge is defined as including 'any owner or other person for the time being possessed of or beneficially interested in the goods'. There is therefore an element of choice as to the identity of the importer in relation to any particular transaction.

In practice, the importer is generally taken as being the person named as such on the SAD (Single Administrative Document). Care needs to be taken in selecting the importer, to ensure that it is someone capable of recovering the tax concerned as input tax (i.e. someone involved in the supply chain, not a mere carrier, etc.), and to avoid any unintended side effects in relation to the place of supply (see 5-280 below).

Legislation: CEMA 1979, s. 1(1)

VAT Reporter: ¶63-760

5-180   Value on importation

The value of imported goods for VAT purposes is generally the same as the value for duty purposes plus (if not already included) taxes, duties, etc. arising prior to or because of the importation, and all commission, packing, insurance, transport, etc. costs up to the place of importation. If a further destination of the goods within the EC is known at the time of importation, the value for VAT purposes includes the further transport, etc. costs in so far as they result from the transport of the goods to that further destination. If the value is based on the price at which they are supplied, this is generally reduced to take account of any prompt payment discount.

International Trade

The value for customs purposes is generally based on the price at which the associated transaction is taking place. Where this is inappropriate, there are other possible bases, such as the transaction value of identical or similar goods, or a computed value based on cost.

Importing computer software

Standard software packages available 'off the shelf' are taxed as goods. This means that import VAT is due and is based upon the customs/importation value which is 'the price actually paid or payable for both the software and the carrier medium'.

Bespoke software packages are taxed as services. Import VAT is not due but the reverse charge applies.

Works of art

The reduced importation value for works of art, etc. from 4 January 2011 is 25 per cent of the full value, giving an effective VAT rate of five per cent.

As an anti-avoidance measure, works of art are subject to the full rate of VAT (or, rather, full value) if exported from the UK and reimported within 12 months. By concession announced on 15 April 2002, HMRC will continue to apply the reduced rate (or reduced value) to such imports unless the importer has artificially arranged the export and reimportation in order to take advantage of the reduced rate.

Legislation: VATA 1994, s. 21

Other material: Notice 252; Notice 702, Section 3 and 7

VAT Reporter: ¶63-740; ¶63-750

5-200 Reliefs – general

There are three main kinds of relief from VAT on the importation of goods from outside the EC:

(1) suspension of the charge – the charge is not removed, but is suspended while the goods are in some kind of suspension regime (such as warehousing). The liability crystallises, and VAT becomes payable, as and when the goods are removed from the suspension regime for free circulation in the UK;

(2) temporary import reliefs – under these, certain goods brought temporarily to the UK escape the liability to VAT on importation altogether, provided that all appropriate conditions are met and the goods are subsequently re-exported. If the goods remain in the UK beyond the permitted period, a UK VAT liability then arises; and

(3) absolute reliefs – in some cases, there is no liability to VAT on the importation.

The reliefs available are mentioned in 5-220–5-240 and 5-260 below. Detailed coverage of these reliefs is beyond the scope of this work.

VAT Reporter: ¶63-920

Other material: Notice 702, Section 5

5-220 Reliefs – suspension

VAT on importation of goods from outside the EC into the UK is suspended in the following main cases:

(1) importation into a free zone – in this instance, the importation VAT is due only when the goods are removed from the free zone for home use. Details are in *Free Zones: Guidance Notes for Users*, available from HMRC;

(2) importation into a customs and/or excise warehouse – in this case, importation VAT becomes payable, if at all, when the goods are removed from the warehouse for home use;

(3) inward processing relief; and

(4) transit and transhipment.

VAT Reporter: ¶63-830; ¶63-840

5-240 Reliefs – temporary import relief

Relief is available for various goods temporarily imported into the UK, including:

(1) certain personal effects temporarily imported;

(2) commercial vehicles and aircraft;

(3) goods for removal to another EC Member State;

(4) containers and pallets; and

(5) various goods specified in the legislation.

In each case, there are a number of conditions to be met, security may be required, and VAT becomes due if the goods remain in the UK beyond a specified period or the conditions for relief are otherwise breached.

VAT Reporter: ¶63-820

5-260 Reliefs – absolute reliefs

There are a number of absolute reliefs from VAT on importation from outside the EC, including the following:

International Trade

(1) No import VAT is due on a consignment to a designated customer of goods worth under £18 (£15 from 1 November 2011). The relief does not apply to excise goods (alcohol, tobacco, perfumes or toilet waters, etc.). This relief applies across the EC although each State may have different monetary values. It was announced in the Chancellor's Autumn Statement, November 2011, that the relief would not apply to goods sent from the Channel Islands to the UK from 1 April 2012.

(2) Visual and audio materials produced by the UN.

(3) Qualifying goods by reference to the use or purpose to which they will be put in the UK. These are identified in Manuals Vol V1-18 para 5.7.

(4) Certain personal property imported by persons entering the UK to take up permanent residence.

(5) Awards: decorations, cups, medals, etc. for recipients or presenters of awards.

(6) Inherited property.

(7) Diplomats, international organisations and visiting forces are excused import VAT subject to conditions.

(8) Reimportation by a person who is not a taxable person and who previously exported the goods, without having been altered, where they have previously borne VAT (which has not been repaid) within the EC and various detailed conditions are met.

(9) Duty free allowances for travellers.

(10) Importations of gold by central banks.

(11) Small consignments of goods of a non-commercial character – this means a consignment with a value below £40.

(12) Imports of heat or cooling, natural gas and electricity through certain systems and networks.

In each case, detailed conditions must be met, and appropriate documentation completed, in order to qualify for relief.

VAT Reporter: ¶63-810

Other material: Manuals Vol V1-18 Sections 5 and 6

5-280 Removal from warehouse, etc.

Import VAT on UK goods placed in warehouse is due on their removal for home use. Any sales which have taken place in the warehouse are ignored.

However, if the goods are processed in the warehouse so as to lose their character, or mixed with UK produced goods so that they are no longer identifiable, the position is different. In this case, import VAT is no longer due on their removal from warehouse. However, if they are supplied while in warehouse, VAT is due on the last such supply to take place, and is payable by the person removing the goods for home use. See 3-340 for an anti-avoidance measure.

VAT Reporter: ¶63-730

5-300 Summary

This section has reviewed the basic rules for the imposition of VAT on the importation of goods from outside the EC into the UK. In most instances, the mechanics of this will be handled for traders by freight forwarders, etc. The important points for traders to bear in mind are to ensure that the right person is named as importer, that the place of supply provisions are properly recognised for any supply by the importer, and that appropriate evidence is held for recovery of input tax (see 6-500).

INTRA EC TRADE IN GOODS

5-320 Introduction

This section explains the incidence of VAT on the sale of goods between EC States and how this fits in with the main VAT system. It also covers the registration requirement for unregistered businesses and other entities acquiring goods in the UK from elsewhere in the EC.

If goods are purchased in one EC State and taken to another EC State they are called 'acquisitions'. The term 'imports' is reserved for goods that are purchased from outside the EC and brought into the EC.

5-340 General outline

The general rule for goods supplied within the EC is that they are taxed in the Member State to which they are dispatched. This is, of course, automatic where goods are supplied within a Member State, and goods imported from outside of the EC are taxed on entry into the Member State of arrival, as explained in the previous section.

The system for intra-EU trade is generally as follows:

(1) the supplier in the Member State of dispatch can zero-rate his supply, but only if he is supplying to a VAT-registered customer and quotes the customer's VAT registration number on his invoice (see 5-320);

(2) the customer is liable to account for VAT in the Member State of arrival on his 'acquisition' of the goods;

(3) the supplier in the Member State of dispatch must have and retain documentary evidence that the goods have left the Member State;

International Trade

(4) to enable the authorities to verify that acquisition tax is properly accounted for, the supplier must submit periodic EC sales listings to which the authorities in the Member State of arrival have access (see 9-540);

(5) a supplier dispatching significant quantities of goods to unregistered persons in another Member State may become liable to register for VAT there, and account for that Member State's VAT on these supplies (see 5-400(4)); and

(6) some unregistered entities acquiring significant quantities of goods from suppliers in other Member States may become liable to register for VAT in respect of these acquisitions. They are then liable to account for their own country's VAT on the acquisitions.

The scheme of the legislation on acquisitions is covered in more detail below.

Legislation: Directive 2006/112, art. 31–34 and 40; VATA 1994, s. 13; *Value Added Tax Regulations* 1995 (SI 1995/2518), reg. 134

Cases *Teleos v R & C Commrs* (Case C-409/04) [2005] BVC 253; *JP Commodities Ltd* [2007] BVC 4,047; *JP Commodities Ltd v R & C Commrs* [2007] EWHC 2474 (Ch); [2008] BVC 683

Other material: Notice 725, Section 2

VAT Reporter: ¶64-200

5-360 Acquisition – normal procedure

The most common case is that where a UK business purchases goods from a supplier elsewhere in the EC who ships the goods to the UK customer.

Five tests for charging acquisition VAT

The liability to pay acquisition VAT arises when:

(1) there is an acquisition of goods in the UK (see 5-380 and 5-440);

(2) the acquisition does not involve the supplier in making a UK supply (i.e. it is not caught by the UK's distance selling rules or by the rules for supplies of installed goods – see 5-400);

(3) the person making the acquisition does so in the course of a business, or in the course of a non-business activity of a company, club, etc.;

(4) the person making the acquisition is a taxable person (i.e. someone who is already registered for VAT, or is liable to be registered, whether under the ordinary VAT system or under the rules for registration of persons making significant UK acquisitions); and

(5) the acquisition is not exempt or zero-rated.

It is interesting to note that, unlike the corresponding provisions for import VAT (see 5-080), the acquisition provisions provide relief for an acquisition of goods covered by the exemption provisions. This is presumably based on the notion that such goods supplied from another

Member State will usually be exempt in that State also, so will carry similar underlying VAT to that borne by competing UK products.

Legislation: VATA 1994, s. 10 and 31(1)

Other material: Notice 725, Section 7

VAT Reporter: ¶64-200

5-380   Meaning of acquisition

An 'acquisition of goods' arises where goods are removed from one Member State to another and:

(1)   the movement involves a supply by the person dispatching the goods; or

(2)   the person is moving his own goods from one Member State to another.

A taxable person moving his own goods from one Member State to another is deemed to make a supply to himself in the Member State of dispatch and an acquisition in the Member State of arrival (see 3-200).

However, a movement of own goods to another Member State for processing and return is not treated as involving a supply.

It will be seen from the above that a transaction which is deemed not to be a supply, such as the provision of an industrial sample (see 3-160), does not give rise to an acquisition either.

Consignment and call-off stocks

Consignment stocks are goods transferred to another Member State to meet future supplies. The important feature is that the movement of the goods occurs before customers are found. By doing this the owner of the stock is making an acquisition in the EC State to which the goods are transferred and must account for VAT there.

Call-off stocks are goods transferred to a customer in another Member State in order that the customer may 'call off' stock as they are required. The transfer to another Member State is an acquisition in the destination Member State. Accounting for VAT on the acquisition is not consistent throughout the EC as some States require the customer to account for the tax and others require the transferee to do it.

Legislation: VATA 1994, s. 11(3)

Other material: Notice 725, para. 15.2 and 3

VAT Reporter: ¶64-220

International Trade

Importance of identifying the acquisition

An Austrian company, K, bought goods from Italian or Dutch firms. K immediately sold them to another Austrian company, EMAG Handel Eder OHG ('EMAG'). Likewise, EMAG straightaway sold the goods on to its customers.

The goods were transported from the Netherlands or Italy to Austria. They were delivered to EMAG or direct to EMAG's customers in Austria.

K accounted for Austrian VAT in respect of its sales to EMAG. EMAG reclaimed this tax as input tax and levied VAT when it invoiced its customers, the final consumers.

The Austrian authorities disallowed EMAG's claim to recover the tax charged by K. Their grounds were that, as 'all the transactions took place in Italy or the Netherlands' Austrian VAT was not due on the sale by K to EMAG. Thus EMAG was not entitled to reclaim the VAT concerned. EMAG appealed and the Austrian Courts referred the issue to the ECJ.

The ECJ was asked whether both the purchase by K and its sale to EMAG would be exempt as intra-Community acquisitions.

The ECJ ruled that, when there are successive supplies, as there were in this case, only one of the transactions will qualify as an intra-Community acquisition. It is necessary to identify the transaction concerned.

Another case provides more guidance on how to do this.

A firm in the Netherlands, Euro Tyres, sold tyres to companies in Belgium. Before taking delivery from Euro Tyres, the Belgium company (Middleman) sold the tyres to another firm in Belgium (the final buyer). Middleman sent its lorry and driver to collect the tyres from the Netherlands. The tyres were then delivered direct to the final buyer.

In this case there were two successive supplies – the supply by Euro Tyres to Middleman followed by the supply by Middleman to the final buyer. The CJEU decided the intra-Community acquisition was the supply by Euro Tyres to Middleman. Its reasons for this were as follows:

> 'The exemption of the intra-Community supply of goods became applicable only if the right to dispose of the goods as owner had been transferred to the person acquiring the goods … In circumstances such as those at issue, in which the person acquiring the goods, having obtained the right to dispose of the goods as owner in the member state of the first supply, expressed his intention to transport those goods to another member state and presented his VAT identification number attributed to that other state, the intra-Community transport should be ascribed to the first supply …'

Legislation: Directive 2006/112, art. 20; VATA 1994, s. 11

Other material: Notice 725, para. 7.1

Cases *EMAG Handel Eder OHG v Finanzlandesdirektion für Kärnten* (Case C-245/04) [2006] ECR I-3227; *Euro Tyre Holding BV v Staatssecretaris van Financiën* (Case C-430/09) [2011] BVC 257

VAT Reporter: ¶64-220

5-400 Exceptions from normal procedure

The basic definition of an acquisition would cover any movement of goods within the EC. There is power to extend the same reliefs for acquisitions as apply for certain imports (see 5-430).

(1) New means of transport

A new means of transport delivered from one Member State to another bears VAT in the Member State in which it is registered, even if the person to whom it is delivered is not a taxable person. Where the customer is a taxable person, the normal rules apply. Where the customer is not a taxable person, he is liable to account for VAT in the State of registration of the means of transport. The person making the acquisition must notify HMRC within seven days of their arrival, and pay the tax due within 30 days of receiving a demand for it.

The supplier of the goods must hold appropriate evidence that tax has been accounted for in the other Member State (where the acquirer is not a taxable person) in order to zero-rate the supply.

A UK supplier of a new means of transport for acquisition in another Member State may need to charge UK VAT in the first instance, pending receipt of evidence that acquisition tax has been accounted for. HMRC can refund the tax at a later date, on receipt of a claim accompanied by suitable evidence.

Meaning of new means of transport

A new means of transport is, broadly, a new ship, aircraft or land vehicle. Excluded from the definition are ships less than 7.5 metres long, aircraft less than 1,550 kilograms in take-off weight, and land vehicles of less than 48cc (or electric vehicles using less than 7.2 kilowatts).

A ship or aircraft is new if, measured from the date of its first entry into service, it is less than three months old or has been used for less than 100 hours or 40 hours respectively.

A land vehicle is new if, measured from the date of its first entry into service, it is less than six months old or has travelled less than 6,000 kilometres.

The ECJ has ruled that an assessment of whether or not something was 'new' had to be made at the time of supply of the new means of transport, and not when it arrived in the Member State of destination.

International Trade

Member State of acquisition

A new car purchased in Germany was brought to and registered in the UK before being taken to Spain where it was normally kept. The First Tier Tax Tribunal ruled that "the car was "consumed" in the UK by being brought here and registered here". Consequently there was an acquisition in the UK upon which VAT was due.

Legislation: VATA 1994, s. 10, 40 and 95; *Value Added Tax Regulations* 1995 (SI 1995/2518), reg. 146

Other material: Notice 728

VAT Reporter: ¶64-380

Cases: *X v Skatteverket* (Case C-84/09) [2010] ECR I-11645; *Feltham* [2011] UKFTT 612 (TC); [2011] TC 01455

(2) Excise goods

As a general rule, when goods liable to excise duty (such as tobacco products, alcohol, etc.) are delivered by a supplier in another Member State to a UK customer, this will involve a taxable supply in the UK under the distance selling rules (see 3-920). This is because no turnover limit applies for the distance selling of excise goods.

In the rare case where the seller is not making the supply by way of business (or is otherwise not registrable in the UK), the customer (including a private individual) is obliged to notify the acquisition and account for VAT on it.

It follows that the only way in which excise goods can enter the UK from elsewhere in the EC without payment of UK VAT (and duty) is if a private individual collects them personally from elsewhere in the EC and brings them back for his own private use.

Legislation: VATA 1994, s. 10 and Sch. 2; *Value Added Tax Regulations* 1995 (SI 1995/2518), reg. 36 and 135

Other material: Notice 725, para. 6.7

VAT Reporter: ¶64-360

(3) Distance selling

The broad aim of these provisions is to prevent consumers in different Member States from using mail order, etc. to obtain goods at lower rates of VAT (they are perfectly at liberty to achieve this end by travelling and buying in person). They apply where a business in one Member State takes orders from an unregistered customer in another Member State, and delivers goods to that customer in that other Member State.

The general method of accomplishing this aim is to provide that a person selling significant quantities of goods to unregistered persons in a particular Member State must register there, and charge that State's VAT on these sales.

The significant points for distance selling are as follows:

(1) these rules do not apply to the supply of a new means of transport or excise goods – there are special rules for these, covered above;

(2) nor do they apply where there is a deemed supply on a movement of the trader's own goods from one EC location to another, without any actual supply;

(3) if the customer is registered for VAT in the State of delivery, the distance selling rules do not apply. Instead, the supply will be zero-rated in the State of dispatch and the customer will be liable to pay VAT on an acquisition in the State of delivery;

(4) the rules only apply if the supplier makes sufficient distance sales to the State of delivery to become liable to register there. Liability to register in the UK as a distance seller is covered at 8-530ff. There are similar rules in other EC Member States;

(5) a supplier elsewhere in the EC whose distance sales to the UK are such as to render it liable to register for UK VAT (or which has opted to register for VAT in the UK as a distance seller) is deemed to make these supplies in the UK, even though delivery commences elsewhere, and must charge UK VAT on them; and

(6) similarly, a UK supplier shipping goods to unregistered persons in another EC State in which it is (or is obliged to be) registered as a distance seller is treated as making its supplies in the Member State of delivery, and must account for that country's VAT on them. If the overseas registration is voluntary rather than compulsory, the UK supplier must also give written notice to HMRC of the overseas registration in order to avoid being liable to pay UK VAT as well. This notification must be made within 30 days of the first supply made under the voluntary registration, and the trader must provide evidence of the voluntary registration.

Legislation: *Value Added Tax Regulations* 1995 (SI 1995/2518), reg. 98

Other material: Notice 725, para. 6

VAT Reporter: ¶63-240

(4) Supplies on intra-EC journeys

Where goods are supplied during passenger transport within the EC, the supply is treated as made in the Member State of departure. Goods for consumption during the journey are treated as being supplied outside the Member States and are relieved of VAT. For return trips, the outward and return stages are treated separately.

Legislation: *Value Added Tax (Place of Supply of Goods) Order* 2004 (SI 2004/3148)

Other material: Single Market 4650 manual

VAT Reporter: ¶63-220

International Trade

(5) Triangulation

The position becomes most complicated in the case of chain transactions. For instance, a UK business might sell goods to a German company, which resells them to a French company, with delivery directly from the UK to France. Specialist advice should be taken by businesses involved in such transactions.

There is a special treatment available for certain three-party chains. The effect is to ignore the intermediate supplier, and let the customer account for VAT on the acquisition of goods in the UK, so that the intermediate supplier does not need to register for VAT.

This special treatment applies when the following conditions are met:

(1)   the movement of the goods: the goods must move from one Member State to another and must not originate in an EC State where the intermediate supplier is registered for VAT;

(2)   the supply chain: there must be a supply of goods from an original supplier to an intermediate supplier taxable in a different State, who resupplies the goods to a person registered for VAT in another Member State;

(3)   if the supply had been made directly by the original supplier to the final customer, the final customer would have made an acquisition in the State concerned; and

(4)   the invoice issued by the intermediate supplier must be endorsed 'VAT: EC Article 28 Simplification Invoice';

(5)   intermediate suppliers to the UK must notify HMRC that they are using this simplification procedure.

Where these conditions are met, the supply by the intermediate supplier is ignored and the final customer is treated as acquiring the goods in the State where the final customer belongs (except for acquisition registration purposes).

When triangulation goes wrong, the intermediary is liable to account for VAT. The intermediary must account for VAT in the EU State which issued the VAT number used to buy the goods free of VAT. This liability may only be reduced by the amount of VAT, if any, accounted for in the EU State to which the goods were delivered.

Legislation: VATA 1994, s. 14; *Value Added Tax Regulations* 1995 (SI 1995/2518), regs. 11, 17 and 18

Cases: *Mexcom Ltd* [2010] UKFTT 163; [2010] TC 00468; *Staatssecretaris van Financiën v X and fiscale eenheid Facet-Facet Trading* (Joined Cases C-536/08 & C-539/08) [2012] BVC 248

Other material: Notice 725, The Single Market, Section 13

VAT Reporter: ¶64-280

(6) Registration number not issued by State to which goods delivered

Special arrangements apply to an acquisition involving three EU States. This is not triangulation.

A UK business may use its VAT number to acquire goods from a business in another State. Subject to the usual conditions, the supplier will not charge 'VAT'. However, instead of the good being delivered to the UK, they are sent to a third State. There are then two acquisition and two tax liabilities as follows:

(1) the UK business that used its VAT number to acquire the goods without paying 'VAT' must account for acquisition tax in the UK;

(2) there is an acquisition in the State to which the goods were delivered and tax must be accounted for there.

The acquisition tax accounted for in the UK is not input tax. Instead the UK business is given credit for any tax accounted for in the State to which the goods were delivered.

Other material: Revenue and Customs Brief 20/11

Legislation: VATA 1994, s. 10

Cases: *Staatssecretaris van Financiën v X and fiscale eenheid Facet-Facet Trading* (Joined Cases C-536/08 & C-539/08) [2012] BVC 248

5-420 Registration in respect of acquisitions

A person in business in the UK, and certain other persons, can become liable to register for VAT in the UK if its acquisitions from other Member States exceed a certain threshold. The limits are in Hardman's Tax Rates and Tables 19-080 or Key Data 1-140(3) (measured from 1 January in the year concerned).

This liability to register affects all businesses, and also any body corporate, club, association, organisation or other unincorporated body carrying on non-business activities.

The liability to register in respect of acquisitions is covered in more detail at 8-430ff.

Legislation: VATA 1994, s. 10(3) and Sch. 2

Other material: Notice 700/1, Sections 5 and 6

VAT Reporter: ¶64-300

International Trade

5-440   Place of acquisition

If the goods are removed to the UK (the normal case), then the acquisition takes place in the UK.

The other instance, where an acquisition might be deemed to take place in the UK, arises where a person accepts an intra-EC delivery of goods in another Member State, but quotes his UK VAT registration number to enable his supplier to zero-rate the supply. In this instance, an acquisition is deemed to take place in the UK unless the acquirer can show that he has actually paid acquisition tax in the Member State of delivery.

This facilitates the policing of the system, since the supplier will have included the UK registration number on his EC Sales Listing (9-540).

An acquisition may be treated as made outside the UK if the acquired goods are within a fiscal warehousing regime, or are placed therein before being resupplied (see 3-350).

Legislation: VATA 1994, s. 13

Other material: Single Market VATSM335 manual

VAT Reporter: ¶64-225

5-460   Time of acquisition

An acquisition is deemed to take place on the earlier of:

(1)   the date when the supplier issues an invoice and the date when the goods are removed. The date of payment for the supply is ignored;

(2)   the fifteenth day of the month following that in which the chargeable event occurs, i.e. the first removal of the goods involved in the transaction which gives rise to the acquisition; and

(3)   the issue of a VAT invoice by the supplier

Legislation: VATA 1994, s. 12

Other material: Notice 725, para. 7.3

VAT Reporter: ¶64-320

5-480   Value of acquisition

The value of an acquisition is the value of the transaction under which it takes place. This will normally be the value of the consideration, whether monetary or non-monetary.

There are special provisions to cover special cases (gifts, connected persons, etc.) on similar lines to those relating to supplies of goods.

Legislation: VATA 1994, s. 20, Sch. 7

Other material: Notice 725, Section 8

VAT Reporter: ¶64-340

5-500 Summary

The above sets out the main rules relating to intra-EC acquisitions, the possible requirement to register in respect of acquisitions, and the interaction of the acquisition head of charge with the VAT system as a whole.

EXPORTS

5-550 Exports of goods

There is a general zero-rating whereby, if a person supplies goods by way of export from the EC (or by delivery to a taxable person elsewhere in the EC who makes an acquisition of the goods), that supply is zero-rated.

The export of goods by a charity is deemed to be a zero-rated supply made in the UK in the course or furtherance of a business. This enables charities exporting goods for relief purposes to recover input tax on them.

The form of words used in granting the zero-rating is such that it is not sufficient merely to export the goods in order to qualify for zero-rating. The zero-rating only applies if HMRC 'are satisfied' that the supplier has exported the goods.

HMRC are generally only prepared to be satisfied that the goods have been exported if the supplier retains evidence of this in a form specified by them. Evidence which might be sufficient to satisfy a court that the goods have been exported has in the past been insufficient to ensure zero-rating if it does not take the form specified by HMRC.

The scope for obtaining zero-rating on the basis of evidence accepted by the tribunals and courts, although not falling within the categories stated by HMRC, has improved following a line of cases on the jurisdiction of the tribunals which commences with *Brookes*. The first specifically concerned with evidence for export is *G McKenzie & Co Ltd* where the appellant made supplies of silver to customers in Bangladesh. The Bangladesh customer had a licence to import lead/flux solder, and the silver was oxidised to give it the appearance of lead. The export documentation described the goods as lead/flux solder.

International Trade

157

HMRC refused zero-rating for the supplies on the grounds that they were not satisfied that the goods had been exported, and that the documentation misdescribed the goods and so failed to meet the conditions laid down in Notice 703.

In a preliminary hearing on jurisdiction, the tribunal decided that HMRC's decisions that they were not satisfied on the question of export, or with the documentation, were 'prior decisions' within VATA 1994, s. 84(10). As such, they fell within the tribunal's jurisdiction. As these were both matters within the discretion of HMRC, the tribunal only had supervisory jurisdiction. The effect was that the tribunal could decide whether HMRC had acted reasonably in their decision whether to accept the evidence provided and, if it decided that they had not, it could set aside their decision. It could not merely substitute its own judgment for that of HMRC.

The conclusion must be that it is advisable, wherever possible, to obtain evidence of export of the kind specified by HMRC but, if this cannot be done, this is no longer absolutely fatal to the zero-rating.

Legislation: VATA 1994, s. 30(5) and (6)

Cases: *C & E Commrs v Henry Moss of London Ltd* (1980) 1 BVC 373; *Brookes* [1995] BVC 681; *G McKenzie & Co Ltd* [1995] BVC 827

Other material: Notice 703

VAT Reporter: ¶20-125

5-570 Evidence of export

The type of evidence required by HMRC varies according to the manner in which the goods are exported. Details of the necessary proof of export are summarised below.

A common feature of the various proofs of export required is that they are generally obtainable only at the time when the export takes place. For instance, if the export is a postal export of goods requiring a customs declaration, the evidence required is a certificate of posting. The Post Office is scarcely likely to issue such a certificate at some later date.

Any trader who exports goods will therefore be well advised to make a careful study of Notice 703, as it relates to the particular form of export, and ensure that arrangements are in hand to ensure that proper evidence of export is obtained, and retained.

For exports to other EC countries, zero-rating is only available if the customer is a taxable person. This must be evidenced by stating the customer's VAT registration number on the tax invoice.

Forms of evidence

HMRC always expect that ordinary commercial documentation, such as contracts, copy correspondence, copy invoices and consignment notes, etc. will be available for inspection. In addition, they look for positive proof of export clearly identifying the particular goods exported and the manner of export, as summarised below. If such additional proof is not held, zero-rating may well be denied.

The additional proof may take the form of primary evidence (documents issued by actual shippers, such as shipping lines and airlines) or secondary evidence (documents issued by freight forwarders, etc. who arrange exports for a number of exporters).

Sea freight

The normal evidence is a copy of the shipped bill of lading or sea waybill certifying actual shipment, or equivalent documentation provided by the shipping company. Bills of lading or sea waybills showing receipt for shipment may also be accepted, provided that evidence of actual shipment can be obtained if required by HMRC for a particular consignment.

Air freight

In this case, the evidence required is a copy of the air waybill, endorsed with the flight prefix and number and the date and place of departure.

Groupage or consolidation transactions

These arise where goods are exported using a freight forwarder, who may consolidate a number of smaller parcels into a single consignment. In this case, the freight forwarder will normally hold bills of lading, etc. dealing with the consignment as a whole, and showing him as consignor. The trader should obtain from the freight forwarder a certificate of shipment showing details of the export vessel or aircraft, place of departure, date of departure, identification number of bill of lading, etc. identifying number of container, etc. and a full description of the goods (including quantity, weight and value).

Postal exports, etc.

For letter post, certificate of posting is required. If the value of the package exceeds £100, and a customs declaration is required, an export label (Form VAT 444) must be fixed to the package.

Where the export is by parcel post, a HMRC Pack must be completed. The receipt copy of this, signed by the collecting driver or by the Post Office counter clerk, combined with the Parcel Force statement of account listing each export, comprise the required evidence of export.

There are similar arrangements for exports via courier and fast parcels services other than those operated by the Post Office, and for certain exports via British Rail.

International Trade

Special procedures

There are a number of special procedures for particular types of export, such as exports of computer software, exports to oil rigs, exports from free zones, etc. These are covered in Notice 703.

Time Limits

Evidence of export must be obtained within three months of the date of the supply, except when the supply involves supplies of goods for processing prior to export when the time limit is increased to six months.

Legislation *Value Added Tax Regulations* 1995 (SI 1995/2518), reg. 129

Other material: Notice 703, section 6; Notice 703, para. 3.5

Cases *Teleos v R & C Commrs* (Case C-409/04) [2005] BVC 253; *JP Commodities Ltd* [2007] BVC 4,047; *JP Commodities Ltd v R & C Commrs* [2007] EWHC 2474 (Ch); [2008] BVC 683

VAT Reporter: ¶63-080

5-590   Export by another

Supplies of goods for export can in some instances be zero-rated even though the export is not carried out by the supplier.

In the case of a supply to an overseas trader who arranges exportation, zero-rating is available provided that:

- the exporter keeps a separate record of the transaction including evidence (such as the order) that the supply is made to an overseas trader;
- the goods are exported within one month of the time of supply;
- valid proof of export (see above) is obtained within three months of the export; and
- the goods are not used in the UK between leaving the exporter's premises and exportation taking place.

Where the trader requires evidence to zero-rate a supply, such evidence needing to be obtained by another, special care is needed to ensure that the evidence is in fact obtained. When dealing with strangers, it will often be wise to require a deposit equivalent to the VAT which would be due if zero-rating did not apply, returning this only when the evidence is provided.

Legislation *Value Added Tax Regulations* 1995 (SI 1995/2518), reg. 129

Other material: Notice 703, para. 6.9;

VAT Reporter: ¶63-080

5-610 Miscellaneous

Ship's and aircraft's stores

Supplies of goods can be zero-rated if the goods are shipped for use as stores on a ship or aircraft with a non-UK destination, provided that certain conditions are fulfilled.

VAT Reporter: ¶63-320

Legislation: VATA 1994, s. 30(6)(b)

Other material: Notice 703, Section 10

Forfeiture

Where a supply of goods is zero-rated as an export, and they are subsequently found in the UK, the goods are liable to forfeiture.

Legislation: VATA 1994, s. 30(10)

VAT Reporter: ¶63-540

Services

It should be noted that the zero-rating for exports applies only to supplies of goods. There is no general zero-rating for 'exports' of services, although some international supplies of services are relieved from UK VAT by being treated as made outside the UK (see 3-940ff.).

Emission allowances

From midnight 30 July 2009 until 31 October 2010, the rate of VAT on emission allowances or 'carbon credits' traded in the UK was zero per cent.

The zero rate applied to any transaction in EU emissions allowances and transferable units issued pursuant to the Kyoto Protocol. This included over the counter spot trades, transactions for future delivery and options. Cross-border transactions are not affected.

From 1 November 2010 this was replaced by the reverse charge. The reverse charge requires the customer to account for VAT and also puts a joint and several liability on traders on the supply chain where VAT remains unpaid.

Other material: Revenue and Customs Brief 46/09; Revenue and Customs Brief 28/10; Revenue and Customs Brief 35/10

Legislation: VATA 1994, s. 55A

VAT Reporter: ¶24-300

International Trade

Interest may become chargeable if correct documentation not available timeously

In *C & E Commrs v Musashi Autoparts (Europe) Ltd (formerly TAP Manufacturing Ltd)*, the trader failed to convince the Court of Appeal that interest should not be payable when they had failed to produce the correct documentation showing that goods had left the UK. The goods were zero-rated and VAT was not accounted for even though the documentation was not available in the three months allowed. The documentation was later – after the raising of the assessment by HMRC – produced. To quote Pill LJ in his summing up, 'I am pleased to have been able to reach a conclusion which gives an incentive to the keeping of good records; zero-rating from the start, which good records permits, will prevent the liability to interest which arose in this case'.

The assessment for interest was raised not because the trader failed to have the evidence, but because he failed to adjust his VAT account after three months – the time allowed for obtaining the evidence. The trader should have accounted for the correct amount of VAT after three months and subsequently, when the documentation was available and the goods could be zero-rated, readjusted the VAT account accordingly.

Legislation: VATA 1994, s. 30(10)

Cases: *C & E Commrs v Musashi Autoparts (Europe) Ltd (formerly TAP Manufacturing Ltd)* [2004] BVC 127; *R (on the application of Teleos plc) v C & E Commrs* [2005] BVC 93; [2005] BVC 253; (Case C-409/04) [2008] BVC 705

VAT Reporter: ¶60-637

INTERNATIONAL SERVICES

5-630 Introduction

It should never be assumed that services provided from the UK to someone in another country are outside the scope of UK VAT. Conversely, it should not be assumed that services received in the UK from abroad are not liable to VAT.

In order to know how to account for VAT it is necessary to determine the 'place of supply'. This is the location at which goods or services are supplied or deemed to be supplied.

Once the place of supply has been determined, it is the VAT regulations that pertain in the country where the place of supply is situated that apply. Thus, if the place of supply is outside the EC, there is no VAT due. If the place of supply is in an EC Member State, it is necessary to consider and apply the regulations of the State concerned.

Certain factual information is required to determine how and where to account for VAT on international services. The required information is some or all of the following:

(1)   whether the recipient is, or is not, a business;

(2)   where the supplier belongs;

(3)   where the customer belongs; and

(4)   a proper understanding of the services concerned.

Each of these items has implications for the VAT liability of the services and on where, and by whom, VAT should be accounted.

EC Sales Lists

UK businesses supplying services to business customers in other EU States must also complete an EC Sales lists. See also 9-540.

5-650   Identifying business customers

The documentary evidence required to prove that the recipient of a service varies a little according to whether the recipient belongs in the EC or outside the EC.

If the recipient belongs in the EC, that person's valid VAT number is sufficient evidence to substantiate that they are a business. When there isn't a VAT registration number, other evidence such as 'certificates from fiscal authorities, business letterheads or other commercial documents indicating the nature of the customers' activities' will normally be acceptable.

If the recipient belongs outside the EC, the supplier of the service may rely on a 'VAT number, or a similar number attributed to the customer by the country of establishment and used to identify businesses' as evidence that the customer is a business. Alternatively 'any other proof which demonstrates that the customer' is a business is acceptable.

Non-business customers

Any recipient of a service who cannot prove they are a business is presumed to be a non-business customer.

Other material: Notice 725, para. 2.7

Legislation: Council Implementing Regulation (EU) No 282/2011, art. 18

5-670   Place of belonging

Where the recipient of the service belongs is often clear. Difficulties arise when the recipient is a business with several branches or fixed establishments. Then it is necessary to identify the place of belonging of the branch or fixed establishment to which the service is supplied.

The rules for establishing where the recipient belongs are explained at 3-950.

5-690   Basic rule

The basic rule under both UK and EC VAT law is the same. The place of supply is determined by reference to where the supplier or customer 'belongs'. Where the work is actually done is not normally relevant. When it is relevant and other variations to the basic rule are explained below in 5-710.

When the service is supplied to a 'relevant business' customer for the purposes of that person's business, the place of supply is where the customer 'belongs' (see flowchart at 5-983). The effect of this is that the supplier does not charge VAT, but VAT is normally due in the State where the recipient 'belongs'. If the recipient 'belongs' outside the EC, there is no VAT due.

When supplying services to customers that are not 'relevant business' customers, the basic rule is that the place of supply is where the supplier 'belongs'. The effect of this is that the supplier must charge VAT according to the rules in the State where he or she 'belongs'.

> ### Example
>
> Anthony is a freelance secretary and registered for VAT. His office is in Worcester, where he lives. He provides secretarial services to a business in France. The business is registered for TVA. Anthony carries out this assignment in France.
>
> Whilst in France Anthony provides some interpretation services to a former UK policeman, Philip, who is resident in France.
>
> The secretarial services for the French business are deemed to be supplied in France because this is where the customer belongs. The services are liable to French TVA and this is accounted for by the French business using the 'reverse charge' procedure
>
> As Philip is non-business customer, the place of supply of the interpretation services is the UK because this is where Anthony belongs. Consequently these services are liable to UK VAT.

Legislation: VATA 1994, s. 7A and Sch. 4A; Directive 2006/112, art. 43

Other material: Notice 741A, Section 5

VAT Reporter: ¶65-545

5-710   Variations to the basic rule

There are three sets of exceptions to the basic rule. There are the general exceptions that apply in all cases, exceptions for services supplied to business customers and exceptions when dealing with non-business customers.

General exceptions applying in all cases

The general exceptions are set out in the order in which they appear in the legislation. They may be referred to in flowchart 5-985.

Services relating to land

Services connected with land are treated as being supplied where the land concerned is located, regardless of where the supplier and customer belong, or where the services are performed.

The services covered are:

(1)   the grant, assignment or surrender of interests in or rights over land, options to obtain an interest in or right over land, licences to occupy land, and contractual rights exercisable over or in relation to land;

(2)   accommodation in hotels or similar, holiday accommodation and camping or seasonal caravan facilities (see 15-200);

(3)   works of construction, demolition, alteration, repair, etc. of any building or civil engineering work; and

(4)   services such as those supplied by estate agents, auctioneers, architects, surveyors, engineers and others involved in matters relating to land.

Following negotiations with other EU States, HMRC issued further information in August 2012 about land related services. In particular HMRC changed its treatment of the following services:

(1)   Stands at exhibitions and conferences – Stand space supplied 'with accompanying services as package' would no longer be treated as a land related service.

(2)   Storage of goods – This is not a land related service unless the goods are stored in a 'specific area' and the owner of the goods is granted 'exclusive use' of this area.

(3)   Access to airport lounges – This is changed to a land related service.

Affected businesses may take three months from 2 August 2012 to implement the changes.

Legislation: VATA 1994, Sch. 4A, para. 1

Other material: Notice 741A, Section 6; Revenue and Customs Brief 22/12

Passenger transport

Transporting passengers – and their accompanying luggage – is made in the country in which it takes place. If more than one country is involved, the services are apportioned in the ratio of the distance travelled in each.

Part of a journey between two places in the same country may take place outside the territorial jurisdiction of that country. When this happens, the journey is treated as wholly within the country concerned so long as there was no stop or break in another country.

Legislation: VATA 1994, Sch. 4A, para. 2

Other material: Notice 741A, Section 10

Hiring of means of transport

The short term hire of a means of transport is made in the country in which the means of transport is actually put at the disposal of the customer.

'Short term hire' is where a vessel is hired for a continuous period not exceeding 90 days and for other means of transport a period not exceeding 30 days.

Legislation: VATA 1994, Sch. 4A, para. 3

Other material: Notice 741A, Section 7

Restaurant and catering services

These services are supplied in the country in which the services are physically carried out – other than when they are part of an EC on-board supply (see below).

Legislation: VATA 1994, Sch. 4A, para. 5

Other material: Notice 741A, Section 9

EC on-board restaurant and catering services

When, during the intra-EU transport of passengers, restaurant or catering services are supplied on board a ship, aircraft or train as part of the transport service, the place of supply is the EU State of departure.

An intra-EU transport of passengers is a passenger transport movement that begins and ends in the EU without a stop outside the EU where passengers may disembark.

Legislation: VATA 1994, Sch. 4A, para. 6

Other material: Notice 741A, Section 9

Hiring of goods

This includes the hiring of goods other than a means of transport.

The place of supply is determined according to the normal rules, but in certain circumstances is varied for relevant business customers.

The additional rules for relevant business customers are concerned with use and enjoyment of the services concerned. If, according to the normal rules, the place of supply is the UK but the services are 'effectively used and enjoyed' in a non-EU country, the place of supply is that non-EU country. Conversely, the place of supply can be the UK when, according to the normal rules, the place of supply is a non-EU country but the services are 'effectively used and enjoyed' in the UK.

Legislation: VATA 1994, Sch. 4A, para. 7

Other material: Notice 741A, Section 16

Telecommunications and broadcasting services

These are services of transmission, emission or reception of signals, writing, images and sounds or information of any nature by wire, radio, optical or other electromagnetic systems. It includes the related transfer or assignment of the right to use 'capacity' for said transmission, emission or reception and access to global information networks. Radio and television broadcasting services are not defined.

The place of supply is determined according to the normal rules, but in certain circumstances is varied for relevant business customers.

The additional rules for relevant business customers are concerned with use and enjoyment of the services concerned. If, according to the normal rules, the place of supply is the UK but the services are 'effectively used and enjoyed' in a non-EU country, the place of supply is that non-EU country. Conversely, the place of supply can be the UK when, according to the normal rules, the place of supply is a non-EU country but the services are 'effectively used and enjoyed' in the UK.

Legislation: VATA 1994, Sch. 4A, para. 8

Other material: Notice 741A, Section 16

Exceptions when supplying business customers

These exceptions are set out in the order in which they appear in the legislation. They apply when the recipient is a business. More information is in flowchart 5-987.

Electronically supplied services

An electronically supplied service is something which 'in the first instance is delivered over the internet or an electronic network ... and ... the nature of the service in question is heavily dependent upon information technology for its supply'.

Examples are as follows:

- website supply, web-hosting and distance maintenance of programmes and equipment;
- supplies of software (including updates);
- supplies of images, text and information, and the making of databases;
- supplies of music, films and games (including games of chance and gambling games);
- supplies of political, cultural, artistic, sporting, scientific and entertainment broadcasts (including broadcasts of events);
- supplies of distance teaching.

The place of supply is determined according to the normal rules, but in certain circumstances is varied for relevant business customers and non-business customers (for non-business customers, see below).

International Trade

167

The additional rules for relevant business customers are concerned with use and enjoyment of the services concerned. If, according to the normal rules, the place of supply is the UK but the services are 'effectively used and enjoyed' in a non-EU country, the place of supply is that non-EU country. Conversely, the place of supply can be the UK when, according to the normal rules, the place of supply is a non-EU country but the services are 'effectively used and enjoyed' in the UK.

Legislation: VATA 1994, Sch. 4A, para. 9

Other material: Notice 741A, Section 16

Admission to cultural, educational and entertainment activities, etc.

The place of supply is varied for 'services in respect of admissions' to certain events or performances. The events and performances concerned are as follows:

- cultural, artistic, sporting, scientific, educational, entertainment or similar events (including exhibitions and fairs); and
- services ancillary to the above.

The place of supply for 'services in respect of admission' is where the event takes place.

For these purposes 'right of admission' is allowing persons to attend a live event. EC regulations outline the essential characteristics as 'right of admission to an event in exchange for a ticket or payment' which includes a subscription, season ticket or periodic fee. In particular this applies to the following:

- shows, theatrical performances, circus performances, fairs, amusement parks, concerts, exhibitions and other similar cultural events;
- sporting events such as matches and competitions.

Legislation: VATA 1994, Sch. 4A, para. 9A

Other material: Notice 741A, Section 8

Exceptions for non-business customers

Exceptions which apply when supplying non-business customers are set out below in the order in which they appear in the legislation. See flowchart 5-987.

Intermediaries

An intermediary is a person who:

'… arranges supplies between two other parties; a supplier and that supplier's customer. Intermediaries may be referred to as brokers, buying or selling agents, go-betweens, commissionaires or agents acting in their own name (undisclosed agents). Payments for their services are often described as commission' (Notice 741, para. 11.1).

The place of supply of intermediary services to non-business customers is the same as the principal service.

Legislation: VATA 1994, Sch. 4A, para. 10

Other material: Notice 741A, Section 12

Transport of goods

It is necessary to distinguish between the intra-Community transport of goods and other movements of goods.

There is an intra-Community transport of goods when the transportation 'begins in one Member State and ends in another' EU State. When these services are supplied to a non-business customer, the place of supply is the EU State in which the transportation begins.

In other instances, the supply is made in the country in which it takes place. If more than one country is involved, the services are apportioned in the ratio of the distance travelled in each.

Part of a journey between two places in the same country may take place outside the territorial jurisdiction of that country. When this happens, the journey is treated as wholly within the country concerned so long as there was no stop or break in another country.

Legislation: VATA 1994, Sch. 4A, para. 11 and 12

Other material: Notice 741A, Section 11

Ancillary transport services

Ancillary transport services are such services as loading, unloading, handling or similar.

These are treated as being made where the services are physically supplied.

Legislation: VATA 1994, Sch. 4A, para. 13

Other material: Notice 741A, Section 11

Valuation services

Such services to a non-business customer take place where the services are physically performed.

Legislation: VATA 1994, Sch. 4A, para. 14

Cultural, educational and entertainment services

For the following, the place of supply is where the event takes place:

International Trade

169

(1)   cultural, artistic, sporting, scientific, educational or entertainment services;

(2)   services relating to exhibitions, conferences or meetings;

(3)   services ancillary to supplies under (1) and (2) above (including services of organising them).

The underlying principle is that live events should be taxed where they take place.

Legislation: VATA 1994, Sch. 4A, para.14A

Other material: Notice 741A, Section 8

Electronic services

Electronic services supplied by a person belonging outside the EU to a non-relevant business customer in the EU are supplied where the customer belongs. The supplier may have to register in the EU (see 18-070).

Legislation: VATA 1994, Sch. 4A, para. 15

Other material: Notice 741A, Section 17

Other services to non-business customers belonging outside the EU

When the customer is not a relevant business customer and belongs outside the EU, the place of supply of certain services is where the customer belongs. Thus, the services are deemed to be supplied outside the EU. The services to which this applies are as follows:

'(a)   transfers and assignments of copyright, patents, licences, trademarks and similar rights,

(b)   the acceptance of any obligation to refrain from pursuing or exercising (in whole or in part) any business activity or any rights within paragraph (a),

(c)   advertising services,

(d)   services of consultants, engineers, consultancy bureaux, lawyers, accountants, and similar services, data processing and provision of information, other than any services relating to land,

(e)   banking, financial and insurance services (including reinsurance), other than the provision of safe deposit facilities,

(f)   the provision of access to, and of transport or transmission through, natural gas and electricity distribution systems and the provision of other directly linked services,

(g)   the supply of staff,

(h)   the letting on hire of goods other than means of transport,

(i)   telecommunication services (as to the meaning of which see paragraph 8(2)),

(j)   radio and television broadcasting services, and

(k)   electronically supplied services (as to the meaning of which see paragraph 9(3) and (4)).'

Previously, these were commonly known as the 'Schedule 5 services'.

The supply of staff can include 'the supply of self-employed persons'. However there is little information available about when this should apply.

Legislation: VATA 1994, Sch. 4A, para. 16

Other material: Notice 741A, Section 15

Cases: *Von Hoffman v Finanzamt Trier* (Case C-145/96) [1997] BVC 562; *ADV Allround Vermittlungs AG v Finanzampt Hamburg-Bergedorf* (Case C-218/10) 26 January 2012

5-730   Types of services in the EC

From 1 July 2011 the Council Implementation Regulation (EU) No 282/2011 is in force throughout the EC.

One of its functions is to serve as an interpretation rule for many types of supplies of services.

The following are covered:

- Restaurant and catering services – Article 6
- Electronically supplied services – Article 7
- Assembling machinery – Article 8
- Sales of certain options – Article 9
- Assigning television broadcasting rights in respect of football matches – Article 26
- Organising funerals – Article 28
- Translation service – Article 29
- Services of intermediaries – Articles 30 and 31
- Cultural, artistic, sporting scientific, educational, entertainment and similar services – Article 32 et seq.
- Ancillary transport services – Article 34
- Valuations of, and work on, moveable property – Article 34
- On board restaurant and catering services – Article 35 et seq.
- Hiring of means of transport – Article 38 et seq.

Legislation: Regulation 282/2011, art. 6, art. 7, art. 8, art. 9, art. 28, art. 29, art. 30, art. 32, art. 34, art. 35, art. 38

VAT Reporter: ¶65-510

5-750   Reverse charge, etc.

When a UK business buys services from a business belonging overseas, it is necessary to consider the 'reverse charge'. The 'reverse charge' is a VAT liability imposed upon the UK buyer or recipient of the services. This charge is not peculiar to the UK. It applies throughout the EC (see 3-220).

International Trade

When invoicing overseas businesses and VAT is not chargeable because the place of supply is where the recipient belongs, the invoice should be endorsed 'Reverse charge supply' (see 9-300).

See also flowchart ¶5-986.

5-770   Pre-January 2010

Before January 2010 the basic rule for the place of supply of a service was that a service was supplied where the business providing the service belonged. There were variations to this. The variations are summarised in the flowchart at 5-970.

The changes introduced on 1 January 2010 and 1 January 2011 are summarised above.

[This page is intentionally blank]

International Trade

FLOWCHARTS

5-900   Selling goods to other EC States

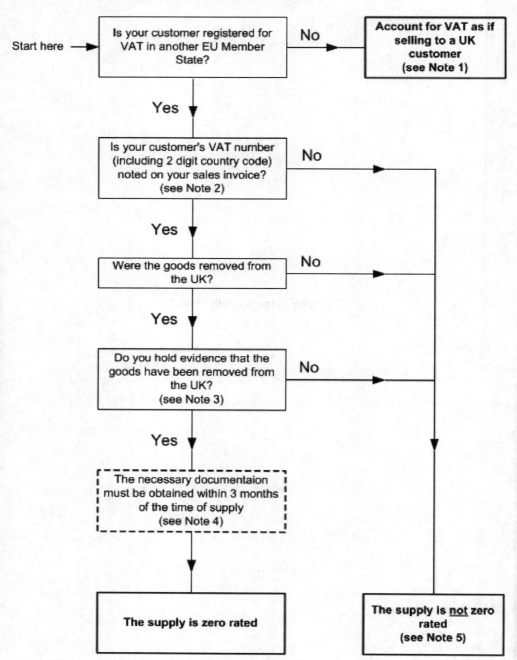

Start here →

Is your customer registered for VAT in another EU Member State?

No → Account for VAT as if selling to a UK customer (see Note 1)

Yes ↓

Is your customer's VAT number (including 2 digit country code) noted on your sales invoice? (see Note 2)

No →

Yes ↓

Were the goods removed from the UK?

No →

Yes ↓

Do you hold evidence that the goods have been removed from the UK? (see Note 3)

No →

Yes ↓

The necessary documentaion must be obtained within 3 months of the time of supply (see Note 4)

↓

The supply is zero rated

The supply is **not** zero rated (see Note 5)

Notes

(1) Selling goods to EU customers who are not VAT registered

Goods despatched to other EC Member States to customers who are not VAT registered are liable to UK VAT. They will be liable to the appropriate rate of UK VAT. Exceptions to this include:

(a) goods supplied and installed in another EC Member State;
(b) new means of transport;
(c) goods liable to excise duty;
(d) 'distance sales' above a certain level – see Notice 725, para. 6.5.

(2) Verifying the customers VAT number

The validity of a VAT registration number belonging to a customer in another EU Member State may be checked with the National Advice Service or by visiting HMRC's website. See 1-730.

(3) Evidence of the goods leaving the UK

'The evidence you obtain as proof of export, whether official or commercial, or supporting must clearly identify:

* the supplier;
* the consignor (where different from the supplier);
* the customer;
* the goods;
* an accurate value;
* the export destination; and
* the mode of transport and route of the export movement.'

Notice 703, para. 6.5

(4) Time limit for obtaining proof of exportation

There is a strict time limit for obtaining proof of 'exportation' to another EC Member State. It is as follows:

'In all cases the time limit for removing the goods and obtaining valid evidence of removal will begin from the time of supply. For goods removed to another EC Member State the time limits are as follows:

* three months (including supplies of goods involved in groupage or consolidation prior to removal); or
* six months for supplies of goods involved in processing or incorporation prior to removal.'

Notice 725, para. 4.4

(5) Failure to meet all the conditions

Unless all conditions are complied with, VAT must be accounted for as if the goods were sold to a UK customer

(6) Further information

For further information see Notice 725.

International Trade

175

5-970 Place of supply of services – exceptions to the basic rule which apply pre-1 January 2010

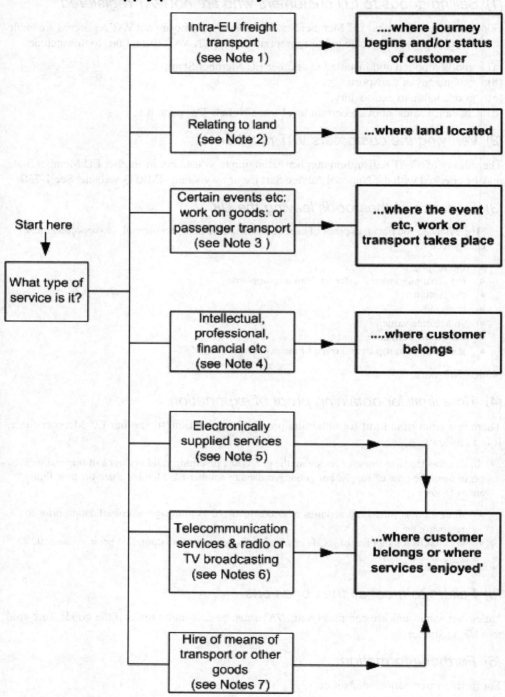

Start here
↓

What type of service is it?

→ Intra-EU freight transport (see Note 1) → ....where journey begins and/or status of customer

→ Relating to land (see Note 2) → ...where land located

→ Certain events etc: work on goods: or passenger transport (see Note 3) → ...where the event etc, work or transport takes place

→ Intellectual, professional, financial etc (see Note 4) → ....where customer belongs

→ Electronically supplied services (see Note 5) →

→ Telecommunication services & radio or TV broadcasting (see Notes 6) → ...where customer belongs or where services 'enjoyed'

→ Hire of means of transport or other goods (see Notes 7) →

Notes

(1) Intra-EU freight transport

This category includes transporting goods between EU States, related ancillary services and services of arranging these supplies.

(2) Relating to land

This category includes the following:

(a)   grants, assignments or surrender of interests in land;
(b)   works of construction, demolition, alteration, etc.; and
(c)   services of estate agents, architects, engineers, etc.

(3) Services supplied where performed

This category includes the following:

(a)   cultural, artistic, sporting, scientific, educational and entertainment services;
(b)   exhibitions, conferences and meetings;
(c)   valuation of, or work on, goods;
(d)   transport of passengers.

(4) Intellectual, professional, financial, etc.

This category includes the following:

(a)   copyright, patents, licences, etc.;
(b)   advertising;
(c)   consultants, engineers, lawyers, accountants, etc.;
(d)   banking, financial and insurance;
(e)   staff;
(f)   hire of goods (but not a means of transport).

(5) Electronically supplied services

This category includes on-line supplies of the following:

(a)   relating to websites;
(b)   software;
(c)   images, text, information, etc.;
(d)   music, films and games (including games of chance and gambling games);
(e)   political, cultural, artistic, sporting, scientific, etc. broadcasts;
(f)   distance teaching.

(6) Telecommunication services and radio or TV broadcasting

This category includes the transmission, emission or reception of signals, etc. and radio or television broadcasting.

International Trade

(7) Hire of means of transport or other goods

According to whether the goods are used outside the EU or in the UK, the letting on hire of a means of transport or other goods may be where the services are enjoyed.

(8) Legislation

The relevant statutory provision is *VAT (Place of Supply of Services) Order* 1992 (SI 1992/3121).

[This page is intentionally blank]

International Trade

5-983 Place of supply of services – basic rule

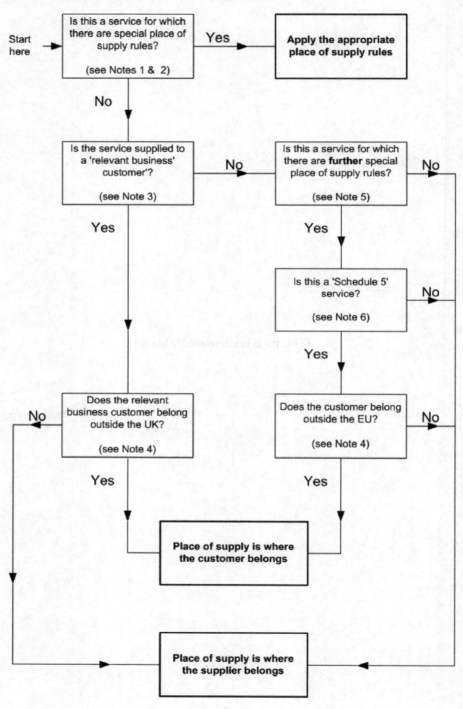

Notes

(1) Supplier belongs in UK

This flowchart is for use when the person supplying the service belongs in the UK.

(2) Services for which there are special place of supply rules (see 5-710)

There are special place of supply rules for the following services:

(a)   services relating to land;
(b)   passenger transport;
(c)   hiring of means of transport;
(d)   restaurant and catering services;
(e)   on-board restaurant and catering services in the EC;
(f)   hiring of goods*;
(g)   telecommunication and broadcasting services*;
(h)   admissions and ancillary services to cultural, educational and entertainment services, etc. (for business customers);
(i)   electronically supplied services* (for business customers);

* 'use and enjoyment' may determine place of supply.

(3) 'Relevant business' customer

For these purposes, a 'relevant business' customer is a–

(a)   person registered for 'VAT' in another EU State; or
(b)   taxable person.

A taxable person is 'any person who, independently, carries out in any place any economic activity, whatever the purpose or results of that activity'.

(4) Place of belonging (see 3-950)

The place of belonging is normally the principal place of business. However, it can also be where the body is legally constituted or when the customer has more than one 'fixed establishment', the establishment most directly associated with receiving the supply.

'Individuals receiving supplies in a non-business capacity are treated as belonging in the country where they have their usual place of residence' (Notice 741, para. 3.5).

(5) Recipient is not a 'relevant business' customer – special place of supply rules (see 5-710)

When the recipient or customer is not a 'relevant business' customer, there are special place of supply rules for the following services:

International Trade

181

(a) intermediaries;
(b) transport of goods (including intra-EU movements);
(c) ancillary transport services;
(d) valuation of, or carrying out work on, goods;
(e) cultural, educational and entertainment services etc.;
(f) electronic services;
(g) other services.

(6) Other services (see 5-710)

These are services which, before 1 January 2010, were commonly referred to as 'Schedule 5' services. They are as follows:

(a) copyright, patents, licences, etc.;
(b) accepting an obligation to refrain from pursuing a business activity, etc.;
(c) advertising;
(d) consultants, engineers, lawyers, accountants, etc.;
(e) banking, financial and insurance;
(f) providing access to natural gas and electricity distribution systems;
(g) supply of staff;
(h) hire of goods (but not a means of transport);
(i) telecommunication services;
(j) radio and television broadcasting services;
(k) electronically supplied services.

[This page is intentionally blank]

International Trade

5-985 Place of supply of services – exceptions to the basic rule, from 1 January 2010

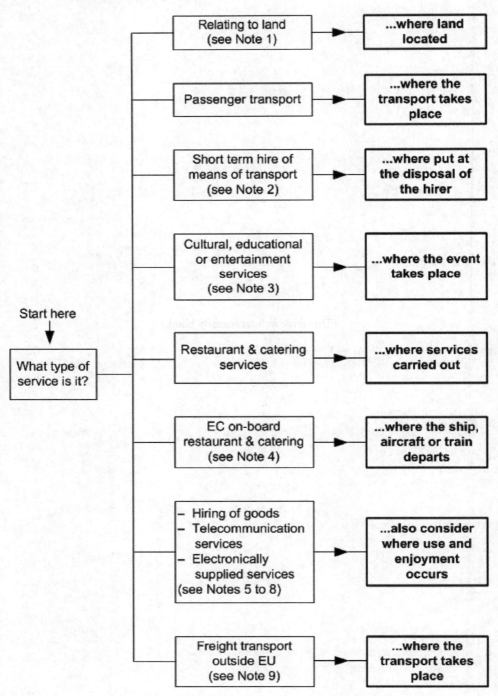

Notes

(1) Relating to land

This category includes the following:

(a)   grants, assignments or surrender of interests in land;
(b)   works of construction, demolition, alteration, etc.; and
(c)   services of estate agents, architects, engineers, etc.

(2) Short term hire of means of transport

Short term hire is for a period not exceeding 90 days or 30 days for a vessel and other means of transport respectively.

(3) Cultural, educational and entertainment services, etc.

This category also includes fairs, exhibitions and services ancillary to the main event.

From 1 January 2011 the special rules vary according to the status of the customer. For business customers only admissions and services ancillary to admissions are taxable where the event takes place. For non-business customers all relevant services are taxable where the event takes place.

(4) EC on-board restaurant and catering services

This is on-board restaurant and catering during an 'intra-EC passenger transport operation'. An 'intra-EC passenger transport operation' is a journey which commences and ends in the EU. If part of the journey takes place outside the EU, this is ignored unless there is a stop outside the EU at which passengers may embark or disembark.

(5) Hire of goods

This category does not include means of transport.

(6) Telecommunication services and radio or TV broadcasting

This category includes the transmission, emission or reception of signals, etc. and radio or television broadcasting.

(7) Electronically supplied services

This category includes on-line supplies of the following:

(a)   relating to websites;
(b)   software;
(c)   images, text, information, etc.;
(d)   music, films and games (including games of chance and gambling games);
(e)   political, cultural, artistic, sporting, scientific, etc. broadcasts;
(f)   distance teaching.

International Trade

185

(8) Where 'use and enjoyment' takes place

The 'use and enjoyment' conditions apply to the hire of goods, telecommunication services and radio or TV broadcasting and electronically supplied service. It varies the place of supply when 'use and enjoyment' is in the UK but, by applying the basic rule, the place of supply would be outside the EU. The reverse situation is also affected by these rules.

(9) Freight transport outside the EU

From 15 March 2010 transport services supplied wholly outside the EU for a UK business are not liable to UK VAT. This is a concession applied by HMRC.

(10) Further information

For further information, see 5-710.

[This page is intentionally blank]

International Trade

5-986 Services imported into the UK – Accounting for VAT

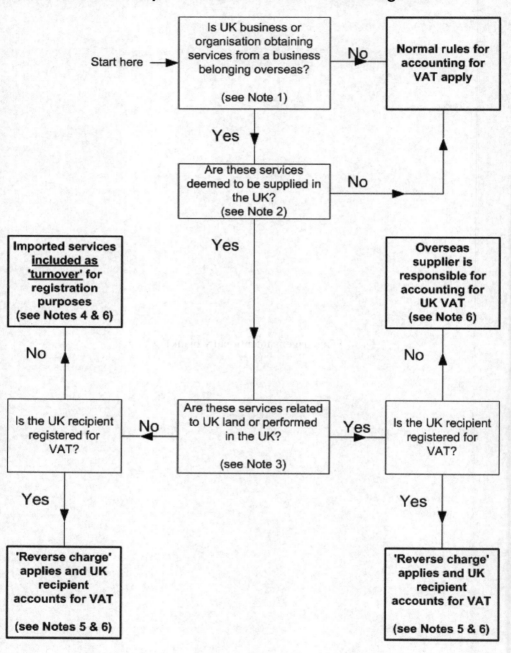

Notes

(1) Affected UK businesses or organisations

Any person (including those who are not registered for VAT) who carries out an 'economic activity' in the UK may be affected by the 'reverse charge' regulations.

An 'economic activity' is defined as 'all activities of producers, traders and persons supplying services including mining and agricultural activities and activities of professions'. This includes the exploitation of tangible and intangible property for the purposes of obtaining income from it.

(2) Services supplied outside UK

The 'reverse charge' does not apply to any services for which the place of supply is outside the UK. For information about place of supply of imported services see 5-710.

(3) Services related to UK land or performed in the UK

These are services which are taxable according to where the land is situated, where the services are performed and, with vi to viii, where they are 'effectively used and enjoyed' in the UK. They are listed in Parts 1 & 2 of Schedule 4A, VATA 1994. Briefly they are as follows:

(i)   services relating to UK land or buildings;
(ii)   passenger transport;
(iii)   short-term hire of a means of transport;
(iv)   restaurant and catering services (including those served on a ship or aircraft during an intra-EU passenger transport operation);
(v)   short-term hire of a means of transport;
(vi)   telecommunication and broadcasting services, and
(vii)   admissions and ancillary services to cultural, educational and entertainment services;
(viii) electronically supplied services.

(4) 'Reverse charge' and people who are not registered for VAT

"If you are not already UK VAT registered … the value of … [the "reverse charge"] supplies must be added to the value of your own taxable supplies in determining whether you should be registered for UK VAT. … if you make no taxable supplies yourself you will still be … [liable to register] … if the value of your imported services exceeds the registration limits." (Notice 741A, para 18.10.3)

(5) UK recipient accounts for VAT

The UK recipient must for '… output tax, calculated on the full value of the supply … received …'. This tax may be reclaimed as input tax according to the normal rules.

(6) Transitional arrangements

The 'reverse charge' does not apply if VAT was accounted for in another EU State under the provision in force before 1 January 2010 (*Finance Act* 2009, Sch. 36, para. 19).

International Trade

189

(7) Overseas supplier may have to register for VAT

'If you … belong outside the UK and supply services whose place of supply is in the UK, you may be liable to register for VAT in the UK (subject to the relevant current registration threshold)'. (Notice 741A, para 2.14)

(8) Further information

HMRC's information on the 'reverse charge' is in Notice 741A, s. 18 (January 2010 edition). The 'reverse charge' legislation is VATA 1994, s. 8.

[This page is intentionally blank]

International Trade

5-987 Place of supply of services, not supplied to a relevant business customer – exceptions to the basic rule

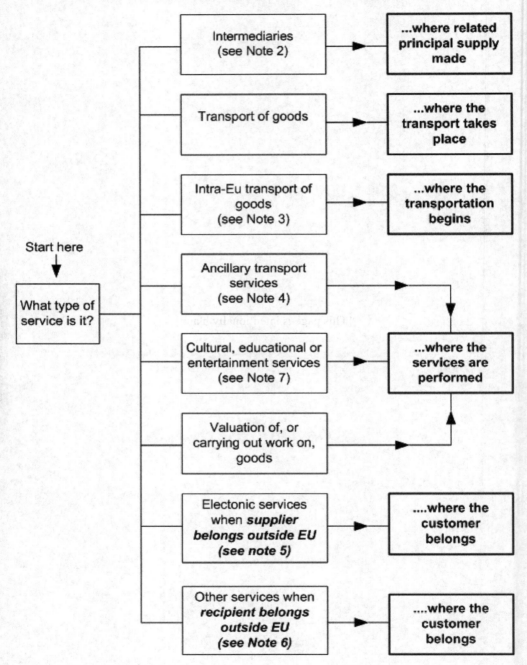

Notes

(1) Status of customer

These exceptions apply when the customer is not a 'relevant business customer'.

(2) Intermediaries

Intermediaries are agents and the like who facilitate the making of supplies/sales by others.

(3) Intra-EU freight transport

Intra-EU freight transport is transporting goods between EU States, related ancillary services and services of arranging these supplies.

(4) Ancillary transport services

This category includes loading, unloading, handling and similar activities relating to the transport of goods.

(5) Electronically supplied services

This category includes on-line supplies of the following:

(a) relating to websites;
(b) software;
(c) images, text, information, etc.;
(d) music, films and games (including games of chance and gambling games);
(e) political, cultural, artistic, sporting, scientific, etc. broadcasts;
(f) distance teaching.

(6) Other services (see 5-710)

These are the services which, before 1 January 2010, were commonly referred to as 'Schedule 5' services. They are as follows:

(a) copyright, patents, licences, etc.;
(b) accepting an obligation to refrain from pursuing a business activity, etc.;
(c) advertising;
(d) consultants, engineers, lawyers, accountants, etc.;
(e) banking, financial and insurance;
(f) providing access to natural gas and electricity distribution systems;
(g) supply of staff;
(h) hire of goods (but not a means of transport);
(i) telecommunication services;
(j) radio and television broadcasting services;
(k) electronically supplied services.

International Trade

(7) Cultural, educational and entertainment services, etc.

From 1 January 2011 the special rules vary according to the status of the customer. For non-business customers all relevant services are taxable where the event takes place. For business customers only admissions and services ancillary to admissions are taxable where the event takes place.

(8) Further information

For further information, see 5-710.

Input Tax Recovery – Partial Exemption

RECOVERY OF VAT ON SUPPLIES TO THE BUSINESS, ACQUISITIONS AND IMPORTATIONS

6-000   Overview

Traders are obliged to account for VAT on taxable supplies which they make. They can also recover VAT charged to them on supplies which they obtain, and on imports of goods from outside the EC and acquisitions of goods from within the EC.

The purpose of this section is to explore the reasons for this curious state of affairs, and to outline the rules for reclaiming tax on business expenses.

The main technical areas covered are:

(1)   the concept of exact proportionality;

(2)   the meaning of input tax, and the circumstances in which it arises;

(3)   input tax which cannot be deducted;

(4)   evidence requirements for the deduction of input tax;

(5)   recovery of input tax arising when not a taxable person;

(6)   recovery of input tax by non-UK taxable persons, and recovery of input tax from other Member States by UK taxable persons; and

(7)   how input tax is reclaimed.

6-040   Concept of exact proportionality

Perhaps the most important underlying concept of VAT is the concept of exact proportionality. This is embodied in art. 2 of Directive 67/227 (the first directive) as follows:

'The principle of the common system of value added tax involves the application to goods and services of a general tax on consumption exactly proportional to the price of the goods and services, whatever the number of transactions which take place in the production and distribution process before the stage at which the tax is charged.'

The intention, therefore, is that the amount of tax ultimately levied should relate to consumption in Member States, and be exactly proportional to the price ultimately paid by consumers.

This might be achieved by levying tax only on supplies made to final consumers, but this presupposes that the trader could identify whether a customer was a final consumer or another business, and that HMRC could verify that tax was being levied on all supplies to final

Input Tax Recovery

consumers. It is because this is impossible to do that the particular tax mechanism has been selected.

Note: The concept of exact proportionality in this context should not be confused with the wider concept of proportionality in European law, that the legislative means used to achieve an objective should not be out of proportion to the end in view.

Legislation: Directive 67/227, art. 2

VAT Reporter: ¶1-100

6-080 Tax mechanism

The mechanism in fact adopted is to charge tax on all taxable supplies, whether to businesses or to consumers, but to allow businesses which themselves make taxable supplies to deduct tax suffered on expenses from the tax which they have to pay. In theory, this should lead to the ultimate collection of an amount of tax exactly proportional to the price paid by the final consumer.

Example: collection of VAT

Suppose that Ann produces goods (without incurring any expenses!), and sells them to Brian for £50 plus VAT. Brian sells them to Chris for £75 plus VAT, who in turn sells them to a consumer for £100 plus VAT. The liabilities to account for VAT by the different traders are as follows:

	£
Ann	
Tax on supply to Brian (£50 × 20%)	10.00

	£
Brian	
Tax on supply to Chris (£75 × 20%)	15.00
Less: Tax on purchase from Ann	(10.00)
	5.00

	£
Chris	
Tax on supply to consumer (£100 × 20%)	20.00
Less: Tax on purchase from Brian	(15.00)
	5.00
Price paid by consumer (£100 + £20.00 VAT)	£120.00
Tax collected (£10.00 + £5.00 + £5.00)	£20.00

It might be thought that the tax in the above example was collected in three tranches, one from each trader. In fact, that is not the case. The likelihood is that the supply to the final consumer will take place in a different tax period from the earlier supplies. It is therefore likely that HMRC will have refunded to Chris the tax of £15 on his purchase from Brian before the final supply is made. At that point, therefore, the tax collected from Ann and Brian is equal to the tax refunded to Chris and, in effect, the goods have not yet borne any VAT.

It is only when the final supply is made to the consumer that the tax 'sticks', becoming accountable by Chris on a supply to a person who cannot recover it. As Chris has already reclaimed the tax on the purchase of the goods, he must account to HMRC for the whole £20. Tax which cannot be recovered by anyone is colloquially known as 'sticking tax'.

VAT Reporter: ¶1-100

6-120   Output tax and input tax

The basic mechanism, therefore, is that traders must account for tax (known as output tax) on supplies which they make, and can set against it, tax suffered (known as input tax) on the supplies which are made to them and on their imports and acquisitions of goods.

This is done by setting the two against one another on periodical returns, and paying the difference to HMRC. If input tax for a period exceeds output tax, HMRC repays the difference to the trader.

The effect of this mechanism is that no net amount should accrue to HMRC until such time as supplies are made to final consumers. Final consumers for this purpose includes businesses which make exempt supplies, rather than taxable ones, and are unable to recover tax on their expenses.

As will be seen in this section, some tax does in fact accrue to HMRC along the way, for a variety of reasons. These include rules preventing the deduction of input tax for certain categories of expenditure and the incidence of tax on supplies to exempt businesses which themselves make supplies to taxable businesses, thus giving rise to 'hidden' tax in the expenses of those taxable businesses.

Another common reason for tax being gathered before the stage of final consumption is failure by taxable traders to understand and to observe the rules for the deduction of input tax. Substantial unnecessary liabilities often arise because of failures of administration, or inattention to the VAT consequences in structuring projects, business entities, or whole businesses.

The most important area of planning for VAT is the structuring of business affairs so as to avoid unnecessary sticking tax within the business sector; relatively little can be done in terms of mitigating liability at the stage of final consumption. This careful structuring of the intermediate stages is not only a perfectly legal manner of minimising tax liabilities, it is also a laudable activity, in that it helps the tax to fulfil its basic purpose by meeting more effectively the concept of proportionality as expressed in the first directive.

VAT Reporter: ¶1-100

Input Tax Recovery

6-160 Basic rules for deduction of input tax

The basic rules on the deduction of input tax are set out schematically in the flow chart at 7-900

Broadly speaking, tax is only deductible by a trader who is a taxable person, on supplies made to him (or importations or acquisitions of goods by him) which are used for the purposes of his taxable activities. Input tax is normally reclaimed from HMRC by means of periodical VAT returns, and proper evidence must be held in respect of the tax reclaimed.

There are special procedures for recovery of input tax by a person who is no longer registered for VAT, or who carries on business outside the UK.

If supplies, etc. are used partly in making taxable supplies, and partly for non-business purposes or in making exempt supplies, only a proportion of the tax suffered can be reclaimed.

Tax on certain business expenses (such as purchase of motor cars or business entertaining) cannot be reclaimed.

These broad principles are expanded below.

Legislation: VATA 1994, s. 24–26

VAT Reporter: ¶19-000

6-180 Input tax recovery on overseas supplies

A taxable person may reclaim input tax incurred in respect of supplies made overseas if the supply would have been taxable if made in the UK.

Conversely, input tax incurred in connection with supplies made overseas that would be exempt if made in the UK is not automatically reclaimable.

Other material: Notice 700, para. 10.2

VAT Reporter: ¶64-400; ¶63-790

Legislation: VATA 1994, s. 26(2)

6-200 Definition of input tax

The only tax which may be recovered by a taxable trader is that which falls within the definition of 'input tax'. Input tax is defined as follows:

'... "input tax" in relation to a taxable person, means the following tax, that is to say–

(a)   VAT on the supply to him of any goods or services;

(b)   VAT on the acquisition by him from another Member State of any goods; and

(c)   VAT paid or payable by him on the importation of any goods from a place outside the Member States,

being (in each case) goods or services used or to be used for the purpose of any business carried on or to be carried on by him ...'

Conditions to reclaim VAT

It follows from this definition that a number of conditions must be met before a person can treat tax as input tax:

(1)   the person must be a taxable person;

(2)   there must be either a supply made to that person (rather than to someone else) or an importation (or acquisition) of goods in respect of which that person is to pay any VAT arising;

(3)   tax must actually arise on the supply or importation (or acquisition);

(4)   tax on supplies, etc. used for the provision of directors' domestic accommodation is expressly excluded from the definition of input tax. This is replaced by measures affecting business/private assets from 1 January 2011; and

(5)   the supply or importation (or acquisition) must be used (or intended for use) for the purposes of a business which the person carries on, or intends to carry on in the future.

Other material: Budget No 2 2010 Notice 42; Revenue and Customs Brief 53/10

Legislation: VATA 1994, s. 24

VAT Reporter: 19-000

'Blocked' input tax

Even where these conditions are met, so that the tax ranks as input tax, some or all of it may still be non-deductible (i.e. 'blocked'), and this aspect is considered later, e.g. relating to entertainment, motor cars and second-hand goods at 6-280. However, there is no possibility of tax being deductible unless it meets the basic criteria set out above, and these are explored in more detail below.

(1) Taxable person

A UK taxable person is a person who is registered for VAT in the UK, or is required to be registered. United Kingdom VAT is also deductible by a non-UK taxable person if, broadly, that input tax would have been recoverable if that trader was established in the UK (see 6-740). Similarly, a UK taxable person can recover certain VAT suffered in other EC States (see 6-780).

Input Tax Recovery

The concept of a taxable person is dealt with more fully at 3-700ff. and registration for VAT is dealt with separately at 8-000ff.

Legislation: VATA 1994, s. 3(1)

VAT Reporter: ¶140

(2) Supply, acquisition or importation

It is implicit in the definition of input tax that a supply, acquisition or importation must actually take place for any 'tax' which is sought to be reclaimed to be input tax.

Transactions which do not amount to supplies are covered at 3-280ff. It is worth recording here that problems frequently arise in respect of transfers of businesses as going concerns, and abortive supplies.

Transfer of a going concern

As indicated at 3-540, the transfer of a business as a going concern does not amount to a supply for VAT purposes.

Consequently, no tax is recoverable in respect of such a transaction, even if the vendor purports to charge VAT. The rules for determining whether a transfer of assets amounts to a going concern transfer are covered at 18-500ff. Careful attention should be given to transactions which may fall within these provisions, as the amounts involved can be substantial.

Abortive supplies

The position relating to abortive supplies should be noted by any business which is asked to pay a deposit when ordering supplies. If the supply does not ultimately take place, for whatever reason, then any 'tax' element of the deposit will cease to be regarded as tax, and it will be clear that no supply has been made to the customer. It is therefore impossible for there to be any input tax in the hands of the customer in respect of the failed transaction, and no refund can be obtained from HMRC. In some cases, however, it may be possible to argue that a supply was made in return for the deposit itself, as when a hotelier kept a room available, and charged for this, even though the customer did not turn up to occupy it.

If tax has already been reclaimed in respect of the proposed supply, it must be repaid. Normally, this should not give rise to problems. The supplier should return any moneys paid to the customer, and issue a credit note to cancel any tax invoice which has been issued. However, it may be that the supplier has become insolvent, or disappeared, in which case the customer will be out of pocket. The effect is to transfer some of the possible loss arising from the insolvency or disappearance from HMRC to the customer.

It should be noted that there is no possibility of obtaining bad debt relief (see 9-520) for 'input tax' paid over in respect of an abortive supply, as bad debt relief relates only to output tax on supplies made by the claimant.

Cases: *Howard* (1981) 1 BVC 1,155; *C & E Commrs v Bass Plc* [1993] BVC 34

VAT Reporter: ¶10-000

(3) Supply to taxable person/acquisition or importation by taxable person

Where input tax refund is sought in respect of a supply, it is essential that the supply is made to the taxable person rather than some other person. This does not necessarily mean that the supply must be paid for by the taxable person, or that all supplies for which a person pays rank as supplies made to that person.

This principle was exemplified by a tribunal case concerning a distributor of lubricants for cars. The distributor provided a guarantee for users of the lubricants whereby, if the engine or gearbox of the customer's car had to be repaired, the distributor would meet the cost on presentation of a receipted garage bill.

The distributor had reclaimed VAT shown on invoices against which it had made payments to customers. HMRC disallowed the tax, and the distributor appealed against this decision. The tribunal held that the supplies made by garages in repairing the vehicles were made to the customers, with whom the garages had made their contracts. There was no contractual nexus between the distributor and the garages. As the supplies were not made to the distributor, it could not treat the tax on the bills as input tax.

If the distributor had contracted with the garages for the repair of the vehicles, the supply of the repairs would have been made to the distributor and so could have ranked as input tax in its hands.

In order to recover input tax on an importation of goods from outside the EC, or an acquisition from within the EC, the importation or acquisition must have been made by the claimant (see also (8) below).

Cases: *Normal Motor Factors Ltd* (1978) 1 BVC 1,068

VAT Reporter: ¶19-015

(4) Contracts of indemnity

The payment by the distributor in the case referred to above was made to the customer under a contract of indemnity. The making of a payment in consummation of such a contract does not generally involve the making of a supply, although the initial making of the contract may well do.

For example, when an insurance policy is issued, the insurer makes a supply of insurance to the insured. When a claim is made in respect of the policy, and the insurer pays over a sum of money, this is a payment under a contract of indemnity and does not involve the making of a supply.

Input Tax Recovery

The money paid over may then be used by the insured to purchase, say, replacements for goods which have been destroyed. This involves a supply of the goods to the insured, not to the insurer, even though the insurer is footing the bill.

VAT Reporter: ¶19-110

(5) Supply paid for by third party

Arrangements whereby supplies are paid for by someone other than the recipient of the supply are fairly common, and do not arise solely in respect of insurance policies.

For instance, property lease agreements frequently permit the tenant to carry out improvements to the let property, subject to approval by the landlord, and provide for the tenant to reimburse any professional costs incurred by the landlord in the course of negotiations connected with these matters. In such a case, the supplies of surveyors, lawyers, etc. made to the landlord may be paid for by the tenant, but tax on such supplies is not input tax in the hands of the tenant.

The meeting of such costs by a tenant is normally treated as additional rent.

Similarly, under many tenancy agreements (particularly in connection with agricultural holdings), certain works to the property may be the legal responsibility of the landlord, but with a right to recover a proportion of reasonable costs incurred from the tenant. In such a case, the supplies are made to the landlord, with no onward supply by the landlord to the tenant. Consequently, only the landlord can treat the tax on the supplies as input tax.

Frequently, the landlord is unable to recover input tax, since he makes only exempt supplies. As the amounts involved can be large, significant amounts of sticking tax can arise. Sometimes, this could be avoided, while retaining the same commercial effect, if agreements were differently drawn up at the outset.

Other material: Notice 742, para. 10.8; HMRC Manuals Vol V1-3 section 7.2

VAT Reporter: ¶19-015

(6) Legal services relating to insurance claims

When claims are made against people who have insured against such claims, and the claims are resisted, lawyers are often engaged to handle the matter. It is accepted by HMRC that the supply by the lawyer, in this instance, is made to the policyholder rather than to the insurance company, even though the insurance company instructs the lawyer on behalf of the policyholder and the insurance company is ultimately responsible for the lawyer's fees.

An employee was charged with causing death by dangerous driving. The insurance policy in force covered both business and private use of the vehicles together with legal costs insurance. The insurance company paid for the legal representation but Jeancharm was required to pay the VAT and then attempted to reclaim this as input tax. Allowing the appeal, the Tribunal held that the question to be posed was whether the insurance policy had been taken out for the purposes of the business. In this instance, the legal costs insurance was an intrinsic part of the company's car insurance policy.

Other material: Notice 701/36; HMRC Manuals Vol V1-3 section 13

Cases: *Jeancharm Ltd (t/a Beaver International)* No. 18,835; [2005] BVC 4,038

VAT Reporter: ¶19-110

(7) Supplies obtained by employees/supplies benefiting others

As a rule, when supplies are ordered by employees of a taxable person for that person's business, it will be clear that the supplies are obtained on behalf of the employer and so no difficulty should arise over the deduction of related input tax. For instance, if a buyer for XYZ Electronics Ltd orders 200,000 printed circuit boards from a supplier, no one will be in any doubt that the contract is really between XYZ Electronics Ltd and the supplier, and the transaction will proceed accordingly.

There are occasions when employees may obtain supplies in their own right and recharge them to the employer. The most common of these are dealt with on a concessionary basis.

If an employee on a business trip obtains accommodation and meals for business reasons and the business bears the full cost, the tax can be treated as input tax even if the supply was made, in the first instance, to the employee. This will not enable tax to be recovered for business entertaining, as such tax is specifically treated as non-deductible, but it does prevent tax on ordinary subsistence expenses from being disallowed on a technicality.

Where the employer is involved in the contractual arrangements then input tax is deductible notwithstanding that the supplies are, in the first instance, received by employees.

Road fuel purchased by employees

A special provision applies where employees buy road fuel for business journeys, and the business reimburses the actual expenditure. In addition, tax can be reclaimed on a reasonable petrol element of mileage allowances paid to employees in respect of business mileage (see 1-703 and Hardmans 19-280).

Following the case of *EC Commission v United Kingdom*, in which the Commission challenged this system and the ECJ found in favour of the Commission, this system was amended so that in order to reclaim the associated input tax on a supply of road fuel, the VAT invoice must be obtained by the business.

Supplies benefiting others

Disputes can arise when supplies obtained benefit more than one person – particularly, if the greater benefit is perceived to be received by someone other than the person paying for the supplies. It appears that, provided that the payer is a party to the contract under which

Input Tax Recovery

the supplies are made, and also receives some discernible benefit, the payer can be treated as having received the supplies and so, in principle, as entitled to recover the related input tax. This is to be contrasted with the position where the person paying has no contractual relationship with the supplier, in which case input tax recovery is unlikely.

There is further clarification in the judgment of the House of Lords in the *Redrow* case, reported more fully below. The position seems to be that, where a person contracts with a supplier of services, and pays for the supply, the tax on the supply is input tax in the hands of the person contracting and paying. Input tax recovery then depends on whether the use of the supply in the hands of the payer is for the payer's business of making taxable supplies, and does not depend upon the use made by any other person benefiting from the supply. However, this must be contrasted with the position where a person pays for supplies contracted for by another person. In this case, there is no supply to the payer, so there can be no input tax in the payer's hands.

Legislation: *Value Added Tax (Input Tax) (Reimbursement by Employers of Employees' Business Use of Road Fuel) Regulations* 2005 (SI 2005/3290)

Cases: *Leesportefeuille 'Intiem' CV v Staatssecretaris van Financiën* (Case 165/86) (1989) 4 BVC 180; *EC Commission v United Kingdom* (Case C-33/03) [2007] BVC 864; *P & O Ferries Dover Ltd* [1992] BVC 955; *The Plessey Co Ltd* [1996] BVC 2,074

Other material: Notice 700/64, para. 8.6 et seq.

VAT Reporter: ¶19-071

Redrow case

The case of *C & E Commrs v Redrow Group Plc* concerned a business promotion scheme whereby Redrow, a housebuilder, offered to pay the estate agents' fees on the sale of their existing houses for people who bought a new house from Redrow. A crucial point was that the estate agents were instructed by Redrow. However, Redrow only became liable to pay for the estate agents' services if the customers, having sold their existing houses, bought a new one from Redrow. In practice, the estate agents also entered into agreements with the customers whereby the customers would pay for their services if Redrow did not become liable to pay the fees.

Tribunal

The tribunal found that the estate agents made their supplies to Redrow in those instances where it was Redrow which paid for their services.

High Court

HMRC argued that Redrow only became liable to pay the fees if the customer actually proceeded with the purchase of the new house. At the time of supply (i.e. the time when the estate agent invoiced Redrow), it was not certain that this would happen. Thus, at the time of supply, the destination of the supply depended upon a contingent future event over which neither party (i.e. Redrow and the estate agent) had any control. The VAT legislation did not contemplate a retrospective alteration to the destination of a supply by reference to subsequent events. This was an issue which the tribunal had not properly addressed.

The court opined that the reason why the tribunal did not address this question was that it was a point not raised before it.

It went on to find that the question of whether the supply was made to Redrow was a question of fact for determination by the tribunal. It had approached that question on the basis of the evidence available at the time of supply, and this was the correct approach. There was ample unchallenged evidence on which the tribunal could conclude that the estate agents had made supplies to Redrow, and the court would not disturb this decision. Furthermore, had it been necessary, the court would have been prepared to make the same finding on the evidence. The tribunal's comment that it might be necessary to await events in a particular case to determine whether the supply was to Redrow was superfluous to its decision, and the court therefore ignored it.

HMRC also contended (citing *BLP Group Plc v C & E Commrs*) that, for input tax to be recoverable, there must be a direct and immediate link between the supply concerned and the ultimate taxable transaction. They did not challenge the fact that Redrow received the supplies for the purposes of its business (which had been conceded before the tribunal), but argued that the lack of a direct link with a taxable transaction rendered the input tax non-deductible.

The court held that this was again a question of fact, and the tribunal had clearly found that there was such a direct and immediate link. The court would have been prepared to make a similar finding had that been necessary.

Court of Appeal

The Court of Appeal took a different view. It derived from BLP the view that, in order to decide to whom the estate agents' services were to be treated as made for VAT purposes, it was necessary to identify with what transaction the supply had a direct and immediate link. It also referred to dicta in *C & E Commrs v Robert Gordon's College* at p. 33F that 'for the purposes of the European VAT legislation, it is not permissible to take a global view of a series of transactions in the chain of supply'.

The court considered that (barring a tripartite contract) the notion of one supply being made to two persons would only be relevant where the two customers not only had a mutuality of interest in receiving the service, but there was also a single transaction in relation to which they shared that interest. In the present case, there were two such transactions, the sale of the customer's house and the sale of Redrow's house. Although Redrow's motive was to facilitate the sale of its house, the estate agent's services were in fact used in the sale of the customer's house. As such they must be regarded as supplied to the customer, so HMRC's appeal would be allowed.

Input Tax Recovery

House of Lords

The Law Lords unanimously disagreed with the Court of Appeal's reasoning.

The *BLP* case dealt with an entirely different question from that under consideration here. It was concerned with the attribution of input tax as between the making of taxable and exempt supplies. The input tax in that case was disallowed because it was directly linked with the making of an exempt supply. However, if it had not been directly linked with any particular supply, it would in principle have been allowable, subject to the partial exemption method in force, since the court had made it clear elsewhere that tax on overhead costs 'for the purposes of the person's taxable transactions' was deductible.

The question in this case was, not the attribution of input tax once it existed, but whether there was input tax in Redrow's hands which, in turn, depended on whether Redrow had received taxable supplies for the purposes of its business.

HMRC's approach was to describe the services as being the ordinary services of an estate agent instructed to sell his client's house, then ask themselves to whom these services were supplied. Inevitably, they concluded that they were supplied to the owner of the house. However, this was because the way they framed the question dictated the answer. However, if the services were described as those of an estate agent instructed to sell a third party's house, the answer was different. The description of the services and the identity of the recipient each depended upon the other, and neither could be ascertained independently.

The proper approach was to start with the claim for input tax deduction, and identify the payment of which the tax formed part. If the supply was to be paid for by someone else, the taxpayer had no claim for deduction of the tax (*Note: I think that this can only be the case where that other person is making the payment under a direct contractual relationship with the supplier. The position is different if the other person's relationship is only with the claimant, as under a contract of indemnity, in which case the other person makes the payment as agent for the claimant, who is deemed to make the payment for these purposes*). If the supply was to be paid for by the claimant, the question to be asked was: 'did he obtain anything at all used or to be used for the purposes of his business in return for that payment?' This could include, not only the right to receive goods or services directly, but also the right to have goods delivered or services rendered to a third party.

In the present case, Redrow did not merely derive a benefit from the services rendered to the householders, but also selected and instructed the agents. The court concluded that Redrow received supplies of services from the agents in return for the consideration paid. Consequently, the tax was input tax in the hands of Redrow and, since the supplies were clearly used for the purposes of Redrow's taxable supplies, it was deductible.

In essence, the Lords were saying that the agents provided two services, one to the householder and one to Redrow. However, since a supply of services only exists for VAT purposes where there is consideration, it was only when it was known who was liable to pay for the services that it could be determined which of the two was supplied for VAT purposes.

While HMRC accept the judgment of the House of Lords (as they must) they have emphasised that they see it as applying only in cases where the person paying the supplier is doing so under a contractual relationship with the supplier. In particular, they do not accept the proposition that anyone who pays the supplier automatically becomes the recipient of the supply concerned.

Cases: *C & E Commrs v Redrow Group Plc* [1999] BVC 96; *BLP Group Plc v C & E Commrs* (Case C-4/94) [1995] BVC 159; *C & E Commrs v Robert Gordon's College* [1996] BVC 27

VAT Reporter: ¶19-015

(7A) Mobile phones involving non-business use

HMRC have published their policy where businesses provide employees with mobile phones for business use in Notice 700, s. 12A (presumably, these guidelines apply, mutatis mutandis, where phones are provided for business use by proprietors/partners).

Phone cost

VAT on the cost of purchasing the mobile phone, and of connecting it to the network (or keeping it connected) can be wholly treated as input tax, provided that it includes no 'free-calls' element, whether or not employees are permitted to use their phones for private calls.

Call charges: private calls not permitted

If the business operates a clear policy of not permitting employees to make private calls on the mobile phones provided for business use, then the whole of the VAT on call charges may be treated as input tax. This applies even if, in practice, the business does not seek to police the system so as to prevent minimal private use.

Call charges: employees charged for private calls

If the business permits private calls, but charges employees for these, it may again treat all of the VAT on call charges as input tax. However, it must account for output tax on the charges to employees for the private calls.

Call charges: free private calls permitted

If the business allows employees to use their mobile phones to make private calls and does not make a charge for this, HMRC expect the VAT on call charge costs to be apportioned, with only the business element treated as input tax. They will accept any method of apportionment which they consider produces a fair and reasonable result. As an example, they suggest an analysis of a sample of bills over a reasonable period, with the proportion derived from this being used for future input tax recovery purposes.

HMRC do not consider it appropriate to obtain full input tax recovery, and account for output tax on private calls, when there is no actual charge for private calls.

Input Tax Recovery

Connection/purchase costs including calls element

Where the charge for the purchase of the phone and/or connection charge includes an element of 'free' calls, HMRC expect an apportionment to be made with the calls element dealt with on the lines set out above, depending on the policy which the business adopts in respect of private calls.

Other material: Notice 700, s. 12A

VAT Reporter: ¶19-085

(8) Importation by taxable person

VAT on the importation of goods from outside the EC ranks as input tax in the hands of the taxable person concerned if it is paid or payable by the taxable person.

VAT on importation is payable as if it were a duty of HMRC. It is therefore payable by the 'importer'. This term is defined as follows:

'"importer", in relation to any goods at any time between their importation and the time when they are delivered out of charge, includes any owner or other person possessed of or beneficially interested in the goods and, in relation to goods imported by means of a pipe-line, includes the owner of the pipe-line.'

It follows that, in relation to any particular importation, a number of different persons may each be entitled to act as importer. As some of these (such as the carrier of the goods) will usually not be in a position to reclaim the VAT, it is important to ensure that care is taken in deciding who is to act as importer for VAT purposes.

HMRC will regard as the importer for VAT purposes the person named on the import entry documentation as such. Since this documentation must be completed and passed to HMRC before the goods can enter the UK, the decision needs to be taken in advance.

Legislation: CEMA 1979, s. 1; VATA 1994, s. 1(4)

(9) Tax properly chargeable

The tax which can be treated as input tax is the tax properly due on the supply, acquisition or importation concerned. While this seems straightforward, it gives rise to problems in practice.

It is not uncommon for VAT to be charged on transactions where it is not due, usually because of difficulties in understanding the law and a desire by the supplier to 'play safe' in cases where the customer can recover any tax due. In such instances, the tax cannot be treated as input tax in the hands of the customer, as it is not properly chargeable on the transaction.

In *Genius Holding BV v Staatssecretaris van Financiën*, subcontractors acted in error in charging the firm VAT. The firm deducted the VAT as input tax and were subsequently assessed for the deducted tax by the Dutch tax authorities. The Dutch court asked the

European Court of Justice to rule whether under Directive 77/388 (now Directive 2006/112) the right to deduct tax arose if the tax was payable only because it was mentioned on an invoice. The ECJ ruled that tax could only be deducted as far as it was legally due, regardless of the amount shown on an invoice. This was the opposite view to that recorded in the opinion of advocate general. The ECJ emphasised that the taxable person was only entitled to deduct 'value added tax due or paid … in respect of goods or services supplied or to be supplied to him by another taxable person.' Therefore, if the tax were wrongly charged it could not be said to have been 'charged in respect of goods or services supplied or to be supplied to [the trader]' and no right to deduction would follow. This interpretation of art. 17(2)(a) best prevents tax evasion.

Legislation: Directive 2006/112, art. 114

Cases: *Genius Holding BV v Staatssecretaris van Financiën*(Case 342/87) [1991] BVC 52

VAT Reporter: ¶19-070

(10) Domestic accommodation for directors

Tax on supplies, etc. used in providing domestic accommodation for directors is deemed not to be input tax, and so cannot be reclaimed.

This rule applies where:

(1) supplies, acquisitions or imports are to be used by a company in connection with the provision of accommodation by the company; and

(2) the accommodation is used or to be used for the domestic purposes of a director of the company, or of a person connected with a director.

A director includes an owner/manager who is not formally a director and, in the case of a company managed by its members rather than by a board of directors, a member of the company. A person connected with a director is a director's spouse, and a relative or the spouse of a relative of the director or the director's spouse.

This exclusion from the definition of input tax appears to apply whether or not the company receives consideration for the provision of accommodation, although its validity in that case appears questionable.

From 1 January 2011

Special measures for apportioning input tax incurred on land and buildings used for both business and non-business purposes were introduced with effect from 1 January 2011. These encompass accommodation provided for directors and are explained at 6-830.

When the special measures were announced, HMRC advised that 'the legislation relating to recovery of VAT on directors' accommodation will then be redundant as the implementation … will ensure no entitlement to any VAT recovery on the private use of directors' accommodation'.

Input Tax Recovery

Legislation: VATA 1994, s. 24(3) and (7)

VAT Reporter: ¶105(12)

(10A) Farmhouses – special rules

HMRC have guidelines, agreed with the National Farmers' Union, in respect of the deduction of input tax on the costs of work done to farmhouses. The guidelines distinguish between input tax on repairs, maintenance and renovations and that on improvements. They are only guidelines, and HMRC may seek different treatments on the facts of particular cases.

In the case of repairs etc., if the farmhouse is occupied by the taxable person (sole trader or a partner in a partnership), the occupant being actively engaged in running the farm, 70 per cent of the input tax can be deducted. However, if the occupant is only engaged part-time in farming HMRC expect the deduction to be considerably less, probably around 10 per cent to 30 per cent.

In the case of alterations, such as building an extension, HMRC say that the treatment will depend upon the dominant purpose of the works. If the dominant purpose is business, 70 per cent may be deducted. If it is not they expect a deduction of 40 per cent or less.

These guidelines do not apply to farmhouses occupied by directors of companies. HMRC consider that the provisions concerning input tax and directors' accommodation (see (10) above) limit the input tax recovery in this case, and only allow recovery to the extent of business use of the rooms concerned, backed by suitable records.

Special measures for apportioning input tax incurred on land and buildings used for both business and non-business purposes and costing more than £250,000 were introduced with effect from 1 January 2011. These measures can apply to farmhouses. See also 6-830.

Legislation: VATA 1994, s. 24(3)

Other material: HMRC Manuals Vol V 1-13 section 14.9

VAT Reporter: ¶19-125

(11) Business use

Tax on supplies obtained by (or importations or acquisitions by) a taxable person cannot rank as input tax unless the goods or services concerned are used, or to be used, for the purposes of a business carried on or to be carried on by that person.

The concept of 'business' is considered at 3-760.

It should be noted that the supplies concerned do not have to be put to business use immediately, provided that they are intended for business use and business use ultimately occurs. It is now established that the test is a subjective one of purpose. However, it should be noted that a tribunal will, perfectly understandably, consider the known facts in order to deduce the purpose for which the supplies were obtained rather than relying on the unsupported assertions of the trader. A long delay before supplies are put to business use, or use in the meantime for some non-business purpose, will inevitably weaken the case for treating the associated tax as input tax.

Another interesting point is that tax on supplies to be used for the purposes of a business not yet operating ranks as input tax. Thus, a taxable person with an existing business ought to have little difficulty in recovering tax on preparatory expenses of a new business not yet commenced, but to be operated by the same person. This view is supported by both UK and EC case law.

The European Court of Justice has held that a preliminary activity of commissioning a report on the profitability of a proposed desalination plant amounted to a business activity, with a right of deduction of input tax, even though the report's findings were such that the company did not proceed with the business. Thus, it is possible to have a business with a right to input tax deduction even though no taxable supplies are ever made.

This applies even though, by the time the case comes to be considered by the tax authorities, the business has already failed without making taxable supplies, provided that there is evidence that the original intention of making taxable supplies was genuine.

Cases: *Ian Flockton Developments Ltd* [1987] 3 BVC 23; *Haydon-Baillie* (1986) 2 BVC 208,095; *Rompelman v Minister van Financiën* (Case 268/83) (1985) 2 BVC 200,157; *Intercommunale voor Zeewaterontzilting (INZO) v Belgian State* (Case C-110/94) [1996] BVC 326; *Finanzamt Goslar v Breitsohl* (Case C-400/98) [2000] ECR I-4321

VAT Reporter: ¶19-020

6-240 Apportionment of input tax

If tax arises on a supply, acquisition or importation used partly for business purposes and partly for other purposes, the tax must be apportioned. Only that part which is referable to business use can be treated as input tax.

No particular mechanism is laid down in the law for making such an apportionment but see 6-840 and 15-610 for details of the 'Lennartz mechanism'.

Legislation: VATA 1994, s. 24(5)

Other material: HMRC Manuals Vol V1-13 section 5

VAT Reporter: ¶19-040; ¶140

6-260 Appeals in respect of input tax

There is a special provision affecting appeals to the tribunal on some matters concerning the deduction of input tax.

Input Tax Recovery

The provision applies to appeals against decisions as to the use to which the relevant inputs are put, and especially whether or not these are business uses. It only applies if the input tax arises on a supply, etc. of 'something in the nature of a luxury, amusement or entertainment'.

The effect of the provision is to prevent the tribunal from allowing the appeal unless it finds that the decision by HMRC is one which was unreasonable (or would have been unreasonable if HMRC had had information which is before the tribunal, but could not have been notified to HMRC at the time of the decision).

This restriction on the powers of the tribunal in input tax appeals may be invalid as being inconsistent with the EC legislation.

Indeed, a tribunal held that, once it finds that there is an entitlement to input tax deduction under the EC legislation, it is bound to apply this directly and take no account of the UK provision purporting to restrict its application.

For appeals and reviews see 19-000ff.

Legislation: VATA 1994, s. 84(4)

Cases: *Myatt & Leason (a firm)* [1996] BVC 2,611

VAT Reporter: ¶62-200

'BLOCKED' INPUT TAX

6-280 Supplies on which tax is non-deductible

Although the general rule is that input tax is, in principle, deductible by a taxable person when making his VAT returns, there are a number of occasions when the tax cannot be deducted. In particular, there are a number of categories of supply (or importation) the tax on which is specifically treated as non-deductible. These are:

(1) purchase of a motor car for use in the business – except in cases where absolutely no non-business use is allowed, permitted or possible (6-300);

(2) most business entertainment (6-320);

(3) certain fittings acquired by the builder of a new house, etc. (6-340);

(4) goods acquired under a second-hand goods scheme (6-360);

(5) certain imports of goods partly owned by another (6-380);

(6) purchases within the scope of the tour operators margin scheme (16-890); and

(7) purchases by persons using the flat rate scheme – although there is an exception for certain capital assets with a capital VAT inclusive value of £2,000 or more (16-820).

Input tax made non-deductible in this way is colloquially referred to as having been 'blocked'.

VAT Reporter: ¶19-004

6-300   Motor cars

Input tax on the purchase, acquisition or importation of a motor car is generally blocked. Hire purchase counts as purchase and the tax on the acquisition of a car by hire purchase is blocked.

Occasions when the blocking of input tax does not apply, so that the tax may be deducted, are:

(a)   any car purchased 'primarily' for use:

    (i)   as a taxi;
    (ii)   as a self-drive hire car; or
    (iii) for driving instruction;

(b)   'stock-in-trade' cars;
(c)   any car purchased for a wholly business purpose – there must be no non-business use;
(d)   purchase of a new car by a person whose sole taxable supplies involve the letting of cars on hire to another taxable person, whose business in turn consists mainly of providing motor cars, broadly, to disabled persons in receipt of a mobility allowance;
(e)   a vehicle whose carrying capacity is reduced to less than 12 passengers because it is equipped with facilities for persons in wheelchairs;
(f)   purchase, acquisition or importation of a new car for transfer to another EC State under a deemed zero-rated supply.

There may be an output tax liability when the input tax on a car is reclaimable. For example, when a demonstrator car is made available to a salesman who is permitted to use the car privately. The private use creates an output tax liability. See 4-840.

Legislation: *Value Added Tax (Input Tax) Order* 1992 (SI 1992/3222), art. 7

Other material: Notice 700/64, Section 3 and Notice 728, Section 7

VAT Reporter: ¶19-073

Self-drive hire

There is relief for cars that are intended to be used for short-term hire. Hire terms are normally under 30 days and not more than 90 days to any one hirer in a 12-month period. A car is not disqualified from the relief merely because the hirer is a corporate body and the car is driven by employees.

Other material: HMRC Manual, Vol. V1-13, Chapter 2A, para. 18.5

VAT Reporter: ¶19-073

Input Tax Recovery

'Stock-in-trade' cars

A 'stock-in-trade' car is:

(a) a car produced by a manufacturer who intends to sell it within 12 months of its manufacture; or

(b) a new or 'qualifying' second-hand car acquired by a dealer for the purpose of resale and intended to be re-sold within 12 months.

Most second-hand cars bought by dealers are not 'stock-in-trade' cars because they are not qualifying cars.

VAT Reporter: ¶19-073

Purchase, etc.

There is no blocking of input tax on the purchase, importation or acquisition of a car where it is wholly for business use. If there is any non-business use at all (including use by an employee for private purposes, such as home to work journeys), then blocking continues. In practice, this means that leasing companies can recover the VAT on cars purchased for leasing, but most others continue to suffer blocking of input tax. See flowchart 7-905.

The tribunals have tended to take a very strict view of the blocking of input tax where the car is intended to be available for any non-business use. However, they have allowed input tax deduction where, on the evidence, no non-business use had taken place and the trader had genuinely attempted (albeit unsuccessfully in one case) to make the car unavailable for non-business use by restricting the insurance cover to business use only. However, it should be noted that it will be unwise to restrict the insurance cover in this way, and risk an uninsured loss, if any non-business use is in fact contemplated as an outside possibility.

Intention to use or make available?

Mr Upton traded as 'Fagomatic' and deals with cigarette vending machines in London. He purchased a motor car that he intended to use solely in the business and reclaimed the input tax. The car was insured for both business and private use although the insurance broker was aware that it was not Mr Upton's intention to use the car privately.

HMRC assessed to recover the input tax, the case went to Tribunal and Mr Upton won but HMRC appealed to the High Court where the decision was reversed. Mr Upton appealed and lost.

The Court of Appeal decided that the Tribunal erred in law. The Tribunal considered that if a person intended to use a car exclusively for the purposes of the business, then he could not intend to make it available to himself for private use. The intention to use, in para. (2E)(a), was not, the Court of Appeal ruled, the same as the intention specified in para. (2G)(b) – to make available for use.

Mr Upton had bought the car and had insured it for private use. In doing this, he had effectively made the car available to himself for private use, even if he had no intention of so using it. In order to reclaim the input tax on a car. the vehicle must be rendered unavailable in some way for private use.

It is understood that during the hearing of the case, HMRC suggested that an employee could keep the keys to the business car and the car stored away from the business or home premises of the trader. The car would then be unavailable for private use.

This decision may increase the difficulty that a sole trader will have in reclaiming the input tax on the purchase of a car.

The car has to be unavailable for private use. It is possible that HMRC will accept that this is by the trader making certain that the vehicle is legally unavailable – by, for example, having business only use on the insurance policy. To make the vehicle physically unavailable (locking it up?) would be difficult for a sole trader.

See *Value Added Tax (Input Tax) Order* 1992, (SI 1992/3222); art. 7(2E)(a) and (2G)(b).

Other material: Notice 700/64, para. 3.5 and 3.6

VAT Reporter: ¶19-075

Hire or leasing

Only 50 per cent of the VAT on the lease of a car is recoverable. This restriction is essentially to take account of the private use which may be made of the vehicle.

Full input tax recovery is allowed for a car leased 'primarily' for use:

- as a taxi; or
- for driving instruction.

When a car is hired for 10 days or less, 100 per cent recovery of the VAT may be made providing that the car is used solely for business purposes during that period. This does not apply to cars hired to replace cars in for servicing, etc.

Under a contract hire agreement, a charge is made for the lease of the car together with a charge for servicing and maintenance. It is only the lease charge which suffers the 50 per cent restriction, the servicing/maintenance element being recoverable in full, providing that it is separately identified.

Further consideration

Input tax recovery is not restricted for 'non-qualifying' cars. A 'non-qualifying' car is one for which input tax recovery was blocked prior to the car being supplied by way of a leasing contract. The status should be discernable from the leasing invoice. The invoice should state whether the car is a 'qualifying' or 'non-qualifying' car.

Input Tax Recovery

Other material: Notice 700/64, Section 4

VAT Reporter: ¶19-073

'Motor car'

A motor car is defined as a vehicle of a kind normally used on public roads which has three or more wheels and either:

(1) is constructed or adapted solely or mainly for the carriage of passengers; or

(2) has to the rear of the driver's seat roofed accommodation which is fitted with side windows or which is constructed or adapted for the fitting of side windows.

Certain vehicles which might otherwise fall within this definition are specifically taken out of it, as follows:

(1) vehicles capable of accommodating only one person (e.g. a racing car);

(2) vehicles which meet road-safety regulations and are capable of carrying 12 or more persons; this includes vehicles that can carry fewer than 12 passengers solely because they have been adapted for wheelchair users.

(3) vehicles of not less than three tonnes unladen weight;

(4) vehicles having a payload of one tonne or more;

(5) caravans, ambulances and prison vans;

(6) vehicles constructed for a special purpose other than the carriage of passengers, and having no passenger accommodation except such as is incidental to that purpose.

See flowchart 7-910.

Motor car further defined

HMRC have issued clarification of their interpretation of the definition of a motorcar. This guidance is needed partly because of the car-derived van market. The VAT on a car is blocked unless certain conditions are in place whereas the VAT on a van may be reclaimed subject to the normal rules.

One difficult area concerns vehicles that are designed initially as cars and then amended to be vans. The exterior has remained the same – looking like a car – but the interior has been changed to serve the function of a van.

HMRC have said that they will not regard such a vehicle as a motor car if:

- the technical criteria specified in HMRC guidance are met by the manufacturer. These criteria relate to how any adaptations to the vehicle have been effected; and
- the adaptations make the vehicle a commercial vehicle. As such, the removal of a bench seat or similar from what is a two-seater car would not automatically be enough; and
- the space behind the front row of seats is highly unsuitable for carrying passengers.

A list of acceptable vehicles is available on HMRC's website.

The second area that is causing concern is that of combination vans.

These look like vans but are designed with seats to enable the carriage of passengers. These are, according to HMRC, motorcars except:

- larger vehicles with a payload of more than one tonne;
- those vehicles where the goods load area when compared with the passenger area makes the carriage of goods the predominant use for the vehicle.

HMRC state that if a combination van was purchased and it does not fall within the two exceptions above, it is a motor car. Any business that has reclaimed the input tax on such a vehicle should adjust their VAT account. It seems harsh that a business that has in good faith reclaimed the input tax on a combination van that is now adjudged not to meet the criteria brought out by HMRC should have to repay input tax.

The whole question of what is a motor car and how it is available for private use is fraught with problems. It is helpful in terms of legal certainty and legitimate expectations that HMRC review their guidance regularly in conjunction with the motor manufacturers and produce a list of models that are acceptable. This list is available from the National Advice Service and should be accessible through their website.

Legislation: *Value Added Tax (Special Provisions) Order* 1995 (SI 1995/1268), art. 2

Cases: *Wood* [1997] BVC 4,085; *Thompson* [1997] BVC 4,077; *Oliver* [1997] BVC 4,112; *Southern UK Breeders* [1998] BVC 4,055; *Grace* [1998] BVC 4,059

Other material: List of car derived vans and combi-vans, accessed via *www.hmrc.gov.uk/vat/sectors/motors/what-is-car.htm*

VAT Reporter: ¶19-072

6-320 Business entertainment

According to the courts, to 'entertain' is 'to give people free meals and to give them free accommodation'. In *BMW (GB) Ltd v C & E Commrs*, Keen J said 'I conclude therefore that the crucial characteristic of "entertainment" within the phrase "business entertainment" is that it is provided to a person or persons who enjoy it free of charge'.

Free entertainment or free hospitality becomes 'business entertainment' when it is provided in connection with a business.

For these purposes, entertainment and hospitality are the same thing. There is no distinction between circumstances that are referred to as 'business entertainment' and 'business hospitality'. See flowchart 7-915.

Input Tax Recovery

Input tax incurred on 'business entertainment' is not recoverable. This is because of art. 5(3) of *Value Added Tax (Input Tax) Order* 1992 (SI 1992/3222).

Entertainment for overseas clients

Following the ECJ case of *Danfoss A/S and AstraZeneca A/S v Skatteministeriet*, HMRC have decided that some VAT incurred when entertaining overseas clients is reclaimable. HMRC have invited affected businesses to submit claims for such input tax.

The important principles to consider are:

- There is no change to rules concerning entertaining UK customers.
- Only in the most exceptional circumstances will businesses be able to reclaim VAT when paying for overseas customers to attend a hospitality event (e.g. golf days or trips to sporting events).
- Entertaining overseas customers must be necessary for and contribute to the smooth running of the payer's business.

Cases: *Danfoss A/S and AstraZeneca A/S v Skatteministeriet* (Case C-371/07) [2009] BVC 781

Other material: Revenue and Customs Brief 44/10; *www.hmrc.gov.uk/news/ ent-claim-input-tax.htm*

Apportionment

The matter of apportionment of business entertainment was considered in *Thorn EMI Plc v C & E Commrs* [1994] BVC 133. The case was to do with hospitality chalets constructed by Thorn EMI at air shows. Although the chalets were mainly used for business entertainment, there was some other business use. In HMRC's opinion, none of the input tax was recoverable because the chalets were predominantly used for business entertainment. The Court of Appeal disagreed. It allowed Thorn EMI to apportion the input tax between the business entertainment and the general business use. The input apportioned to general business use was recoverable subject to the normal rules.

Directors and partners

Where entertainment is provided only for directors or partners of a business, the VAT incurred is not deductible because HMRC consider that the goods or services are not used for a business purpose.

HMRC accept that where partners or directors attend a staff function with other employees, the associated input tax is not blocked.

Staff acting as hosts

Staff 'entertainment' which is incidental to the provision of hospitality to others is trapped by reg. 5(3) and cannot be recovered.

Staff entertainment

There have been a series of cases connected with the right to recover input tax incurred on entertainment primarily for the benefit of the staff. These have considered whether input tax must be apportioned when guests are present at staff functions, and what happens when guests are asked to pay.

Before input tax on staff entertainment can be reclaimed it is necessary to establish that the entertainment was for the purposes of the business. The 'purposes of the business' are described in HMRC publications as being when an employer entertains employees to reward them for good work or to maintain and improve staff morale. Events such as staff parties, team building exercises, staff outings etc. are considered to be such events.

When the guests go free

In *KMPG (a firm)*, the appellants held dinner-dances at their different offices for their staff. The staff were invited to bring guests. The purpose of the dinner-dance was to express thanks to the staff for their work and to maintain and improve staff relations. The dinner-dances were free to the staff and the guests.

The Tribunal found that the dinner-dances were used to maintain and improve staff relations. This was indisputably for the purpose of KMPG's business.

HMRC sought to disallow a proportion of the input tax for the dinner-dances on the grounds that KMPG provided business entertainment to the non-paying guests. KMPG sought to reclaim all the input tax because the dinner-dances were primarily for the staff.

The Tribunal decided in favour of HMRC. It ruled that the input tax apportioned to the cost of entertaining the guests was not recoverable.

When the guests pay

In *Ernst & Young*, the appeal was against an assessment disallowing input tax incurred on a range of nine events involving staff entertainment. Based upon the natures of the events, the entertainment issues were sub-divided as follows:

(a)   supplies to staff;
(b)   supplies to guests;
(c)   supplies to partners.

With regard to supplies to staff the Tribunal allowed the appeal. This was on the grounds that the entertainment was provided for the benefit of the staff. The business purpose was that it improved and maintained staff morale, encouraged team and relationship building and communication. It was also a means of recognising achievement and rewarding staff. Examples of events used for these purposes were team lunches, counselling meals, lunches for audit teams and departmental lunches.

Input Tax Recovery

There was also a Christmas party attended by partners and staff who paid £10 each and guests who were charged £15 each. HMRC sought to disallow the input tax apportioned to the guests but after making an allowance for the output tax accounted for on the amounts paid by the guests.

The amount paid by the guests did not cover the cost. The Christmas party cost Ernst & Young £82.50 per head whereas the guests paid £15.

The Tribunal decided that the guests were not receiving entertainment or hospitality from Ernst & Young when they attended the Christmas party. This was because the guests paid. The Tribunal considered that although the charge to guests was nominal 'it was not so small that one could say that the meal was effectively supplied free of charge'. As a result, Ernst & Young were able to recover input relating to the guests but they also had to account for output tax on the income from guests.

The supplies to the partners were in connection with a two and a half day conference which was attended by 400 partners from 26 offices. The conference included a cabaret which took place after dinner on the second day. The Tribunal agreed with HMRC that the cabaret was pure entertainment and that it was not incurred for the purposes of the business. Thus, the input tax relating to the cabaret was not reclaimable.

Miscellaneous

It should be noted that the blocking applies to all supplies used for business entertainment purposes, not merely supplies of catering services, etc. Expenditure relating to the acquisition and maintenance of a race horse has been held to fall into the business entertainment category, where one purpose of the expenditure was to enable representatives of the company to take potential customers to the races.

If a business holds a stock of goods used for business entertainment and also for other purposes, the proportion of input tax relating to non-entertainment use may be recovered subject to the normal rules.

Where input tax has been blocked on goods used for business entertainment, a corresponding relief is given on the subsequent supply of those goods (see 14-800).

Legislation: *Value Added Tax (Input Tax) Order* 1992 (SI 1992/3222), art. 5(3)

Cases: *C & E Commrs v Shaklee International* (1981) 1 BVC 444; *BMW (GB) Ltd v C & E Commrs* [1997] BVC 400; *KMPG (a firm)* [1997] BVC 2,469; *Ernst & Young* [1997] BVC 2,541; *British Car Auctions Ltd* (1978) VATTR 56

Other material: Notice 700/65 'Business Entertainment'

VAT Reporter: ¶19-006

6-340   Fittings in new buildings

There are provisions to prevent the use of the zero-rating relief for sales of new houses from being exploited by incorporating into the building, prior to sale, certain fixtures, etc. which would attract VAT if supplied separately. These rules apply when a taxable person constructs a building to be used (wholly or partly) as a dwelling, with the intention of selling it or of granting a major interest in it (broadly, a lease for a term greater than 21 years). This provision is illustrated by the flow chart at 7-920.

In these circumstances, the taxable person concerned is prevented from reclaiming input tax on the purchase or importation of goods to be incorporated in the building (or in that part to be used as a dwelling, and so qualify for zero-rating), other than materials (such as bricks and mortar), builder's hardware, sanitary ware and other items of a kind ordinarily installed by builders as fixtures. In addition, tax on these items cannot be reclaimed if they are:

(1)   finished or prefabricated furniture, other than furniture designed to be fitted in kitchens. This prevents the builder from deducting input tax in respect of fitted wardrobes, etc. Note, however, that many built-in wardrobes making use of alcoves, etc. inherent in the design of the building are not regarded as 'furniture', so no blocking of input tax arises. HMRC also accept that a base unit incorporating a wash hand basin fitted in a bathroom, etc. does not amount to fitted furniture. However, they consider that other base units are fitted furniture;

(2)   materials for the construction of fitted furniture, other than kitchen furniture;

(3)   electrical or gas appliances but not the following:

- appliances designed to heat space or water (or both) or to provide ventilation, air cooling, air purification, or dust extraction;
- in a building designed as a number of dwellings, a door-entry system, a waste disposal unit or a machine for compacting waste;
- a burglar alarm, a fire alarm, or fire safety equipment or designed solely for the purpose of enabling aid to be summoned in an emergency; or
- a lift or hoist;

(4)   carpets or carpeting material.

Legislation: *Value Added Tax (Input Tax) Order* 1992 (SI 1992/3222), art. 6

Cases: *McLean Homes Midland Ltd v C & E Commrs* [1993] BVC 99

Other material: Notice 708 'Building and Construction'

VAT Reporter: ¶33-305

6-360   Goods supplied under second-hand goods scheme

Where goods are sold under the second-hand goods scheme, and provided that all conditions for the use of the scheme are met, the vendor charges tax only on the margin which he has made on the sale.

The purchaser of goods sold under the scheme is prohibited from deducting any input tax in respect of the purchase.

If the goods are for use in the purchaser's business, rather than for resale to the public, the purchaser may prefer to buy the goods outside of the second-hand goods scheme, thus avoiding the unnecessary creation of sticking tax.

Example: second-hand goods scheme

Bert Cod is a freelance fisherman, and is registered for VAT. He wishes to buy a boat for use in his business. Harry Tub is prepared to sell him a second-hand boat for £21,000. Harry is selling the boat under the second-hand goods scheme for boats. He bought it for £15,000, and the sale price of £21,000 includes £1,000 in respect of VAT (£1,000 is VAT at 20% included in the profit margin (£21,000–£15,000)). Harry therefore expects to receive £20,000 net after paying the VAT to HMRC.

The net cost to Bert of buying the boat under the second-hand goods scheme will be £21,000, as he cannot reclaim any of the VAT on the purchase. Bert would do better to buy the boat from Harry outside of the scheme, for £20,000 plus £4,000 VAT. Bert would be able to reclaim the VAT, so his net cost would be £20,000, while Harry would still receive the same net price.

More information on the second-hand goods scheme is given at 16-430ff.

VAT Reporter: ¶48-630

6-380   Certain imports of goods

There is a special provision blocking the deduction of input tax arising on the importation of goods where:

(1)   at the time of importation the goods belong wholly or partly to some person other than the importer;

(2)   the purposes for which they are to be used include non-business purposes either of the taxable person or of the other person wholly or partly owning them; and

(3)   the identification of tax on supplies (other than general overheads) used in making both exempt and taxable supplies.

In order to prevent an effective double charge to VAT, HMRC have power to allow a refund (or partial refund) if they are satisfied that a double charge would otherwise arise. If they agree to make such a payment, it is made to the taxable person separately from his ordinary VAT payments or repayments made via his VAT returns.

Legislation: VATA 1994, s. 27

VAT Reporter: ¶19-004

6-420   Use to which supplies are put

Even where the basic rules relating to input tax are met, the trader may be prevented from deducting some or all of the input tax arising on supplies to him and importations of goods by him.

As seen above, wholly non-business use of the supplies prevents the tax on them from falling within the definition of input tax. There are further provisions restricting the right to deduct input tax so that, broadly, only tax on supplies and importations used in making taxable supplies may be deducted. Input tax on supplies used in making exempt supplies is, in principle, non-deductible.

More specifically, the deduction of input tax is restricted to that attributable to:

(1)   the making of taxable supplies;

(2)   the making of supplies outside of the UK which would be taxable if they were made within the UK; or

(3)   the making of certain other supplies outside the UK and certain exempt supplies designated by treasury order.

Specified supplies for (3) above include certain insurance and financial transactions, and arrangements therefore, supplied to persons outside the EC or in connection with the export of goods from the EC, if these supplies are exempt or would be if made in the UK.

Input tax must be attributed as between the types of supplies made by the trader, and business activities not giving rise to supplies, by reference to the use to which they are put. The detailed 'partial exemption' rules for making this attribution are contained in regulations, and are extremely complex. They are covered at 6-950ff.

The amount of 'exempt input tax' for the period must be ascertained and disallowed. However, if it falls below the de minimis limit (see 7-520) it can be deducted.

The rules on partial exemption need to be understood and applied by any business which makes exempt supplies, even such occasional supplies as an exempt sale of business premises.

Legislation: VATA 1994, s. 26(2); *Value Added Tax (Input Tax) (Specified Supplies) Order 1999 (SI 1999/3121)*

VAT Reporter: ¶19-004

Input Tax Recovery

EVIDENCE FOR DEDUCTION OF INPUT TAX

6-460 Requirement

Before a trader may deduct tax as input tax, he must hold evidence in support of the claim. Furthermore, the evidence must take a specified form which varies depending upon the manner in which the input tax arose.

Legislation: *Value Added Tax Regulations* 1995 (SI 1995/2518), reg. 29

Other material: Notice 700, para. 19.7

VAT Reporter: ¶19-000

6-480 Tax on supplies

Input tax most commonly arises in respect of supplies received from other taxable persons. In this instance, the evidence which must be held to support the claim to deduct the VAT is a VAT invoice issued by that other trader. The VAT invoice must be in the right form, containing all the particulars required on a VAT invoice (9-280). If the invoice is technically defective in some way, HMRC may cancel the deduction of the VAT and recover it from the trader.

HMRC have power to accept evidence which does not fully meet the criteria laid down, but this is rarely exercised except in respect of minor technical defects (but see 6-580 below).

VAT Reporter: ¶19-000

6-500 Imports of goods

Where input tax relates to an import of goods from outside the EC, it is necessary to hold the import VAT certificate, showing the claimant as importer, consignee or owner, showing the tax due, and authenticated or issued by the proper officer. This document will normally be the monthly certificate issued by HMRC directly to the importer.

It is vital to ensure that import entry documents are properly made out, so that the certificate is issued to the correct person.

Other material: Notice 702, Section 8

VAT Reporter: ¶63-790

6-520 Imports of services

Where input tax arises under the reverse charge procedure on certain imports of services, the trader must hold an invoice from the supplier. This will substantiate the value attributed to the supply, and hence the amount of tax, which will be important if only a part of it can be reclaimed.

Other material: Notice 741A, Section 18

VAT Reporter: ¶19-000

6-540   Removal of goods from warehouse

In order to deduct tax paid to HMRC on the removal of goods from warehouse, the claimant must hold a document authenticated or issued by the proper officer showing the claimant's particulars and the amount of tax due on the goods.

Other material: Notice 702, Section 8

VAT Reporter: ¶55-202

6-560   Acquisition of goods from elsewhere in the EC

Where input tax arises on an acquisition of goods from elsewhere in the EC, the claimant must hold the invoice, etc. issued by the supplier, quoting the customer's UK VAT registration number and other specified information.

Other material Notice 725, para. 6.7

VAT Reporter: ¶55-800

6-580   Other evidence

As indicated above, HMRC have power to accept other evidence for the deduction of tax. This power has been exercised as follows:

(1)   an invoice made out to an employee is acceptable evidence in the case of subsistence expenses and petrol; and

(2)   a tax invoice is not required for expenditure below £25 on telephone calls from public or private telephones, purchases through coin operated machines, or car park charges.

HMRC can be asked to accept alternative evidence in particular cases, and they must act reasonably in the exercise of their discretion.

Broadly, this means that a trader who has evidence that a taxable supply has been received, and was received from a taxable person (someone registered for VAT, or liable to be registered), is entitled to recovery of input tax even without a VAT invoice.

Input Tax Recovery

The situation is tightened for businesses operating in the following trade sectors:

(1)   computers (including parts, accessories and software);

(2)   telephones (including parts and accessories);

(3)   alcohol products;

(4)   oils held out as road fuel (including bulk supplies).

The tightening is to require evidence, not only that the supply took place, but also that it was bona fide in nature. Essentially, this is about making sure that the supplier is who they say they are, and that they can properly make the supply (for instance, they are supplying goods which they own, not goods which they have stolen).

Cases: *Best Buys Supplies Ltd v R & C Commrs* [2011] UKUT 497 (TCC); [2012] BVC 1,501

Other material: Notice 700, para. 19.7.5, Statement of Practice March 2007 VAT Strategy – Input tax deduction without a valid VAT invoice

VAT Reporter: ¶19-001

6-600   Need to obtain evidence

Because of the stringent evidence requirements, it is vital that the trader ensures that the evidence is always obtained, that it is correct and meets all the formal requirements, and that it is preserved.

It is essential that incoming tax invoices are checked to ensure that they meet all of the criteria laid down, particularly where they are for large amounts.

Traders who import goods need to see that the entry documents are properly completed and that the import VAT certificates are obtained and retained.

VAT Reporter: ¶19-011

PRE-REGISTRATION AND PRE-INCORPORATION SUPPLIES/POST-DE-REGISTRATION SUPPLIES

6-640   Relief available

Relief is available for certain input tax incurred prior to registration (or, in the case of a limited company, prior to incorporation) and after de-registration. This tax would not, in principle, be deductible as the trader will not have been a registered taxable person at the time when the tax arose. Consequently, there are special provisions to give effect to the relief. The rules are illustrated in the flow chart at 7-925.

In each case, there are a number of conditions to be met and, even if these are met, the relief remains at the discretion of HMRC.

Legislation: *Value Added Tax Regulations* 1995 (SI 1995/2518), reg. 111

VAT Reporter: ¶19-130

6-660   Pre-registration supplies

The tax which can be reclaimed is:

(1)   tax on supplies of goods within four years before registration, if the goods are still on hand at the date of registration, either in their original state or incorporated into other goods. However, this does not include goods which are within the scope of the Capital Goods Scheme (see 7-760); and

(2)   tax on supplies of services obtained within six months before the registration date (not the date when the business started).

In order to reclaim the tax, the trader must hold ordinary evidence for deduction of input tax. In addition, the trader must make a list of all the services in respect of which a claim is made, showing their description, date of purchase and (if appropriate) the date of their disposal. A service would be disposed of if it consisted of work done on goods which were then sold.

Where a claim includes input tax relating to supplies of goods obtained before registration, the trader must compile a stock account showing quantities purchased, quantities used in making other goods, date of purchase and date of disposal (either of original goods or of goods made from them).

HMRC have announced their position that the ordinary partial exemption rules, and particularly the de minimis limits, do not apply to claims for pre-registration input tax. Pre-registration input tax attributable to exempt supplies is not recoverable, but does not go to swell the exempt input tax measured against the de minimis limits for the initial return period in which pre-registration input tax is claimed.

Other material: Notice 700/1, para. 4.2

VAT Reporter: ¶19-130

6-680   Pre-incorporation supplies

A company can reclaim input tax on supplies obtained on its behalf prior to its incorporation. The tax covered is the same as that for pre-registration supplies.

In order to qualify for this relief, certain extra conditions need to be met. The supplies must have been obtained for the benefit of the company or in connection with its incorporation. The person who obtained the supply must have become a member, officer or employee of the

Input Tax Recovery

company, and must not have been a taxable person at the time of the supply or importation. The company must have reimbursed the person who acquired the supplies, or given an undertaking to do so. The goods or services must have been obtained for the purposes of a business to be carried on by the company, and must not have been used (even temporarily) for any other purpose.

The evidence required is as for pre-registration inputs (i.e. normal input tax evidence plus a list of services and/or a stock account).

VAT Reporter: ¶19-138

6-700   Re-registration following de-registration

VAT accounted for on assets when a business de-registers may, subject to conditions, be reclaimed if or when the business registers again for VAT. In order to do this the usual conditions apply and the claimant must have proof of paying this VAT to HMRC when the business de-registered.

Assets within the capital goods scheme are considered separately. They are not within the scope of the regulation allowing businesses to reclaim VAT incurred on assets held at registration. Instead any claim for input tax when re-registering is calculated, and only allowable, using the capital goods scheme.

Other material: Revenue and Customs Brief 01/12

6-720   De-registration: relief in respect of services

HM Revenue and Customs also have power to refund tax incurred after de-registration has taken place where this relates to services (but not goods) obtained for the purposes of the business which the person carried on while registered. Relief for such input tax is at the complete discretion of HMRC.

Typically, relief is given in respect of services such as those of accountants and lawyers involved in closing the business down, or disposing of it. Normal evidence for input tax deduction must be held.

If possible, the claim should be made by including the tax as input tax on the trader's final VAT return. If this is not possible (e.g. because the work is not done, or a tax invoice is not received, until later), the trader should contact the HMRC with a view to making a separate claim on Form VAT 427. The claim must be made within four years of the date on which the input tax arises. See flowchart 7-930.

Other material: Notice 700/11

VAT Reporter: ¶44-030

6-730   Input tax relating to supplies made before registration

It has been held that input tax arising after registration for VAT cannot be recovered if the inputs have, in effect, been resupplied before registration. Thus, input tax recovery was disallowed on post-registration inputs to the extent that the onward supplies were paid for before the date of registration.

Cases: *Schemepanel Trading Ltd v C & E Commrs* [1996] BVC 304

VAT Reporter: ¶19-134

MISCELLANEOUS

6-740   Repayments to non-UK traders

There are also provisions permitting repayments of input tax to traders established elsewhere in the EC and to traders established outside the EC.

A claim can be made if the claimant:

(1)   has no UK business establishment; and

(2)   does not make supplies in the UK, other than certain supplies connected with international freight transport or supplies of services treated as made in the UK merely because that is where the recipient belongs (see 3-980(4)).

No input tax will be repaid under these provisions if the claimant intends to use the inputs in making a UK supply, or to export them from the UK (in either of these cases UK VAT registration is the proper mechanism to obtain a refund). Input tax will only be repaid if it would have been repaid to a similar trader registered for VAT in the UK.

The treatment of claims by partially exempt businesses has long been unclear. The European Court of Justice has now confirmed that, in principle, an apportionment must be made for inputs used both in making taxable supplies and in making exempt supplies. The basic entitlement depends upon the categorisation of the supplies made in the claimant's own Member State, but may be reduced if there is a different classification for similar supplies in the Member State whose tax is claimed. See flowchart 7-935.

Non-EU businesses

Non-EU businesses must make claims to HMRC on Form VAT 65A, enclosing a certificate of status (Form VAT 66A) authenticated by the trader's own tax authority, and original invoices, etc. The year for these claims ends on 30 June. Claims must be made by the following 31 December. See flowchart 7-940.

Input Tax Recovery

A non-EU business is not entitled to a refund unless, if registered for VAT in the UK, the non-EU business would be entitled to claim the VAT concerned as input tax. The Upper Tribunal endorsed the First Tier Tribunal view of this as follows:

'The Tribunal correctly stated the "basic requirement" as that found in regulation 186. This required the claimant to show that the tax sought to be relieved "would be input tax of his were he a taxable person in the UK".'

EU businesses

Claims made on or after 1 January 2010 must be made online via the tax authority in the EU State in which the business is established. That tax authority is then responsible for forwarding the claim electronically to HMRC who will process it and make the refund.

A claim can be made for a calendar quarter or for a full calendar year. There is a time limit for making these claims. It is 30 June following the relevant calendar year.

Before 1 January 2010 claims had to be made to HMRC on Form VAT 65, enclosing a certificate of status (Form VAT 66) authenticated by the trader's own tax authority, and original invoices, etc.

Legislation: *Value Added Tax Regulations* 1995 (SI 1995/2518), reg. 173–194

Cases: *Ministre du Budget, Ministre de l'Économie et des Finances v Société Monte Dei Paschi Di Siena* (Case C-136/99) [2000] ECR I-6109; *SRI International v R & C Commrs* [2011] UKUT 240 (TCC); [2011] BVC 1,643

Other material: Notice 723; Notice 723A

VAT Reporter: ¶66-030; ¶66-500

6-780   Repayment of input tax to UK traders by other EC States

Claims submitted after 1 January 2010

HMRC have a system whereby a business established in the UK that has incurred input tax in another Member State can submit an electronic claim via the UK – the Member State of Establishment (MSEST). This will then be forwarded to the Member State of Refund (MSREF). The claimant will receive an electronic notification from the MSEST that the claim has been forwarded and will then receive a further notification from the MSREF that the claim has been received. This system applies to all claims submitted from 1 January 2010, including claims for refunds in relation to VAT incurred before that day.

How to make a claim

Use the standardised form available on the UK Government Gateway or HMRC's VAT online services.

An agent may submit the claim but will themselves have to have the relevant permissions and be registered as the agent with HMRC.

All claims are made electronically. There is no facility for making paper claims.

Language

Most Member States will accept the reclaim submitted in English.

Evidence needed

It is necessary to have the original invoices and other documents to support the claim although most of these will not need to be sent to the Member State of Refund.

Some Member States require documents to be scanned and submitted with the application. Usually these involve invoices for fuel over €250 and other invoices with a value of more than €1,000 (or the equivalent if not a Member State in the Eurozone).

Each Member State should have a website with details of their requirements.

Time limits

The claim must be made within nine months of the end of the calendar year in which the input tax was incurred. This is usually the date on the invoice rather than the date when the supplier was paid.

The claim must not be for more than one calendar year or less than three months (unless that is all that is left of the relevant calendar year).

Decision – time limits

The Member State of Refund will send an email confirming receipt of the claim. That may take up to 15 days.

A decision on the claim will be made within four months. If further information is required, they will ask for it within the four months and there is one month to supply it. They will then have up to eight months after they have received the claim to make a final decision.

Payments and time limits

Payments will be made by credit transfer – usually in the currency of the Member State of Refund.

Refunds will be paid:

- within four months and ten days of receiving the claim (providing there has been no request for further information), or
- within eight months and ten days of receiving the claim where there has been a request for further information.

Input Tax Recovery

Appeals

Any appeal about the reclaim must be made under the rules of the Member State of Refund – HMRC cannot and will not intervene on behalf of any UK trader.

Each MSREF should have procedures whereby VAT, penalties and interest may be recovered from any claimant submitting a fraudulent, or incorrect, application.

Information for agents

HMRC have issued online guidance, 'VAT EU refunds for agents and advisers'.

It is important to look at this information before attempting to sign up for the service because there are several details that are needed from each client. Subsequently, the client will be sent a letter giving a unique code needed by the agent that remains valid for 30 days.

Existing agents have been given the option of reclaiming EU VAT on behalf of clients. New agents should register for dealing with both EU refunds and other VAT online services for a client through the HMRC website. Registration via the Government Gateway is only for VAT online – not for EU refunds.

Other material: Notice 723; Notice 723A; *www.hmrc.gov.uk/news/vat-eu-changes.htm*

VAT Reporter: ¶66-010

6-800   Manner of claim for input tax deduction

As a general rule, deduction of input tax is claimed by including the VAT on the periodic VAT return form for the period in which the claimed VAT arises. In some cases of difficulty, and if authorised by HMRC, an estimated claim may be made and then rectified on a subsequent return.

In the case of pre-registration or pre-incorporation input tax, the tax should be included on the trader's first VAT return. For VAT on supplies of services obtained after de-registration, the VAT should be included on the final VAT return if possible, or otherwise claimed separately using Form VAT 427.

In no case may input tax be reclaimed unless the necessary evidence is held to support the refund. If the evidence is not to hand at the time when the relevant return has to be submitted, it should in strictness be notified separately to HMRC (either by letter or using Form VAT 652). In practice, it will often be included as input tax on a later return, and HMRC have indicated that they will not normally see this as giving rise to a serious misdeclaration penalty. Such late input tax claims have been implicitly approved of in a number of tribunal decisions. However, a claim cannot be made more than four years after the tax point for the input concerned.

Legislation: *Value Added Tax Regulations* 1995 (SI 1995/2518), reg. 29 and 29(1A)

VAT Reporter: ¶19-000

6-810 Funded Pension Schemes

Normally, there are two legal entities when a funded pension scheme is formed as a trust. These are the employer's business and the trust.

Subject to the normal rules, an employer may reclaim input tax incurred on fees charged by third parties for managing/administering a funded pension scheme. The third party will often also provide investment advice to the pension fund. The employer may not reclaim any VAT charged on the investment advice.

When management/administration services and investment advice are provided for a single fee or are not quantified separately there has been a long running policy of dividing the input tax '30/70'. This is 30 per cent for administration and 70 per cent for investment advice. The employer is allowed to treat 30 per cent as input tax.

It was proposed that from 1 January 2006 HMRC's administrative practice of splitting relevant input tax '30/70' would be further restricted as follows:

> 'Third parties providing both investment and administration services who are able to determine the actual values of each must provide separate invoices to trustees and employers showing the actual value of services provided. Where third parties are genuinely unable to determine separate values for investment and administration services, HMRC will continue to accept use of the 30/70 split, but only where the third parties are administering the pension scheme fully or providing the bulk of the administration of the scheme.'

Following discussions with representatives of the asset management industry these proposals were delayed until a future date.

Other material: VAT Notice 700/17 'Funded Pension Schemes'

VAT Reporter: ¶19-162

ASSETS USED FOR BUSINESS AND NON-BUSINESS PURPOSES

6-820 Introduction

There are several matters to be considered when dealing with input tax on assets which are used both for business and private purposes.

Private use is normally using the asset 'for the private purposes of the trader or his staff'. HMRC do not rule out that there may be other uses 'wholly outside the purposes of the taxpayer's enterprise or undertaking' which qualify as private use.

The matters to be taken into account when dealing with the purchase of business/private assets are as follows:

(1)   Purchases of land, buildings, civil engineering works, ships, boats and aircraft must be dealt with in a particular manner.

(2)   Various choices may be made when dealing with other assets.

6-830   Land, buildings, civil engineering works, ships, boats and aircraft

For expenditure incurred on these assets on or after 1 January 2011 the following applies:

*   Input tax must be apportioned between business and private use of the asset concerned. Only the business proportion is reclaimable.
*   If the asset concerned costs more than a certain amount there will be on-going adjustments to reflect the changes in business/private use. These adjustments will be made using the Capital Goods Scheme – see 7-775.

The assets to which the Capital Goods Scheme adjustments apply are as follows:

(1)   Land, buildings and civil engineering works costing more than £250,000 (excluding VAT).

(2)   Aircraft, boats, ships or other vessels costing more than £50,000 (excluding VAT).

These regulations also encompass refurbishments, alterations and extensions to buildings, civil engineering works, aircraft, ships etc. Before 1 January 2011 there were no special arrangements for dealing with input tax incurred on these assets. It was dealt with in the same way as that incurred on other assets.

Other material: Revenue and Customs Brief 53/10; VAT Information Sheet 06/11

Legislation: VATA 1994, s. 5A and 5B; *Value Added Tax Regulations* 1995 (SI 1995/2518), reg. 113 and 115

6-840   Other assets

Introduction

A VAT-registered person who acquires assets (except, from 1 January 2011, those in 6-830) which will be used for business and private/non-business purposes may choose how to account for input tax and output tax. The options are as follows:

(1) Reclaim no input tax and in turn do not account for output tax on private/non-business use or when the asset is disposed of.

(2) Reclaim only a proportion of the input tax relating to the business use (see 6-240) and account for output tax when the asset is disposed of.

(3) For some assets, reclaim input tax in full, account for output tax on the private/non-business use and when the asset is disposed of (the Lennartz procedure).

See flowchart 7-943 Goods for business and non-business/private use.

The choice must be made when input tax is incurred. If it is not, HMRC consider that the person concerned must use option 2.

Other Material: VAT Information Sheet 14/07 Assets used partly for non-business purposes

VAT Reporter: ¶19-040

Reclaim input tax in full, account for output tax as relevant

This is frequently referred to as 'The Lennartz Procedure' after a European Court of Justice case.

The dispute concerned whether or not a German businessman was entitled to reclaim in full input tax paid on the purchase of a car which he used for both business and private purposes.

The ECJ decided that Mr Lennartz could reclaim the input paid on his car in full. The quid pro quo was that he would have to account for VAT on the private use. This would be an output tax charge. The principles espoused by the ECJ were as follows:

> 'A taxable person using goods for the purposes of an economic activity ... had a right ... to deduct input tax in accordance with the *(normal)* rules ... however small the proportion of business use ... output tax to be charged for the private use.'

Non-business use from 22 January 2010

For the purposes of Lennartz accounting, non-business use is private use by the 'trader or his staff'. Following an ECJ case in 2009, it is clear that Lennartz accounting is not, and never was, available if the non-business use is different from this.

HMRC are applying the ECJ ruling strictly with effect from 22 January 2010.

To smooth the transition to new narrower understanding of when Lennartz may be used, HMRC are operating two concessions. These are as follows:

(1) permitting persons already using Lennartz for a non-qualifying asset to continue the process through to its ultimate conclusion;

Input Tax Recovery

(2) persons who have entered into 'binding commitments for projects' which did (but no longer do) qualify for Lennartz accounting may apply to HMRC to proceed with this method of accounting for VAT.

Assets for which Lennartz may be used

The goods for which Lennartz cannot be used are those for which input tax recovery is blocked, e.g. cars and business entertainment. Also, it may not be used when there is no entitlement to reclaim input tax (e.g. the asset is used wholly for making exempt supplies).

In *Seeling*, the ECJ decided that where a taxable person received supplies of construction services that resulted in the creation of a new business asset, then the resulting asset could be brought within the Lennartz mechanism. HMRC interpret this as meaning that where any services are used in creating a new asset, for example new moveable goods or buildings or annexes, etc. to existing buildings, that asset may be brought into the Lennartz mechanism. The Lennartz mechanism is only available for services that result in the creation of new goods.

Amount of non-business use/private use

The non-business/private use does not have to exceed a certain level in order to apply Lennartz. The goods may be overwhelmingly used for private purposes. However, there must be some genuine business use of the goods. When there is not, input tax is not recoverable and Lennartz cannot be applied.

Make the decision at the outset

HMRC's view is that Lennartz cannot be applied retrospectively. The registered person must opt for Lennartz at the outset. This is when the input tax which they wish to claim in full is incurred.

Time span

The output charge due on the private use of the goods is payable throughout the 'economic life' of the goods/asset concerned. The 'economic life' is 60 months.

When Lennartz was available for land and buildings the 'economic life' of these was normally 120 months. It may have been less than 120 months when, at the start of the 'economic life', the interest in land had less than 120 months to run. Then the 'economic life' equalled the period of the lease.

The 'economic life' begins when the goods are 'first used for any purpose'.

Particular circumstances

The Lennartz procedure legislation is not straightforward. There are several circumstances when Lennartz is applicable or may be used. The relevant situations can be categorised as follows:

- goods purchased on or after 1 November 2007;
- enhancement expenditure;
- transitional arrangements for those already using Lennartz.

Examples of each situation are given below.

Example – goods purchased after 1 November 2007

An environmental engineer travels the country monitoring toxic emissions from industrial plants. The monitoring process is normally continuous over a period of 24 or 48 hours. The engineer needs to be on site during the monitoring process. He decides to buy a motor home for £100,000 plus £17,500 VAT. It will provide him with on-site accommodation and work space. He and his family will use the motor home at other times for holidays, week-end breaks, etc.

The engineer's VAT periods are calendar quarters. The motor home is purchased on 1st December 2007. It is used over the next few months as follows:

Period ending –	31 Dec 2007	31 Mar 2008	30 Jun 2008
business use (B)	2	16	7
private use (P)	8	4	21
private use % $(P/(B + P) \times 100)$	80%	25%	75%

VAT due on the private use is calculated as follows:

Period ending –	31 Dec 2007	31 Mar 2008	30 Jun 2008
No. of months	1	3	3
Value of private use –	$\frac{1}{60} \times £100,000 \times 80\%$	$\frac{3}{60} \times £100,000 \times 25\%$	$\frac{3}{60} \times £100,000 \times 75\%$
	= £1,333.33	= £1,250.00	= £5,000.00
VAT due at 17.5%	= £233.33	= £218.75	= £875.00

Note – The number of months is reduced for the period ending 31 December 2007 because two months of the period had elapsed before the vehicle was purchased.

Example – enhancement expenditure

On 1 January 2008, a VAT-registered vehicle repair business moved into a new workshop and storage area. The unit is about 100 square metres. About 20 square metres will house the proprietor's personal collection of classic car memorabilia. The collection is not part of the business. The building was purchased freehold and cost £200,000 plus VAT.

The proprietor opts to reclaim input tax in full and use Lennartz to account for output tax on the private use. The VAT quarters end on 31 March, 30 June, 30 September and 31 December.

Input Tax Recovery

The VAT due for the private use for periods 31 March 2008, 30 June 2008 and each subsequent period is as follows:

Period ending –	**31 Mar 2008**	**30 Jun 2008**
Private use ($\frac{20 \text{ sq mtrs}}{100 \text{ sq mtrs}} \times 100$)	20%	20%
Value of private use –	$\frac{3}{120} \times £200{,}000 \times 20\%$	$\frac{3}{120} \times £200{,}000 \times 20\%$
	= £999.99	= £999.99
VAT due at 17.5%	= £174.99	= £174.99

In 2009, the building is extended mainly to house a newly-acquired collection of memorabilia. However, it is also an opportunity to alter the layout of the business. By moving the office into the new extension, the workshop is increased and made more efficient. The office is about 15 per cent of the floor area of the extension. The extension costs £90,000 plus VAT. Again, the proprietor chooses to use Lennartz. The extension is first used on 1 April 2009.

The charge for the private use of the extension is calculated as follows:

3 month period	
Private use	85%
Value of private use –	$\frac{3}{120} \times £90{,}000 \times 85\%$
	= £1,912.50
VAT due at 17.5%	= £334.68

The output due in the period ending 30 June 2009 (and subsequent periods unless there are any relevant changes) is £174.99 and £334.68 for the original building and extension respectively.

Note – The charges for the original building and extension are calculated separately. The original building and extension have separate economic lives. Thus, the charges begin and (unless the economic life is disrupted) end at different times.

Example – transitional arrangements for those already using Lennartz

On 1 January 2005 a VAT-registered engineering business moved into new premises. The unit is about 100 sq meters. Initially about 20 sq meters is used to house the proprietor's personal collection of war memorabilia. In September 2005, more of the building was used for the collection – approximately 30%.

The collection is not part of the business. The building was purchased freehold and cost £200,000 plus VAT.

The proprietor opts to reclaim input tax in full and use Lennartz to account for output tax on the private use. The VAT quarters end on 31 March, 30 June, 30 September and 31 December.

The VAT due for the private use for periods 31 March 2005, 30 June 2005 and each subsequent period up until 1 November 2007 is as follows:

Period ending –	31 Mar 2005	30 Jun 2005	30 Sep 2005
Private use –	20%	20%	30%
Value of private use – (per month)	$\dfrac{1}{240} \times £200{,}000 \times 20\%$	$\dfrac{1}{240} \times £200{,}000 \times 20\%$	$\dfrac{1}{240} \times £200{,}000 \times 30\%$
	= £166.66	= £166.66	= £250.00
Value per quarter	£499.98	£499.98	£750.00
VAT per quarter (@ 17.5%)	= £87.50	= £174.99	= £131.25

The figure of 240 in the table is 240 months (or 20 years), the maximum economic life over which HMRC permitted private use liability under the Lennartz mechanism to be calculated before the new legislation was introduced.

A series of steps are then necessary to determine the 'economic life' for calculating private use liability post-1 November 2007. These steps are as follows:

Step 1 Value of deemed supplies pre-1 November 2007

	Private use	Number of months	Value per month	Grossing up	Total value of private liability
1 Jan to 30 Jun 2005	20%	6	£166.66	$(£166.66 \times 6) \times \dfrac{100}{20}$	£4,999.80
1 Jul 2005 to 31 Oct 2007	30%	28	£250.00	$(£250 \times 28) \times \dfrac{100}{30}$	£23,333.33
					£28,333.13

Step 2 – Post-1 November 2007 'economic life'

The period of the economic life remaining after 1 November 2007 is calculated as follows:

$$120 \text{ months} \times \frac{(\text{cost of goods} - \text{value of private liability to 31 Oct 2007})}{\text{cost of goods}}$$

$$= 120 \times \frac{(£200{,}000 - £28{,}333.13)}{£200{,}000}$$

$$= 103 \text{ months}$$

Step 3 – Post-1 November 2007

Use 'economic life' of 103 months for calculating private use liability post-1 November 2007.

Legislation: Directive 2006/112, art. 26(1)(a); *Value Added Tax Regulations* 1995 (SI 1995/2518), reg. 116A et seq.; VATA 1994, Sch. 4, para. 5(4)

Input Tax Recovery

239

Cases: *Lennartz v Finanzamt München III* (Case C-97/90) [1993] BVC 202; *P Charles & TS Charles-Tijmens v Staatssecretaris van Financien* (Case C-434/03) [2005] ECR I-7037; *Seeling v Finanzamt Starnberg* (Case C-269/00) [2003] BVC 399; *Vereniging Noordelijke Land-en Tuinbouw Organisatie v Staatssecretaris van Financiën* (Case C-515/07) [2009] ECR I-839

Other material: VAT Information Sheet 14/07; HM Revenue and Customs Brief 02/10; VAT Information Sheet 06/11

VAT Reporter: ¶19-040

PARTIAL EXEMPTION

6-950   Introduction to partial exemption

The basic structure of VAT has been covered in previous divisions. Traders must account for VAT on taxable supplies which they make, and can recover the input tax suffered on supplies made to them, and on importations and acquisitions of goods. Traders who only make exempt supplies cannot register for VAT, and so cannot recover tax suffered on their expenses.

The position is fairly straightforward, therefore, for traders who only make taxable supplies, and very straightforward for those who only make exempt supplies.

Many traders make taxable supplies and also make exempt supplies, and for them the position is more complex. Clearly, if a trader making both kinds of supply was allowed to recover all input tax, this would cause a distortion of competition compared with a trader making the same kind of exempt supplies but not making any taxable supplies.

In order to meet this circumstance, there is a set of rules for determining the amount of input tax which can be recovered by a trader who makes both types of supply. Such a trader is referred to as being partially exempt, and the rules concerned are referred to as the partial exemption rules. The general objective is to allow a partially exempt trader to recover tax on supplies relating to the making of taxable supplies, but to prevent the recovery of input tax which relates to the making of exempt supplies.

VAT Reporter: ¶19-400

6-990   Partial exemption practicalities

While this is a simple enough idea in the abstract, its practical implementation is a notoriously complex area.

Partial exemption is not a matter which concerns only a few traders. Most traders make exempt supplies at one time or another, and some such supplies can be substantial in relation to the size of the business. Typical exempt supplies which can give rise to partial exemption problems include:

(1)   sale of business premises or land;

(2)   sale and leaseback of business premises or land;

(3)   subletting of business premises; and

(4)   sale of shares or securities (e.g. sale of a subsidiary company).

Because most businesses are likely to be involved in exempt supplies at some time, it follows that people in business need at the least to have a general awareness of partial exemption, so that advice can be sought when needed. Those businesses which regularly make exempt supplies need a proper understanding of the rules. This part of the commentary provides an overview of the partial exemption rules, and goes into them in a little more detail.

It should be noted that the application of the rules to any particular business is very much a matter for detailed analysis of the activities and accounting systems of that business. 'Off the peg' solutions are not appropriate in the area of partial exemption; 'tailor made' is not a luxury, but a necessity.

VAT Reporter: ¶19-415

7-030   Partial exemption legislation

The basic principle of the UK legislation on partial exemption is that the input tax which is recoverable by a trader is that which relates to the making of taxable supplies. HMRC may also make regulations setting out detailed rules to give effect to this principle. References in this part of the commentary to regulations are to these regulations unless otherwise indicated.

Legislation: Directive 2006/112, art. 173; VATA 1994, s. 26; *Value Added Tax Regulations* 1995 (SI 1995/2518), reg. 99–116

Other material: Notice 706 and 706/2

VAT Reporter: ¶19-420

7-070   Overview of the partial exemption rules

The general principle is that the input tax for which a trader may obtain credit is that which is attributable to the making of:

(1)   taxable supplies; or

(2)   supplies treated as made outside the UK which would be taxable if made inside the UK (this heading includes certain supplies made in warehouse); or

(3)   other supplies made outside the UK and certain exempt supplies designated by the Treasury.

Input Tax Recovery

Specified supplies for (3) above include certain insurance and financial transactions, and the making of arrangements therefore, supplied to persons outside the EC or in connection with the export of goods from the EC, if these supplies are exempt or would be if made in the UK *Value Added Tax (Input Tax) (Specified Supplies) Order* 1999 (SI 1999/3121).

Any other input tax is, in principle, non-deductible.

The regulations provide that this basic rule is to be implemented by analysing input tax according to the use to which the related supplies or importations are put. Tax on supplies used solely in making taxable supplies is deductible, while that on supplies used solely in making exempt supplies or for a separable business activity which does not involve the making of supplies is, in principle, non-deductible.

Some supplies obtained will inevitably not fall into one category or the other, being used in support of the business activities generally. The tax on such supplies is referred to colloquially as 'residual input tax', being tax which cannot be directly attributed either to the making of taxable supplies or the making of exempt supplies. The relative use of supplies used in making both taxable and exempt supplies must be ascertained, and residual input tax must then be allocated between making taxable supplies and making exempt supplies in the proportion arrived at.

In principle, the input tax attributed to the making of taxable supplies, either directly or indirectly, is deductible while that attributed to making exempt supplies (referred to as exempt input tax) is non-deductible. However, if the exempt input tax falls below the de minimis limit, it too may be deducted.

Example: basic partial exemption calculation

To summarise the points above, each trader is obliged to analyse input tax as far as possible according to the use to which the related supplies are put, then to reallocate residual input tax between taxable and exempt input tax as follows:

	Total input tax	*Taxable input tax*	*Exempt input tax*	*The residual input tax*
Primary attribution	X	X	X	X
Secondary attribution of residual input tax, according to relative taxable and exempt use	–	X	X	(X)
Final attribution	X	X	X	–

If the exempt input tax so calculated is sufficiently small, the whole of the input tax for the period can be recovered (see 7-520). Otherwise, only the taxable input tax can be recovered and the exempt input tax is non-deductible.

This calculation must be done for each VAT return period. At the end of the trader's VAT year, the calculation must be reworked for the year as a whole to calculate the amount of input tax finally deductible. Any under or over-payment arising from the calculations for the return periods is adjusted on the first return of the next VAT year.

As indicated above the system of partial exemption is based upon an analysis of input tax. This must be carried out by any trader who incurs input tax in connection with current or future exempt supplies in order to determine whether there is to be any restriction on the recovery of input tax and, if so, the amount of the restriction.

The provision requires the trader to identify importations, acquisitions and supplies received for each period, and then provides for the VAT to be regarded as deductible or non-deductible according to the use to which the supplies are put. It states that VAT is deductible in respect of supplies 'used or to be used by him exclusively in making taxable supplies', but not in respect of supplies 'used or to be used by him exclusively in making exempt supplies, or in carrying on any activity other than the making of taxable supplies'. The treatment of VAT on supplies not used in making either taxable or exempt supplies is considered separately at 7-700.

VAT on supplies 'partly used or to be used by him in making both taxable and exempt supplies' must also be identified, and a further apportionment made in respect of it. Before dealing with this attribution of residual input tax, it is first necessary to consider the primary attribution of tax on supplies used exclusively in making taxable, or exempt, supplies.

Legislation: VATA 1994, s. 26; *Value Added Tax (Input Tax) (Specified Supplies) Order* 1992 (SI 1999/3121); *Value Added Tax Regulations* (SI 1995/2518), reg. 101

Other material: Notice 706, Section 2

Cases: *C & E Commrs v UBAF Bank Ltd* [1996] BVC 174

VAT Reporter: ¶19-410

7-110   Attribution of input tax

At first sight, there seems little difficulty caused by the need to attribute input tax to either taxable or exempt supplies, it appears to be an administrative matter. There are, however, several areas that need closer attention either because the purchases are used in making both exempt and taxable supplies or because the purpose of the transaction is more difficult to ascertain. See flowchart 7-960.

Attributing input tax to taxable or exempt supplies

Most important when dividing the input tax is the liability of the supply which consumes the relevant expenditure. Input tax is analysed solely according to the use made, or to be made, of the expenditure in making taxable or exempt supplies. In *BLP Group* the court ruled that the right to deduct input tax depended upon a 'direct and immediate link' between expenditure

Input Tax Recovery

and the taxable transaction. It follows that the principle of a 'direct and immediate' link must be considered when attributing input tax to either taxable or exempt supplies.

HMRC's views on the attribution of input tax were expressed in HM Revenue and Customs Brief 31/07. These are as follows. Costs are therefore 'used' to make taxable supplies of goods or services within the meaning of the partial exemption regulations, if they:

- have a direct and immediate link with the taxable transaction (see *BLP* Case C-4/94);
- are borne directly by the cost components of a taxable transaction (see *Midland Bank Plc* Case C-98/98), and
- are costs of the various components of the price (see *DA and EA Rompelman* Case 268/83). These are different aspects of a single test to determine whether VAT is recoverable.

In applying these ECJ principles, HMRC's view is that in order for costs to be a cost component of a taxable transaction, the costs should normally be reflected in the selling price of the taxable transaction. In other words, there is an objective test for determining VAT recovery, in that VAT on costs is not recoverable unless the costs are reflected in the selling price of the taxable supply.

Importance of intention

A point worth noting is that the attribution of input tax is based, in some circumstances, on intended future use of the inputs concerned and not simply on the status of the first supply made (*Briararch*). It was held in these cases that where inputs were used in making an exempt supply, but there was an intention to make a subsequent taxable supply, the input tax must be apportioned. It was not to be attributed wholly to the first exempt supply.

See also 7-495 and 7-500 for the position where there is a change of use of the inputs, or where the use to which the inputs are to be put is initially unclear.

Inputs used in making supply versus inputs resulting from supply

C & E Commrs v Midland Bank Plc (Case C-98/98) [2000] BVC 229 concerned the treatment of input tax on legal costs incurred by Samuel Montagu & Co Ltd, a member of Midland's VAT group.

Samuel Montagu acted for a US company in connection with a bid to take over a company listed on the London stock exchange, and related transactions. Various things went wrong and, as a result, Samuel Montagu found itself involved in protracted litigation.

It was common ground that Samuel Montagu was supplying 'Schedule 5 services' to its US client. Under the UK law as it stood at the time such supplies were zero-rated (under the law as it stands now they would be treated as made in the US, and so outside the scope of UK VAT but with a right of input tax recovery).

Midland recovered the whole of the input tax on the legal costs, on the basis that they were wholly attributable to the supplies made to the US client. HMRC took the view that the input tax on the costs was not wholly attributable to these supplies, but should be treated as residual, which gave rise to a far lower rate of recovery. Midland appealed to the VAT and Duties Tribunal, where HMRC lost and subsequently HMRC took the case to the High Court. The High Court sent a reference for a preliminary ruling to the ECJ.

The ECJ concluded that the basic right to deduct arose once there was a direct and immediate link (as determined by the national court) with taxable output transactions.

However, full deduction by a person making both taxable and exempt transactions was not permissible unless the inputs concerned represented a cost of actually carrying out taxable transactions. If they were merely consequential upon the carrying out of taxable transactions, as opposed to part of the costs of carrying them out, the input tax was residual and must therefore be recovered according to the person's partial exemption method.

Cases: *C & E Commrs v Midland Bank Plc* (Case C-98/98) [2000] BVC 229; *C & E Commrs v Briararch Ltd; C & E Commrs v Curtis Henderson Ltd* [1992] BVC 118; *BLP Group Plc v C & E Commrs* (Case C-4/94) [1995] BVC 159; *Rompelman v Minister van Financiën* (Case 268/83) (1984) 2 BVC 200,157

VAT Reporter: ¶19-550

Other material: HM Revenue and Customs Brief 31/07; Notice 706, Section 3

How to assess 'use'

Subject to the relevant regulation, there are occasions when input tax should be apportioned on the basis of use. When considering how to quantify use, the Court of Appeal said as follows:

> 'in assessing that use, and its extent, consideration is not limited to physical use. The assessment must be of the real economic use of the asset, that is to say having regard to economic reality, in the light of the observable terms and features of the taxpayer's business'

Cases: *R & C Commrs v London Clubs Management* [2011] BVC 406

ATTRIBUTION OF RESIDUAL INPUT TAX

7-250 The standard method

Once a primary attribution of input tax has been made, there will almost certainly remain an amount of residual input tax which has not been allocated specifically to the taxable input tax or exempt input tax categories. It is then necessary to make a secondary analysis to allocate residual input tax between the making of taxable and exempt supplies.

The proportion of residual input tax attributed to taxable supplies, and hence regarded as deductible, is the proportion which taxable turnover bears to total turnover.

The sum of the input tax directly attributed to exempt supplies, and the exempt proportion of residual input tax, is referred to as 'exempt input tax'.

Input Tax Recovery

> ### Example: attribution of residual input tax – standard method
>
> ProRata Ltd has the following results:
>
> | | £ |
> |---|---|
> | Taxable outputs | 500,000 |
> | Exempt outputs | 100,000 |
>
> | Input tax used for: | £ |
> |---|---|
> | Taxable supplies | 35,000 |
> | Exempt supplies | 2,500 |
> | Both types of supplies | 12,000 |
>
> The deductible proportion of residual input tax is:
>
> $$\frac{500,000}{500,000 + 100,000} = 84\%$$
>
> $84\% \times £12,000 = £10,080$
>
> | The exempt input tax is: | £ |
> |---|---|
> | Wholly exempt | 2,500 |
> | Residual input tax (£12,000 – £10,080) | 1,920 |
> | | 4,420 |

It will be noted that, in the above example, the percentage of taxable to total supplies is 83.33333 per cent. This is rounded up to 84 per cent (in favour of the trader) because the legislation requires that this be rounded up to the nearest whole percentage number. For a standard format for operating the standard method, see 7-975.

Legislation: *Value Added Tax Regulations* 1995 (SI 1995/2518), reg. 101

VAT Reporter: ¶19-459

'Residual input tax' above £400,000 on average

The rounding up referred to above is no longer available when the 'residual input tax' is on average £400,000 or more per month. When rounding up is not available the percentage is expressed to two decimal places.

Legislation: *Value Added Tax Regulations* 1995 (SI 1995/2518), reg. 101

Standard Method override

The final calculation may need to be adjusted by reference to the 'standard method override'. See 7-530.

Legislation: *Value Added Tax Regulations* 1995 (SI 1995/2518), reg. 101

Other material: Notice 706, Section 4

VAT Reporter: ¶19-450

7-260 Mandatory variations

There are mandatory variations to the standard partial exemption method.

When one or more of the mandatory variations applies, a business using the standard partial exemption method must apportion the residual input in the following order:

- first to strip out an amount calculated according to the mandatory variation;
- to apportion the remainder under the normal standard method calculation.

A business which also has non-business activities will also need a further preliminary stage to identify and strip out 'non-business' tax.

Variations to the standard method

Persons using the standard method must vary the standard method methodology for the following:

(1) supplies made from an establishments located outside the UK;

(2) other financial services (mainly financial instruments such as shares and bonds);

(3) investment gold.

The mandatory variations were more extensive before April 2009. The pre-April 2009 variations also encompassed supplies made outside the UK, which would be taxable if made in the UK and certain 'specified' supplies. These are now encompassed by the standard method.

Cases: *Kretztechnik AG v Finanzamt Linz* [2006] BVC 66

VAT Reporter: ¶19-684

Varying the methodology

This methodology applies to supplies made from establishments outside the UK and other financial services. The variation for supplies of investment gold is dealt with separately.

A business to which this mandatory variation applies must carry out a two-stage calculation for partial exemption purposes. Apportionment of input tax is carried out in two steps as follows:

(a) Input tax relating to supplies from establishments outside the UK and other financial services must be ring fenced and recovered on the basis of use. Also these supplies are excluded from the standard method calculation.

(b) Other input tax is attributed to taxable and exempt supplies using the standard method.

This methodology must be used even when the place of supply of the services concerned is the UK.

Input Tax Recovery

247

Legislation: *Value Added Tax Regulations* 1995 (SI 1995/2518), reg. 101(8)

Other material: VAT Information Sheet 04/09

Investment gold

The standard method may not be used to calculate input tax incurred in making supplies of investment gold. There are special rules about reclaiming input tax incurred on some of the goods and services that are directly attributable to exempt supplies of investment gold.

Legislation: *Value Added Tax Regulations* 1995 (SI 1995/2518), reg. 103A

Other material: Notice 702/21, Section 5

VAT Reporter: ¶19-684

Special partial exemption methods

In some cases, special methods (see 7-310ff.) may already deal specifically with out of country supplies etc., in which case no special action is needed.

In others, HMRC advise that a reg. 103 apportionment by use must be carried out, with the agreed special method then applied to the remaining input tax.

It was held that non-UK supplies in respect of which input tax credit is available for attributable inputs were not to be included in the calculation of the deductible proportion of input tax under the standard method. The legislation was amended to allow HMRC to authorise 'combined methods' that take account of input tax recoverable on overseas supplies. The 'combined method' is one method that takes into account both recovery of input tax on overseas supplies and a special method dealing with recovery of UK input tax.

Cases: *C & E Commrs v Liverpool Institute for Performing Arts* [2001] BVC 333 (HL)

7-270 Exclusions from turnover under standard method

Certain potentially distortive amounts of turnover are to be excluded from the formula for the apportionment of residual input tax under the standard method. These are amounts resulting from:

(1) supplies of capital goods used for business purposes;

(2) non-taxable amounts relating to the supply of goods on which input tax deduction was blocked (e.g. sale of a business car);

(3) self-supplies;

(4) certain financial and property supplies which are incidental to the trader's business, as follows:

    (a) zero-rated supplies of dwellings and of residential and charitable buildings;

(b)   zero-rated supplies of financial services to persons overseas;

(c)   exempt land supplies;

(d)   taxable supplies of the freeholds of new commercial buildings, etc.;

(e)   taxable land supplies which would be exempt except for the fact that the option for taxation has been exercised; and

(f)   exempt supplies of financial services.

It should be noted that the supplies mentioned at (4) above are only excluded from the calculation if they are incidental to the trader's business. If they form part of the main business activity they will continue to be included.

In *Régie Dauphinoise – Cabinet A Forest SARL v Ministre du Budget* (Case C-306/94) [1996] BVC 447, Advocate General Lenz considered what constituted 'incidental transactions'. At para. 47, he suggested that: 'An exact determination of the extent of incidental transactions is … not possible.' He continued at para. 48 that in order to be 'incidental' transactions would:

> '… have a certain link with the taxable person's other activity but do not form a direct part thereof. They require the use of the relevant business assets only to a slight extent. They may not exceed the extent of the actual activity.'

Although Advocate General Lenz suggested that any incidental transaction should not exceed the extent of the actual activity, this may not be in a merely financial measure. It is possible that a trader has a large valued one-off transaction which could still be considered to be incidental to the main business.

Following *Empresa de Desenvolvimento Mineiro SGPS SA (EDM) v Fazenda Publica (Ministerio Publico, intervener)* (Case C-77/01), it is now clear that the relevant financial transactions may be 'incidental' even when they are the main source of income. The deciding factor is not the amount received but whether the transactions concerned utilise 'only a very limited use of assets or services subject to value added tax'. If so they should be excluded from the partial exemption standard method fraction used to apportion partly recoverable input tax.

Bingo promoters in Spain operated from rooms providing playing facilities, a bar and/or restaurant. These promoters were required by law to return as winnings a fixed percentage of the bingo card price. When calculating their partial exemption recovery percentage, the promoters considered they should exclude the winnings from the calculation. The CEJ agreed. The court ruling was correct to exclude 'for the purposes of calculating the deductible proportion of VAT, the portion, fixed in advance by legislation, of the bingo card price which must be returned to players as winnings'.

Legislation: *Value Added Tax Regulations* 1995 (SI 1995/2518), reg. 101(3)

Cases: *Régie Dauphinoise – Cabinet A Forest SARL v Ministre du Budget* (Case C-306/94) [1996] BVC 447; *Empresa de Desenvolvimento Mineiro SGPS SA (EDM) v Fazenda Publica (Ministerio Publico, intervener)* (Case C-77/01) [2004] ECR I-4295; *International Bingo Technology SA v Tribunal Económico-Administrativo Regional de Cantaluña (TEARC)* (Case C-377/11) judgment delivered 19 July 2012

VAT Reporter: ¶19-460

Other material: Notice 706, para. 4.4; VAT Information Sheet 04/09

Input Tax Recovery

7-280 Provisional recovery option

For partial exemption years commencing on or after 1 April 2009, a partially exempt business may avoid making the standard method calculations each quarter. Instead, it may do the following:

- Each period use a fixed percentage to apportion residual input tax. The fixed percentage is taken from the annual adjustment for previous partial exemption year.
- Make the annual adjustment calculations in the normal way.

The decision to do this must be made when completing the return for the first period in the partially exemption year. Whatever is done for this period must be followed for the subsequent periods in the same partial exemption year. Changing the methodology after completing the return for the first period is not permissible.

Example

Pru has been partially exempt for many years. In the partial exemption year to 30 April 2009, Pru recovered 29 per cent of its residual input tax. Pru chooses to us this new 'fixed percentage' recovery option for the year to 30 April 2010.

Input tax attributable to quarter ending–	31 Jul 09 £	31 Oct 09 £	31 Jan 10 £	30 Apr 10 £	Totals £
taxable supplies	15,000	9,000	12,000	9,000	45,000
exempt supplies	2,000	3.000	2,500	4,000	11,500
both exempt and taxable supplies *(residual tax)*	1,500	2,000	3,000	1,750	8,250
	18,500	14,000	17,500	14,750	64,750
Input tax attributable to supplies	2,000	3,000	2,500	4,000	11,500
Residual tax (71%)	1,065	1,420	2,130	1,243	5,858
exempt input tax	3,065	4,420	4,630	5,243	17,358
Input tax attributable to taxable supplies–	15,000	9,000	12,000	9,000	45,000
Residual tax (29%)	4,354	580	870	508	2,393
Reclaimable input tax	15,435	9,580	12,870	9,508	47,393
exempt input tax within 'de minimis' limits–	£0	£0	£0	£0	£0
Total reclaimable	15,435	9,580	12,870	9,508	47,393

Annual Adjustment			
Sales, ye 30th April 2010	taxable	£900,000	
	exempt	£325,000	
		£1,225,000	
PE recovery %		£900,000 =	73.47%
		£1,225,000 (rounded up)	74%
Input tax attributable to taxable supplies–	b/d		£45,000
Residual tax attributable to taxable supplies		(£8,250 × 74%)	6,105
Reclaimable input tax			£51,105
less claimed during the year	b/d		47,393
Annual adjustment		(payable to HMRC)	3,713

Legislation: *Value Added Tax Regulations* 1995 (SI 1995/2518), reg. 101

Other material: VAT Information Sheet 04/09

OTHER METHODS

7-310   Use of other special methods

HMRC may approve the use of a partial exemption method other than the standard method. As a general rule, direct attribution will still be required where possible, and the variation of method will relate to the way in which residual input tax is apportioned. However, different methods may also be approved for the apportionment of the whole of the input tax. See flowchart 7-965.

If a non-standard method is required, it is mandatory to obtain written approval from HMRC.

HMRC will only approve a special method if the applicant declares that the method is 'fair and reasonable'. HMRC have issued a draft declaration in HM Revenue and Customs Brief 23/07. See flowchart 7-967 – Partial exemption special methods – considerations and formalities.

HMRC say that a special method is liable to be fair and reasonable if it:

- can be operated by the business;
- can be checked by HMRC; and
- produces a fair result.

Certain trade sectors

Special methods for certain trade sectors have been agreed by the trade bodies concerned. Details of these methods are in Notice 700/57.

Separate framework documents have been issued for higher education institutions and housing associations.

Legislation: *Value Added Tax Regulations* 1995 (SI 1995/2518), reg. 102(1), (5)

Other material: Notice 700/57; HM Revenue and Customs Brief 23/07; Framework for HEI partial exemption special methods (March 2011) www.hmrc.gov.uk/menus/frame-hei-march11.pdf; Framework for Housing Association partial exemption special methods (June 2010) www.hmrc.gov.uk/menus/frame-hei-apr10.pdf

VAT Reporter: ¶19-480

Shortcomings in the approval letter

On occasions, input tax will be incurred which is not covered or otherwise referred to within the terms of the approval letter. There is a regulation intended to provide 'certainty and clarity to businesses and HMRC' as to what to do in these circumstances.

This applies to input tax not 'prescribed in whole or in part' by the special method concerned. When there is input tax which does not fit within the approved attribution measures or falls within regs. 103, 103A or 103B, it must be apportioned on the basis of use. This only applies to the part or proportion of the input tax which is not covered by the approved special method. Regulations 103, 103A and 103B apply to attributing input tax to supplies made outside the UK, investment gold and incidental financial transactions respectively.

Special method override

A special method may be displaced by a method of apportioning input tax that is more acceptable to HMRC. The enforced change may not be backdated: it is effective from a current or future date only.

Before an authorised special method may be overridden, there must be grounds for believing the method used does not 'fairly and reasonably represent the extent to which goods or services are used … in making taxable supplies'. A notice forcing the business concerned to deal with its input tax recovery in different way may then be issued. The notice should contain the following information:

(a)   reasons why a notice has been issued;
(b)   the effect of the notice.

When HMRC issue an override notice, they are not required to tell the recipient what method should be used to determine a fair and reasonable attribution of input tax to taxable supplies.

Essentially, the effect of the notice is to force the business concerned to calculate its input tax recovery according to the 'extent to which the goods and services are used ... in making taxable supplies'. Somehow, one must decide to what extent costs are used to generate taxable supplies.

For the same reasons and in the same way, a taxpayer may serve a notice on HMRC that the special method in use does not produce a fair and reasonable result. A taxpayer's notice is only effective when 'the Commissioners approve' it.

HMRC's new policy is to issue an override notice in any circumstances when:

- 'they have clear evidence that the current special method is not fair and there is a significant loss of revenue'; and
- 'direction of another special method is not appropriate'.

Legislation: *Value Added Tax Regulations* 1995 (SI 1995/2518), reg. 102C, 102, 102A

Cases: *Vision Express (UK) Ltd* [2009] BVC 2,223

Other material: Notice 706, Sections 6 and 7

VAT Reporter: ¶19-517

Incorrect 'fair and reasonable' declaration

If HMRC determine that the 'fair and reasonable' declaration made when the special method was approved was 'incorrect' they may take action to correct the situation.

If HMRC consider that due to an incorrect declaration too much input tax was reclaimed they may serve notice directing that henceforth input tax recovery must be determined on the basis of 'use'. They may also assess for the excessive claims in earlier periods.

Legislation: *Value Added Tax Regulations* 1995 (SI 1995/2518), reg. 102(11) and 102B

7-330 Use-based methods

Methods frequently used include:

(1) transaction count – relating the attribution of input tax to the relative numbers of taxable and exempt transactions, rather than their relative values;

(2) staff count – relating the attribution of input tax to the relative numbers of staff employed on different activities (this may be appropriate where the bulk of the unattributed VAT relates to resources used on a per capita basis, such as office equipment, telephones, etc.);

(3) attribution by reference to floor areas occupied for different purposes;

Input Tax Recovery

(4)   cost centre accounting – using the methods already adopted by the business for attributing expenses between its various activities for internal accounting purposes; and

(5)   a mixture of the above – for instance, the attribution may be made mainly on the basis of cost centre accounting, with a further attribution on some other basis in those sections dealing with both taxable and exempt supplies.

Apart from establishing the amount of input tax finally recoverable by the business, a major priority in selecting a method of attribution must be to minimise the administrative effort involved, by making use of existing information where possible.

VAT Reporter: ¶19-505

7-350   Imposition or termination of method

HMRC have power to impose a partial exemption method. If HMRC seek to use this power, the trader has a right of appeal to a tribunal.

HMRC may direct the use of a special method if it is considered that a more 'fair and reasonable' attribution of input tax would result. The aim of the direction is to achieve an equitable result; it is not merely to reduce the amount of input tax reclaimable by the trader. Prior to the imposition of a special method, HMRC usually attempt to reach an agreement with the trader regarding any proposed changes.

In practice, the result of an imposed special method is usually to reduce the amount of input tax which the trader may reclaim.

Businesses have some rights, duties and expectations in situations where HMRC attempt to impose a special method:

* there is no retrospection (the direction must be from a current or future date);
* to be effective, the direction must be clear and unambiguous (this was decided by the Court of Session in Scotland in the case of *Kwik-Fit (GB) Ltd v C & E Commrs* [1998] BVC 48;
* the trader has the right of appeal to the VAT and Duties Tribunal;
* the method must be used until HMRC agree or direct the termination of its use.

Cases: *Kwik-Fit (GB) Ltd v C & E Commrs* [1998] BVC 48

Legislation: *Value Added Tax Regulations* 1995 (SI 1995/2518), reg. 102(1), (3) and (4)

Other material: Notice 706, para. 6.9

VAT Reporter: ¶19-495

Termination of a method

In *Banbury Visionplus Ltd* [2006] BVC 2,246, the appellants used an approved partial exemption special method based on floor area. In January 2004, HMRC wrote to the appellants terminating the permission to use this special method. They did not impose a different special method. The effect was that each business had then to use the standard method.

The VAT and Duties Tribunal considered the following:

- its jurisdiction in appeals such as this;
- whether the termination of the special method secured a fair and reasonable attribution of input tax.

It was decided that the jurisdiction of the Tribunal is limited to determining if the discretionary powers in reg. 102 was properly exercised. In simple terms, this means considering if HMRC acted reasonably when using their powers to terminate the use of the special method.

The appellants lost their appeal. The Tribunal decided that HMRC's decision was taken and carried out in a fair and reasonable manner. They took six months to inquire into the use of the special method and the officer concerned did not close his mind to the use of a different special method.

Legislation: VATA 1994, s. 26(3) and 83(1)(e)

Cases: *Banbury Visionplus Ltd* [2006] BVC 2,246

VAT Reporter: ¶19-495

7-370   Normal features of a special method

Direct attribution

There are some similarities between a special method and the standard method. HMRC do not normally allow a special method unless it incorporates the direct attribution of input tax used exclusively in making taxable or exempt supplies. Special methods are mainly concerned with apportioning the residual input tax.

Residual input tax

A trader is allowed to devise any 'fair and reasonable' method for the apportioning of residual input tax. The method should be agreed with HMRC and the trader has the right of appeal to the VAT and Duties Tribunal.

Mandatory variations

The mandatory variations described in ¶7-260 also apply to special partial exemption methods.

Annual adjustment

Provisional calculations are carried out period-by-period with a final 'annual' adjustment. The annual adjustment periods are the same as for the standard method unless other arrangements are authorised by HMRC.

Input Tax Recovery

Commencement date

Special methods may only be used from a current or future date. HMRC do not authorise their retrospective use although the relevant regulation appears to give them the discretion so to do.

It used to be allowed that a trader who applied to use a special method during the partial exemption year could be given authorisation and allowed to use the method from the start of their year. This has been made stricter. A trader who receives authorisation to use a special method during their tax year may be allowed to backdate its use to the start of their tax year. It is common for this to be allowed, but it is a discretionary matter.

Cessation date

A trader cannot unilaterally stop using a special method. The agreement of HMRC must be sought and obtained. A date of cessation should be agreed.

A tribunal ruled that a special method had to continue until a change was negotiated and agreed with HMRC even when an ECJ decision had direct implications for the method concerned.

Comment

It is essential that any method be verifiable. Authorisation to use a special method is unlikely to be forthcoming unless it can be checked and verified by reference to the business and the business records.

It is particularly important that the apportionment of residual input tax is readily checkable.

It would be ill advised to suggest a special scheme on the basis of a one-off sample. The aim is to devise a method that reflects the pattern of business and can be demonstrated to do so.

Cases: *Mercedes-Benz Financial Services Ltd* [2010] UKFTT 332 (TC); [2010] TC 00617

Other material: Notice 706, para. 6.4

VAT Reporter: ¶19-480

7-380 Special methods – the right of appeal

The role of the VAT and Duties Tribunals when HMRC reject a proposed special method was considered in *DCM (Optical Holdings) Ltd*.

The essential issue was whether or not the Tribunal could overturn HMRC's decision to reject a special method put forward by a taxpayer. HMRC argued that the Tribunals had only a supervisory role in these appeals. This would mean that they were restricted to deciding if HMRC's decision was unreasonable. The Tribunals could 'review the ... refusal in a Wednesbury context as being justified or not, but no further'.

DCM (Optical Holdings) Ltd maintained the Tribunals had greater rights when hearing these appeals. The First Division, Inner House, Court of Session found in favour of DCM (Optical Holdings) Ltd. The Court of Session described the role which Tribunals should play in appeals when HMRC reject a proposed special partial exemption methods as follows:

> '... a tribunal ... had no power itself to devise a special method and impose it on the parties. That, however, does not mean I that the only alternatives open to a tribunal are to accept a proposed method in all its particulars or reject it outright ... A method might be proposed ... which might ... be acceptable ... subject to modification ... These required modifications might become evident in the course of the hearing ... alternatively, the tribunal after deliberation might return with an indication to parties that it was minded to approve the method but only subject to identified modifications. Provided that the appellant was prepared, even subject to reservation of any right of further appeal, to accept these modifications, a tribunal would be entitled to approve the method so modified. We prefer this indication of the tribunal's powers ...'

The Court of Sessions remitted the DCM (Optical Holdings) Ltd appeal to the Tribunals which must now decide it along these lines.

Cases: *DCM (Optical Holdings) Ltd* [2006] BVC 2,708; *Associated Provincial Picture Houses Ltd v Wednesbury Corporation* [1948] 1 KB 223

CHANGE OF USE

7-470   Special provisions

There are special provisions to cover the position where input tax is attributed to an intended taxable supply but, in the event, the supply or importation on which the tax arose is actually used in respect of an exempt supply. There are similar provisions to deal with input tax attributed to an intended exempt supply if the supply, etc. is then used in respect of a taxable supply.

If input tax is attributed to one type of supply and, within six years and before the supply or importation is used for the originally intended purpose, it is used in making the other type of supply, the input tax attribution must be reviewed. The input tax deduction must be adjusted to that which would have applied under the method in use at the time of the original attribution. Where input tax was originally attributed as exempt input tax, and the supply or importation is redirected to taxable use, the trader must make an application to HMRC for repayment of the tax originally disallowed.

These 'redirection' provisions apply both to directly attributed input tax and to residual input tax. What happens, in effect, is a reworking of the whole partial exemption calculation for the period in which the initial deduction occurred.

The regulations do not make it clear whether this recalculation is for the longer period concerned, or merely for the return period. The better view is that it is for the longer period. See flowchart 7-970.

Input Tax Recovery

Legislation: *Value Added Tax Regulations* 1995 (SI 1995/2518), reg. 108 and 109

Other material: Notice 706, Section 11

7-495   Change of use following use for originally intended purpose

There are a number of cases on the consequences of a change in the use of inputs following use for the original purpose, the most notable being those of *Pembridge Estates Ltd* and *C & E Commrs v University of Wales College of Cardiff*. Also, of relevance is the case of *C & E Commrs v Briararch Ltd* which established that, when an attribution of input tax is made, account should be taken of intended future use as well as any known immediate use.

The rules which emerge from these cases may be summarised as follows:

(1)   a provisional attribution must be made in the prescribed accounting period in which the input tax arises, based on actual and intended use as known at that time;

(2)   when the annual adjustment is made for the longer period, the provisional attribution must be reviewed taking into account actual and intended use as known at the end of the longer period;

(3)   if within six years, and before the originally intended use takes place, the inputs are put to a different use, the original attribution is to be reviewed;

(4)   in certain cases involving land and computer equipment the original attribution is, in any case, reviewed slice by slice over a five or ten-year period under the capital goods scheme (7-760ff.); and

(5)   otherwise, the attribution as determined at the end of the longer period is final.

Cases: *Pembridge Estates Ltd* [1993] BVC 777; *C & E Commrs v University of Wales College of Cardiff* [1995] BVC 211

VAT Reporter: ¶19-550

7-500   Speculative property developers

HMRC have guidance on the attribution of input tax incurred by property developers in advance of making supplies, including input tax relating to projects which do not proceed.

It is important to note that the guidance is specifically concerned with the position where a developer incurs costs in connection with potential projects but is uncertain whether the resultant supplies (should the project proceed) will be taxable or exempt. The position where the nature of the supplies is known from the outset (such as in the case of a developer whose sole intention is to build and sell new houses, making zero-rated supplies) is the same as it has always been – input tax should be attributed to the intended type of supply when it is incurred. In this case, no subsequent adjustment is needed unless an actual supply is made which is different in liability from that originally intended.

The guidance is concerned with the initial attribution of input tax when the nature of the expected supplies is uncertain, the treatment of abortive projects, and the occasions when re-attribution is required. It seems applicable in principle to all cases where the position is initially uncertain, not just cases involving property developers.

Initial attribution

Where a developer is investigating potential projects (looking at locations or sites and assessing their suitability, seeking customers, etc.) without a clear idea of the precise nature of the supplies which will ultimately be made, and so of their VAT liability status, HMRC accept that this is a business activity and that the tax on the costs incurred is input tax in the hands of the developer. Since this input tax cannot be clearly linked with either taxable outputs or exempt outputs, it must be classed as residual. The extent of recovery will then be determined under the developer's partial exemption method.

Abortive projects

Where a particular project does not proceed, so that no supply is made by the developer, no further adjustment is required for input tax on costs relating to that project alone. Input tax on inputs which are diverted for use in another project will need to be re-attributed according to the nature of that other project.

Re-attribution of input tax

 The Value Added Tax Regulations provide for re-attribution of input tax where, after the initial attribution of the input tax and both:

- within six years of the initial attribution; and
- before the originally intended supplies are made,

either there is a change of intention or the trader uses the inputs in making a supply of a different nature from that initially intended. In such a case, a fresh attribution must be made, and an appropriate adjustment made in the current period to reflect the new attribution.

Where input tax has been treated as residual because the nature of the expected supplies was uncertain, and a decision is taken to proceed with a particular project, the original input tax must then be re-attributed according to the nature of the supplies which will result from the project.

HMRC expect that the decision to proceed will normally become firm at or about the time when the land is acquired (although this may not always be the case).

In cases where taxable supplies are expected, but these depend on the exercising of the option for taxation, HMRC consider that the tax cannot be re-attributed to taxable supplies until the option has in fact been exercised. They rely on the case of *Lawson Mardon Group Pension Scheme* in support of this view.

Input Tax Recovery

259

Cases: *Lawson Mardon Group Pension Scheme* [1993] BVC 892; *C & E Commrs v Curtis Henderson Ltd* [1992] BVC 118

Other material: VAT Information Sheet 08/01, December 2001; Notice 706, Section 11

Legislation: The *Value Added Tax Regulations* 1995 (SI 1995/2518), reg. 108 and 109

VAT Reporter: ¶43-260

7-510 House-builders – change of plans

It is possible that a builder constructs a dwelling – or dwellings – and is unable to sell it. Thus, it is decided to let the property before finally selling it.

Adjusting past returns

By letting a dwelling before making a zero-rated sale, the registered person triggers reg. 108 of the *Value Added Tax Regulations* 1995 (SI 1995/2518). This imposes an obligation to adjust claims made in previous periods when there is a change of plans.

Regulation 108 applies when an intended zero-rated disposal (e.g. the sale of a new dwelling) is proceeded by exempt supplies (e.g. the letting of the property). An adjustment is not necessary if the dwelling is let as holiday accommodation because these lettings are taxable.

This regulation overrides the normal four-year cap. It is necessary to consider making adjustments to periods beginning up to six years earlier.

How to calculate the adjustment

Adjustments due in these circumstances are calculated by making partial exemption calculations. The calculations which need to be made vary according to circumstances.

A builder who was partially exempt in the periods which need to be adjusted has to revise his previous workings. The original workings must be revisited and reworked to take account of the change in circumstances. The adjustment is the difference between the two sets of workings.

Many builders will not have been partially exempt or made partial exemption calculations for the periods which need to be adjusted. These must calculate the adjustment in the following manner:

(a) applying the partial exemption standard method to the periods which must be adjusted; or

(b) for these periods only, using a simpler method authorised by HMRC.

The simplified method cannot be used by a builder who was already partially exempt and making the necessary calculations.

HMRC's policy is to 'accept any clawback calculation provided it fairly reflects the use of costs in making taxable supplies'. They suggest this can be done by using 'reasonable estimates and valuations' of the total rental income and eventual sale price.

Example

Harry, a small speculative builder, has one new house unsold. He intends to let it for two years at £750 per month until market conditions improve. Eventually, he hopes to sell it for £250,000. His VAT periods ends on 31 December.

He paid no VAT on the land purchase. The total input tax claimed was £10,000 in the year to 31 March 2006 and £12,000 in the year to 31 December 2007.

The input tax attributable to the rents and which may have to be repaid is as follows:

$$\text{Repayable \%} \quad \frac{\text{total rents}}{\text{(selling price + total rents)}} = \frac{(24 \times £750)}{(£250,000 + £750 \times 24)} = 6.7\%$$

Adjustment for	2006	2007
	(£10,000 × 6.7%)	(£12,000 × 6.7%)
	(£670)	(£804)

(Note – it is necessary to consider all input tax for the years concerned, not merely that incurred on the direct costs.)

Finally, it is necessary to consider the 'de minimis' limits to decide if these amounts must be paid to HMRC.

'Simple check for de minimis'?

HMRC have put forward a quick test for 'de minimis'. This appears to presume that a dwelling has an economic life of 10 years, presumably because this dovetails with other adjustments – namely the Capital Goods Scheme and Lennartz accounting.

With this quick test, the exempt use is calculated as follows:

$$\frac{\text{Number of years let \%}}{10 \text{ years}}$$

For Harry in the example above, this would be (2 years ÷ 10 years) % i.e. 20%.

This percentage may be used to calculate the exempt input tax for the affected periods and when the exempt input tax is within the 'de minimis' limits an adjustment is not required. Better calculations must be made when the 'de minimis' limit is exceeded.

Input Tax Recovery

Current and future periods

The above adjustments only apply to past periods. An affected house builder must adopt and apply a partial exemption method for current and future periods. This will be the standard method unless a special method is agreed with, and authorised in advance, by HMRC.

Other material: VAT Information Sheet 07/08; Notice 706, Section 11

Legislation: *Value Added Tax Regulations* 1995 (SI 1995/2518), reg. 108

VAT Reporter: ¶19-580

COMPUTATION PRINCIPLES

7-520   De minimis limit

If a trader incurs exempt input tax, that input tax is non-deductible in principle. However, if the exempt input tax falls below the de minimis limit, then the trader's input tax for the period concerned is treated as wholly attributable to the making of taxable supplies, and so as being deductible.

The standard de minimis test

The exempt input tax falls below the de minimis limit if:

(1)   it is less than £625 per month on average (£7,500 per annum); and

(2)   it does not exceed 50 per cent of total input tax.

Exempt input tax for this purpose is the aggregate of:

- input tax directly attributed to exempt supplies; and
- the portion of residual input tax attributed to exempt supplies.

Example: de minimis limit for partial exemption

Becket Ltd has the following input tax analysis for the 12-month period ending on 31 March 2005:

	£
Taxable input tax	20,000
Exempt input tax	5,500
Total input tax	25,500

The company's exempt input tax is less than £625 per month on average (£7,500 for a 12-month period) and less than half the total input tax. Consequently, the exempt input tax is treated as attributable to taxable supplies, having fallen below the de minimis limit, and the whole of the input tax for the period can be recovered.

Alternative 'de minimis' tests

Alternative simplified 'de minimis' tests were introduced for partial exemption years beginning on or after 1 April 2010. The simplified 'de minimis' tests are targeted at businesses whose total input tax is less than £625 per month on average. These tests avoid the need for detailed partial exemption calculations.

Like the standard 'de minimis' test, the new tests must be considered every VAT period, and then applied to the year as whole (the annual adjustment).

If during any period (or complete year) the parameters allowing a business to use the simplified tests are contravened, the business must revert to carrying full and detailed partial exemption calculations (i.e. the standard method) for the period or year concerned.

See flowchart at 7-985 for details of the calculations needed.

Annual 'de minimis' test

Following a year in which the 'de minimis' limits were not exceeded, certain businesses may operate for the next year on the basis that they will again not exceed these limits. These businesses may choose to forego 'de minimis' tests each period. Instead, they apply the 'de minimis' only once when completing an annual calculation at the end of the year.

This option is restricted to businesses whose total input tax is usually less than £1m.

Legislation: *Value Added Tax Regulations* 1995 (SI 1995/2518), reg. 105A and reg. 106

Other material: Notice 706, Section 9; VAT Information Sheet 04/10 Partial Exemption – changes to the de minimis rules

VAT Reporter: ¶19-430

7-530   Calculation of tax

The calculation of deductible input tax is, in principle, an annual calculation. The final calculation is normally done for a VAT year to 31 March, 30 April or 31 May, depending upon the trader's VAT quarter. This may vary, as discussed below.

Although the final calculation is for a full year, a provisional calculation must be made for each return period. This provisional calculation follows the same basic rules as the annual calculation.

After the VAT year is over, the trader must aggregate the figures from the provisional calculations made for the separate return periods, and make a final calculation for the year as a whole. The input tax deductible for the year as a whole is calculated and compared with that actually deducted in the return periods. Any under or over-deduction is then entered on the first VAT return of the next year, or the last return for the year concerned.

Input Tax Recovery

Example: provisional and final calculations

A trader's input tax analysis for the VAT year to 31 March 2005 is as follows:

Quarter to	Taxable input tax £	Exempt input tax £	Below de minimis?	Deductible input tax £
30/6/04	6,200	1,900	No	6,200
30/9/04	6,100	1,450	Yes	7,550
31/12/04	8,450	1,600	Yes	10,050
31/3/05	4,200	1,850	Yes	4,200
	24,950	6,800		28,000

The annual adjustment is as follows:

	£
Taxable input tax	24,950
Exempt input tax	6,800
Total	31,750
Exempt input tax is no more than both £625 per month and 50 per cent of all the input tax	£7,200

	£
Therefore tax recoverable	31,750
Tax previously recovered	(28,000)
Giving a further deduction of	3,750

This further deduction of £3,750 should be entered on the trader's VAT return for the quarter to 30 June 2005.

Legislation: *Value Added Tax Regulations* 1995 (SI 1995/2518), reg. 101(1)(g)

VAT Reporter: ¶19-459

Standard method override

The final calculation may need to be made by reference to the 'standard method override'. See flowchart 7-980.

This does not apply to traders using a special partial exemption method (see 7-310ff.). It only applies to a standard method trader if that trader's residual input tax for the year is greater than £50,000 (or, in the case of a company capable of inclusion in a VAT group but not so included, greater than £25,000).

When making its final calculation for the VAT year, an affected business must calculate its input tax recovery for the year as a whole, not only under the standard method but also by reference to the use and intended use of the inputs concerned (see 7-330).

An adjustment must be made if the use based result is 'substantially' different from the standard method result. The difference is substantial if:

(1)   it exceeds £50,000; or

(2)   it exceeds 50 per cent of residual input tax and also exceeds £25,000.

Smaller businesses should not be affected by this. The provisions seem to be particularly aimed at cases where schemes are arranged so that inputs are obtained in one tax year and used wholly for taxable purposes in that tax year, but the main use of the inputs takes place in later years for exempt purposes.

Exempt input tax within de minimis limits

The standard method override adjustment is triggered by input tax attributable to exempt supplies. If there is none, as is the case when, because of the 'de minimis' limits, all input tax is deemed to be attributable to taxable supplies, the override provision does not apply. This was the ruling of the VAT and Duties Tribunal in *Camden Motor (Holdings) Ltd*. HMRC have not yet announced if they will be appealing against this decision.

Legislation: *Value Added Tax Regulations* 1995 (SI 1995/2518), reg. 107

Other material: Notice 706, Section 5

Case: *Camden Motor (Holdings) Ltd* No. 20,674 [2008] BVC 2,442

VAT Reporter: ¶19-470

7-560   Tax years and longer periods

As indicated at 7-530 above, a trader is normally required to make a provisional attribution of input tax for each prescribed accounting period (i.e. VAT return period), and then review this for a 'longer period'. A business which regularly incurs exempt input tax will almost always have a longer period which is the same as its VAT tax year.

The tax year is a period of 12 months ending on 31 March, 30 April or 31 May, depending upon the business's VAT accounting period. For a business making monthly returns, the tax year will normally end on 31 March.

A trader's first tax year is the first 'full' tax year (the part year from the date of registration to the normal tax year-end being known as the 'registration period'). HMRC have the power to approve or direct a different first tax year.

A different tax year is sometimes used in order to have a tax year which corresponds with the business's financial year.

In the normal course of events, a trader's longer period is the same as the tax year. However, a different longer period may be used by mutual consent of the trader and HMRC.

Input Tax Recovery

Legislation: *Value Added Tax Regulations* 1995 (SI 1995/2518), reg. 99(1) and (3)–(7)

Other material: Notice 706, Section 10

VAT Reporter: ¶19-520

7-580   Incurring exempt input tax for the first time

If a trader incurs exempt input tax, and did not incur exempt input tax in the preceding VAT tax year, the longer period runs from the beginning of the VAT period in which exempt input tax was first incurred to the end of the tax year, rather than covering the whole tax year.

Example: longer periods

PX Ltd's VAT accounting periods are based on calendar quarters, and its VAT year runs to 31 March. Its exempt input tax for the three years to 31 March 2005 is as follows:

Year to 31 March	2003	2004	2005
	£	£	£
Quarter to:			
30 June	–	–	–
30 September	–	–	5,000
31 December	–	2,000	6,000
31 March	–	4,500	–

As the company incurred no exempt input tax in the year to 31 March 2003, it is not concerned with the partial exemption rules for that year.

It will be concerned with partial exemption for the year to 31 March 2004, since it incurred exempt input tax in the quarter to 31 December 2003. It must make a provisional attribution for that quarter, and a final attribution for its longer period. As there was no exempt input tax incurred in the year to 31 March 2003, the longer period runs from 1 October 2003 (the start of the accounting period in which exempt input tax was first incurred) and ends on 31 March 2004 (the end of the tax year).

The company must also make provisional attributions for the quarters to 30 September 2004, 31 December 2004 and 31 March 2005. As it incurred exempt input tax in the previous tax year, the longer period for its final calculation in this case runs from 1 April 2004 (the start of the tax year) to 31 March 2005 (the end of the tax year).

There is a special rule for a trader who incurs exempt input tax only in the last accounting period of the tax year, and did not incur exempt input tax in the previous tax year. In this case, no longer period applies, so the provisional calculation for the accounting period is also the final calculation. This generally works against the trader's interests, since it prevents the use of the de minimis limits at 'full year' rates.

Legislation: *Value Added Tax Regulations* 1995 (SI 1995/2518), reg. 99(3)–(7)

VAT Reporter: ¶19-520

7-600   Newly registered businesses

As indicated at 7-530 above, the period from registration to the beginning of the first full tax year is known as the 'registration period'.

If a business incurs exempt input tax in its registration period, the longer period which applies runs from the first day on which exempt input tax is incurred and finishes at the end of the following 31 March, 30 April, or 31 May when the normal tax year would end.

> ### *Example: newly registered business*
>
> Newly-Reg Ltd is registered for VAT with effect from 1 August 2005. It makes returns for quarters ending on 31 October, etc. Its registration period therefore runs from 1 August 2005 to 30 April 2006, and its first tax year starts on 1 May 2006.
>
> The company incurs exempt input tax for the first time on 1 March 2006, and its exempt input tax for the months of March and April 2006 totals £1,400. Its taxable input tax for those months totals £28,000.
>
> The provisional calculation for the quarter ending on 30 April 2006 shows that exempt input tax is below £625 per month on average (3 × £625 = £1,875). Consequently, the exempt input tax is treated as attributable to taxable supplies, and can be recovered on the VAT return for that quarter.
>
> However, the company must make a final calculation based on the longer period from 1 March 2006 to 30 April 2006. As the exempt input tax exceeds £625 per month on average (2 × £625 = £1,250, compared with exempt input tax of £1,400), the de minimis limit is exceeded and the exempt input tax cannot be deducted. The company must pay back the exempt input tax by way of an adjustment on its return for the quarter to 31 July 2006.

It follows that the longer period of such a business will almost invariably be shorter than the combined lengths of the accounting periods affected, making it more difficult to meet the de minimis limits.

In the case of a business which is late in registering for VAT, and has an initial return period longer than six months, there is provision for this long period to be broken up into three-monthly chunks for partial exemption purposes.

In *Dunn* [1997] BVC 4,080, the trader was registered with effect from 1 January 1994. On appeal to the tribunal, it was held that the appellant's first tax year began on 1 April 1994. Thus, the initial 'longer period' or registration period was from 1 January 1994 to 31 March 1994.

Input Tax Recovery

Example

Fred registers belatedly. His first return VAT period runs from 1st October 2004 to 31 July 2006. The first normal return will be for the three months to 31 October 2006. The 21-month return covers a special accounting period which must be subdivided into the following 'periods':

'Longer period' 1:

(a) 1 October 2004 to 31 January 2005; and

(b) 1 February 2005 to 30 April 2005.

'Longer period' 2:

(a) 1 May 2005 to 31 July 2005;

(b) 1 August 2005 to 31 October 2005;

(c) 1 November 2005 to 31 January 2006; and

(d) 1 February 2006 to 30 April 2006.

'Longer period' 3:

1 May 2006 to 31 July 2006.

Fred's initial 'longer' period is from 1 October 2004 to 30 April 2005.

'Longer period' 2 is from 1 May 2005 to 30 April 2006.

'Longer period' 3 starts on 1 May 2006 and will run to 30 April 2007.

Legislation: *Value Added Tax Regulations* 1995 (SI 1995/2518), reg. 99(1)(e) and (4)

Other material: Notice 706, para. 10.7

VAT Reporter: ¶19-520

7-610 Newly registered businesses – calculations

Often, the partial exemption standard method does not work well with newly registered businesses. This is because their sales may not have started or fluctuate wildly.

Until 1 April 2009, the only alternative to using the standard method was to agree a special partial exemption method with HMRC. This has been relaxed in two situations. The two situations are as follows:

• When a partially exempt business registers for VAT.

• When an already registered business becomes partially exempt.

For the 'registration period' and the next partial exemption year, the business concerned has an alternative to using the standard method (or applying for a special method). The alternative is to reclaim VAT on the basis of the use to which the VAT bearing costs are put.

A similar choice exists for business which become partially exempt whilst being VAT-registered. For its initial partial exemption 'year', the business concerned may choose to not use the standard method (or applying for a special method) and instead reclaim VAT on the basis of the use.

HMRC's brief description the use based procedure is as follows:

'In simple terms, the principle of use means examining the main categories of business expenditure and determining how they relate to business supplies. In many ways, this is no more than an exercise in cost accounting.'

For more information about use based methods see 7-330.

Example

Property Owner Ltd is not trading nor is it VAT-registered. It owns a development site. Planning consent has been obtained for housing. Property Owner plans to build the housing – some of which it will sell and some which it will let. Its business plan is as follows:

- To build a total of 50 houses.
- To let 10 and sell 40.
- The first income not expected until April 2010.

Property Owner registers for VAT before building work starts. The agreed registration date is 1 May 2009. Its VAT periods will end on the calendar quarters. Its first periods and initial partial exemption 'year' will be as follows:

(1)   Period 1 – 1 May 2009 to 30 June 2009.

(2)   Period 2 – quarter ending 30 September 2009.

(3)   Period 3 – quarter ending 31 December 2009.

(4)   Period 4 – quarter ending 31 March 2010.

(5)   Initial partial exemption 'year'/registration period – 1 May 2009 to 31 March 2010.

The standard partial exemption method is not appropriate for these periods as there will not be any income until April 2010. Instead, Property Owner opts to apply the use based method. As a result, the partial exemption workings will be as follows:

Input tax on –	Period 1	Period 2	Period 3	Period 4
	£	£	£	£
direct costs of houses for sale	10,000	8,500	11,000	9,000
direct costs of houses for letting	2,000	3,000	2,500	4,000
other costs	1,500	2,000	3,000	1,750
	13,500	13,500	16,500	14,750

Input tax attributable to taxable supplies –	direct costs	2,000	3,000	2,500	4,000
	other costs	300	400	600	350
exempt input tax		2,300	3,400	3,100	4,350
Input tax attributable to taxable supplies –	direct costs	10,000	8,500	11,000	9,000
	other costs	1,200	1,600	2,400	1,400
Reclaimable input tax		11,200	10,100	13,400	10,400
exempt input tax within 'de minimis' limits –		0	0	0	0
Total reclaimable		11,200	10,100	13,400	10,400

Notes

(1) Input tax on other costs apportioned in the ratio of number of houses to be sold (40) to the number to be let (10).

(2) Using the same methodology the 'annual' adjustment will be nil.

Legislation: *Value Added Tax Regulations* 1995, reg. 101

Other material: VAT Information Sheet 11/09

7-620 Business ceasing to be registered

As would be expected, where a person ceases to be a taxable person and so is de-registered, the longer period ends on the day when the person ceases to be taxable.

Legislation: *Value Added Tax Regulations* 1995 (SI 1995/2518), reg. 99(6)

VAT Reporter: ¶19-520

7-640 Approval of different longer period

A different longer period from those set out above can be used if this is approved by HMRC. However, they do not have power to direct that a different longer period be used against the trader's will.

Legislation: *Value Added Tax Regulations* 1995 (SI 1995/2518), reg. 99(7)

VAT Reporter: ¶19-520

NON-SUPPLY ACTIVITIES AND SELF-SUPPLIES

7-700   Non-business activities

It is essential that all input tax associated with non-business activities is eliminated before applying any partial exemption method. Consequently there is a two stage process for partially exempt businesses that also have non-business activities. These businesses must first quantify and disallow input tax relating to the non-business activities. Only after doing this may they carry out the necessary partial exemption calculations.

Businesses and organisations that face this dilemma may apply to HMRC to use a single 'special method' to quantify how much input tax is attributable to non-business activities, exempt supplies and taxable supplies. The input tax attributable to non-business activities is not reclaimable and that attributable to exempt supplies in only reclaimable if it is within the de minimis limits.

Combined 'special methods' of this type are allowable under the partial exemption regulations from 1 January 2011. If approved they will be similar to and subject to many of the conditions applying to partial exemption special methods.

Legislation *Value Added Tax Regulations* 1995 (SI 1995/2518), reg. 102ZA

Other material: Revenue and Customs Brief 47/10

VAT Reporter: ¶19-600

7-720   Self-supplies

It should be borne in mind that input tax arising on self-supplies must be brought into the partial exemption calculations (although the self-supplies themselves are excluded from turnover under the standard method). This can arise in respect of imports of services, on the acquisition of a business as a going concern by a partially exempt group of companies (see 17-840ff.), and on certain matters relating to land and buildings (see 15-150ff.).

Input tax on a self-supply cannot be attributed to the self-supply itself.

Legislation: *Value Added Tax Regulations* 1995 (SI 1995/2518), reg. 104

VAT Reporter: ¶12-795

Input Tax Recovery

CAPITAL GOODS SCHEME

7-760   Introduction to the capital goods scheme

Further complications have been introduced for input tax in the form of the capital goods scheme.

The purpose of the scheme is to prevent partially exempt traders from making full recovery of input tax on major acquisitions by putting them wholly to taxable use in the period of acquisition, then switching them to exempt use.

The method adopted is to allow the initial deduction (or disallowance) to be made in the ordinary way, but to review this in later periods and make adjustments to the initial deduction in the light of subsequent use.

Legislation: *Value Added Tax Regulations* 1995 (SI 1995/2518), reg. 112–116

Other material: Notice 706/2

VAT Reporter: ¶19-800

7-770   Capital item

The term 'capital item' was considered in *Shurgard Storage Centres UK Ltd (t/a West London Self-storage Centre)*. The VAT and Duties Tribunals explained it as follows:

'The phrase "capital item" means … an item which the owner "uses in the course or furtherance of his business, otherwise than solely for the purpose of selling" such use, properly understood connotes use, as a capital item for making taxable supplies within the business.'

Cases: *Shurgard Storage Centres UK Ltd (t/a West London Self-storage Centre)*No. 20,797 [2009] BVC 2,139

Legislation: *Value Added Tax Regulations* 1995 (SI 1995/2518), reg. 112(2)

7-775   Assets used for business and private purposes

From 1 January 2011 the Capital Goods Scheme will apply to certain assets used both for business and private purposes. The relevant assets are land, buildings, civil engineering works, boats and aircraft.

Legislation: *Value Added Tax Regulations* 1995 (SI 1995/2518), reg. 113

Other material: VAT Information Sheet 06/11

7-780   Input tax affected under capital goods scheme

The capital goods scheme applies to input tax on the supply or importation of:

(1)   computer equipment costing £50,000 or more. The £50,000 limit is applied to each item of equipment separately. A system consisting of a number of items each costing less than £50,000 is not affected, even though the total system cost may exceed £50,000;

(2)   land, buildings, parts of buildings, and certain extensions or alterations, costing £250,000 or more. The scheme applies to both freehold and leasehold acquisitions, and to self-supplies. The extensions and alterations affected are those which increase the floor area of the building by 10 per cent or more;

(3)   the capital goods scheme also applies to civil engineering works costing £250,000 or more, whether bought in or constructed by the trader, and to any buildings refurbished or fitted out at a capital cost of £250,000 or more (regardless of any change in floor area);

(4)   aircraft costing £50,000 or more;

(5)   ships, boats or other vessels costing £50,000 or more.

The expenditure to be taken into account in considering the thresholds includes whether or not it would normally be considered to be capital expenditure, consideration in the form of rent paid or payable more than 12 months in advance, or invoiced for a period in excess of 12 months.

Self-storage infrastructure

All supplies of self-storage are standard-rated from 1 October 2012 (see 15-200). To provide relief for infrastructure installed before then and for which input tax was not reclaimed self-storage operators may select to apply the Capital Goods Scheme to this input tax. The decision to do this must be made before 31 March 2013.

This relief is available for input tax incurred on or in respect of land, buildings, parts of buildings, extensions or alterations and civil engineering works. Other expenditure incurred to make supplies of self-storage does not qualify of this relief.

The advantage of this relief is that it applies to any qualifying infrastructure costing more than £1 (excluding VAT).

When there is qualifying expenditure and the necessary election is made before 31 March 2013, affected businesses apply the 10-year adjustment period and calculate adjustments in the same way as for land etc costing more than £250,000 – see 7-800.

Legislation: *Value Added Tax Regulations* 1995 (SI 1995/2518), reg. 113 and 113A

Other material: Notice 706/2, Section 3 and 4; VAT Information Sheet 06/11

VAT Reporter: ¶19-800

Input Tax Recovery

7-800 Period and manner of adjustment under capital goods scheme

The adjustment period is, broadly, 10 years for land, buildings and civil engineering works; it may be less if the asset is a lease with less than 10 years to run. For all other relevant assets the adjustment period is normally 5 years.

The initial deduction is made in the ordinary way, but must then be reviewed in each of the remaining years (four for computer equipment or an interest in land having less than 10 years to run when acquired, nine for other land) of the adjustment period. In each period, the deductible proportion (using the then current partial exemption method) is calculated for the appropriate proportion of the input tax originally incurred (20 per cent or 10 per cent, depending on the length of the adjustment period). This is compared with the initial deduction and an appropriate adjustment is made. This adjustment is made on the second VAT return after the end of the period to which it relates.

Example: capital goods scheme adjustment

Kapex Ltd acquires a new building for £1 million plus £175,000 VAT. In the year of acquisition, its partial exemption method enables it to recover 60 per cent of the VAT on the building. In the next year, the recovery percentage increases to 70 per cent and in the following year it drops to 55 per cent.

In the first year, Kapex recovers £105,000 of the VAT on the building.

In the next year, it must review the position for £17,500 of the input tax. The current amount recoverable is £12,250, compared with £10,500 originally recovered, so an extra £1,750 can be reclaimed. In the following year, the amount recoverable falls to £9,625, so Kapex must repay £875 of the £10,500 originally recovered.

Where a change in liability arises because of the exercising of the option for taxation for property subject to the capital goods scheme (15-120ff.), the resulting input tax recovery adjustments must be dealt with under the capital goods scheme, not under a 'fair and reasonable' adjustment on opting to tax.

The University of Essex required new student accommodation. A stand alone company, Universal Accommodation Group Ltd (UAG), was formed to acquire the land and build the accommodation. After building the accommodation, UAG granted a long lease to the University. The lease was taxable – 98% zero rated and 2% standard rated because of opting to tax. Later, UAG joined the University of Essex's VAT group.

The First Tier Tribunal ruled that the VAT group was not required to make CGS adjustments because there was a zero-rated supply before UAG joined the VAT group to which all the input tax should be attributed. According to the Tribunal 'the only relevant supply ... was the zero rated supply, and consequently no adjustment falls to be made to the recovery of input tax attributable to that supply'.

Legislation: *Value Added Tax Regulations* 1995 (SI 1995/2518), reg. 114, 115 and 116

Other material: Notice 706/2, Section 6; VAT Information Sheet 06/11

Cases: *C & E Commrs v Trustees for R & R Pension Fund* [1996] BVC 348; *University of Essex* [2010] UKFTT 162 (TC); [2010] TC 00467

VAT Reporter: ¶19-868

7-805   Assets on hand at registration

If a Capital Goods Scheme asset is owned when registering for VAT, there may be ongoing Capital Goods Scheme adjustments. This applies to persons registering on or after 1 January 2011. Prior to this an extra-statuary concession applied to relevant land, buildings or civil engineering works on hand at registration.

Persons in this situation may not have to apply as appropriate 5 or 10 adjustment intervals to the asset concerned. For each full year that the asset is used prior to registration, the number of adjustment periods is lessened by one.

An adjustment is due for each adjustment interval that ends after the date of registration.

Legislation: *Value Added Tax Regulations* 1995 (SI 1995/2518), reg. 114(3D)

Other material: Notice 706/2, para. 8.6; VAT Information Sheet 06/11

7-810   Interaction of adjustments with partial exemption de minimis limit

As noted above, where inputs are subject to the capital goods scheme, the initial recovery (or non-recovery) of input tax is determined by the use to which the inputs concerned are put during the (longer) period within which the input tax is incurred. This is then adjusted, over time, according to the use made of those inputs during subsequent VAT periods.

The tricky bit arises when you consider how to determine the use of these inputs in the future periods. This becomes particularly complicated when you remember that the partial exemption rules include de minimis provisions whereby a relatively small amount of exempt input tax may be ignored, and the taxable person treated as fully taxable.

The main legislation on the determination of use in future periods is as follows:

'Subject to regulation 115(3) and (3B) and paragraphs (2), (A2) and (3) below, for the purposes of this Part, an attribution of the total input tax on the capital item shall be determined for each subsequent interval applicable to it in accordance with the method used under Part XIV for that interval and the proportion of the input tax thereby determined to be attributable to taxable supplies shall be treated as being the extent to which the capital item is used in making taxable supplies in that subsequent interval.'

Input Tax Recovery

275

Exactly how to apply this is problematical, but the following sets out what is understood to be the view taken by HMRC. This view has no real effect on very large partially exempt businesses, but may be of benefit to businesses which are mainly treated as fully taxable, but could be tipped into partial exemption by some large capital expenditure.

The attribution of the tax arising on the initial spend (for instance, £300,000 plus VAT on a property intended for significant exempt use) is dealt with in the ordinary way. This may well breach the de minimis limits and lead to a disallowance of input tax.

When the position is reviewed in later periods, the proportion of taxable use is ascertained by reference to the input tax actually incurred in those periods. The input tax (or proportion of input tax) relating to the item subject to the capital goods scheme is ignored.

The important point is that HMRC consider that the determination of the proportion of use 'in accordance with the method used under Part XIV' includes the application of the de minimis limit to the current exempt input tax.

It follows that, if the business is treated as fully taxable, using the de minimis rules and ignoring the 'reviewed' portion of input tax on the capital goods, then its use of the asset for the period is considered to be fully taxable and it can recover any part of the input tax currently under review which has previously been disallowed.

The important point is that HMRC do not see the 'reviewed' input tax as counting towards the de minimis limit in the subsequent period when the initial recovery is reviewed. This is a pretty difficult concept to get to grips with, but it makes sense. That input tax will have counted towards the de minimis limit in the period when the input tax was originally incurred, and perhaps led to a disallowance of 'revenue' input tax which would normally have been deductible.

Taking it into account a second time for de minimis purposes could amount to a form of double taxation.

Legislation: *Value Added Tax Regulations* 1995 (SI 1995/2518), reg. 116(1)

Other material: Notice 706, para. 9.4

VAT Reporter: ¶19-926

7-820   Disposal, etc. within review period

If an asset to which the capital goods scheme applies is disposed of within the adjustment period, use for the remaining complete intervals of the adjustment period is deemed to be taxable or exempt according to the status of the supply made on disposal of the asset. The appropriate adjustment is made at the same time as the adjustment for the period of disposal.

If a capital item is lost, stolen or destroyed or if a lease expires during the adjustment period, an adjustment is not necessary for the remaining complete intervals.

When a business is transferred as a going concern the transferee takes over responsibility for carrying out the capital goods scheme (CGS) adjustment for any remaining intervals. Since this could result in a new owner having to repay input tax which was reclaimed by the vendor, or in being able to recover additional input tax, warranties and indemnities arranged at the time of the transfer should reflect this.

A provision 'caps' the input tax recovery where an asset is disposed of within the review period. The total recovery of input tax (i.e. initial deduction and the total of adjustments under the capital goods scheme, including the final adjustment) in respect of the asset disposed of cannot exceed the amount of output tax due on the disposal, and any excess recovery must be repaid.

Clearly, this provision would give an unfair result in many circumstances. For instance, if a computer system was bought for £1m plus VAT, used wholly for taxable purposes, then sold after four years for its then market value of £100,000 plus VAT, the capping provision would require the trader, on selling the system, to repay 90 per cent of the input tax originally reclaimed: more than the sale proceeds.

The legislation seeks to cope with this, in a rough and ready way, by providing that capping is to apply 'save as the Commissioners otherwise allow'. HMRC have published a statement of practice indicating how they propose to use this power, either to waive the capping requirement altogether or to limit its effect to what is necessary to prevent the trader from obtaining what they see as 'an unjustified tax advantage'.

Legislation: *Value Added Tax Regulations* 1995 (SI 1995/2518), reg. 114(5A), reg. 115(4), 115(3A) and 115(3B)

Other material: Notice 706/2, Sections 8 and 9

VAT Reporter: ¶19-868

When capping is not applied

HMRC say that they will not require the application of the capping provision at all in the following circumstances:

(1) sales of computer equipment;

(2) where an owner disposes of an item at a loss due to market conditions (such as a general downturn in property prices);

(3) where the value of the item has depreciated;

(4) where the value of the item is reduced for other legitimate reasons (such as accepting a lower price to effect a quick sale);

(5) where the amount of output tax on disposal is less than the input tax claimed only due to a reduction in the VAT rate;

(6) where the item is used only for taxable (including zero-rated) purposes throughout the adjustment period (which includes the final disposal).

Input Tax Recovery

In other words, the provision will generally not be applied, but you cannot know this for certain without checking with HMRC case by case. Normally the cap is only applied in cases of avoidance or abuse.

Extent of capping

Even where the capping provision does have effect, HMRC will not normally require it to be applied to its maximum effect. Rather, they expect the trader to agree with them the amount of the 'unjustified tax advantage'. The kind of circumstance they envisage is where a trader engineers a high value exempt supply of the asset followed by a low value taxable supply of the residual interest in it. They see the 'net tax advantage' as being the amount of input tax recovery relating to the disposal (i.e. the tax relating to the unexpired intervals at the time the disposal is made). They accept that some portion of this does properly relate to the final taxable supply, but they also regard part of it as relating to the large exempt supply which preceded the final disposal, and they suggest apportioning the 'net tax advantage' in the proportion of these taxable and exempt supplies to arrive at the 'unjustified tax advantage'.

If an asset is supplied as part of a transfer of a going concern, the new owner takes over the obligation to make adjustments under the capital goods scheme.

If an asset is lost, stolen, or destroyed (or a short lease expires) no further adjustments are made.

Other material: Notice 706/2 section 8 'Capital Goods Scheme'

VAT Reporter: ¶19-884

7-830   Residential property developers

HM Revenue and Customs have released information about the interaction between residential property developments and the Capital Goods Scheme. In certain circumstances, residential property developments are within the scope of the Capital Goods Scheme.

Residential property developers who grant leasehold interests need to consider the Capital Goods Scheme. This is so even when granting a leasehold interest which is a zero-rated supply.

Other material: Business Brief 23/06 22 December 2006

7-840   Other matters

It should be noted that adjustments under the capital goods scheme may give rise to the need for adjustments to the accounts, and to capital allowances computations for direct tax purposes.

Although the capital goods scheme affects partially exempt traders, this does not mean that fully taxable businesses can ignore it. A person who is fully taxable when the input tax arises but becomes partially exempt during the adjustment period must also apply the scheme. A particular danger is that a fully taxable trader may buy a new building, and then sell it within the adjustment period by way of exempt supply. The remaining intervals will be attributed to exempt use, with significant loss of input tax.

VAT Reporter: ¶19-800

7-880   Conclusion

It is a fundamental underlying principle of VAT that businesses which make taxable supplies should be able to recover input tax incurred in making them, but unable to recover other input tax.

This part of the commentary has reviewed the mechanics by which the UK legislation seeks to achieve this goal.

The most important thing to bear in mind about the UK system (apart from recognising its complexity) is that it is based around an analysis of the input tax incurred by the business. It follows that all traders need to be able to carry out such an analysis even if only to prove that they are not affected by the partial exemption rules, if this is in fact the case.

Input Tax Recovery

FLOWCHARTS

7-900 Is VAT recoverable?

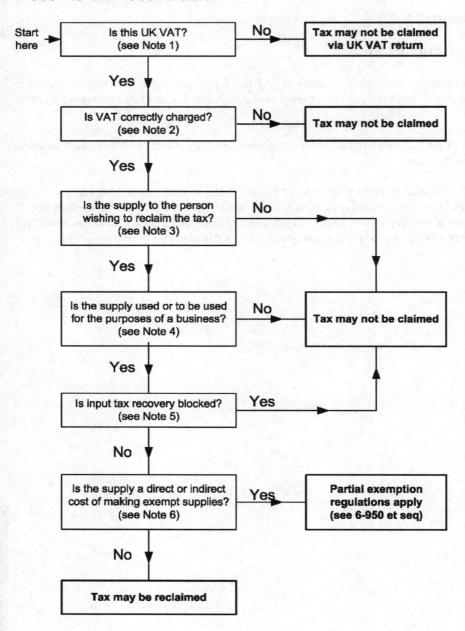

Start here → **Is this UK VAT?** (see Note 1) — **No** → **Tax may not be claimed via UK VAT return**

Yes ↓

Is VAT correctly charged? (see Note 2) — **No** → **Tax may not be claimed**

Yes ↓

Is the supply to the person wishing to reclaim the tax? (see Note 3) — **No** →

Yes ↓

Is the supply used or to be used for the purposes of a business? (see Note 4) — **No** → **Tax may not be claimed**

Yes ↓

Is input tax recovery blocked? (see Note 5) — **Yes** →

No ↓

Is the supply a direct or indirect cost of making exempt supplies? (see Note 6) — **Yes** → **Partial exemption regulations apply (see 6-950 et seq)**

No ↓

Tax may be reclaimed

Notes

(1) Pre-conditions

This flowchart assumes that the person who has incurred the input tax is registered for VAT in the UK and holds the necessary documentation (see 6-460.)

(2) Foreign VAT

VAT incurred in other EU States may be recovered according to the regulations of the State concerned and by making a claim to that State (see 6-780.)

(3) Person to whom the supply is made

The person to whom the supply is made is normally the person who orders the goods or commissions the service in question. It is not necessarily the person who pays for the goods or service. An exception is expenditure by an employee on subsistence expenses or on car fuel (see 6-160 and 6-200).

(4) Non-business expenditure

Input tax incurred for private or non-business purposes is not recoverable. Input tax incurred for business and non-business purposes must be apportioned (see 6-240).

(5) Non-deductible input tax

Certain input tax is not recoverable or blocked (see 6-280).

(6) Exempt supplies

Input tax incurred on costs used to make exempt supplies is not normally recoverable and specific regulations apply (see 6-950).

Input Tax Recovery

7-905 Is VAT on the purchase of a car recoverable?

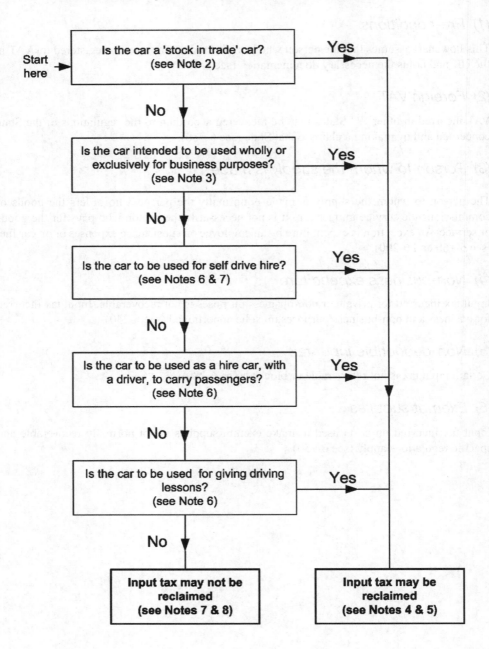

Notes

(1) Cars

For the definition of a car, see 6-300.

(2) 'Stock in trade cars'

'Stock in trade' means obtained by a motor dealer, or produced by a manufacturer, for resale and intended to be sold within 12 months of:

(a)   supply, acquisition or importation by the motor dealer; or
(b)   production by the manufacturer.

(3) Used wholly or exclusively for business purposes

To satisfy this condition, it is necessary to prove that the car is unavailable for private use. Insuring the car for private/business use is normally sufficient to prevent input tax recovery (see 6-300).

(4) Private use

When input tax is reclaimable, tax must be accounted for on any private use. For information, see 3-160 and section 6, Notice 700/64.

(5) Self-supplies

When input tax is recoverable, a change of circumstances can trigger a 'self-supply' tax charge (see 3-200).

(6) Primary purpose

The primary purpose must be 'self drive hire', to give driving lessons or to use as a hire, with a driver, to carry passengers.

(7) Self drive hire

Self drive hire is when the hirer is drives the car and the period of hire is:

(a)   less than 30 consecutive days; and
(b)   less than 90 days in any period of 12 months.

(8) Leasing or hiring a car

Input tax incurred on hiring or leasing is normally limited to 50 per cent recovery (see 6-300).

(9) Cars let to handicapped persons

Input tax may also be reclaimed by a person whose sole taxable supplies involving the letting of cars on hire to another taxable person, whose business in turn consists mainly of providing

Input Tax Recovery

motor cars, broadly, to disabled persons in receipt of a mobility allowance. Further advice should be sought in connection with these situations.

7-910   Is the vehicle a 'motor car'?

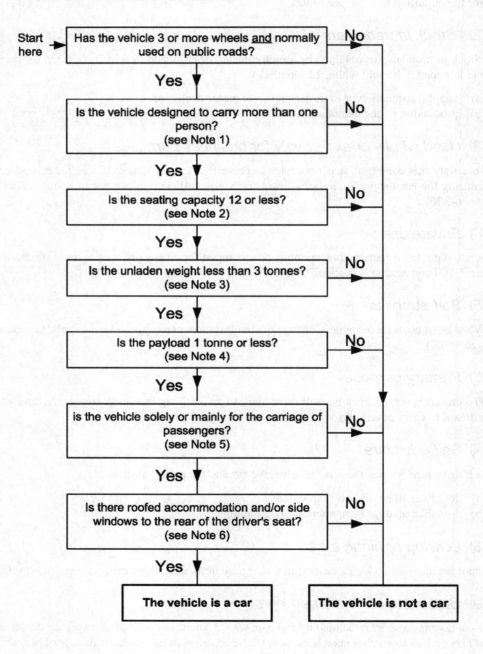

Notes

(1) A vehicle capable of carrying only one person is not a car.

(2) These vehicles must also comply with the requirements of the *Road Vehicles (Construction and Use) Regulations* 1986, Sch. 6.

(3) 'Unladen weight' is defined in the *Road Vehicles (Construction and Use) Regulations* 1986, reg. 3(2), Table.

(4) 'Payload' is the difference between a vehicle's kerb weight and maximum gross weight. These terms are defined in the Table to the *Road Vehicles (Construction and Use) Regulations* 1986, reg. 3(2), Table.

(5) Caravans, ambulances or prison vans are not cars nor are vehicles constructed for a special purpose which is not the carriage of persons and, except for any incidental accommodation, does not have any accommodation for carrying persons.

(6) This includes roofed accommodation that is constructed or adapted for the fitting of side windows.

Input Tax Recovery

7-915   Is input tax on business entertainment recoverable?

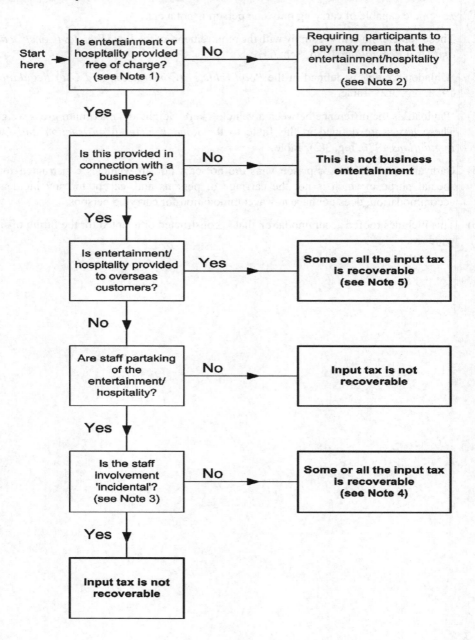

Notes

(1) Free entertainment or hospitality

Free entertainment or hospitality is to give people free meals and/or free accommodation.

(2) Nominal charges

The VAT & Duties Tribunals decided that entertainment was not free when those attending paid an amount which was 'not so small that one could say the meal was effectively supplied free of charge'.

(3) Incidental staff involvement

Input tax may not be recovered when the staff entertainment (e.g. acting as hosts) is incidental to provision of free entertainment/hospitality.

(4) Staff entertainment

Input tax is recoverable if the purpose of entertaining the staff is to reward them for good work or to maintain and improve staff morale.

(5) Overseas customers

In the CEJ case of *Danfoss A/S and Astra Zenica A/S v Skatteministeriet* it was decided that some VAT incurred when entertaining overseas customers is reclaimable – see 6-320.

(6) Further information

For further information, see 6-320.

7-920 Recovery of VAT on building materials used in new dwellings

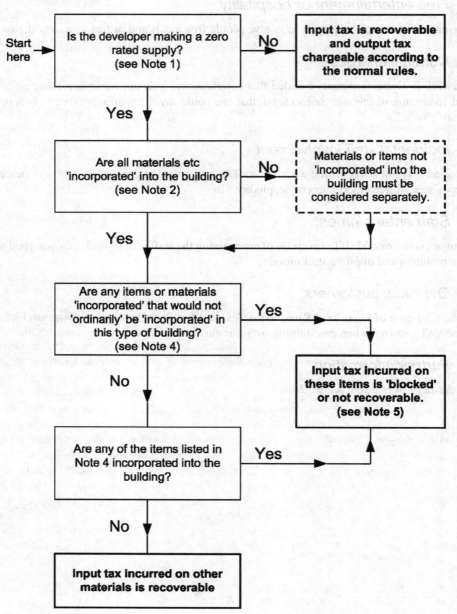

Notes

(1) Zero-rated supplies by building developers

Subject to complying with all the relevant conditions, the first grant of a major interest in a new:

(a)   dwelling(s);
(b)   relevant residential building;
(c)   relevant charitable building,

is a zero-rated supply. For further information, see 13-050.

(2) 'Incorporated'

'Incorporated' is taken to mean fixed to a building, or its site, in such a way that fixing or removal requires the use of tools, result in the need for remedial work to the fabric of the building (or its site) or cause substantial damage to the goods themselves. (see Notice 708, para. 13.3).

(3) 'Ordinarily incorporated'

Any goods that are not 'ordinarily' installed in the type of building concerned may not be zero-rated.

(4) Items for which input tax is not recoverable

The goods or materials for which input tax may not be recovered ('blocked') are as follows:

(a)   finished or prefabricated furniture, other than furniture designed to be fitted in kitchens;
(b)   materials for the construction of fitted furniture, other than kitchen furniture;
(c)   electrical or gas appliances, unless the appliance is an appliance which is:

- designed to heat space or water (or both) or to provide ventilation, air cooling, air purification, or dust extraction; or
- intended for use in a building designed as a number of dwellings and is a door-entry system, a waste disposal unit or a machine for compacting waste; or
- a burglar alarm, a fire alarm, or fire safety equipment or designed solely for the purpose of enabling aid to be summoned in an emergency; or
- a lift or hoist;

(d)   carpets or carpeting material.

(5) Further information

For further information, see Notice 708.

Input Tax Recovery

7-925 Reclaiming pre-registration input tax

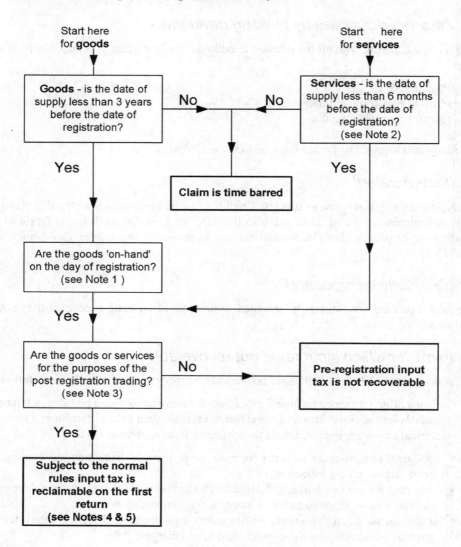

Notes

(1) Goods 'on-hand' on the day of registration

These goods are described by HMRC as follows:

- '… goods you bought for your business … and which you have not yet sold' – para. 4.2, Notice 700/1 Should I be registered for VAT;
- '… either stock for resale or fixed assets …' – Sections 6.5, HMRC Manuals V1-13 VAT – Input Tax.

(2) Services received before registration

Information published by HMRC about these services is as follows:

- '… services, which you received not more than 6 months before your date of registration …' – para. 4.2, Notice 700/1 Should I be registered for VAT;
- '… that services obtained will relate to business activity carried on at the time of registration …' – Sections 6.5, HMRC Manuals V1-13 VAT – Input Tax.

(3) Trading activities

Pre-registration input tax is not recoverable unless the goods or services 'were obtained for the business which is now covered by the VAT registration' – para. 11.2, VAT Notice 700.

(4) Corporate bodies and pre-incorporation input tax

Additional conditions apply to goods and services bought on or before the date of incorporation VAT – see 6-680.

(5) Normal conditions apply

The normal input tax rules apply. The basic rules are set out at 6-160 and 6-640.

Input Tax Recovery

7-930 Reclaiming input tax after de-registration

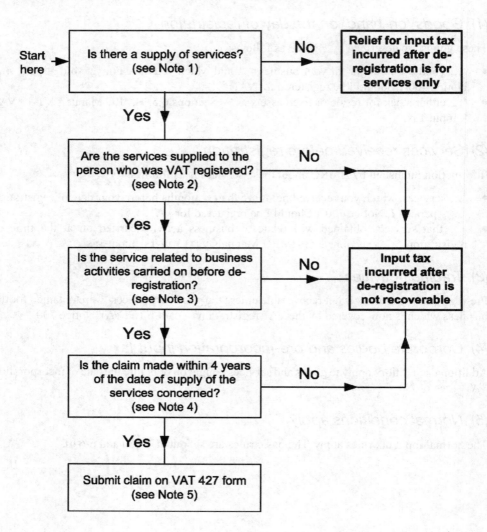

Notes

(1) Services only

Relief for post-registration input tax is for supplies of services only.

(2) To whom supply made

The services must be supplied to the person who was VAT-registered.

(3) Link with pre-registration supplies

Input tax is not recoverable unless the services were received for the purposes of 'taxable business activities'.

'Taxable business activities' are those which were liable to VAT and which were carried on whilst the claimant was VAT-registered.

(4) Time bar

Four year time bar runs from the date of supply of the service.

(5) Making the claim

The original invoice(s) must be sent with Form VAT 427.

Input Tax Recovery

7-935   When a foreign trader may reclaim UK VAT

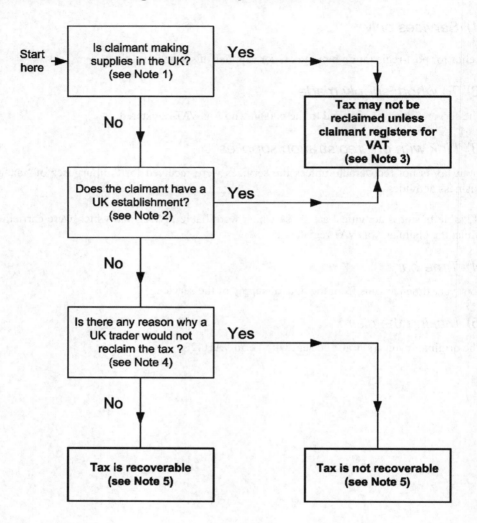

Notes

(1) Supplies in UK

Certain supplies made or deemed to be made in the UK are not taken into account for these purposes. These are supplies of international freight transport or supplies deemed to be made in the UK because this is where the recipient belongs (see 3-980(4)).

(2) Established in UK

A foreign trader with a UK establishment may not reclaim UK VAT in this way.

(3) Foreign person who may register for VAT

Foreign persons making relevant supplies in UK may register for VAT and reclaim VAT in the normal way (see 8-000).

(4) Non-recoverable input tax

A foreign trader may recover input tax in accordance with UK legislation. Thus, the UK blocking orders apply equally to foreign and UK traders (see 6-740).

(5) Making a claim

Time limits and other criteria apply – see 6-740 and 7-940.

7-940 How non-EU businesses may reclaim UK VAT

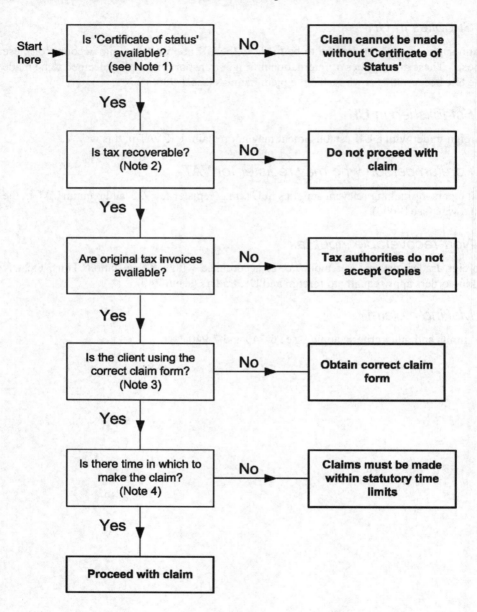

Start here → Is 'Certificate of status' available? (see Note 1)
— **No** → Claim cannot be made without 'Certificate of Status'

Yes ↓

Is tax recoverable? (Note 2)
— **No** → Do not proceed with claim

Yes ↓

Are original tax invoices available?
— **No** → Tax authorities do not accept copies

Yes ↓

Is the client using the correct claim form? (Note 3)
— **No** → Obtain correct claim form

Yes ↓

Is there time in which to make the claim? (Note 4)
— **No** → Claims must be made within statutory time limits

Yes ↓

Proceed with claim

Notes

(1) 'Certificate of Status'

A 'Certificate of Status' is confirmation from the overseas tax authorities that the person making the claim is registered for business in that country.

(2) 'Blocked' tax

Certain tax may not be reclaimed. This is tax:

* incurred on supplies within the scope of the tour operators' margin scheme;
* on intra-EU acquisitions;
* not reclaimable by virtue of the UK regulations;
* below the minimum amount.

(3) Claim forms

Claim Form VAT 65A must be submitted to VAT Overseas Repayment Unit, PO Box 34, Foyle House, Duncreggan Road, Londonderry BT48 7AE, Tel +44 (0) 287137 5100.

(4) Time limits

Claims must usually be made within six months from the end of the year ending 31 July. Interim claims are permissible subject to certain conditions.

(5) More information

For further information, see VAT Notice 723A.

Input Tax Recovery

7-943   Goods for business and non-business/private use

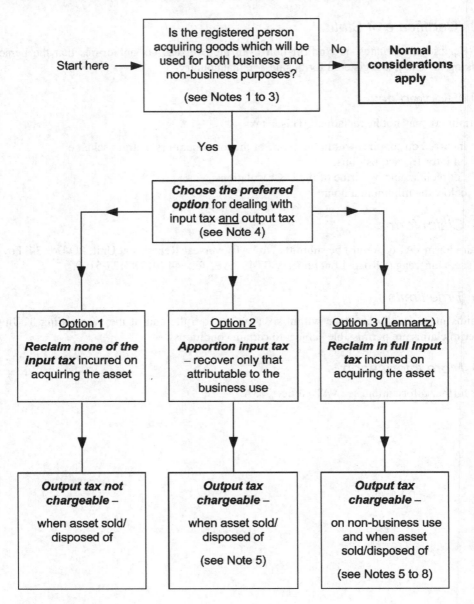

Start here →

Is the registered person acquiring goods which will be used for both business and non-business purposes?

(see Notes 1 to 3)

No → **Normal considerations apply**

Yes ↓

Choose the preferred option for dealing with input tax <u>and</u> output tax (see Note 4)

Option 1

Reclaim none of the input tax incurred on acquiring the asset

Option 2

Apportion input tax – recover only that attributable to the business use

Option 3 (Lennartz)

Reclaim in full input tax incurred on acquiring the asset

Output tax not chargeable –

when asset sold/ disposed of

Output tax chargeable –

when asset sold/ disposed of

(see Note 5)

Output tax chargeable –

on non-business use and when asset sold/disposed of

(see Notes 5 to 8)

Notes

(1) Qualifying assets

Except for items for which input tax recovery is specifically blocked (e.g. cars); most goods qualify for this practice. The goods may be new or old. From 1 January 2011 it may not be used for land, buildings, civil engineering works, ships, boats or aircraft.

(2) Non-business use

For the purposes of Lennartz accounting, non-business use is private use by the 'trader or his staff'. Lennartz accounting does not encompass other non-business use.

(3) Minimal business use

This practice may be used whenever there is some business use. The extent of the business use is immaterial, i.e. there is no de minimis level.

(4) When to choose – one opportunity

It is necessary to select the most suitable option when the relevant input tax is incurred. HMRC consider the decision to be irrevocable.

(5) Sale or disposal of the asset

The normal rules apply for accounting for output tax.

(6) Accounting for output tax on non-business use

Output tax must be accounted for on the non-business usage in the VAT period in which the non-business use takes place.

(7) Transitional rules

Some assets acquired before 1 November 2007 will be subject to transitional rules. Other transitional rules affecting assets which were used for non-business purposes were introduced with effect from 22 January 2010.

(8) Further information

For further information, see VAT Information Sheet 14/07 and HM Revenue and Customs Brief 02/10 Lennartz accounting – new policy following ECJ case; HM Revenue and Customs Brief 53/10 and VAT Information Sheet 06/11,

VAT Reporter: ¶19-040

Input Tax Recovery

7-950   Is the business partially exempt?

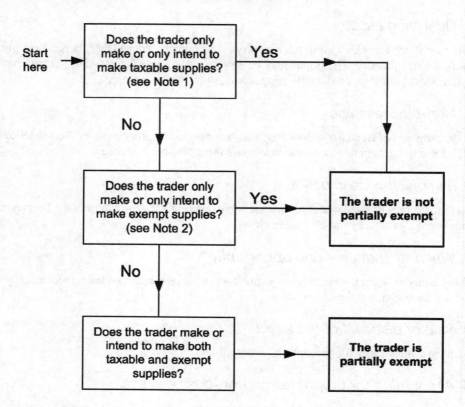

Notes

(1) Taxable supplies

Taxable supplies are goods or services that are liable to standard rate, reduced rate or zero-rate VAT. It includes supplies made outside the UK that would be taxable if made within the UK.

(2) Exempt supplies

Exempt supplies are as defined under group headings in VATA 1994, Sch. 9 as follows:

(1)   Land.

(2)   Insurance.

(3)   Postal services.

(4)   Betting, gaming and lotteries.

(5)   Finance.

(6)   Education.

(7)   Health and welfare.

(8)   Burial and cremation.

(9)   Trade unions and professional bodies.

(10) Sport, sports competitions and physical education.

(11) Works of art, etc.

(12) Fund-raising events by charities and other qualifying bodies.

(13) Cultural services, etc.

(14) Supplies of goods where input tax cannot be recovered.

(15) Investment gold.

7-960　Attributing Input tax

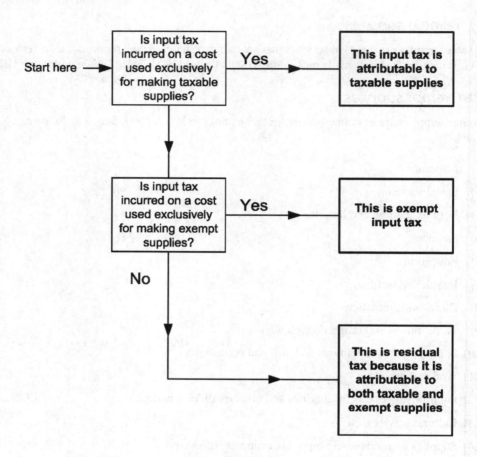

Notes

(1) Non-business activities

Eliminate any input tax attributable to non-business activities at the outset.

(2) 'Out of country' or 'foreign' supplies

Attribute tax to 'out of country' supplies if they would have been taxable or exempt supplies if made in the UK.

(3) Direct link

When attributing input tax to taxable or exempt supplies, it is necessary to establish a direct and immediate link between the expenditure and the onward supply.

7-965   Choosing a method

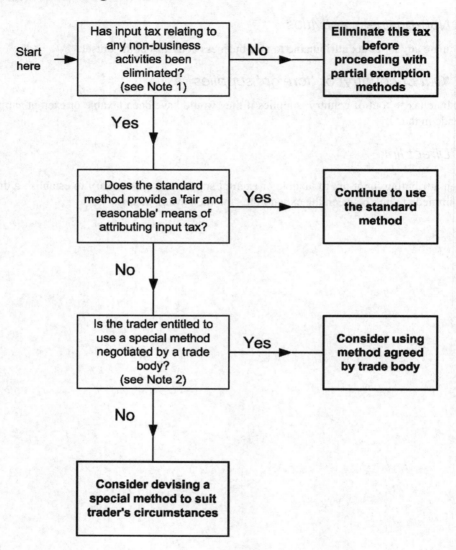

Notes

(1) Non-business activities

For further information about dealing with non-business activities, see 7-700.

(2) Special methods agreed by trade bodies

Details of special methods agreed with trade bodies are published in Notice 700/57.

7-967 Partial exemption special methods – considerations and formalities

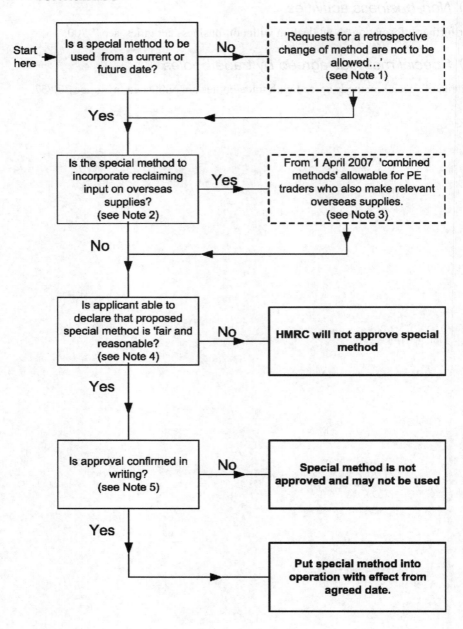

Start here → Is a special method to be used from a current or future date?

— **No** → 'Requests for a retrospective change of method are not to be allowed...' (see Note 1)

Yes ↓

Is the special method to incorporate reclaiming input on overseas supplies? (see Note 2)

— **Yes** → From 1 April 2007 'combined methods' allowable for PE traders who also make relevant overseas supplies. (see Note 3)

No ↓

Is applicant able to declare that proposed special method is 'fair and reasonable? (see Note 4)

— **No** → **HMRC will not approve special method**

Yes ↓

Is approval confirmed in writing? (see Note 5)

— **No** → **Special method is not approved and may not be used**

Yes ↓

Put special method into operation with effect from agreed date.

Notes

(1) Retrospective change of method – further information

'Requests for a retrospective change of method are not to be allowed, except to the extent that a method may be approved with effect from the start of the tax year in which the written application (being the approved application) is received … the retrospective approval of a method may be granted where a partly exempt business has failed to adopt any method to apportion input tax …' (VAT Guidance Manuals Vol V1-15, s. 7. paras. 7.5 & 7.6).

(2) Overseas supplies and input tax recovery

Input tax may be reclaimed for supplies made outside the UK. These are supplies which, if made in the UK, would be taxable. In addition, input tax may be recovered in respect of some specified exempt supplies (*Value Added Tax (Input Tax) (Specified Supplies) Order* 1999 (SI 1999/3121)).

(3) 'Combined methods'

HMRC may approve 'combined methods'. These are partial exemption special methods which include a means of quantifying input tax recovery for 'overseas supplies' for which input tax may be reclaimed.

(4) 'Fair and reasonable declaration' required

HMRC will not approve a special method unless the applicant declares 'to the best of its knowledge and belief' that its proposed special method is fair and reasonable.' HMRC have the power to set aside a method if the person signing the declaration 'knew or ought reasonably to have known that was not fair and reasonable'.

(5) Written approval is mandatory

Special methods must be approved in writing (*Value Added Tax Regulations* 1995 (SI 1995/2518) reg. 102(5)).

(6) Further information

For further information, see Notice 706 and HM Revenue and Customs Brief 23/07, 14 March 2007

Input Tax Recovery

7-970 Change of use

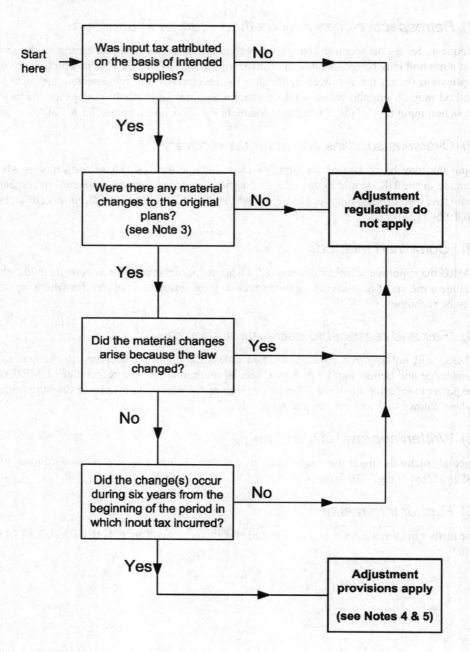

Start here → **Was input tax attributed on the basis of intended supplies?** — **No** →

Yes ↓

Were there any material changes to the original plans? (see Note 3) — **No** → **Adjustment regulations do not apply**

Yes ↓

Did the material changes arise because the law changed? — **Yes** →

No ↓

Did the change(s) occur during six years from the beginning of the period in which inout tax incurred? — **No** →

Yes ↓

Adjustment provisions apply

(see Notes 4 & 5)

Notes

(1) Capital items

These adjustments do not apply to items within the scope of the Capital Goods Scheme (see 7-760).

(2) Input tax attributed to intended supplies

This applies to situations where input tax has been attributed according to an intended use.

(3) Material change

When the supply is obtained the input tax is attributed to future intended taxable supplies, exempt supplies or allocated to residual input tax. Subsequently, the original intention is not fulfilled and the supplies put to a different use.

Example

Gordon, a funeral director and builder, buys a van that he intends to use solely to transport bodies to the Chapel of Rest. The input tax on the van is attributed to exempt supplies. Before he uses the van for his funeral business, he changes his mind and uses it for the building business.

This constitutes a material change. The input tax was attributed on the basis of the intention only to use it for making exempt supplies but prior to such use it was used to make taxable supplies.

---

(4) Consequences of change of intention

The original computations have to be reworked if the initial intention is not fulfilled and the change of use takes place both:

(a)   after the end of the longer period; and

(b)   within the above six-year limit.

(5) Change of intention before the end of the longer period

Any change of intention should be taken into account when calculating the 'annual' adjustment (see 7-470).

Input Tax Recovery

7-975 Partial exemption calculations: Standard Method
DRAFT LAYOUT AND EXAMPLE COMPUTATIONS FOR ANNUAL OR 'LONGER' PERIOD ADJUSTMENT

PERIOD DETAILS —

	Ref
First day —	
Last day —	
Period No —	
Number of months in longer period/tax year —	12 A

INPUT TAX SUMMARY (see 7-110)

	Ref	Totals	31.03.06	Period ending — 31.12.05	30.09.05	30.06.05
Input tax linked **exclusively** to taxable supplies	B	35000	6000	8000	12000	9000
Exempt input tax linked **exclusively** to exempt supplies	C	5100	2000	1000	900	1200
Residual input tax	D	4450	1200	1500	1000	750
TOTALS	E	44550	9200	10500	13900	10950
Input tax claimed each period	F	42070	6720	10500	13900	10950

SUMMARY OF RELEVANT OUTPUTS/TURNOVER (see 7-270)

	Ref	Totals	31.03.06	31.12.05	30.09.05	30.06.05
Taxable supplies/turnover	G	103000	30000	20000	25000	28000
Exempt supplies/turnover	H	66000	20000	15000	14000	17000
TOTALS		169000	50000	35000	39000	45000

APPORTIONMENT OF RESIDUAL INPUT TAX (see 7-250)

		Input tax wholly linked to taxable outputs	Exempt input tax	Residual input tax
b/d B		35000		
b/d C			5100	
b/d D				4450

1. Computation of recovery % —

$$\frac{\text{Taxable outputs (G) \%}}{\text{Taxable outputs (G) + exempt outputs (H)}}$$

$$= \frac{103000}{169000}$$

= 60.95%

Rounded up = 61.00%

2. Re-allocation of residual input tax to —

			Exempt input tax
taxable outputs 61.00%	2715		-2715
exempt outputs 39.00%	1736		-1736
			1736

DE MINIMIS' TESTS (see 7-520)

Test 1

Average exempt input tax per month —

$$\frac{\text{exempt input tax (J)}}{\text{No. of months (A)}} = \frac{6,836}{12} = 569.63$$

Is average less than £625 per month?

Answer Yes or No   YES

Test 2

Half total input tax (E)   22275   K

Is exempt input tax (J) equal to or less than half total input tax (K)?

Answer Yes or No   YES

RECLAIMABLE TAX

Input tax linked to taxable supplies b/d	37,715
Only claim exempt input tax when 'YES' is answer to both 'de minimis' tests	6,836
Total reclaimable in this example	44,550
less input tax claimed during the year or 'longer' period (F)	42,070
ADJUSTMENT	2,480

J   37715

6836

0

Input Tax Recovery

311

7-980   Standard method override

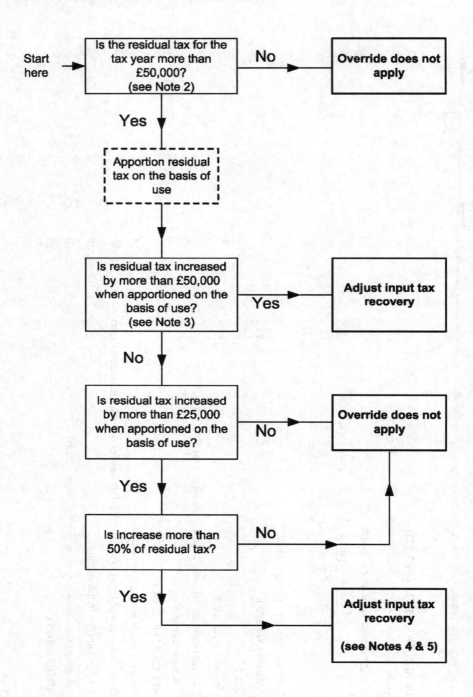

Notes

(1) Relevant input tax

The measure applies to residual input tax incurred during the partial exemption year. Thus, Capital Goods Scheme adjustments should be excluded but the input tax incurred when acquiring a capital item should be included.

(2) When to apply this test

This test is applied at the end of the partial exemption 'year' to the total 'residual' input tax for the year concerned. In some circumstances, a partial exemption 'year' may be less than 12 months.

(3) Calculating 'use'

The object is to compare input tax recovery using the standard method with what it would be if 'residual' input tax were apportioned according to the way in which the relevant costs are used or will be used in the future. Any method may be devised to compute actual 'use' or future 'use' of the relevant costs so long as it 'provides a fair and reasonable attribution of input tax'.

If, when the input tax is incurred, it is intended that the purchases will be included in the transfer of a going concern it is necessary to take into account how the transferee or successor will use the purchases.

(4) The adjustment

The adjustment is the difference between the input tax reclaimed using the standard method and that reclaimable according to 'use'.

(5) Making the adjustment

Any necessary adjustment should usually be declared with the partial exemption annual adjustment.

Input Tax Recovery

7-985 Simplified de minimis tests

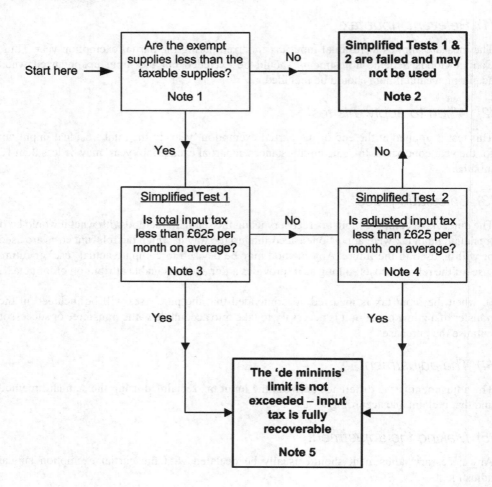

Notes

(1) Taxable and exempt supplies condition

For these purposes, taxable supplies are the total of such supplies made in the UK, supplies made outside the UK which would be taxable if made in the UK and exempt supplies made outside the UK for which input tax is recoverable. Exempt supplies are any supplies that 'are not taxable supplies'.

(2) What to do when business fails simplified test

Whenever the business may not use the simplified tests, it must revert to carrying out standard method calculations. This may be for an individual period or a whole year according to whether the tests are failed for (a) period(s) or the year as a whole.

(3) Total input tax

This is the total input tax incurred in the period or partial exemption year but excluding blocked input tax (e.g. business entertainment).

(4) Adjusted input tax

Adjusted input tax is the total input tax less that 'exclusively' attributable to the taxable supplies. In effect the adjusted input tax is the sum of the residual tax and that 'exclusively' attributable to exempt supplies.

(5) Annual adjustment

An annual adjustment is required at the end of the partial exemption 'year'. If the 'year' as a whole fails the simplified tests, standard method workings must be done.

(6) Legislation

The new regulations implementing these tests is VAT Regulations 1995 (SI 1995/2518), reg. 105A.

(7) Further information

For further information, see VAT Information Sheet 04/10 (March 2010) – VAT: Partial Exemption – changes to the de minimis rules.

Input Tax Recovery

Registration and Deregistration

REGISTRATION

8-000 Introduction to registration

Businesses making UK supplies

Persons carrying on businesses of making taxable supplies in the United Kingdom (often referred to as traders) are generally obliged to register with Her Majesty's Revenue and Customs. However, not everyone who makes taxable supplies by way of business is forced to register. If the volume of taxable supplies is below certain registration limits, set out at Hardman's Tax Rates and Tables 19-080 or Key Data 1-140, then the trader is not obliged to register for VAT.

A trader who wishes to register, but is not obliged to register, can apply for registration. If HMRC (or, on appeal, a Tax tribunal) are satisfied that the trader is carrying on a business and either makes taxable supplies already or intends to do so in the future, then the trader is entitled to registration. Similarly, registration can also be obtained by a person with a UK business establishment who makes (or intends to make) supplies overseas which would be taxable if made in the UK.

Internal market – special rules

There are special rules requiring registration of UK businesses and other organisations receiving acquisitions of goods from elsewhere in the EC. There are also rules requiring businesses involved in distance selling to the UK or supplying telecommunication services to the UK to register. See 8-430, 8-530 and 8-640.

This section sets out the main rules on registration under each of these heads, the time limits therefore, and various other matters concerned with registration.

VAT Reporter: ¶5-050

REGISTRATION – UK SUPPLIES

8-040 Taxable turnover

The rules for determining whether a trader's business is sufficiently large to make registration mandatory are based upon the trader's taxable turnover. This refers to the amount of the trader's taxable supplies (including zero-rated supplies) in a given period. Consequently, it is not a measure of the size of the trader's business in terms of the net income which can be derived from it, but a measure of the volume of supplies which are made to others.

Example: turnover versus profit

Smith is a self-employed window cleaner. She employs no staff and her total annual sales are £12,000. Her net annual profit is £10,000.

Jones runs a shop. His annual sales are £60,000. By the time he has paid for the goods which he sells and covered his overheads, his net annual profit is also £10,000.

Although Smith and Jones have equivalent businesses in terms of the income which they derive from them, Smith's is only one-fifth the size of Jones's in terms of turnover.

Because the limits are based on turnover, their application is to some extent uneven as between different types of business. Differences can also arise depending on how activities are organised. For instance, consider two labour only building subcontractors, each with annual sales of £50,000. Neither of them is obliged to register for VAT. But if they choose to go into partnership, their combined turnover will exceed the turnover limit (see 8-070) and they will be obliged to register.

Strictly speaking, turnover for VAT includes all taxable supplies made in the course of a business, except that supplies of goods which are capital assets of the business may be ignored in determining whether the turnover limits have been reached. However, capital supplies of land which are taxable at the standard rate may not be ignored.

Example: computation of turnover

Newman is a self-employed debt collector with turnover (for the year to 30 April 2011) of £65,000. He sells his van for £9,000 and buys a new one. Although the sale of the van is a taxable supply, Newman can leave it out of his turnover for VAT registration purposes, so he does not need to register for VAT.

If Newman disposed of commercial property which was under three years old or subject to an option to tax it would be 'turnover' for VAT purposes.

Legislation: VATA 1994, Sch. 1, para. 1(7) and (8)

Other material: Notice 700/1 para. 2.4

VAT Reporter: ¶43-002

Registration of racehorse owners

HMRC will register racehorse owners who comply with conditions agreed with the Thoroughbred Horseracing and Breeding Industry. The basic principles are that the owner or owners must be registered with Weatherbys under the Orders and Rules of Racing and have a sponsorship agreement registered at Weatherbys or can demonstrate that their horse racing generates business income.

Not all racehorse owners need to use or should use the special scheme. The scheme is intended for those for whom racehorse ownership is a separate venture and not part of a business which is, or should be VAT-registered.

Other material: Notice 700/67 .

VAT Reporter: ¶43-895

8-070   Turnover limits: general

Broadly speaking, a person is liable to register for VAT in respect of UK supplies if he makes taxable supplies and his taxable turnover has exceeded the historic turnover limit, or there are reasonable grounds for believing that it will exceed the future turnover limit which applies where there are reasonable grounds for supposing that the trader's taxable turnover within the next 30 days alone will exceed the annual turnover limit (see flowchart 8-950).

These turnover limits are based on the actual value of taxable supplies made, whether standard-rated or zero-rated. It is not permissible to reduce the turnover for any notional figure of VAT included in it. In allocating supplies to particular periods, the ordinary VAT time of supply rules apply. However, a person who is not registered for VAT cannot issue an invoice which meets the technical definition of a tax invoice, so the date of invoicing does not affect the time of supply. In general, a supply is treated as made at the earlier of the date when the supply is actually made and the date when the payment is received for it.

When certain services (see 3-980) are acquired from overseas by a person carrying on a business in the UK, they are treated as supplies in the UK and, thus, add to the recipient's taxable turnover. These supplies count when checking whether the registration limits have been exceeded.

In the case of a commercial group of companies, each company is treated separately for registration purposes as each is a separate person. However, if group treatment has been applied for and obtained (17-080ff.), the whole of the group turnover will need to be considered.

Legislation: VATA 1994, s. 8, Sch. 1 and 5

VAT Reporter: ¶43-025

8-100   Annual turnover limit: historic

A trader who makes taxable supplies over a 12-month period which exceed the annual turnover limit is liable to register for VAT, and must notify HMRC of the liability to register (see 8-220 below). This is a running 12-month period, not an accounting or any other sort of year.

In order to comply with this requirement, it is essential to maintain turnover records on the basis of calendar months.

However, if at the required registration date HMRC are satisfied that turnover for the year then commencing will not exceed the annual turnover limit, there is no liability to be registered. HMRC's satisfaction (or otherwise) as to future turnover must be determined as at the date of required registration, on information available to them as at that time, so this provision is unlikely to be of assistance in cases involving late notification.

The historic turnover limit must be considered at the end of each calendar month, and is based on taxable turnover for the 12 months then ending. If the trader's turnover for the 12 months has exceeded the annual turnover limit (see Hardman's Tax Rates and Tables 19-080 or Key Data 1-140), then registration is required.

Legislation: VATA 1994, Sch. 1, para. 1(1)(a) and (3)

Other material: Notice 700/1 para 2.3

Cases: *Gray v C & E Commrs* [2000] BVC 396

VAT Reporter: ¶43-025

8-130 Notification: historic turnover

Where a trader has become liable to register for VAT because of the historic turnover limit, he must notify HMRC of this within 30 days from the end of the calendar month for which the relevant turnover limit was exceeded. HMRC must then register him with effect from the end of the month following that in which the turnover limit was exceeded. However, registration can take effect from an earlier date if HMRC and the trader jointly agree to this.

The trader need not be registered if he can satisfy HMRC that his turnover for the forthcoming 12 months will not exceed the de-registration limit (see Hardman's Tax Rates and Tables 19-100 or Key Data 1-280).

Example: date of registration

Terence has taxable turnover for the 12 months ending on 30 September 2011 of £78,000. This is in excess of the then annual turnover limit and so he is liable to register for VAT. He must notify HMRC of his liability to register by 31 October 2011, and they must register him with effect from 1 November 2011.

It is important to monitor taxable turnover and, if registration becomes necessary, to make the appropriate notification on time. If the trader knows that he has to account for VAT on his sales, he can often recover the money from his customers. But it is hard (and often impossible) to go back after the event and ask for VAT on top of the price already agreed and paid. Furthermore, there are penalties for late notification (10-100) even if there is no loss to the revenue. It should be noted that, where any VAT chargeable would be recoverable by customers, it is still the normal policy of HMRC to seek to recover the tax from the supplier.

Both the basic loss which can arise from late registration and the penalty which can arise mean that it is bad policy for a trader to leave it to his accountant to tell him when he should register. Often, the accountant to a small business will only see the books once a year, and it may be many months after the year-end before he sees them and works out the turnover.

Turnover needs to be monitored monthly. In practice, this generally means that it needs to be done by the trader rather than by his accountant. The accountant who leads his client to believe otherwise may be doing him a disservice.

Legislation: VATA 1994, Sch. 1, para. 5

Other material: Notice 700/1, para. 3.2

VAT Reporter: ¶43-150

8-160   Turnover limit: future

If a trader makes taxable supplies and there are reasonable grounds for supposing that his taxable supplies in the next 30 days alone will exceed the annual turnover limit, he becomes liable to register for VAT. He must then notify HMRC of his liability to register (see 8-220 below).

Because of this requirement, it is not sufficient for a trader to monitor the turnover which he has achieved, and register after he has exceeded the historic turnover limit for the first time. He must constantly look forward and register if it seems likely that he will exceed the turnover limit in the future (this should not be too difficult, given the high amount of anticipated turnover for a 30-day period).

Legislation: VATA 1994, Sch. 1, para. 1(1)(b)

Other material: Notice 700/1, para. 2.3

VAT Reporter: ¶43-025

8-190   Notification: future turnover

A person who becomes liable to register for VAT because of anticipated turnover for a future period of 30 days must notify HMRC of this by, at the latest, the end of the 30-day period. They must then register him from the start of 30 days or, if agreed by HMRC and by the trader, from some earlier date. In practice, this may often mean that almost immediate notification is necessary.

Legislation: VATA 1994, Sch. 1, para. 6

Other material: Notice 700/1, para. 3.2

VAT Reporter: ¶43-002

8-220 Registration procedure

When a person becomes liable to register for VAT, he must notify HMRC of this fact. In doing this, he is obliged to use the VAT registration form VAT 1. In addition, if the trader is a partnership, form VAT 2 must be completed. This gives details of all of the partners.

A trader who makes zero-rated supplies and wishes to apply for exemption from registration on that ground (see 8-290 below) can indicate this fact in a box provided on the form for this purpose.

On-line registrations

Most applications for registration may be completed on-line. The notable exceptions are VAT groups and overseas businesses. HMRC aim to make registration on-line mandatory from August 2012.

Postal registrations

The completed application form should be submitted to the Registration Unit (see Hardman's Tax Rates and Tables 19-805 or Key Data 1-705). Never send a VAT 1 form to the VAT Central Unit at Southend or the Shipley payment office – indeed, never send anything to either of these places except for a VAT return and the related payment.

Forms VAT 1, VAT 1W and VAT 2 may be obtained from the National Advice Service or printed from HMRC's website.

Welsh-speaking traders can, if they prefer, use form VAT 1W instead of form VAT 1. This is the equivalent form but printed in Welsh. It is not clear whether this facility is available generally, or only in Wales.

See flowcharts 8-980 and 8-995.

Legislation: *Value Added Tax Regulations* 1995 (SI 1995/2518), reg. 5(1)

VAT Reporter: ¶43-175

8-230 Voluntary registration

A trader who already makes taxable supplies, but is not obliged to register for VAT by reason of either the historic or future turnover limits, can still seek registration if he wishes to do so.

Provided that the trader can satisfy HMRC that taxable supplies are being made in the course of business, they are obliged to make the registration.

The application for registration by a trader seeking voluntary registration should be made in the same way as a trader who is obliged to register (see 8-220 above). The only differences are that the voluntary registrant does not have to submit his application by a particular day and that he will find it easier to send a covering letter explaining his business need for registration. In most cases, this is a matter of saying that taxable supplies are being made, and the trader wishes to recover input tax.

Although HMRC are not obliged to allow a voluntary registration to have retrospective effect, they are normally prepared to do so. However, as a matter of policy, they do not allow retrospection in excess of four years.

Planning considerations

A business making taxable supplies to other taxable businesses will generally be better off if it registers for VAT, even if its turnover is not such as to make this mandatory. This enables it to recover input tax on its costs, while the output tax which it charges can be recovered by its customers.

A new business supplying the general public may often wish to defer registration, and it is possible to make considerable supplies free of VAT before registration becomes mandatory (see 8-070). Care may sometimes be needed to avoid permanent loss of input tax on services acquired before registration (see 6-660).

Where there are genuine taxable supplies made in the course of business and the trader wishes to be registered for VAT, HMRC must register the trader if application for registration is made. This can be exploited by small businesses which make essentially exempt supplies. If the business also makes some taxable supplies, the trader can insist on registration. If input tax attributable to the exempt supplies falls below the partial exemption de minimis limit (see 7-520), the whole of the trader's input tax can be recovered.

Legislation: VATA 1994, Sch. 1, para. 9(a)

Other material: Notice 700/1, para. 2.10, Should I be registered for VAT?

VAT Reporter: ¶43-225

8-260 Intending trader registration

A person who does not yet make taxable supplies, but intends to do so, can also apply to be registered for VAT. Such a person will typically have started business already but still be at the stage of developing products or markets, so that taxable supplies have yet to be made.

If HMRC (or a Tax tribunal) are satisfied that taxable supplies are intended to be made, they must allow such a registration. In reaching a decision, they will tend to look for such things as the existence of business premises or of firm orders for the ultimate product. The more evidence which can be produced of a genuine taxable business activity, the better.

Provided that there is a genuine intention to make taxable supplies by way of business, input tax recovered under an intending trader registration can be retained even if the proposed venture proves abortive and no supplies are actually made.

HMRC have guidelines for the required evidence that will establish firstly, that there is a business and secondly, that the trader intends to make taxable supplies.

The evidence could include the following:

- copies of invoices, for example from an accountant or business adviser;
- details of efforts made to secure finance for the project;
- details of any contracts for supply or receipt of goods or services;
- details of actual or proposed advertising;
- details of any application for planning permission;
- business plan or minutes of meetings or the like.

HMRC will examine this evidence to determine that the supplies to be made will be taxable supplies, not exempt supplies. Thus, they will be specially vigilant where the business will be making supplies of land and property. They will need to be satisfied that the relevant supplies will be taxable, not exempt.

It should be noted that the intention of making taxable supplies confers a right of registration, and consequent input tax recovery, even if the business has in fact failed, and the prospect of making supplies has vanished, by the time HMRC consider the case.

A trader who has not yet made any taxable supplies, and so is seeking registration as an intending trader, must indicate the expected annual value of taxable supplies, and when these may commence.

HMRC are reviewing the level of evidence required for an 'intending trader' in the light of the assessment of risk posed by making VAT registration easier.

Legislation: VATA 1994, Sch. 1, para. 9(b)

Cases: *Merseyside Cablevision Ltd* (1987) 3 BVC 596; *Rompelman v Minister van Financiën* (Case 268/83) (1984) 2 BVC 200,157; *Intercommunale voor Zeewaterontzilting (INZO) (in liquidation) v Belgian State* (Case C-110/94) [1996] BVC 326; *Finanzamt Goslar v Breitsohl* (Case C-400/98) [2000] ECR I-4321

VAT Reporter: ¶43-250

8-290 Exception from registration

A trader who makes only zero-rated supplies can, if he wishes, apply to be excepted from registration even though his taxable turnover exceeds the registration limits. This allows a trader who would only be reclaiming tax from the revenue, not paying tax into it, to escape from the administrative requirements of VAT registration. The cost to him is the input tax which he would otherwise be able to reclaim.

In fact, exception from registration can be sought by a trader who makes some standard-rated supplies, if most of his supplies are zero-rated. Such exception may well be granted if it appears likely that the trader will generally be reclaiming VAT rather than paying it over.

HMRC can withdraw exception from registration at any time. In addition, a trader who is granted exception from registration is obliged to give notification, within 30 days, of any material change in the nature of the supplies which he makes, or of any material alteration in any calendar quarter in the proportion of his taxable supplies which are zero-rated. A trader excepted from registration therefore takes on significant obligations to monitor the potential VAT position, over and above those faced by a below limits unregistered trader.

Legislation: VATA 1994, Sch. 1, para. 14(1)–(3)

Other material: Notice 700/1, para. 2.13

VAT Reporter: ¶43-002

8-320 Overseas supplies, etc.

A trader established in the UK can also be registered for VAT without making any UK taxable supplies. This applies if the trader:

(1)   makes supplies outside of the UK which would be taxable if made within the UK; or

(2)   makes supplies in bonded warehouse which would otherwise be taxable (since these supplies are deemed to take place outside the UK, and so fall within (1) above).

Such a trader can apply to HMRC to be registered for VAT (but is not obliged to register).

A trader who makes no taxable supplies, but does make exempt financial supplies to overseas customers in respect of which input tax is deductible (see 6-420, 14-400) may register in order to recover input tax.

Legislation: VATA 1994, s. 18; VATA 1994, Sch. 1, para. 10

VAT Reporter: ¶43-002

8-350 Previous owner's turnover

There is a special rule for determining taxable turnover for the purposes of the registration limits where a business has been taken over as a going concern. In determining whether the new owner is liable to be registered for VAT, he is deemed to have made the taxable supplies of that business before the transfer as well as after it. Thus, he has to count the previous owner's turnover as well as his own in checking whether he has reached the turnover limits.

This rule applies only if the person who previously carried on the business was himself a taxable person.

There is no provision to enable the new owner of the business to discover the turnover of the previous owner.

Note that the carrying over of the previous owner's turnover position needs to be borne in mind when the trade of a company is transferred under ICTA 1988, s. 343, particularly given the need for the successor company to register for VAT and the penalties for delay in this.

Legislation: VATA 1994, s. 49(1)(a)

Other material: Notice 700/1, para. 2.8

VAT Reporter: ¶43-775; ¶43-002

8-380 Effective date of late registration

A person who becomes liable to register for VAT may not realise this until some time later (in some cases, years later). Where this happens, the liability to be registered will still have existed from the proper time. Furthermore, the trader will (unknowingly) have been a taxable person throughout, since a taxable person is defined as one who makes taxable supplies and either is or is required to be registered.

This applies even if, after the liability to register came about, the person's turnover dropped so that de-registration could have been obtained, and even if the person could have applied not to be registered on grounds of low anticipated turnover. This is because it is a prerequisite for such de-registration or non-registration that HMRC are satisfied that future supplies are likely to be below the de-registration limit, and they cannot have been so satisfied without being provided with the relevant information.

In order to reflect this position, the registration of such a person will be made with retrospective effect to the proper registration date. He will be required to account for any output tax which has become due from that effective registration date. By the same token, he can reclaim input tax arising from then, provided that he holds the necessary evidence for reclaiming the tax.

Apart from the tax itself, a person registering late may be liable to a penalty for late registration. It should also be noted that there is no relief from the tax liability merely because customers would have been able to reclaim any tax charged to them. See 10-100.

Legislation: VATA 1994, s. 3(1); VATA 1994, Sch. 1, para. 1(3) and para. 4(1)

VAT Reporter: ¶43-149

8-390 Incorrect registration date

When the wrong registration date is obtained because of an error made when completing the application, HMRC may use their general care and management powers to allow a change. They state that they will only do this if, when completing the original application, the applicant applied to be registered earlier than they needed to be, a genuine error was made when completing the original application, the business requests the change before the due date for submitting the first return and returns the original VAT registration certificate.

If HMRC make an error when processing the application for registration, they 'can or must correct' the mistake.

In appeals about this, Tribunals have a supervisory role only. They are limited to considering 'whether HMRC...acted in a way in which no reasonable panel of Commissioners could have acted or whether...(HMRC)...have taken into account some irrelevant matter or have disregarded something to which they should have given weight'.

Legislation: VATA 1994, Sch. 1, para. 9

Cases: *Lead Asset Strategies (Liverpool) Ltd v R & C Commrs* [2009] (Lon/2008/0689), *John Dee Ltd v C & E Commrs* [1995] BVC 125

Other material: VAT Guidance Manual V1-28A, Vol 1, para 8.8

8-400 Overseas business trading in the UK

From 1 November 2012 an overseas business making taxable sales in the UK must register for VAT. Such businesses can no longer avoid VAT registration because their taxable sales in the UK are below the VAT registration threshold.

The obligation to register for VAT is triggered by the first sale made in the UK on or after 1 November 2012. Before this date the overseas business did not have to register until its taxable supplies in the UK exceeded the VAT registration threshold.

Common examples of businesses affected by this measure are overseas market traders who sell at UK markets and Southern Ireland services providers like plumbers and builders who do work in Northern Ireland.

Example

O'Leary is a Southern Ireland firm of plumbers. They are registered in Southern Ireland for VAT. For many years they have done some work in Northern Ireland. Normally the sales in Northern Ireland are not more than £10,000 per annum.

Until 1 November 2012 O'Leary has no obligation to register for UK VAT because the value of taxable sales in Northern Ireland is well below the UK VAT registration threshold. Due to the withdrawal of the VAT threshold for overseas businesses making taxable supplies in the UK, O'Leary must register for VAT from the date of its first taxable supply in Northern Ireland after 1 November 2012.

Legislation: VATA 1994, Sch.1 (introduced by FA 2012)

8-410 Registration – overseas traders selling UK goods

There are special provisions requiring UK registration by traders established outside the UK who make UK supplies of goods on which input tax has been, or will be, reclaimed under the special provisions for overseas traders (see 6-740), regardless of the turnover limits and regardless of whether the goods concerned are capital assets.

Legislation: VATA 1994, Sch. 3A

Other material: Notice 700/1, Section 7

VAT Reporter: ¶43-045

REGISTRATION – ACQUISITIONS OF GOODS FROM OTHER EC COUNTRIES

8-430 Introduction to acquisitions of goods from other EC countries

There is a possible liability to register by an organisation not registered for VAT in the UK which acquires goods from EC suppliers. The effect of registration is to bring these acquisitions into the UK VAT net, instead of that of the other EC countries concerned, and prevents substantial 'VAT rate shopping' between Member States.

This provision applies not only to (exempt) businesses, but also to clubs, associations, bodies corporate and unincorporated associations acquiring goods for non-business activities.

If the value (net of VAT) of intra-EC acquisitions by a 'person' since 1 January of a calendar year exceeds the acquisitions limit (see Hardman's Tax Rates and Tables 19-080 or Key Data 1-140), the 'person' becomes liable to register for VAT.

The effects of registration are:

(1) the overseas supplier can zero-rate its supplies, quoting the organisation's UK VAT registration number on its invoice; and

(2) the UK organisation becomes liable to account for UK VAT on its acquisitions from elsewhere in the EC (see 3-240).

This liability to register is illustrated in the flow chart at 8-960.

Other material: Notice 700/1, Section 6

VAT Reporter: ¶64-300

8-450 Persons affected

Businesses which are already registered for VAT are already obliged to account for VAT on acquisitions of goods from elsewhere in the EC.

The liability to register in respect of acquisitions is therefore of importance to persons not already registered, or liable to be registered, for UK VAT. The liability to register applies to:

(1) any person carrying on a business; and

(2) a body corporate, club, association, organisation or unincorporated body carrying on a non-business activity.

Where such a person acquires goods from a taxable person in another Member State, and the place of acquisition is the UK, the transaction counts for acquisition tax purposes.

Legislation: VATA 1994, s. 3 and s. 10(3)(a); Sch. 3

Other material: Notice 700/1, para. 6.1

VAT Reporter: ¶64-300

8-470 Acquisitions limit

A person becomes liable to register in respect of acquisitions from elsewhere in the EC if:

(1) at the end of any month, the value of acquisitions from the previous 1 January to the month end exceeds the annual acquisitions limit (see Hardman's Tax Rates and Tables 19-080 or Key Data 1-140); or

(2)   at any time, there are reasonable grounds for believing that the value of acquisitions in the following 30 days will exceed the annual acquisitions limit.

The value of acquisitions for this purpose is reckoned exclusive of any overseas VAT charged. Acquisitions of new means of transport, and of excise goods, are ignored as there are alternative provisions rendering these liable to UK VAT (see 5-400).

A person who becomes liable to register because of past acquisitions has 30 days from the end of the month in which the limit was exceeded in which to notify HMRC, and they must register him from the end of the month following that in which the limit was exceeded (or a mutually agreed earlier date).

A person who becomes liable to register because of anticipated acquisitions must notify HMRC of this before the end of the 30-day period concerned, and they must register him from the beginning of that period (or a mutually agreed earlier date).

Where a taxable person becomes liable to register in respect of zero-rated acquisitions, he may apply for exemption from registration.

Legislation: VATA 1994, Sch. 3, para. 8

Other material: Notice 700/1, para. 2.3

VAT Reporter: ¶64-300

8-490 Voluntary registration

It is also possible to register voluntarily in respect of acquisitions, or intended acquisitions, regardless of the amounts involved. This may be advantageous either because the rates of VAT are higher in the supplier countries, or as a matter of administrative convenience where it is expected that the registration thresholds will in any case be exceeded before long.

HMRC may impose conditions on such a voluntary registration.

Legislation: VATA 1994, Sch. 3, para. 4

VAT Reporter: ¶64-300

8-510 Ceasing registration

Persons registered solely because of the level of acquisitions must de-register if the acquisitions cease. They may also de-register when the value of acquisitions falls below the registration threshold. However, this is subject to the following conditions:

(1)   they have not exceeded the acquisitions threshold in the previous calendar year; and

(2)   they are able to satisfy HMRC that they will not exceed the threshold in the current year.

Voluntary registrations may not be cancelled for at least two years. The registration cannot be cancelled until 1 January following the second anniversary of the registration date.

Legislation: VATA 1994, Sch. 3, para. 6, 7

Other material: Notice 700/11, Section 4

VAT Reporter: ¶64-300

REGISTRATION – DISTANCE SELLING TO THE UK

8-530 General

As discussed at 3-920(6), a trader established elsewhere in the EC can become liable to register for VAT in the UK in respect of sales of goods to UK customers who are not registered for VAT. The place where such supplies are deemed to be made is then the UK, and the overseas supplier must account for VAT accordingly.

The distance selling registration provisions apply to a person who makes relevant supplies, being supplies of goods which involve the removal of the goods to the UK from another Member State, and their acquisition in the UK by a person who is not a taxable person.

The rules governing liability to register as a distance seller are illustrated in the flow chart at 8-970.

Legislation: VATA 1994, Sch. 2, para. 10

Other material: Notice 700/1, Section 5

VAT Reporter: ¶43-030

8-550 Distance selling limit

A person who is not otherwise liable to register for VAT becomes liable to register on a day when the total value of his relevant supplies to the UK since the previous 1 January exceed the distance selling threshold (see Hardman's Tax Rates and Tables 19-080 or Key Data 1-140).

The value of relevant supplies for this purpose is reckoned exclusive of any overseas VAT charged.

Notification must be made to HMRC within 30 days from the time when the liability to register arose, and they must register him with effect from the day when the liability arose (or from a mutually agreed earlier date).

Legislation: VATA 1994, Sch. 2, para. 1(1) and 3

Other material: Notice 700/1, para. 2.3

VAT Reporter: ¶43-175

8-570 Excise goods

A person who makes such supplies of excise goods (i.e. goods liable to a duty of excise, such as tobacco products, alcoholic beverage, petrol, etc.) becomes liable to register as soon as such supplies are made. There is no turnover limit for excise goods.

The same notification and registration rules apply as for registration when the turnover limit is exceeded.

Legislation: VATA 1994, Sch. 2, para. 1(3)

VAT Reporter: ¶63-280

8-590 Voluntary registration

A person belonging in another Member State who has elected to treat his UK distance sales as taking place outside that State becomes liable to register in the UK when he makes such a supply.

The same notification and registration rules apply as for the other categories of distance selling registration.

A person intending to make an election to treat his UK distance sales as made outside his own Member State, or who has made such an election, and intending to make distance sales to the UK, may request registration as a distance seller, and HMRC may impose conditions on such a registration. However, if the person also qualifies for voluntary registration as a UK intending trader or as a person making supplies outside the UK and having a business establishment in the UK, he will be registered under VATA 1994, Sch. 1 rather than Sch. 2.

A person who has registered on the basis of an intended election, or intended distance sales to the UK, must notify HMRC within 30 days of the intended election or sales taking place (VATA 1994, Sch. 2, para. 5(2), (3)).

Legislation: VATA 1994, Sch. 2, para. 1(2) and. 4

8-610 Ceasing registration

A person ceases to be registrable if a position arises where he is neither obliged, nor able, to register under any of the UK VAT provisions, taking each separately. He must notify HMRC of this within 30 days of ceasing to be registrable.

A person who ceases to be liable to be registered may have his registration cancelled, provided he is not liable to be registered under other provisions. Also, HMRC may cancel the registration of a person who has registered voluntarily, and who has failed to make the intended election or supplies, or has breached any conditions imposed.

Legislation: VATA 1994, Sch. 2, para. 5(1) and (4), 6 and 7

Other material: Notice 700/11, Section 3

VAT Reporter: ¶43-930

8-620 Registration of UK suppliers in other Member States

A UK trader making distance sales to other Member States, but not compulsorily registered there, can make elections similar to those mentioned in 8-590 above. Distance sales to the other Member States concerned are then treated as made in those Member States and not in the UK.

Such an election must be notified to HMRC within 30 days before the date on which the first supply under it is to be made, and the trader must within 30 days of making that first supply provide documentary evidence of having notified the other Member State of the election. If the election is subsequently withdrawn, the trader must notify HMRC of this within 30 days before the first supply intended following such withdrawal. However, the withdrawal cannot take effect before 1 January which is, or follows, the second anniversary of making the first supply under the election.

A trader voluntarily electing to treat distance sales to another Member State as being made in that State is, therefore, bound by that election for a period of two to three years.

Legislation: VATA 1994, s. 7(5); *Value Added Tax Regulations* 1995 (SI 1995/2518), reg. 98

Other material: Notice 725, para. 6.5

VAT Reporter: ¶43-046

REGISTRATION – NON-EC SUPPLIERS OF ELECTRONIC SERVICES

8-630 Special scheme for non-EC suppliers of electronic services

Supplies of certain electronic services by non-EC businesses to EC consumers are taxable in the EC (see 3-980(5)). Normally, this would involve such suppliers needing to register in each Member State.

Instead, there is a special scheme under which such suppliers can:

(a) electronically register for VAT in a single EC State;
(b) electronically make declarations of tax due throughout the EC on a single return made to the State of registration.

It is then the responsibility of the State of registration to distribute the VAT to the appropriate Member States.

Legislation: VATA 1994, Sch. 3B

Other material: VAT Information Sheet 7/03

VAT Reporter: ¶43-047

OTHER MATTERS RELATING TO REGISTRATION

8-640 Joint and several liability

In the normal course of events, the only person responsible for paying to HMRC the VAT on a taxable supply is the supplier.

This is amended for supplies of:

(a) computers and computer equipment, including parts, accessories and software;
(b) telephones and telephone equipment, including parts and accessories.

Budget 2007 amended the list of goods in s. 77A(1) of VATA 1994 to which these provisions apply. The changes apply from 1 May 2007.

The amendment takes into account that technological developments mean that electronic equipment is becoming more capable of a range of functions. Hence the Order extends the definition of 'telephone' and 'computer' to include any goods that are made or adapted for these uses. In addition, it indicates that certain goods may fall into more than one category. It stipulates that 'satnav' equipment is to be regarded as being within the definition of a computer for the purpose of the Order. This is the first use to be made of the power to make such an Order contained in s. 77A(9) of VATA 1994.

Businesses which receive a supply of such items become jointly and severally liable for the VAT on the supply of them if they 'knew' or 'had reasonable grounds to suspect' that the VAT on the supply of them had not or would not be paid. The potential liability extends to any supply of the items concerned within the supply chain, not just the supply under which the business received the items.

Rebuttable presumption

There is a (rebuttable) presumption that a business 'knew' or 'had reasonable grounds to suspect' that VAT would not be paid if it purchased the items:

(a)   for less than the lowest open market value of them; or

(b)   for less than a price paid for them earlier in the chain.

The presumption will be rebutted, in particular, where it can be shown that the price of the items related to some factor other than failure to pay VAT.

This presumption does not in any way restrict the more general meaning of the test (i.e. you can still be caught if the transaction looked dodgy, even if you paid a full price).

Following the *Finance Act* 2007, HMRC are altering the 'rebuttable presumption' rule in s. 77A(6).

The rule is that HMRC are allowed to presume that a business had reasonable grounds to suspect VAT would go unpaid if specified goods were purchased for less than the market value or less than the price payable for them by a previous supplier. The business needs to be able to prove that the low price payable was unconnected with a failure to pay VAT in order to rebut this presumption.

The new sections contained in s. 77A(9A) and (9B) will allow the Treasury to extend or otherwise alter the circumstances in which a person may be presumed to have reasonable grounds for suspecting that VAT will be unpaid elsewhere in the supply chain.

Where a person is caught by the new provisions, HMRC may issue a liability notice. The person will then be jointly and severally liable with the supplier for the VAT due on a supply of the items. The VAT due is the output tax arising, less any input tax credit properly available to the supplier.

As a general rule, traders should be able to avoid the risk of falling within these provisions where they can show that they have taken reasonable steps to verify the legitimacy of their suppliers and customers.

Public Notice, VAT Notice 726, Joint and Several Liability in the supply of specified goods, gives HMRC's views on the measures.

ECJ puts legislation in question

The UK are likely to have to amend this legislation following the European Court of Justice ruling in the cases of *C & E Commrs v Optigen Ltd*, *C & E Commrs v Fulcrum Electronics Ltd*, *C & E Commrs v Bond House Systems Ltd*.

These were all cases involving a so-called carousel fraud. The appeals were joined together in a reference to the ECJ for a preliminary ruling. See also 11-620.

The main question referred was:

Is the entitlement of a trader to deduct input tax on a transaction to be judged by:

(a) only the particular transaction, including the trader's purposes in entering into the transaction; or

(b) the totality of transactions, including subsequent or circular transactions of which the trader has no knowledge and/or means of knowledge; and/or

(c) the fraudulent acts and intention, whether prior or subsequent to the transaction, of others in the circular chain of whose involvement the trader is unaware and of whose acts and intentions the trader has no knowledge; and/or

(d) some other, and if so what, criteria?

The ECJ has ruled that the right to reclaim VAT in these types of cases may only be limited or removed if the trader had knowledge or had the means of knowledge about the fraud.

This indicates that businesses affected will have to make sure that some effort has been made to check that a transaction is bona fide. It is notable that in this situation, it will be necessary to have information about both the supplier and the customer.

The care needed is likely to include the usual checks made on new customers:

• credit checks including taking up credit references;
• identification of personnel involved akin to the need for such action in the 'money laundering' legislation;
• address and office checks;
• trading history;
• verification of VAT number – see Hardman's Tax Rates and Tables 19-860 or Key Data 1-730.

It would appear that there would also need to be similar checks put in place for new suppliers since the transactions affected may be part of a chain of supply.

Legislation: VATA 1994, s. 77A

Cases: *C & E Commrs v Optigen Ltd* [2006] BVC 119; *C & E Commrs v Fulcrum Electronics Ltd* [2006] BVC 119; *C & E Commrs v Bond House Systems Ltd* [2006] BVC 119

Other material: Notice 726

VAT Reporter: ¶43-300

8-660 Requirement for security

Although it is not strictly a registration matter, it is worth noting that HMRC have power to require security from a taxable person. Making taxable supplies without providing the security required under this provision is a criminal offence punishable by a fine at level 5 on the standard scale contained in the *Criminal Justice Act*.

Security is normally required only where the taxable person (or its managers), or an associated business, has a history of failing to pay VAT to HMRC. It may also be required in the case of an overseas business with no UK establishment or agent.

HMRC may also require security on the basis of the possible insolvency, disappearance, etc. of entities with which the trader deals.

Legislation: VATA 1994, s. 72(11)

VAT Reporter: ¶43-830

Amount of security

Where quarterly returns are submitted, the usual practice is to require security equal to the estimated net liability of about six months. In cases where monthly returns are made, the security demanded usually only covers the estimated net liability for a period of four months.

VAT Reporter: ¶43-830

Appeals

The First-tier Tax Tribunal has a supervisory jurisdiction. The appellant will need to show that HMRC:

- acted unreasonably;
- took account of irrelevant matters; or
- disregarded a matter that should have been taken into account.

VAT Reporter: ¶43-830

Checklist

When a person is served with a notice to give security, the following should be considered:

- request a review of both the decision to give security and the quantum required;
- lodge an appeal;
- consider asking to submit monthly returns in order to lower the amount of security required; and
- if the compliance record improves, ask HMRC to review their decision and consider appealing against the new decision.

Legislation: VATA 1994, Sch. 11, para. 4(2)

Other material: Notice 700/52 Notice of requirement to give security

VAT Reporter: ¶43-830

8-680 Tax representatives

A person who is liable to be registered for VAT in the UK, but who has no UK business establishment, may be required by HMRC to appoint a UK VAT representative. Such a VAT representative is responsible for his principal's compliance with UK VAT requirements, and is jointly and severally liable for any VAT and penalties due.

HMRC can only direct the appointment of a VAT representative in the case of a non-EC trader, and then only if the trader's own country does not have mutual assistance arrangements with the UK for the recovery of VAT, exchange of information and administrative co-operation concerning indirect taxation.

A person who fails to appoint a VAT representative when so directed may be required to provide such security as HMRC think fit.

Legislation: VATA 1994, s. 48

VAT Reporter: ¶43-860

8-700 Changes in circumstances

A person who is registered for VAT is obliged to notify HMRC of such changes as changes of name, constitution or ownership of the business, and any other changes which may necessitate the variation of the register or cancellation of the registration. Notification must be made within 30 days after the change.

Legislation: *Value Added Tax Regulations* 1995 (SI 1995/2518), reg. 5(3)

Other material: Notice 700, para. 26.3

VAT Reporter: ¶43-200

8-720 Scope of registration and person registered

When a person is registered for VAT, the registration covers all of that person's business activities and, in the case of a partnership, covers activities of other partnerships having the same partners (see 3-720 and 3-740). This is because it is the partners themselves who are registered for VAT rather than the partnership as such.

Although a change in partners does not trigger a new registration, merely an amendment to the register, a change from a partnership to a sole trader, or vice versa, does involve a new registration and all of the formalities of de-registration and notification of liability to register must be observed.

In the case of a group of companies for which group treatment has been obtained, the registration of the representative member of the group covers the activities of all of the companies within the group (17-080ff.).

In the case of a company organised in divisions, it is possible to arrange for each division to be entered in the register so that separate returns can be submitted but there is still, in principle, a single registration covering all of the divisions.

A club, association, etc. is registered in its own name. Responsibility for meeting VAT obligations rests with its president, chairman, treasurer, etc. or, if none, its committee or, if none, with every member.

Legislation: VATA 1994, s. 46(1) and (3); *Value Added Tax Regulations* 1995 (SI 1995/2518), reg. 8

VAT Reporter: ¶43-135

8-740 Splitting a business to avoid registration

A business making standard-rated supplies to the public (or to entities which cannot recover any VAT charged) will generally be better off if it does not have to register for, and charge, VAT. A very large business does not usually have any option in this matter. A smaller one has some options, if it makes its arrangements with care.

VAT Reporter: ¶43-650

Splitting whole business

The most obvious route is to operate two or more similar businesses through separate legal entities, each having taxable turnover below the VAT registration threshold (see Hardman's Tax Rates and Tables 19-080 or Key Data 1-140). If, say, a business which would have annual turnover of £85,000 can instead be operated as two businesses, each with turnover of £42,500, this can result in an output tax saving of £14,166 per annum (£85,000 × 16). The effect on profitability will depend on the amount of input tax recovery foregone. Clearly, the benefit will be greater for a service business with little in the way of inputs than for a business which buys and sells standard-rated goods.

It is absolutely essential, if this sort of split is attempted, that there is a genuine separation. This can be difficult in practice, despite operating separate bank accounts, etc. because of the need to present a credible impression to customers of the businesses while making it clear that there are two or more businesses (probably trading from the same premises). It is also necessary to be alert for any taxable supplies passing between the businesses, which might make it necessary for one or more of them to register.

VAT Reporter: ¶43-650

339

Division of functions

Another approach often used in services industries where the ultimate provision of service is done by a single individual is to reflect this in the way that the legal entities are organised, having one entity providing central resources used by a number of self-employed individuals who provide services to the public.

For instance, instead of having a single hairdressing business employing stylists, it is perfectly possible to have a business providing such central resources as a salon, bulk buying facilities, and central booking, with the delivery of services to the public done by self-employed stylists who buy the resources they need from the central business.

Similarly, a number of self-employed cab drivers might make use of the facilities of a central booking organisation.

Once again, great care is needed in setting up such arrangements to ensure that, not only is the desired result achieved, but it is properly documented and can be shown to be achieved. There are many similarities between these modes of organisation and others which have quite different VAT effects. It is necessary to ensure that:

(1)   the service providers are, indeed, self-employed; and

(2)   in their self-employed capacity, they are providing the final services direct to the public, rather than them providing services to the central organisation which re-supplies them to the public.

An example of a case in which self-employed hairdressers were found to have made their supplies directly to the public is that of *C & E Commrs v MacHenrys (Hairdressers) Ltd* [1993] BVC 43.

Another important case, though not directly concerned with this sort of arrangement, is that of *C & E Commrs v Music and Video Exchange Ltd* [1992] BVC 30, which illustrates the importance of the legal arrangements entered into by the parties in determining the treatment which applies in cases which are susceptible to a number of different interpretations. However, the contractual arrangements will not always be decisive in determining the supply position, especially if (as is often the case) they are open to more than one interpretation. In such cases, it is for the tribunal to determine what supplies are made, and by whom, as a question of fact.

It should be noted that, under arrangements of this sort, the central organisation may well need to register for VAT and charge VAT on some or all of the services provided to the self-employed service providers. The VAT saving which arises is on the 'value added' by the service providers.

In particular, HMRC take the view that in most cases involving hairdressers, chair rental charges by the salon owner represent consideration for a taxable supply of facilities, rather than for an exempt supply of a licence to occupy land.

In the case of hairdressers, it is common to seek to structure matters so that at least part of the supply by the central organisation is exempt from VAT, as the grant of a licence to occupy land, in the form of a chair rent. There have been conflicting decisions on the success of such schemes over the years. However, in *Simon Harris Hair Design Ltd* [1996] BVC 4,260 the tribunal held that there was a single standard-rated supply of services. Although there was a charge for the use of facilities (such as shared junior staff, etc.) and a separate charge for the exclusive use of the chair, the tribunal considered that the use of the chair was a supply ancillary to the other facilities, was not economically dissociable from the supply of the other facilities, and was subsumed within the supply of the other facilities. Following this decision, HMRC take the view that, where stylists are working in open plan salons and clearly making using of general facilities, such as junior staff, basins, and hair dryers, there is a single taxable supply. One way of circumventing this decision may be to have one entity supply the licence to occupy land, and a separate entity provide the other facilities: if there are two suppliers, it can hardly be said that there is only one supply.

Cases: *C & E Commrs v MacHenrys (Hairdressers) Ltd* [1993] BVC 43; *C & E Commrs v Music and Video Exchange Ltd* [1992] BVC 30; *C & E Commrs v Reed Personnel Services Ltd,* [1995] BVC 222; *Simon Harris Hair Design Ltd* [1996] BVC 4,260

VAT Reporter: ¶43-650

Deciding if there is more than one business

'In deciding whether two businesses were carried on separately, a tribunal should examine the substance and the reality and could only conclude that there were separate taxable entities if the so called businesses were sufficiently at arm's length from one another, and had normal commercial relationships each with the other'. The above guidance was given in the case of *Burrel.*

However, the High Court did not give guidance on the facts which should be taken into account in cases like this.

The VAT Tribunals applied this guidance in the case of *Mr D Harris t/a Fellows Sandwich Bar and Mrs M Harris t/a Fellows Bistro.*

In this case, the more salient facts taken into account by the Tribunal were as follows:

- '… the nature of the businesses'. They were (both) in the catering business.
- 'they operated from the same premises under the terms of a common business lease held jointly by the Appellants.'
- 'the operations were dependent upon the shared facilities …'
- 'the success of the businesses was critically reliant on the skills and expertise of Mr Harris …'
- how the purchase and sale of the businesses was represented in the respective documentation.
- 'the physical, legal and human resource infrastructure for the two businesses ...'
- 'the different working practices … were ones of form rather than substance.'

- 'Mrs Harris' weekly payment ... for the share of premises costs remained constant ... [and] ... was not calculated from the costs of the actual resources consumed'.

The Tribunal decided that 'the substance and reality of Fellows Bistro and Sandwich Bar was that it was single business'.

This case is a salutary lesson in the problems associated with, and dangers arising from, splitting a business.

Anti-avoidance measure – direction to treat two or more businesses as one

There is a special provision to counter attempts to avoid registration by splitting a business activity among several legal entities, each with turnover below the VAT registration threshold.

This entitles HMRC to make a direction treating the persons named in it as being one person for VAT purposes, and so liable to be registered with effect from the date of direction. Further persons can, if necessary, be added to the direction and such additions to an existing direction can have retrospective effect.

HMRC's policy is to issue such directions when the following conditions apply:

(1) The separation is artificial.

(2) The separation results in an avoidance of VAT.

(3) The parties involved are closely bound by financial, economic and organisational links.

(4) The other legal requirements are satisfied.

The legal requirements for making a direction are as follows:

(1) each person named therein makes taxable supplies; and

(2) the activities in the course of which the supplies are made form part of a business described in the direction, the remaining activities of that business being carried on by the other persons named in the direction; and

(3) when the whole of the activities of the business are considered together, the person carrying it on is liable to be registered for VAT.

A 2011 example of HMRC's attempts to make a direction to treat two businesses as one is in *Forster* where an appellant carried on a bed and breakfast business whilst her husband, son and the appellant in partnership carried on a farming business.

Legislation: VATA 1994, Sch. 1, para. 2

Other material: Notice 700/1, Section 13

VAT Reporter: ¶43-680

Cases: *Burrell (t/a the Firm) v C & E Commrs* [1998] BVC 3; *Harris (t/a Fellows Sandwich Bar) and Harris (t/a Fellows Bistro)* Decision No 20235; [2007] BVC 4,111; *Cringan* [1992] BVC 721; *Spence* [1991] BVC 1,330; *Horsman* (1990) 5 BVC 904; *Hundsdoerfer* (1990) 5 BVC 886; *Knights* (1990) 5 BVC 803; *Turner* Decision No 19,076; [2005] BVC 4,089; *Francis* Decision No 19919; [2007] BVC 4,051; *Forster* [2011] UKFTT 469 (TC),[2011] TC 01319

8-760   Deferring registration

With a turnover limit for registration purposes of £73,000 per annum (from 1 April 2011), it is tempting to advise a new business which is clearly going to exceed that figure to register from the outset and have done with it.

Where the business is primarily selling to registered businesses which can reclaim any tax charged this is clearly the best advice, but for businesses dealing directly with the public – particularly service businesses – there may be worthwhile savings from deferring registration.

The amount of VAT-free turnover which can be obtained before registration is rather higher than might be expected from a cursory glance at the registration provisions.

Deferment and potential savings

Assume that a new business expects to turn over up to £50,000 per month and that the business proprietor makes no other taxable supplies. The proprietor is aware of the VAT rules and is prepared, initially, to take time off if need be to prevent turnover exceeding £73,000 (from 1 April 2011) in any 30-day period, so is not caught by the future turnover test.

In month 1, turnover is £50,000. Neither test is triggered.

In month 2 it is £50,000 again. This time, the historic turnover test is triggered, and the trader must register from the end of month 3 (but not earlier, so long as he continues to keep turnover down to avoid the 30-day look-ahead).

Thus, the trader has three months of turnover at £50,000, totalling £150,000, before needing to register. The value of this will depend upon the amount of input tax foregone as a result of deferring registration. Bear in mind that input tax can be reclaimed, on registration, for goods acquired in the previous four years and still on hand, and for some pre-registration services (but not any arising more than six months before registration) (see 6-660).

Types of business

Deferment of registration is least valuable for businesses with high levels of input tax, such as those dealing in standard-rated goods. Benefits are more likely for those with low inputs, such as:

• service industries supplying consumers, such as hairdressers, etc.;

343

- service industries serving exempt businesses, such as a consultant to certain financial sector businesses; and
- businesses with standard-rated outputs but zero-rated inputs, such as restaurants.

Legislation: VATA 1994, s. 49(1)(a), Sch. 1, para. 1(1)

VAT Reporter: ¶43-000

8-770 Transfer of registration number

Where a business is transferred as a going concern, and the transferor ceases to be registered for VAT, it is possible for the registration number to be transferred to the transferee by mutual consent of the parties (see 18-600).

VAT Reporter: ¶43-775

8-780 Partnerships: registration in name of firm

The VAT registration of a partnership may be made in the name of the firm, rather than of the partners. This is to avoid the need to reregister the entity every time there is a change in the partners.

However, changes in the partners must still be notified to HMRC. If a person leaves a partnership, the retiring partner continues to be treated as a partner for VAT purposes, and so liable for any VAT due from the partnership, until notification is made.

It should be noted that, where a sole trader takes a partner, or where the retirement of a partner leaves the business as a sole trader business, the change is between a partnership entity and a non-partnership entity. In this case, the old registration ceases and a new one comes into being. All the usual requirements for notification, etc. apply and, if they are not complied with on time, penalties can arise.

If there are two partnerships, each having the same partners, they are effectively regarded as a single person for VAT purposes, so that a single registration covers both partnerships. However, two limited partnerships are regarded as separate, even though they are of identical composition, if the limited partners are different in each case. The limited partners are not regarded as carrying on the business of the firm in partnership, so the composition of the partnerships has to be considered by reference to the general partners, and excluding the limited partners.

Where it is necessary for HMRC to give any notice to a partnership, such as a notice of assessment, this can be done by a notice addressed to the firm. It is not necessary to make separate notification to each partner.

Legislation: VATA 1994, s. 45

Other material: Notice 700, Section 26

Cases: *Beaton, Snelling & Co* (1986) 2 BVC 208,116; *C & E Commrs v Glassborow* (1974) 1 BVC 4; *Saunders and Sorrell* (1980) 1 BVC 1,133

VAT Reporter: ¶43-300

8-790   Supplies contracted before registration

A trader is liable to account for VAT on all supplies made on or after the effective date of the registration. With one qualification, the normal time of supply rules (see 4-020) are used to determine if a supply takes place before or after registration. The qualification concerns tax invoices.

Someone who is not VAT-registered cannot issue a tax invoice. Thus, invoices issued before registration do not create tax points. These invoices should be ignored for determining the time of supply.

Continuous supplies

A business making continuous supplies must normally account for tax on all payments received after registration (see 4-280 for special tax point rules). The exception is when the supplies concerned ceased prior to registration. This was decided in *BJ Rice & Associates v C & E Commrs*.

Cases: *BJ Rice & Associates v C & E Commrs* [1996] BVC 211

VAT Reporter: ¶43-075

8-800   Penalties

A person who is late in notifying liability to register can incur a civil penalty. This, together with the changes to be implemented at a date after 1 April 2009, is discussed at 10-100ff.

VAT Reporter: ¶43-858

8-810   Death, insolvency and receivership

Where a sole proprietor dies or becomes bankrupt, the person carrying on the business must notify the appropriate VAT office within 21 days). Until such time as someone else is registered in respect of the business the Commissioners may treat as a taxable person anyone carrying on the business.

If a company becomes insolvent the person carrying on the business must notify the appropriate VAT office) within 21 days. If the business continues, deregistration is not required as the company is treated as a continuing taxable person even though a receiver or a liquidator has been appointed. The receiver or liquidator is required to inform HMRC of their appointment on Form VAT 769. The statement of affairs (if available) and the certificate of appointment should be attached. Any supplies made by the liquidator, receiver or administrator are made by them as an agent of the company. VAT invoices are issued by the company. The VAT status of the company is unaffected by its going into liquidation, etc.

If the business is not continued the normal procedures for cancellation of registration apply. An administrative receiver is a taxable person and must account for VAT but a receiver responsible for realising a fixed charge over a specific asset is not a taxable person. However, where the receivership is exercised over a property subject to the option to tax, the receiver must still account to HMRC for the VAT element of rents collected by them in respect of that property (*Sargent v C & E Commrs* [1995] BVC 108).

Legislation: *Value Added Tax Regulations* 1995 (SI 1995/2518), reg. 9

Other material: Notice 700, para. 26.7

Cases: *Sargent v C & E Commrs*[1995] BVC 108

VAT Reporter: ¶43-872

DEREGISTRATION

8-830 Compulsory deregistration

Deregistration is compulsory if:

(a) a business ceases, i.e. if a taxable person sells or closes down the business;
(b) the legal status of the business is changed, i.e. a sole proprietor takes another person into partnership (but it is possible to transfer the registration);
(c) a person registered as an intending trader no longer intends to make taxable supplies. An intending trader may thus be compulsorily deregistered if the intention to make taxable supplies ceases;
(d) a person registered under para. 9A of Sch. 1 (i.e. because of supplies of goods in warehouse or outside the UK) stops making or intending to make such supplies;
(e) the registration was void from the start.

A person is not able to be deregistered if he is liable for registration under any other provision of VATA 1994, e.g. because of acquisitions of relevant goods from other Member States.

It is not always easy to decide when a business has ceased. If a business ceases temporarily, but the taxable person intends to resume in the not too distant future, then deregistration is not necessary. A business may also cease to be registrable in certain unexpected circumstances. For example, if the nature of the business changes (or legislation changes) so that all supplies become exempt, deregistration will be compulsory.

HMRC may cancel a registration 'with effect from the day on which the registered person ceased to be liable or entitled to be registered'. They may not do it from any other date except a 'later date agreed between them and the registered person'.

Legislation: VATA 1994, Sch. 1, para. 11, 12 and 13

Cases: *Gardner & Co* [2011] UKFTT 470 (TC), [2011] TC 01320

Other material: Notice 700/11, para. 2.1

Notification period

A person who is liable for compulsory deregistration under any of the items above must notify the appropriate VAT office within 30 days. Where a business has ceased, deregistration is effective from the day on which the business ceased or from a mutually agreed later date. Where a registration was void from the start it is cancelled from the date of registration

Legislation: VATA 1994, Sch. 1, para. 11

8-840 Voluntary deregistration

Voluntary deregistration is possible if certain conditions are fulfilled. If a taxable person can satisfy the Commissioners that taxable supplies in the next 12 months will not exceed the deregistration threshold (see 19-080 or Key Data 1-280) voluntary deregistration will be allowed.

Voluntary deregistration is not permitted if the reason turnover will not exceed the threshold is that:

- the person plans to stop trading during the next 12 months; or
- the person plans to sell the business; or
- the person plans temporarily to cease making taxable supplies for 30 days or more.

Legislation: VATA 1994, Sch. 1, para. 4(3)

Other material: Notice 700/11, para. 2.2

8-850 How to deregister

A person wishing to deregister should write or send form VAT 7 to the Grimsby deregistration unit (see 1-705). If the Commissioners accept the application to deregister, the person will be sent a formal notice of cancellation showing the date of cancellation. The person is also required to complete a final VAT return. The final return must be completed even if there is no VAT due.

8-860 Consequences of deregistration

There are a number of consequences, some obvious and some not, of deregistration:

(a) the person must not issue any more VAT invoices. Where invoices are issued under self-billing arrangements customers must be informed immediately to stop issuing invoices relating to that person;

(b) the person must not charge VAT on any supplies made;

(c) VAT records must be retained. The business must also keep a list of business assets on hand at the time of deregistration, including their values;

(d) partly exempt businesses must make a final adjustment on their final VAT return;

(e) adjustments may also be necessary if retail schemes are used;

(f) the business may be liable to pay VAT on stocks and assets on hand at the time of deregistration;

(g) some VAT incurred after deregistration may be reclaimed (see 6-720 and flowchart 7-930).

VAT Reporter: ¶43-920

8-870 Accounting for VAT on stocks and assets on hand

The requirement to account for VAT on stocks and assets on hand at the time of deregistration is because the law deems such assets to be supplied in the course or furtherance of a business, unless:

(a) the business is transferred as a going concern;

(b) the business becomes bankrupt or insolvent and is carried on by a liquidator, administrator or receiver; or

(c) the tax on the deemed supply would not be more than £1,000.

If VAT is payable on stocks or assets on hand at the time of deregistration, it is payable on the price that would have to be paid (excluding VAT) to purchase identical goods at the time of supply. The goods must be identical in every respect including age and condition to the goods concerned. If the value of identical goods cannot be ascertained, then VAT is payable on the cost of purchasing similar goods. If it is not possible to establish a value using either identical or similar goods, VAT must be paid on the cost of producing the goods concerned at the time of deregistration.

Legislation: VATA 1994, Sch. 4, para. 8(1) and Sch. 6, para. 6

Other material: Notice 700/11, Section 6

8-880 Land and buildings on hand

Land and buildings on hand at deregistration are subject to the same principles and possible charges as other stock and assets.

HMRC explain when VAT is due on land and buildings at deregistration as follows:

'You will have to account for VAT on these assets if the following conditions are met:

- you were entitled to claim input tax on their acquisition or on their construction where that construction created a new building, or acquired them as a transfer of a going concern and a predecessor owner was entitled to claim input tax,
- your supplies of them, if made, would be taxable (for example because you have opted to tax) ...'

For further information about this and farmers using the agricultural flat rate scheme go to VAT Notice 742, para 7.8 and VATSC23600.

Other material: Notice 742, para 7.8; VATSC23600

Registration and Deregistration

FLOWCHARTS

8-950 Liability to register

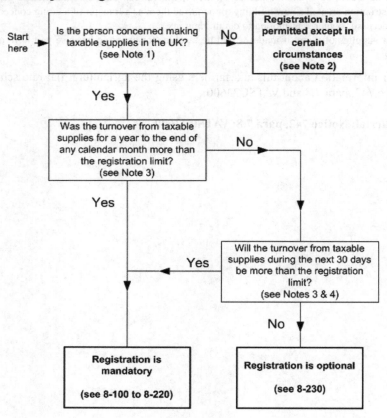

Notes

(1) Taxable supplies

A supply is taxable if it is liable to zero per cent, five per cent or the standard rate of VAT. For further information about supplies, see 3-120.

(2) Registration when making no taxable supplies

Subject to HMRC's discretion, registration is permitted in the following circumstances:

- before taxable supplies commence (see 8-260); and
- when the only supplies are certain supplies made outside the UK (see 8-320).

(3) Taxable turnover

Certain disposals of capital assets are not turnover for these purposes. For further information, see 8-040 and 8-070.

(4) Future supplies

Taxable supplies expected to arise during the forthcoming 30 days must be considered. For further information, see 8-160 and 8-190.

8-960 Liability to register

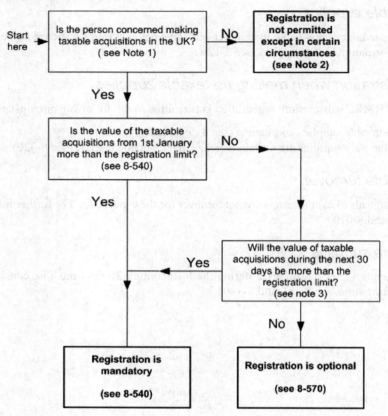

Notes

(1) Taxable acquisitions

Taxable acquisition are goods 'imported' from another EU State and which are liable to zero per cent, five per cent or the standard rate of VAT. For further information about supplies, see 5-600.

(2) Registration before acquisitions making when making no taxable supplies

Subject to HMRC's discretion, registration is permitted before acquisitions are made (see 8-570).

(3) Future acquisitions

Acquisitions expected to take place during the forthcoming 30 days must be considered. For further information, see 8-470.

8-970 Liability to register – distance selling

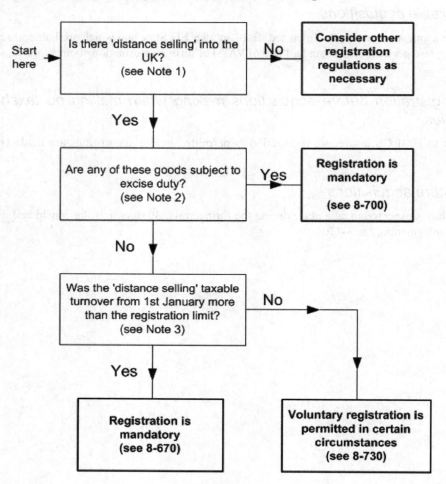

Start here → **Is there 'distance selling' into the UK?** (see Note 1) — No → **Consider other registration regulations as necessary**

↓ Yes

Are any of these goods subject to excise duty? (see Note 2) — Yes → **Registration is mandatory** (see 8-700)

↓ No

Was the 'distance selling' taxable turnover from 1st January more than the registration limit? (see Note 3) — No →

↓ Yes

Registration is mandatory (see 8-670)

Voluntary registration is permitted in certain circumstances (see 8-730)

Notes

(1) Distance selling

'Distance selling is when a taxable person in one European Community (EC) Member State supplies and delivers goods to a customer in another EC Member State and the customer is not:

- registered for VAT; or
- liable to be registered for VAT.' (Notice 700/1, para. 5.1).

(2) Excise goods

Goods liable to excise duty are most commonly tobacco and alcohol products.

(3) Taxable turnover

With certain exceptions, these are sales which would be liable to zero per cent, five per cent or the standard rate of tax when bought from a UK trader. For more information, see 8-040.

8-980 Registering for VAT – use the correct form

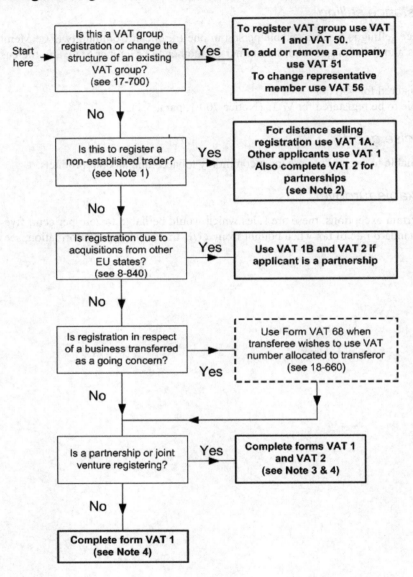

Start here → Is this a VAT group registration or change the structure of an existing VAT group? (see 17-700)

Yes → To register VAT group use VAT 1 and VAT 50. To add or remove a company use VAT 51 To change representative member use VAT 56

No ↓

Is this to register a non-established trader? (see Note 1)

Yes → For distance selling registration use VAT 1A. Other applicants use VAT 1 Also complete VAT 2 for partnerships (see Note 2)

No ↓

Is registration due to acquisitions from other EU states? (see 8-840)

Yes → Use VAT 1B and VAT 2 if applicant is a partnership

No ↓

Is registration in respect of a business transferred as a going concern?

Yes → Use Form VAT 68 when transferee wishes to use VAT number allocated to transferor (see 18-660)

No ↓

Is a partnership or joint venture registering?

Yes → Complete forms VAT 1 and VAT 2 (see Note 3 & 4)

No ↓

Complete form VAT 1 (see Note 4)

Notes

(1) Non-established traders

A non-established trader is someone who is:

(a)   not normally resident in the UK;
(b)   without a business establishment in the UK; and
(c)   not incorporated in the UK if the trader is a company.

(2) Distance selling

'Distance selling is when a taxable person in one European Community (EC) Member State supplies and delivers goods to a customer in another EC Member State and the customer is not:

- registered for VAT; or
- liable to be registered for VAT.' (VAT Notice 700/1, para. 5.1).

For more information, see 8-530.

(3) Joint ventures

Normally, joint ventures are registered as if a partnership. For further information, see 17-050.

(4) Welsh forms

The following forms are available in Welsh:

- VAT 1;
- VAT 1A;
- VAT 1B;
- VAT 1TR;
- VAT 2;
- VAT 68.

The Welsh version is denoted by 'W' (e.g. VAT 1(W)).

Registration and Deregistration

357

8-990 Checklist for completing Form VAT 1

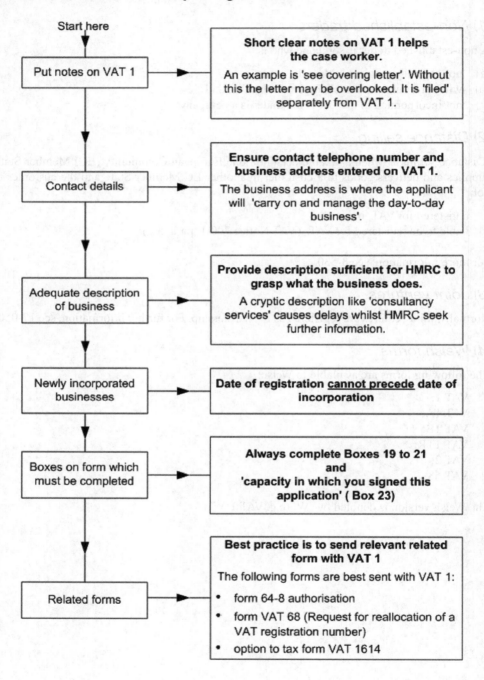

Start here

Put notes on VAT 1 → **Short clear notes on VAT 1 helps the case worker.**
An example is 'see covering letter'. Without this the letter may be overlooked. It is 'filed' separately from VAT 1.

Contact details → **Ensure contact telephone number and business address entered on VAT 1.**
The business address is where the applicant will 'carry on and manage the day-to-day business'.

Adequate description of business → **Provide description sufficient for HMRC to grasp what the business does.**
A cryptic description like 'consultancy services' causes delays whilst HMRC seek further information.

Newly incorporated businesses → **Date of registration cannot precede date of incorporation**

Boxes on form which must be completed → **Always complete Boxes 19 to 21 and 'capacity in which you signed this application' (Box 23)**

Related forms → **Best practice is to send relevant related form with VAT 1**
The following forms are best sent with VAT 1:
- form 64-8 authorisation
- form VAT 68 (Request for reallocation of a VAT registration number)
- option to tax form VAT 1614

[This page is intentionally blank]

8-995 Errors to be avoided when completing Form VAT 1

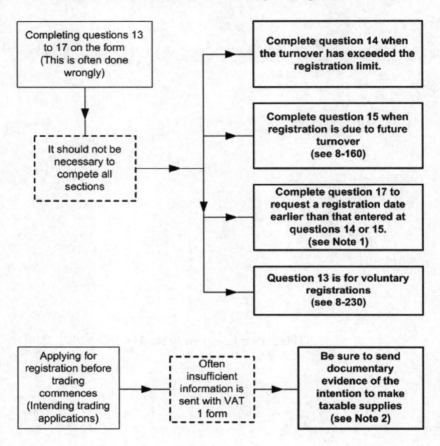

Notes

(1) Earlier registration date

With the agreement of HMRC, the registration date may be put back to some time before the mandatory date. According to circumstances, this can be advantageous. It is best to seek advice before making such an application.

(2) Intending trader registrations

The necessary documentary evidence may be copies of contracts, planning permissions, purchase invoices, etc. The purpose is to satisfy the Registration Unit that proper steps are being taken to generate taxable supplies (see 8-260).

Registration and Deregistration

Records and Returns

VAT RECORDS AND RETURNS

9-100 Introduction to VAT records and returns

The purpose of this section is to review the importance of records in the VAT system, and the kinds of records which all traders must keep, and to consider the role of VAT returns in the administration of the tax.

9-130 Importance of records

VAT is ultimately collected at the level of individual supplies, therefore it is important that records should exist of all transactions. This becomes even more important given the provisions for refund of tax, so that one trader may be seeking repayment from HMRC of tax which should have been paid to them by another trader. Not surprisingly, HMRC are anxious to be able to verify that the tax has in fact been paid.

In order to meet this need, HMRC have a general power to require traders to keep such records as they may require.

From the trader's point of view, proper records are important in order to prevent HMRC from making assessments for tax which they might reasonably deduce to be due, but which is not in fact due when the full information is examined. A great many appeals to VAT tribunals fail, not from any technical deficiency in the appellant's case, but purely from lack of evidence as to the transactions which have actually occurred.

The trader also needs to hold evidence when reliefs from tax are sought. Examples include the refund of input tax, and claiming zero-rating for a supply.

In some instances, these evidential requirements are specifically imposed by law. For instance, input tax may not be reclaimed unless the appropriate evidence (such as a valid tax invoice) is held.

In other instances, the holding of evidence is a matter of prudence rather than of strict legal requirement. For instance, some supplies of services are outside the scope of UK VAT if supplied to a person who belongs outside of the UK, but taxable at the standard rate if supplied to someone who belongs in the UK. Although there is no formal requirement as to evidence in such a case, it is wise to retain whatever evidence is available to show where the customer belongs (e.g. business correspondence).

Legislation: VATA 1994, Sch. 11, para. 6(1); *Value Added Tax Regulations* 1995 (SI 1995/2518), reg. 49–55

Other material: Notice 700, Section 19

VAT Reporter: ¶4-620

9-160   General requirements

The general requirements as to record keeping for VAT are set out in the *Value Added Tax Regulations* 1995 (SI 1995/2518). References in this section are to these regulations unless otherwise specified. Each taxable person has an obligation to keep and preserve:

(a)   business and accounting records;
(b)   VAT account;
(c)   copies of all VAT invoices issued;
(d)   all VAT invoices received;
(e)   all certificates prepared for acquisitions of goods from other Member States, or received for supplies of goods or services, in fiscal or other warehousing regimes when the acquisitions or supplies are either zero-rated or are deemed to take place outside the UK;
(f)   documentation relating to acquisitions any goods from other Member States;
(g)   documentation relating to the transfer, dispatch or transportation of goods to other Member States;
(h)   documentation relating to importations and exportations;
(i)   credit notes, debit notes, or other documents received and copies of all such documents issued;
(j)   copy of any self-billing agreement operated;
(k)   when a customer of a business operating a self-billing, the name, address and VAT registration number of the business concerned.

Such records must be preserved for a period of six years, unless HMRC allow a shorter period.

Legislation: *Value Added Tax Regulations* 1995 (SI 1995/2518), reg. 31 and 32

VAT Reporter: ¶4-620

9-190   The VAT account

The required contents of the VAT account are specified in the *Value Added Tax Regulations* 1995 (SI 1995/2518), reg. 32.

The VAT account must be divided into separate parts for the different prescribed accounting periods for which VAT returns are made, and each part is then divided into a tax payable portion and a tax allowable portion.

In the tax payable portion for a period must be entered:

(1)   output tax due for the period on sales, etc.;
(2)   output tax due for the period on acquisitions of goods from other EC States;

(3) earlier output tax errors discovered during the period, where current period adjustment is both permissible and implemented (see 9-410 below);

(4) increases or decreases in output tax arising during the period from changes in the consideration for supplies (e.g. following price adjustments, disputes, retrospective discounts, etc.);

(5) other adjustments to output tax required or allowed under the VAT legislation.

In the tax allowable portion for a period must be entered:

(1) input tax allowable for the period on supplies, etc.;

(2) input tax allowable for the period on intra-EC acquisitions;

(3) earlier input tax errors discovered during the period, where current period adjustment is both permissible and implemented (see 9-410 below);

(4) increases or decreases in input tax arising during the period from changes in the consideration for supplies received (e.g. following price adjustments, disputes, retrospective discounts, etc.);

(5) other adjustments to input tax required or allowed under the VAT legislation.

Examples of adjustments required or allowed under the VAT legislation are:

- partial exemption annual adjustments;
- capital goods scheme adjustments;
- retail scheme annual adjustments;
- bad debt relief claims;
- adjustments under approved estimation.

It will be noted that, where errors are made, they never form part of the formal VAT account as such unless they are corrected under the current period adjustment procedure. However, it will be wise to keep a record of all errors discovered, and of their manner of correction, cross-referenced both to the period when each error was made and to that in which it was discovered.

Legislation: *Value Added Tax Regulations* 1995 (SI 1995/2518), reg. 14 and 32(2)

Other material: Notice 700, section 19

VAT Reporter: ¶55-000

9-220 Special record-keeping requirements

Apart from the records needed by traders generally, traders operating special schemes are usually subject to special record-keeping requirements. These may be specified by HMRC in notices, which have the force of law for this purpose. For instance, a car dealer who wishes to use the second-hand goods scheme for second-hand cars has no legal entitlement to do this unless records are kept in accordance with the scheme rules, providing acquisition and disposal details for each car dealt with under the scheme.

Other areas where special record-keeping requirements arise include:

- retail schemes;
- retail export schemes;
- reclaim of pre-registration input tax;
- bad debt relief claims;
- cash accounting scheme;
- margin schemes.

Legislation: *Value Added Tax Regulations* 1995 (SI 1995/2518), reg. 31(2)

9-250 Period of retention

Business records must be kept for a minimum of six years, unless agreement is reached with HMRC to dispose of them earlier.

Instead of keeping the original records, the trader may be permitted to keep copies on microfilm or microfiche, provided that copies can easily be produced and there are adequate facilities for HMRC officers to view them.

Electronic storage of invoices must meet the ordinary record keeping requirements. That is they must be produced to HMRC within a reasonable period of time either at the main place of business or other reasonable place when required. The data may be compressed provided that its integrity and authenticity can be maintained.

Legislation: VATA 1994, Sch. 11, para. 6(3)

Other information: Notice 700, para. 19.2; Notice 700/63, section 5

VAT Reporter: ¶59-000

9-280 Tax invoices

The most important single document for VAT purposes is probably the tax invoice.

In most cases where taxable supplies are made to other traders, there is a specific requirement to issue a tax invoice.

As far as the customer is concerned, HMRC have an absolute right to require traders to hold specific evidence to support claims for input tax. If the evidence is not held, or is defective in some way, then the input tax concerned cannot be deducted. However, HMRC must act reasonably (6-580).

Proposed changes from 1 January 2013

An EU Directive has been issued on invoicing requirements from 1 January 2013. The few practical changes that the UK must make are highlighted in the relevant sections below. See also 9-300.

(1) Contents of a tax invoice

In the usual case, where the input tax arises in respect of a supply received from another UK trader, the evidence required for input tax deduction is a tax invoice issued by that other trader. In order to be valid, and so capable of supporting a claim for input tax, a tax invoice must show all of the following information (although HMRC have power to authorise suppliers to allow some of the information to be omitted):

(1)   an identifying number which must be sequential and unique;

(2)   the date of the supply;

(3)   the date when the tax invoice is issued;

(4)   the following information about the supplier:

    (a)   name;

    (b)   address; and

    (c)   VAT registration number (prefixed by the letters GB where the supply is made to a person elsewhere in the EC);

(5)   the following information about the recipient of the supply:

    (a)   name (or trading name);

    (b)   address; and

    (c)   in the case of a supply to a person elsewhere in the EC, the customer's VAT registration number (if any) in his EC State;

(6)   a description sufficient to identify the goods or services supplied;

(7)   for each description on the invoice:

    (a)   the quantity of goods, or extent of services, supplied;

    (b)   the rate of VAT applicable; and

    (c)   the amount charged in any currency (net of VAT);

(8)   the total amount charged (net of VAT);

(9)   if a cash discount is offered, the rate of discount;

(10) the total amount of tax chargeable, expressed in sterling;

(11) the unit price must be shown. This applies to countable goods or services. It may be the hourly rate or standard service charge. It will not be a requirement if it is not normally provided in that business sector and is not required by the customer.

An invoice which includes exempt or zero-rated supplies must show separate totals for the different categories.

If the invoice held in support of a claim for input tax fails to show any of the above particulars, it is technically invalid (unless HMRC have allowed the supplier to omit some of the information – but it is difficult to see how the customer can tell) and this may result in the disallowance of the related tax. A consignment note or delivery note issued before the time of supply (e.g. where goods are sold on consignment or on sale or return terms) does not constitute a tax invoice even if it contains all of these details.

HMRC do have power to accept alternative evidence for input tax deduction, instead of insisting on a 'perfect' tax invoice. They also have an obligation to exercise this discretion reasonably, so minor technical deficiencies in invoices should not generally preclude recovery of input tax (see, for instance, *Chavda t/a Hare Wines* where an input tax claim was allowed despite the lack of proper invoices).

Legislation: *Value Added Tax Regulations* 1995 (SI 1995/2518), reg. 14

Other material: Notice 700, para. 16.3

Cases: *Chavda (t/a Hare Wines)* [1993] BVC 1,515

VAT Reporter: ¶55-800

(2) Production of a tax invoice

A trader is obliged to provide his customer with a tax invoice if he:

(1) makes a positive-rated supply in the UK to a taxable person; or

(2) makes a positive-rated supply, or a zero-rated supply of goods for acquisition elsewhere in the EC, to a person in another Member State, or receives a payment on account in respect of such a supply, or intended supply.

However, a tax invoice is not required in the case of a supply in respect of which input tax is 'blocked' (e.g. supplies of business entertainment, etc. – see 6-280ff.), or for supplies under second-hand goods schemes, or for supplies made for no consideration. In the case of blocked input tax, the supplier will frequently not be in a position to know whether or not he is obliged to issue a tax invoice, since this will often depend upon the use to which the supply is put by the customer.

HMRC accept that it is, in practice, impossible to issue a tax invoice at the time of the supply for a supply made under the tour operators' margin scheme (16-890), as the actual margin will not be known until the year-end calculation is carried out.

Where a tax invoice is required, the trader has an obligation to issue it within 30 days after the tax point.

Legislation: *Value Added Tax Regulations* 1995 (SI 1995/2518), reg. 13(1) and (5) and 20

Other material: Notice 700, para. 16.2

VAT Reporter: ¶55-800

(3) Less detailed invoice

A less detailed invoice can be issued, and used to support a claim for input tax if:

- the supplier is a retailer; and
- the value of the supply (including VAT) is less than £250.

The information which must be shown on a less detailed invoice is:

(1)   the name, address and VAT registration number of the supplier;

(2)   the date of the supply;

(3)   a description sufficient to identify the goods or services supplied;

(4)   the total payable, including VAT;

(5)   the rate of tax applicable.

A credit card voucher may be used as a less detailed tax invoice, provided that the retailer adapts it to show the information required. A retailer can also issue a tax invoice in a modified form, if the customer agrees. The modification is to show separate supplies at tax-inclusive values (instead of tax-exclusive), but the total VAT and the total of the VAT-inclusive and exclusive values of supplies at different rates must be shown.

A tax invoice for petrol, derv, etc. may be issued as a less detailed invoice if the value of supply is below £100. If the value is greater than £100, it is permissible to show the vehicle registration number instead of the customer's name and address, and to omit details of the quantity supplied and of the type of supply (sale, hire purchase, etc.).

A cash and carry wholesaler can use till slips as tax invoices provided that he maintains product code lists, provides up-to-date copies of these to all VAT-registered customers, ensures that the till rolls provide the other details required for a tax invoice, and retains copies of till rolls and product code lists for six years.

Legislation: *Value Added Tax Regulations* 1995 (SI 1995/2518), reg. 16(1)

Other material: Notice 700, para. 16.6.1, 16.6.2, 17.1 and 17.2

VAT Reporter: ¶55-800

Proposed changes from 1 January 2013

It is proposed that less detailed invoices may be used more generally – not just by retailers.

Other material: HMRC Technical Note VAT: Changes to VAT Invoice Rules 31 May 2012 *http://customs.hmrc.gov.uk/channelsPortalWebApp/channelsPortalWebApp.portal?_nfpb= true&_ pageLabel=pageLibrary_ConsultationDocuments&propertyType=document&colum ns=1&id=HMCE_PROD1_032093*

(4) Electronic invoicing

The Invoicing Directive states that all Member States must accept electronic invoicing using advanced electronic signature or Electronic Data Interchange (EDI). Other methods may be accepted. The UK will accept:

- Internet-based systems, e.g. XML/XSL (extensible Mark-up/Style-sheet language) messages transmitted using http; EDI files sent under File Transfer Protocol (FTP) or as attachments to emails; free format or structured text sent by email.
- Intermediary service providers. These receive messages in various formats (e.g. EDI, XML/XSL, CSV (comma-separated variables) etc.) as convenient to the supplier, undertake translation and pass them to the customer in a different format as required. They are usually internet-based and on secure websites.
- Bill presentment. Invoices are presented on a website, either hosted by suppliers or their agents. Customers access the website to view the invoice.

Other material: Notice 700/63

VAT Reporter: ¶56-450

Proposed changes

From 1 January 2013, in order to encourage the use of electronic invoicing, the EU rules are to be simplified to prevent the imposition by a Member State of specific conditions. It will be for the business to determine the method used and the only condition is that is that the customer must agree to the use of electronic invoicing.

The business will decide controls to put in place to ensure authenticity of origin, integrity of content and legibility of the invoice which will also create a reliable audit trail between the invoice and the supply of goods or services.

Other material: HMRC Technical Note VAT: Changes to VAT Invoice Rules 31 May 2012 *http://customs.hmrc.gov.uk/channelsPortalWebApp/channelsPortalWebApp.portal?_nfpb=true&_pageLabel=pageLibrary_ConsultationDocuments&propertyType=document&columns=1&id=HMCE_PROD1_032093*

(5) Waiver of requirement for tax invoice

By concession, a tax invoice for subsistence expenses (or for petrol used for business purposes – although this is now covered by legislation) may be made out to an employee, instead of the employer, and a tax invoice is not required for expenditure below £25 on:

(1)   telephone calls from public or private telephones;

(2)   purchases through coin-operated machines;

(3)   car park charges; and

(4)   a single or return toll charge.

In view of the stringent requirements which must be met for a document to be acceptable as a tax invoice, and so capable of supporting a claim for input tax, it is essential that staff involved in authorising payment of, and processing, suppliers' invoices are aware of the requirements and instructed to refuse payment where they are not met. See also 6-200.

Other material: Notice 700, para. 19.7.5

VAT Reporter: ¶55-900

(6) Corporate purchasing cards

HMRC have announced arrangements relating to corporate purchasing cards whereby the card provider can generate the relevant input tax evidence, instead of this being provided directly by the supplier. These arrangements only apply to cards designed for the purpose, not to ordinary credit cards and charge cards (although a modified credit card slip can sometimes substitute for a less detailed invoice: see (3) above).

(7) Credit notes

Commentary on credit notes is at 18-790.

Other material: Notice 701/48 Corporate purchasing cards

9-290 Unauthorised issue of an invoice

Whenever an invoice shows 'VAT' as being payable, the issuer is liable to pay to HMRC the 'VAT' concerned. This is so whether or not the issuer is VAT registered or whether or not the supply takes place.

Under EU legislation, 'any person who mentions the VAT on an invoice' is liable to pay this tax to the relevant authorities.

When the European Court of Justice (ECJ) considered the similar provision in the EU Sixth Directive, it concluded as follows: 'any person who mentions VAT on an invoice or other document serving as an invoice is liable to pay that tax …'

The point is that the tax authorities are entitled to collect any VAT shown on an invoice regardless of the status of the person issuing the invoice, etc.

For penalties incurred see 10-230.

Case: *Staatssecretaris van Financiën v Stadeco BV* (Case C-566/07) [2010] BVC 925

Legislation: VATA 1994, Sch. 11, para. 5; EU Directive 2006/112, art. 203

9-300 Invoices to EU businesses

EU legislation requires cross-border invoices upon which VAT is not charged to be endorsed with a reason.

The wording of the endorsement on the invoice is 'a matter for business and not for HMRC'. The aim is to give 'affected businesses the widest possible discretion'. However, endorsements acceptable to HMRC are to be found in VAT Information Sheet 10/07.

UK businesses are excused from issuing an invoice for exempt supplies when it is not a requirement of the regulations of the EU State in which the customer belongs. Affected UK businesses 'should be guided by their customers'.

See flowchart 9-900 Endorsing invoices to EU businesses. See also 9-280 for electronic invoicing.

Other information: VAT Information Sheet 10/07

Proposed changes from 1 January 2013

Three changes will be introduced with effect from 1 January 2013.

Endorsement of invoices

The intention is to harmonise the endorsements used throughout the EU. The only endorsements which may be used are:

- for exempt supplies – the reference is 'exempt';
- for margin scheme supplies – the reference 'margin scheme: works of art' or, 'margin scheme : antiques or collectors items' or 'margin scheme: second hand goods' or 'margin scheme: tour operators' as appropriate;
- for reverse charge supplies – the reference 'reverse charge';
- for self-billed supplies – the reference 'self billing'.

Time limit

The invoice must be issued by the 15th day of the month following that in which the goods are removed or the services performed.

Invoices for exempt supplies

Customers in other EU States may no longer demand a VAT invoice for exempt supplies from a UK business.

Other material: HMRC Technical Note VAT: Changes to VAT Invoice Rules 31 May 2012 *http://customs.hmrc.gov.uk/channelsPortalWebApp/channelsPortalWebApp.portal?_ nfpb=true&_pageLabel=pageLibrary_ConsultationDocuments&propertyType=document&c olumns=1&id=HMCE_PROD1_032093*

9-310 Self-billing

Arrangements are available whereby the customer generates the tax invoice for the supply.

These arrangements are particularly useful where it is the supplier who calculates the amount of the consideration for the supply, under a pre-agreed formula (such as royalties due under a publishing contract, where it is the publisher who has the information on sales made, and advises the author of the amount of the royalties due).

It is not necessary to obtain HMRC's approval for a self-billing arrangement and such system is not restricted to supplies inside the UK. However, any self-billing process will be invalid unless all the following conditions are fulfilled.

- There must be an agreement in place at the outset between the supplier and the customer. Each must keep a copy of this agreement and produce it if needed.
- The agreement must state that the customer may issue self-bills and that the supplier will accept such bills during the agreement period.
- The agreement period expires at the end of 12 months or at the end of the contract.
- The supplier must be registered for VAT during the period and must not issue VAT invoices for supplies covered by the agreement.
- The self-biller must keep an up-to-date register of supplier who have agreed to self-billing. This must include names, addresses, VAT numbers of the suppliers. It must be available to HMRC when required.
- Any supplier who de-registers or changes his VAT number, must inform the customer immediately.
- Each self-bill must be endorsed '*The VAT shown is your output tax due to HMRC*'.

The normal requirements for the contents of tax invoices apply, so the customer must satisfy himself that he has all relevant information.

The normal procedure is then that the customer generates the tax invoices, retains a copy for himself to act as evidence for his claim for input tax, and provides a copy to his supplier to enable him to account for output tax.

There is a special provision whereby, if a customer using a self-billing arrangement generates a self-billing invoice which understates the tax due, HMRC may elect to recover this from the customer rather than from the supplier.

Legislation: VATA 1994, s. 29; *Value Added Tax Regulations* 1995 (SI 1995/2518), reg. 13(3)

Other material: Notice 700/62

VAT Reporter: ¶56-200

9-340 Authenticated receipts

There is a further procedure used in the construction industry for contracts involving stage payments. Often, the amount due for a particular payment will depend upon work certified by the architect, etc., this information being passed to the customer. The customer then sends payment to the supplier with relevant details. The supplier then issues an authenticated receipt (i.e. a receipt signed by the supplier) to the customer.

This authenticated receipt can be used by the customer as a tax invoice provided that it contains all the necessary details, and that no tax invoice, or document which could be construed as one, is issued in respect of the supply concerned.

It should be noted that, in practice, the authenticated receipts procedure and self-billing procedure can cause a lot of difficulty, particularly in the construction industry, because of different practices adopted by different companies working on the same contract. Some may be used to operating self-billing, others to authenticated receipts, and others to neither of these schemes. Unless some of the companies involved in such a case are able to adapt their accounting systems, some of the conditions for use of the special arrangements are breached.

Legislation: *Value Added Tax Regulations* 1995 (SI 1995/2518), reg. 13(4)

Other material: Notice 700, para. 17.4

VAT Reporter: ¶55-800

9-350   Translation into English

Where a VAT invoice or part of an invoice is in a language other than English, HMRC may issue a written notice requiring an English translation to be provided within 30 days. It is the recipient in the UK of the invoice who has the task of providing the translation.

Legislation: *Value Added Tax Regulations* 1995 (SI 1995/2518), reg. 13B

VAT Reporter: ¶55-800

9-370   Returns

Each trader must make a periodical VAT return to HMRC, showing amounts of output tax to be accounted for and of deductible input tax. The return also gives statistical information on the value of supplies made and received and intra-EC imports and exports of goods. The requirements of HMRC as to the way in which the amounts for supplies made and received are to be arrived at are set out in Notice 700/12.

Generally, returns are submitted quarterly, the quarter end to be used being notified to the trader by HMRC. Traders who regularly receive repayments of VAT (i.e. those who normally make zero-rated supplies) usually make a return each month, rather than each quarter.

In some cases, notably when a business starts or finishes, it may be necessary to submit a return for a non-standard period.

The VAT return must be submitted by the end of the month following the period to which it relates, and any tax shown on it as due to HMRC must be paid to them by the same date. Failure to pay on time any VAT shown as due on a return can give rise to a liability to a surcharge (see 10-120).

Although VAT is normally payable when submitting the return, certain large traders (broadly, those whose net annual liability exceeds £2 million) can be directed to make monthly payments on account (see 9-610 below).

From April 2010, businesses with a turnover above £100,000 and newly registered businesses must submit VAT returns electronically. From April 2012 all businesses must submit VAT returns electronically.

Legislation: *Value Added Tax Regulations* 1995 (SI 1995/2518), reg. 25

VAT Reporter: ¶55-200

Aligning VAT periods

A business may ask HMRC that VAT periods fit in with the business's financial year. Applications should be sent to the Grimsby registration unit (see 1-705).

Other material: Notice 700, para. 20.5; Notice 700/12

VAT Reporter: ¶55-000

Submission of returns

VAT returns should be submitted by post to VAT Controller, VAT Central Unit, BX5 5AT. This is in Shipley. Prior to August 2008, all returns were dealt with at Southend.

If a business needs to send a return by courier, it should be sent to HMRC, Alexander House, Southend, SS99 1AA.

Electronic returns

Electronic VAT returns are submitted via HMRC's website, *www.hmrc.gov.uk*. In addition, traders submitting electronic VAT returns must also pay any money due by electronic means. See 9-580.

Compulsory online filing and electronic payment

Businesses with a turnover of above £100,000 must file returns online and pay tax due electronically for periods from 1 April 2010.

All businesses with a registration date on or after 1 April 2010 must use online filing of VAT returns and an electronic payment system. From April 2012 all businesses must use this system.

Legislation *Value Added Tax Regulations* 1995 (SI 1995/2518), regs. 25 and 25A

Other material: Notice 700/12 Filling in your VAT return

VAT Reporter: ¶55-210

9-390 Estimation of input tax and output tax

HMRC have power to allow a person to submit a return based on an estimate of the input tax and/or output tax due, any discrepancy from the true figures being corrected on the next return or, with the agreement of HMRC, some later return. This can be a valuable facility when negotiating the treatment of transactions with HMRC, to avoid the risk of incurring default interest in the event of temporary underpayments.

Legislation: *Value Added Tax Regulations* 1995 (SI 1995/2518), reg. 28 and 29(3)

Other material: Notice 700, para. 21.2.3

VAT Reporter: ¶55-420

CORRECTION OF ERRORS AND BAD DEBT RELIEF

9-410 Correction of errors

There is specific provision that if an error is made in a return, it is to be corrected in such manner and at such time as HMRC may require.

The general requirements for the correction of errors are set out in Notice 700/45.

Legislation: *Value Added Tax Regulations* 1995 (SI 1995/2518), reg. 34, as amended by the *VAT (Correction of Errors, etc.) Regulations* 2008 (SI 2008/1482)

(1) Making adjustments

HMRC must be informed of net errors amounting to more than £50,000. HMRC must also be notified of net errors that exceed both £10,000 and one per cent of the figure to be declared in Box 6 of the return for the period in which the error(s) is (are) discovered. The voluntary disclosure of the net error(s) should be declared using Form VAT 652, although HMRC will also accept other written notification. Whichever method is used, HMRC require full details of the errors, how they arose, in which period the mistake was made, etc. This form or the written notification must be submitted to regional specialist offices. These offices are listed in VAT Notice 700/45 and see Hardman's Tax Rates and Tables 19-840 or Key Data 1-723.

Form VAT 652 may also be used for lesser errors.

Legislation: VATA 1994, s. 63(8); *Value Added Tax Regulations* 1995 (SI 1995/2518), reg. 34

(2) Errors which may be corrected on a return

If the net amount of errors discovered in a prescribed accounting period (i.e. VAT return period) is £10,000 or less, the trader is entitled to correct them by making an adjustment on the VAT return for that period. Larger errors may also be adjusted in this way if they are both less than £50,000 and one per cent of the figure to be declared in Box 6 of the return for that period. Where this procedure is followed, there is no requirement to notify HMRC of the errors, but they must be separately entered in the VAT account for the period of adjustment (see 9-410 above).

Adjusting errors in the current period (where permissible) affects the calculation of penalties (see 10-120 and 10-140). The amounts involved are treated as being part of the true tax for the period of adjustment, and not for the periods in which the errors arose.

(3) Voluntary disclosure, penalties and interest

A voluntary disclosure will only provide protection from a penalty if it is made at a time when the trader has no reason to know that HMRC are making enquiries into the business affairs.

Following *Wilkinson v IR Commrs*, the practice of not charging default interest on net errors of £2,000 or less separately notified to HMRC is unlawful. Error notifications (voluntary disclosures) requiring an assessment may have default interest added. De minimis errors notified on a VAT return will not attract interest.

(4) Time limits for correcting errors

The time limit for correcting errors was raised from three to four years with effect from 1 April 2009. Only errors made during a specified period may be, or need to be, corrected. Earlier errors are time barred.

The relevant period begins at the end of the VAT period 'for which the return was made'. It finishes at the end of the VAT period during which the capped period elapses.

The legality of the three-year cap on output tax was considered in *Marks & Spencer Plc v C & E Commrs*. The ECJ ruled that 'in the interests of legal certainty ... a national limitation period of three years ... appeared reasonable'. This case caused the British Government to introduce a transitional period to allow a limited number of claims which were submitted or would have been submitted around the time of the introduction of the three-year cap. The transitional period applied from 4 December 1996 to 30 June 1997 and claims were permitted to be submitted for a period ending 30 June 2003.

The three-year cap on input tax claims was introduced with effect from 1 May 1997. Some claims for input tax incurred before then have not been settled. In February 2006, the Court of Appeal ruled that this regulation introduced '... without any transitional period ... must be disapplied'. The appellants' claim lodged in October 2000 for input tax incurred over three years earlier was allowed. The Court declined to decide on dates of the transitional period.

Records and Returns

The House of Lords has now considered the effect and the legitimacy of transitional arrangements as applied to input tax reclaims. Of particular concern was whether or not the introduction of the three-year cap for input tax claims met the legitimate expectations of businesses and whether the means of making the rules allowed for legal certainty.

In a decision that upheld the view of the taxpayer, the House of Lords has ruled that the legitimate expectations of the taxpayer were not met. In order to give businesses legal certainty, there should have been a transitional period fixed in advance. The House of Lords has indicated what should now happen.

The conclusions may be summed up in the words of Lord Hope of Craighead when speaking of the transitional period.

> '... I would hold that the period has not yet begun and that it is for Parliament or the Commissioners, if they choose to do so by means of an announcement disseminated to all taxpayers, to introduce prospectively an adequate transitional period. Until that is done the three year time limit must be disapplied in the case of all claims for deduction of input tax that had accrued before the introduction of the time limit.' – Lord Hope of Craighead at para. 12. *Fleming (t/a Bodycraft) v R & C Commrs; Conde Nast Publications v R & C Commrs* [2008] UKHL 2; [2008] BVC 221

Transitional period – claims for pre- 1996 and 1997 output and input tax

Budget 2008 considered the above case and introduced a further period during which businesses may make claims for overdeclared output tax or underclaimed input tax during the period before the three-year cap was introduced.

Businesses have until 31 March 2009 in which to submit claims to HMRC for underclaimed input tax for accounting periods ending between 1 April 1973 and 1 May 1997. Businesses have a similar period in which to submit claims for overdeclared output tax for accounting periods between 1 April 1973 and 4 December 1996.

Cases: *Marks & Spencer Plc v C & E Commrs* (Case C-62/00) [2002] BVC 622; *Fleming (t/a Bodycraft) v R & C Commrs; Conde Nast Publications v R & C Commrs* [2008] UKHL 2; [2008] BVC 221

Other material: Revenue and Customs Brief 38/08; Notice 700/45; Business Brief 27/02, 7 October 2002; Budget 2008 Notes BN78; Revenue and Customs Brief 43/10; flowchart at 9-840

Legislation: *Value Added Tax Regulations* 1995 (SI 1995/2518), reg. 29(1A)

VAT Reporter: ¶55-250

9-420 Unjust enrichment

HMRC Guidance Manuals describe unjust enrichment as follows:

'... we use the phrase 'unjust enrichment' to describe the situation where payment of a claimant's claim for a refund would put him in a better economic position than he would have been if he had not mistakenly accounted for the tax, in other words, where he would get a 'windfall' profit ...'

'Unjust enrichment' only applies to cases within VATA 1994, s. 80. This was decided in *Marks & Spencer Plc v C & E Commrs; University of Sussex v C & E Commrs*. The Court of Appeal concluded as follows:

'The defence of unjust enrichment applied only to claims for overpayments under s. 80(3) of the 1994 Act ... the defence was introduced from 1 January 1990.'

Section 80 is the provision under which wrongly charged output tax may be reclaimed. Late input tax claims are dealt with under *Value Added Tax Regulations* 1995 (SI 1995/2518), reg. 29. This is clear from *Marks & Spencer Plc v C & E Commrs; University of Sussex v C & E Commrs*. The Court of Appeal concluded that:

'the university's 'late' claim for payment of input tax fell to be considered under reg. 29(1) of the 1995 regulations and not as overpaid tax under s. 80 of the 1994 Act.'

See flowchart 11-750 When unjust enrichment applies.

In *Société Camateb v Directeur Général des Douanes et Droits Indirects*, the ECJ ruled that a Member State could only resist repayment if the charge had been borne in its entirety by another person and that reimbursement to the trader would constitute unjust enrichment. HMRC explain this in their Guidance Manuals as follows:

'... principles of Community law tell us that unjust enrichment can only be successfully invoked where it can be shown that someone other than the claimant effectively bore the burden of the tax.'

From *Société Camateb*, it is also clear that if only part of the charge had been passed on, a claimant should be reimbursed to the extent of the part not passed on. Where the charge has been passed on, but domestic law permits the trader to claim that the illegal levying of the charge has caused him damage which excludes unjust enrichment, the national court must give such appropriate effect to the claim.

Cases: *Marks & Spencer Plc v C & E Commrs; University of Sussex v C & E Commrs* [2004] BVC 151; *Société Camateb v Directeur Général des Douanes et Droits Indirects* (Joined Cases C-192/95–C-218/95) [1997] ECR I-165

Legislation: VATA 1994, s. 80

Other material: *HMRC Guidance Manual* Vol V1–33 (Refunds: unjust enrichment) Section 3.3; Revenue and Customs Brief 38/08

VAT Reporter: ¶55-435

Burden of proof

In *Computeach International Ltd*, the tribunal considered that in the context of VAT, the concept of unjust enrichment was a European one. The Tribunal decided that the burden of proof was upon HMRC to show that the appellant would be unjustly enriched by a repayment. To do this, they need to show that the VAT was paid by customers.

Cases: *Computeach International Ltd* [1995] BVC 931

VAT Reporter: ¶55-435

Restrictions on claims – VATA 1994 s. 80(3A)–80(3C)

Any loss or damage to the taxpayer arising from wrong assumptions about tax liability is to be ignored in considering unjust enrichment, except for the 'quantified amount'. This is the amount (if any) 'shown by the taxpayer to constitute the amount that would appropriately compensate him for loss or damage shown to have resulted ... from the making of the mistaken assumptions'.

In effect, a person who has wrongly accounted for output tax must be able both to show that this has ultimately caused him loss, and also be able to prove the amount of that loss. If he cannot do both, then his loss is ignored in determining any unjust enrichment.

In *Marks & Spencer Plc v C & E Commrs*, Marks & Spencer submitted a claim to recover tax wrongly accounted for on its jaffa cakes. After a lengthy hearing in 1996, the VAT & Duties Tribunal found that Marks & Spencer's customers bore the brunt of the tax charge. However, they agreed a refund of 10 per cent of the claim as being the tax borne by M&S. 'Unjust enrichment' would occur if more than this was refunded. Marks & Spencer subsequently conceded this. However, M&S appealed to the House of Lords on other grounds and the matter was referred to the European Court of Justice.

Cases: *Marks & Spencer Plc v C & E Commrs* [2005] BVC 503

When unjust enrichment does not apply

A business cannot be unjustly enriched by a repayment if it passes this on to its customers. Where repayments are allowed on the basis that they will be repaid to customers, HMRC have power to agree reimbursement arrangements with the trader, including documentation, monitoring arrangements, etc.

A claimant who fails to reimburse customers within the agreed time scale must notify HMRC and repay to HMRC any tax not refunded to its customers. Previously, HMRC had to assess to recover this tax.

Claims made before 26 May 2005 were not restricted or affected by unjust enrichment. This was decided in *Marks & Spencer Plc v C & E Commrs*.

Before 1 September 2005, it was the case that 'unjust enrichment' applied only to periods in which a trader paid tax to HMRC. Another amendment does away with this discriminatory interpretation of VATA 1994, s. 80.

Legislation: *Value Added Tax Regulations* 1995 (SI 1995/2518), reg. 43D; *Value Added Tax Regulations* 1995 (SI 1995/2518), Pt. VA

Cases: *Marks & Spencer Plc v C & E Commrs* [2009] BVC 106

VAT Reporter: ¶55-435

Case example

In *Global Self-Drive Ltd*, Global submitted a claim to recover tax wrongly accounted for on insurance. It was advised by the National Advice Service as follows:

> '... the Voluntary Disclosure team would not pay a claim that would result in the Appellant's unjust enrichment, for example, where you have passed on the VAT on [sic] to your customer but are unable, or do not intend, to pass on to them any repayment resulting from the claim.'

With this in mind, Global reduced the claim to £19,183. As best they could they eliminated the tax charged to VAT-registered customers.

Revenue refused Global's claim for two reasons. These were as follows:

(a) Global used 'a number of unsubstantiated assumptions' to calculate the claim;
(b) refunding the tax would result in 'unjust enrichment' of Global.

The 'unsubstantiated assumption' to which Revenue objected was an estimate of the proportion of customers that were VAT-registered. According to the Tribunal, this did not infringe the requirement that a claim must be calculated by reference to such documentary evidence as is in the possession of the claimant. Of this condition the Tribunal said as follows:

> 'That wording does not preclude a claim based on documentary evidence but (in part) also based on best judgement assumptions made by the claimant.'

With regard to the 'unjust enrichment' issue Global adduced evidence to show that prices were not increased in 1993 when VAT was added to the insurance charge. However, the Tribunal was not satisfied there was 'a reduction in (profit) margins in the period from 7 October 2000 to 6 October 2003, with which the claim is concerned'. However, if the profit margins had been reduced, the Tribunal acknowledged there wouldn't have been any 'unjust enrichment'.

With such claims, it is for Revenue to prove, rather for the claimant to disprove, 'unjust enrichment'. In this case, it was for 'Customs to establish, on the whole of the evidence ...' that it was the customer, not Global, that suffered the relevant tax charge. The Revenue failed to do this and the Tribunal allowed the claim.

Cases: *Global Self-Drive Ltd* [2006] BVC 2,020

VAT Reporter: ¶55-435

9-430 Interest on overpaid VAT

Where VAT is overpaid as a result of an error by HMRC, they are liable to pay interest on it. Broadly speaking, this interest runs from the date when the amount shown as due on a payment return was paid or, in the case of a repayment return, the date when the repayment of the amount should have been authorised. However, delays due to a failure by the taxable person to provide information required to verify the claim, or unreasonable delays in making either the repayment claim or the claim for statutory interest, are left out of account.

HMRC's view is that statutory interest is 'demonstrably part of the taxable income of the business and therefore chargeable to direct tax'.

Rate of interest charged

From 7 January 2009, the rate of interest awarded will be amended 13 working days after the meeting of the Monetary Policy Committee of the Bank of England.

From September 2009 the rates of interest will be as follows:

- For late payments of VAT the interest rate charged will be the Bank of England rate plus 2.5.
- The interest paid by HMRC on overpayments (whether caused by an official error or not) will be the Bank of England rate minus 1 with a minimum rate of 0.5 per cent.

For interest rate tables see Hardman's Tax Rates and Tables 19-560 and 19-590 or Key Data 1-560.

Questions have been put before the CEJ for a preliminary ruling on whether this interest should be calculated as simple or compound interest. . The CEJ decided that it "… was for national law to determine in compliance with the principles of effectiveness and equivalence whether the principal sum must bear'simple interest', 'compound interest' or another type of interest". The cases will now be considered by the Upper Tax Tribunal in the light of this ruling.

Legislation: VATA 1994, s. 78; *The Taxes and Duties (Interest Rate) (Amendment) Regulations* 2009 (SI 2009/2032)

Cases: *Littlewoods Retail Ltd v R & C Commrs* [2011] BVC 14; (Case C-591/10) judgment delivered 19 July 2012; *Grattan plc v R & C Commrs* [2011] UKUT 399 (TCC); [2011] BVC 1,730

Other material: Revenue and Customs Brief 14/09 VAT repayment claims and Statutory Interest – treatment for the purposes of direct tax

VAT Reporter: ¶60-680

9-440 Default interest

The provisions normally apply to tax paid late.

Interest will arise in cases where:

(1) an assessment is made to recover extra tax for a period for which a return has already been made, or an assessment in lieu of a return issued;

(2) a voluntary disclosure is notified to HMRC on Form VAT 652 – see 4-900;

(3) no VAT return is submitted resulting in an assessment being raised and paid that is later found to be too low.

As a general rule, default interest runs from the due date for the submission of the VAT return for the period concerned until the date when the person pays the tax. However, if the assessment is to recover tax which has been incorrectly repaid by HMRC, interest runs from seven days after the date when HMRC issued a written instruction authorising the repayment. In the case of the issue of an invoice by an unauthorised person, interest runs from the date of the invoice.

The rate of interest is fixed by Treasury order, and is intended to reflect commercial rates of interest. The rates and their period of application are in the checklist at Hardman's Tax Rates and Tables 19-560 or Key Data 1-420.

Default interest does not rank as an allowable expense for income tax and corporation tax purposes (ICTA 1988, s. 827(1)).

However, a tribunal has held that balancing errors which relate to the same period must be set off against each other, interest being due only on the net underdeclaration, if any.

Commercial restitution

HMRC state that, by concession, they will generally assess default interest only where this is necessary in order to achieve commercial restitution. For instance, if a business has failed to charge VAT but, if charged, this would have been recoverable by the customer, they will generally not assess for default interest.

Rate of interest charged

From 7 January 2009, the rate of default interest charged will be amended 13 working days after the meeting of the Monetary Policy Committee of the Bank of England.

For interest rates charged, see Hardman's Tax Rates and Tables 19-560 or Key Data 1-420.

Legislation: VATA 1994, s. 74 and *Taxes and Duties (Interest Rate) (Amendment) Regulations* 2008 (SI 2008/3234)

Cases: *London Borough of Camden* [1993] BVC 1,004

Other material: VAT Notice 700/43 Default Interest

VAT Reporter: ¶60-630

9-445 Repayment supplement

A repayment supplement is added to certain late repayments of VAT shown as repayable on a VAT return. In order to qualify for such a supplement, the return must have reached HMRC by the due date.

Repayment supplement is then due if HMRC fail to issue the written instruction directing the making of the repayment within 30 days of the later of:

(1) the end of the period concerned; and

(2) the date when HMRC received the return.

Ignored periods

In determining whether the instruction is issued within the 30-day period, certain periods are ignored. These periods are those taken in making reasonable enquiries about the return, or correcting errors in the return, and periods in which the trader has failed to submit other returns, or pay the tax due on them or on assessments issued by HMRC, or comply with the conditions concerned with the production of documents or the giving of security.

The period needed for the making of reasonable enquiries is, in effect, determined by HMRC. The 30-day clock generally stops when HMRC actually make contact with the trader.

Also, the Treasury has power to make a statutory instrument directing that any specified period be ignored. This power might be used in the event, say, of a prolonged civil service strike.

How the repayment supplement is paid

The payment is made with the payment of the relevant return. It is calculated as the greater of five per cent of the return or £50.

HMRC have the discretion to award a greater, ex-gratia payment in certain cases.

Overstated claim

If the return overstates the amount of the repayment due by more than the greater of five per cent of the amount actually due and £250, no supplement is payable.

Tax-free treatment

A repayment supplement is not liable to corporation tax or income tax.

See flowchart 9-990.

Legislation: ICTA 1988, s. 827(2); VATA 1994, s. 79

Other material: Notice 700/58

VAT Reporter: ¶60-650

9-450 Payment by cheque

HMRC have announced that from 1 April 2010 all cheque payments by post will be regarded as being received by HMRC on the date when cleared funds reach HMRC's bank account. Since a cheque takes three working days to clear, this means that people will have to be aware that cheques must be sent about a week before the end of the month in which the payment is due. Penalties are liable to be incurred for late payments.

Other information: *www.hmrc.gov.uk/payinghmrc/vat.htm*

9-460 Payment by credit card

It is possible to pay the tax using debit or credit cards. A note of caution, however, is that the use of a credit card will incur a 1.4 per cent charge from HMRC. Using a debit card does not incur a charge.

In order to use this facility, it is necessary to have the credit or debit card details and the relevant VAT number available. The payment is made via BillPay – a Santander Corporate Banking facility.

HMRC provide a telephone help line at 0845 302 1423 between 8 am and 5 pm.

Other information: *www.hmrc.gov.uk/payinghmrc/vat.htm*

9-480 Payment by credit transfer

Paper VAT returns

HMRC accept payment through the Bankers Automated Clearing System (BACS), bank giro credit transfer and Clearing House Automated Payment System (CHAPS).

By concession, seven extra calendar days are allowed for the return and payment to reach HMRC when payment is made by the above methods. HMRC do not subscribe to the Faster Payment System operated by certain banks.

The following apply:

- The seven day extension will be applied automatically any time payment is made by these means.
- Payment must be in HMRC's bank account on or before the 7th calendar day. If this falls on a weekend, payment must be received by the Friday. If it falls on a bank holiday, payment must be received by the last working day prior to the bank holiday.
- People using the Annual Accounting scheme are not given this concession.

- Traders in the Payment on Accounts Scheme and rendering quarterly returns will not get this concession.
- If the return or payment are received late, the normal default system applies.
- For payments by Bank Giro, a book of paying in slips and counterfoils may be obtained by telephoning 01702 366376 or 01702 366314.

Electronic VAT returns

Traders submitting electronic returns must pay by BACS, CHAPS, Bank Giro and direct debit. Payment by cheque is not allowed.

Other material: Notice 700, para. 21.3; *www.hmrc.gov.uk/vat/pay-howto.htm; www.hmrc.gov.uk/payinghmrc/news-fps.htm*

VAT Reporter: ¶55-395

9-490 Monthly payments on account by large traders

There are provisions under which certain businesses have to make monthly payments on account during a prescribed accounting period. Any balance is settled when the return for the period is submitted. This affects businesses whose net VAT payments exceed £2 million per annum. Payments of account begin in the quarter following that in which you exceeded the threshold. From 1 June 2011 the threshold increases to £2.3 million.

A first payment on account is required by the end of the month following the first month of the prescribed accounting period and the next a month later. The balance is settled by submission of the return by the due date.

The payments on account required at the end of the first and second months of a VAT quarter are each one twenty-fourth of the annual liability, estimated by reference to a particular year's liability. This is using a year-end of 30 September, 31 October or 30 November to coincide with the prescribed accounting periods. This sets the payments of account for the year beginning on the following April, May or June respectively.

HMRC have power to require that payment is made by electronic means, and the usual seven-day extension of time for payment by such means (9-480) no longer applies to those subject to such directions.

If the net VAT liability in a subsequent 12-month period falls below £1.6 million (from 1 June 2011 this is £1.8 million), the business concerned may apply to revert to the normal procedures.

Legislation: VATA 1994, s. 28; *Value Added Tax (Payments on Account) Order* 1993 (SI 1993/2001)

Other information: Notice 700/60

VAT Reporter: ¶55-410

9-520   Bad debt relief

Bad debt relief is available when:

(a)   at least six months have elapsed since the later of the date of the original supply or the due date for payment;

(b)   tax has been accounted for and paid to HMRC;

(c)   the supplier has formally written off the debt for VAT purposes (see below); and

(d)   the supplier holds the necessary records.

When these conditions are met, the supplier can recover from HMRC the VAT originally accounted for on the supply by including an equivalent amount in the input tax box of his VAT return. If payments are subsequently received in respect of the debt, the VAT element must be repaid to HMRC.

It is not necessary to write off the debt for commercial accounting purposes in order to obtain VAT bad debt relief (although HMRC are likely to dispute a claim unless some identification of it has been made within the accounting records to facilitate identification of subsequent payments received as triggering repayment of relief). Instead, the trader must enter the debt in a 'VAT: refunds for bad debts' account, which may be maintained outside the main accounting system.

Bad debt relief may be claimed up to four years and six months after the later of the date of supply or the due date for payment. The four-year-and-six-month time limit applies to claims due on or after 1 October 2005. Previously, the limit had been three years and six months.

For adjustments when a lesser amount is accepted in full and final settlement see 4-590.

See flowchart 9-880 Claiming bad debt relief.

Legislation: *Value Added Tax Regulations* 1995 (SI 1995/2518), reg. 165 to 172B

Other material: Notice 700/18 HM Revenue and Customs Brief 18/2009, 31 March 2009, VAT – Implications to the bad debt relief conditions as a result of the Tribunal decision in Times Right Marketing Ltd; *www.hmrc.gov.uk/vat/managing/reclaiming/bad-debts.htm*

VAT Reporter: ¶18-900

Payments on account

Where payments on account have been received, the amount on which relief can be claimed is reduced accordingly. If there have been a number of supplies and payments, the payments are attributed to the earliest supplies on a first in, first out basis. Where more than one supply was made on a particular day, payments are split between these supplies pro rata. If a payment has been specifically allocated by the customer, and represents full payment for the supply concerned, this allocation takes precedence.

A firm of solicitors dealt with insurance claims. Where applicable when the main invoice was paid by the insurers, a VAT registered customer was sent a VAT only invoice from the solicitors and told that this VAT was reclaimable as input tax. When any of these 'VAT only' invoices remained unpaid the solicitors claimed bad debt relief for the whole amount. The lower Tribunal determined that this was incorrect and that the amount should be treated as VAT inclusive as part payment of the total consideration. This decision was reversed by the Upper Tax Tribunal.

In the case of supplies under the second-hand goods scheme or the tour operator's margin scheme, the amount of the claim is the VAT fraction of the margin, or the VAT fraction of the outstanding debt, whichever is lower.

Cases: *Simpson & Marwick v R & C Commrs* [2011] UKUT 498 (TCC); [2010] UKFTT 380 (TC); [2011] TC 00662

Other material: Notice 700/18, para. 3.2

Legislation: *Value Added Tax Regulations* 1995 (SI 1995/2518), reg. 170

VAT Reporter: ¶18-950

Bad debts account

The information to be recorded in respect of each claim made is as follows:

(1) For each taxable supply on which the claim is based:
   (a) the amount of tax chargeable;
   (b) the period in which the tax was accounted for and paid to HMRC;
   (c) the date and number of the related tax invoice, or other information showing the time, nature and purchaser of the supply;
   (d) any payment received for the supply.

(2) The outstanding amount to which the claim relates.

(3) The amount of the claim.

(4) The period in which the claim is made.

All relevant records must be kept for four years from the date of the claim.

Legislation: *Value Added Tax Regulations* 1995 (SI 1995/2518), reg. 168 and 169

VAT Reporter: ¶18-983

Effect of claim on customer

The customer must repay any input tax re-claimed if the debt remains unpaid after six months, even if the supplier has not claimed bad debt relief. If the customer subsequently makes payment, the input tax can be claimed again on the return covering the date of payment.

HMRCs have announced a concession whereby the input tax clawback is not required in relation to insolvent businesses.

Legislation: *Value Added Tax Regulations* 1995 (SI 1995/2518), reg. 172F to 172J

Other material: Notice 700/18, Section 4

VAT Reporter: ¶18-915; ¶18-917

Assigned debts

There are further complications when the supplier assigns a debt (as when debts are factored).

When bad debt relief is initially claimed, the amount claimable is calculated by reference to all payments made by way of consideration for the supply, not just those amounts received by the claimant. Consequently, if the claimant has assigned the debt before making the claim, amounts received by the assignee must be taken into account in fixing the amount of the claim.

Although amounts received by an assignee of a debt before a bad debt relief claim is made must be brought into account in fixing the amount of the claim, subsequent receipts by an assignee do not count in determining whether the claimant must then repay some, or all, of the amount claimed.

The bad debt relief claimant must adjust his claim if payment is subsequently received by an assignee to whom he is connected. Assignments made to unconnected third parties will not be affected. Whether any person is connected is determined by reference to ICTA 1988, s. 839.

Legislation: *Value Added Tax Regulations* 1995 (SI 1995/2518), reg. 171

Other information: Business Brief 27/03, 10 February 2003

VAT Reporter: ¶18-955

Non-monetary consideration

Although the UK legislation is framed in terms of supplies made for a consideration in money, the European Court of Justice held that relief is also due in the case of supplies made for non-monetary consideration. The UK legislation gives statutory effect to this.

Cases: *Goldsmiths (Jewellers) Ltd v C & E Commrs* (Case C-330/95) [1997] BVC 494

VAT Reporter: ¶18-987

Transfer of a business as a going concern

If the transferee takes over the transferor's VAT registration number, the transferee takes over the transferors right to bad debt relief on respect of earlier supplies made. The transferor's liability to repay input tax previously claimed on supplies received but not paid for is also transferred.

VAT Reporter: ¶18-980

Goods sold under hire purchase or conditional sale agreements

A refund for bad debts in respect of goods supplied on hire purchase, conditional sale or credit sale is available when customers default on payment.

To calculate bad debt relief, it is necessary to apportion payments received to interest charges and consideration for the goods according to the commercial method used by the business concerned.

Repossessed goods

Goods repossessed under the terms of hire purchase or conditional sale agreement are normally resold. When bad debt relief is claimed, VAT must be accounted for when the goods are resold. See 3-580 Credit sale goods are not repossessed because the buyer owns the goods.

Following a High Court ruling, the proceeds arising from the sale of repossessed goods are ignored when computing bad debt relief. The High Court ruled that the consideration paid by the customer/hirer did not include the amount obtained when the car was resold. Its view was as follows:

'The resale proceeds are not paid by the hirer; still less are they paid by the hirer as consideration for the supply. Nor is the redelivery of the car any part of the consideration for the supply.'

It follows that the resale value is not part of the consideration and should not be taken into account when calculating bad debt relief.

Legislation: *Value Added Tax Regulations* 1995 (SI 1995/2518), reg. 170A

Cases: *Abbey National Plc v C & E Commrs* [2005] EWHC 1187 (Ch); [2005] BVC 348; *General Motors Acceptance Corporation (UK) Plc v C & E Commrs (GMAC)* [2004] BVC 611

Other material: HM Revenue and Customs Brief 14/2007, 14 February 2007; Notice 700/18, para. 3.5

VAT Reporter: ¶18-951

EC SALES LISTS AND INTRASTAT

9-540   Statistical returns for intra-EC trade

As well as the normal VAT returns, businesses making cross-border sales within the EC may have to make one or both of the following returns:

(1)   EC sales lists ('ESL') giving details of movement of goods to other EC States and sales of services to certain customers in other EC States;

(2)   Supplementary Statistical Declarations (INTRASTAT) providing further information about shipments of goods within the EC.

An ESL is sometime referred to as 'recapitulative statements' or 'summary statements'.

(1) EC Sales List (ESL)

An ESL return is necessary in certain circumstances when a UK business supplies relevant goods or services to a business in another EC State. The relevant circumstances are as follows:

(1)   the recipient is VAT registered in the EC State concerned;

(2)   the services are not liable to UK VAT because the 'reverse charge' applies;

(3)   the goods are zero rated in the UK because there is an acquisition in another EC State and VAT must be accounted for in the State concerned.

The purpose of the ESL is collect information about the person to whom the goods and services are supplied and a limited amount of information about the sales. It is necessary to declare the VAT registration number of the recipient, the values of the sale(s) and indicate if the sale was of goods or services.

Monthly, quarterly or annual filing

The default position is that an ESL should be submitted monthly. Persons who must file ESLs because of supplying services may choose between monthly or quarterly filing.

Variations apply to persons supplying goods to other EC States. The variations are as follows:

(1)   Quarterly returns may be made if the value of the goods to be declared in the quarter is less than £70,000 (£35,000 from 1 January 2012) and this has been the case for the previous four quarters. If in any quarter this limit is exceeded, the person concerned may make that return as normal. Thereafter they must file monthly returns.

(2)   Annual returns may be made in only two circumstances. In both circumstances the values of goods to be declared must be less than £11,000 per annum and also, there must not be any intra-EU supplies of new means of transport. Then HMRC may allow the following small businesses to file an annual ESL:

   (a)   a business whose taxable supplies are less than the registration threshold plus £25,500 per annum;

   (b)   a business making annual returns and whose taxable supplies are less than £145,000 per annum.

Delivery costs must be included when considering the value of the goods to be declared on an ESL.

Time limits for filing

An ESL must be filed within 14 or 21 days of the end of the period for which it is due. These time limits apply to paper returns and on-line filing respectively.

Records and Returns

Transfer of own goods

The permanent transfer of own goods to another EC branch, etc. involving the acquisition of the goods in the other Member State gives rise to a deemed supply of the goods in the UK. The trader must record this on the ESL in the same way as any other supply, citing his own registration number in the other EC State.

New means of transport

Where a new means of transport is supplied to a person not registered for VAT for acquisition in another Member State, the UK supplier must submit Form VAT 411 within 42 days of the end of the calendar quarter concerned.

See flowcharts 9-920 Frequency of submission for EC Sales lists; 9-940 Requirement to submit EC Sales lists.

Legislation: *Value Added Tax Regulations* 1995 (SI 1995/2518), reg. 22(1)

Other material: Notice 725, Section 17

VAT Reporter: ¶55-200; ¶13-466

(2) Supplementary Statistical Declarations (INTRASTAT)

The Supplementary Statistical Declaration (SSD) or Intrastat is a monthly return detailing all movements of goods between the UK and other EC States. It covers transfers between branches of the same business as well as purchases and sales of goods, and provides the information needed for the trade statistics.

Although the requirement to provide Intrastat declarations is not strictly a VAT matter, the main rules are outlined below. HMRC may use the data collected for Intrastat purposes for VAT purposes.

The obligation to submit declarations arises separately for imports and exports and depends on the value of the movements.

From 1 January 2010 the threshold for arrivals was *increased* to £600,000 and that for dispatches *reduced* to £250,000. These limits are the same for the year from 1 January 2011 and for the year from January 2012.

The Intrastat declaration must give details of each shipment, including such matters as the detailed trade classification of the goods, quantities, shipping costs, countries of departure and arrival, etc.

Businesses that have arrivals or dispatches less than £16 million are not required to provide details of delivery terms, e.g. carriage, insurance, freight.

From March 2012 the time limit for declarations was reduced to 21 days, prior to this it was the end of the month following the reference period.

Movements of goods excluded from Intrastat declarations

The following movements of goods should not be included on the declaration:

(1) goods dispatched to another EC country for a period less than two years, if they would qualify for temporary importation relief if arriving from outside the EC (e.g. exhibition goods);

(2) goods transferred temporarily for hire, lease or loan, or for use in carrying out a service in another EC State;

(3) industrial or commercial samples sent to actual or potential customers free of charge;

(4) goods sent to another EC State for examination, analysis or testing followed by return or destruction, or the return of such goods after testing, etc;

(5) dispatches of goods (other than excise goods or new means of transport) to unregistered customers.

See flowcharts 9-960 Intrastat obligations – goods coming to the UK; 9-980 Intrastat obligations – goods leaving the UK.

Other material: Notice 725, Section 18

Legislation: *Statistics of Trade (Customs and Excise) Regulations* 1992 (SI 1992/2790); Statutory Instrument 2008/2847

VAT Reporter: ¶64-600

(3) Electronic submission of returns

These returns often consist of large amounts of detailed information. From 1 April 2012 paper returns are being withdrawn and arrangements must be made to submit the material online.

In order to do so, the business must enrol for the service via the Government Gateway (*www.gateway.gov.uk*).

It is possible to appoint an agent to submit the returns as well as complete form 101 online or select the upload facility for bulk files using either the CSV or XML format.

VAT Reporter: ¶64-800

9-560 Register of temporary movements of goods

The movement of a business's own goods from one EC State to another generally gives rise to a deemed supply in the State of departure and an acquisition in the State of arrival. However, certain temporary movements of goods are excepted from this procedure.

In order that such temporary movements can be controlled, it is a requirement that the taxable person keeps a register of them, giving dates of removal and return, details of the goods, and of processing of them, etc.

Legislation: *Value Added Tax Regulations* 1995 (SI 1995/2518), reg. 33

VAT Reporter: ¶63-380

ASSESSMENTS

9-580 When HMRC can make a VAT Assessment

HMRC can make a VAT assessment where:

(a) a person has failed to make VAT returns;
(b) a person has failed to keep the relevant documents or has failed to make available the facilities for HMRC to check the accuracy of VAT returns submitted;
(c) HMRC consider a VAT return to be incomplete or incorrect;
(d) a VAT repayment or refund has been made that should not have been made;
(e) a VAT credit has been given that should not have been given;
(f) a VAT-registered person is unable to account for goods that he has imported or acquired or had supplied to him;
(g) fiscal warehousing errors.

In all the above cases, the assessment must be made to HMRC's best judgment and must be notified to the person assessed.

Supplementary assessments

HMRC can make a supplementary assessment for the same period where they consider the original assessment to be inadequate. They may also withdraw the original assessment and issue a new one for an increased amount. Any amended or increased assessment must be made within the normal time limits except in certain circumstances. Subject to the overriding four-year limit where HMRC find new facts, they may make a further assessment outside the normal two year limit for assessments. Such an assessment must be made within one year of the facts upon which the assessment is based coming to HMRC's attention. In addition the 20-year limit detailed below may also apply (see 9-600).

Reducing or withdrawing assessments

Only a validly made assessment may be reduced. Where a lower amount is due than has been already assessed, but the existing assessment is invalid, that assessment must be withdrawn and a replacement issued. The replacement must be made within the normal time limits.

Stocks of goods

One important point which is often overlooked is the power of HMRC to make assessments, with no evidence that taxable supplies have been made, if the trader is simply unable to account for the whereabouts of goods.

If a trader has acquired or imported goods, HMRC may require him to account for those goods. If he is unable to prove that the goods:

(1)   have been supplied by him; or

(2)   are available to be supplied by him; or

(3)   have been exported from the UK otherwise than by way of a supply; or

(4)   have been lost or destroyed;

then HMRC may make an assessment to the best of their judgment based on the tax which would have been chargeable if the goods had been supplied by the trader.

In effect, the trader is asked to prove a negative. It is therefore important to retain adequate stock records, having regard to the nature and size of the business, and particularly to keep some record of events which might explain stock losses (spoilage, theft, etc.).

Legislation: VATA 1994, s. 73

VAT Reporter: ¶58-000 and ¶53-900

9-600 Time limits for making assessments

Time limits run from either the end of a VAT return period or from the date of an event (for example, the date of a control visit, the date of death or the date the goods were acquired or imported). This should exclude the last day of the return period or the date of the event itself.

Two-year and one-year time limits

An assessment may be made within:

(1)   two years of the end of the period; or if later

(2)   one year from when HMRC consider they have sufficient evidence of facts to make an assessment. This has been considered in several Tribunal and Court cases including *Lazard Bros & Co Ltd* [1996] BVC 2,418 and *C & E Commrs v Post Office* [1995] BVC 292.

Four-year limit

From 1 April 2009, an overriding four-year cap applies except in cases involving dishonest conduct, fraud, failure to register and unauthorised issue of invoices. Prior to this date, there was a three-year cap. Relevant assessments may not be raised on or after 1 April 2009 for a VAT period which ended on or before 31 March 2006.

20-year limit

There is a 20-year limit for cases involving:

(a)   loss of VAT caused deliberately;
(b)   participation in a transaction knowing it was intended to bring about loss of VAT;
(c)   loss of VAT through a failure to comply with an obligation to register for VAT;
(d)   loss of VAT attributable to an undisclosed tax avoidance scheme.

Death

Assessments cannot be made more than four years after death.

Global assessments

For global assessments generally, the time limit runs from the end of the first VAT period included in the assessment.

Supplementary assessments

A supplementary assessment must be made within the same time limits as the original assessment.

Assessments where the VAT-registered person is unable to account for goods

Assessments made where a person is unable to account for goods imported, acquired or otherwise supplied to him must be made within four years of the importation, acquisition or supply. This is extended to 20 years in circumstances detailed above.

Legislation: VATA 1994, s. 73(7) and 77

Cases: *Lazard Bros & Co Ltd* [1996] BVC 2,418; *C & E Commrs v Post Office* [1995] BVC 292

Other material: Notice 915 – Assessment and time limits: Statement of Practice

VAT Reporter: ¶58-005

9-620   Date, and period of assessment

Date of assessment

HMRC's policy is that an assessment is made when it is 'sent by us, by post, hand, fax or email, to the last known address of the taxpayer'.

Statement of Practice for Tax Assessments is intended to avoid ongoing disputes about when an assessment was made as arose in numerous cases.

Period to be assessed to recover repayments

The period which should be assessed when HMRC are seeking to 'recover money paid, repaid or credited to taxpayers in error' remains unclear following *C & E Commrs v Croydon Hotel & Leisure Co Ltd*, *C & E Commrs v Laura Ashley* and *DFS Furniture Co Plc v C & E Commrs*. Each case has provided different guidance.

Cases: *C & E Commrs v Croydon Hotel & Leisure Co Ltd* [1996] BVC 394; *C & E Commrs v Laura Ashley* [2004] BVC 260; *DFS Furniture Co Plc v C & E Commrs* [2004] BVC 666

Other material: Notice 915; Business Brief 25/04, 14 September 2004

VAT Reporter: ¶58-240

9-640   Checking VAT assessments

The following is a checklist to see if the assessment is valid.

(1)   Has the assessment been addressed to the correct person? The assessment is only valid if it is in the name of the right VAT-registered person and shows the correct address.

(2)   Have HMRC used best judgment in making the assessment? 'Best judgement' has been examined at some length in Tribunal and Court cases. In *Van Boeckel v C & E Commrs*, it was said '... the commissioners will fairly consider all material placed before them and, on that material come to a decision which is one which is reasonable and not arbitrary as to the amount of tax which is due. As long as there is some material on which the Commissioners can reasonably act then they are not required to carry out investigations which may or may not result in further material being placed before them."

A later case considered the way in which the Tribunal should look at instances where the appellant claimed that best judgment had not been used by HMRC. *Rahman (t/a Khayam Restaurant) v C & E Commrs* said that:

(a)   the tribunal should not invalidate an assessment merely because it disagrees as to how the judgment should have been exercised;

(b)   if the assessment is shown to be wholly unreasonable or not bona fide it may be set aside;

(c)   it should be assumed that HMRC have made an honest and genuine attempt to reach a fair assessment; the debate before the tribunal should centre upon whether the amount of the assessment is sustainable in the light of the material available. An assessment may be adjusted rather than set aside.

It is difficult to show that HMRC have not used best judgment. There must be actual evidence of this rather than a feeling that HMRC have been difficult. It must also be remembered that HMRC are only obliged to look at the evidence put before them when making the assessment, therefore it is too late to bring new facts before the Tribunal. Any new facts or evidence must be made known to HMRC before a tribunal hearing, possibly as part of the local reconsideration of the assessment.

(3)   Does the assessment cover the right period and does this match up with any back-up schedules provided? A global assessment covering a number of periods can be acceptable if analysed period by period in an accompanying schedule.

(4)   Has the assessment been made within the relevant time limits?

(5)   Have the correct grounds for the assessment been given. For example, check that an assessment for over-claimed input tax has not been put as an assessment for under-declared output tax.

In a case involving a repayment return, the Upper Tribunal, made the following observations:

'The return will show the amount of tax that the taxpayer says the Commissioners owe him. If they dispute that amount they have a public law obligation to explain why (see Lightman J at [26] in *Tradecorp* and Arden LJ in *BUPA* at [44 et al]). There can only be three reasons: (1) they dispute the amount of output tax in the return, (ii) they dispute the amount of input tax claimed, or (iii) they say that there is some arithmetic error in arriving at the net amount payable. The resolution of (i) and (ii) is reserved to the appeals process and will ordinarily be covered by section 83(1)(b) and (c) …'

(6)   Is the assessment correct in law? Check the dates of any changes in VAT rates, etc. and whether the assessment may be incorrect in European law.

(7)   Is the assessment arithmetically correct? HMRC do make mistakes.

(8)   Has the 'error' previously been discussed with HMRC? If the error or the facts relating to the error have been discussed with HMRC or otherwise brought to their attention, there may have been a misdirection. See ¶9-780.

Cases: *Van Boeckel v C & E Commrs* (1980) 1 BVC 378; *Rahman (t/a Khayam Restaurant) v C & E Commrs* [1998] BVC 323; *Benridge Care Homes Ltd (t/a Benridge Rest Home) v R & C Commrs* [2012] UKUT 132 (TCC); [2012] BVC 1,708

VAT Reporter: ¶58-002

ASSURANCE VISITS

9-660   Assurance visits by HMRC

HMRC are enabled to inspect premises, assets and records for most taxes including VAT. A visit may cover several taxes. HMRC have the right to see all records and inspect all computers without the right of appeal from the taxpayer. Although there is no right of appeal, the occupier can refuse entry to the premises and prevent the inspection being completed. If the inspection has been authorised by a First-tier Tribunal, there is a penalty for such an obstruction.

Taxpayers must be given seven days' notice of the meeting and will be able to arrange the timing of the meeting to suit themselves, not only to suit HMRC. A shorter period before the meeting is possible by agreement.

Any arranged meeting will take place at a time and place to be agreed There is, however, a ban on HMRC officers inspecting purely private dwellings without consent.

It is possible that HMRC will make unannounced visits, usually when there are reasons to suspect fraud, dishonest conduct and the like. In these cases, each visit must be authorised by a specially-trained officer.

HMRC issue information to taxpayers explaining why a visit is being made and the information that is required. These 'factsheets' are detailed in Revenue and Customs Brief 36/10.

Place of visit

Visits by HMRC are normally carried out at the principal place of business; usually the address at which the business is registered for VAT purposes. Where other premises are also used for business purposes, such as a factory unit, warehouse or branch, the officer may also wish to visit these premises.

The main reasons for wishing to visit the principal place of business and where necessary any other premises occupied by the business, are so that the officer can:

(a)   confirm the existence of a bona fide business; and
(b)   satisfy himself that the activities actually carried out are fully reflected in the business records and the returns submitted

Where the place of business is not suitable for the examination of the business records the officer may agree, once the place of business has been seen, to carry out the rest of the visit at some more appropriate venue.

Legislation: *Finance Act* 2008, Sch. 36

Other information: Revenue and Customs Brief 36/10; Notice 989

Records and Returns

9-680   Information from third parties

HMRC have the right to ask taxpayers and third parties for more information and documents relevant to a tax position. This requires HMRC to issue a formal notice and the taxpayer and the third party have the right of appeal against this procedure. Unless it is deemed inappropriate – presumably in instances where criminal activities are suspected – the taxpayer is asked to give permission for HMRC to seek information from a third party.

Penalties will be levied where a person:

- fails to comply with the information notice;
- conceals, destroys or otherwise disposes of documents required by an information notice, or
- conceals, destroys or otherwise disposes of documents that they have been notified are, or are likely to be, required by an information notice.

If HMRC need a formal notice for information issued without permission from the taxpayer, there is the possibility of asking a First-tier Tribunal to issue such a notice. Failure to meet the obligations of the notice will result in a penalty.

Finance Act 2009 extended these powers for HMRC. They are able to require a third party to give contact details for those in debt to HMRC.

Legislation: *Finance Act* 2009, s. 96, Sch. 49; *Finance Act* 2008, Sch. 36

Other information: a podcast at *www.hmrc.gov.uk/podcasts/index.htm*; *www.hmrc.gov.uk/ about/new-compliance-checks.htm*

9-700   Record of compliance visits, etc.

One form of record which is not required by law, but which is invaluable in practice, is a record of dealings with HMRC.

It is vital that evidence be held of all rulings made by HMRC, to prevent tax being levied retrospectively where the trader has acted on the basis of an incorrect ruling. It is also useful to have a record of when visits have been made, the identity of the visiting officers, and of what information has been disclosed to them.

It is also important to bear in mind that matters may be deemed to have been agreed at compliance visits, such as amendments to partial exemption methods, because of a subsequent course of dealing, even though such changes have never been documented.

If there is a retrospective VAT liability due to errors of treatment in some area, it will often be possible to persuade HMRC to levy the tax only from a current date, or from the date of the last control visit, if it can be shown that the area concerned has been specifically covered on assurance visits.

Cases: *Julian Hodge Bank Ltd* [1993] BVC 897

9-710 Officer's powers during a visit

An officer's powers during a compliance visit are wide. For example, an officer can:

(1) require the opening of a gaming machine;

(2) take samples of goods. This may be necessary to check whether a supply is, say, zero-rated, e.g. whether water's purity is within the standard in VATA 1994, Sch. 8, Grp. 2, item 2(a). The trader should receive compensation if the sample is not returned within a reasonable time and in good condition;

(3) require the production of certain documents;

Powers to require the production of documents relating to refunds for bad debts and the flat-rate scheme for farmers are in the *Value Added Tax Regulations* 1995 (SI 1995/2518), reg. 169(2), and 211 respectively.

HMRC can also take all or part of the records back to the local VAT office for further examination and provide a receipt. Generally, HMRC only use this power of removal if it is absolutely essential;

(4) require the trader to account for goods which were supplied to him or acquired or imported by him. The trader can account for goods by proving that:

  (a) he supplied them,
  (b) he has them available to be supplied or used in the business,
  (c) he has removed them from the UK, or
  (d) they were lost or destroyed.

This test is especially common for goods which are capable of non-business use, e.g. a table or heater; and

(5) start work on issuing an assessment for a penalty if a person obstructs an officer while inspecting business premises and records.

Legislation: FA 2008, Sch. 36, para. 39; VATA 1994, s. 73(7), Sch. 11, para. 8 and 9

Cases: *Foster* (1984) 2 BVC 205,016

COPING WITH VAT

9-720 Objectives

All businesses need to ensure that they protect themselves adequately against the build-up of unforeseen VAT liabilities, and associated penalties. The four-year time limit for claiming repayments of VAT overpaid (see 9-410(5)) means that businesses also need to be vigilant to identify overpayments before they go out of time. The precise means of doing this will vary depending upon the size and nature of the business. The main objectives to be achieved are the same for all businesses:

- ensure that the accounting systems and procedures bring together the VAT information accurately, and quickly enough to submit returns on time;
- ensure that finance is available to pay VAT on time;
- identify any areas where there is any doubt as to the liability of transactions, and obtain formal rulings on these from HMRC;
- ensure that there is a means of spotting doubtful areas in the future, and obtaining suitable clearances;
- review major transactions (especially property transactions) and lines of business to establish whether a better VAT position than at present might be achieved; and
- establish a plan to review the VAT position from time to time, even if no major changes are immediately apparent.

VAT Reporter: ¶160

9-740 Establishing VAT awareness

If VAT is to be a necessary (but not costly) evil, rather than a large and unexpected extra cost, it needs to be considered before transactions and agreements are put in place.

In order to achieve this, those making decisions affecting the VAT position – who usually have no connection either with VAT or with direct financial functions generally – need to be persuaded to look at VAT early on. The first step for this is that those involved with VAT need to see themselves as involved in getting the best results for their business, not just recording transactions after the event.

The best way of bringing VAT into the decision-making process then varies from company to company. Obvious strategies involve talking to people in departments unknowingly involved with VAT, talking to central management, and talking to both. Whatever method suits the organisation, those involved with VAT are not simply entitled to create VAT awareness. HMRC have made it their duty to do so.

VAT Reporter: ¶160

9-760 Rulings and non-statutory clearances by HMRC

HMRC give 'rulings' to non-business persons and 'non-statutory clearances' to businesses.

As well as providing some protection against liability for the tax itself, the obtaining of a ruling or non-statutory clearance should give protection against a penalty. The trader will have made a full disclosure of the relevant facts to HMRC, so should be able to rely on the statutory defence of disclosure.

Non-statutory clearances

Clearances will be provided to businesses:

- on areas of material uncertainty arising within four Finance Acts of the introduction of any new legislation; and
- on legislation older than this where there is material uncertainty around the tax outcome of a real issue of commercial significance to the business itself determined by reference to the scale of the business and the impact of the issue upon it.

Supplier or recipient of the supply

A clearance on a liability issue should normally be requested by the supplier. However, questions regarding input tax recovery should be made by the recipient of the supply.

How to apply for a clearance

Large businesses should send their applications to their Client Relationship Manager. Other applications should be submitted to HMRC Clearances Team, Alexander House, 21 Victoria Avenue, Southend on Sea, Essex SS99 1BD.

HMRC say that applications will be dealt with more efficiently if submitted by email to hmrc.southendteam@hmrc.gsi.gov.uk Any email application must be accompanied by a copy of the checklist (see below).

Advance notification of any particularly sensitive issues may be discussed prior to submission.

Required information

In addition to the name of the business, their VAT number and ensuring that any authority to act is in place it will be important to emphasise that the concern about the VAT matter or liability is because any publicly available information does not cover the point or is not sufficiently clear.

Cover Sheet

HMRC ask that each application for a non-statutory clearance should have the following checklist completed and attached as a cover sheet to the application.

Annex A - Checklist for non-statutory clearance applications

Please use this checklist when deciding which documents to attach to your email application, or print and include as a cover sheet where you do not send it electronically.

Check that you have included information that is relevant and available for your clearance application and indicate with a tick (☑) items that are included. It helps us if you follow the order set out below in your clearance application letter and in the way that you group any supporting documents.

1. Information about the applicant and the application:	
1.1 Name and address of the person carrying on the business (and name of the business if different) and relevant customer identification number in full, e.g. Unique Taxpayer Reference, VAT Registration Number	
1.2 Your contact details (if you are acting on behalf of a client) and authority to act for the client where it has not yet been sent to us	
1.3 A brief indication of the subject of the application. Fuller details should be provided under the appropriate headings below	
2. Information about the transaction(s):	
2.1 The details of which tax (es) the application refers to	
2.2 The reasons why the business is undertaking the transaction	
2.3 The relevant facts about the transaction, set out chronologically as transaction steps, so that we have enough information to provide the clearance response, e.g. what was supplied, price, contract terms etc.	
2.4 The answer sought – set out your view of the tax consequences of the transaction and the issues you want us to consider	
2.5 The proposed date of the transaction if it has not yet happened, and supporting information, such as a draft contract where available	
2.6 Any details that are contingent, e.g. on future events or the consent of others	
3. Information about commercial background:	
3.1 Explain the significance of the tax result in achieving the desired outcome	
3.2 Explain why you chose this form of transaction over another that could achieve the same commercial result, where you have considered alternative forms	
3.3 Details of how the transaction will be accounted for where relevant to the tax consequences	
3.4 Details of any related clearances (both statutory and non-statutory) including the relevant clearance references where known	
3.5 For queries which relate to direct tax legislation that is older than four Finance Acts, details of the commercial significance to the business of the issue	
4. Information about legal points:	
4.1 Outline the specific legislation at issue	
4.2 Details of why you believe the application of the legislation is open to possible different interpretations, summary of those different interpretations, and why the tax consequences are uncertain, including reference to our published guidance or to case law	
4.3 Any legal advice you have already received and you are content to disclose	
4.4 Details of any relevant previous advice you have received from HMRC	
4.5 Details of how you intend to use the clearance, such as for public documents	

Appeals against decisions

Appeals may be made to the Tax Tribunal. However, HMRC state in their material that such an appeal may only be made after the supply has taken place.

Time for response from HMRC

It is claimed that the normal situation will allow HMRC to supply a clearance – a definitive yea, nay or maybe – within 28 calendar (not working) days. A major facet of the new Clearance Service will be that the speed of response from HMRC will be reasonably assured – they claim!

Other information: *www.hmrc.gov.uk/cap/links-dec07.htm*

Other material: Revenue and Customs Brief 20/08

Rulings for non-business persons

The following information is based upon material in Notice 700/6. HMRC state that the procedures in this notice only apply to non-business persons from April 2008. Businesses seeking to confirm the treatment of transactions with HMRC should use the non-statutory clearance service detailed above.

HMRC state that:

'It [Notice 700/6] tells you what you need to do to obtain a binding ruling ... in relation to a particular transaction, on which you can rely'

When HMRC will not give a ruling

In the following situations, HMRC will not usually provide a ruling:

- On matters 'that do not involve genuine points of doubt or difficulty ...'
- To hypothetical or 'what if' questions.
- When HMRC consider that the point or issue is covered in a VAT Notice or other material published by them. HMRC state that they 'will refer you to the relevant publications and indicate where you will find the answer.' This is not a new or uncommon practice.

HMRC will not usually provide a general ruling.

Who may rely on a ruling?

'Normally, only the individual taxpayer for whom the request for a ruling was made may rely upon it'. HMRC therefore expect to be informed when the intention is that a ruling will be passed to other businesses or a trade organisation. It is acknowledged that a ruling is not restricted to the individual taxpayer when:

- 'we agree a ruling with a trade body';
- 'where the ruling is about a particular type of product or activity';
- any relevant correspondence 'clearly states otherwise'.

If a ruling is obtained by one business, it is necessary to obtain separate clearance from HMRC before applying this decision to other, albeit associated, businesses. In this situation, the written application should, where possible, include a copy of the original ruling. There should also be confirmation that the associated, or indeed unrelated, business 'operates in precisely the same way' or an explanation of the differences.

This may be particularly relevant when there is a transfer of a going concern.

Notice 700/6 does not say whether any ruling remains binding when the business to whom the ruling has been given is the subject of a transfer of a going concern.

No help for tax planning?

HMRC do not give approval for general tax planning schemes and further tell taxpayers and others that any suggestion that a tax-planning scheme has HMRC approval should be treated with care.

HMRC will not provide a ruling where they 'suspect the transactions are part of a tax avoidance scheme'.

To whom a ruling will be given

The policy of HMRC is to give a ruling in the following circumstances:

- 'normally ... it is the supplier who should ask for a ruling on the liability to tax of goods or services';
- 'if it is an enquiry about tax recovery, then it is the customer who should apply'.

This policy sometimes causes problems. It is hoped that the National Advice Service will review their very strict application of the policy regarding not giving rulings to recipients of supplies. If the supplier is wrong and an incorrect amount of tax is levied, customers find it difficult or impossible to correct the situation after payment has been made.

To obtain a ruling

The person concerned with making the supply should write to the appropriate VAT office.

Any application should include:

- details of the person for whom the ruling is sought (including any VAT registration number);
- the full facts of the situation together with all associated documents;
- a clear explanation of the precise point(s) for which clearance is required; and
- in cases where professional advice has been sought, there must also be included the reason for the uncertainty and details of any alternative interpretations considered.

In cases where there is any doubt about whether or not something is relevant, HMRC say that the details should be disclosed.

In addition, HMRC ask that the person asking for the ruling:

- confirms that 'to the best of your knowledge and belief, the facts you have given are correct and that the full facts and relevant information have been disclosed';
- explains the use to be made of the ruling;
- provides an estimate of the financial implications arising from any decision that may be given. HMRC state that this is so they can 'target their resources appropriately';
- provides details (quoting in full) of 'any transactions (proposed or actual) related to, consequent upon, or forming part of a series with the transaction in respect of which a ruling is sought, whether or not these transactions are certain to take place'.

In addition, HMRC ask that taxpayers or their advisers 'put all of their cards face up on the table' when seeking a ruling. Qualified professionals will find that a little perturbing since professional standards of institutes and associations require nothing less.

Advance rulings

HMRC will only give an advance ruling if they are satisfied that the transaction 'will indeed take place'. They ask for the following additional information in regard to advance rulings:

- a copy of the final draft contract;
- as far as possible, details of all the parties involved.

It is possible that a ruling is given before contracts are finalised. Such decisions are based on the facts as relevant and known at the time. If the eventual transaction or contract differs materially from the information provided HMRC will not be bound by the ruling. They advise that 'you should come back to us to review our ruling where the relevant terms of the contract have changed'. It is also advisable that a further ruling be applied for if a 'significant period of time' elapses between obtaining the decision and the transaction taking place.

HMRC's other requirements regarding applying for rulings must also be complied with.

Other material: Notice 700/6

VAT Reporter: ¶3-790

9-780   Incorrect advice from HMRC

It is well established that the trader cannot, in law, rely on rulings/non-statutory clearances made by HMRC, since it is not open to the trader to rely on the doctrine of estoppel against the Crown.

The best way of dealing with this, where significant amounts of tax are involved, is to provide the facts in writing, and to obtain a written ruling or non-statutory clearance. The response should be checked carefully, to ensure that it is indeed clear and unambiguous. A decision to the effect that, if condition X is met then treatment Y applies, is of little value if the real enquiry is whether condition X is met.

Records and Returns

HMRC may not abide by any ruling or decision given by them if they can show that full information was not given. This may result in the ruling being retrospectively withdrawn. This matter was taken to Judicial Review in the case of the Medical Protection Society Ltd where HMRC won. The case of Corktech involved advice given by the National Advice Service where the Appellant could not prove to the satisfaction of the Court that incorrect advice had been given.

Where HMRC provides incorrect information or advice

HMRC have stated their policy on their website as follows:

'There may be a small number of cases where we provide information or advice that is incorrect in law. Where this happens, we will be bound by such advice provided that it is clear, unequivocal and explicit and you can demonstrate that:

- you reasonably relied on the advice;
- where appropriate, you made full disclosure of all the relevant facts: and
- the application of the statute would result in your financial detriment.

Where this is the case, to apply the statute may be so unfair that it could amount to an abuse of power. But, where we have given incorrect information or advice, our primary duty will always remain to collect the correct amount of tax as required by the law and therefore there will be some circumstances where we will not be bound by the advice we have given.

Where we provide you with erroneous advice that is binding on us and subsequently notify you that it is incorrect, the established legal position is that you will only be required to start accounting for tax on the correct basis from the date of notification. All cases will be subject to any statutory time limits.

Misunderstanding

There may be certain circumstances where you have misunderstood the law and applied the wrong tax treatment when carrying out a transaction or providing information or payment to HMRC. In these circumstances, the wrong amount of tax has been collected. As HMRC has a duty to collect the correct amount of tax as required by law, the situation must be rectified for the past and for the future in order to ensure that the law is applied correctly. However, in rectifying the situation, HMRC will be bound by considerations of public law for example to treat taxpayers fairly.'

The new policy for dealing with occasions when HMRC are responsible for a tax loss is now only available on the website. It is being removed from the printed material published by HMRC.

The old policy spelled out succinctly in the Parliamentary statement is replaced by a wordy policy document. It is couched in and littered with statements which will inevitably deter those who believe that a tax loss has arisen because of bad or incorrect advice received from HMRC. For instance, HMRC previously accepted responsibility when their advice was 'clear and unequivocal', henceforth they will not do so unless their advice was 'clear, unequivocal and explicit'. In future, taxpayers must also 'demonstrate' that they 'reasonably relied on the advice'.

From 1 January 2012, any appeal regarding incorrect advice from HMRC and the refusal of HMRC to stand by that advice has to be appealed through the Upper Tax Tribunal as a Judicial Review matter.

Other material: *www.hmrc.gov.uk/pdfs/info-hmrc.htm*; Technical Note 14 December 2010 'Admin Law' manual 1000 and 'Admin Law' manual

Cases: *R (on the application of the Medical Protection Society Ltd) v R & C Commrs* [2009] EWHC 2780 (Admin); [2009] BVC 943; *Corkteck v R & C Commrs* [2009] EWHC 785 (Admin); [2009] BVC 378

9-800 Changes to interpretation of the law

Changes in interpretation of the law usually arise because of litigation. Appeals by taxpayers do from time to time establish that HMRC have been applying the law incorrectly. When this occurs, HMRC are forced to change their policy. The change is announced in a Revenue and Customs Brief, VAT Information Sheet and VAT Notes.

When litigation forces a change in policy, HMRC operate in the following manner:

(a) announce the date from which businesses will be expected to apply the change;
(b) errors made before the date upon which HMRC expect businesses to implement the change need not be corrected;
(c) businesses may choose to correct errors made before the date from which HMRC expect the change to be applied. Only corrections taking account of over payments and under payments will be accepted – also, they must be made within the requisite time limits; and
(d) the above principles will be applied in cases where HMRC use their discretion not to collect any arrears which may be due in these circumstances.

Other material: Revenue and Customs Brief 24/11

VAT Reporter: ¶55-250

9-810 Responsibility and awareness

Once it is established that the systems in force cope with VAT as well as is reasonably possible, it is necessary to ensure that this continues to be the case.

Ideally, someone within the business should have overall charge of VAT matters. In the case of a one-man business, this is an extra burden on the one man, but he is aided by his detailed knowledge of the business.

Large organisations may be able to train someone in VAT, or recruit a specialist from outside, but that person may have difficulty in getting to know exactly what is going on in all parts of the business. It is essential that managers and decision makers should be aware of the importance of identifying the VAT treatment before transactions are entered into, and encouraged to consult with the person responsible for VAT at an early stage. They should be particularly aware of the general triggers indicating possible problem areas.

It is also essential that someone should monitor *VAT Notes*, which HMRC send to traders with VAT return forms, as HMRC regard receipt of this publication as the time by which traders should be fully aware of policy changes announced in it.

It will never be possible to eliminate errors entirely, but the risk of error and the consequences can be reduced to manageable proportions. Valuable cost savings can often be discovered in the process.

Duty of senior accounting office of large qualifying company.

This is a new requirement put in place by *Finance Act* 2009.

It affects UK registered companies with a turnover of more than £200 million or gross assets of £2 billion (this could be a Group). A senior accounting officer (SAO), the director or officer with overall responsibility for the financial accounting arrangements, must be appointed.

The company must notify HMRC of the SAO each financial year. It is the duty of the SAO to ensure that reasonable steps are taken to put appropriate tax accounting arrangements in place and provide a certificate to HMRC.

The guidance available states that:

'For VAT the tax accounting arrangements in scope would be those that:

- Produce any numbers or figures feeding through into the VAT returns for the year.
- Any of the 2010 tax accounting arrangements that have an impact on the VAT figures for a period falling partly in 2009.
- Any of the 2010 tax accounting arrangements that have an impact on earlier financial years, i.e. where there is a review of historic returns for voluntary disclosure purposes.'

Penalties are put in place. These are:

- there could be a penalty of £5,000 assessable on the SAO if they fail to comply with the main duty;
- there could be a penalty of £5,000, again assessable on the SAO, if they fail to provide the requisite certificate or if they provide an incorrect certificate;
- there could be a penalty where a company fails to notify HMRC of the name/s of the person who was the SAO throughout the financial year.

Legislation: *Finance Act* 2009, s. 92, Sch. 46

Other material: Revenue and Customs Brief 37/09 *Duties of Senior Accounting Officer of large qualifying companies*; HMRC Guidance Note 17 August 2009

9-820   Conclusion

VAT is complex, substantial and ubiquitous. It is a fact of business life. The best, and cheapest, way of dealing with it is to recognise its existence and to recognise it in the decision making and administrative processes of the business. Ignoring it is a costly mistake.

Records and Returns

FLOWCHARTS

9-840   Correcting errors

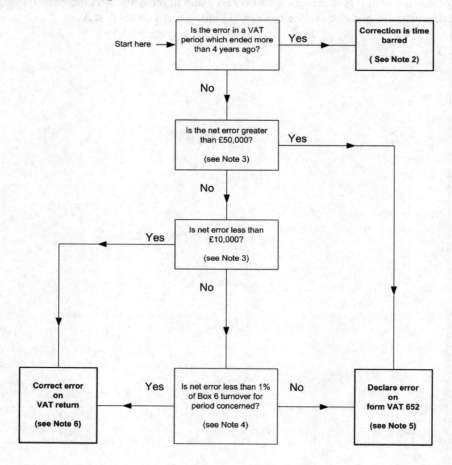

Notes

(1) Revised regulations

More generous regulations for correcting errors came into force on 1 July 2008.

(2) Time-barred adjustments

Normally, input tax or output tax errors cannot be corrected if they occurred in a VAT period which ended more than four years ago.

(3) Net error

For these purposes, the net error is the aggregate of all input tax and output tax errors discovered during the same VAT period.

(4) One per cent of turnover limit

The value against which the net error must be measured is as follows:

$$1\% \times \text{VAT-exclusive turnover for the relevant VAT period.}$$

VAT-exclusive turnover is the amount to be entered in Box 6 of the return for the relevant period.

The relevant VAT period concerned is the one in which the errors are discovered.

(5) When to use form VAT 652

Form VAT 652 must be used to declare errors that they may not be corrected on a return.

(6) How to correct errors

The net payment or repayment should be incorporated into the return for the period in which the error(s) is (are) discovered.

Legislation: *Value Added Tax Regulations* 1995 (SI 1995/2518), reg. 34, 35

Records and Returns

413

9-860 When unjust enrichment applies

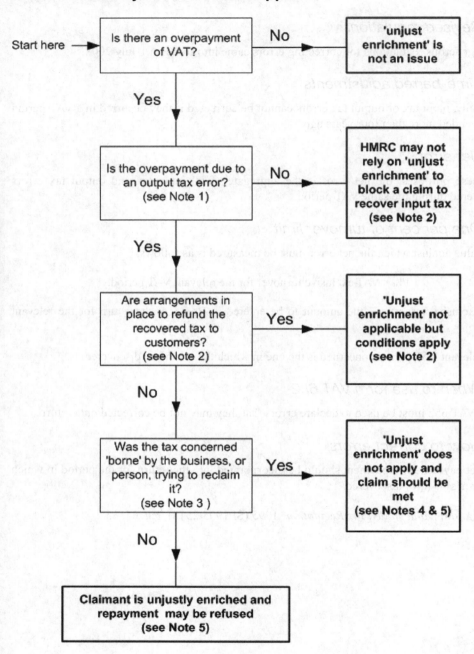

Notes

(1) When unjust enrichment applies

'Unjust enrichment' applies to overpayment of output tax (*Marks & Spencer Plc v C & E Commrs; University of Sussex v C & E Commrs* [2004] BVC 151). Input tax claims cannot be denied on the grounds of 'unjust enrichment'.

(2) Refunding tax to customers

There is no unjust enrichment when the reclaimed output tax is refunded to customers. This should normally be done in accordance with the relevant regulations.

(3) Claimant effectively bore the burden of the tax

'… principles of Community law tell us that unjust enrichment can only be successfully invoked where it can be shown that someone other than the claimant effectively bore the burden of the tax.' (VAT Guidance Manuals Vol V1-33 (Refunds: unjust enrichment) Section 3.3).

(4) Loss and damage suffered by claimant

Any loss of damage caused to the claimant by charging output tax when it was not due can only be taken into account only to the extent that it is quantifiable (*Marks & Spencer Plc v C & E Commrs* [1999] BVC 107).

(5) Unjust enrichment

'In simple terms, we use the phrase "unjust enrichment" to describe the situation where payment of a claimant's claim for a refund would put him in a better economic position than he would have been if he had not mistakenly accounted for the tax, in other words, where he would get a "windfall" profit …' (*VAT Guidance Manuals* Vol V1-33 (Refunds: unjust enrichment) Section 3.3).

Records and Returns

9-880 Claiming bad debt relief

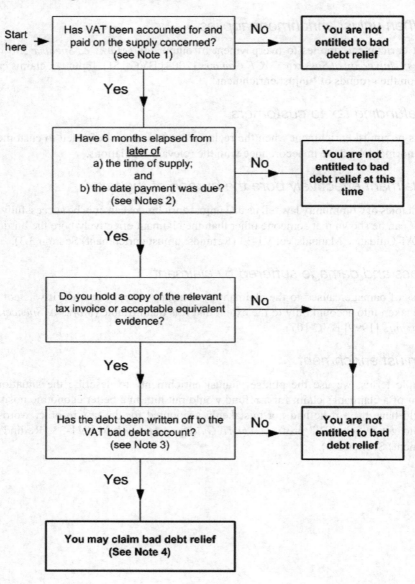

Start here → Has VAT been accounted for and paid on the supply concerned? (see Note 1)

No → You are not entitled to bad debt relief

Yes ↓

Have 6 months elapsed from <u>later of</u> a) the time of supply; and b) the date payment was due? (see Notes 2)

No → You are not entitled to bad debt relief at this time

Yes ↓

Do you hold a copy of the relevant tax invoice or acceptable equivalent evidence?

No →

Yes ↓

Has the debt been written off to the VAT bad debt account? (see Note 3)

No → You are not entitled to bad debt relief

Yes ↓

You may claim bad debt relief (See Note 4)

Notes

(1) Accounting for and paying VAT

VAT bad debt relief is conditional upon the claimant having already accounted for and paid the tax to HMRC. By concession, traders in the annual accounting scheme may account for output tax and claim bad debt relief in the same VAT return.

(2) Capping

Bad debt relief must be claimed within four years and six months of the later of:

*   the time of the supply; and
*   the due date for payment.

(3) VAT bad debts refunds account

A debt is regarded as written off for VAT bad debt relief purposes once it has been entered into this VAT Bad Debts Refunds Account (see 9-520).

(4) Amount of relief

Only the VAT element of an outstanding debt can ever be claimed. If a customer disputes the liability of a supply, it is important to remember that whatever amount is recovered is regarded as VAT-inclusive.

Legislation: *Value Added Tax Regulations* 1995 (SI 1995/2518), Part XIX

9-900 Endorsing invoices to EU businesses

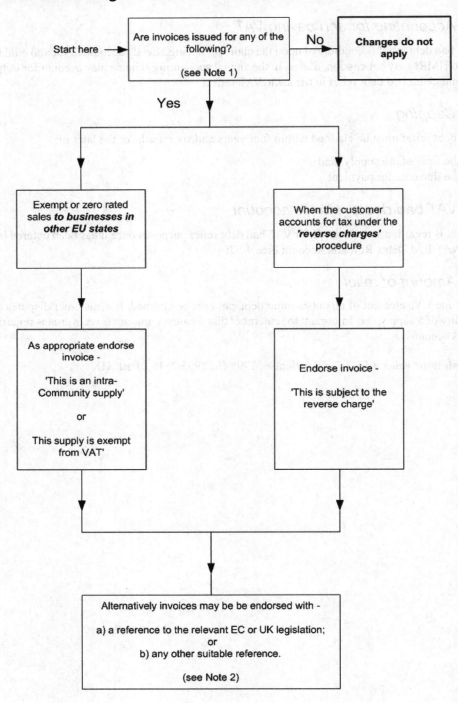

Start here → Are invoices issued for any of the following?

(see Note 1)

No → **Changes do not apply**

Yes

Exempt or zero rated sales *to businesses in other EU states*

As appropriate endorse invoice -

'This is an intra-Community supply'

or

This supply is exempt from VAT'

When the customer accounts for tax under the *'reverse charges'* procedure

Endorse invoice -

'This is subject to the reverse charge'

Alternatively invoices may be be endorsed with -

a) a reference to the relevant EC or UK legislation;
or
b) any other suitable reference.

(see Note 2)

Notes

(1) Affected supplies

It is necessary to endorse an invoice to a business in another EU State when invoicing for any of the following:

- intra EC supplies of goods and services;
- supplies where the customer accounts for the VAT;
- margin scheme sales of second-hand goods, works of art, antiques and collectors items;
- travel related supplies that fall within the scope of the Tour Operators Margin Scheme.

(2) Appropriate endorsement

Originally businesses were given as much flexibility as possible in deciding a suitable endorsement. It is proposed to change this from 1 January 2013. From then the only acceptable endorsements should be as a follows:

- 'Exempt' – for exempt supplies;
- 'Self-billing' – for self-billed supplies;
- 'Margin scheme: works of art', 'Margin scheme: antiques or collectors items,'' Margin scheme: second-hand goods' or 'Margin scheme: tour operators' – for the appropriate margin scheme.

(3) Legislative references

For further information, see VAT information sheet 10/07 – Changes to VAT invoicing with effect from 1 October 2007.

(4) Further information

For further information, see VAT information sheet 10/07 – Changes to VAT invoicing with effect from 1 October 2007 and VAT: changes to VAT invoice rules (published 31 May 2012).

9-920 Frequency of submission for EC Sales lists

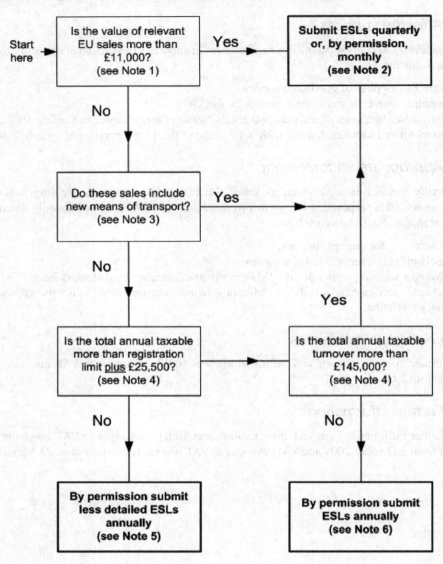

Notes

(1) EU sales

For these purposes, EU sales are sales of goods or services to persons registered in other Member States.

(2) EU Sales of goods

At the end of any month, the annual EU sales must be less than £11,000. Alternatively, the limit may be applied at the start of a year when there are reasonable grounds for believing that the value will be less than £11,000 in the year concerned.

(3) Normal frequency

ESLs are normally submitted monthly or quarterly. Suppliers of goods exceeding £70,000 in a quarter must submit monthly ESLs.

(4) When EU sales include new means of transport

Persons making EU sales of new means of transport (see 5-400) may not make annual or less detailed ESLs.

(5) Annual taxable turnover

This is the total of taxable supplies made in the past year or the year which is about to begin.

(6) Less detailed ESLs

Less detailed ESLs (see 9-540) may be made by persons whose annual taxable turnover does not exceed the sum of the registration limit and £25,500. An application to do so must be submitted to the National Advice Service.

(7) Persons submitting Annual ESLs

Applications to submit ESLs annually must be made to the National Advice Service.

Legislation: *Value Added Tax Regulations* 1995 (SI 1995/2518), Part IV

Other material: Notice 725, Section 17

Records and Returns

421

9-940 Requirement to submit EC Sales lists

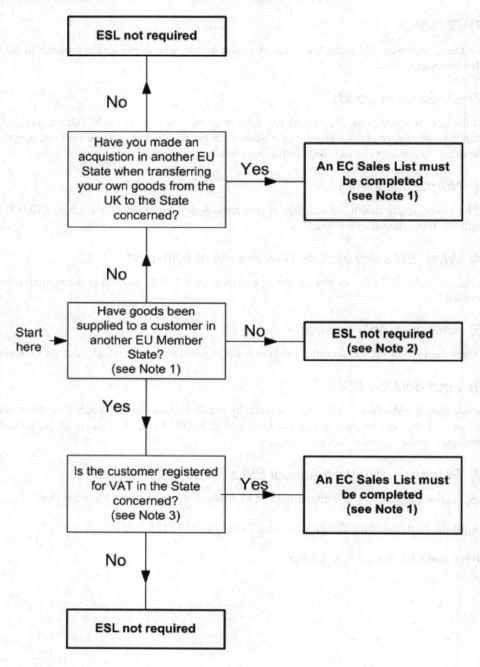

Notes

(1) Use of ESL

The information supplied on ESLs is used to control and verify the VAT on movements of goods and supplies of services within the EU.

ESLs must be completed by UK VAT-registered persons who supply goods or services to other Member States to persons who are registered for VAT.

(2) Supplies of services

From 1 January 2010, ESLs must be completed by VAT-registered persons who supply services to businesses or organisations registered in another EU State.

(3) Customers in other EU Member States who are not VAT-registered

Sales to customers in other EU States who are not VAT registered are not declared on ESLs.

(4) Acquisitions involving own goods

The transfer of goods within the same legal entity from one EC Member State to another is deemed to be a supply of goods for VAT purposes. There is an acquisition in the State to which the goods are transferred (see 5-380).

Legislation: *Value Added Tax Regulations* 1995 (SI 1995/2518), Part IV

Other material: Notice 725, Section 17

9-960 Intrastat obligations – goods coming to the UK

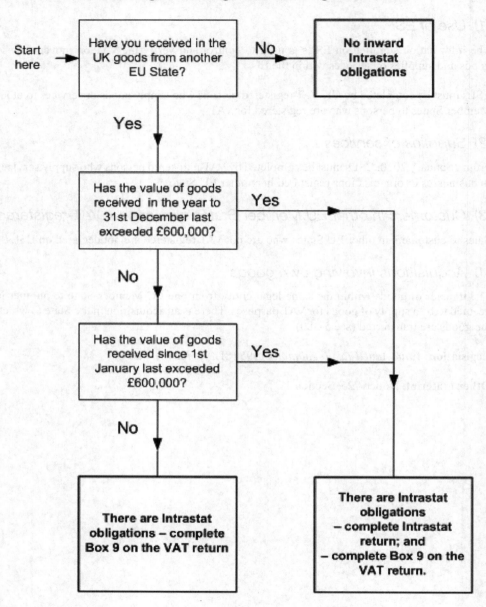

Start here → Have you received in the UK goods from another EU State?

No → **No inward Intrastat obligations**

Yes ↓

Has the value of goods received in the year to 31st December last exceeded £600,000?

Yes →

No ↓

Has the value of goods received since 1st January last exceeded £600,000?

Yes →

No ↓

There are Intrastat obligations – complete Box 9 on the VAT return

There are Intrastat obligations – complete Intrastat return; and – complete Box 9 on the VAT return.

9-980   Intrastat obligations – goods leaving the UK

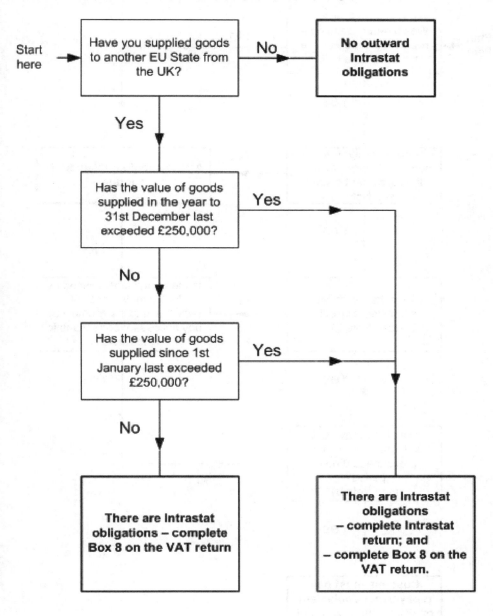

9-990   Entitlement to a repayment supplement

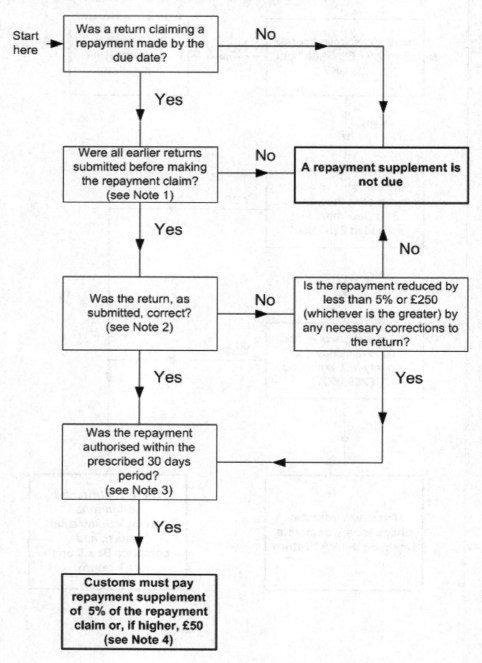

Notes

(1) Outstanding returns

A repayment supplement is not due if earlier returns are outstanding when HMRC receive the repayment return.

(2) Corrections to returns

Only correct repayment returns, and those requiring minimal corrections, qualify for a repayment supplement.

(3) 30-day period during which repayment must be authorised

A repayment supplement is due when the repayment is not authorised within 30 days of HMRC receiving the return. The following periods are omitted from the 30-day period:

- the time taken by HMRC to make reasonable enquiries to be satisfied that the claim is legitimate and accurate; and
- to correct errors or omissions on the return.

(4) Further information

For further information, see 10-140.

Other material: Notice 700/58

Records and Returns

Penalties and Tax Avoidance

THE PENALTY REGIME

10-000 Introduction

The formation of HMRC in 2005 heralded a review of the sanctions which could be imposed when taxpayers failed to provide HMRC with complete and accurate information. To this end, HMRC published a consultation document in December 2006 entitled *Modernising Powers, Deterrents and Safeguards: a new approach to penalties for incorrect tax returns.*

Subsequently, the necessary legislation was introduced in FA 2007, s. 97. More changes were brought in by FA 2008, s. 123.

The aim of the changes is to introduce a single civil penalty regime for all tax returns with the onus on encouraging compliant behaviour.

Other material: Compliance handbook manual

VAT Reporter: ¶59-600

10-010 Broad principles

A penalty may be triggered when there is an inaccuracy that leads to a potential loss in revenue for HMRC. The types of behaviour that lead to an inaccuracy have been banded into three:

(1)   the inaccuracy is caused by the failure of the person giving the information to HMRC to take reasonable care;

(2)   the inaccurate information has been deliberately given to HMRC;

(3)   the inaccurate information has been given deliberately to HMRC and the offence has been compounded by the action being concealed.

Failure to take reasonable care

HMRC say that taking reasonable care depends on the individual's abilities and circumstances. They do not expect the same level of expertise from a self-employed and unrepresented individual compared with a multi-national company. They liken a careless act to that of the general law of negligence, citing a 1856 case: 'Negligence is the omission to do something which a reasonable man, guided upon those considerations which normally regulate the conduct of human affairs, would do, or doing something which a prudent and reasonable man would not do. The defendants might be liable for negligence, if, unintentionally, they omitted to do that which a prudent and reasonable person would have done or did that which a person taking reasonable care would not have done.'

For example, it is assumed that a reasonable person would take advice, keep complete and accurate records and be aware of the need to register for VAT. A person who fails to do so because he has lacked care would be subject to a maximum penalty of 30% of the lost revenue.

Mistake by temporary bookkeeper

In *Express Foods* HMRC queried a refund claimed on a VAT return. After checking the return, the appellant's accountant stated that the correct refund was £20,578 less than that claimed. The appellant's accounts administrator had been on holiday and a replacement had covered her absence. The over-claim resulted from transposition and timing errors made by the temporary replacement who was unfamiliar with the accounting system. Some invoices for zero-rated purchases had been entered with a nil figure in the 'net' column and the full amount in the 'VAT' column. Some sales invoices had not been updated to the customers' ledgers until after the VAT return was completed. The First-tier Tribunal decided that the appellant's actions did not demonstrate reasonable care in completing the return, so it had been careless within the meaning of FA 2007, Sch. 24, para. 3(1)(a) and was liable to the penalty under Sch. 24, para. 1 of 15 per cent of the potential lost revenue of £20,578. This was the minimum percentage applicable for an unprompted disclosure.

Legislation: FA 2007, Sch. 24, para. 3(1)(a)

Cases: *Blyth v Birmingham Waterworks Co* (1856) 11 Exch 781; 156 Eng Rep 1047; *Express Foods* [2011] TC 00728

Other Material Compliance handbook Para CH 81120

VAT Reporter: ¶59-662

Deliberate action or inaction

This is defined as knowingly and intentionally giving HMRC an inaccurate document.

An example would be deliberately submitting an inaccurate VAT return understating liability. Although this could be fraud it is treated as a civil rather than a criminal matter. HMRC will still treat large frauds as a criminal matter.

The maximum penalty is 70% of the lost tax.

Legislation: FA 2007, Sch. 24, para. 3(1)(b)

VAT Reporter: ¶59-662

Deliberate and concealed action or inaction

This involves the deliberate submission of inaccurate information and some act of concealment such as destroying records, falsifying documents, suppressing takings or similar.

The maximum penalty is 100% of the lost revenue.

Legislation: FA 2007, Sch. 24, para. 3(1)(c)

VAT Reporter: ¶59-662

Mitigation of penalties

The penalties may be mitigated. This mitigation varies according to whether the error was prompted by the intervention of HMRC or was entirely voluntary. Details are in 10-140.

VAT Reporter: ¶59-730

10-020   Assessment of penalties

HMRC have power to assess amounts due by way of civil penalty, default interest or default surcharge. For all practical purposes these assessments are the same as tax assessment.

HMRC have 12 months in which to assess penalties due under the single penalty system introduced by FA 2007. The 12 months run from the end of the appeal period applicable to the assessment (or decision) correcting the inaccuracy. When there is no assessment it runs from the date on which the inaccuracy or understatement is corrected.

It appears, from *Dollar Land (Feltham) Ltd v C & E Commrs*, that once the basic liability to a penalty, etc. is established, the decision whether to assess is not a matter which is appealable to the tribunal. If HMRC act unreasonably in imposing the penalty which is legally due, the only remedy is by way of judicial review.

Legislation: VATA 1994, s. 76; FA 2007, Sch. 24, para. 13

Cases: *Dollar Land (Feltham) Ltd v C & E Commrs* [1995] BVC 115

VAT Reporter: ¶57-805

10-030   Naming and shaming

HMRC have been given the power to publicise the name, address, nature of any business and potential lost tax revenue of anyone involved in a *deliberate* action causing a potential loss of VAT revenue exceeding £25,000.

There will be no published details of anyone who has made a full disclosure, either unprompted or prompted in a time considered appropriate by HMRC. Details must be published within 12 months from the relevant penalty becoming final and may only be published for 12 months from when first published.

This power is detailed in the *Finance Act* 2009 and will come into force by Statutory Instrument for periods after 1 April 2010.

Legislation: *Finance Act* 2009, s. 93

VAT Reporter: ¶59-629

10-040   Interaction of penalties

It will have been seen that, in some cases, the same act or omission is capable of attracting more than one of the penalties available to HMRC.

Penalties and Tax Avoidance

The general principle of the various penalties (except for default interest on tax) is that they are mutually exclusive. It is up to HMRC to decide which kind of penalty they will seek.

It seems that, in practice, HMRC will normally seek to use the penalty provision most closely suited to the nature of the offence, rather than that which involves the highest amount of penalties. However, it should not be presumed that this will always be the case, as there would then be no purpose in the degree of overlap provided in the law.

Legislation: FA 2007, Sch. 24, para. 12

VAT Reporter: ¶60-610; ¶59-600

10-100   Late notification

Introduction

As has been seen earlier, a trader who makes taxable supplies is obliged to notify HMRC if these supplies exceed the registration limits, so that a VAT registration can be effected. Also, a trader who is exempted from registration by HMRC must notify a change in the nature of supplies made. There is a penalty for failure to make these notifications to HMRC by the proper date.

For registrations due on or before 31 March 2010 the old penalty system applies whilst for registrations due on or after 1 April 2010 the new penalty system applies.

Going concern transfers

There is a liability to a penalty for a person who becomes liable to register on acquiring a business as a going concern and fails to do so timeously.

VAT Reporter: ¶43-025

Registration date 31 March 2010 or earlier

The penalty under this superseded system is the greater of:

(1)   £50; and

(2)   a percentage of the tax due from the date when the trader should have been registered to the date when proper notification is made (or, if earlier, the date when HMRC become aware of the liability to be registered by some other means).

The percentage rate for this purpose depends on the length of the delay in notification, as follows:

Length of delay	Percentage
9 months or less	5
9–18 months	10
over 18 months	15

The penalty is based on the net tax due for the penalty period (i.e. output tax less input tax), not on the total output tax due. It applies not only to 'black economy' traders who are discovered by HMRC, but also to traders who register in the ordinary way but are late in doing this. See flowchart at 11-820.

Legislation: VATA 1994, s. 67

Other material: Notice 700/41

VAT Reporter: ¶60-480

Statutory defence

The late registration penalty is not due if the trader can satisfy HMRC or, on appeal, a VAT tribunal, that there is a reasonable excuse for the failure. The reasonable excuse defence applies to several of the civil penalties, and is discussed separately below.

VAT Reporter: ¶60-490

Mitigation

The penalty can be mitigated by up to 100 per cent by HMRC or, on appeal, the tribunal).

Legislation: VATA 1994, s. 70

VAT Reporter: ¶60-480

Registration date 1 April 2010 or later

The new penalty regime applies to the 'failure to notify' for periods on or after 1 April 2010.

There is not a penalty when the taxpayer has a reasonable excuse for registering at the correct time. A 'reasonable excuse' does not include 'an insufficiency of funds ... unless attributable to events outside' the control of the person concerned, relying 'on any other person to do anything' unless reasonable care is taken to avoid failure or when the reasonable excuse ceased unless remedial action is taken 'without unreasonable delay'.

In other circumstances, the penalty is a percentage of the tax unpaid due to failure to register at the correct time.

HMRC also have the power to make an unqualified mitigation in 'special circumstances'. 'Special circumstances' do not include the inability to pay or that the error giving rise to the penalty may be balanced by an over-payment by another person.

HMRC have issued the following table indicating the levels of penalty and mitigation:

433

Why you failed to notify us	Disclosure	Minimum penalty	Maximum penalty
Reasonable excuse		No penalty	No penalty
Not deliberate	Unprompted	0% within 12 months of tax being due, otherwise 10%	30%
	Prompted	10% within 12 months of tax being due, otherwise 20%	30%
Deliberate	Unprompted	20%	70%
	Prompted	35%	70%
Deliberate and concealed	Unprompted	30%	100%
	Prompted	50%	100%

Other material: HM Revenue and Customs Brief 30/10; *www.hmrc.gov.uk/compliance/cc-fs11.pdf*

VAT Reporter: ¶43-858

10-120   Late returns/default surcharge

Late returns and/or payments are subject to penalties. This system is being revised as part of the consolidated penalty system. According to the consultation document issued in December 2009, HMRC anticipate that legislation to bring in the new system will be enacted during 2010. Until then the system described below continues.

Default

Traders who are late in submitting returns, or who submit returns on time but neglect to pay the tax due, are subject to penalties. If either the return or the payment is not received by HMRC by the due date, the trader is 'in default'.

Surcharge liability notice

When a trader is in default, HMRC may issue a surcharge liability notice (SLN) specifying a surcharge period commencing with the date of the notice and ending on the anniversary of the last day of the period for which the default arose. However, if the period of default falls within an existing surcharge period, that surcharge period is extended (i.e. the further surcharge period may be regarded as beginning before the date when the SLN is issued).

Amount of penalty

If the trader is in default again within the surcharge period, he is liable to a default surcharge of two per cent of the outstanding VAT for the period, being that part of the liability for the period which is not paid by the due date. A second default in a surcharge period attracts a surcharge at five per cent, a third at 10 per cent, and any further defaults at 15 per cent. There is a minimum surcharge of £30.

In practice, HMRC do not normally assess a surcharge at the two per cent or five per cent rates if the amount of it is less than £400.

Repayment return

If there is no outstanding VAT (for instance, in the case of a repayment return), no surcharge is due. However, HMRC can still issue a SLN initiating or extending a surcharge period.

Payments on account

The default surcharge also applies to payments on account by large traders (9-610).

Defences to the surcharge

A trader who is in default is not liable to a surcharge, or to the issue of a SLN, if he can satisfy HMRC or the tribunal:

(1)   that the return (and payment) was dispatched at such a time and in such a manner that it was reasonable to expect that it would be received by HMRC by the due date; or

(2)   that there was a reasonable excuse for the default.

If HMRC impose a breach of regulations penalty, the default does not count for surcharge purposes.

Help for small businesses

The first default by a business with a turnover of less than £150,000 does not result in HMRC issuing a surcharge liability notice. Instead, the business should receive a letter from HMRC offering help and assistance. As a surcharge may not be imposed until after a surcharge liability notice has been issued this allows 'extra time to sort out any short-term difficulties before formally entering the default surcharge system'.

Legislation: VATA 1994, s. 59

Other material: Notice 700/50

VAT Reporter: ¶60-450

10-140   Inaccuracies on returns, assessments, other claims etc.

Introduction

The penalty levied for inaccuracies on returns is different according to when the inaccuracy occurred. The determining factor is whether the inaccuracy occurred before or after April 2009.

Penalties and Tax Avoidance

435

Penalties for returns submitted and assessments issued after 1 April 2009

Incorrect returns incur a penalty when the prescribed accounting period commenced on or after 1 April 2008 and the return is due to be filed on or after 1 April 2009. The penalty is a percentage of the loss of revenue to HMRC because of the actions of the taxpayer concerned. The legislation refers to 'the potential loss of revenue' (PLR) being the additional tax payable as a result of correcting the error.

Assessments

When HMRC issue an assessment which, unbeknown to them, is too low, the recipient has 30 days in which to advise HMRC of the higher and correct liability. If this is not done within 30 days of the assessment, a penalty is triggered. This is normally treated as 'careless behaviour'.

Experience since April 2009 has shown that this penalty is applied both to assessments issued because a return has not been rendered and to assessments issued following an assurance visit or investigation.

Mitigation

The penalties may be mitigated. The maximum mitigation varies according to how and when HMRC are notified as follows:

Penalised behaviour	Maximum penalty, without disclosure, based on PLR	Minimum penalty, with prompted disclosure, based on PLR	Minimum penalty, with unprompted disclosure, based on PLR
Careless	30%	15%	Nil
Deliberate but not concealed	70%	35%	20%
Deliberate and concealed	100%	50%	30%

An error which occurred despite the taxpayer taking reasonable care should not incur a penalty so long as HMRC are notified promptly.

HMRC also have the power to make an unqualified mitigation in 'special circumstances'. 'Special circumstances' do not include the inability to pay or that the error giving rise to the penalty may be balanced by an over-payment by another person.

HMRC have the power to suspend for up to two years a penalty due as a result of a 'careless' error.

Voluntary disclosure of errors made on returns

The system for adjusting errors made on returns is as described at 9-410. Previously, complying with these regulations ensured that there was not a penalty when an error on a return was voluntarily disclosed to HMRC. There is no such certainty under the new penalty regime.

Delay in declaring tax due

Where an inaccuracy results in an amount of tax being declared later than it should have been, the potential loss in revenue is:

- five per cent of the delayed tax for each year; or
- a percentage of the delayed tax for each separate period of the delay of less than a year equating to five per cent per year.

Example

A trader included on his VAT return for the three months to last 31 December £70,000 of input tax for which the VAT invoice was dated four days after that 31 December.

This resulted in an underpayment of VAT for that period. However the error corrected itself because the same amount was excluded from the input tax in the following VAT return.

HMRC may assess a penalty of 1.25 per cent of £70,000.

Legislation: FA 2007, Sch. 24

Other material: Revenue and Customs Brief 15/11; *www.hmrc.gov.uk/compliance/cc-fs7.pdf*

VAT Reporter: ¶60-002

Misdeclaration – prior to April 2009

What constitutes a misdeclaration

A serious misdeclaration may arise when:

(1) a VAT return is submitted which understates a person's VAT liability, or overstates entitlement to a repayment of VAT; or

(2) HMRC make an assessment which is less than the tax due and the person concerned fails to take all reasonable steps to point this out to HMRC within 30 days of the date of the assessment.

In order to attract a penalty, the error must be above certain limits. Also, a misdeclaration will not attract a penalty if it is protected by one or other of the statutory defences (see 10-140).

The amount potentially subject to penalty is the amount of tax which would have been lost had the errors not been discovered; this is the net amount of any underdeclaration for the period.

Penalties and Tax Avoidance

Magnitude of the error

In order to establish whether a misdeclaration attracts penalties, it is necessary to see if the net underdeclaration of liability (or overstatement of repayment due) for the period concerned exceeds either of the two limits. These are the lesser of £1,000,000 and 30 per cent of the 'relevant amount' for the period.

The 'relevant amount' when the misdeclaration arises because of an incorrect return is the 'gross amount of tax' (or GAT) for the period, being the sum of:

(1)   the total amount of input tax which should have been shown on the return; and

(2)   the total amount of output tax which should have been shown on the return.

Where the misdeclaration results from failure to tell HMRC that an assessment is incorrect, the 'relevant amount' is the 'true amount of tax' being the net liability or repayment which should have been shown on the return for the period (i.e. the difference between the amounts at (1) and (2) above). See para. 9-410.

Example

A trader's VAT return (as revised for all errors which may originally have been in it) shows the following amounts of tax:

	£
Output tax	12,000
Input tax	4,500

The thresholds for SMP are:

(1) Errors in return:

   £12,000 + £4,500 = £16,500 @ 30% = £4,950

(2) Assessment understated:

   £12,000 − £4,500 = £7,500 @ 30% = £2,250

The underdeclaration used in applying these tests is the net underdeclaration for the period concerned, taking account of errors in favour of HMRC. Thus, if a trader inadvertently omits a week's results, involving output tax of £500 and input tax of £300, the underdeclaration is the £200 difference between the two, not the £500 of output tax omitted.

Rate of misdeclaration penalty

When a misdeclaration penalty arises, there is an automatic penalty of 15 per cent of the tax underdeclared.

Statutory defences

A person who makes a serious or persistent misdeclaration will not be liable for a penalty:

(1)   if it can be shown that there is a reasonable excuse for the underdeclaration; or

(2)   if the trader notifies HMRC of the underdeclaration before they discover it, and at a time when he had no reason to believe that they were making enquiries into his tax affairs.

For the defence of disclosure to succeed, the trader must give full information about the underdeclaration to HMRC. In order to avoid a penalty, it is necessary to disclose details of the mistakes to HMRC before they start enquiries into the VAT affairs of the business. Usually, HMRC consider that enquiries have begun when they make an appointment to inspect the business records. However, HMRC will accept voluntary disclosures after this point provided they have no reason to believe that the errors were discovered earlier and disclosure was only made because of the projected visit, or the disclosure during or after the visit was prompted by their enquiries into the business affairs.

Concessionary defences

There are two concessionary defences.

A serious misdeclaration penalty will not normally be applied where an error is made which is corrected by an equal and opposite error in the following period. This could arise, for instance, in the case of a supply made in one period and included on the return for the next.

A serious misdeclaration penalty will not normally be applied to an error discovered before the due date for submission of the return for the next prescribed accounting period. Hence the length of time of the period of grace varies as to whether returns are submitted monthly, quarterly or annually.

Mitigation

Penalties can be mitigated by up to 100 per cent by HMRC or, on appeal, the tribunal.

Claims for VAT refunds from outside the UK

Businesses based outside the EU are liable for penalties for incorrect claims for UK VAT refunds under the EC 13th Directive (86/560/EEC) for years starting after 1 July 2009.

EU businesses making claims for UK VAT refunds under EC 8th Directive are liable for penalties for incorrect claims submitted for years on or after 1 January 2009.

For the rate of penalty see the table above.

Other material: VAT Notice 700/42

Legislation: VATA 1994, s. 63 and 70

VAT Reporter: ¶60-030 and ¶60-036

Penalties and Tax Avoidance

10-160 Persistent misdeclaration

For filing dates due after 1 April 2009, this penalty is repealed and there is no direct equivalent. Such errors will henceforth be dealt with under the 'Inaccuracies on Returns' system. See 10-210 below.

Legislation: VATA 1994, s. 64 and 70

VAT Reporter: ¶60-060

10-190 Failure to submit EC Sales Lists

Failure to submit an EC Sales List (ESL) by the due date can give rise to a civil penalty at a daily rate.

If an ESL is not submitted by the due date, HMRC may issue a notice. If the ESL is not submitted within a further 14 days, then a penalty will be due. Penalties can also be levied (regardless of whether the first late ESL attracts a penalty) for any further late ESLs until 12 months have elapsed without an ESL being submitted late.

The penalty is at a rate of £5 per day for the first default, £10 per day for the second, and £15 per day for any subsequent ones. The maximum penalty is 100 days' worth, and the minimum is £50.

Legislation: VATA 1994, s. 66

VAT Reporter: ¶60-130

Other material: Notice 725, para. 17.12

10-210 Inaccuracies in EC Sales Lists

A penalty can be imposed where there is a 'material inaccuracy' in an EC Sales List (ESL; also known as an EC sales statement). A material inaccuracy is defined as the inclusion or omission of information, as a result of which the ESL is misleading in any material respect.

When a first material inaccuracy is discovered, HMRC may issue a written warning. If a further material inaccuracy is discovered on an ESL due for submission within the two years following the issue of the warning, a further warning may be issued. If a further material inaccuracy is discovered on an ESL due in the next two years, a penalty of £100 is due.

Legislation: VATA 1994, s. 65

Other material: Notice 725, para. 17.12

VAT Reporter: ¶60-100

10-230   Unauthorised issue of invoices

Where a person who is not registered for VAT, or otherwise authorised to issue VAT invoices (e.g. a receiver selling business assets owned by a taxable person can validly issue a tax invoice), issues an invoice which purports to include VAT, he is liable to a penalty.

If the relevant invoice is issued on or after 1 April 2010 the matter is dealt with under the new system.

From 1 April 2010

From 1 April 2010, this penalty is included in the 'Wrong doing penalties'. There is a penalty of between 10 per cent and 100 per cent of the VAT shown on the invoice. The level of the penalty depends on whether the offence was committed deliberately and whether there were attempts to conceal the offence.

The following table indicates the level of penalty that will be assessed:

Reason for wrongdoing	Disclosure	Minimum penalty	Maximum penalty
Reasonable excuse		No penalty	No penalty
Non-deliberate	Unprompted	10%	30%
	Prompted	20%	30%
Deliberate	Unprompted	20%	70%
	Prompted	35%	70%
Deliberate and concealed	Unprompted	30%	100%
	Prompted	50%	100%

There is a defence of 'reasonable excuse'.

Pre April 2010

The penalty was the greater of £50, or 15 per cent of the purported tax (whether or not the amount of 'tax' was shown separately). The criteria for determining the penalty, and any mitigation, was the same as for the late notification penalty. There was a defence of 'reasonable excuse'.

Legislation: VATA 1994, s. 67; FA 2008, s. 123, Sch. 41, para. 2

Other material: Revenue and Customs Brief 52/09

VAT Reporter: ¶60-535

Penalties and Tax Avoidance

10-260   Incorrect certificates

Certain zero-ratings and reduced ratings (particularly in connection with property) depend upon the supplier obtaining a certificate of use from the customer. If an incorrect certificate is used, HMRC may assess the customer for a penalty of 100 per cent of the tax 'saved' by the issue of the certificate.

Reasonable excuse

The usual statutory defence of reasonable excuse applies for this penalty.

Legislation: VATA 1994, s. 62

Other material: Notice 708, para. 16.8

VAT Reporter: ¶60-200

10-290   Breaches of regulations

There are penalties for breaches of VAT regulations of any kind.

The amount of penalty varies with the type and frequency of the breach concerned. The basic penalty is at a rate of £5 per day while the breach continues. This is increased to £10 per day if there has been an earlier breach of the same regulation within the previous two years, and £15 per day if there has been more than one such earlier breach.

In some cases, this basic daily penalty is increased to a daily percentage of the tax involved, if this is greater. The percentage rises in line with the number of previous breaches, in exactly the same way as the basic daily penalty. The possible percentages are $\frac{1}{6}$ per cent, $\frac{1}{3}$ per cent and ½ per cent. The equivalent annual rates are approximately 61 per cent, 122 per cent and 183 per cent.

The offence of failing to preserve records for the required period gives rise to a fixed penalty of £500.

An assessment for a daily penalty is subject to a maximum of 100 times the daily amount.

No penalty can be imposed under this provision, other than for failure to keep records or failure to notify end of liability or entitlement to be registered, unless HMRC have given the trader written warning concerning compliance with the requirement concerned within two years preceding the assessment.

An offence which has given rise to a criminal conviction, or a penalty for civil fraud or serious misdeclaration, cannot also be treated as a breach of regulations.

Summary of breaches and penalties

The following table shows the types of regulatory breach and the penalties which attach to them.

Breach	Penalty
Failure to notify cessation of taxable supplies	Fixed daily rate
Failure to make records	Fixed daily rate
Failure to retain records	£500
Failure to furnish information and documents	Fixed daily rate
Failure to make a VAT return by the due date	Greater of fixed daily rate and tax-geared percentage rate
Failure to pay the tax due on a VAT return by the due date	Greater of fixed daily rate and tax-geared percentage rate
Any other breach of regulations	Fixed daily rate

The amount of tax on which the tax-geared percentages are to be based is the tax shown as due on the return for the period concerned. If no return has been made, it is the amount assessed as due for the period by HMRC.

The levels of penalties can be altered by statutory instrument, to take account of inflation.

A statutory defence is provided whereby no penalty is due if the trader can satisfy HMRC (or a tribunal) that there is a reasonable excuse for the breach.

Legislation: VATA 1994, s. 69 and 76(2)

VAT Reporter: ¶60-580

10-320   Failure to disclose VAT avoidance scheme

There are penalties for not notifying HMRC 'within the prescribed time, and in such form and manner as may be required' by the regulations. The penalties are as follows:

(a)   up to £5,000 for non-designated schemes (hallmarked schemes);
(b)   15 per cent of the 'tax saving' for designated schemes (listed schemes).

There is the usual 'reasonable excuse' defence. These penalties do not apply if the person concerned is convicted of an offence or is assessed for evasion under VATA 1994, s. 60.

Legislation: VATA 1994, Sch. 11A, para. 10

VAT Reporter: ¶60-604

Other material: Notice 700/8, Section 12

Other information: *www.hmrc.gov.uk/avoidance/aag-disclosure.htm#4*

10-350 Transactions in gold – breach of record keeping requirements

A civil penalty may be imposed if a trader fails to comply with the requirements of the scheme for exempt transactions in investment gold. The penalty cannot exceed 17.5 per cent of the value of transactions to which failure relates.

Defences to the penalty include:

(1) the trade satisfies HMRC (or on appeal a tribunal) that he has a reasonable excuse for the failure; or

(2) generally over three years have elapsed from the event giving rise to the penalty.

The penalty can be mitigated by HMRC.

Legislation: VATA 1994, s. 69A and 70(1)

Other material: Notice 701/21, section 9

VAT Reporter: ¶60-550

10-380 Failure to furnish Intrastat declarations

A failure to furnish an Intrastat declaration, or to provide information requested by HMRC in connection with the administration of the Intrastat system, is a criminal offence and can attract a fine up to £2,500 (being level 4 in the standard scale). Thus, HMRC generally issue a caution to a person who is liable to such a penalty.

A defence to such a fine relating to an Intrastat is that the accused took all reasonable precautions and exercised all due diligence to avoid committing the offence.

A trader who knowingly or recklessly makes a false Intrastat return, or falsifies a return, is:

(a) on summary conviction, liable to a fine up to £2,500 and/or three months' imprisonment; and

(b) on indictment, liable to an unlimited fine and/or imprisonment up to two years.

Legislation: CEMA 1979, s. 167; *Statistics of Trade (Customs and Excise) Regulations* 1992 (SI 1992/2790), reg. 6 and 12

Other material: Notice 60, para. 3.4

VAT Reporter: ¶60-155

10-410   Breaches of walking possession agreements

A person who breaches an undertaking given in a walking possession agreement may be liable to a penalty equal to half of the VAT, or amount recoverable as VAT, which the person in default has refused or neglected to pay. There is a defence of 'reasonable excuse'.

Legislation: VATA 1994, s. 68

VAT Reporter: ¶60-560

10-440   Civil tax evasion

Introduction

Civil fraud arises where a person takes steps, or omits to take steps, in order to evade tax and his conduct 'involves dishonesty'.

The penalty for civil fraud is 100 per cent of the tax involved. This may be mitigated by up to 100 per cent, either by HMRC or, on appeal, by a tribunal, in recognition of cooperation given by the trader in the investigation into the true tax position. The standard of proof, in the event of an appeal, is the civil standard (balance of probabilities), but the burden of proof lies with HMRC. See flowchart 11-830.

Mitigation

In considering the amount of penalty due, HMRC will start from the basic amount of 100 per cent of the tax involved and consider mitigation of:

- up to 40 per cent, for an early and truthful explanation of why arrears arose and the true extent of them; and
- up to 40 per cent, for fully embracing and meeting responsibilities under the new procedure by, for example, supplying information promptly, including full written disclosure, attending meetings and answering questions.

In most cases, therefore, the maximum mitigation is 80 per cent of the penalty. HMRC will consider further mitigation in exceptional circumstances, such as where the trader has made a full and unprompted voluntary disclosure.

Although it seems unlikely that HMRC will take criminal proceedings where this procedure has been commenced, and is complied with by the trader, they clearly retain the right to do so in cases where they think fit. They state that they will consider criminal action where the person makes any incorrect disclosures or materially false statements are made.

FA 2007 changes

Many of the situations where this penalty would have been assessed are being covered in the new penalty system (e.g. inaccuracies on documents; late notification). This penalty

Penalties and Tax Avoidance

remains almost as a catch all base line that may be invoked for such matters as evading import VAT.

Legislation: VATA 1994, s. 60 and 70

Other material: Notice 300 June 2009 Statement of Practice

VAT Reporter: ¶59-750

10-470   Investigation and fraud

From 1 September 2005, there is a single Civil Investigation of Fraud procedure for HMRC.

All taxes and penalties for tax fraud are covered by the new procedure except HMRC Duties Civil Evasion Penalties.

One chance

Where HMRC consider there has been some fraud or wrongdoing, the taxpayer (or should that be non-payer?) will be given a single opportunity to make a full disclosure of the wrong doing. This disclosure must cover all irregularities. Following this admission of culpability, it is said by HMRC that the whole investigation and settlement will work more quickly, advantageously and efficiently for all parties concerned.

However, if an incomplete disclosure is made or the taxpayer decides not to admit irregularities, HMRC will conduct their own investigation. In such cases, formal assessments will be issued; payment of unpaid tax and interest will be sought; and penalties imposed are liable to be higher than in cases where the taxpayer disclosed the underdeclarations.

Code of Practice 9

This is the procedure used in cases where fraud is suspected. The 'Code of Practice 9' is in the notice that accompanies the letter informing a person that irregularities are suspected.

The procedure is as follows:

- After an initial explanatory letter, the procedure commences with a meeting, not a taped interview.
- At the meeting, the trader will be asked for yes or no answers to four formal questions concerning their VAT affairs (see below), essentially inviting the trader to admit that there have been underdeclarations and that the trader is aware of these. There are separate questions concerned with other taxes.
- The officer will explain why it is believed that the underdeclaration arises from dishonest conduct but will not give full details of the suspected irregularities.
- If the trader declines to co-operate in the procedure, or states that there are no underdeclarations, HMRC will normally revert to the existing Notice 730 procedure and carry out their own investigation.

- If the trader co-operates with the procedure, the next stage is for the trader (or his representative) to produce a disclosure report, including a full schedule of irregularities.
- HMRC may carry out selective checks on the information provided in the report.
- The intention is that it should then be possible for HMRC and the trader to reach agreement as to the amount of underdeclarations and of interest and penalties due, and to agree a timetable for payment.
- In the absence of agreement, the trader retains the right to appeal to a First-tier Tax Tribunal against the amount of any tax liability or penalty.

The four VAT questions

The questions which will be asked at the initial meeting are:

(a)   Have any transactions been omitted from, or incorrectly recorded in, the books and records of (name of legal entity) with which you are (responsible status)?
(b)   Are the books and records you are required to keep by HMRC for (name of legal entity) with which you are (responsible status) correct and complete to the best of your knowledge and belief?
(c)   Are all the VAT returns of (name of legal entity) with which you are (responsible status) correct and complete to the best of your knowledge and belief?
(d)   Were you aware that any of the VAT returns were incorrect or incomplete at the time when they were submitted?

Disclosure reports

Disclosure reports prepared by advisers will have to cover both direct and indirect taxes.

Content of disclosure report

The disclosure report should contain the following:

- A brief history of the business.
- The nature of the irregularities and how they came about.
- The extent of the irregularities.
- Steps taken to verify amounts with supporting documentation and any assumptions made.
- A detailed schedule of the irregularities for each period involved for each tax.

HMRC will expect the initial meeting to agree a timetable for preparing the disclosure report. Normally, this will be expected to be within six months of the initial meeting.

Payments on account

HMRC will invite the person to make payments on account during the period of investigation. Any payments on account will reduce the interest assessed.

Human Rights issues

HMRC state that safeguards have been built into the procedure to ensure that it is compliant with the Human Rights Act.

Penalties and Tax Avoidance

Other material: Business Brief 18/05, 16 September 2005; Code of Practice 9 [2009] – April 2009; Notice 161 Investigation into traders with suspected serious indirect tax irregularities

10-500   When officers of a company are liable for a penalty

In a case where the trader is a company, it is open to HMRC to issue a notice transferring liability for some or all of certain penalties to an officer of the company. Written notice must be given to the officer.

The penalties for which HMRC have these powers are:

- Inaccuracies on returns – 10-140
- Late registration – 10-100
- Unauthorised issue of an invoice – 10-230
- Civil tax evasion – 10-440

The penalty may only be transferred to an officer when HMRC can show that:

- the officer gained personally from the deliberate wrongdoing, or
- the company is insolvent, or
- there are grounds to think that the company will become insolvent.

In a 2005 civil evasion penalty case, *Wood*, the company had paid low centrally issued assessments instead of completing VAT returns and paying the correct liability. The company subsequently went into liquidation. HMRC said that the tax owed was £117,931.

HMRC assessed two directors each for 50 per cent of the penalty for dishonest evasion of VAT. At appeal, it came to light that one of the directors knew that the centrally issued assessments understated the true liability but authorised their payment. He wilfully closed his eyes to his responsibilities. This director withdrew his appeal. The second director showed that he did not know of the true situation until after the event. He was not dishonest and his appeal succeeded.

See flowchart 11-840.

Legislation: VATA 1994, s. 61; FA 2007, Sch. 24, para. 19; FA 2008, Sch. 41, para. 22

Cases: *Wood* [2005] BVC 4,017

Other material: Revenue and Customs Brief 52/09

VAT Reporter: ¶59-790; ¶60-022

10-530   Criminal tax evasion

Criminal fraud arises, broadly, where a person knowingly takes steps to evade tax, or to enable another person to do so.

The penalties for criminal fraud apply not only to the concealment of liability to account for tax, but also to such matters as the overstatement of claims for the repayment of input tax.

A criminal fraud penalty can only arise as a result of criminal proceedings, in which case the level of penalty depends whether the conviction secured is a summary conviction (i.e. before magistrates) or a conviction on indictment (i.e. before a jury). In either case, the penalty consists of a fine and/or imprisonment.

On summary conviction, the maximum term of imprisonment is six months, and the maximum fine is the greater of the statutory maximum (£5,000) or three times the tax involved.

On conviction on indictment, the maximum term of imprisonment is seven years, while the level of fines is unlimited.

Legislation: VATA 1994, s. 72

VAT Reporter: ¶60-710

10-560   Reasonable excuse defence

Prior to the integrated penalty system introduced by HMRC in FA 2007 the 'reasonable excuse' defence was the main method of appealing against the imposition of a VAT penalty. In the new integrated system it has a more limited scope.

2007 onwards integrated system

Reasonable excuse is only a defence against two penalties.

These are:

* Late registration – 10-100
* Unauthorised issue of an invoice – 10-230.

The reasonable excuse defence is not available where the behaviour that caused the penalty was deliberate.

The term 'reasonable excuse' has not been defined in the legislation. However, the legislation does specify that the following are not to give rise to a reasonable excuse:

(1)   an insufficiency of funds to pay any tax due unless attributable to events outside the person's control; and

(2)   where the taxpayer relied on another person, unless the taxpayer took reasonable care to avoid the relevant act or failure.

If a reasonable excuse is accepted but the excuse ceases, the taxpayer will be treated as continuing to have a reasonable excuse if the act is remedied without unreasonable delay after the excuse ceases.

Penalties and Tax Avoidance

Penalties imposed under the pre-2007 integrated system

The term 'reasonable excuse' has not been defined in the legislation. However, the legislation does specify that the following are not to give rise to a reasonable excuse:

(1)　an insufficiency of funds to pay any tax due; and

(2)　the fact of reliance on another to perform any task, or dilatoriness or inaccuracy on the part of the person relied upon.

There have been hundreds of cases on what can amount to a reasonable excuse, many apparently conflicting with one another. Each case depends on its own facts. A comprehensive review of the cases is beyond the scope of this Service, but a few main points emerging are covered below.

Obviously, ignorance of the law is not an acceptable defence, although in some instances it has been accepted that the rules are so complex that they have themselves caused confusion.

Case law

(1) The reasonable businessman in a similar situation test

This has been accepted in many instances as the test of whether or not there is a reasonable excuse. It was formulated in two cases: *Appropriate Technology* and *Clean Car Co Ltd*.

These involved the serious misdeclaration penalty but may equally be applied in relation to other penalties.

The test to be applied in *Appropriate Technology* was:

> 'Would a reasonable and conscientious businessman who knew all the facts of the case and who was alive to the need to comply with one's responsibilities in regard to the rendering of VAT returns, consider that the taxpayer in acting as it did in the circumstances in which it had found itself, had acted with due care in the preparation of the return?'

In the *Clean Car Co Ltd* case, it was held that in providing a 'reasonable excuse' defence, Parliament must have intended that the question whether a particular trader had a reasonable excuse should be judged by the standards of reasonableness which one would expect to be exhibited by a taxpayer who had a reasonable attitude to his duties as a taxpayer but who, in other respects, shared such attributes if the particular appellant as the tribunal considered relevant to the situation being considered. This attitude to what constitutes reasonableness goes back to *DPP v Camplin*.

It was thus indicated that age, experience, health, particular misfortunes in business or personal problems are all capable of building towards a reasonable excuse but that a total lack of concern about tax matters is not acceptable.

The overwhelming impression is that all factors, no matter how insignificant by themselves, should be joined together to give a whole picture. When preparing a defence, do not leave anything out. Personal factors may be as valid as the business situation.

(2) Lack of money

Lack of money is ruled out by statute as a defence. But *C & E Commrs v Steptoe* eventually succeeded. The criteria to look at is whether or not a reasonably prudent business person would have got into the situation and to consider any underlying reasons for the lack of money. The taxpayer must show reasonable foresight and due diligence.

In *Steptoe*, a main customer did not pay on time. The situation was totally outside the control of the taxpayer and he was not able to foresee it. There have been cases since where it has been decided that if customers habitually pay late, this is foreseeable and the taxpayer has not established a reasonable excuse. 'Everything, as so often, depends on the facts of the case', said Kennedy J in *Steptoe*.

(3) Ignorance of the law

It seems that, while ignorance of basic VAT law will not give rise to an excuse, ignorance of more complex matters can do so. Some regard will be had to the age and background of the trader in determining the level of knowledge which may reasonably be expected. Relevant cases include *Geary*, *Jenkinson* and *Moseley*.

(4) Reliance on another

Although reliance on another cannot of itself give rise to a reasonable excuse, this is not to say that there can never be a reasonable excuse where there is reliance on another. The main test seems to be whether, had the trader himself acted in the same way as the person relied upon, he would have had a reasonable excuse. Also, in cases where the person relied upon was unexpectedly unable to carry out the task concerned, reasonable excuses have often been found provided reasonable steps were taken to make other arrangements. See also *Bowen*.

Legislation: VATA 1994, s. 71(1); FA 2008, Sch. 41, para. 20

Cases: *Appropriate Technology* [1991] BVC 571; *Clean Car Co Ltd* [1991] BVC 568; *DPP v Camplin* [1978] All ER 168; *C & E Commrs v Steptoe* [1991] BVC 3; *Geary* (1987) 3 BVC 546; *Jenkinson* (1987) 3 BVC 729; *Moseley* (1990) 5 BVC 1,308; *Bowen* (1987) 3 BVC 647

VAT Reporter: ¶59-665

10-590   Appeals

Appeal against the imposition of a penalty or the level of mitigation allowed by HMRC may be made to the Tax Tribunal. See 19-000ff.

VAT Reporter: ¶61-420; ¶61-300

Penalties and Tax Avoidance

TAX AVOIDANCE

10-620   Introduction

HM Revenue and Customs are committed to fighting all forms of tax avoidance. The specific measures being taken include action to combat specific schemes in certain areas of VAT, the need to notify HMRC that certain schemes are being used or contemplated and also measures to fight the large scale avoidance of VAT in the EU.

10-650   Specific avoidance measures

Anti-avoidance measures targeted at specific matters or issues are dealt with in the relevant sections. The main measures are as follows:

- group registrations – see 17-350 and 17-400;
- partial exemption – see 6-950 et seq;
- splitting businesses to avoid VAT – see 8-860;
- transfer of a going concern – see 18-120 et seq;
- valuation – see 4-720 et seq;
- change of use of a zero-rated relevant residential or charity building – see 15-280;
- option to tax anti-avoidance measure – see 15-300;
- splitting supplies – see 11-650.

10-680   Introduction to notification of tax avoidance schemes

It is mandatory to notify HMRC that certain tax avoidance schemes are being implemented. The measures apply when relevant schemes are used in periods starting on or after 1 August 2004. This includes instances when the scheme 'started before 1 August 2004'.

As appropriate notification must be in writing within 30 days of the following:

- the due date for submission of the return to which the scheme applies;
- the date of the claim;
- following a direction that a number of taxpayers should be treated as a single business for VAT purposes, the due date of the first return.

Suitable notifications must be posted or emailed to:

VAT Avoidance Disclosure Unit
Anti Avoidance Group (Intelligence)
HMRC
1st Floor
22 Kingsway
London WC2B 6NR

The email address is vat.avoidance.disclosures.bst@hmrc.gsi.gov.uk.

Information about disclosure of VAT avoidance schemes sent to other addresses will not be considered to have been validly made.

The regulations subdivide tax avoidance schemes into listed schemes and hallmarked schemes. Listed schemes are those described as such in the regulations.

Legislation: *VAT (Disclosure of Avoidance Schemes) Regulations* 2004 (SI 2004/1929)

Other material: Notice 700/8; Business Brief 14/05, 27 July 2005

VAT Reporter: ¶55-220

10-710   Notifying listed schemes

Not all businesses must notify HMRC that they are using a listed scheme. It is only businesses with a turnover of more than £600,000 that must do so. The turnover limit is suitably adjusted according to circumstances.

Listed schemes are each given a designated number. When notifying HMRC, it is only necessary to quote the designated number. The notification should be 'prominently headed with: Disclosure of use of listed scheme – Notification under para. 6(2) of Sch. 11A to 1994'.

The listed schemes are as follows.

(1)   First grant of a major interest in a building.

(2)   Payment handling services.

(3)   Value shifting.

(4)   Leaseback agreement.

(5)   Extended approval period.

(6)   Groups: third party supplies.

(7)   Training and education by a non-profit making body.

(8)   Training and education by a non-eligible body.

(9)   Cross-border face value vouchers (from 1 August 2005).

(10) The surrender of relevant lease (from 1 August 2005).

Legislation: *Value Added Tax (Disclosure of Avoidance Schemes) (Designation) Order* 2004 (SI 2004/1933)

Other material: Notice 700/8

VAT Reporter: ¶55-222

10-740   Notifying hallmarked schemes

It is not always necessary to notify HMRC that a hallmarked scheme is being used. It is only businesses with a turnover of more than £10 million that must do so. The turnover limit is suitably adjusted according to circumstances.

A hallmark scheme exists when its main purpose, or one of its main purposes, is to gain a 'tax advantage'. These arrangements normally have particular 'hallmarks'. The current 'hallmarks' are entitled as follows.

(1)   Confidentiality conditions.

(2)   Sharing a tax advantage.

(3)   Contingent fees.

(4)   Prepayments between connected persons.

(5)   Funding by share subscriptions or loans.

(6)   Off-shore loops.

(7)   Property transactions between connected persons.

(8)   Issue of face value vouchers.

For these purposes, a 'tax advantage' includes the following:

(a)   the output tax declared on a return is less than it otherwise would have been;

(b)   a repayment is claimed that:

- would not otherwise have obtained;
- is larger than it would otherwise have been;
- is obtained earlier than it would otherwise have been;

(c)   input tax is recovered before the supplier has to account for output tax, and the period between the two events is longer than it otherwise would have been;

(d)   schemes that are intended to reduce any persons irrecoverable VAT (1 August 2005).

Notification should be 'prominently headed with: Disclosure of use of hallmarked scheme – Notification under paragraph 6(3) of Schedule 11A to the VAT Act 1994'. A notification is only valid when all the following information is provided:

- 'information demonstrating how the scheme works' together with details of 'how the involvement of any party to the scheme contributes to the obtaining of the tax advantage';
- 'a statement as to which hallmark or hallmarks are included in or associated with the scheme'; and
- 'a statement as to which legislation you rely upon for the tax advantage'.

Legislation: VATA 1994, Sch. 11A, para. 6(3)

Other material: Notice 700/8

VAT Reporter: ¶55-222

11-600 Abuse of law

The ECJ have ruled that there could be an abuse of law where intermediate companies or actions are put in place that have no purpose other than to obtain a tax advantage.

- An exempt bank tried to recover otherwise irrecoverable input tax on construction of call centres by using a series of intermediate companies.
- A university tried to recover otherwise irrecoverable input tax on the renovation of two derelict buildings using a lease and lease-back arrangement.
- A private hospital attempted to use a large prepayment to an associated company for the future delivery of drugs, etc. in order to recover otherwise irrecoverable input tax.

The questions

The ECJ was asked to determine whether these sort of transactions could be termed supplies of goods or services and an economic activity for VAT purposes even if the only reason for the transaction was to obtain a tax advantage.

Secondly, it was asked to rule on whether the right of a taxable person to deduct input tax was precluded where the relevant transaction was an abusive practice – an abuse de droit.

The answers

The first answer was straightforward enough. These sort of transactions could be termed economic activities.

The second response was more of a ground-breaking decision. It could be an abuse of right – or law – and the right of the taxable person to deduct input tax could be prevented.

When is it an abuse?

There are two conditions about which the national court must be satisfied in order to decide that such a situation constitutes an abuse of law.

(1) The transactions must result in a tax advantage, the grant of which would be contrary to the purpose of the relevant provisions of the Directive 2006/112.

(2) It must be apparent from a number of objective factors that the essential aim of the transactions is to obtain a tax advantage.

Subsequent action

Transactions involved in such a practice must be redefined so as to re-establish the situation that would have prevailed in the absence of the transactions constituting the abusive practice. This process was followed in *Redcats (Brands) Ltd*.

Sanctions allowed

The tax authorities may demand with retroactive effect repayment of the deductions in relation to any abusive practice less any output tax that has been charged.

Objective criteria

The judgment is an objective, not a subjective approach.

Some Officers of HMRC appear to have the mindset that if they feel that any sort of tax benefit has been gained – no matter how or why – then it is fair game to have a go at the punter, threaten 'Abuse of Law', probably raise some sort of assessment and wait for the cheques to start pouring in.

Further developments – Weald Leasing

Weald Ltd purchased goods that were then leased to Suas Ltd. Suas in turn leased the goods to two companies that were associated with Weald but which were part of a separate Churchill VAT group making mainly exempt supplies of insurance and had a VAT recovery rate of something less than one per cent. Suas made a small profit on the transactions. The rents charged to Suas were 10 per cent or less per year of the costs of the assets. The money to purchase the leased goods was loaned to Weald by companies in the Churchill group. Weald did not pay interest on the loans (it surrendered to the other group companies the corporation tax losses), it reclaimed the input tax and charged Suas VAT on the rents. VAT was charged by Suas on the leases to the insurance companies. The assessments raised by HMRC amounted to some £1.7 million. The Tribunal decided in favour of Weald saying that the arrangements did not constitute an abuse of rights. Evidently, HMRC do not agree! This is an instance of 'watch this space' in order to determine the correct situation.

The ECJ issued its preliminary ruling in December 2010. It found that this did not represent an abusive practice.

New dwellings – granting a major interest before letting

Letting unsold new dwellings prior to making a zero-rated grant of a major interest triggers a VAT adjustment (see 7-470). This can be avoided by making a zero-rated grant to an associated person prior to letting the property. HMRC do not generally regard this as an abuse of law. In their view, it 'does not produce a result contrary to the purpose of the legislation'. However, they consider granting a major interest in order to recover input tax incurred on repairs, maintenance and the like is an abuse of the law.

Lower Mill Estate Ltd ('Lower Mill')

Lower Mill owned land with planning permission for the erection of dwellings that 'shall be occupied for holiday accommodation only'. There was an associated construction company, Conservation Builders Ltd. The same person owned all the shares in both companies. The land was marketed by Lower Mill Estates Ltd, which also ran the on-site sales operation. Conservation Builders Ltd constructed the new homes. The marketing involved proposing to buyers that they should buy the land and construction work separately. The promotional material included 'Frequently asked questions' which explained the rationale for separate contracts as follows:

'Why are the land and construction contracted separately?

Because the land sale is subject to VAT but the construction works on the new dwelling by Conservation Builders Ltd is free of VAT (zero-rated).'

HMRC maintained this was an abuse practice. Lower Mills appealed.

The Upper Tax Tribunal ruled against HMRC. It reasoned that based upon previous case law there are two criteria which must be satisfied before there is abusive practice. The first criteria to consider is whether the arrangements achieve a tax advantage which is contrary to the purposes of the relevant legislation. The second criteria is deciding if the essential aim of the arrangements is to gain a tax advantage.

In *Lower Mills*, the first criteria was not satisfied. The tax advantage was not contrary to the legislation because the same tax advantage could be gained in other ways and referred to as the 'self build' model

The 'self build model' envisaged a person buying a building plot with all its planning restrictions from Lower Mills and contracting with an unconnected building firm to construct. The services of that building firm would be zero rated. If this was not contrary to the VAT legislation, the Upper Tribunal concluded that the Lower Mill scheme by which the same amount of tax was payable could not be contrary to the underlying purposes of the legislation.

Cases: *Halifax Plc, Leeds Permanent Development Services Ltd, Country Wide Property Investments Ltd v C & E Commrs* (Case C-255/02) [2006] BVC 377; *University of Huddersfield Higher Education Corporation v C & E Commrs* (Case C-223/03) [2006] BVC 377; *BUPA Hospitals Ltd, Goldsbourough Developments Ltd v C & E Commrs* (Case C-419/02) [2006] BVC 377; *Redcats (Brands) Ltd* [2006] BVC 2,754; *R & C Commrs v Weald Leasing Ltd* (Case C-103/09) [2011] BVC 118; *Lower Mill Estate Ltd v R & C Commrs* [2011] BVC 1,554

Other material: HM Revenue and Customs Brief 54/08

VAT Reporter: ¶36-975

11-620   Carousel and Missing Trader Frauds

This is the type of VAT fraud that is being reported from many Member States. Belgium and the Netherlands have done a lot of work in identifying the fraud in two high risk areas, computer parts (the Netherlands) and mobile phones (Belgium).

A trader registers in one country in order to obtain goods VAT free, often from a second Member State. The registered trader does not account for tax in the correct way and disappears before the tax authorities carry out any control visits or checks.

At its most extreme, it involves the same goods circulating from State to State sometimes being taken outside the EU, with VAT being stolen on each leg of the journey. This has been named a 'carousel' fraud carried out by disappearing traders.

See also 8-760.

Measures to fight these crimes

The measures are:

- clarification of powers for HMRC to inspect goods;
- power for HMRC to direct additional record keeping;
- changing the person responsible for accounting for and paying VAT on the sale of certain goods; and
- joint and several liability for certain goods.

Clarification of powers for HMRC to inspect goods

This measure clarifies the power that HMRC have to enter premises and inspect goods. It emphasises that HMRC officers have the right to mark goods inspected and to record details of the goods by any means including electronic scanning of barcodes. The identifying marking is on outside packaging and does not, according to advice received by HMRC, affect the value of the goods.

Although the measure is currently aimed at businesses dealing in goods identified as being at risk from the carousel fraud, HMRC say that they would use the same powers in combating other areas involving non-compliance of VAT.

Power for HMRC to direct additional record keeping

This is aimed at the identification of supplies upon which VAT may go unpaid. These supplies include mobile phones and computer chips but the measure will also be used in any other case where HMRC has reasonable grounds to believe that the additional records may help in the identification of goods at risk.

HMRC have been granted powers to insist that traders keep records of such things as identification numbers for goods. Mobile phones, for example, have IMEI numbers.

HMRC will direct that the business must keep such additional records from a future date. A Notice of Direction will be issued to the business.

Penalty regime

This measure is supported by a penalty regime. The penalty is £200 each day where the business fails to comply with the direction, up to a maximum of 30 days. The 30-day period will start running from the date upon which the direction takes effect.

Any business will have the right to appeal to the VAT and Duties Tribunal against the issue of a direction and the imposition of any penalty.

The person responsible for accounting for and paying VAT on certain goods

Businesses buying and selling any of the following must be made aware that from 1 June 2007 VAT should be accounted for using the reverse charge system. The goods affected are:

(a) Mobile telephones. For this purpose, mobile phones include BlackBerrys and pay-as-you-go phones but exclude mobile phones sold with airtime contracts.

(b) Computer chips. These are described as integrated circuit devices such as microprocessors and central processing units in a state prior to integration into end user products.

De minimis

The de minimis limit is £5,000. This applies to the total value of goods subject to the reverse charge supplied together and detailed on a single invoice. Amounts less than this are subject to the normal VAT accounting rules.

Checks

Retailers and wholesalers are expected to carry out relevant checks on customers to establish whether the customer is VAT-registered and is purchasing the goods for a business purpose. Retailers may have difficulty in doing this and in such cases should charge VAT in the normal way. VAT numbers of customers should be obtained and verified where necessary (for example, with new customers). HMRC expect retailers who have checks in place for money laundering or fraud purposes to apply similar checks to customers who exceed the de minimis limits. There will be challenges from HMRC to any attempts to manipulate the de minimis limit.

The system

When such specified goods are purchased by a VAT-registered business, the purchaser will account for VAT on the sale. The supplier will not charge VAT but will specify on the invoice that the reverse charge applies. The right to input tax recovery remains unchanged. Sales to non-business customers are not affected, normal VAT rules apply.

HMRC have issued a statement of practice regarding input tax deduction that is to be to be applied in cases where there is no valid VAT invoice. This tightens up on the procedure for accepting 'other evidence' for goods that may be part of a carousel fraud. See 6-580.

Reverse charge sales list

Any business affected by this measure must maintain reverse charge sales lists detailing the customers to whom they have supplied goods under this scheme and the amount supplied. The business must register for an on-line Government account via the Government Gateway. Persons who already have Government Gateway User IDs may merely add this service to the ones they already use. Further information is available online via HMRC website.

Penalties and Tax Avoidance

Joint and several liability for certain goods

This affects trade in the following goods:

- telephones, telephone parts and accessories; and
- computer equipment, parts, accessories and software.

When a business receives a supply of specified goods or services and knew or had reasonable grounds to suspect that VAT on these goods or services would go unpaid, it may be held liable for the tax due if the supplier defaults. Notice 735 gives full details.

The relevant Order that takes into account that technological developments mean that electronic equipment is becoming more capable of a range of functions. Hence the Order extends the definition of 'telephone' and 'computer' to include any goods that are made or adapted for these uses. In addition, it indicates that certain goods may fall into more than one category. It stipulates that 'satnav' equipment is to be regarded as being within the definition of a computer for the purpose of the Order. This is the first use to be made of the power to make such an Order contained in s. 77A(9) VATA 1994.

Rebuttable presumption

In tandem with this measure, HMRC are altering the 'rebuttable presumption' rule in s. 77A(6). The rule is that HMRC are allowed to presume that a business had reasonable grounds to suspect VAT would go unpaid if specified goods were purchased for less than the market value or less than the price payable for them by a previous supplier. The business needs to be able to prove that the low price payable was unconnected with a failure to pay VAT in order to rebut this presumption. The new sections contained in s. 77A(9A) and (9B) allows the Treasury to extend or otherwise alter the circumstances in which a person may be presumed to have reasonable grounds for suspecting that VAT will be unpaid elsewhere in the supply chain. This measure is included in the *Finance Act* 2007.

Further developments

The High Court sent a reference for a preliminary ruling to the ECJ in the case of *Teleos* in which HMRC had attempted to assess Teleos and Others for tax amounting to several million pounds even though it was recognised that Teleos, etc. were in no way connected with the VAT fraudsters. The ECJ held:

- The term 'dispatched' means that the right to dispose of the goods as owner has been transferred to the purchaser and the supplier establishes that those goods have physically left the territory of the Member State of supply.
- The tax authorities cannot require a trader who acted in good faith and submitted evidence establishing at first sight his right to the exemption of an intra-Community supply of goods subsequently to account for VAT on those goods where the evidence is found to be false but the supplier has no part in the tax evasion provided also that 'the supplier took every reasonable measure in his power' to check the evidence.
- A declaration by the purchaser concerning intra-Community acquisition may constitute additional evidence tending to show that the goods have left the country, but this is not

conclusive proof for the exemption of VAT For further information regarding evidence required to prove that goods have been exported, see 5-570.

In *Blue Sphere Global Ltd*, the High Court emphasised that in these cases the burden of proof is on HMRC to show that the business did, could have or should have known that it was part of a fraud.

Legislation: VATA 1994, s. 77A and 77A(9); *Value Added Tax (Amendment of section 77A of the Value Added Tax Act 1994) Order* 2007 (SI 2007/939)

Cases: *C & E Commrs v Optigen Ltd* [2006] BVC 119; *C & E Commrs v Fulcrum Electronics Ltd* [2006] BVC 119; *C & E Commrs v Bond House Systems Ltd* [2006] BVC 119; *R (on the application of Teleos Plc) v C & E Commrs* (Case C-409/04) [2008] BVC 705; [2005] BVC 253; [2005] BVC 93; *Blue Sphere Global Ltd v R & C Commrs* [2009] EWHC 1150 (Ch); [2009] BVC 580

Other material: Budget Notice 2007 60: Statement of Practice March 2007 VAT Strategy – Input tax deduction without a valid VAT invoice; Notice 735 VAT Reverse Charge for Mobile Phones and Computer Chips; Notice 700/21 (2008) para. 2.5 – Keeping VAT Records

VAT Reporter: ¶1-840

11-640   Anti-forestalling measures

Change of rate 2010–11

Measures to thwart manipulation of the tax point rules to gain an advantage by paying at 17.5 per cent rather than 20 per cent are in *Finance (No. 2) Act* 2010. These measures have effect from 22 June 2010. The rules are the same as when the standard VAT rate was increased from 15 per cent to 17.5 per cent in January 2010.

The anti-avoidance provisions (or forestalling measure as it is termed in the legislation) are targeted at transactions involving persons who are not able to reclaim (fully or partly) input tax.

The forestalling provisions are subdivided into parts. There are provisions dealing with supply of goods or services and alternative provisions covering the grant of a right to goods and services.

Goods and services

A person supplying goods or services is caught by the forestalling provisions when the following conditions apply:

(1)   the recipient of the supply is unable to reclaim any, or only some of the tax, charged;

(2)   the basic tax point or time of supply is on or after 4 January 2011;

(3)   due to a prepayment or issue of an invoice, one or more actual tax points occurs before 4 January 2011; and

(4)   one or more of these conditions applies:

   •   the consideration for the supply is more than £100,000;

461

- the supplier and recipient are connected;
- a prepayment is financed by the supplier or a person connected to the supplier, and
- an invoice is issued before 4 January 2011 with payment not due for six months or more.

See Flowchart 11-880.

Rights to goods and services

In the main, the measures applying to the grant of a right to received goods or services largely mirror those applying to a person supplying good or services. In these circumstances, the conditions which trigger the forestalling provisions are as follows:

(1) the recipient of the supply is unable to reclaim any, or only some, of the tax charged;

(2) the time of supply (basic tax point) for the underlying goods or services is on or after 4 January 2011;

(3) the grant of the right to these goods or services is before 4 January 2011;

(4) the underlying goods or services will be supplied at a discount or free of charge; and

(5) one or more of these conditions applies when:

- the consideration for the supply is more than £100,000;
- the grantor and the person to whom the right is granted are connected; and
- payment made in respect of the grant is financed by the grantor or a person connected to the grantor.

The provisions are suitably amended to entrap a series of grants relating to the same, or substantially the same, goods and services.

The supplementary charge

When the forestalling provisions apply, the person making the supply (not the recipient of the supply) incurs a further tax liability. There is a supplementary charge which nullifies the tax saving.

The supplementary charge is due on 4 January 2011 or, as applicable, when a right to receive goods or services is exercised. If de-registration happens before this, the supplementary charge must be declared on the final return.

Other material: *www.hmrc.gov.uk/budget2010/bn44.htm*; HM Revenue and Customs Brief 52/10

Legislation: *Finance Act* 2009, s. 9(2); *Value Added Tax Regulations* 1995 (SI 1995/2518), reg. 15A

Budget 2012

Alterations to listed building – anti-forestalling measure

Anti-forestalling measures aimed at approved alterations (and the materials used) made to listed building after 1 October 2012 apply from 21 March 2012. The aim is to negate arrangements made to avoid paying 20 per cent VAT on relevant work carried out, including the materials used, on or after 1 October 2012. Such measures normally involve creating tax points by issuing invoices or making payments before the rate change.

The relevant work to which these measures apply are 'approved alterations' which, under extant legislation, are zero rated (see 15-380).

When the anti-forestalling measure is triggered, standard rate VAT is due on relevant work (and materials used) done on or after 1 October 2012. This tax charge incurs on 1 October 2012 and must be accounted for by the person doing the work.

For construction services the charge will apply to the proportion of such services performed on or after 1 October 2012. For goods the charge will apply to the extent that they are incorporated into the building on or after 1 October 2012.

Self-storage – anti-forestalling measure

Anti-forestalling measures aimed at self-storage provided from 1 October 2012 apply from 21 March 2012. The aim is to negate arrangements made to avoid paying 20 per cent VAT on self-storage facilities made available from 1 October 2012. Such measures normally involve creating tax points by issuing invoices or making payments before the rate change

When the anti-forestalling measure is triggered, amounts paid in advance for post 1 October 2012 storage is liable to 20 per cent VAT. This tax charge incurs on 1 October 2012 and must be accounted for by the person supplying the self-storage.

The charge will apply to the proportion of such services performed on or after 1 October 2012. For grants of the right to receive supplies of self storage-facilities the charge will apply to the extent that the services are carried out on or after 1 October 2012.

Legislation *Finance Act* 2012 Sch. 27; *Value Added Tax Regulations* 1995 (SI 1995/2518), reg. 15B

11-650   Splitting supplies to avoid VAT

Measures to prevent businesses splitting a single standard rated supply of services in order to zero rate one or more component parts apply from the Royal Assent of the 2011 Finance Act. These changes are a direct result of the 'Telewest' scheme. By separating the supply of its in-house magazine from its package of television services, Telewest was able to zero rate the magazine. This practice was disliked by HMRC.

This measure is triggered when:

(a)   there is a supply of zero-rated printed matter which is connected to a 'separate' standard or reduced rate service;

(b)   the printed matter and relevant services are provided by different suppliers;

(c)   there would be single reduced or standard rated supply if both printed matter and connected services were provided together by the same person.

For the relevant flowchart see 11-890.

Legislation: VATA 1994, Sch. 8, Grp. 3, Note (2)

Cases: *Telewest Communications plc v C & E Commrs* [2005] BVC 156

VAT Reporter: ¶57-820

Penalties and Tax Avoidance

FLOWCHARTS

11-820   Late registration penalty – for a registration date of 31 March 2010 or earlier

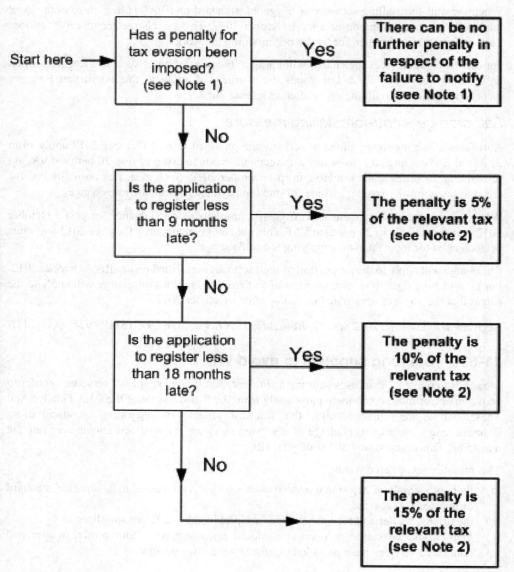

Start here → Has a penalty for tax evasion been imposed? (see Note 1)

Yes → There can be no further penalty in respect of the failure to notify (see Note 1)

No ↓

Is the application to register less than 9 months late?

Yes → The penalty is 5% of the relevant tax (see Note 2)

No ↓

Is the application to register less than 18 months late?

Yes → The penalty is 10% of the relevant tax (see Note 2)

No ↓

The penalty is 15% of the relevant tax (see Note 2)

Notes

(1) Tax evasion penalties

Failure to register may be 'tax evasion'. When it is dealt with as such and the relevant penalty imposed (see 10-600), there cannot also be a late registration penalty.

Legislation: VATA 1994, s. 67(9)

(2) Relevant tax

The late registration penalty is a percentage of the 'relevant tax'. The 'relevant tax' is the net amount of VAT due for the period from date when the person concerned should have registered to the date when HMRC are notified, or otherwise become fully aware, of that person's obligation to register.

(3) Reducing the penalty

The late registration penalty is waived if the person has a reasonable excuse (see 10-100) for not registering at the correct time. It may also be mitigated.

(4) More information

For further information on the late registration penalty, refer to 10-100.

Penalties and Tax Avoidance

11-830   Civil Penalty for tax evasion

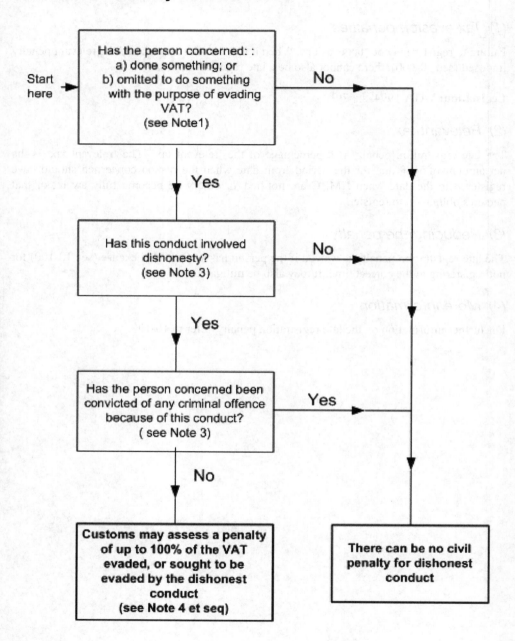

Start here →

Has the person concerned: :
a) done something; or
b) omitted to do something
with the purpose of evading
VAT?
(see Note1)

No

Yes

Has this conduct involved
dishonesty?
(see Note 3)

No

Yes

Has the person concerned been
convicted of any criminal offence
because of this conduct?
(see Note 3)

Yes

No

**Customs may assess a penalty
of up to 100% of the VAT
evaded, or sought to be
evaded by the dishonest
conduct
(see Note 4 et seq)**

**There can be no civil
penalty for dishonest
conduct**

Notes

(1) Evading VAT

'Evading VAT' encompasses all the following situations:

- overstated input tax;
- understated output tax;
- when a return has not been made, paying an assessment which is less than the full amount due for period concerned;
- obtaining an incorrect payment from HMRC;
- improper DIY Housebuilder;
- bad debt relief;
- refunds in relation to 'new means of transport' supplied to other Member States;
- refunds involving acquisitions from other EU States;
- repayments obtained by businesses not established in the UK.

(2) Amount evaded

The amount of VAT evaded or sought to be evaded is either:

(a) the sum of any falsely understated output tax and any falsely over-claimed input tax; or
(b) the amounts of falsely claimed refunds or repayments.

(3) 'Dishonesty'

A person is considered to be 'dishonest' when 'according to the ordinary standards of reasonable and honest people that what he was doing would be regarded as dishonest'. 'Dishonesty' is to be given the same meaning as for the *Theft Act* 1968.

(4) Interaction with criminal prosecutions

If HMRC choose to proceed with a criminal prosecution, they cannot also impose this penalty.

Legislation: VATA 1994, s. 60(6)

(5) Defence does not include 'reasonable excuse'

The 'reasonable excuse' defence is not applicable to this penalty.

(6) Mitigation

This penalty may be mitigated. HMRC do not normally grant a reduction of more than 75 per cent.

(7) Finance Act 2007 changes

Many of the situations to which this penalty would apply are now within the scope of the new penalty system. This penalty remains almost as a catch all.

Penalties and Tax Avoidance

(8) Further information

For further information, see 10-440.

Cases: *Gandhi Tandoori Restaurant* (1989) 4 BVC 535

Other material: VAT Notice 730; Notice 300 June 2009 Statement of Practice

[This page is intentionally blank]

11-840 Apportioning a civil evasion penalty to an 'officer' of the company

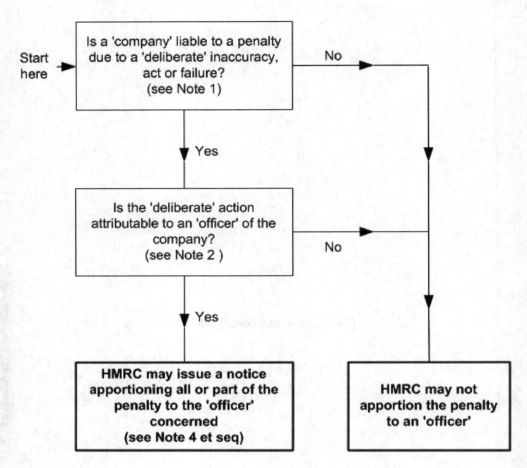

Notes

(1) Relevant penalties

The penalties which may be apportioned to an 'officer' are as follows:

- inaccuracies on returns and other claims (see 10-140)
- late notification of an obligation to register (see 10-100)
- unauthorised issue of a VAT invoice (see 10-230)
- civil evasion penalty (see 10-440)

(2) Civil evasion penalty (VATA 1994, Section 60)

The criteria applicable to when this penalty may be transferred to an officer is not dealt with here.

(3) 'Officer' of a company

An 'officer' of a 'body corporate' is a director (including shadow director) or secretary. In other cases, a director, a secretary, a manager or any other person purporting to manage the company's affairs is an 'officer'.

(4) 'Written notice' requirement

HMRC must 'specify by written notice to the officer' the proportion of the penalty which they seek to recover from the person concerned.

(5) Legislation

FA 2007, Sch 24, para. 19 & FA 2008, Sch. 41, para. 22.

Penalties and Tax Avoidance

11-860   Abuse of Law: four questions to be considered

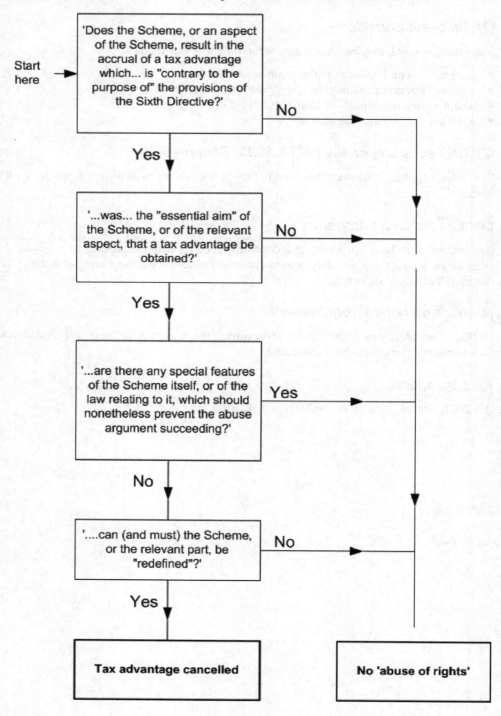

Notes

(1) Terminology

The EU principle permitting HMRC, on occasions, to nullify VAT planning is commonly referred to as 'abus de droit', 'abuse of rights', abuse of law or an abusive practice.

(2) Source of questions

'The abuse issue can usefully be considered by answering four questions ...' (*WHA Ltd v R & C Commrs* [2007] EWCA Civ 728; [2007] BVC 695). The four questions used above are taken from this judgment.

(3) Overlapping questions

'While one can analyse the issue in this case by breaking it down into these four questions, it is right to acknowledge that the answers may overlap to some extent, and that it may be a matter of opinion as to which question a particular argument or point goes ...'

(4) Bona fide commercial transactions

'... the European Court drew a distinction between transactions entered into "in the context of normal commercial operations" and those entered into "solely for the purpose of wrongfully obtaining advantages provided for by Community law". The latter type of transaction is capable of constituting an abuse ...' (*WHA Ltd v R & C Commrs* [2007] EWCA Civ 728; [2007] BVC 695).

(5) Further information

For further information, see 'Abuse of law' 11-600.

Penalties and Tax Avoidance

11-880 Change of rate – anti-avoidance forestalling measures

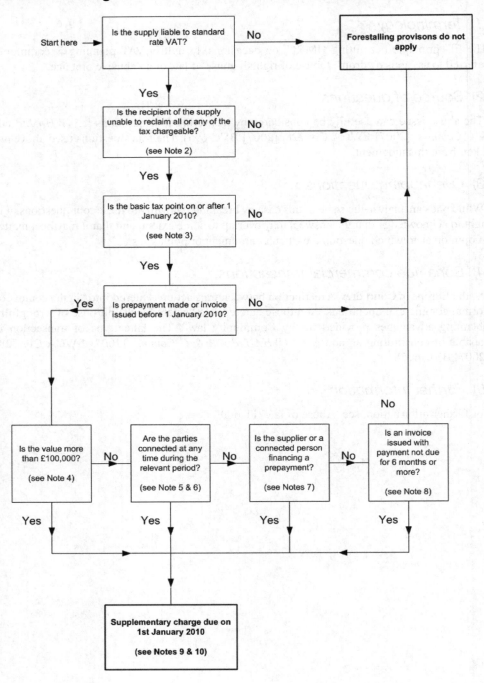

Notes

(1) Grant of a right to goods and services

Granting a right to goods and services is subject to conditions not encompassed by this flowchart.

(2) Affected persons

Persons who are able to reclaim in full tax chargeable on the supply concerned are not affected by the forestalling legislation. Affected persons are those who are not able to reclaim 'all of the VAT on the supply', e.g. businesses making exempt supplies.

(3) Basic tax point for supplies 'listed' in forestalling legislation

The forestalling legislation determines the basic tax point for the following:

(a)   a supply of services (i.e. continuous supplies);
(b)   a supply arising from the grant of a major interest in land;
(c)   a supply of water other than:

- distilled water, deionised water or water of similar purity; or
- bottled water.

(d)   a supply of:

- coal gas, water gas, producer gases or similar gases; or
- petroleum gases, or other gaseous hydrocarbons, in a gaseous state.

(e)   a supply of power, heat, refrigeration or ventilation; and
(f)   a supply of goods together with services in the course of the construction, alteration, demolition, repair or maintenance of a building or civil engineering work.

(4) Supplies of £100,000 or more

The value is the aggregate of any invoices or prepayments made which establish one or more actual tax points occurring before 4 January 2011. This includes related invoices or payments which are part of the same tax avoidance 'scheme'.

(5) Period during which 'connected persons' status applies

The relevant period is from the date of an actual tax point and 4 January 2011.

(6) 'Connected persons'

'Connected persons' are as defined in s. 839 of *Income and Corporation Taxes Act* 1988.

Penalties and Tax Avoidance

(7) Supplier finances prepayment(s)

A supplier may finance a prepayment by providing the recipient of the supply with any of the following:

- a loan;
- providing security for a loan;
- providing consideration for the issue, or acquisition by any person, of shares or securities for raising funds; or
- any transfer of assets or value to generate funds for these purposes.

'Connected persons' condition applies from when payment received or invoice issued to 3 January 2011.

(8) Letting, hiring or rental of assets

An exception applies to the letting, hiring or renting of assets when normal commercial practice is to invoice, or pay, in advance for a period of up to one year. These transactions are not subject to a supplementary charge.

(9) Supplementary charge

The supplementary charge is 2.5 per cent and is accounted for by the supplier of the affected goods or services. The value for this charge is the amounts subject to 17.5 per cent VAT.

(10) Further information

The relevant legislation is *Finance (No. 2) Act* 2010, Sch. 2. For other information see Notice 700/8.

[This page is intentionally blank]

Penalties and Tax Avoidance

11-890 Splitting supplies – anti-avoidance measure

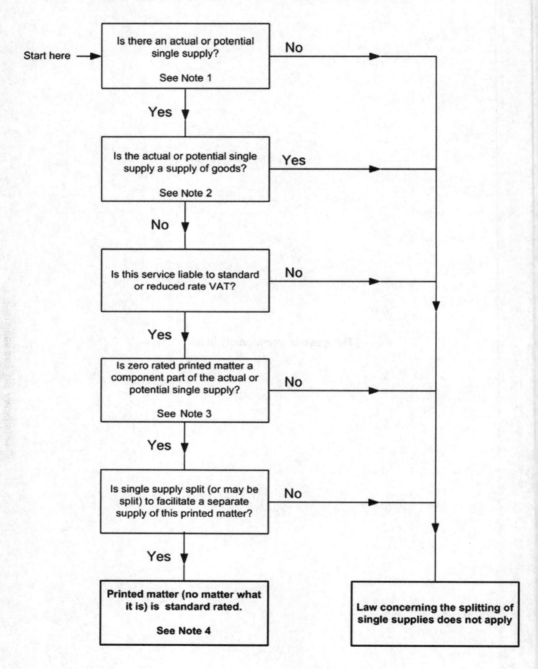

Notes

(1) Actual or potential single supply

This anti-avoidance measure entraps connected supplies of goods and services.

Supplies of goods and services may be connected when supplied separately by different persons. They are connected when, if they were to be supplied together by the same business, they would be categorised as a single supply for VAT purposes. This is the actual or potential single supply for these purposes.

For more information with identifying single supplies see 3-820.

(2) Definition of services

A service is 'anything which is not a supply of goods but is done for a consideration' (VATA 1994, s. 5(2)(b)).

(3) Zero rated printed matter

See 12-900 and Notice 701/10 Zero Rating of Books etc for information about zero rated printed matter.

(4) Affected supplies

This anti-avoidance measure applies to affected supplies made on or after 19 July 2011.

Penalties and Tax Avoidance

Zero-rate, Reduced Rate, Exemption

ZERO-RATING

12-000 Meaning of zero-rating

The general rule for determining the liability to VAT for a supply is that the standard rate of VAT applies unless the supply is explicitly included in a category which qualifies for relief. Probably the most important relief is zero-rating.

If a supply falls into a zero-rated category, then it is treated as a taxable supply, but the VAT due is calculated at a rate of zero per cent. Thus, the supplier does not have to account for any VAT on the supply. However, since it is a taxable supply, the supplier can register for VAT (indeed must, if taxable turnover exceeds the registration limits) and so can recover input tax incurred on supplies obtained for the business.

The effect of this is that zero-rated supplies reach the consumer free of VAT, except to the extent that the supplier's costs include items on which the deduction of input tax is specifically blocked (e.g. purchase of a motor car for business use). This is in contrast with exempt supplies, where there is always a hidden VAT cost, being the irrecoverable VAT element of underlying costs.

VAT Reporter: ¶20-000

12-100 Basic provisions

Zero-rating applies under UK law by VATA 1994, s. 30. This section sets out the consequences of zero-rating applying to a supply, provides certain general zero-ratings in respect of exports of goods, and specifies that supplies listed in VATA 1994, Sch. 8 are also to be zero-rated.

There is special provision that a supply of services of producing goods by applying a process to goods owned by someone else is zero-rated if a supply of the finished goods would be zero-rated.

VATA 1994, Sch. 8 contains the bulk of the law on zero-rating. It consists of a series of 'Groups', each of which contains a number of 'items' specifying supplies which are to be zero-rated. The Groups are structured so as to contain items which are linked in some general way. For instance, the Group headed 'Books, etc.' provides zero-rating for supplies of books and also for supplies of newspapers. Essentially, the zero-ratings for supplies of published material are contained in this Group.

Legislation: VATA 1994, s. 30 and Sch. 8

VAT Reporter: ¶20-100

12-200 Interpretation of zero-rating Groups

Although each zero-rating Group has a heading, these headings are of no legal force. The headings are there merely to assist in identifying which Groups may provide zero-rating for a particular supply. In order to determine whether a zero-rating does in fact exist, it is necessary to study the items within the Groups, to see whether the supply fits precisely into one or other of the descriptions.

Furthermore, there are notes to each Group which amplify or modify the meanings of the zero-ratings contained in the items, and these must be studied as well to see whether zero-rating is available.

Since the UK zero-rating provisions do not generally derive from the EC legislation, but are derogations from it, they must be interpreted in accordance with UK principles. However, the provisions for zero-rating exports of goods, and various other supplies connected with international trade, do arise from the EC legislation, so that recourse can be had to this in interpreting the legislation.

Legislation: VATA 1994, s. 96(9) and (10)

12-300 Outline of Groups

This section provides an outline of the zero-rating provisions. The general zero-rating for exports of goods is covered in the International Trade section (see 5-040ff.). There is a series of sections covering each of the zero-rating Groups. In each case, reference is made to the notices and leaflets published by HM Revenue and Customs which give their views on the application of the zero-rating concerned.

The zero-rating Groups, covered later in this section, are as follows:

- Grp. 1 – food;
- Grp. 2 – sewerage services and water;
- Grp. 3 – books, etc.;
- Grp. 4 – talking books for the blind and handicapped and wireless sets for the blind;
- Grp. 5 – construction of dwellings, etc.;
- Grp. 6 – protected buildings;
- Grp. 7 – international services;
- Grp. 8 – transport;
- Grp. 9 – caravans and houseboats;
- Grp. 10 – gold;
- Grp. 11 – bank notes;

- Grp. 12 – drugs, medicines, aids for the handicapped, etc.;
- Grp. 13 – imports, exports, etc.;
- Grp. 14 – tax free shops;
- Grp. 15 – charities, etc.; and
- Grp. 16 – clothing and footwear.

Legislation: VATA 1994, Sch. 8

Other material: Notice 701/39 ('VAT Liability Law')

VAT Reporter: ¶20-100

ZERO-RATING GROUPS

12-800   Group 1 – food

Zero-rating is available, in principle, for supplies falling within four general items. However, there are a series of excepted items which cannot be zero-rated even though they fall within the general items (unless they are also included in a further list of items which override certain of the exceptions). Supplies in the course of catering can never be zero-rated.

Changes introduced with effect from 1 October 2012 standard rated or ended uncertainty about some aspects of the following:

- sports drinks – see excepted items below;
- hot take-away food – see hot food below;
- eating areas for customers of fast food outlets and/or other persons supplying take -away food – see premises (take-away food) below.

General items

The general items for which zero-rating is available are:

(1)   food of a kind used for human consumption (but not if supplied in the course of catering);

(2)   animal feeding stuffs;

(3)   seeds or other means of propagation of plants used as food for consumption by humans or by animals; and

(4)   live animals of a kind generally used as, or yielding or producing, food for human consumption.

Excepted items and items overriding exceptions

Those items which cannot be zero-rated even though they fall within the general items are listed below. Exceptions to the exceptions (which fall back into zero-rating) are shown in italics.

Zero-rate, Reduced Rate

483

The items which cannot be zero-rated are:

(1)   ice cream, ice lollies, frozen yogurt, water ices and similar frozen products, and prepared mixes and powders for making such products. *Frozen yogurt can still be zero-rated if it is unsuitable for immediate consumption when frozen*;

(2)   confectionery (which, in principle, includes chocolates, sweets and biscuits; drained, glacé or crystallised fruits; and any item of sweetened prepared food normally eaten with the fingers) but not including cakes and not including biscuits except biscuits wholly or partly covered with chocolate or with some product similar in taste and appearance. *Drained cherries and candied peels remain zero-rated*;

(3)   beverages chargeable with a duty of excise specifically charged on spirits, beer, wine, made-wine or preparations thereof;

(4)   other beverages, including fruit juices and bottled waters, and syrups, concentrates, essences, powders, crystals or other products for the preparation of beverages. *Tea, maté, herbal teas and similar products, and preparations and extracts thereof, remain zero-rated, as do cocoa, coffee and chicory and other roasted coffee substitutes, and preparations and extracts thereof, and milk and preparations and extracts of meat, yeast, egg or milk*;

(5)   'sports drinks' intended to enhance performance, accelerate recovery after exercise or build bulk. This includes concentrates, syrups, essences powders or crystals from which 'sports drinks' may be prepared;

(6)   any of the following when packaged for human consumption without further preparation:

   (a)   potato crisps, potato sticks, and potato puffs;
   (b)   similar products made from potato, or from potato flour or potato starch;
   (c)   savoury products obtained by the swelling of cereals or cereal products; and
   (d)   salted or roasted nuts other than nuts in shell;

(7)   pet foods, if canned, packaged or prepared; packaged foods (other than pet foods) for birds other than poultry or game; and biscuits and meal for cats and dogs (whether or not packaged, etc. and whether or not the animals concerned are pets); and

(8)   goods which are canned, bottled, packaged or prepared for use in home brewing or wine making.

Other material: Notice 701/14; Notice 701/15

(1) Catering

As indicated above, supplies in the course of catering can never fall within the zero-rating, even though they would otherwise fall within one or more of the general items.

Supplies in the course of catering specifically include supplies for consumption on the premises where the supply is made, and also supplies of hot food wherever it is to be consumed.

They also include supplies which are, in the general sense of the term, made in the course of catering. The tribunals have generally taken this to mean that the food is to be consumed in conjunction with some other event or function.

Snack bars, catering services and similar

A CEJ case in 2011 cast doubt upon the liability of hot take away food supplied by snack bars, etc. The ruling concerned whether take away food is the supply of goods or services. They decided it was the supply of goods. The CEJ concluded that: 'the supply of food or meals freshly prepared for immediate consumption from snack stalls or mobile snack bars or in cinema foyers is a supply of goods ... the elements of supply of services preceding and accompanying the supply of the food are not predominant'.

By comparison they concluded that normally a party catering service is a supply of services as this often offers delivery in 'closed warmed receptacles or reheated by him on the spot' and 'may include elements to enable consumption, such as the supply of crockery, cutlery or even furniture'. They ruled that:

> 'In the light of those considerations, it must be considered that, except in cases in which the caterer does no more than deliver standard meals without any additional service elements, or in which other special circumstances show that the supply of the food represents the predominant element of the transaction, the activities of a party catering service are supplies of services ...'

HMRC maintain this does not alter how UK VAT is applied to take away food. Their view is that 'the ECJ judgement has no implications for the UK treatment of supplies of hot food and businesses should continue to treat their supplies in accordance with the published guidance'.

Cases: *C & E Commrs v Cope* (1981) 1 BVC 430; *Finanzamt Burgdorf v Bog* (Case C-497/09) Judgment delivered 10 March 2011

Other material: Revenue and Customs Brief 19/11; Notice 709/1, section 1

VAT Reporter: ¶20-300

(2) Hot food

Pre-1 October 2012

'Hot food' means food which has been heated to a temperature above the ambient temperature to enable it to be eaten while hot, and is still above ambient temperature when provided to the customer. Zero-rating remains for food that happens to be hot when sold, if the purpose of heating it was not to enable its consumption while hot. In applying this test, it is necessary to look at the intentions of the supplier, not those of the customer.

The *Pimblett* case was concerned with the liability status of sales of pies, which were generally hot at the time of sale. The tribunal found as a fact that the vendor's purpose in heating the pies was to demonstrate that they were fresh, rather than to enable their consumption while hot. However, it then decided that many customers bought the hot pies (and some insisted on

Zero-rate, Reduced Rate

having pies which remained hot rather than others which had cooled) in order to consume them while hot. Consequently, it decided that some of the supplies made by the company were made in the course of catering. The High Court overturned this decision, holding that the motives of the customers were of no relevance when the motives of the supplier had already been determined. The Court of Appeal upheld the High Court's decision. This decision was followed in the case of *Lutron Ltd*.

The factors which are taken into account by HMRC in determining if hot food may be zero-rated include the following:

- Type of outlet – if advertised as a take-away food outlet, supplies of hot food will be standard-rated.
- What happens to the food between the time it is cooked or heated and the time it is handed to the customer – if efforts are made to keep it hot, this may be an indicator for standard rating, whereas if it is left to cool naturally for a period of time this may be an indicator for zero-rating.
- Type of packaging used – if food is packaged to retain heat, this would be an indicator for standard rating. However, the reverse does not necessarily apply, since food intended for immediate consumption will often be sold in packaging that is not heat retentive.
- Availability of condiments, napkins and utensils – this would be an indicator for standard rating.
- The way in which the food is advertised and promoted, including in-store signage and any wording shown on packaging.
- Food hygiene regulations – HMRC accept that in some cases food may be kept hot partly for the purpose of complying with food hygiene regulations. However, the requirement to comply with these regulations will often not be an aim in itself for the supplier, but merely a consequence of supplying food for consumption whilst hot or warm. If this is the case, then the supplies will be standard-rated.
- Palatability – if an item is generally accepted to be unpalatable when cold, this would be an indicator for standard rating. However, the reverse does not necessarily apply – the fact that an item remains palatable when cold does not preclude the possibility that it has been heated for the purpose of enabling it to be consumed hot.

More information is included in HMRC Manuals but it must be remembered that these are indicators of HMRC's interpretation, not pure law.

Each case must be looked at on its own facts. It is the purpose of the supplier when making the supply that matters. In some cases the supplier has proven to the satisfaction of a Tribunal that their purpose when supplying hot take-away food was not to serve hot food as such but to ensure that the food had its final cooking – the purchase by the customer of the hot food was merely a secondary result of this final cooking.

From 1 October 2012

The following are standard-rated:

- food provided hot for the purpose of allowing it to be eaten hot (the current situation);
- cooked, heated or reheated to order;

- kept hot – where the natural process of cooling is delayed. This will include products kept in heated cabinets, hot plates, heat lamps, etc. Pasties etc will be zero-rated when they are hot but cooling naturally in racks but standard-rated when kept in heated cabinets;
- provided in heat-retaining packages or other packaging specifically designed for hot food – for example foil lined packaging;
- advertised, marketed or promoted in any way that indicates that it is supplied hot.

Cases: *John Pimblett & Sons Ltd v C & E Commrs* (1987) 3 BVC 161; *Lutron Ltd* (1989) 4 BVC 685

Other material: Notice 709/1, section 4; HMRC Manual VFOOD 4260; HMRC Manual VFOOD 4620; HMRC Manual VFOOD 4280

Legislation: VATA 1994, Sch. 8, Grp. 1, Notes (3B), (3C) and (3D)

VAT Reporter: ¶20-300

(3) Premises (takeaway food)

Clearly, if food is served in a restaurant, it is intended to be consumed on the premises where the supply takes place. This puts beyond doubt the VAT treatment of most supplies of meals (as opposed to the raw material for making meals).

Difficulties can arise where cold food is supplied for more or less immediate consumption, but not for consumption in an area which is owned by the supplier. It is then necessary to consider what is meant by the term 'premises'. The areas to be considered are the unit from which the retailer makes supplies together with other areas set aside for the consumption of food.

The legislation was altered with effect from 1 October 2012 to ensure that eating areas in places such as food courts and motorway services which have several outlets were brought within the meaning of 'premises'.

Unit from which the retailer makes supplies

HMRC changed their policy on the interpretation of 'premises' after the Court of Appeal ruled that they were wrong. The appeal, by Compass Contract Services UK Ltd concerned the supply of cold food to people at BBC Television Centre.

HMRC said that because the food was supplied in an area to which people have restricted access, all supplies of food and drink, whether hot or cold, were standard-rated. The interpretation of food consumed 'on the premises' and being standard-rated as supplies of catering, encompassed the whole site.

Compass sold food from six outlets in BBC Television Centre. There were no facilities for eating the food at the outlets. Customers simply bought the goods and took them away. Compass successfully persuaded the Court of Appeal that the supply of cold take-away food was not a supply of catering and should be zero-rated.

Zero-rate, Reduced Rate

The Court of Appeal ruled that a retailer occupies only the unit from which the sales are made. However, any facilities provided to allow the customer to eat the food will extend the area considered to be 'premises' and mean that such food will be standard-rated. Hence a sandwich bar with some nearby tables will have to standard-rate food consumed at those tables.

HMRC now accept that similar supplies of cold take away food, even in an area to which there is restricted access, may be zero-rated. Restricted access areas include such places as football stadia, theme parks, factories and the like.

This brings HMRC's interpretation of 'on the premises' to be the same whether access to the general area is restricted (people have specific permission to be in the area such as an office block or theme park) or unrestricted (anyone can visit the area, such as railway stations, shopping arcades and similar).

Areas set aside for the consumption of food – from 1 October 2012

Where a retailer makes provision for customers to eat the food (e.g. tables on the pavement outside the premises) the area set aside is considered to be part of the seller's premises. Therefore the food concerned is consumed on the supplier's premises and liable to standard-rate VAT. However, there has been much litigation about this.

From 1 October 2012 the statutory definition of premises is amended to include 'any area set aside for the consumption of food by that supplier's customers, whether or not the area may also be used for customer of other suppliers'. The purpose of the change is to end doubt about the status for these purposes of food courts in shopping areas and similar shared eating areas such as motorway service stations, airports, railway stations, etc. Henceforth they are by statutory definition areas 'set aside for the consumption of food'.

Cases: *Bristol City Football Supporters Club* (1975) 1 BVC 1,035; *James* (1977) 1 BVC 1,056; *Armstrong* (1984) 2 BVC 205,046; *Crownlion (Seafood) Ltd* (1985) 2 BVC 205,332; *Sims (t/a Supersonic Snacks)* (1986) 2 BVC 208,114; *Mowbray* (1986) 2 BVC 208,122; *Compass Contract Services (UK) Ltd v R & C Commrs* [2006] BVC 569

Other material: Notice 709/1, section 3

Legislation: VATA 1994, Sch. 8, Grp. 1, Note (3A)

VAT Reporter: ¶20-300, ¶20-325

(4) Delivered food

Where the supplier of food undertakes to deliver it to the premises of the customer, it could be argued that the supply was made on the premises of the customer for consumption there, and so was done in the course of catering. In one case, the supplier arranged for a taxicab to deliver the food to the houses of customers. However, the cab driver was paid for the delivery of the food by the customer, and not by the appellant. In this case, it was held that the supply was not made on the premises of the customer, and so the supply was not regarded as made in the course of catering.

The position where, say, sandwiches are delivered to office workers (the supplier providing the transportation) is a difficult question.

If the supplier's representative, on arriving at the office block, stands in the street and shouts that the sandwiches are there, so that someone comes out and collects them, then the supply is presumably made outside of the premises where the sandwiches are intended to be consumed.

On the other hand, if the supplier's representative goes into the office block to hand over the sandwiches (particularly, if they are taken round to the individuals who ordered specific items), then it might be argued that the premises where the supply took place were the office block, and so the supply was made in the course of catering. However, in one case of this sort a tribunal has held that the supplies were not made in the course of catering.

Although this could be a difficult area, it seems that HMRC generally take a pragmatic approach, and avoid distortion of competition with sandwich bars which do not provide delivery services, by regarding such supplies as not made in the course of catering even if the supplier delivers the sandwiches.

This is just as well, since a similar problem could easily arise in respect of grocers who provide delivery services.

Cases: *Levy (t/a Becket's Diner)* (1985) 2 BVC 205; *Cooper* (1987) 3 BVC 1,364

VAT Reporter: 20-325

Other material: Notice 709/1

VAT Reporter: ¶20-300

12-850   Group 2 – sewerage services and water

(1) Sewerage services

Zero-rating applies to supplies of services of:

(1)   the reception, disposal or treatment of foul water or sewage in bulk; and

(2)   the emptying of cesspools, septic tanks or similar receptacles used otherwise than in the course of carrying on in the course of business a relevant industrial activity. A relevant industrial activity is one described in Divisions 1–5 of the Standard Industrial Classification.

(2) Water

Zero-rating also applies to the supply, for non-industrial purposes, of water (other than distilled water, deionised water, etc.). However, supplies of water in beverages excluded from the 'Food' zero-rating are not zero-rated. Supplies of heated water are excluded from the zero-rating.

The zero-rating does not apply to a supply for use in a 'relevant industrial activity', being an activity in Divisions 1–5 of the Standard Industrial Classification.

Other material: Notice 701/16

VAT Reporter: ¶20-450

12-900 Group 3 – books, etc.

This zero-rating covers supplies of books, booklets, brochures, pamphlets, leaflets, newspapers and periodicals, printed music (and other forms of music reproduced on paper), maps, and ancillary objects (such as covers and cases) supplied with the zero-rated items and not charged for separately. Plans and drawings for industrial purposes, etc. are expressly excluded from the zero-rating.

Essentially, the zero-rating sets out to relieve from tax most printed matter, while retaining the tax charge for items such as commercial stationery, advertising posters, etc. It has been held that, to rank for zero-rating as a leaflet, the item concerned must be limp, and generally must be printed on unlaminated paper. This prevents zero-rating for many menus, price lists, etc.

HMRC argue that items of stationery are outside of the zero-rating, even if they take the form of books, etc. This view is supported by *C & E Commrs v Colour Offset Ltd* [1995] BVC 31, where it was held that the supply of a blank diary was not within the zero-rating for supplies of books. The term 'book' was to be taken as meaning something to be read or looked at.

By concession, supplies of loose-leaf books in instalments are treated as zero-rated even if the individual items supplied do not themselves amount to books.

Cases: *Panini Publishing Ltd* (1989) 4 BVC 704; *C & E Commrs v Colour Offset Ltd* [1995] BVC 31

Other material: Notice 701/10; Revenue and Customs Brief 04/12

VAT Reporter: ¶20-600

12-950 Group 4 – talking books for the blind and handicapped and wireless sets for the blind

This zero-rating covers supplies (including hire) of certain goods to the Royal National Institute for the Blind, the National Listening Library and similar charities. It also covers supplies (including hire) to any charity of certain equipment which is to be lent, free of charge, to blind persons.

The equipment covered where supplies are to RNIB, etc. are machines for the recording and reproduction of tapes for use by the blind or severely handicapped. Such equipment needs to be specially adapted for use for the blind and handicapped (i.e. unsuitable for other use) except in the case of equipment for making the recordings, where relief is available provided that the only actual use is for the blind and handicapped. Zero-rating is also available for a supply of the repair or maintenance of such equipment.

In order to be regarded as a charity, a body does not necessarily have to be registered as such with the Charity Commissioners and, according to HMRC, the supply of sound recording equipment for the production of voluntary bodies producing talking newspapers, etc. for the blind is zero-rated.

In order to benefit from the zero-rating, the charity should provide the suppliers with a certificate specifying the use to be made of the equipment. Examples of such certificates may be found in Notice 701/6 Supplement – charity funded equipment for medical, veterinary uses.

Supplies to charities of wireless receiving equipment, or of cassette (but not reel to reel) tape recorders are zero-rated provided that the equipment is for free loan to the blind.

Other material: Notice 701/1 – Charities; Notice 701/6 Supplement – charity funded equipment for medical, veterinary uses

VAT Reporter: ¶50-320

13-050   Group 5 – construction of dwellings, etc.

Zero-rating is provided for:

(1)   supplies in the course of constructing of some new buildings;

(2)   civil engineering work necessary for the development of a permanent park for residential caravans;

(3)   when carried out for a housing association, converting a non-residential building into dwellings or a building to be used for a relevant residential purpose; and

(4)   the sale of the freehold or long lease (more than 21 years or, in Scotland, 20 years or more) of a qualifying building by the person constructing it.

For further details, see 15-000ff.

Legislation: VATA 1994, Sch. 8

Other material: Notice 708

VAT Reporter: ¶21-350

Zero-rate, Reduced Rate

13-100   Group 6 – protected buildings

Zero-rating is available for supplies of certain protected buildings, see 15-160. Some alteration work is also zero-rated until 1 October 2012, see 15-380.

Legislation: VATA 1994, Sch. 8, Grp. 6

Other material: Notice 708

VAT Reporter: ¶21-400

13-350   Group 7 – international services

(1) Work on goods for export

The zero-rating is available for a supply which consists of work carried out on goods provided that:

(1)   the goods have been obtained or acquired within the EC, or imported into the EC, for the purpose of having the work carried out and then being exported from the EC; and

(2)   the goods are in fact exported either:

  (a)   by or on behalf of the supplier of the services; or

  (b)   if the customer belongs outside the EC, by or on behalf of the customer.

Legislation: VATA 1994, Sch. 8, Grp. 7, item 1

VAT Reporter: ¶65-520

(2) Making arrangements for certain international supplies

Zero-rating is available for the making of arrangements for:

(1)   an export of goods from the EC;

(2)   a supply of services of carrying out work on goods which is itself zero-rated under item 1 above; or

(3)   a supply of services which is deemed to take place outside the EC.

Zero-rating is not available in respect of insurance or financial services.

Legislation: VATA 1994, Sch. 8, Grp. 7, item 2; VATA 1994, Sch. 9, Grp. 2 and 5

13-400   Group 8 – transport

The zero-ratings fall into five main categories:

(1)   supplies of ships and of aircraft;

(2)   supplies of lifeboats;

(3)   supplies of public transport services;

(4)   supplies of freight transport and related supplies; and

(5)   certain supplies by tour operators outside the EC.

Legislation: VATA 1994, Sch. 8

(1) Supplies of ships and aircraft

The zero-rating applies to ships and aircraft above a certain size (see below) and not designed or adapted for use for recreation or pleasure. The supplies which are zero-rated are:

(1)   the supply of the ship or aircraft;

(2)   the repair or maintenance of the ship or aircraft;

(3)   the letting on hire of the ship or aircraft;

(4)   the chartering of the ship or aircraft, unless the services provided under the charter consist wholly of one or more of the following, wholly performed in the UK:

    (a)   transport of passengers;
    (b)   accommodation;
    (c)   entertainment; or
    (d)   education; and

(5)   parts and equipment of a kind ordinarily installed or incorporated in the propulsion, navigation or communication systems, or the general structure, of a qualifying ship or aircraft.

The ships and aircraft to which this zero-rating applies are ships of a gross tonnage of 15 tons or more, and aircraft of a weight of 8,000 kilograms or more, provided that they are neither designed nor adapted for use for recreation or pleasure.

HMRC maintain that use or intended use does not affect the qualifying status. It is the nature of the original design and any subsequent alterations that provide the key to determining the VAT liability of a ship or boat.

The definition of 'aircraft' which may be zero-rated was changed from 1 January 2011. It is no longer based on weight but instead on the status of the customer. Supplies of aircraft will be zero-rated only when used by airlines operating for reward primarily on international routes.

Legislation: VATA 1994, Sch. 8, Grp. 8, items 1 and 2

Other material: Notice 744C; *www.hmrc.gov.uk/budget2010/bn39.htm*

VAT Reporter: ¶22-310

(2) Lifeboats, etc.

Zero-rating is also available for supplies of lifeboats, and related supplies, to a charity providing rescue or assistance at sea. The supplies zero-rated are the supply, repair or maintenance of:

(1)   a lifeboat;

(2)   carriage equipment designed solely for the launching and recovery of lifeboats;

(3)   tractors for the sole use of the launching and recovery of lifeboats; or

(4)   winches and hauling equipment for the sole use of the recovery of lifeboats.

There are additional zero-ratings for supplies connected with the construction, repair, etc. of slipways for lifeboats, and with spares, etc. for lifeboats and related equipment.

In each case, it is a condition for zero-rating that the supply be made to an appropriate charity.

Legislation: VATA 1994, Sch. 8, Grp. 8, item 3

Other material Notice 701/1, para. 6.1.7

VAT Reporter: ¶22-325

(3) Public transport supplies

Zero-rating is provided for supplies of public transport of passengers within the UK and outside it. Zero-rating is available within the UK for the transport of passengers:

(1)   in any vehicle, ship or aircraft designed or adapted to carry 10 or more passengers – the Upper Tax Tribunal decided that when a vehicle had been adapted to carry nine people instead of the original 10 for which it had been designed, the zero-rating was lost;

(2)   by the Post Office; or

(3)   on any scheduled flight.

Zero-rating is also available for a supply of the transport of passengers from a place within the UK to a place outside it, or vice versa, to the extent that the supply takes place within the UK. Zero-rating in this instance is not dependent on either the nature of the vehicle used or on the identity of the supplier.

Cruises, etc.

The treatment of various cruises and waterborne functions such as business entertainment, wedding receptions, etc. has been problematical, and has given rise to litigation.

If the various elements of the package are supplied for a single consideration, all elements being integral to the main supply, and without some tariff whereby the charges are varied depending on the taking up or non-taking up of the different elements, HMRC see a single supply. If the essential nature of the supply is passenger transport, then the whole supply is zero-rated. If the essential supply is the provision of a function, etc. and the transport element is minor and incidental to this, then the whole supply is standard-rated. Where the different elements are separately negotiable and priced there is normally a number of separate supplies, liable to VAT according to their nature.

For HMRC guidance on this, see Notice 744A Passenger Transport.

Excluded supplies

The following supplies are specifically excluded from the public transport zero-rating:

(1) transport in any vehicle to, from or within a place of entertainment or cultural, historical, etc. interest by a person who supplies a right of admission or use of facilities there, or a person connected with him;

(2) transport in a motor vehicle between a car park and an airport passenger terminal by the person who supplies parking facilities or a connected person; and

(3) transport in an aircraft where the flight is held out as providing entertainment or amusement, or the experience of flying (either generally or in a particular aircraft).

Whether persons are connected is determined by ICTA 1988, s. 839.

Legislation: VATA 1994, Sch. 8, Grp. 8, Note (4)

Other material: Notice 744A

Cases: *C & E Commrs v Peninsular and Oriental Steam Navigation Co Ltd (No. 2)* [1996] BVC 206; *Virgin Atlantic Airways Ltd* [1996] BVC 2,644; *Davies (t/a Special Occasions/2XL Limos) v R & C Commrs* [2012] UKUT 130 (TCC); [2012] BVC 1,699

VAT Reporter: ¶22-225

(4) Freight transport and related supplies

Various zero-ratings are provided in connection with freight transport to and from the EC and with ship and aircraft handling, etc.

Ship or aircraft handling

The handling of ships or aircraft in a port, a customs and excise airport, or outside the UK is zero-rated.

This zero-rating only applies if the ship or aircraft is one whose supply would be zero-rated (i.e. it meets the size requirement and is not adapted for pleasure). However, there is an alternative zero-rating for handling of non-qualifying craft, provided that the customer belongs outside the UK and receives the supply for the purposes of his business.

Zero-rate, Reduced Rate

495

Handling or storage of goods

The handling or storing goods at a port, a customs and excise airport, or outside the UK is zero-rated.

There is further zero-rating for similar supplies relating to goods imported into the EC, or to be exported from the EC, at the place of import or export or in connection with their transport from or to that place, and for the supply of transporting them from or to the place of import or export.

Pilotage, salvage and stowage

Supplies of pilotage, salvage and towage are zero-rated. There is no restriction on the type of vessel or the place of performance for this zero-rating to apply.

Surveying and classification

Supplies of or in connection with surveying ships or aircraft, or classifying them for the purposes of a register, are zero-rated if:

(1)   a supply of the ship or aircraft would be zero-rated; or

(2)   the supply is to a person outside the UK who receives the supply for the purposes of his business.

Making arrangements for zero-rated supplies and supplies of space

The supply of making arrangements for any of the above supplies is zero-rated, as is the supply of making arrangements for the supply of space in a ship or aircraft. However, the latter zero-rating only applies if the ship or aircraft is such that the supply of it would be zero-rated or the customer belongs outside the UK and receives the supply in a business capacity.

Air navigation services

Air navigation services has the same meaning as in the *Civil Aviation Act* 1982. It includes the provision of information and directions furnished, issued or provided with the navigation or movement of aircraft.

Legislation: VATA 1994, Sch. 8, Grp. 8, items 5–12

Other material: Notice 744C; Notice 744B, Section 3; Revenue and Customs Brief 13/10

VAT Reporter: ¶22-425

(5) Supplies by tour operators

The supply by a tour operator of a designated travel service is zero-rated to the extent that the service is enjoyed outside the EC (16-890).

VAT Reporter: ¶54-450

13-450   Group 9 – caravans and houseboats

VATA 1994 provides zero-rating, broadly, for supplies of caravans and houseboats likely to be used as private residences, putting these on the same basis for VAT as private houses.

The zero-rating applies to supplies of:

(1)   caravans exceeding the size permitted for towing on roads by a motor vehicle of unladen weight below 2,030 kilograms (raised to 3,500 kilograms from 1 October 2012). These are caravans greater than:

    (a)   7 metres in length; or
    (b)   2.55 metres in width;

in addition from 6 April 2013, caravans with these characteristics may not be zero-rated unless they were or are manufactured to a specific British Standard. This is standard BS3632:2005. Some second-hand caravans may have been manufactured to an earlier British Standard – BS3632. These caravans may be zero- rated if occupied before 6 April 2013.

From 6 April 2013, other caravans of this type are liable to 5 per cent VAT – see 13-995;

(2)   a houseboat designed or adapted for use solely as a place of permanent habitation and not having means of self-propulsion, or readily adaptable for self-propulsion; and

(3)   an undivided share in, or possession (without ownership) of, such caravans and houseboats.

'Dutch barges' and similar vessels

Dutch barges and similar vessels designed and supplied for use as the permanent residence of the customer benefit from the zero-rating. Vessels less than 15 gross tonnes can never be zero-rated and therefore this provision does not apply to the majority of narrow boats.

Certain supplies of services and goods to the owners of such vessels may also be zero-rated. These supplies include repairs and maintenance of the vessel (not domestic fittings); modification of the vessel provided that it remains a qualifying ship after modification; parts installed for the propulsion, communications, navigation or structure of the ship (not including domestic fittings).

Removable contents

The zero-rating does not extend to the supply of removable contents of caravans and houseboats, unless they would qualify for zero-rating if incorporated in a house (see 13-050(5)).

Accommodation exclusion

There is also a specific exclusion from zero-rating for the supply of accommodation in a caravan or houseboat, which is presumably intended to ensure that the supply of holiday accommodation in this way remains standard-rated. It is difficult to see how this exclusion

Zero-rate, Reduced Rate

can be expected to work in law, particularly regarding the supply of possession without ownership (usually letting) of the goods concerned. In each case, this will inevitably involve the possibility of there being a supply of accommodation. On the words of the law itself, therefore (as opposed to the intentions of those drafting it), it seems likely either that all hire of such goods is zero-rated, or that all such hire is standard-rated.

Legislation: VATA 1994, Sch. 8, Grp. 9

Cases: *Talacre Beach Caravan Sales Ltd v R & C Commrs* (Case C-251/05) [2007] BVC 366; *R & C Commrs v Stone* [2008] BVC 635

Other material: Notice 701/20; Revenue and Customs Brief 38/09 8 July 2009 *'Dutch barges' and similar vessels*; Revenue and Customs Brief 20/10 VAT: *Zero-rating – Changes to zero-rating on Caravans*

VAT Reporter: ¶22-775

13-500   Group 10 – gold

Group 10 zero-rates supplies of gold held in the UK between Central Banks and members of the London Gold Market.

Legislation: VATA 1994, Sch. 8, Grp. 10

Other material: Notice 701/21

VAT Reporter: ¶22-875

13-550   Group 11 – bank notes

Group 11 is of interest mainly to the Bank of England and the Scottish banks, and zero-rates the issue of bank notes by banks.

Legislation: VATA 1994, Sch. 8, Grp. 11

VAT Reporter: ¶22-975

13-600   Group 12 – drugs, medicines, aids for the handicapped, etc.

The reliefs in Group 12

The zero-ratings provided by Group 12 are multifarious, tightly defined, and highly specialised.

The group zero rates a number of supplies of goods and services for use by people who are ill or are handicapped. The supply must be made to the individual concerned for their personal use.

Medicines prescribed by doctors, dentists and other professionals who are permitted to prescribe drugs and dispensed by chemists are zero-rated. The zero-rating of prescriptions issued by 'other professionals' came into effect on 2 December 2009. Changes in Scotland in 2011 made it necessary for dispensing doctors in Scotland to register for VAT.

In the case of handicapped persons, the scope is widened slightly as some supplies may be for their domestic use or to a charity which makes it available to the handicapped person. It should be noted that, to the extent that zero-rating is given for supplies of goods designed or adapted for use by handicapped persons, the tribunals have tended to take a narrow view and deny zero-rating where items have been of particular use to handicapped persons but also of use to the population generally (see, for instance, *Portland College*).

The supplies which can qualify for zero-rating are tightly defined, but include items such as specialised equipment, modifications to buildings, etc. Qualifying goods supplied directly by doctors are zero-rated in the same way as those supplied by pharmacists.

Details are set out in Notice 701/7.

The meaning of 'handicapped'

Handicapped is defined as 'chronically sick or disabled'. This is further refined by HMRC as being a person:

- with a physical or mental impairment that has long term adverse effect upon the ability to carry out everyday activities;
- with a chronic sickness such as diabetes;
- who is terminally ill.

It is not considered to include a person who is temporarily incapacitated or disabled.

Legislation: VATA 1994, Sch. 8, Grp. 12

Cases: *Portland College* [1993] BVC 827

Other material: Notice 701/7; VAT Information Sheet 05/11; Revenue and Customs Brief 41/11

VAT Reporter: ¶50-340

13-650   Group 13 – imports, exports, etc.

Group 13 provides certain peripheral zero-ratings in relation to international trade.

Imported goods not yet entered

A supply of goods in the UK is zero-rated if the goods have been imported from outside the EC but have not yet been entered, and they are supplied under an agreement which requires the purchaser to make the entry.

Zero-rate, Reduced Rate

Supplies for defence projects and visiting forces

Supplies of goods or services relating to defence projects under international collaboration agreements, made to or by overseas bodies, authorities or traders are zero-rated.

Jigs and tools, etc. for manufacture of goods for export from EC

The supply to an overseas authority, body or trader of jigs, patterns, templates, etc. used in the UK solely for the manufacture of goods for export to a place outside the EC are zero-rated.

Legislation: VATA 1994, Sch. 8, Grp. 13

VAT Reporter: ¶63-520

13-700   Group 14 – tax-free shops

The provisions relating to tax-free shops (or duty free) were abolished from 1 July 1999.

VAT Reporter: ¶23-430

13-750   Group 15 – charities, etc.

Group 15 zero-rates a number of supplies to or by charities and related bodies. However, it should be noted that it does not provide any general zero-rating for matters relating to charities. In the main, charities are subject to exactly the same VAT rules as other entities.

What is a 'charity?'

According to HMRC:

> 'There is no distinction for VAT purposes between those charities that are registered with one of the charity regulators and those that are not. However, charities not registered with a regulator who want to claim VAT relief may need to demonstrate to Customs that they have "charitable status" through recognition of that charitable status by the Inland Revenue.'

Supplies by charities, etc.

There is a zero-rating for supplies by charities of goods which have been donated to them for sale, provided that the supply results from the goods being made available to the general public, and does not result from some pre-agreed arrangement.

The zero-rating applies to the hire of goods as well as the sale of them. The goods can be offered to two or more 'specified persons', being people who are handicapped or in receipt of certain means-tested benefits, rather than to the public at large. The zero-rating is available to a 'profits to charity' person, being someone who has given a written undertaking to donate profits from the supplies concerned to charity, or whose profits from such supplies are otherwise payable to charity. Item 1A.

The export of goods by a charity is also zero-rated. If the export does not involve a supply in the ordinary sense, there is deemed to be a zero-rated supply. This might help with the recovery of input tax by charities in some circumstances.

Legislation: VATA 1994, s. 30(5); VATA 1994, Sch. 8, Grp. 15, items 1 and 3

VAT Reporter: ¶50-000

Other material: *R & C Commrs Guidance Manual* V1–9 s. 7 and 8; Notice 701/1

Supplies to charities

Donation of goods

The donation of goods to a charity for sale, hire or export (or to a taxable person for sale, the profits of sale being covenanted to a charity) is zero-rated. Once more, this may create a deemed supply where there might not otherwise be a supply in the ordinary sense.

Advertising services

The conditions for zero-rating advertising services to charities are as follows:

(1) zero-rating applies to all charity advertising, not just advertisements for a qualifying purpose;

(2) zero-rating is available for advertisements (or the supply of the right to advertise) in all media;

(3) zero-rating is available for supplies of the design or production of advertisements intended to be promulgated via any medium of public communication;

(4) however:

   (a) zero-rating is not available where any of the persons reached by the advertisement are selected by or on behalf of the charity. This excludes direct mailing and telesales from the zero-rating;

   (b) supplies connected with the charity's own website are specifically excluded. However, zero-rating would apply to a supply of advertising on someone else's website;

   (c) supplies to a charity used directly by the charity to produce its own advertisement are specifically excluded from zero-rating. This prevents a charity from claiming zero-rating on its own overheads used in producing advertisements.

Fund-raising

Certain paper and other products are zero-rated when supplied to a charity due to an Extra Statutory concession (see Notice 48 para. 3.3). The relevant products are as follows:

(a) Lapel stickers or other lapel attachments given as a token or acknowledgement of a donation. The items must have no intrinsic value and be of low cost to the charity.

(b)   Collecting receptacles meeting all the following conditions:

- manufactured specifically for collecting donated money;
- used solely for collecting money for charity;
- clearly marked for 'collecting for a named charity';
- secured by lock or tamper evident seal.

(c)   Bucket lids intended to provide a secure lid for buckets used solely for collecting donations for charity.

(d)   Pre-printed letters appealing for donations.

(e)   Envelopes for forwarding donations or sending out letters appealing for donations as long as the envelopes concerned are over-printed with details of the relevant appeal.

(f)   Pre-printed collecting envelopes normally delivered and collected by hand to private homes to request donations.

(g)   Stewardship envelopes for planned giving so long as they are pre-printed with the name of the place of worship or charity.

This relief does not cover 'general stationery supplied to charities'.

Supplies of medicinal products are zero-rated if made to a charity providing care, medical or surgical treatment, or medical research, if the medicines are to be used for these purposes. There is a similar zero-rating for a supply to a charity of a substance directly used for synthesis or testing in the course of medical or veterinary research.

Legislation: VATA 1994, Sch. 8, Grp. 15, items 2, 9 and 10

Other material: Notice 701/58; Notice 701/1; HM Revenue and Customs Brief 25/10

VAT Reporter: ¶50-570; ¶50-555; ¶50-585

Supplies to eligible bodies or for donation to eligible bodies

The supply of certain goods for donation to an eligible body (such as a Health Authority, etc.) is zero-rated provided that the purchase is made with funds provided from a charity or from voluntary contributions, as is a supply to such a body which is using funds from such sources to make the purchase. Also, a supply to an eligible body which is a charitable institution providing care or medical or surgical treatment for handicapped persons is zero-rated regardless of the source of the funds. The goods concerned are mainly medical goods and vehicles adapted for the carriage of handicapped persons. The supply of goods for these purposes includes hire, and zero-rating is also available, under similar conditions, for the repair of eligible goods owned by a relevant body and associated supplies of goods.

The zero-rating of supplies for donation under these headings is not available if the donee is not a charity and has contributed to the funds.

Legislation: VATA 1994, Sch. 8, Grp. 15, items 4, 5, 6 and 7

Other material: Notice 701/1

VAT Reporter: ¶50-440

13-800   Group 16 – clothing and footwear

Group 16 zero-rates supplies of children's clothing, protective boots and helmets for industrial use, and motor cycle helmets.

Legislation: VATA 1994, Sch. 8, Grp. 16

Other material: Notice 714 (children's clothing); Notice 701/23 (protective clothing)

VAT Reporter: ¶24-075

REDUCED RATE

13-900   Overview

The reduced rate of VAT, currently five per cent, applies to the following groups of supplies.

Group 1 – Domestic fuel or power.
Group 2 – Energy saving materials: installation.
Group 3 – Grant funded installation of heating equipment, security goods or connection of gas supply.
Group 4 – Women's sanitary products.
Group 5 – Children's car seats.
Group 6 – Residential conversions, etc.
Group 7 – Residential renovations and alterations.
Group 8 – Contraceptive products.
Group 9 – Welfare advice or information.
Group 10 – Installation of mobility aids for the elderly.
Group 11 – Smoking cessation products.
Group 12 – Caravans – from 6 April 2013.

Legislation: VATA 1994, Sch. 7A

VAT Reporter: ¶32-000

13-910   Group 1 – Domestic Fuel or power

The following are fuel and power for this purpose:

- coal, coke and other solid fuel held out for sale solely for that purpose;
- coal gas, water gas, producer gases or similar gases;
- petroleum gases, or other gaseous hydrocarbons whether in a gaseous or liquid state;
- fuel oil, gas oil or kerosene; and
- electricity heat or air conditioning.

Zero-rate, Reduced Rate

This fuel liable to the reduced rate applies when it is supplied for 'domestic use' or non-business use by a charity.

'Domestic use' encompasses the following:

(1) A dwelling.

(2) Communal residential accommodation including:

    (a) children's homes;

    (b) homes providing personal care for those in need because of old age, disability, past or present dependence on alcohol or drugs, or past or present mental disorder;

    (c) hospices;

    (d) residential accommodation for students or school pupils;

    (e) residential barracks;

    (f) residential accommodation for religious orders; and

    (g) institutions which are the sole or main residence of at least 90 per cent of residents.

(3) Self-catering holiday accommodation advertised or held out as such.

(4) Caravans.

(5) Houseboats designed or adapted as a place to live and not being capable of self-propulsion or capable of being readily adapted for self propulsion.

'Domestic use' excludes:

- use at a hospital, a prison or similar institution; and
- an hotel, or inn or similar establishment.

'Non-business use by a charity' means a building used in either or both of the following ways:

(a) otherwise than in the course or furtherance of a business;

(b) as a village hall or similar in providing social or recreational facilities for a local community.

Small quantities of fuel

Certain small quantities of fuel are always regarded as being for 'domestic use'.

Apportionment

If 60 per cent or more of a given delivery is for qualifying use, then the whole delivery may be treated as being for a qualifying use. If less than 60 per cent is for a qualifying use, then the supply must be apportioned.

Protection for the supplier

In cases where there is any doubt about the entitlement to the reduced rate, the supplier must obtain a certificate from the customer confirming the entitlement.

Legislation: VATA 1994, Sch. 7A, Grp. 1

Other material: Notice 701/19 Fuel and Power

VAT Reporter: ¶32-250

13-920   Group 2 – Energy-saving materials: installation

The service of installing certain energy-saving materials or equipment in residential accommodation or buildings used solely for relevant charitable purposes, is liable to the reduced rate of tax. The relevant materials are also liable to the reduced rate of tax but only when supplied by the person installing them.

The buildings affected are those listed at 13-910 but excluding self-catering holiday accommodation. For this section, 'caravans' are limited to those which are used as a place of permanent habitation.

The relevant 'energy-saving materials' are as follows.

(1)   Insulation for walls, floors, ceilings, roofs or lofts or for water tanks, pipes or other plumbing fittings.

(2)   Draught stripping for windows and doors.

(3)   Central heating system controls (including thermostatic radiator valves).

(4)   Hot water system controls.

(5)   Solar panels.

(6)   Wind turbines.

(7)   Water turbines.

(8)   Ground source heat pumps (from 1 June 2004).

(9)   Air source heat pumps (from 7 April 2005).

(10) Micro-combined heat and power units (from 7 April 2005).

(11) Boilers fuelled solely by wood, straw or similar vegetable matter (from 1 January 2006).

Legislation: VATA 1994, Sch. 7A, Grp. 2

Other material: Notice 708/6 Energy-saving materials

VAT Reporter: ¶32-005

13-930   Group 3 – Grant funded installation of heating equipment, security goods or connection of gas supply

Subject to certain conditions, the reduced rate applies to the installation or work in connection with the following:

Zero-rate, Reduced Rate

- 'heating appliances';
- mains gas supply;
- central heating systems;
- 'renewable source heating system'; and
- 'security goods'.

The 'heating appliances' to which this relief applies are as follows:

- gas room heaters with thermostatic controls;
- electric storage heaters;
- closed solid fuel fire cassettes;
- gas-fired boilers;
- oil-fired boilers; and
- radiators.

A 'renewable source heating system' means a space or water heating system which uses energy from:

(a)   renewable sources, including solar, wind and hydroelectric power; or

(b)   near-renewable resources, including ground and air heat.

'Security goods' are defined as follows:

- locks and bolts for windows;
- locks, bolts and security chains for doors;
- spy holes; and
- smoke alarms.

Conditions

The goods and services referred to above are not liable to the reduced rate unless supplied to a 'qualifying person'. A 'qualifying person' is an individual aged 60 or more. It may also be someone in receipt of one of the following benefits.

(1)   Council tax benefit under Pt. VII of the *Contributions and Benefits Act*.

(2)   Disability living allowance under Pt. III of the *Contributions and Benefits Act* or Pt. III of the *Northern Ireland Act*.

(3)   Any element of child tax credit other than the family element, housing benefit or income support under Pt. VII of the *Contributions and Benefits Act* or Pt. VII of the *Northern Ireland Act*.

(4)   An income-based Jobseeker's Allowance within the meaning of s. 1(4) of the *Jobseekers Act 1995* or art. 3(4) of the *Jobseekers (Northern Ireland) Order 1995*.

(5)   Disablement pension under Pt. V of the *Contributions and Benefits Act*, or Pt. V of the *Northern Ireland Act*, that is payable at the increased rate provided for under s. 104 (constant attendance allowance) of the Act concerned.

(6)   War disablement pension under the *Naval, Military and Air Forces Etc. (Disablement and Death) Service Pensions Order 1983* that is payable at the increase.

Further, the work must be done to the home or main residence of the 'qualifying person'.

Consideration liable to reduced rate

Not all the consideration for the supply may be liable to the reduced rate. The reduced rate only applies to the consideration 'funded by a grant made under a relevant scheme'. Additional consideration is liable to the standard rate of tax.

Leasing arrangements for central heating systems

Leasing arrangements utilised to help fund the installation of a central heating system comprise of two supplies. There is the standard-rated supply to the leasing company and the second supply by the leasing company to the 'qualifying person'. Subject to the other conditions applying, the supply by the leasing company to the 'qualifying person' is liable to the reduced rate.

Legislation: VATA 1994, Sch. 7A, Grp. 3

Other material: Notice 708/6 Energy-saving materials

VAT Reporter: ¶32-030

13-940   Group 4 – Women's sanitary products

Women's sanitary products are defined as follows.

(1)   Products that are designed, and marketed, as being solely for use for absorbing, or otherwise collecting lochia or menstrual flow.

(2)   Panty liners, other than panty liners that are designed as being primarily for use as incontinence products.

(3)   Sanitary belts.

The reduced rate does not apply to protective briefs or any other form of clothing.

Legislation: VATA 1994, Sch. 7A, Grp. 4

Other material: Notice 701/18 Women's sanitary protection products

VAT Reporter: ¶32-230

13-950   Group 5 – Children's car seats

The reduced rate applies to supplies of children's car seats. A child is a person aged under 14.

A 'children's car seat' is defined as follows:

• a safety seat;

- the combination of a safety seat and a related wheeled framework;
- a booster seat; or
- a booster cushion.

A seat is a 'safety seat' when it complies with the following conditions:

- designed to be sat in by a child in a road vehicle;
- designed so that, when in use in a road vehicle, it can be restrained:
  - by a seat belt fitted in the vehicle; or
  - by belts, or anchorages, that form part of the seat being attached to the vehicle; or
  - in either of those ways; and

- incorporating an integral harness, or integral impact shield, for restraining a child seated in it.

A wheeled framework is 'related' to a safety seat if the framework and the seat are each designed so that:

- when the seat is not in use in a road vehicle, it can be attached to the framework; and
- when the seat is so attached, the combination of the seat and the framework can be used as a child's pushchair.

'Booster seat' means a seat designed:

- to be sat in by a child in a road vehicle; and
- so that, when in use in a road vehicle, it and a child seated in it can be restrained by a seat belt fitted in the vehicle.

'Booster cushion' means a cushion designed:

- to be sat on by a child in a road vehicle; and
- so that a child seated on it can be restrained by a seat belt fitted in the vehicle.

Legislation: VATA 1994, Sch. 7A, Grp. 5

Other material: Notice 701/23 Protective equipment

VAT Reporter: ¶32-240

13-960   Group 6 – Residential conversions, etc.

The reduced rate of VAT applies to certain residential conversions. For details, see 15-400.

Legislation: VATA 1994, Sch. 7A, Grp. 6

Other material: Notice 708 Buildings and construction

VAT Reporter: ¶32-400

13-970   Group 7 – Residential renovations and alterations

The reduced rate applies to supplies of building services (and related goods) in the course of the alteration (including extension), or renovation, of qualifying building that have been unoccupied for two years or more. See 15-400. Qualifying buildings are as follows:

(a)   a single household dwelling;
(b)   a multiple occupancy dwelling; and
(c)   a building, or part of a building, which, when last lived in, was used for a relevant residential purpose.

A dwelling can also qualify if:

• there has been a period of at least two years when it has not been lived in;
• a person, whose occupation of the building ended the period of not being lived in, acquired it before starting to live there, and acquired it at a time when it had not been lived in for at least two years;
• no works of renovation or alteration were carried out in the two years ending with the acquisition;
• the supply is made to a person whose occupation brought the period of non-occupation to an end and who also acquired the building as described above; and
• the works are carried out within one year after the acquisition of the building.

Constructing, renovating or converting a building into a garage as part of the renovation of a property also qualifies for the reduced rate.

There are many detailed conditions for this relief which must be met.

Prior to 1 January 2008, the period when the building had to be unoccupied for this relief was three years.

Legislation: VATA 1994, Sch. 7A, Grp. 7

Other material: Notice 708 Buildings and construction

VAT Reporter: ¶32-400

13-975   Group 8 – Contraceptives

Contraceptive products, other than relevant exempt supplies, are subject to the reduced rate of VAT. Relevant exempt supplies are exempt supplies of goods in any hospital, etc. in connection with medical or surgical treatment.

Legislation: VATA 1994, Sch. 7A, Grp. 8

VAT Reporter: ¶32-500

13-980   Group 9 – Welfare advice

Certain welfare advice or information provided by a charity or a state regulated private welfare institution or agency is liable to the reduced rate of VAT. 'State Regulated' has the same meaning as in Grp. 7 (health and welfare) of Sch. 9 (see Note (8) of that Group).

The welfare advice or information must directly relate to:

- the physical or mental welfare of elderly, sick, distressed or disabled persons; or
- the care or protection of children and young persons.

Not included in the reduced rate are supplies that would be exempt as education if they were made by an eligible body, such as: supplies of goods unless such supplies are wholly or almost wholly for the purpose of conveying the advice or information; or supplies of advice or information provided solely for the benefit of a particular individual or according to his or her personal circumstances.

Legislation: VATA 1994, Sch. 7A, Grp. 9

Other material: Notice 701/2, Section 5

VAT Reporter: ¶32-530

13-985   Group 10 – Reduced rate for supply and installation of mobility aids for the elderly

These are defined as the 'Installation of mobility aids for the elderly'. Mobility aids are defined as follows: grab rails, ramps, stair lifts, bath lifts, walk-in baths fitted with sealable doors, built-in shower seats or showers containing built-in shower seats.

This is not a radical change especially as persons who are 'chronically sick' (i.e. a condition which the medical profession treats as a chronic sickness, such as diabetes) are already entitled to have many of these installed at zero per cent. Information about when zero per cent VAT applies is given in VAT Notice 701/7 – VAT reliefs for disabled people. When five per cent applies to mobility aids for the elderly is explained further in flowchart 14-960.

Legislation: VATA 1994, Sch. 7A, Grp. 10 (Installation of mobility aids for the elderly)

Other material: Notice 708, section 26

13-990   Group 11 – Smoking cessation products

The Budget 2007 introduced a one-year period starting on 1 July 2007 when the reduced rate of VAT would be applied to over-the-counter sales of smoking cessation products. This period was extended beyond 1 July 2008 in the 2008 Budget.

Prescription supplied smoking cessation products continue to be zero-rated.

Legislation: VATA 1994, Sch. 7A, Grp. 11

Other material: Revenue and Customs Brief 48/07 26 June 2007; Budget 2008 Notes BN 77

VAT Reporter: ¶32-540

13-995   Group 12 – Caravans

From 6 April 2013 the reduced rate applies to supplies of certain caravans exceeding the size permitted for towing on roads by a motor vehicle of unladen weight below 3,500 kilograms. These are caravans greater than:

(a)   7 metres in length; or

(b)   2.55 metres in width.

The reduced rate does not extend to the supply of removable contents unless they would qualify for zero-rating if incorporated in a house. There is also a specific exclusion for the supply of accommodation in these caravans. This is presumably intended to ensure that the supply of holiday accommodation in this way remains standard-rated.

For caravans manufactured to BS3632:2005, see 13-450.

EXEMPTION

14-100   Overview

The exemption schedule operates on similar lines to the zero-rating schedule. If a supply falls within one of the categories listed in the Groups (but not in their headings, which are merely to help in identification of potential exemptions), then the supply is exempted.

If a supply falls within an exemption category and also within a zero-rating category, then it is treated as zero-rated rather than exempt, since a supply falling within a zero-rated category is treated as zero-rated whether or not tax would otherwise be chargeable on it.

The exemption Groups are:

- Grp. 1 – land;
- Grp. 2 – insurance;
- Grp. 3 – postal services;
- Grp. 4 – betting, gaming and lotteries;
- Grp. 5 – finance;
- Grp. 6 – education;
- Grp. 7 – health and welfare;
- Grp. 8 – burial and cremation;
- Grp. 9 – subscriptions to trade unions, professional and other public interest bodies;
- Grp. 10 – sport, sports competitions and physical education;

Zero-rate, Reduced Rate

- Grp. 11 – works of art, etc.;
- Grp. 12 – fund-raising events by charities and other qualifying bodies;
- Grp. 13 – cultural services, etc.;
- Grp. 14 – supplies of goods where input tax cannot be recovered; and
- Grp. 15 – investment gold.

If a supply is exempt from VAT, no VAT is chargeable on it. However, the supplier is not entitled to deduct input tax incurred in connection with an exempt supply (subject to the partial exemption rules – see 6-950ff.), so this input tax forms part of the costs of the business.

A person whose only supplies are exempt is not entitled to register for VAT.

Apart from the exemptions listed above, HMRC acknowledge that there is an exemption arising directly from the sixth VAT directive, for supplies of goods used wholly for exempt activities or in respect of which no input tax has previously become deductible. This was established by the European Court of Justice judgment in *EC Commission v Italian Republic*. This is implemented in UK law with effect from 1 March 2000.

Legislation: Directive 2006/112, art. 136; VATA 1994, s. 26, 30(1) and Sch. 9

Cases: *EC Commission v Italy* (Case C-45/95) [1997] BVC 536

VAT Reporter: ¶27-000

EXEMPT GROUPS

14-200   Group 1 – land

Group 1 exemption covers the grant, assignment or surrender of:

(1)   any interest in land;

(2)   any right over land; or

(3)   any licence to occupy land.

For further information on which land transactions are exempt, standard-rated or zero-rated, see 15-000 et seq.

Election to waive the exemption/option for taxation

It is possible to elect to waive the land exemption (otherwise known as the option for taxation). The effect is to make exempt supplies into taxable supplies. This is covered at 15-300ff.

VAT Reporter: ¶35-000

14-250   Group 2 – insurance

This covers the provision of insurance or reinsurance and the provision of various intermediary services.

Most intermediary services provided by insurance brokers or insurance agents are covered, but not market research, promotional activities, etc, valuation or inspection services, or supplies of loss adjusters, etc. (except where handling a claim with full written authority to conclude it).

Certain internet websites promoting insurance products provide a form of intermediary services. These are the 'click-thru' links to insurance companies or brokers. The Court of Appeal ruled in April 2010 that such services were exempt. According to HMRC the companies that appealed were 'doing much more than providing a mere click-thru facility to a broker or insurance company (that is, they were not acting as a mere conduit)'. HMRC has published guidance as to when they will accept that a click-thru insurance website is making exempt supplies.

Legislation: VATA 1994, Sch. 9, Grp. 2

Cases: *Insurancewide.com Services Ltd v R & C Commrs* [2009] BVC 412; *Trader Media Group Ltd v R & C Commrs* [2009] BVC 412; *R & C Commrs v InsuranceWide.com Services Ltd* [2010] EWCA Civ 422; [2010] BVC 606

Other material: Revenue & Customs Brief 31/10 (HMRC position following the Court of Appeal judgement in Insurancewide/Trader Media Group); Notice 701/36

VAT Reporter: ¶40-000

14-300   Group 3 – postal services

This covers supplies of the conveyance of postal packets by the Post Office, and the supply by the Post Office of services in connection with the conveyance of postal packets (other than the hire of goods).

This exemption was examined by the ECJ in the case of *TNT Post UK Ltd v R & C Commrs* (Case C-357/07) [2009] BVC 389. It ruled that:

'The exemption provided for in Article 13(A)(1)(a) of Sixth Directive 77/388 applies to the supply by the public postal services acting as such – that is, in their capacity as an operator who undertakes to provide all or part of the universal postal service in a Member State – of services other than passenger transport and telecommunications services, and the supply of goods incidental thereto. It does not apply to supplies of services or of goods incidental thereto for which the terms have been individually negotiated.'

The principal taxable services supplied by the Royal Mail are as follows:

- All individually negotiated services;

Zero-rate, Reduced Rate

- Parcelforce services;
- Door-to-door (unaddressed mail);
- Mailroom services.

Royal Mail start charging tax on theses services from 1 February 2011. Full details of the taxable services are available in a HMRC technical note entitled 'VAT – Postal services' published in March 2010.

Legislation: VATA 1994, Sch. 9, Grp. 3

Other materials: Revenue and Customs Brief 64/09: *VAT treatment of postal services: decision of the European Court of Justice in the case of TNT Post UK Ltd*

VAT Reporter: ¶27-200

14-350   Group 4 – betting, gaming and lotteries

This applies to supplies of:

(1)   the provision of facilities for placing bets;

(2)   the provision of facilities for playing games of chance;

(3)   the granting of a right to take part in a lottery.

However, excluded from the exemption are charges for admission to any premises, subscriptions to clubs, and supplies made through gaming machines, or of gaming machines. Until 27 April 2009, some participation fees (e.g. for playing bingo) were liable to standard rate VAT. However, there is ongoing litigation (the Rank case) regarding the liability of participation fees for playing mechanised cash bingo (MCB).

The net takings (i.e. 'amount put into the machine less the amount returned by the machine as winnings to players') of a gaming machine are liable to VAT. A gaming machine is one constructed for playing a game of chance and where the element of chance is provided by the machine. This would include such machines as one arm bandits and video games.

The statutory definition of a gaming machine was revised with effect from 6 December 2005 (with some further adjustment 1 November 2006) in line with the *Gambling Act* 2005. The definition is intended to maintain the status quo and to avoid some machines being liable to VAT and certain excise duties.

'Electronic lottery terminals' gaming machines

These are gaming machines called 'electronic lottery terminals' by manufacturers – it does not affect the terminals for Lotto, the National Lottery. Takings from such machines are exempt because players are participating in a lottery. However, this was in doubt until the Tax Tribunal decided the matter in 2009. Due to the uncertainty, some operators may have wrongly accounted for tax on the takings. Claims to correct this may be made subject to the usual time constraints etc.

Legislation: VATA 1994, Sch. 9, Grp. 4

Cases: *Oasis Technologies (UK) Ltd* [2010] TC 00581

Other material: Notices 701/13; 701/26; 701/27; 701/28; HM Revenue and Customs Brief 63/08 7 January 2009, *VAT – Rank Group Plc – Mechanised cash bingo and gaming machine takings, 2009 Budget Notice 73*; HM Revenue and Customs Brief 75/09; 01/2011

VAT Reporter: ¶27-300

14-400   Group 5 – finance

This provides exemption for a wide range of financial transactions, including loans, dealings in money, the sale of stocks and shares, etc.

The exemption applies to supplies deemed to be made in the UK. As a general rule, the place of supply will be outside the UK if there is a non-EC customer or an EC customer receiving the supply in a business capacity. Where the customer is based outside the EC, or the supply is directly linked with the export of goods from the EC, related input tax will be recoverable for a supply which would be exempt under this head if made in the UK (see 6-420).

A trader who makes no taxable supplies, but makes exempt supplies of this type in respect of which input tax is deductible, may register for VAT notwithstanding the lack of taxable supplies.

Other material: Notice 701/49

VAT Reporter: ¶40-000

(1) Item 1 – dealings in money, etc.

Exemption is provided for supplies of the issue, transfer or receipt of money, security for money, or any note or order for the payment of money, and for any dealings with these things.

'Money' includes all legal tender, including foreign currency, while securities for money includes such things as bills of exchange, local authority bills, etc. However, shares and securities which used to be securities or secondary securities under the former *Exchange Control Act* 1947 are excluded from this item and dealt with separately under item 6 (see below). This takes out of the item 1 exemption such things as stocks and shares.

Also, supplies of coins or banknotes as collectors' pieces or investment articles are excluded from exemption under this or any other item in Grp. 5.

Legislation: VATA 1994, Sch. 9, Grp. 5, item 1

VAT Reporter: ¶40-000

(2) Item 2 and 2A – supplies of credit

The making of any advance or the granting of credit is exempt. Interest received, being the consideration for the granting of credit, therefore represents consideration for an exempt supply.

The exemption encompasses the management of credit by the person granting the credit.

Following *C & E Commrs Electronic Data Systems Ltd*, HMRC stated that services such as supplies of loan arrangements and execution services where the payment or transfer of funds is central to the supply are exempt. EDS supplied loan arrangement and execution services to banks in relation to the granting of personal loans. These services included a staffed call centre, printing and dispatch of documentation, the transfer of funds via BACS following the release of loans and administrative work in handling loan accounts and repayments. The Court of Appeal decided that EDS supplied an exempt service aptly described as 'loan arrangements and execution services'.

Legislation: VATA 1994, Sch. 9, Grp. 5, item 2 and 2A

Cases: *C & E Commrs v Electronic Data Systems Ltd* [2003] BVC 451

VAT Reporter: ¶53-775

(3) Item 3 and 4 – instalment credit

The provision of instalment credit is exempt where a separate charge for credit is made and disclosed to the customer, and covers hire purchase, conditional sale and credit sale agreements.

Where goods are sold, and payment is deferred, a separate charge for the deferment of payment is therefore regarded as consideration for a separate supply of the facility to defer payment. If no separate charge is made, the whole of the consideration is seen as relating to the supply of the goods, and as attracting tax, or not, according to the status of that supply.

There is a further exemption for the provision of administrative arrangements, documentation, and the transfer of title in respect of such an agreement, provided that the consideration for this is separately disclosed and does not exceed £10.

Legislation: VATA 1994, Sch. 9, Grp. 5, item 3 and 4

(4) Item 5 – finance commissions and making of arrangements

There is an exemption for intermediary services, being services of bringing together persons wishing to buy financial services with those who provide them. For these purposes, intermediary services do not included market research, product design, advertising and promotional or similar services.

This exemption applies to intermediary services supplied in connection with the following:

- dealings in money (1 above);
- supplies of credit but not the management of credit (2 above);
- instalment credit (3 above);
- securities (6 below).

Qualifying intermediary services are exempt 'whether or not any ... transaction is finally concluded' by the parties involved.

An intermediary service is categorised according to 'its overall character and not the presence of certain services'.

As a result of the litigation, a body that introduces its members, supporters or customers to a credit card provider and undertakes work preparatory to the provision of the credit card is regarded as providing exempt negotiation or intermediary services.

Portfolio management

Management of investments ('portfolio management') by financial advisers normally includes an annual review of the client's portfolio. The review usually includes re-considering the needs of the clients concerned, checking that the investment portfolio is in line with the client's needs and making necessary changes to keep the portfolio in line with those needs. The fee for the annual review is normally fixed in advance. In a case involving Deutsche Bank, the CEJ ruled that portfolio management is a single taxable service. At the time of writing HMRC had not announced from when affected persons should begin accounting for VAT on portfolio management services.

Debt negotiation

Debt negotiation services provided by an intermediary are treated as exempt supplies following the VAT and Duties Tribunal case of *Debt Management Associates Ltd*. 'Debt negotiation services' are considered to be services of mediation between a debtor and creditor for payment of a debt. The intermediary will have no interest of his own in the terms of the contract but will act between the parties and attempt to mediate a change to any payment terms in place.

The ECJ decided that debt collection services are standard-rated. HMRC interpret 'debt collection' as including all services connected with the collection of payments on behalf of a creditor. The European understanding of 'debt collection' includes any process of collecting payments even where the payment is not overdue. However, where the collection of a payment is ancillary to other payment-related transactions – for example the movement and settlement of payments between bank accounts – the charge will continue to fall within the VAT exemption.

Bloomsbury Wealth Management are independent financial advisers. They appealed against HMRC's ruling that their initial and annual fee for dealing with investments were taxable. The First-tier Tribunal allowed Bloomsbury's appeal and ruled that Bloomsbury provided 'exempt intermediary services to its client'. At the time of writing it is not known if HMRC will appeal.

Zero-rate, Reduced Rate

517

Insolvency practitioners

Following the case of *Paymex Ltd* HMRC accepted that the services of an insolvency practitioner when conducting and supervising Individual Voluntary Arrangements is an exempt supply. HMRC have confirmed that *Paymex* applies to:

- individual voluntary arrangements;
- company voluntary arrangements;
- partnership voluntary arrangements; and
- protected trust deeds (applicable in Scotland).

This includes both the nominee services in making the arrangements and also the supervisory service of collecting and distributing the money to creditors in accordance with the agreement reached.

Legislation: VATA 1994, Sch. 9, Grp. 5, item 5

Cases: *C & E Commrs v FDR Ltd* [2000] BVC 311; *C & E Commrs v Institute of Directors* [2003] BVC 112; *Debt Management Associates Ltd* [2003] BVC 4,055; *R & C Commrs v AXA UK plc* (Case C-175/09) [2011] BVC 35; *Paymex Ltd* [2011] UKFTT 350 (TC); [2011] TC 01210; *Bloomsbury Wealth Management LLP* [2012] UKFTT 379 (TC); [2012] TC 02063; *Finanzamt Frankfurt am Main V-Höchst v Deutsche Bank AG* (Case C-44/11) Judgment delivered 19 July 2012

Other material: Business Brief 30/03, 24 December 2003; Revenue and Customs Brief 54/2010; Revenue and Customs Brief 27/11; Revenue and Customs Brief 36/11; Revenue and Customs Brief 03/12

(5) Underwriting

The underwriting of a service which is exempt because it is within item 1 or item 6 of the exemption schedule (see Dealings in money, etc. above and Securities below) is also exempt.

Legislation: VATA 1994, Sch. 9, Grp. 5, item 1 and 6

(6) Items 6 and 7 – securities

Item 6 exempts the supply of the issue, transfer or receipt of, or any dealing with, any security or secondary security.

In broad terms, it covers such financial instruments as:

(1) stocks and shares, bonds, notes (other than promissory notes), debentures, shares in an oil royalty;

(2) a document which gives the bearer the right to receive a stated sum of money, with or without interest, and which can be transferred by delivery (with or without endorsement);

(3) a bill, note or other obligation of the Treasury or of any Government, other than legal tender of any part of the world, which is transferable by delivery (with or without endorsement);

(4)   letters of allotment, etc;

(5)   unit trust units.

Legislation: VATA 1994, Sch. 9, Grp. 5, item 6 and 7

(7) Item 8 – operation of bank accounts, etc.

The supply of operating a current, deposit or savings account is exempt.

Legislation: VATA 1994, Sch. 9, Grp. 5, item 8

(8) Item 9 – management of unit trust scheme, etc.

The management of authorised unit trust schemes, or of trust-based schemes within FSMA 2000, s. 237(3) and s. 239(3)(a), is exempt.

Changes from 1 October 2008

The management of trust-based schemes is no longer exempt.

The management of open-ended investment companies remains exempt but this service is moved to item 9 from item 10.

The management of the following becomes exempt:

(a)   an authorised open-ended investment company; or

(b)   an authorised unit trust scheme; or

(c)   a Gibraltar collective investment scheme that is not an umbrella scheme; or

(d)   a sub-fund of any other Gibraltar collective investment scheme; or

(e)   an individually recognised overseas scheme that is not an umbrella scheme; or

(f)   a sub-fund of any other individually recognised overseas scheme; or

(g)   a recognised collective investment scheme authorised in a designated country or territory that is not an umbrella scheme; or

(h)   a sub-fund of any other recognised collective investment scheme authorised in a designated country or territory; or

(i)   a recognised collective investment scheme constituted in another EEA state that is not an umbrella scheme; or

(j)   a sub-fund of any other recognised collective investment scheme constituted in another EEA state.

Legislation: VATA 1994, Sch. 9, Grp. 5, item 9; *Value Added Tax (Finance) (No. 2) Order* 2008 (SI 2008/2547)

Zero-rate, Reduced Rate

(9) Item 10 – closed investment companies

Changes from 1 October 2008

The legislation is amended to make the management of a closed-ended collective investment undertaking exempt.

The management of open-ended investment companies remains exempt but this service is moved to item 9 above.

Other material: Notice 701/49 Finance and Securities

14-450   Group 6 – education

Exemption applies, in broad terms, to education or training provided by schools, universities and other 'eligible bodies', and supplies of research by one eligible body to another. Exemption also applies to certain ancillary supplies, and also the provision of facilities by youth clubs to their members.

Education, training and research

The main exemption covers the supply by an 'eligible body' of:

(1)   education or vocational training; or

(2)   research, if provided to another 'eligible body'.

The term 'eligible body' covers:

(1)   various kinds of schools within the meaning of the *Education Acts* 1944 to 1993 and related legislation which are subject to state regulation;

(2)   UK universities and colleges, institutions, schools or halls of such universities;

(3)   institutions defined in the *Further and Higher Education Act* 1992 and related legislation;

(4)   certain public bodies, such as Government departments, local authorities and other bodies acting under an enactment for public purposes, otherwise than for profit, and performing functions similar to those of a Government department or local authority; or

(5)   a body which:

(a)   is precluded from distributing any profits;

(b)   does not distribute any profits; and

(c)   applies any profits from exempt educational supplies to the continuance or improvement of such supplies and does not use them to subsidise some other purpose.

A body teaching English as a foreign language (EFL) is also an 'eligible body', but only in respect of its supplies insofar as they consist of the teaching of EFL.

A university trading company may, subject to conditions, also be accepted by HMRC as an 'eligible body'. HMRC applied this policy from 11 March 2010.

Closely related supplies

This exemption also covers the supply of goods or services closely related to an exempt educational supply either directly to the students concerned (whether by the eligible body providing the education, etc. or by some other eligible body), or by another eligible body to the one providing the education, etc.

Government funded training

The provision of vocational training (including related goods and services essential thereto and supplied directly to the trainee) ultimately funded under:

- Section 2 *Employment and Training Act* 1973;
- Section 1A *Employment and training Act (Northern Ireland)* 1950;
- Section 2 *Enterprise and New Towns (Scotland) Act* 1990;
- Part i or Part ii of the *Learning and Skills Act* 2000 when provided by the Learning and Skills Council for England or the National Council for Education and Training for Wales.

The exemption only covers the amount received from those bodies; any additional fee or charge must be considered separately.

Private tuition

Exemption is also provided for private tuition by an individual teacher, acting independently of any employer, in subjects ordinarily taught in schools or colleges. See flowchart 14-955.

Examination services

The supply of examination services is exempt if supplied either by an eligible body or to an eligible body, or supplied to a person receiving education or training which is either exempt or provided otherwise than in the course of a business.

Youth clubs

There is exemption for the provision of facilities by a youth club (or association of youth clubs) to its members, or by an association of youth clubs to members of clubs which are its members.

Legislation: VATA 1994, Sch. 9, Grp. 6

Other material: Notice 701/30 Education and vocational training; Revenue and Customs Brief 09/10 VAT status of University trading subsidiary companies; Information Sheet 03/10 VAT status of University trading subsidiary companies

VAT Reporter: ¶50-630

Zero-rate, Reduced Rate

521

14-500   Group 7 – health and welfare

A number of supplies connected with the provision of health and welfare services, and related goods are exempt.

(1) Items 1 to 3 – supplies by doctors, etc.

Supplies of medical services, by persons enrolled on certain registers, such as the register of medical practitioners or the dentists' register are exempt.

Medical services are defined as those services intended principally to protect (including maintain or restore) the health of an individual. The supplies are made by qualified doctors, dentists, ophthalmic or dispensing opticians, nurses, midwives, health visitors, ancillary dental workers, hearing aid dispensers, and those enrolled in a register under the *Health Professions Order* 2001. From 1 May 2007, certain supplies by health professionals are no longer considered to be 'medical' services and will be standard-rated. See below.

The exemption includes supplies by a person not on one of these registers, where the services are wholly performed or directly supervised by a person who is so enrolled.

The qualified supervisor need not be physically present at all times for the work of an unqualified person to be seen as being directly supervised, provided that there are suitable controls in place.

Supplies of prostheses services by dental technicians are exempt as are supplies of services (other than the hire of goods) by pharmaceutical chemists. This latter exemption covers such supplies as pregnancy testing, acting as locum to a dispensing chemist, and supplies covered by NHS payments such as rota payments.

There are special considerations relating to dental practices, which have a number of special forms of organisation.

Legislation: Directive 2006/112, art. 132(1)(c); VATA 1994, Sch. 9, Grp. 7, item 1

Cases: *Elder Home Care Ltd* [1994] BVC 709; *Barkworth v C & E Commrs* (1988) 3 BVC 391

VAT Reporter: ¶28-500

Personally administered drugs and appliances

The treatment of drugs and appliances personally administered, injected or applied to patients by general practitioners has been decided by the Courts. HMRC's view that this forms part of the doctor's overall exempt supply of medical services was upheld.

The House of Lords drew heavily on the guidance given by the Court of Justice in *Card Protection Plan Ltd*. The situation was correctly classified by the NHS – a single supply of services – and should not artificially be subdivided.

Cases: *Dr Beynon and Partners v C & E Commrs* [2003] BVC 127; *Card Protection Plan Ltd v C & E Commrs* [2001] BVC 158

Other material: Notice 701/57

VAT Reporter: ¶28-500

Non-medical services

Following the decision of the ECJ in *d'Ambrumenil; Dispute Resolution Services Ltd v C & E Commrs* the VAT treatment of services by health professionals that are not medical services was amended.

VAT is chargeable on:

- pre-employment medicals;
- medical reports in connection with personal injury litigation and professional medical negligence;
- medical reports to assess a person's entitlement to a war pension or similar benefit.

Medical services where the principal purpose is the protection, maintenance or restoration of the health of the individual are exempt from VAT.

Medicals to assess the level of insurance premiums are no longer exempt as a medical service. However, following *Morganash Ltd* they may be exempt as an insurance related service.

Liability of services and goods

Advice in Information Sheets 03/06 and 12/06 concerning the liability of certain supplies made by doctors is summarised in the table below.

Service, etc. provided	VAT liability
'Medical services (including drugs administered in the course of treatment) …' '… primary health care … by doctors … using … professional skills, training and knowledge …'	Exempt
'Drugs and appliances dispensed to patients for their personal use … under the NHS arrangements.'	Zero-rated
'All take-away drugs supplied privately by doctors …'	Standard-rated (Note – these drugs can be exempt when an 'integral part of a private medical service')
Signing passport applications	Standard-rated
'Medico legal services that are predominantly legal rather than medical …'	Standard-rated
'Clinical trials or market research for drug companies that do not involve the care or assessment of a patient'	Standard-rated
Paternity testing	Standard-rated

Zero-rate, Reduced Rate

Cases: *d'Ambrumenil; Dispute Resolution Services Ltd v C & E Commrs* (Case C-307/01) [2005] BVC 741; *Morganash Ltd* [2007] BVC 2,184

Other material: Business Brief 29/03, 16 December 2003; Information Sheets 03/06, 12/06 and 05/07; HMRC Revenue and Customs Brief 06/07; Notice 701/57 Health Professionals

VAT Reporter: ¶43-866

(2) Item 4 – provision of care

The provision of care, or medical or surgical treatment, and connected supplies of goods, in a hospital or state-regulated institution is exempt. A state-regulated institution is one approved, licensed or registered under relevant social legislation or exempted from obtaining such approval or registration by the relevant legislation.

Examples of such institutions include a hospital or hospice, nursing homes, a children's home, residential homes for the disabled, elderly or infirm residents, residential homes for people with past or present dependence on alcohol or drugs, or a past or present mental disorder, a nursery, creche or playgroup, an after-school club or similar provider of non-residential care for children. The institution may be either commercial or carry out its activities on a charitable basis.

The exemption covers such supplies as accommodation, catering, medical services, nursing services, drugs and appliances. For childcare and certain welfare services provided by local authorities, see 17-730.

HMRC consider that 'care' encompasses looking after the generality of a person's physical, personal and domestic needs. It includes the medical treatment, protection control and guidance of the individual. In a tribunal case, it was decided that this 'care' does not have to be as in inpatient but should be a treatment that would ordinarily be regarded as a treatment in a hospital.

In situations where there are other services provided, the contract for the 'care' of the patient will have to be examined to determine whether a single or multiple supply is being made. For example, the provision of payphones in a residential home is likely to be a separate supply as would the hosting of children's parties by a playgroup.

Legislation: VATA 1994, Sch. 9, Grp. 7, item 4

Other material: Notice 701/37

Cases: *Coleman* [1993] BVC 1,020; *Poole General Hospital* [1993] BVC 990

VAT Reporter: ¶28-535

(3) Item 9 – welfare services

The supply of welfare services by a charity, a public body or a state regulated private welfare institution or agency. 'State regulated' refers to the obligation under social care legislation for providers of certain care and welfare services to register with, and be regulated by, national bodies established for the regulation and inspection of care services. Such a business is not 'state regulated' until its registration has been approved by the relevant authority. In some instances, the business concerned may rely on an extra-statutory concession to exempt its services whilst its registration is being approved.

'Welfare services' means services that are directly concerned with the provision of care, treatment or instruction designed to promote the physical or mental welfare of elderly, sick, distressed or disabled persons. It includes the care and protection of children and young persons. The provision of spiritual welfare by a religious institution as part of a course of instruction or a retreat (not a holiday or recreation) is also included.

Subject to complying with certain conditions domiciliary care may be an exempt supply.

Cases: *Watford and District Old People's Housing Association Ltd (t/a Watford Help in the Home Service)* [1998] BVC 2,351

Other material: Notice 701/2 Welfare

Legislation: VATA 1994, Sch. 9, Grp. 7, item 9

VAT Reporter: ¶28-535

(4) Items 5, 6, 7, 8 and items 10 and 11 – miscellaneous

The following are exempt:

(1) medical deputising services;

(2) supplies of human blood, blood-derived therapeutic products, human organs or tissue for diagnostic or therapeutic purposes or medical research;

(3) the supply of goods and services incidental to the provision of spiritual welfare by a religious community, if made to a resident member of the community for a subscription, etc. and made otherwise than for profit;

(4) the supply of transport, in specially designed vehicles, for sick or injured persons (i.e. ambulance services).

Legislation: VATA 1994, Sch. 9, Grp. 7, item 5–11

VAT Reporter: ¶28-450

Zero-rate, Reduced Rate

14-550   Group 8 – burial and cremation

Supplies of the disposal of the remains of the human dead, and the making of arrangements for and in connection with such disposal are exempt.

Legislation: VATA 1994, Sch. 9, Grp. 8

Other material: Notice 701/32

VAT Reporter: ¶52-300

14-600   Group 9 – subscriptions to trade unions, professional and other public interest bodies

Exemption is provided for supplies made in return for subscriptions by:

(1)   trade unions;

(2)   professional associations;

(3)   learned societies and the like;

(4)   certain trade associations;

(5)   bodies which are made up of the exempt bodies above and which have the same objectives; and

(6)   bodies which have objects which are in the public domain and are of a political, religious, patriotic, philosophical, philanthropic or civic nature.

In each case, the body seeking exemption must be non-profit making.

Exemption does not apply to supplies involving a right of admission to premises, events or performances if non-members can also attend but have to pay.

Certain membership subscriptions can often be apportioned according to the benefits received. This is an advantage when some of the benefits are zero-rated (e.g. an in-house journal or magazine). The apportionment is permitted by Extra-Statutory Concession. The concession may not be applied retrospectively.

Other material: Notice 701/5 Clubs and Associations; Notice 48 Extra-Statutory Concessions, para. 3.35; Revenue and Customs Brief 06/09 20 February 2009 Claims for retrospective application of Extra-Statutory Concession 3.35.

VAT Reporter: ¶50-827; ¶29-050

Legislation: VATA 1994, Sch. 9, Grp. 9

(1) Trade unions

A trade union is a body whose members are employed, and whose main object is to negotiate pay and conditions of service on their behalf.

(2) Professional associations

A professional association is a body which restricts its membership wholly or mainly to individuals who have, or are seeking a qualification appropriate to the practice of the profession concerned.

The question whether something is a profession has been narrowly interpreted by the tribunals. Occupations which have been held not to be professions include cleaning, funeral directorship and employment agency and consultancy.

HMRC interpret the requirement that membership be limited 'wholly or mainly' to individuals to be that significantly more than 50 per cent are individuals. Their policy is that if 75 per cent of members are individuals, this satisfies the requirement. In order to determine whether there is the required limitation in membership, it is necessary to look to see what actually happens in practice. The mere note in the constitution that there is a limitation does not carry the day if the practice is not followed through.

Cases: *The British Institute of Cleaning Science Ltd* (1985) 2 BVC 205,373; *National Association of Funeral Directors* (1985) 2 BVC 205,391; *The Institute of Employment Consultants Ltd* (1987) 3 BVC 1,312

Other material: *Customs Guidance Manuals* Vol V1-7 Liability Chapter 24 Section 4.3

Legislation: VATA 1994, Sch. 9, Grp. 9

(3) Learned societies

A learned society is a body whose primary purpose is the advancement of a particular branch of knowledge, or the fostering of professional expertise. It must restrict its membership wholly or mainly to individuals, and those individuals must be persons whose past or present professions or employments are linked with the objects of the association.

The comments at (2) above on the restriction of membership apply equally to learned societies.

(4) Representational trade associations

A representational trade association is a body whose primary purpose is to make representations to Government on legislation and other public matters affecting the business or professional interests of its members. Membership must be restricted wholly or mainly to persons whose business or professional interests are directly connected with its objects. However, membership does not need to be restricted to individuals.

Zero-rate, Reduced Rate

14-650 Group 10 – sport, sports competitions and physical education

This applies to the right to enter a sporting competition where all entry fees are returned as prizes, and also the right to enter a sporting competition promoted by a non-profit-making body established for the purposes of sport or physical recreation. However, the latter exemption does not apply if the competition involves the free use of facilities for the use of which the body normally makes a charge.

Supplies of sporting services

The exemption only applies where supplies of sporting services are made to individuals. In the case of a members' club, the exemption only applies to supplies made to members (whose membership must be for a period of three months or more); for other non-profit-making organisations exemption applies to supplies to any individual.

It can be difficult in some instances to decide whether a membership scheme is in existence. In one case, a tribunal decided that the issue of privilege cards, entitling holders to various discounts, did not amount to a membership scheme, even though the holders of the cards were referred to as members.

This exemption covers supplies of services closely linked with and essential to sport or physical education in which the individual takes part. The supply of residential accommodation, catering and transport are specifically excluded. If the subscription covers both exempt sporting services and other facilities an apportionment must be made.

Complex restrictions apply to this exemption. The exemption excludes bodies which are 'subject to commercial influence' within, broadly, the three years prior to the supply for which exemption is sought. A body is subject to commercial influence if it receives a supply of land or the occupation of land, or pays an emolument related to its profit or gross income, to an associated person including an officer or a shadow officer.

Non-members and sports fees

In June 2011 the first tier tax tribunal decided that fees (e.g. green fees) paid to a non-profit making sports club by non-members were exempt. HMRC have announced that they are seeking leave to appeal.

All-inclusive membership fees paid to leisure trusts

HMRC have amended their view that all-inclusive membership fees paid to a non-profit making body providing leisure services are fully taxable. Such fees should be exempt. Supplies made by commercial organisations are not affected and remain standard-rated. This came into effect on 1 April 2009. This only affects non-profit making bodies including leisure trusts. All-inclusive membership fees are exempt. If these organisations now make exempt and standard-rated supplies, they will have to apply the partial exemption rules. It may be necessary to consider amendments to any Capital Goods Scheme calculations (see Notice 706/2 – the Capital Goods Scheme).

In most cases, the customer who purchases an all-inclusive membership package will have access to a range of leisure centre facilities. If purchased on an individual basis, many of these facilities would be exempt as 'services closely linked with and essential to sport or physical education in which the individual is taking part'. Therefore, it has been decided that where an all-inclusive membership package has the same aim, the same tax treatment should apply. If the main reason that the customer purchases an all-inclusive package is to use the sports facilities, other subsidiary benefits of the membership, such as use of the sauna (usually standard-rated), will be regarded as incidental and the package will be exempt. If the main reason the customer purchases the all-inclusive package is to make use of standard-rated facilities, the whole supply is standard-rated.

Affiliation fees paid to Sports governing bodies

Following the ruling by the ECJ in *Canterbury Hockey Club* (Case C-253/07) HMRC have accepted that affiliation fees charged by sports governing bodies are exempt even when supplied to corporate persons and unincorporated associations when the supplies are

- closely linked and essential to sport;
- supplied by non-profit making organisations; and
- the true beneficiaries are individuals taking part in sport.

From 1 September 2010 these supplies must be exempted from VAT. When the supply is to a commercial profit making organisation, the beneficiary test will not be met and the supply will continue to be standard rated.

Legislation: VATA 1994, Sch. 9, Grp. 10; *Value Added Tax (Sport, Sports Competitions and Physical Education) Order* 1999 (SI 1999/1994)

Cases: *Basingstoke & District Sports Trust Ltd* [1996] BVC 2,373; *Canterbury Hockey Club v R & C Commrs* (Case C-253/07) [2008] BVC 824; *The Bridport and West Dorset Golf Club Ltd* [2011] UKFTT 354 (TC); [2011] TC 01214

Other material: Notice 701/45 Sport; Revenue and Customs Brief 37/10 – VAT: Leisure Trusts providing all inclusive membership schemes; Revenue and Customs Brief 15/10 VAT – Changes to treatment to Sports related services following EC judgement in Canterbury Hockey Club; Revenue and Customs Brief 30/11

VAT Reporter: ¶29-150

14-700   Group 11 – works of art, etc.

This applies to the disposal of certain works of art, etc. exempted from capital taxes when disposed of by private treaty sale, or by way of acceptance in lieu of tax, under the douceur arrangements.

Zero-rate, Reduced Rate

Legislation: VATA 1994, Sch. 9, Grp. 11

Other material: Notice 701/12

VAT Reporter: ¶29-250

14-750 Group 12 – fund-raising events by charities and other qualifying bodies

Exemption is provided for the supply of goods or services in connection with a one-off fund-raising event (such as a fête, performance, etc.) by:

(1) a charity, if the event is organised for charitable purposes by one or more charities;

(2) a trade union or professional body within 14-600 above, or certain bodies with objects of a 'public' nature (VATA 1994, s. 94(3)), if the event is organised solely for the benefit of the body concerned;

(3) by a non-profit making body established principally to provide facilities for participating in sport of physical education;

(4) an eligible body providing cultural services which are exempt (see 14-780).

In the case of a charity, relief is also available for supplies by a wholly owned subsidiary which has agreed in writing to transfer the whole of its profits to the charity.

Exemption is available in principle for any event, including an event accessible via electronic media, which is held by a charity or qualifying body primarily to raise money. Exemption is available provided that the body does not hold more than 15 similar events at the same location in a 12-month period and, in applying this test, events raising less than £1,000 (gross) in any week are ignored.

Exemption is not available where accommodation is provided, unless the accommodation is merely incidental to the event and does not exceed two nights in total.

There is a general proviso that exemption does not apply to any supply where this would be likely to create distortions of competition such as to place a commercial enterprise carried on by a taxable person at a disadvantage.

Charity challenge events

Charities that organise – directly or through a trading subsidiary – charity challenge events such as treks, cycle tours, mountain adventures and the like, should review the VAT treatment of such events because it is unlikely that they fall within the VAT exemption for fund-raising.

Events that include a package of both travel and accommodation or bought-in accommodation; or more than two nights accommodation from a charity's own resources do **not** fall within the exemption.

Legislation: VATA 1994, Sch. 9, Grp. 12

Other material: Notice 701/1; Notice 709/6; Revenue and Customs Brief 36/08 *VAT treatment of Charity Challenge Events*

VAT Reporter: ¶50-872

14-780   Group 13 – cultural services, etc.

Cultural bodies – exemption for admissions

Admission charges to cultural events or sights are exempt in certain circumstances. This hinges on the nature of the event or sight and the status of the cultural body.

The events and sights which are within the scope of the exemption are as follows:

(a)   theatrical, musical or choreographic performances of a cultural nature; and
(b)   museums, galleries, art exhibitions and zoos.

For admission fees to these events to be exempt, the person staging it must be an 'eligible body'. An 'eligible body' is defined as an organisation that:

(a)   is precluded from distributing, and does not distribute, any profit it makes;
(b)   applies any profits made from supplies of a description falling within item 2 to the continuance or improvement of the facilities made available by means of the supplies; and
(c)   is managed and administered on a voluntary basis by persons who have no direct or indirect financial interest in its activities.

Most litigation has been about condition (c).

In the *Zoological Society of London* case, the ECJ ruled that for these purposes management and administration is the role of taking 'decisions of the last resort concerning the policy of the body, particularly in the financial area and … higher supervisory tasks'. Characteristically, this is 'the taking, rather than the implementation, of policy decisions and accordingly takes place at the highest level'.

Bournemouth Symphony and *Longborough Festival* were about what is or is not a 'direct or indirect financial interest'. The main principles established by the Courts were as follows:

(a)   a 'flat-rate remuneration at a proper rate' does not give an employee a financial interest and 'if remuneration is to constitute a financial interest, it must be either results-based in some way or at such a high rate as to be a disguised means of distributing profit';
(b)   'financial interest' meant an interest leading to 'the enrichment of the person' concerned.

HMRC has published its policy for deciding when there is or is not a 'financial interest'.

'It is now our view that a person who is managing and administering the cultural body can be seen to have a direct or indirect financial interest in its activities only when

Zero-rate, Reduced Rate

531

- the person receives any payments for services supplied to the cultural body above the market rate, paid as routine overheads, or receives any payments which are profit-related (whether below, at or above the market rates); and
- there is a link between the payments and the persons participation in the direction of the cultural body's activities.

This means that payments to individuals for services of managing and administering the body are not financial interests if:

- they are allowed by the constitution;
- the recipient is excluded from any decision- making regarding the award of any contract to themselves;
- the payments are not above the market rates; and
- are not linked to profits.

There is no financial interest where the only potential – for example, where a risk is undertaken or guaranteed – so that guarantor only stands to lose money and not gain money as a result.'

Legislation: Directive 2006/112, art. 132(1)(n)); VATA 1994, Sch. 9, Grp. 13

Cases: *C & E Commrs v Zoological Society of London* [2002] BVC 414; *Bournemouth Symphony Orchestra v C & E Commrs* [2005] BVC 547; *R & C Commrs v Longborough Festival Opera* [2006] BVC 839

Other material: Notice 701/47

VAT Reporter: ¶50-880

14-800 Group 14 – supplies of goods where input tax cannot be recovered

There is exemption for the supply of goods if:

(1) input tax arose (or will arise) on the supply of the goods to the relevant supplier or a predecessor (or on the importation or acquisition of the goods); and

(2) the whole of this input tax was non-deductible; and

(3) the supply being made is not one which would be an exempt land supply but for the exercise of the option for taxation by the supplier.

A predecessor of the supplier is someone who supplied the goods to the supplier free of VAT under the 'transfer of a going concern' rules or the VAT grouping rules. In the case of a chain of transfer of going concern or VAT group transactions, this is extended back along the chain until the original purchaser of the goods under a taxable transaction is found.

Input tax on the purchase, etc. is non-deductible if it is attributable to exempt supplies under the partial exemption rules, or it is specifically blocked under the rules relating to business entertainment, fittings in new houses, or motor cars (other than cars for resale). The exemption does not apply to goods which are already eligible for the second-hand goods margin scheme.

Where exempt input tax is actually recovered because of the partial exemption de minimis limit, it continues to be regarded as non-deductible for the purposes of this exemption.

Where the goods concerned are subject to the capital goods scheme, so that a taxable supply of them would give rise to partial recovery of the original input tax, the exemption does not apply.

Legislation: VATA 1994, Sch. 9, Grp. 14

VAT Reporter: ¶29-500

14-850 Group 15 – investment gold

There is exemption for supplies of 'investment gold'. Investment gold is defined in the exemption group, and is generally gold in bar or wafer form (as opposed to jewellery) having a minimum level of purity, or certain gold coins. Unusually, an exemption applies to the importation of investment gold as well as its supply or acquisition in the UK.

There are complex related provisions, maintaining zero-rating for supplies within the London Bullion Market, retaining the reverse charge in the case of taxable gold supplies, providing an option for taxation, etc.

Legislation: VATA 1994, Sch. 9, Grp. 15

Other material: Notice 701/21; Notice 701/21A

VAT Reporter: ¶29-550

14-900 Cost sharing exemption

The cost sharing exemption is intended to benefit charities and also businesses making exempt supplies. It will facilitate a supply chain through which these persons may gain by joining together and buying services in bulk without incurring additional VAT liabilities. The facility is not available for buying goods in bulk.

Subject to quite stringent conditions, charities and/or relevant businesses may form a separate independent legal entity ('a cost sharing group') to buy services for them. The 'cost sharing group' buys in the relevant services and in turn supplies them to its members.

The supply of the relevant services by the cost sharing group to its members will not be liable to VAT. It will be an exempt supply.

By forming a cost sharing group participating members will be able to benefit from economies of scale when buying relevant services without incurring more VAT on the supply of the services by the cost sharing group to its members.

This measure was introduced by *Finance Act* 2012

Legislation *Finance Act* 2012, s. 197

Zero-rate, Reduced Rate

533

FLOWCHARTS

14-955   When private tuition may be an exempt supply

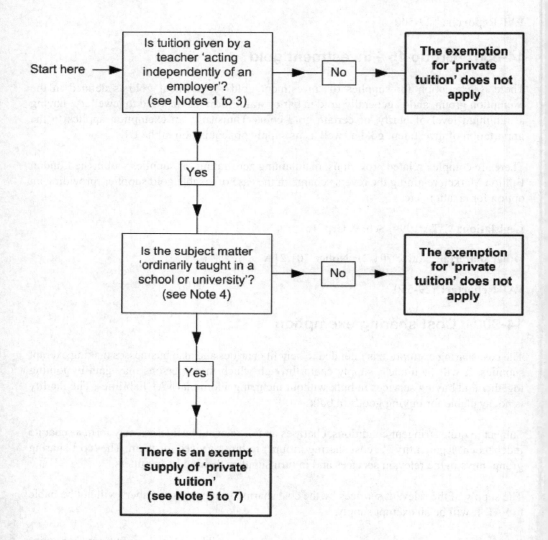

Start here →

Is tuition given by a teacher 'acting independently of an employer'?
(see Notes 1 to 3)

No → **The exemption for 'private tuition' does not apply**

Yes ↓

Is the subject matter 'ordinarily taught in a school or university'?
(see Note 4)

No → **The exemption for 'private tuition' does not apply**

Yes ↓

There is an exempt supply of 'private tuition'
(see Note 5 to 7)

Notes

(1) Acting 'independently of an employer'

A teacher is acting 'independently of an employer' when he or she is a sole proprietor or partner. It is only tuition supplied personally by this person which is within the scope of the exemption.

(2) Directors/employees of limited companies

A teacher who is employed by a limited company is not 'acting independently of an employer' and 'this applies even if the teacher concerned is the sole shareholder of the company'. (*VAT Guidance Manuals* Vol 1-7 Ch. 21 Section 7.5).

(3) Scotland

The matter of 'private tuition' and 'one man' companies was considered in Scotland in *R & C Commrs v Empowerment Enterprises Ltd* [2006] CSIH 46; [2007] BVC 878. The Court of Session confirmed that exemption is only available to sole proprietors and partners.

(4) Subjects 'ordinarily taught in school or university'

'A reasonable test … is whether the subject is taught in a number of schools or universities on a regular basis. In practice, the vast majority of structured courses delivered by an individual teacher are likely to meet this criterion.' (*VAT Guidance Manuals* Vol 1-7 Ch. 21 Section 7.3).

(5) Apportionment

A sole proprietor or partnership employing teachers needs to quantify the income arising from tuition given by their employees. The employer may use 'any fair and reasonable method to apportion their supplies … If this is impractical, they may treat all their supplies as taxable regardless of who actually delivers it'. (*VAT Guidance Manuals*, Vol 1-7 Ch. 21 Section 7.4).

(6) Goods or other services

Goods and other services supplied in conjunction with 'private tuition' are not necessarily exempt.

(7) Further information

For further information see Notice 701/30 Educational and vocational training.

Zero-rate, Reduced Rate

14-960   Reduced rate for mobility aids for the elderly

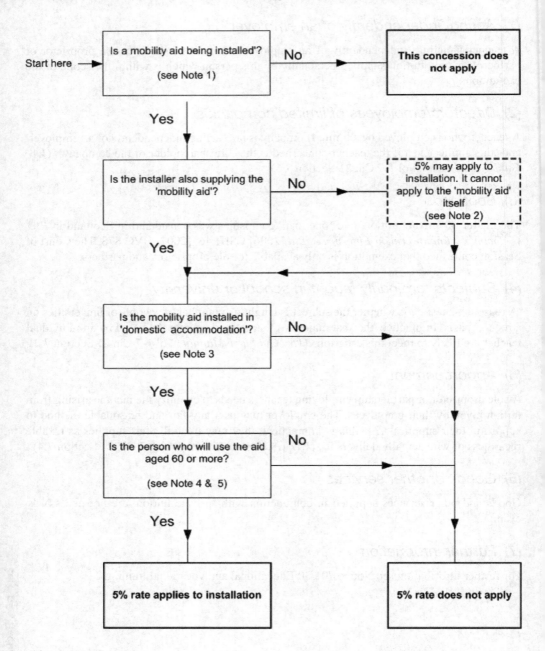

Start here → **Is a mobility aid being installed'?** (see Note 1) → **No** → **This concession does not apply**

Yes

Is the installer also supplying the 'mobility aid'? → **No** → 5% may apply to installation. It cannot apply to the 'mobility aid' itself (see Note 2)

Yes

Is the mobility aid installed in 'domestic accommodation'? (see Note 3) → **No**

Yes

Is the person who will use the aid aged 60 or more? (see Note 4 & 5) → **No**

Yes

5% rate applies to installation

5% rate does not apply

Notes

(1) Mobility aids. Mobility aids are grab rails, ramps, stair lifts, bath lifts, walk-in baths fitted with sealable doors and built-in shower seats or showers containing built-in shower-seats.

(2) Mobility aids not liable to five per cent unless supplied by installer. Only when supplied and installed by the same person both the service of installation and the aid itself qualify for five per cent VAT. With other arrangements, the mobility aid will not qualify for five per cent VAT.

(3) Domestic accommodation. 'Domestic accommodation' is 'a building, or part of a building, that consists of a dwelling or a number of dwellings'.

(4) Aged 60 or more. This is the age at the time of supply of the mobility aid.

(5) HMRC expect the supplier to obtain a written declaration confirming the name, address and age of the beneficiary.

Zero-rate, Reduced Rate

Land, Property and Construction

LAND, PROPERTY AND CONSTRUCTION

15-000   Introduction

This section provides an overview of the application of VAT as it affects the construction, alteration and repair of buildings and the sale and letting of land and buildings.

Property and construction is a notoriously difficult and complex area of VAT, and businesses will be well advised to take professional advice before undertaking even the simplest of property-related transactions. The purpose of this section is to provide a general introduction to the subject, and is a guide to the factors that must be taken into consideration when dealing with property transactions and developments.

It is necessary to consider property transactions and construction services separately.

15-020   Introduction to land transactions

Transactions in land are normally exempt from VAT unless specifically standard- or zero-rated. Certain transactions may be converted to standard-rated supplies by use of the 'option to tax' provisions. The reduced rate of VAT does not apply to land transactions.

15-040   Meaning of land

'Land' is regarded as including buildings, structures, natural objects attached to the land, etc. so long as they remain attached. An interest in land or a right over land is a legal interest such as the freehold, a lease or tenancy, or a right to remove minerals from it.

Other material: Notice 742, para. 2.1

VAT Reporter: ¶13-542

15-060   Transactions in land

Land transactions include the grant, assignment or surrender of:

(1)   any interest in land;

(2)   any right over land; or

(3)   any licence to occupy land.

As a matter of principle, a right to call for, be granted or surrender such an interest, right or licence is itself an interest in land, and so capable of falling within the exemption. However, in Scotland such a personal right is not considered to be a right over land, and the legislation therefore makes specific provision bringing such a right within the exemption.

Some supplies falling within these categories are excluded from the exemption (see below).

Major interest

A major interest means a freehold interest or a lease or a tenancy for a term exceeding 21 years. In Scotland, 'freehold interest' is replaced by the interest of the proprietor of the *dominum utile* or in the case of land not held on feudal tenure, the estate or interest of the owner.

Legislation: VATA 1994, s. 96(1)

VAT Reporter: ¶33-155

Licence to occupy land

The exemption does not extend to all licences relating to land, but only to a licence to occupy the land.

A licence to occupy land is a licence falling short of a legal interest in the land. It must relate primarily to occupation of the property, rather than to doing something else which happens to involve going on to the land, and it must be possible to identify the land concerned.

HMRC's interpretation of 'licence to occupy land'

According to HMRC there is a licence to occupy land when a 'licensee is granted right of occupation' of:

- a defined area of land (land includes buildings);
- for an agreed duration;
- in return for payment; and
- has the right to occupy that area as owner and to exclude others from enjoying that right.

All four conditions must be met.

Characteristics of a 'licence to occupy land'

In *Sinclair Collis Ltd v C & E Commrs*, Sinclair Collis Ltd provided, operated and maintained cigarette vending machines for the sale of cigarettes in public houses, clubs and the like. Sinclair Collis could select the site for the machines and under the agreement the site owner could not unreasonably refuse permission for any change of siting. The agreement was for a period of two years during which time Sinclair Collis had the right to install and operate the machines which remained the property of Sinclair Collis.

In 1996, HMRC decided that these agreements should be exempt under the Sixth Directive (now Directive 2006/112). Sinclair Collis appealed saying that the supplies were taxable. The VAT and Duties Tribunal agreed with Sinclair Collis; this was overturned by the High Court. The Court of Appeal subsequently agreed with the High Court and so Sinclair Collis appealed to the House of Lords. The House of Lords sent a reference for a preliminary ruling to the ECJ asking if such an agreement was capable of amounting to the letting of immovable property within the meaning of art. 13(B)(b).

The ECJ found that:

> 'it is settled that the fundamental characteristic of the letting of immovable property for the purposes of art 13(B)(b) of the Sixth Directive (now Directive 2006/112 art. 135(1)(l), 135(2) lies in conferring on the person concerned, for an agreed period and for payment, the right to occupy property as if that person were the owner and to exclude any other person from enjoyment of that right (see to that effect *Goed Wonen para. 55 and C & E v Cantor Fitzgerald International* [2002] BVC 9).'

Thus, the arrangement between Sinclair Collis and the site owners was not the letting of immovable property. There were no rights of possession or control to Sinclair Collis other than those expressly set out in the agreement between the parties.

Hairdressers

The 'rent-a-chair' type of licence agreements have caused many disputes with HMRC. Although some have been successful in persuading the VAT and Duties Tribunals that the agreement amounts to a licence to occupy a specific area of land, see *Quaife*. This is now very unusual. The tendency is that such agreements should be regarded as taxable licences to trade even when a specific chair is assigned to the self-employed hairdresser.

Changes from 1 October 2012

Following the Budget 2012 the Finance Act included a measure that all such hairdresser chair rental agreements be subject to VAT from 1 October 2012. The measure included the letting of a 'whole floor, separate rooms or clearly defined area' when the lessor also provides 'hairdressing services' to the lessee. For these purposes hairdressing services means providing 'a hairdresser's assistant or cashier, the booking of appointments, the laundering of towels, the cleaning of the facilities ... the making of refreshments and other similar services'.

Consideration for the supply

The manner in which the consideration for the supply is calculated does not affect the nature of the supply made. For instance, in one case involving the grant of a concession to operate shops, the consideration for which was calculated as a percentage of sales from those shops, it was held that the substantive supply made amounted to a licence to occupy land and so was exempt. Great care is needed in the case of such supplies to ascertain exactly what rights, etc. are granted.

Legislation: Directive 2006/112 art. 135(1)(l), 135(2); VATA 1994, Sch. 9, Grp. 1, item 1(ma)

Cases: *Sinclair Collis Ltd v C & E Commrs* [2003] BVC 374; *Quaife* [1983] 2 BVC 208,010; *British Airports Authority v C & E Commrs* [1976] 1 BVC 97

VAT Reporter: ¶33-185

Other material: Notice 742, para. 2.5

15-080   Variations of leases

The variation of a lease may result in it being regarded as having been surrendered and a new lease granted. This is a very complex area of land law and professional advice should be sought in respect of the specific variation being made and the consideration being given. The VAT liability of consideration paid by a tenant to a landlord for the variation of the terms of a lease will follow that of any rent due under the lease.

If the correct analysis is that there has been a surrender of the existing lease and the grant of a new lease, then whether there is a VAT liability on the grant of the new lease depends upon whether an election to waive the exemption has been made.

Other material: Notice 742, para. 10.5

VAT Reporter: ¶34-775

15-100   Inducements, reverse premiums and reverse assignments

Offering an inducement to a prospective tenant to take a lease may be a supply of services by the prospective tenant to the landlord. The service supplied is not the grant of an interest in land. A reverse premium is where a landlord pays a tenant in order to induce the tenant to enter into a lease of the landlord's property.

In June 2005, HMRC revised its policy in respect of 'lease obligations, to which tenants are normally bound'. They no longer regard such obligations as an inducement creating a taxable supply by the prospective tenant to the landlord.

The policy concerning 'lease obligations, to which tenants are normally bound' is as follows:

'There will be a taxable supply only where payment is linked to benefits a tenant provides outside normal lease terms. However, merely putting such a benefit as an obligation in a lease will not mean it ceases to be a taxable supply.'

A tenant may provide 'benefits … outside normal lease terms' by agreeing to make improvements/refurbishments to the property or by 'acting as anchor tenant'. Improvements/refurbishments may be 'carrying out building work to improve the property …' or carrying out fitting-out work or refurbishment works for which the landlord has responsibility and is paying the tenant to undertake.

HMRC's views on reverse assignments is as follows:

'A reverse assignment is where a tenant pays a person in order to induce that person to take an assignment of the existing lease.

Mirror Group and *Cantor Fitzgerald International* were both references from the High Court under Article 177 of the EC Treaty (now Article 234) to the ECJ for preliminary rulings on points of law that involved property deals. The cases were not joined although the ECJ issued the rulings on the same day and both of the cases involved Article 13B(b) of the Sixth Directive.

The facts

Mirror Group entered into an agreement with Olympia & York Canary Wharf Ltd (in administration), whereby a total of about £12 million plus VAT could be paid to Mirror Group. Part of this payment would be as an inducement to take a lease and part as an inducement to take up an option for leases. The sum of £6.5 million was deposited in an account so that when the current leases ended and Mirror Group had to enter into new leases, the money, or part of the money, would be released.

Prior to the transactions, Mirror Group had no interest in the land.

Cantor Fitzgerald International agreed to take over a lease on some property from Wako International (Europe) Limited (Wako) in return for a payment of £1.5 million.

Prior to the transaction, Cantor Fitzgerald had no interest in the property.

The problem

Were these payments liable to VAT or were they exempt under Article 13B(b)?

The law

Article 6 of the Sixth VAT Directive states that any transaction that does not constitute a supply of goods is a supply of services and that services may include "obligations to refrain from an act or to tolerate an act or situation".

Article 13B(b) of the Sixth VAT Directive allows the letting or leasing of immovable property to be an exempt supply.

The rulings

In the case of the payments to Mirror Group, it was decided that neither payment constituted consideration for supplies under Article 13B(b). It was not specified exactly what supplies were actually made by Mirror Group. It was sufficient for the ECJ to rule that the supplies were not exempt under this legislation because Mirror Group did not have an interest in the land prior to the transactions.

In the second case, it was ruled that the acceptance for a consideration of an assignment of the lease of a property in this situation was not exempt because again Cantor Fitzgerald did not have an interest in the land prior to the transaction.

These cases must be distinguished from the situation in *Lubbock Fine*. Neither Mirror Group nor Cantor had any interest in the land. Lubbock Fine was in possession of a lease and thus had an interest in land at the start of proceedings.'

See flowcharts 18-900, 18-905 and 18-910.

Legislation: Directive 2006/112, art. 135(1)(l), 135(2)

Cases: *Mirror Group Plc v C & E Commrs* (case C-409/98) [2002] BVC 16; *Lubbock Fine & Co v C & E Commrs* (case C-63/92) [1993] BVC 287; *Cantor Fitzgerald International v C & E Commrs* (case C-108/99) [2002] BVC 9

Other material: Business Brief 12/05, 15 June 2005; HMRC Guidance Manuals Vol V1–8, Section 2.2

VAT Reporter: ¶34-800

15-120 Release of restrictive covenants

The release of a restrictive covenant over land involves the grant of an interest in or right over the land, and so the supply made is exempt from VAT unless the supplier has opted for taxation.

Other material: Notice 742 para. 10.6

VAT Reporter: ¶33-327

15-140 Joint ownership

The legal position where property is owned jointly is far from being clear. This has not mattered unduly in the past, when land transactions have generally been exempt or zero-rated for VAT purposes. The introduction of standard rating for many property transactions, and particularly the option for taxation, means that VAT must now be brought into consideration where property is owned jointly.

It is also necessary to consider the position where there is a difference between the legal ownership of land (i.e. the names on the deeds) and the beneficial ownership. This deems a 'grant', etc. to be made by the person to whose benefit the consideration for the grant, etc. accrues.

The 'person to whom the benefit accrues' was considered in *Abbey National v C & E Commrs* [2005] BVC 331. The High Court endorsed the view that 'accrues' may be interpreted as a right to receive rental income. Thus, for VAT purposes the 'beneficial owner', and the person who must account for VAT, is the person to whom the proceeds accrue.

HMRC normally want joint owners to register as a partnership. This may be a convenient solution for VAT purposes but the joint owners should be sure that they are registering 'as if they were a partnership' rather than as an actual partnership in order to avoid prejudicing their position for other purposes.

If the theoretical difficulties of joint ownership are recognised in advance, they can often be resolved by agreeing a suitable treatment with HMRC. Where the joint owners are on good terms, this is usually the best practical solution, and avoids the cost of litigation.

In the case of joint owners who are at odds with each other, this sort of solution may not be available. It seems likely to be this sort of case which will lead to litigation to resolve (or confuse) the technical position.

Cases: *Abbey National v C & E Commrs* [2005] BVC 331

Legislation: VATA 1994, Sch. 10, para. 40

VAT Reporter: ¶33-150

Other material: Notice 742, Section 7; Guidance Manuals Vol V1–8 Section 4.2

15-160   Zero-rated supplies of buildings

Introduction

In order to qualify for zero-rating, the transaction must involve the first grant of a major interest in a new dwelling, relevant residential building or building for charitable use. Further restrictions apply in respect of substantially reconstructed listed buildings.

When the major interest is a lease, zero-rating only applies to the premium payable or, where there is no premium payable, to the first rent payment.

Checklist

Within each category, there are certain conditions and reservations. Anyone dealing with potentially zero-rated land transactions should check the following carefully:

(1) the required grant of a major interest is made by the appropriate person;

(2) that a new dwelling, relevant residential building or building for charitable use is being created, and

(3) the required certificate is obtained for relevant residential buildings or buildings for charitable use.

In the case of a building for relevant residential or charitable use, the supplier must hold a certificate of use issued by the customer, before the supply is made, in order to qualify for zero-rating.

See flowcharts 15-570 and 18-920.

What is 'new'

'New' is not defined in the legislation.

For the purposes of the zero-rating schedule, a 'new' building may be created by the following:

- the creation of an entire building;
  the demolition, or almost complete demolition, of an existing building and the erection of another building;
- an enlargement to an existing building to the extent that the enlargement creates an additional dwelling or dwellings;
- certain annexes to buildings used for charitable purposes;
- conversion of a non-residential building;
- renovation of a disused residential building; and
- a substantially reconstructed protected building.

VAT Reporter: ¶33-605; ¶33-327

The creation of an entirely new building

This is self-evident. If there has been a building on the site, it should have been demolished to ground level although any cellars, basement or concrete base may have been retained.

The demolition, or almost complete demolition, of an existing building and the erection of another building

The complete demolition of an existing building is self-evident. However, there are occasions when a building is not completely demolished. In such instances, a single façade, or double façade on a corner site, may be retained where it is a condition of the planning permission granted. Any demolition work should have been completed before work on the new structure started.

In *Clarke* a condition of the planning consent was that certain walls had to be retained. The amount to be retained was such that the rebuild was not a 'new' building. In the event the wall to be retained fell down and had to be rebuilt. The First Tier Tribunal disregarded this. They ruled that what matters is the amount to be retained under the terms of the planning permission. The Trustees of the Eaton Mews Trust were successful in showing that although the planning permission did not specify that a certain wall was to be retained, it did refer to the plans showing the retained wall submitted with the application. The Tribunal accepted that this was 'planning permission'.

Other material: Notice 708, para. 3.2.3

Cases: *Clarke* [2010] TC 00552; [2010] UKFTT 258 (TC); *Trustees of the Eaton Mews Trust* [2012] TC 01943; [2012] UKFTT 249 (TC)

Legislation: VATA 1994, Sch. 8, Grp. 5, Note (18)

An enlargement to an existing building to the extent that the enlargement creates an additional dwelling or dwellings

This would include situations where, for example, a flat is constructed on top of an existing building or a semi-detached dwelling is constructed using a wall of an existing building as the party wall. It is essential that the existing building is enlarged or extended and not merely rearranged. If the existing building is a residential building, the new dwelling must be wholly within the extension, that is, not the conversion of an attic or similar.

Legislation: VATA 1994, Sch. 8, Grp. 5, Note (16)(b)

Other material: Notice 708, para. 3.2.45

Certain annexes to buildings used for charitable purposes

The whole annex must be intended for a relevant charitable purpose (see below). The annex must be capable of functioning independently although may share supplies of power and water with the main building. The new structure must neither be the main entrance to the existing building nor must the existing building provide the main entrance to the annex.

There is no statutory definition of annex (or extension) for these purposes. Whether something is an annex (or extension) is normally a matter of fact and degree based upon what was there before and after the construction was carried out. The decision must be made based upon the following:

'... the answer must be given after an objective examination of the physical characters of the building or buildings at the two points in time, having regard (inter alia) to similarities and differences in appearance, the layout, the uses for which they are physically capable of being put and the functions which they are physically capable of performing. The terms of planning permissions, the motives behind undertaking the works and the intended or subsequent actual use are irrelevant, save possibly to illuminate the potential for use inherent in the building or buildings.'

Legislation: VATA 1994, Sch. 8, Grp. 5, Note (16)(c) and (17)

Other material: Notice 708, para. 3.2.3

Cases: *Cantrell (t/a Foxearth Lodge Nursing Home) v C & E Commrs* [2003] BVC 196

Conversion of a non-residential building

In order to qualify as a non-residential building, the existing structure must never have been designed or adapted for use as a dwelling, a number of dwellings or relevant residential purpose (see below).

Care must be taken when dealing with the conversion of a building that has been or is part non-residential and part residential. Incorporation of a residential part with what was a non-residential area of the building into a dwelling may result in that dwelling not being a 'new' dwelling. Blom-Cooper indicates that where a building is already part residential, the conversion of the non-residential part could not be treated as 'converting ... a non-residential part of a building' unless the result of that conversion was to create an additional dwelling or dwellings.

HMRC have stated that they do not consider that the CA decision concerning Jacobs, a DIY housebuilder has any impact in similar situations where a developer converts a mixeduse building into dwellings and the number of dwellings post conversion is greater than that pre-conversion. Items 1(b) and 3(a) of Group 5 to Schedule VATA 1994 restricts the zero-rating to dwelling(s) derived from the conversion of the non-residential part. They are maintaining their policy that where developers are concerned the zero-rate will not apply to any dwelling that utilises any part of the original residential part of the building.

Cases: *C & E Commrs v Blom-Cooper* [2003] BVC 416; *Ivor Jacobs* [2005] BVC 690

Legislation: VATA 1994, Sch. 8, Grp. 5, items 1(b) and 3(a) and Note (9)

Other material: Notice 708, para. 5.3

Renovation of a disused residential building

A building that was once either designed or adapted as a residential building may be brought back into the housing stock. In order to be within the scope of the zero-rating schedule, it must have been constructed more than 10 years before the grant of the major interest and no part of it used as a dwelling or for a relevant residential purpose during these 10 years.

A developer can zero-rate his sale of a renovated house provided the sale takes place after the dwelling has been empty, or not used as a dwelling, for 10 years. This means a developer who does renovation work before the building has been empty for 10 years may still zero-rate his sale provided the renovated home has been an empty dwelling for 10 years when he sells it. It is the developer's responsibility to hold proof that their claim for input tax can be verified. HM Revenue and Customs will accept evidence which, on the balance of probabilities, shows that the building has been an empty home for at least 10 years. The evidence can include electoral roll and council tax data, information from utilities companies, evidence from empty-property officers in local authorities, or information from other reliable sources. If a developer holds a letter from an empty-property officer certifying that a home has been empty for 10 years or will have been empty for 10 years at the time of sale, no other evidence is needed. If an empty-property officer is unsure about the length of time a home has been empty, he should write with his best estimate and HMRC may than call for other supporting evidence.

Legislation: VATA 1994, Sch. 8, Grp. 5. Note (7)

Other material: Notice 708, para. 5.3.2

'Substantially reconstructing' a listed building

The supply by the owner of a protected qualifying building (i.e. a dwelling, relevant residential purpose building, or a building used solely for a charitable purpose) of a major interest in it is zero-rated if the supplier has substantially reconstructed the building.

From 1 October 2012 the two tests used to determine if a protected building has been substantially reconstructed are abolished. They are replaced by a single test and some transitional reliefs.

The single test introduced by FA 2012 means a protected building is only 'substantially reconstructed' when:

> 'the reconstructed building incorporates no more of the original building (that is to say, the building as it was before the reconstruction began) than the external walls, together with other external features of architectural or historic interest.'

Transitional reliefs

Subject to conditions, a protected building is also 'substantially constructed' when either of two transitional tests apply. The transitional tests are as follows:

(1)   When written contracts were entered into, or listed building consent was applied for, before 21 March 2012, there is a substantial reconstruction when at least three-fifths of the total work done to the building (measured by cost) could be zero-rated under the transitional rules for 'approved alterations' – see 15-380.

(2)   In other circumstances a building is 'substantially reconstructed' when:

   (a)   at least 10 per cent of the reconstructions (measured by cost) was completed by 21 March 2012; and

   (b)   if written contracts had been entered into, or listed building consent was applied for, before 21 March 2012, at least three-fifths of the total work done to the building (measured by cost) would be zero-rated under the transitional rules for 'approved alterations' – see 15-380.

Pre-October 2012

The substantially reconstructed building must also meet one of the following conditions:

(1)   at least 60 per cent of the works carried out to effect the reconstruction measured by reference to cost, must be such that they qualify for zero-rating under the further zero-rating for the services of builders, etc. covered below. However, architects' fees, etc. which are specifically excluded from zero-rating, are left out of this calculation and Notice 708; or

(2)   the reconstructed building must incorporate no more of the original building than the external walls and other external features of architectural or historic interest.

If either of these tests is met, then the sale of the building, or the letting of it under a major interest lease, will amount to a zero-rated supply. As for new dwellings, only the premium or first rental is zero-rated for a leasehold supply.

See flowchart 15-610.

Cases: *Cheltenham College Enterprises Ltd* [2010] UKFTT 118 (TC); [2010] TC 00429

Legislation: VATA 1994, Sch. 8, Grp. 6, item 1;

VAT Reporter: ¶34-200

Other material: Notice 708, Section 10

Qualifying buildings

Dwelling

A building is designed as a dwelling or a number of dwellings where in relation to each dwelling the following conditions are satisfied:

- the dwelling consists of self-contained living accommodation;
- there is no provision for direct internal access from the dwelling to any other dwelling or part of a dwelling;
- the separate use, or disposal of the dwelling is not prohibited by the terms of any covenant, statutory planning consent or similar provision; and
- statutory planning consent has been granted in respect of that dwelling and its construction or conversion has been carried out in accordance with that consent.

A dwelling includes a garage constructed at the same time for occupation with it. However, it does not include a house whose occupation throughout the year is prevented by the terms of tenure or of a planning permission, covenant, etc.

A dwelling includes a garage constructed at the same time for occupation with it. However, it does not include a house whose occupation throughout the year is prevented by the terms of tenure or of a planning permission, covenant, etc.

The Upper Tribunal has concluded that 'separate use' means 'separate from' and that the purpose of this condition is 'to prevent zero-rating unless the new subsidiary dwelling could, in accordance with planning permission, be used independently'. That the new structure may be used as for and as a 'separate household' is not sufficient.

'Separate use' may not be allowed by the planning consent. In a case involving a new flat, it was sufficient to deny zero-rating. The offending condition in the planning consent read as follows:

> 'The ... flat shall be ancillary to the residential use of *(the existing dwelling)* ... and shall not be occupied other than by visiting friends and members of the family of the occupier of *(the*

existing dwelling) … To ensure that … (*the flat*) … remains as ancillary accommodation to and dependent upon (*the existing dwelling*) …'

'Extra care' accommodation

'Extra care' accommodation is commonly 'self contained flats, houses, bungalows or maisonettes that are sold or let with the option for the occupant to purchase varying degrees of care to suit his or her needs as and when they arise'. These are often built in the grounds of care homes and similar establishments.

For planning purposes, local authorities often classify care accommodation as 'Use Class C2'. This makes no difference to the VAT liability which should be determined in the usual way.

Cases: *Bracegirdle v R & C Commrs* [2009] BVC 4,038; *R & C Commrs v Lunn* [2009] UKUT 244 (TCC); [2010] BVC 1,503

Legislation: VATA 1994, Sch. 8, Grp. 5, Note (7)

Other material: Notice 708, para. 14.2.1; Revenue and Customs Brief 47/11

VAT Reporter: ¶21-350

Relevant residential purpose

Use for a relevant residential purpose means use as:

(1)   a home or other institution providing residential accommodation for children;

(2)   a home or other institution providing residential accommodation with personal care for persons in need of personal care by reason of old age, disablement, past or present dependence on alcohol or drugs or past or present mental disorder;

(3)   a hospice;

(4)   residential accommodation for students or school pupils;

(5)   residential accommodation for members of any of the armed forces;

(6)   a monastery, nunnery or similar establishment; or

(7)   an institution which is the sole or main residence of at least 90 per cent of its residents.

However, use as a hospital, a prison or similar institution, or an hotel, inn or similar establishment is specifically excluded from the definition.

The zero-rating is available for a building, or part of a building, intended solely for qualifying use. HMRC interpret 'solely' as being 95% or more. If part of the building is intended solely for qualifying use and part is not, an apportionment must be made.

Cases: *C & E Commrs v Link Housing Association Ltd* [1992] BVC 113

Legislation: VATA 1994, Sch. 8, Grp. 5, Note (6)

Other material: Notice 708, para. 14.6; Revenue and Customs Brief 33/10

VAT Reporter: ¶33-450

Relevant charitable purpose

Use for a relevant charitable purpose means use by a charity:

(1)   otherwise than in the course of a business; or

(2)   as a village hall or similarly in providing social or recreational facilities for a local community.

The zero-rating is available for a building, or part of a building, intended solely for qualifying use. If part of the building is intended solely for qualifying use and part is not, an apportionment must be made.

The zero-rating may also apply to an annex capable of functioning independently although it may share supplies of power and water with the main building. The new structure must not be the main entrance to the existing building nor the existing building provide the main entrance to the annex.

The way in which 'solely' is interpreted and quantified changed with effect from 1 July 2009. However, the old and new methods are both available during the transitional year ending on 30 June 2010.

Until 30 June 2009

By extra-statutory concession, non-qualifying use up to 10 per cent of the total may be ignored, and zero-rating obtained despite such non-qualifying use. This concession has generally been applied by comparing the amount of time the building was used solely for non-business purposes with the total time it was available for use.

HMRC have made available alternative methods for calculating the extent of non-business use, although specific permission is required to use the alternative methods of calculation.

Extra-statutory concession 3.29 is as follows:

'Charities can now calculate the extent of qualifying non-business use by reference to time, floor space, or the number of people using the building. The non-qualifying use of the building will be disregarded provided that –

- the building is used solely for non-business activity for 90 per cent or more of the time it is available for use;
- 90 per cent or more of the floor space of the building is used solely for non-business activity; or
- 90 per cent or more of the people using the building are engaged solely in non-business activity.

The above method can only be applied to the building as a whole, apart from the time-based method which can also be applied to parts of the building. In addition, permission must be sought from Customs to use any of the methods, except the time-based method when applied to the whole building.'

From 1 July 2009

From 1 July 2009, the extra-statutory concession is removed. HMRC interpret 'solely' as meaning that the relevant charitable use must be at least 95 per cent. However, the relevant charitable use may be quantified using any 'fair and reasonable' method.

Transitional period

During the year to 30 June 2010, charities may choose between the concession used to 1 July 2009 and the replacement interpretation operative from this date. If choosing to use the redundant concession, there must be a 'meaningful' start to the construction work or, if buying a completed building, a 'meaningful' deposit paid before 30 June 2010.

Other material: Notice 708, Section 14.7; Notice 48, para. 3.29; Revenue and Customs Brief 39/09; VAT Information Sheet 08/09; HM Revenue and Customs Brief 26/10

Legislation: VATA 1994, Sch. 8, Grp. 5, Note (6)

VAT Reporter: ¶33-475

15-180   Certificate of use

The grant of a major interest in new relevant residential accommodation or a building to be used for charitable purposes may only be zero-rated if, before the grant is made, a certificate of use is issued by the person who will be using the building.

The form of certificate required is shown in Notice 708.

If an incorrect certificate is issued, the person issuing it is liable to a penalty equal to the relief incorrectly given.

Legislation: VATA 1994, s. 62

Other material: Notice 708, Section 16

VAT Reporter: ¶33-825

15-200   Standard-rated supplies of land

There are two reasons why a transaction in land may be standard-rated. Firstly, it may be standard-rated because the law stipulates that it is not zero-rated and is not exempt. Secondly, it may gain standard-rating because the owner has elected to waive the exemption – or opted to tax the land.

The law stipulates that the following supplies are neither zero-rated nor exempt. Thus, they become standard-rated.

Freehold sale of new building, etc.

The freehold supply of a partly completed or new building (other than a dwelling or a building for relevant residential or charitable use) or civil engineering work is excluded from exemption.

A building is 'new' for three years from the earlier of the date when a certificate of practical completion is issued or the date when it is first fully occupied.

The supply of a long lease of a building is not excluded from exemption under this head. Great care is needed when advising on this, as it is not uncommon for a person granting or assigning a very long lease (say 999 years) to refer to the transaction as a 'sale' of the building, which may give the adviser the false impression that a freehold supply is intended.

It follows that the freehold sale of a new commercial building gives rise to a standard-rated supply, while the letting of it (or sale of a lease) gives rise to an exempt supply. Once the building has ceased to be 'new' (when it is over three years old), either the sale or letting of it will be exempt, unless the building is subject to an election to waive the exemption.

For grants made on or after 10 April 2003, the whole of the consideration will be taxable under this rule if the original grant was made while the building was new. This corrects a defect in the original legislation whereby, if the tax point for part of the consideration was deferred until the building was no longer new, under the tax point rules for cases where part of the consideration is uncertain at the time of the supply, that part was regarded as consideration for an exempt supply (see 4-180).

Legislation: VATA 1994, Sch. 8, Grp 5, Notes (2)–(6)

Other material: Notice 742, Section 3

VAT Reporter: ¶34-525

Supplies under developmental leases, etc.

A supply under a developmental lease, tenancy, etc. is excluded from exemption.

Legislation: VATA 1994, Sch. 9, Grp. 1, item 1(b)

VAT Reporter: ¶34-901

Supplies of sporting rights

The supply of an interest in or right over land which consists of a right to take game or fish is excluded from exemption. This clearly applies to a supply consisting only of the sporting rights, but the UK law takes this further.

On a supply other than a freehold sale of land, if the interest supplied includes valuable sporting rights, an apportionment is required so that the sporting rights element is taxed. Whether this apportionment provision is compatible with the general principles of VAT law is open to question. It seems inconsistent with the notion that a single supply is being taxed.

Legislation: VATA 1994, Sch. 9, Grp. 1, item 1(c)

Other material: Notice 742, Section 6

Cases: *Skatteministeriet v Henriksen (Case 173/88)* (1989) 5 BVC 140

VAT Reporter: ¶34-902

Hotel accommodation

The provision of sleeping accommodation, accommodation in rooms provided with sleeping accommodation (i.e. a suite), or accommodation provided for the purpose of catering in a hotel, inn, boarding house or similar establishment is excluded from exemption.

'Similar establishment' includes such premises as certain service flats, where sleeping accommodation is provided with or without food preparation facilities, if the accommodation is held out as being suitable for use by visitors or travellers.

Accommodation provided in a hotel, etc. is taxable even if the customers concerned are in long term occupation of the accommodation. However, some relief will then be available by way of the value of supply provisions (see 4-860).

Where a conference room is hired for a meeting or similar organised by a third party and where meals and sleeping accommodation are provided under the 24-hour delegate rate, from 19 January 2006 HMRC, will accept that each should be treated as separate supplies.

The room hire will be exempt (except where an option to tax is in place) and the other supplies are taxable. Where there is one consideration paid for supplies having different liabilities a fair and reasonable apportionment should be made.

Legislation: VATA 1994, Sch. 9, Grp. 1, item 1(d)

Other material: Notice 709/3, Section 2 and 3

Cases: *McGrath v C & E Commrs* [1992] BVC 51

VAT Reporter: ¶34-904

Holiday accommodation

The provision of holiday accommodation is excluded from exemption. This is expressed as excluding the supply of 'any interest in, right over or licence to occupy holiday accommodation', so covers rather more than the direct supply of holiday accommodation to holidaymakers.

In this context, 'holiday accommodation' includes accommodation in a building, caravan, houseboat, or tent which is advertised or held out as holiday accommodation or as suitable for holiday or leisure use, other than accommodation in a hotel, etc. However, it does not follow that once a building has been held out as suitable for holiday accommodation, some future supply of it for other purposes, having no connection with the advertisement or holding out of the property, is also excluded from exemption. The subsequent supply must be considered on its own merits.

The exclusion is not limited to living accommodation, but can also act to prevent exemption for the supply of other accommodation, such as a beach hut.

The exclusion covers the outright freehold sale of a new building (less than three years old) where a covenant or planning permission prevents the purchaser from occupying the property throughout the year. It also includes the granting of a tenancy, etc. under which the tenant is permitted to erect and occupy holiday accommodation.

However, the freehold sale of a holiday property over three years old qualifies for exemption, as does a premium on the granting of a tenancy, lease or licence over such a property.

The tribunal decided in *Ashworth* [1996] BVC 2,110 that it was not enough for a restriction on all year round use to make a property 'holiday accommodation'. There must be other elements present. HMRC will also consider if the property is part of a holiday complex, if the property is marketed as holiday accommodation and any restrictions imposed by the planning authority or developer.

Legislation: VATA 1994, Sch. 9, Grp. 1, item 1(e)

Other material: Notice 709/3, Section 5

Cases: *Cooper & Chapman (Builders) Ltd v C & E Commrs* [1993] BVC 11; *Poole Borough Council* [1992] BVC 755; *Ashworth* [1996] BVC 2,110

VAT Reporter: ¶34-906

Seasonal pitches for caravans

There is an exclusion for the supply of seasonal pitches for caravans and for the supply of facilities at caravan parks to the occupants of these pitches.

The exclusion applies where a caravan pitch is supplied for a period less than a year or, if supplied for a longer period, where some covenant, planning permission, etc. prevents the customer from living in a caravan on the pitch throughout the period for which the pitch is provided.

From 1 March 2012 a pitch on a holiday site occupied by an employee as his or her principal place of residence is exempt.

Legislation: VATA 1994, Sch. 9, Grp. 1, item 1(f); VATA 1994, Sch. 9, Grp. 1, Note (14)

Other material: Notice 701/20, para. 4.1; Revenue and Customs Brief 05/12

VAT Reporter: ¶34-914

Camping and tent pitches

The provision of pitches for tents, or of camping facilities, is excluded from exemption.

Legislation: VATA 1994, Sch. 9, Grp. 1, item 1(g)

Other material: Notice 709/3, para. 6.1

VAT Reporter: ¶34-920

Parking facilities

The granting of facilities to park vehicles is normally standard rated.

A common exception to this is when parking arrangements are acquired with or linked to an agreement to buy or rent a dwelling. These parking rights may be exempt or zero-rated depending on circumstances.

Local authorities

Local councils had always accounted for VAT on these charges until the *Fazenda Pública* Case. After this, 127 local authorities claimed a total of £129 million in VAT repayments on the grounds that these parking charges by local authorities, acting as bodies governed by public law should not have been subject to the tax. HMRC refused the claims.

It was established that the local authorities were right, except where the lack of tax on the charges would lead to significant distortion of competition. The High Court sent a reference to the ECJ for a preliminary ruling on this.

The ECJ ruled that:

- The 'distortion of competition' should be decided by the activity itself without the evaluation of any local market in particular.
- 'Would lead to' must be interpreted as meaning not only actual competition but also potential competition, where such potential competition is a real possibility not merely a hypothetical situation.

- 'Significant' means that actual or potential distortion must be more than negligible.

The matter has been returned to the High Court to resolve.

Excess charges

HMRC have considered the matter of excess charges imposed on motorists for various infringements of parking rules both in Local Authority owned facilities and in other car parks.

It has been decided that where the excess charge is a penalty for infringement of the contract for parking facilities, that charge is not liable to VAT.

In a case in which the owner of a car park engaged a company to manage the car park, excess charges collected and retained by the company managing the site were liable to VAT. The Upper Tribunal ruled that the company managing the site had to account for VAT on the excess charged because it had no interest in the land and the excess charges which it retained were further consideration for the services which it supplied to the owner of the car park.

Cases: *Dowse* (1973) 1 BVC 1,012; *R & C Commrs v Isle of Wight Council* (C-288/07) [2008] BVC 799; *Fazenda Pública v Camara Municipal do Porto* (C-446/98) [2001] BVC 493; *Vehicle Control Services Ltd* [2012] UKUT 130 (TCC); [2012] BVC 1,690

Legislation: VATA 1994, Sch. 9, Grp. 1, item 1(h)

VAT Reporter: ¶10-602; ¶34-924

Other material: HM Revenue and Customs Brief 57/08; Notice 742, Section 4

Right to fell timber

The granting of a right to fell or remove standing timber is excluded from exemption.

VAT Reporter: ¶34-928

Legislation: VATA 1994, Sch. 9, Grp. 1, item 1(j)

Storage of aircraft and boats

The granting of facilities for housing or storing aircraft, or for mooring, anchoring, berthing or storing ships, boats, and other vessels is excluded from exemption. This is the case even if the vessel concerned is used as a permanent residence.

Other material: Notice 742, para. 3.1

Cases: *Roberts* [1992] BVC 738

Legislation: VATA 1994, Sch. 9, Grp. 1, item 1(k)

VAT Reporter: ¶34-932

Self storage

From 1 October 2012, the self storage of goods (but not the stabling of animals) is excluded from the exemption and is standard-rated. This includes self storage in a container, any other fully enclosed structure, unit or building.

The latest legislation also includes some concessions and an anti-avoidance measure. These are as follows:

(1) self storage provided to a charity which uses this 'otherwise than in the course of a business" remains exempt unless the supplier has opted to tax;

(2) when there is a grant of a building of which part of the building is self storage, the self storage is not caught by this piece of legislation when it is 'ancillary' to the other use of the building. The self storage remains exempt unless the supplier opts to tax;

(3) the anti-avoidance measure applies when self storage is supplied to a 'connected person' and the lessor is required to make Capital Goods Scheme adjustments (see 7-760) in respect of these facilities. This ensures the supply of self storage to the 'connected person' is exempt. The lessor is unlikely to be able change this because of another anti-avoidance measure (see 15-300).

Legislation: VATA 1994, Sch. 9, Grp. 1, item 1(ka)

Boxes at theatres, etc.

The grant of a right to occupy a box, seat, or other accommodation at a sports ground, theatre, concert hall or other place of entertainment is excluded from exemption.

VAT Reporter: ¶34-936

Legislation: VATA 1994, Sch. 9, Grp. 1, item 1(i)

Sporting facilities

The supply of facilities for playing any sport or participating in physical recreation is excluded from exemption, except for lettings in excess of 24 hours and certain lettings to schools, etc.

The exclusion in respect of sporting facilities does not apply if the granting of the facilities is:

(1) for a continuous period of use greater than 24 hours; or

(2) for a series of 10 or more periods of any duration, where each is for the same activity and at the same place, the interval between periods is never less than one day or more than 14 days, the fee relates to the whole series and is evidenced by a written agreement, the use of the facilities is exclusive to the customer, and the customer is a school, club, association, or organisation representing clubs and associations.

Commercially operated sports leagues are not considered to be making an exempt supply of a pitch – football or the like – instead, HMRC regard the service as a standard rated composite supply.

Other material: HMRC Brief 04/11; Notice 742, Section 5

Legislation: VATA 1994, Sch. 9, Grp. 1, item 1(m)

VAT Reporter ¶34-940

Hairdressers' rental agreements

See 15-060 for details of the changes introduced in 2012 making hairdressers' chair rentals standard-rated.

Legislation: VATA 1994, Sch. 9, Grp. 1, item 1(ma)

Option to acquire taxable interest

The grant of a right (including an equitable right, a right under an option and, in relation to land in Scotland, a personal right) to be granted an interest, etc. the supply of which would be excluded from exemption is itself excluded from exemption.

Other material: Notice 742, para. 7.4

Legislation: VATA 1994, Sch. 9, Grp. 1, item 1(n)

VAT Reporter: ¶34-942

15-220   Exempt supplies of land

The basic rule is that the grant, assignment or surrender of any interest in, or right over, land or of any licence to occupy land is an exempt supply unless specifically standard-rated or zero-rated – see above and flowchart 15-630.

Legislation: VATA 1994, Sch. 9 Grp. 1

VAT Reporter: ¶33-327

15-260   Input tax recovery

When exempt supplies are made, the partial exemption situation must be considered (see 6-950 et seq). Property transactions may also be affected by the capital goods scheme which affects relevant land transactions costing more than £250,000 (see 7-760).

Property supplies can be taxable (either standard-rated or zero-rated), or exempt. Frequently, the most important issue is the recoverability, or otherwise, of input tax arising, and this depends on the liability of the supplies made.

Other material: Notice 706, Section 11

15-280   Miscellaneous land-related transactions

Change of use of a zero-rated relevant residential or charitable building

The entitlement to zero-rating by a person who constructs or purchases a new relevant residential or new charitable building depends upon the intended use of the building. The change of use of such a building (whether with or without a change in ownership) can trigger anti-avoidance provisions designed to negate the benefit of the zero-rating. These apply if the change occurs within ten years of the completion of the building.

When the change takes place there is a deemed self-supply to recover some or all of the tax that would have been charged on the new building.

The method of calculation is amended from 1 March 2011 for buildings completed on or after 1 March 2011 and when the change in use occurs after this date.

Legislation: VATA 1994, Sch. 10, para. 35–39

Other material: VAT Information Sheet 04/11; HMRC Business Brief 13/11

VAT Reporter: ¶50-280

Liability of service charges

It is common for property to be let in return for a rental and for the lease to provide for payment of a service charge in addition, to cover costs associated with the general running of the property, maintenance of common areas, etc. As a general rule, the service charge is seen as being additional consideration for the landlord's supplies under the lease, and so will be exempt or standard-rated depending whether the landlord opted for taxation. In the case of residential property, it will always be exempt, as an option for taxation is ineffective in such cases.

Domestic accommodation

This treatment of service charges payable to freeholders, or to independent service companies, has given rise to anomalous treatment in the case of domestic accommodation. Occupants of flats, etc paying service charges to freeholders or service providers other than their landlords have faced a VAT cost, while those paying them to their landlords have not. A concession applies, under which all service charges in respect of domestic accommodation can be exempted. Service charges for non-domestic accommodation are not affected by this concession, and

561

their liability is determined in accordance with the rules set out above. Service charges in respect of holiday lettings have always been and remain standard-rated.

Following the European Court of Justice case of *RLRE Tellmer Property sro v Financni reditelstvi v Ústí nad Labem* (Case C-572/07) [2010] BVC 802, there was concern that all tenants would have to pay VAT on service charge payable to the landlord for the upkeep of common areas. After considering the ECJ judgment, HMRC have concluded that they need not change the way in which VAT is accounted for service charges. HMRC decided that changes were not necessary because in *RLRE Tellmer* tenants had the right to engage someone other than the landlord to clean, etc the common areas. Most UK tenants do not have this choice. They are bound by the lease to rely on the landlord to maintain the common areas.

However, in the case of service charges in respect of freehold property, there is no supply of land to which the service charge can be attributed, with the result that it becomes consideration for a standard-rated supply of the underlying services provided. Also, there are many instances where the service charge is payable, not to the landlord, but to a separate entity (often a company set up for the purpose) acting in its own right. Again, the charges are, in principle, consideration for a taxable supply of services.

Other material: Notice 48, Extra statutory concessions, para. 3.18; HMRC Brief 67/09 issued on 27 October 2009; Notice 742, Sections 11 and 12

VAT Reporter: ¶37-550

Cases: *RLRE Tellmer Property sro v Financni reditelstvi v Ústí nad Labem* (Case C-572/07) [2010] BVC 802

Caravan sites

It is common for caravan site proprietors to recharge the following costs to caravan owners:

- business rates;
- water/sewerage rates;
- one-off charges such as first time connection to gas, electricity, water and sewerage.

The proprietor of the site must account for VAT on these as if they are additional rent receipts. Consequently the VAT liability is the same as the underlying rent. If the rent is standard rated, the above recharges are also standard rated.

When site owners charge caravan owners for 'the actual consumption of water and sewerage for individual pitches (that is, through metering at the individual pitch)' the supply of water and/or sewerage is zero rated.

An extra statutory concession by which VAT was not chargeable on the above was withdrawn with effect from 1 January 2012.

Other material: HMRC Brief 37/11

Milk quotas

It is possible to transfer milk quotas without the need to attach them to specific land. HMRC have issued guidance identifying three possible ways of transferring quota, and their view of the VAT treatments:

(1) land is sold or leased with quota attaching to it. This is seen as a single supply of land, and is therefore regarded as exempt or standard-rated depending whether the landlord has opted for taxation. HMRC say that this applies even if separate sums are agreed and shown on the invoice in respect of the land and the quota;

(2) if quota is transferred in isolation, this is a supply of services and, as it does not fall within any exemption or zero-rating (not being an interest in land), it is standard-rated;

(3) if quota is transferred with a grazing licence, HMRC see two supplies, a zero-rated supply of animal feed under the licence and a standard-rated supply of quota.

Other material: HMRC manuals Vol V1–7 Liability Chapter 1 part G (Milk Quotas); Notice 742

VAT Reporter: ¶15-670

Land swaps/non-monetary consideration

It is not unusual for transactions to be carried out which involve swaps of land, with no monetary consideration passing. Care is needed in determining the terms of the contract as, in the absence of any specific provision, there seems to be no legal basis on which a person making a standard-rated supply of land can require his customer to pay the VAT amount.

The potential problem here is concerned with the relationship of the parties to the contract as much as with anything HMRC might do. The solution is to cover the matter in the contract.

VAT Reporter: ¶12-329

Dedication of roads and sewers, etc.

The VAT position of a developer who dedicates the roads and sewers on a new estate to the local authority, or carries out works under an agreement with the planning authority, are now discussed.

When the new VAT and property rules were first introduced, HMRC took the view that these transactions involved the developer in making taxable supplies to the local authority.

They have since modified their position, and their current view as detailed in Notice 742 Section 8 is set out below:

'8. Developers' Agreements

8.1 Dedicating or vesting new roads or sewers

Agreements drawn up between developers, local authorities and water sewerage undertakers make provision for a wide variety of land, buildings and works to be provided, at the developer's expense, in connection with the granting of planning permission for the development.

If you, as a developer, dedicate or vest, for no monetary consideration:

(a) a new road (under the provisions of the Highways Act 1980 or the Roads (Scotland) Act 1984); or

(b) a new sewer or ancillary works (under the provisions of the Water Industries Act 1991 or the Sewerage (Scotland) Act 1968),

it is not a supply by you. No VAT is chargeable to the local authority or sewerage undertaker.

The input tax you incur on the construction of such works is attributable to your supplies of the development that is served by the road or sewer. For example, if your supplies of the land or buildings are taxable supplies, such as new houses, then the input tax you incur on constructing the roads and sewers is recoverable according to the normal rules. Where you make exempt supplies you will not be able to recover all your input tax.

8.2 Transfers of common areas of estates to management companies

As a developer of a private housing or industrial estate you may transfer, for a nominal monetary consideration, the basic amenities of estate roads, footpaths, communal parking and open space to a management company that will maintain them. This is not a supply, but the input tax you incurred on the building costs is attributable to the supplies of the land and buildings of the development itself.

8.3 Planning gain agreements

As a developer you may provide many other types of goods and services free, or for a purely nominal charge, to the local or other authority under section 106 of the Town and Country Planning Act 1990 or other similar agreements. These agreements are sometimes described as 'planning gain agreements'.

Such goods and services may include buildings such as community centres or schools, amenity land or civil engineering works. Alternatively, they may be in the form of services such as an agreement to construct something on land already owned by the authority or a third party. Any such provision of goods or services is not a supply for a consideration to the local or other authority, or to the third party. Consequently, no VAT is chargeable by you on the handing over of the land or building or the completion of the works. However, the input tax you incur is attributable to your supplies of land and buildings on the development for which the planning permission was given.

8.4 Agreements with the Highways Agency

When a development is undertaken, there may need to be road improvements. These road improvements will normally be undertaken in one of the following ways:

8.4.1 Works carried out by the Highways Agency

The Highways Agency will arrange for the works to be carried out. Under Section 278 of the Highways Act 1980, the Highways Agency may then recover from you, the developer, the costs incurred by the Highways Agency on certain road improvements. These costs will normally include irrecoverable VAT that has been charged to the Highways Agency by a contractor. As there is no supply between the Highways Agency and yourself, but merely a reimbursement by you of VAT inclusive costs, you are not entitled to recover the VAT element as your input tax.

8.4.2 Works carried out by the developer

If you, the developer, are permitted by the Highways Agency to carry out the works at your own cost, then there is no supply by you of the works to the Highways Agency. This is because you do not receive any consideration for the works from the Highways Agency. However, you may recover the input tax as attributable to your own ultimate supply of land and buildings from the development. For example, if the development is a taxable supply you can recover all the input tax.

8.5 What if I am required to make a cash contribution?

You may be required to pay sums of money, or sums of money in addition to buildings or works, to a local authority or a third party under section 106 of the Town and Country Planning Act 1990 and other similar agreements. You may, for example, pay money towards the future maintenance of a building or land, or as a contribution towards improvement of the infrastructure. Such sums are not consideration for taxable supplies to you by the local authority or by the third party.'

Other material: Notice 742, Section 8

VAT Reporter: ¶37-275

OPTION TO TAX

15-300   The option for taxation

The election to waive exemption (or option for taxation) was introduced on 1 August 1989, major revisions were made from 1 June 2008.

The option for taxation is exercised in relation to land or buildings specified by the person making the election, who must give written notice of it to HMRC. Once the option is exercised, the land exemption ceases to apply to supplies of the land or building concerned by the person exercising the option.

The option for taxation is irrevocable in principle, but see (6) and (7) below.

Further details about the option and its use are given below. See flowchart 18-935.

(1)   Scope of the option for taxation

The election to waive the exemption may be made with respect to a specified area of land, a building, an interest in part of a building or a planned building. When the option is exercised in respect of a building, it applies to all of the land within the curtilage of the building.

For the purposes of this, the following are treated as one building:

(1)   buildings linked internally;

(2)   buildings linked by a covered walkway;

(3)   complexes consisting of a number of units grouped round a fully-enclosed concourse.

Modifications from 1 June 2008

When an option is made in respect of land, it will henceforth apply to 'any building that is (or is to be) constructed on the land'. Prior to 1 June 2008, there was some doubt about this.

Although opting to tax land will henceforth entrap any buildings constructed on the land, there is a facility for excluding new buildings from the effect of the original option to tax. This can only be done by notifying HMRC at the proper time and on the correct form.

It was the case that an option made in respect of a building was regarded as ceasing when or if the building was demolished. HMRC say that for options made before 1 June 2008, this practice will continue 'as a transitional rule, provided that it is clear from your notification … that the option was made on the building only …'

Buildings are now defined as including any 'enlarged or extended building' and 'an annexe to a building'.

Henceforth, not all 'covered walkways' are regarded as forming a link such that the buildings are treated as single building for these purposes. The revised legislation excludes this when the 'covered walkway' is one 'to which the general public have reasonable access'.

There is also a relaxation for buildings linked after completion. If an internal link or covered walkway is put in place after the buildings are completed, the building will not be treated as a single building.

Legislation: VATA 1994, Sch. 10, para. 18 and 27

Other material: VAT Information Sheet 03/08; Notice 742A, Section 2

VAT Reporter: ¶35-015

(2)   Notification of the option for taxation

Opting to tax is a two-stage process. Stage one is making the decision to opt to tax. Stage two is notifying HMRC.

An option to tax must be made from a current or future date as an option to tax cannot be exercised retrospectively. The option to tax is effective from the 'start of the day on which it is exercised or the start of any later day specified in the option'.

An option to tax is not effective unless notified to HMRC on the correct form within 30 days from the effective date. From 1 June 2008, HMRC have discretion to accept belated notifications. They may accept notification 'at the end of such longer ... as the Commissioners may in any particular case allow'. HMRC's policy for belated notifications prior to 30 June 2008 is explained in Business Brief 13/05, 5 July 2005.

In some circumstances, it is necessary to obtain HMRC's permission to opt to tax. Without it, the option to tax is not effective.

When to seek HMRC's permission

If the person wishing to opt to tax has made (or will make) during a specified period an exempt supply of the land or building which they wish to opt to tax, it is necessary to obtain HMRC's permission to opt to tax. The specified period is the 10 years ending on the day before the option to tax is due to have effect.

HMRC's permission may be automatic. The circumstances when it is automatic are set out in Notice 742A, para. 5.2:

5.5 How do I apply for permission?

The following statement has the force of the law
An application for prior permission to opt to tax *(for the purpose of paragraphs 28 and 29 of Schedule 10 to the Value Added Tax Act 1994)* must be made on form **VAT 1614H** and must contain the information requested on that form.

You can download application form VAT 1614H from *www.hmrc.gov.uk* or obtain it from our advice service on 0845 010 9000.

When permission is not automatic, HMRC must be sent sufficient information for their purposes. The form used to obtain permission is intended to be sufficient for these purposes. HMRC will only grant permission when they are satisfied that to do so will 'result in a fair and reasonable attribution of input tax' – see below. A Tribunal determined that HMRC should only take into account supplies and input tax which the person wishing to opt to tax has made, incurred or is expected to do so in the future. How other parties to the transaction are affected is not relevant.

The form with which to seek permission (automatic or otherwise) is available on HMRC's website: VAT Form 1614A; Notice 1614H.

Other material: Notice 742A; VAT Information Sheet 03/08; VAT Form 1614A; Notice 1614H

Cases: *British Eventing Ltd* [2010] TC 00664

VAT Reporter: ¶35-085

Legislation: VATA 1994, Sch. 10, para. 19, 20 and 27–30

(3) Input tax arising before the option is exercised

There is a general rule that input tax which pre-dates the effective date of the option cannot become recoverable as a result of the option. However, some input tax may be recoverable because of the application of the Capital Goods Scheme or, alternatively, a HMRC concession.

The Capital Goods Scheme requires 10 'annual' adjustments to input tax recovery to reflect the change of use of a building. When any of these occur after opting to tax, the adjustment will normally result in more input tax being recovered.

For buildings/land not subject to the Capital Goods Scheme, HMRC operate a concession, explained as follows: '... so as to ensure equity of treatment with land and buildings that fall within the CGS, we normally allow recovery of that part of the input tax on land or a building which does not fall within the CGS to the extent to which it will be used in making taxable supplies. In this situation, you should identify the capital expenditure on goods and services which will be used in whole or part in making future taxable supplies, then agree a fair and reasonable recovery of the related input tax. This should be calculated over a 10-year period to ensure consistency with the CGS, although recovery will be through a one-off credit on the first return following the option to tax.'

See 7-760.

VAT Reporter: ¶35100

Other material: *HMRC Guidance Manuals* Vol V1–8 Section 22.13.1; Notice 742, Section 9

(4) Cases where the option is ineffective

Even if the option is exercised, it is ineffective in respect of the following supplies which continue to be exempt or, possibly, zero-rated (for definitions of dwelling, relevant residential purpose and relevant charitable purpose, see 15-160):

(1) the supply is of a building intended for use as a dwelling;

(2) buildings to be converted to dwellings or for use solely for a relevant residential purpose;

(3) the supply is of a building intended for use solely for a relevant residential purpose, and the customer has issued a certificate to that effect;

(4) the supply is of a building intended for use solely for a relevant charitable purpose (other than as an office), and the customer has issued a certificate to that effect;

(5) the supply is to a relevant housing association which has issued a certificate stating that the land will be used for the construction of buildings for use as dwellings or for a relevant residential purpose;

(6) the supply is to an individual who intends to use it for the construction of his own dwelling; or

(7) the supply is of a pitch for a residential caravan or of facilities for mooring a houseboat.

The option is also ineffective for certain supplies between connected persons (see (8) below), and certain other supplies where the property is used for non-taxable purposes (see (9) below).

Converting buildings – prior to 1 June 2008

If a non-residential building is to be sold and converted to dwellings or used for a relevant residential purpose, it is possible for the vendor and the purchaser to agree that the option to tax will be effective. They have to do so in a written agreement before the sale takes place. It is not possible to have this agreement if the sale is to a housing association.

Following the tribunal decision in *S E H Holdings Ltd*, HMRC have issued clarification of their policy concerning the disapplication of the option on the ground that a building, or part, is intended for use as a dwelling. If the immediate purchaser does not intend to use the building himself as a dwelling, nor to convert the building to a dwelling himself for sale or letting, then the option is not to be disapplied. This means that if A, who has opted for taxation, sells a building to B, who resells it to C, and it is C who intends to convert the building for use as a dwelling, VAT will be due on the sale from A to B. B cannot validly opt for taxation (so that the VAT charged by A will be an irrecoverable cost in his hands), unless C intends to make a zero-rated supply of the converted dwelling and B and C agree in writing that the option should apply. HMRC indicate that, where VAT will become a cost in this way, businesses should contact the National Advice Service, which may be a hint of the possibility of some flexibility in applying the rules.

Converting buildings – post-1 June 2008

An option to tax a building to be converted to a dwelling or solely for use as relevant residential accommodation is nullified when the buyer gives the seller a suitable certificate by the required time. A suitable certificate is one which confirms that the buyer intends to convert the building to, and use it as, a dwelling or relevant residential accommodation. This certificate must be given 'before the price for the grant … is legally fixed, e.g. by exchange of contracts, letters or missives, or the signing of heads of agreement'. Draft certificates are available on HMRC website – Forms 1614G, 1614F, Notice VAT 1614D.

The revised legislation permits a series of certificates when a building changes hands one or more times before being acquired by the person who will convert it to and use it as a dwelling or relevant residential accommodation.

An intermediary buying a building to sell to someone who will convert it to a dwelling or relevant residential accommodation may receive from his or her buyer a certificate as described above. After receiving this, the intermediary may issue a similar certificate to the person from whom they are buying the building concerned. If there are several intermediaries, this can develop into a chain of certificates.

Used solely for a relevant purpose

In certain circumstances the option to tax is only disapplied when the building concerned is, or will be, used 'solely' for a relevant purpose. The 'solely' condition is met when other use is less than 5%. HMRC accept that the 'solely' condition is met when the relevant use of the building by a charity or relevant residential user is 95% or more.

Legislation: VATA 1994, Sch. 10, para. 5–11

Cases: *S E H Holdings Ltd* [2001] BVC 2,093

Other material: Notice 742A, Section 3; VAT Information Sheet 03/08; HM Revenue and Customs Brief 08/2010; Revenue and Customs Brief 33/10

VAT Reporter: ¶34-510

(5) Apportionment of rents

Rent apportionments are not required for wholly commercial properties. The whole of the rent is either taxed or not, depending whether the option is in force at the time of supply. In a case where the property is part living accommodation and part commercial (e.g. a public house), the rent for the living accommodation is always exempt and is not affected by an option to tax.

VAT Reporter: ¶34-965

(6) Revoking the option to tax

There are three situations when an option to tax is or may be revoked:

(1) during an initial cooling-off period;

(2) in specific situations, automatically after six years; or

(3) after 20 years.

The cooling-off period during which the option may be revoked is six months (until 31 May 2008, this was three months). There are conditions that must be fulfilled if the option is to be revoked during this period.

The automatic revocation after six years is a new (1 June 2008) concept. It applies to instances where the person who opted to tax has held no relevant interest in the land or buildings for a continuous period of six years.

After 20 years, the option may be revoked, provided certain conditions are met or permission is received from HMRC.

For more details regarding all these situations, see the flowchart 'Revoking the Option to Tax' at 15-680.

VAT Reporter: ¶35-060

Legislation: VATA 1994, Sch. 10, para. 23, 24, 25, 26

Other material: Notice 742A, Section 8; VAT Information Sheet 03/08; VAT Information Sheet 12/09

(7)   Real estate elections

To ease the administration of opting to tax on a property-by-property basis, HMRC have always accepted global elections. By making a global election, the person concerned opted to tax all their properties at a stroke.

Global elections were not statutory. However, they are being superseded by a statutory single election system. These are being called 'real estate' elections. This facility was introduced with effect from 1 June 2008.

Like global elections, a 'real estate' option to tax avoids the need to make an election for each and every property added to a person's property portfolio. It works by automatically opting to tax all land or buildings acquired by the person concerned after he or she has made this election.

When making a real estate option to tax, special consideration must be given to options already made and the portfolio at the time of making this election. These issues are considered in the flowchart at 15-710.

Another important principle of a real estate election is the way in which it operates in respect of the affected land or buildings. The real estate election is applied to the property portfolio concerned as if an option to tax was made on a property-by-property basis. As a result of this, the 'individual' options to tax may be revoked on a property-by-property basis.

Although a real estate election allows elections to be revoked on a property-by-property basis, the real estate election itself may not be revoked. However, HMRC may cancel it when the person concerned repeatedly does not comply with the applicable terms and conditions.

Other principles of a 'real estate' option to tax are as follows:

- some options to tax are automatically revoked by making 'real estate' elections. These are ones applying to land in which the person concerned has no legal interest at the time of making the 'real estate' election;
- some individual options to tax continue and are unaffected by the 'real estate' election. These are ones applying to land in which the person concerned has a legal interest at the time of making the 'real estate' election;
- HMRC must be notified with 30 days of making the 'real estate' option to tax and be provided with certain information.

Legislation: VATA 1994, Sch. 10, para. 21 and 22

Other material: Notice 742A, Section 14; VAT Information Sheet 03/08; VAT Information Sheet 12/09

VAT Reporter: ¶35-020

(8) Anti-avoidance – property for ineligible use by grantor, financier or connected person

A restriction on the effect of the option to tax may apply to the land concerned if it is occupied by any of the following:

(1)   the grantor;

(2)   a person who financed the development; or

(3)   a person connected with either of these.

Minor occupation

When the grantor (or someone connected with this person) occupies no more than 2% of the building concerned, this may be ignored. Several conditions must be considered when applying this concession. This concession is available from 1 March 2011.

If the person who financed the development (or someone connected to this person) occupies no more than 10% of the building concerned, or merely occupies 'any part of the land which is not a building', this occupation may be ignored. This concession was introduced with effect from 1 April 2011.

Occupation solely by way of an Automatic Teller Machine ('ATM') may also be ignored.

When the anti-avoidance measure applies

These rules apply only where the land concerned falls within the capital goods scheme in the hands of the grantor at the time when the grant is made, or later in the hands of the grantee. If the property does fall within the capital goods scheme, it is necessary to determine the intentions of the parties at the time when the grant is made. If there is an intention of ineligible occupation at that time, the option does not have effect for supplies made under the grant concerned even if such ineligible occupation never in fact comes about. Conversely, if ineligible occupation was not intended at the time of the grant, the option continues to have effect even if such occupation ultimately comes about. 'Occupation' was considered in the case of *Newnham College* where Lord Hope of Craighead said at 31:

'I do not think that there is much doubt about what the word "occupation" means, although it may be more difficult to apply its ordinary meaning to the facts in some contexts than it is in others. In its ordinary meaning it requires more than just a right to use the land or to enjoy the facilities that are to be found there. Physical presence is an essential element. But there is more to it than that. It requires actual possession of the land, and the possession must have some degree of permanence.'

See flowchart 15-730.

Developer of the land

The legislation is couched in terms of a developer of the land concerned. However, this is defined as anyone in whose hands the land falls within the capital goods scheme, so it is not necessary that there should have been recent development of the property, or that the grantor be the person who carried out any development. The provisions apply equally to an existing building which has been bought under a transaction on which VAT was due.

The provisions are further extended to cover the position where the land concerned is not within the capital goods scheme at the time when the initial grant is made, but is expected or intended to become so.

Person financing development

The definition of a person financing the grantor's purchase or development of the property is widely drawn. It includes a person:

(1)   directly or indirectly providing funds to meet some or all of the cost of purchase or development, or procuring the provision of such funds by another; or,

(2)   directly or indirectly providing funds to discharge liabilities incurred by any person in connection with the grantor's purchase or development of the property, or procuring the discharge of such liabilities by another.

The provision of funds includes the making of loans, the provision of guarantees or other security in relation to loans, the provision of consideration for shares or securities issued at least partly to raise funds for the purchase, etc. It also includes entering into any agreement or understanding (whether or not legally enforceable) to do any of these things. However, there must also be an intention on the part of the financier that the property will be put (or continue to be put) to ineligible use by an occupant connected with the grantor or the financier, at least for a while.

In *Winterthur Life UK Ltd* [1999] BVC 2,093, it was held that the partners in an exempt partnership, who paid contributions to a pension fund and then used this money as a deposit to purchase land, were persons providing finance, notwithstanding that they obtained pension entitlements in return for the contributions. Occupation of part of the property by the partnership was considered to involve occupation by the partners, and the fund's option for taxation was ineffective as regards the supplies to the partnership.

Connected persons

Connected persons are as defined in ICTA 1988, s. 839.

From 15 August 2009, banks are not connected merely because of any government shareholding.

Eligible purpose

Until 31 May 2008

Land and buildings are occupied for an eligible purpose when they are used 'wholly or mainly' for making taxable supplies. This is that the building is used 'wholly or mainly' for a purpose for which the occupier is entitled to reclaim input tax.

HMRC's interpretation of 'mainly' is confusing. Their advice concerning this is as follows:

'a   The term 'mainly' is not defined in law. Current policy is that 80% of the supplies made should give rise to credit for input tax. [HMRC Guidance Manuals Vol V1–8 Section 23.9]

b   'Mainly' means substantially more than half [Notice 742, paragraph 13.10].'

However, occupation of land by a government department is deemed to be occupation for an eligible purpose, as is occupation for non-business purposes by a local authority or other body listed in VATA 1994, s. 33.

Where land is held for occupation, but is not yet in use, it is deemed to be used for the purposes for which it is intended to be used, provided that it has not yet been put to use for some other purpose.

From 1 June 2008

The test is now whether or not land or buildings are used 'wholly, or substantially wholly' for making taxable supplies.

'Wholly' is when the land or buildings are used 100 per cent for making taxable supplies; 'substantially wholly' means the land or buildings are used at least 80 per cent for making taxable supplies.

Legislation: VATA 1994, Sch. 10, para. 15(5)

Cases: *Newnham College Cambridge v R & C Commrs* [2008] BVC 452

Other material: HMRC Guidance Manuals Vol V1–8, Section 23.9; VAT Information Sheet 02/10; Revenue and Customs Brief 03/11; Notice 742A, Section 13

Expectation or intention

The application of the provisions is to be determined as at the time when the grant concerned is made, and depends on the expectations or intentions of the grantor or of someone financing the purchase or development of the property. If either or both expect or intend the property to be (or continue to be) occupied by them or someone connected with them otherwise than for an eligible purpose, the provisions have effect.

Effect of provisions

The effect of these anti-avoidance provisions is to render the option for taxation ineffective for all supplies made under the grant concerned. However, they do not remove the option as such, so it continues to be effective for any subsequent grant in respect of the same land.

Transitional provisions

The anti-avoidance rules do not affect a grant made before 30 November 1999 in pursuance of a written agreement entered into before 26 November 1996, provided that its terms are in accordance with that written agreement. The written agreement does not have to be the final, legally binding, agreement. On 11 February 1997, the Exchequer Secretary told the Standing Committee:

> 'It will apply as long as there is something reasonable in writing. We do not require a lease. We do not even require a drafted lease – heads of agreement, or a letter that indicates a serious intent to lease at a certain level is enough. When the BPF (British Property Federation) raised the issue at a meeting, we agreed to be as flexible and broad as possible.'

Cases: *Winterthur Life UK Ltd* [1999] BVC 2,093

Other material: HC Official Report, Standing Committee B (Eighth Sitting), Col. 291

VAT Reporter: ¶35-030

15-310   VAT groups – opting to tax

An option to tax made by a corporate body also binds any relevant associate. Relevant associate status is acquired in the following circumstances:

- both corporate bodies are members of the same VAT group when the election is made;
- both corporate bodies are members of the same VAT group at any time when the person who made the option to tax holds a relevant interest in the land or buildings concerned;
- by being a member of the same VAT group or another relevant associate of the body which opted to tax at a time when either the body which opted to tax or this other relevant associate held a relevant interest in the land or buildings concerned.

The relevant associate status need not continue indefinitely but may be ended in the ways described in Notice 742A paragraph 6.3ff.

Other material: Notice 742A, para. 6.3; VAT Information Sheet 12/09

Legislation: VATA 1994, Sch. 10, para. 2

15-320   Who can opt for taxation

Nothing is laid down in law in the case of, say, a limited company, as to what individual can elect to waive exemption on behalf of the company. Equally, there is nothing to prevent companies, etc. from making their own rules on this.

Given the irrevocable nature of the option, it is a useful precautionary measure for bodies which own property (even if they have no current intention of opting for taxation) to decide, and record, their internal rules for doing this.

CONSTRUCTION AND BUILDING SERVICES

15-340   Construction services

Although the basic rule is that supplies of carrying out construction works (including repairs) are standard-rated, zero-rating is available for certain supplies and to further complicate matters, some construction services are subject to the reduced rate.

15-360   Zero-rated supplies of construction services

Zero-rating is available for supplies in the course of:

(1)   construction of new buildings designed as dwellings (i.e. houses and flats);

(2)   construction of new buildings intended for certain relevant residential accommodation (e.g. nursing or retirement homes) or charitable use;

(3)   construction of civil engineering works necessary for the development of a permanent park for residential caravans;

(4)   approved alterations to listed buildings designed to remain as, or become, dwellings (see below);

(5)   approved alterations to listed buildings intended for relevant residential accommodation or charitable use (see below); and

(6)   conversion of certain non-domestic buildings to dwellings or relevant residential accommodation only if the customer is a housing association.

For the definition of 'dwelling', 'relevant residential accommodation' and 'charitable use', see above.

Zero-rating applies to the supply, in the course of construction of 1, 2, 3 and 6 above, of:

(1)   services, other than those of an architect, surveyor, consultant, or a person acting in a supervisory capacity; and

(2)   materials, etc. supplied by a person supplying zero-rated services and used in connection with those services. However, fitted furniture (except kitchen furniture), materials for constructing fitted furniture, electrical or gas appliances (other than space or water heaters and certain other items), and carpeting material are all excluded from zero-rating (see also 6-340).

Certificates are required when constructing relevant residential accommodation or a building for charity use (see 15-420). Zero-rating is not available unless the supply is made to the person who is to use the building, and only then if a certificate of use is obtained from the customer before the supply is made. It follows from this that, in the case of such buildings:

(1)   if the owner of the building plans to sell or let it, rather than use it himself, the contractors who construct the building cannot zero-rate their supplies. However, if the developer

makes a zero-rated supply on the sale or letting of the building (see below), he will be able to recover the tax charged as input tax; and

(2)   subcontractors who make their supplies to a main contractor rather than to the owner of the building cannot zero-rate their supplies. However, the main contractor can recover the tax charged as input tax.

It should be noted that the zero-rating only covers supplies in the course of construction of a qualifying building. A qualifying building for these purposes is an entirely new building.

A new building is defined as one not incorporating any part of an existing building other than foundations or a basement, and one or two facades retained as a condition of planning consent. Also, an annex to an existing charitable building will be regarded as a separate building, notwithstanding internal access to the existing building, provided that it is capable of independent operation and has its own external access.

According to circumstances, the first time connection of a dwelling or non-business charity building to a mains electricity or gas supply may be liable to zero or reduced rate. Fewer of these connections qualify for the zero rate with effect from 1 January 2012.

Converting existing buildings

Supplies in the course of conversion of an existing building cannot generally be zero-rated. However, where the person carrying out the construction is a housing association, the contractors can zero-rate their supplies. A 'relevant housing association' is a registered social landlord or a private registered provider of social housing as defined in the various Housing Acts or Housing and Regeneration Acts that, as appropriate, apply in the UK.

See flowchart 15-750.

Legislation: VATA 1994, Sch. 8, Grp.5, items 1, 2 and 3

Other material: Notice 708, Sections 3 and 6; Revenue and Customs Brief 43/11

VAT Reporter: ¶33-775

15-380   Alterations to listed buildings

Changes from 1 October 2012

The zero-rating relief for alterations to listed buildings is removed, except for supplies to which the transitional arrangements apply.

Transitional arrangements

Subject to conditions, certain work may continue to be zero-rated until 30 September 2015. Any work done or performed after this date is standard-rated. It will be necessary to apportion work qualifying for transitional relief but which is not finished on 30 September 2015.

The conditions which must be met for the transitional relief to apply are as follows:

(1) if the pre-1 October 2012 law applied, the work would be zero-rated; and

(2) a written contract for this work was entered into, or listed building consent applied for, before 21 March 2012.

For more information see flowchart at 15-775.

Zero-rated work prior to 1 October 2012

The buildings to which this relief applies are dwellings, relevant residential accommodation and buildings used solely for charitable purposes which are also:

(1) buildings which are listed buildings under the *Planning (Listed Buildings and Conservation Areas) Act* 1990, or its Scottish or Northern Irish equivalents; and

(2) scheduled monuments within the meaning in the *Ancient Monuments and Archaeological Areas Act* 1979 or the *Historic Monuments (Northern Ireland) Act* 1971.

A protected building can include a garage which is occupied in conjunction with the dwelling concerned.

The same general restrictions apply in respect of this zero-rating as in respect of services and related goods for new construction work.

The works in connection with which zero-rating is available are restricted to works carried out in the course of an approved alteration to a protected building. In general, an approved alteration is one which is not permitted to be carried out without the permission of the protecting authority under the relevant planning legislation, and for which such permission has in fact been obtained in advance.

Exceptions to this general rule are:

(1) if the building is an ecclesiastical building in use as such and is a building to which section 60 of the *Planning (Listed Buildings and Conservation Areas) Act* 1990 applies, then *any* works of alteration are regarded as approved alterations; and

(2) if the building is a Crown interest, or Duchy interest, as defined in the relevant planning legislation, then approved alterations are those which could not have been carried out without permission of the protecting authority had it not been such an interest.

The House of Lords has ruled upon a case involving alterations to an outbuilding in the curtilage of a listed building.

The property consisted of a house and an outbuilding within the curtilage of this house. The work was to convert the outbuilding to games and changing facilities and to construct an adjoining indoor swimming pool.

The house was a protected building listed under *Planning (Listed Buildings and Conservation Areas) Act* 1990. As such, alterations could be zero-rated. The outbuilding was not itself listed under the 1990 Act, but was protected as being a structure within the curtilage of a listed building. The two structures were physically separate although linked by a sandstone wall. It was mutually agreed that some of the work was standard-rated. However, HMRC decided that none of the work to the outbuilding could be zero-rated.

Lord Walker divided the key part 'protected building' into three. The structure must be:

- a building;
- designed to remain as or become a dwelling; and
- be a listed building within the meaning of the 1990 Act.

In this case, the outbuilding was not itself listed. In addition, Lord Hoffmann emphasised that two important conditions to be met were that the zero-rating facility is designed to give some relief for owners of a protected building that is designed 'to remain as or become a dwelling house'. The outbuilding was not so destined. It was to be a games facility. Therefore, even if the outbuilding were a listed building, the alterations did not qualify for the relief.

Repair and maintenance

Works of repair and maintenance are specifically excluded from the definition of approved alteration. If the works carried out are partly approved alterations and partly repairs or maintenance, the consideration must be apportioned and tax must be charged on the part relating to the repairs or maintenance

See flowchart 15-770.

VAT Reporter: ¶34-225

Legislation: VATA 1994, Sch. 8, Grp. 6, item 2

Cases: *C & E Commrs v Zielinski Baker & Partners Ltd* [2004] BVC 309

Other material: Notice 708, Section 9

15-400   Reduced rate supplies of construction services

The reduced rate of VAT applies to certain residential conversions and certain residential renovations/alterations.

Residential conversions

The reduced rate for residential conversions applies to supplies of building services and related goods in respect of the following.

(1) Changed number of dwellings conversion: this is a conversion of a building (or part of a building) so that after conversion it contains a different number of single household dwellings from the number it contained before the conversion.

(2) House in multiple occupation conversion: this is a conversion of a building (or part of a building) so that it contains only one or more multiple occupancy dwellings. It does not include conversion for relevant residential use.

(3) Special residential conversion: this is a conversion of premises for use solely for a relevant residential purpose. When last used, the premises should not have been to any extent used for a relevant residential purpose. After the conversion, the premises must be intended to form the 'entirety of an institution' used for a relevant residential purpose.

There are many detailed conditions for this relief which must be met.

Legislation: VATA 1994, Sch. 7A, Grp. 6

Other material: Notice 708, Section 7

VAT Reporter: ¶33-952

Residential renovations and alterations

The reduced rate applies to supplies of building services (and related goods) in the course of the alteration (including extension), or renovation, of qualifying building that have been unoccupied for two years or more. Qualifying buildings are as follows:

(a) a single household dwelling;
(b) a multiple occupancy dwelling; and
(c) a building, or part of a building, which, when last lived in, was used for a relevant residential purpose.

A dwelling can also qualify if:

• there has been a period of at least two years when it has not been lived in;
• a person whose occupation of the building ended the period of not being lived in acquired it before starting to live there, and acquired it at a time when it had not been lived in for at least two years;
• no works of renovation or alteration were carried out in the two years ending with the acquisition;
• the supply is made to a person whose occupation brought the period of non-occupation to an end and who also acquired the building as described above; and
• the works are carried out within one year after the acquisition of the building.

Constructing, renovating or converting a building into a garage as part of the renovation of a property also qualifies for the reduced rate.

There are many detailed conditions for this relief which must be met.

Prior to 1 January 2008, the required period for the building to be unoccupied was three years.

Land, Property and Construction

Legislation: VATA 1994, Sch. 7A, Grp. 7

Other material: Notice 708, Section 8

VAT Reporter: ¶33-952

15-420   Certificate of use

Construction services as detailed above may only be zero-rated or charged at the reduced rate if a certificate of use is provided by the user of the building.

The form of certificate required is shown in Notice 708.

If an incorrect certificate is issued, the person issuing it is liable to a penalty equal to the relief incorrectly given.

Legislation: VATA 1994, s. 62, Sch. 8, Grp. 5, Note 12

Other material: Notice 708, Sections 16 and 18

VAT Reporter: ¶33-825

15-440   Building materials

The zero-rating or reduced-rating of construction services in relation to dwellings or buildings for relevant residential or relevant charitable use is extended to the supply of materials, builders' hardware, sanitary ware or other materials of a kind ordinarily incorporated by builders into the type of building concerned where the supply is made by the person providing the zero-rated or reduced-rate construction services. The same applies in relation to materials, etc. supplied for zero-rated civil engineering work on developing a permanent park for residential caravans.

Thus, a contractor can zero-rate or reduce-rate the supply of 'building materials' when:

- he incorporates those goods in a building; and
- his service of 'incorporating' those goods is zero-rated or charged at the reduced rate.

A contractor must charge VAT when he:

- supplies 'building materials' (or other goods) on their own without incorporating them in a building;
- incorporates 'building materials' in a building and cannot zero-rate or reduce-rate the incorporation services; or
- incorporates in a building goods which are not 'building materials' (unless he can zero-rate or reduce rate the services of incorporating those goods under other rules).

As regards what is 'ordinarily incorporated by builders' into the type of building concerned, there is an old purchase tax case concerning the meaning of 'builders' hardware, sanitary ware and other articles of kinds ordinarily installed by builders as fixtures'. The court had to decide whether built-in dressing-table units fell within this category or whether they constituted furniture. Stamp J held that the 'articles' referred to were 'articles which one would expect a builder to install as fixtures in the ordinary way without special instructions, because a builder when performing his function of building ordinarily installs them'.

Regarding 'materials ordinarily incorporated', in Notice 708, HMRC explains that it sees this term as encompassing goods attached to a building (or its site) that make up 'one whole' with the building. In addition to covering the obvious structure of, and fixtures to, a building, it also covers installed fittings. HM Revenue and Customs accept that an item is 'incorporated' when it is fixed to a building, or its site, in such a way that its fixing or removal would either:

- require the use of tools; or
- result in either:
  - the need for remedial work to the fabric of the building, or its site; or
  - substantial damage to the goods themselves.

HM Revenue and Customs hold the view that 'ordinarily incorporated' means that which in the ordinary course of events would normally be incorporated in the construction of a building of that generic type. In essence, it means the 'norm' for, say, dwellings or churches or schools, etc. HM Revenue and Customs do not split generic types of buildings into subcategories and then conclude that the same item can be 'ordinarily incorporated' in one but not in the other. For example, no distinction is drawn between large detached houses and small terraced houses.

HMRC takes the same approach when determining if the goods themselves are the 'norm' for that type of building. So, for example, a tap would be regarded as being 'ordinarily incorporated' whether it is chromium or gold plated.

Although the Tax Tribunal accepted that a roller blind was 'building materials', HMRC have stated that they do not agree with this and will not apply it to other cases.

Notice 708 provides some useful lists of materials and hardware which, in the opinion of HMRC, do and do not qualify for zero or reduced rating, in an attempt to overcome previous problems of interpretation.

Legislation: VATA 1994, Sch. 8, Grp. 5, note 22

Other material: Notice 708, Section 13; Revenue and Customs Brief 02/11

Cases: *F Austin (Leyton) v C & E Commrs* [1968] 2 All ER 13

VAT Reporter: ¶33-725

Fitted furniture

As indicated above, the installation of fitted cupboards and work surfaces in kitchens is eligible for zero or reduced rating. However, these reliefs are only available where such installation is carried out at the time of the construction of the dwelling. Any installation carried out subsequently is standard-rated, irrespective of whether such work is the fitting of additional units or replacement ones.

Difficulties have been encountered in relation to fitted wardrobes as to whether they constitute 'furniture' or form part of the fabric of the building. In one case, it was held that built-in wardrobes formed by fitting doors across an end wall and two internal walls formed part of the building. The wardrobes concerned included wardrobes which ran the entire length of a wall and wardrobes which included a side end. These wardrobes are described as elaborate, including several shelves and shoe racks.

Cases: *C & E Commrs v McLean Homes Midland Ltd* [1993] BVC 99

Other material: Notice 708, para. 13.5.3

VAT Reporter: ¶33-327

15-450   Tax repayments to DIY housebuilders

There are special rules enabling recovery of VAT on goods (but not on services) by persons building certain buildings otherwise than in the course of a business.

The buildings covered are those for which the construction or sale by the developer can be zero-rated, namely dwellings and certain buildings for relevant residential or charitable use (see 13-050ff.). Input tax repayment is only available if construction of the building is lawful (so appropriate planning permissions must be produced) and all relevant conditions are met.

A single claim must be made in respect of any one building, within three months after completion of construction. It must be accompanied by acceptable invoices. A letter with all the relevant information has been found to be 'an invoice' for these purposes.

Although no VAT can be recovered on services, most services supplied in the course of construction of such a building will be zero-rated (although the DIY builder must issue a certificate of use to obtain zero-rating of building services in connection with a building other than a dwelling). Certain services cannot be zero-rated, such as architects' services and the hire of equipment, so a VAT cost will arise on these.

The DIY builder does not necessarily need to do the building work personally. Specialist help can be hired. In effect, the DIY builder can be acting as main contractor to himself.

Input tax can also be reclaimed in respect of the conversion of certain non-domestic buildings to dwellings. It is essential that any such conversion results in the creation of an additional dwelling or dwellings. A case concerning this matter went through three levels of the Court system. A building had been purchased that was a public house on the ground floor and living accommodation on the first and second storeys. There was a third floor and a cellar not used as residential accommodation. The whole building was converted to one dwelling and a DIY house builders claim for repayment of VAT was submitted. HMRC refused the claim saying that because the conversion of the non-residential part did not result in an additional dwelling or dwellings, the claim was disallowed. The appeal to the VAT and Duties Tribunal succeeded, the High Court agreed with the Tribunal but the Court of Appeal overturned the decision. Lady Jane Blom-Cooper tried to appeal to the House of Lords but was refused permission – hence the matter was finalised, HMRC won.

Legislation: VATA 1994, s. 35; *Value Added Tax Regulations* 1995 (SI 1995/2518), reg. 200; *Value Added Tax Regulations* 1995 (SI 1995/2518), reg. 201

Cases: *Blom-Cooper v C & E Commrs* [2003] BVC 415; *Jennings* [2011] TC 001160; [2011] UKFTT 298 (TC)

VAT Reporter: ¶38-000

Conversions resulting in a changed number of dwellings

Following the Court of Appeal judgment in the case of *R & C Commrs v Jacobs*, HMRC accept that for the purpose of the DIY scheme where a mixed-use building is converted so that an additional dwelling is created, then the VAT incurred on converting the non-residential part may be reclaimed. This reflects an alteration in their previous interpretation whereby the refund was only available where the additional dwelling was created exclusively from the non-residential part of the building.

Cases: *Blom-Cooper v C & E Commrs* [2003] BVC 415; *R & C Commrs v Jacobs* [2005] BVC 690

Other material: Notice 719

VAT Reporter: ¶38-155

Non-residential and residential conversions into one dwelling

Clark provides help to DIY conversions. Before work started the building concerned was partly residential accommodation; the 'residential' part was the garage for an existing dwelling. The conversion created an additional dwelling. The First Tier Tribunal ruled that the claim should be allowed 'subject to an adjustment to exclude ... VAT attributable to the conversion of the garage area'.

Cases: *Clark* [2010] UKFTT 258 (TC); [2010] TC 00552; *Wade* [2011] UKFTT 504 (TC)

Separate use and disposal

For details of this see 15-160.

Holiday Homes

Early in 2010 the Tax Tribunal ruled that the DIY Housebuilders' Scheme encompassed holiday homes built by an individual for a non-business purpose. Prior to this, HMRC would not apply the scheme to holiday homes.

Claims previously rejected were retrospectively accepted. New claims were subject to the four year cap.

Cases: *Jennings* [2010] TC 00362

Other material: Notice 719; HM Revenue and Customs Brief 29/10

VAT Reporter: ¶38-000

15-460   Conclusion

There are many more areas of difficulty in relation to VAT and property. Those mentioned above are merely intended to give an indication of the kinds of pitfalls which abound.

FLOWCHARTS

15-490   Mirror Group

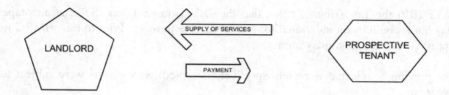

Notes

(1)   Inducement to take a lease

There is a supply of services by the prospective tenant to the landlord. The service supplied is not the grant of an interest in land. At the relevant time, the prospective tenant did not have 'any interest in the immovable property'.

(2)   Further information

For further information about the VAT liability of surrendering leases, see VAT Reporter ¶34-800 and VAT Notice 742, section 10.

15-530   Cantor Fitzgerald

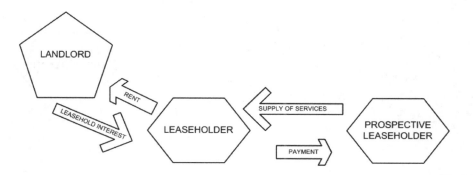

Notes

(1)   Inducement to accept the assignment of a lease

There is a supply of services by the prospective leaseholder to the current leaseholder. The service supplied is not the grant of an interest in land. At the relevant time, the prospective leasee did not have 'any interest in the immovable property'.

(2)   Further information

For further information about the VAT liability of surrendering leases, see VAT Reporter ¶34-800 and VAT Notice 742, Section 10.

15-550   Lubbock Fine

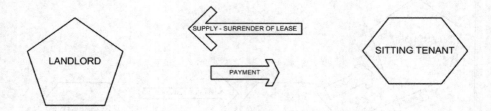

Notes

(1)   Interest in land

The tenant had an interest in the property, a lease. The surrender to the landlord was held to be grant of an interest in land.

(2)   Further information

For further information about the VAT liability of surrendering leases, see VAT Reporter ¶34-675 and VAT Notice 742, Section 10.

[This page is intentionally blank]

15-570 New buildings – when disposals may be zero-rated

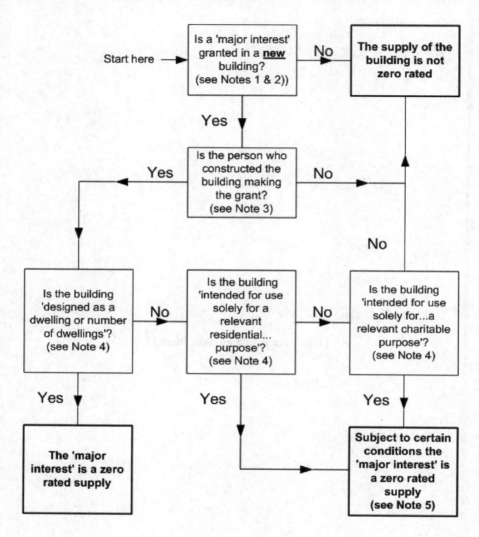

Notes

(1) New buildings

For these purposes, a new building includes the following:

- the creation of an entire new building;
- the erection of a new building following the demolition, or almost complete demolition, of an existing building;
- an enlargement to an existing building to the extent that the enlargement creates an additional dwelling or dwellings;
- certain annexes to buildings used for charitable purposes.

(2) 'Major interest'

'Major interest' means the fee simple or a tenancy for a term certain exceeding 21 years or the equivalent in Scotland.

(3) Person constructing

'You are a "person constructing" a building if, in relation to that building, you are, or have at any point in the past ... acted as a developer – i.e. you physically constructed, or commissioned another person to physically construct, the building (in whole or in part) on land that you own or have an interest in ...' (Notice 708, para. 4.5)

(4) Buildings which may be zero-rated

Only certain buildings may be zero-rated. The buildings concerned are as follows:

- dwellings; or
- those used 'solely for a relevant residential purpose'; or
- those used 'solely for a relevant charitable purpose'.

(5) Other conditions - used solely for 'a relevant residential purpose' or 'a relevant charitable purpose'

These supplies may not be zero-rated unless the supply is made to the person who will use the building for 'a relevant residential purpose' or 'relevant charitable purposes' and that person certifies in advance in writing that the building will be so used.

(6) Further information

For more information, see 13-050 and Notice 708.

15-590 Converted buildings – when disposals may be zero-rated

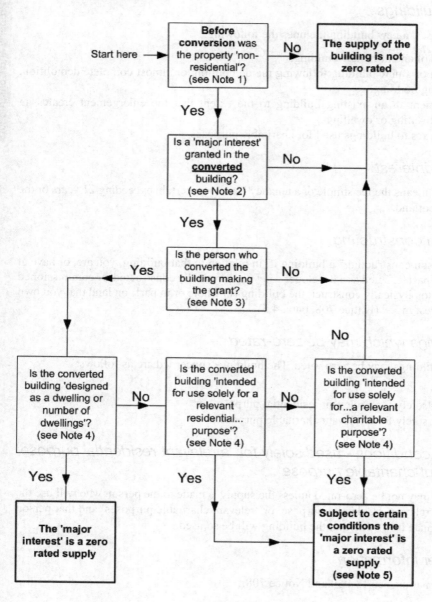

Start here → **Before conversion** was the property 'non-residential'? (see Note 1)

No → **The supply of the building is not zero rated**

Yes ↓

Is a 'major interest' granted in the **converted** building? (see Note 2)

No →

Yes ↓

Is the person who converted the building making the grant? (see Note 3)

No →

Yes ←

No →

Is the converted building 'designed as a dwelling or number of dwellings'? (see Note 4)

No → Is the converted building 'intended for use solely for a relevant residential... purpose'? (see Note 4)

No → Is the converted building 'intended for use solely for...a relevant charitable purpose'? (see Note 4)

Yes ↓

Yes ↓

Yes ↓

The 'major interest' is a zero rated supply

Subject to certain conditions the 'major interest' is a zero rated supply (see Note 5)

Land, Property and Construction

Notes

(1)   Non-residential

For these purposes, a building or part of a building is 'non-residential' if:

(a)   it is neither designed, nor adapted, for use as a dwelling or number of dwellings, or for a relevant residential purpose; or

(b)   it is designed, or adapted, for such use but:

    (i)   it was constructed more than 10 years before the grant of the major interest; and

    (ii)   no part of it has, in the period of 10 years immediately preceding the grant, been used as a dwelling or for a relevant residential purpose.

(2)   'Major interest'

'Major interest' means the fee simple or a tenancy for a term certain exceeding 21 years or the equivalent in Scotland.

(3)   Person converting

'You are a "person converting" a building if, in relation to that building, you are, or have at any point in the past ... acted as a developer – i.e. you physically converted, or commissioned another person to physically convert, a building (in whole or in part) that you own or have an interest in.' (Notice 708, para. 5.5).

(4)   Buildings which may be zero-rated

Only certain buildings may be zero-rated. The buildings concerned are as follows:

- dwellings; or
- those used 'solely for a relevant residential purpose'; or
- those used 'solely for a relevant charitable purpose'.

(5)   Other conditions – used solely for 'a relevant residential purpose' or 'a relevant charitable purpose'

These supplies may not be zero-rated unless the supply is made to the person who will use the building for 'a relevant residential purpose' or 'relevant charitable purposes' and that person certifies in advance in writing that the building will be so used.

(6)   Further information

For more information, see 13-050 and Notice 708.

15-610   Protected buildings – when disposals may be zero-rated

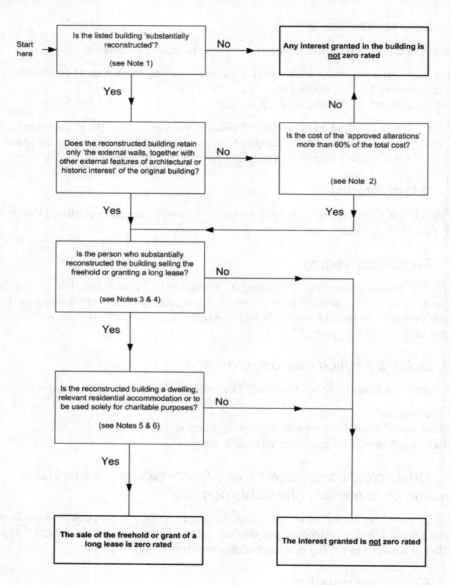

Land, Property and Construction

Notes

(1)   Substantially re-constructed

In Cheltenham College Enterprises the First Tier Tribunal said ' "Substantially reconstructing" clearly does not envisage total rebuilding of the listed property in question ... "substantially" means ... of the most part or at least 50%'.

(2)   Changes from 1 October 2012

This test was discontinued with effect from 1 October 2012 but transitional rules apply until 30 September 2015, see 15-160.

(3)   Approved alteration

An 'approved alteration' is an alteration (not repair or maintenance) for which listed building consent is both needed and has been obtained before the work is carried out.

(4)   Long Lease

A long lease is a lease for a term certain exceeding 21 years or the equivalent in Scotland.

(5)   Person substantially reconstructing

'You are a "person substantially reconstructing" a protected building if, in relation to that building, you are, or have at any point in the past ... acted as a developer – i.e. you physically converted, or commissioned another person to physically convert, a building (in whole or in part) that you own or have an interest in' (Notice 708, para. 10.6).

(6)   Buildings which may be zero-rated

Only certain buildings may be zero-rated. The buildings concerned are as follows:

- dwellings; or
- those used 'solely for a relevant residential purpose' ; or
- those used "solely for a relevant charitable purpose' .

(7)   Other conditions – used solely for 'a relevant residential purpose' or 'a relevant charitable purpose'

These supplies may not be zero-rated unless the supply is made to the person who will use the building for 'a relevant residential purpose' or 'relevant charitable purpose' and that person certifies in advance in writing that the building will be so used.

(8)   Further information

For more information, see 13-100 et seq and Notice 708.

15-630   Exempt supplies of land/buildings

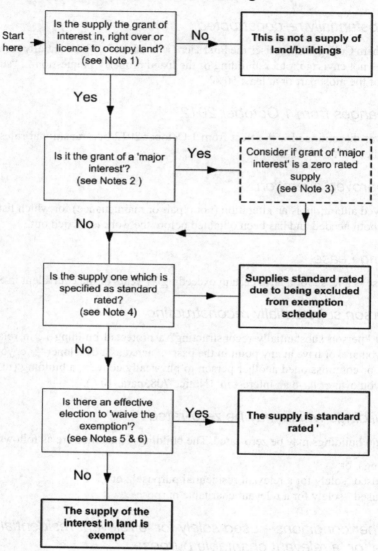

Start here → Is the supply the grant of interest in, right over or licence to occupy land? (see Note 1)

— No → **This is not a supply of land/buildings**

Yes ↓

Is it the grant of a 'major interest'? (see Notes 2)

— Yes → Consider if grant of 'major interest' is a zero rated supply (see Note 3)

No ↓

Is the supply one which is specified as standard rated? (see Note 4)

→ **Supplies standard rated due to being excluded from exemption schedule**

No ↓

Is there an effective election to 'waive the exemption'? (see Notes 5 & 6)

— Yes → **The supply is standard rated '**

No ↓

The supply of the interest in land is exempt

Notes

(1)   Interests in land

Grant includes an assignment or surrender.

(2)   'Major interest'

'Major interest' means the fee simple or a tenancy for a term certain exceeding 21 years.

(3)   Zero-rated supplies of a 'major interest'

Subject to certain conditions, the grant of a 'major interest' in a dwelling, a building used 'solely for a relevant residential purpose' or used 'solely for ... a relevant charitable purpose' is a zero-rated supply.

(4)   Specified standard-rated supplies

The supply of certain interests in land are always standard-rated. This is stipulated by law. The main supplies of this type are as follows:

- freehold disposal of certain new (or partly completed) buildings or civil engineering works;
- rights to take game or fish;
- hotel, inn, boarding house or similar accommodation;
- holiday accommodation and seasonal pitches for caravans and tents;
- parking;
- the right to fell and remove timber;
- housing, storage, mooring for aircraft, ships, etc.;
- facilities for playing sport.

(5)   Standard-rated due to 'waiving the exemption'/opting to tax

VAT may be charged on certain 'interests in land' by the person concerned 'waiving the exemption'. An election to do so is ineffective when an anti-avoidance measure applies or for the following:

- a building (or part of) intended for use as a dwelling, a relevant residential purpose or solely for a relevant charitable purpose (other than as an office);
- a pitch for a residential caravan or facilities for the mooring of a residential houseboat;
- the grant to a relevant housing association for the construction of a dwelling(s) or solely for a relevant residential purpose;
- the grant is made to an individual for him to build a dwelling for use by him.

(6)   Further information

For further information, see 13-050, 13-100. Notice 708 and Notice 742.

15-650   How to opt to tax land or buildings

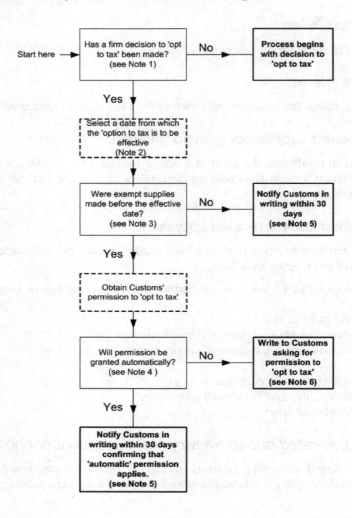

Start here →

Has a firm decision to 'opt to tax' been made?
(see Note 1)

— No → **Process begins with decision to 'opt to tax'**

Yes ↓

Select a date from which the 'option to tax is to be effective
(Note 2)

↓

Were exempt supplies made before the effective date?
(see Note 3)

— No → **Notify Customs in writing within 30 days (see Note 5)**

Yes ↓

Obtain Customs' permission to 'opt to tax'

↓

Will permission be granted automatically?
(see Note 4)

— No → **Write to Customs asking for permission to 'opt to tax' (see Note 6)**

Yes ↓

Notify Customs in writing within 30 days confirming that 'automatic' permission applies.
(see Note 5)

Notes

(1)   Deciding to 'opt to tax'

In *Blythe Limited Partnership v C & E Commrs* [1999] BVC 2,224, the VAT & Duties Tribunals ruled that there is 'a clear distinction between election and notification'. The first stage is making the decision to opt to tax. The second stage is contacting HMRC.

(2)   Effective date

The effective date must be a current or future date as an election to 'opt to tax' cannot be exercised retrospectively.

(3)   Exempt supplies

It is necessary to establish if the person entitled to opt to tax has made, or will make, an exempt of supply of the land or building during the ten years ending on the date that it is intended the option to tax becomes effective.

(4)   Permission granted automatically

There are four situations when HMRC grant permission automatically. These are set out in Notice 742A, para. 5.2.

(5)   Notifying Customs

The election is not effective unless notified to HMRC within 30 days from the effective date. Notification may be made using the Form VAT 1614A or 1614H.

(6)   Seeking Customs' permission

When it is necessary to apply for permission HMRC certain information including a brief description of the future plans for the land or building, details of expected input tax recovery, value of exempt supplies made during the last 10 years, expected taxable supplies and details of anyone who has helped to fund the land or building, or any 'connected person', who is occupying or intends to occupy any part of the land or building.

Fuller information is available in Notice 742A, para. 5.5.

(7)   Further advice and information

Further advice may need to be sought because this is a complicated area. Further information is available in VAT Notice 742A.

15-680   Revoking the option to tax

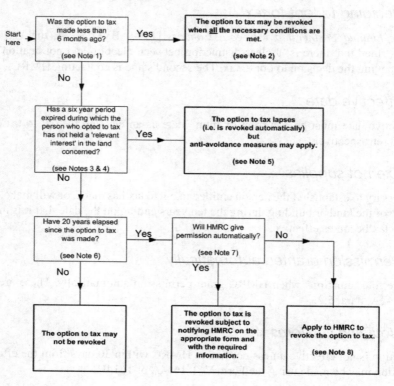

Land, Property and Construction

Notes

(1) Commencement of six-month cooling-off period

The six-month period runs from the date upon which the option to tax had effect.

(2) Conditions for revoking option during six-month cooling-off period

The conditions which must be met to revoke the option to tax during the cooling-off period are as follows:

(1) no use, including your own occupation, has been made of the land since the option to tax had effect. This condition was revoked with effect from 1 April 2010;

(2) no tax has become chargeable on a supply of the land as result of the option;

(3) no input tax is claimed or becomes allowable as a result of the option to tax;

(4) no transfer of a going concern has taken place;

(5) HMRC are notified on the appropriate form.

Legislation: VATA 1994, Sch. 10, para. 23

(3) Six-year period

The six-year period must be continuous. It may commence any time after the option to tax is exercised and effective.

Legislation: VATA 1994, Sch. 10, para. 24

(4) 'Relevant interest'

'Relevant interest' is an 'interest in, right over or licence to occupy the building or land (or any part of it)'.

Legislation: VATA 1994, Sch. 10, para. 24(3)

(5) Automatic revocation anti-avoidance

The revocation is not revoked when, during the relevant six-year period:

(1) the person who opted to tax was a member of a VAT group; and

(2) a relevant associate with an interest in the property left the group without ceasing to be a relevant associate.

Legislation: VATA 1994, Sch. 10, para. 26

(6)   20-year period

The 20-year period starts on the day upon which the option to tax had effect.

Legislation: VATA 1994, Sch. 10, para. 24

(7)   *When HMRC give permission automatically*

(1)   neither the person revoking the election nor any member of the same VAT group has an interest in the property when the option is revoked; or

(2)   when all the following conditions are met:

  (a)   the capital goods scheme does not apply or (from 1 August 2009) the sum of all remaining capital goods scheme adjustments is £10,000 or less;

  (b)   during 10 years prior to revocation, there were no grants for less than open market value nor a grant which will rise to supplies for an inflated consideration after revocation;

  (c)   supplies made before the option will not be attributable a supply, or use of the land and buildings, more than 12 months after the option is revoked.

Legislation: VATA 1994, Sch. 10, para. 25

(8)   *When after 20 years automatic permission does not apply*

HMRC will only give permission when some, but not all, the conditions in Note (7)(b) have been met.

Other information: Notice 742A, Section 8

[This page is intentionally blank]

15-710 Real estate elections

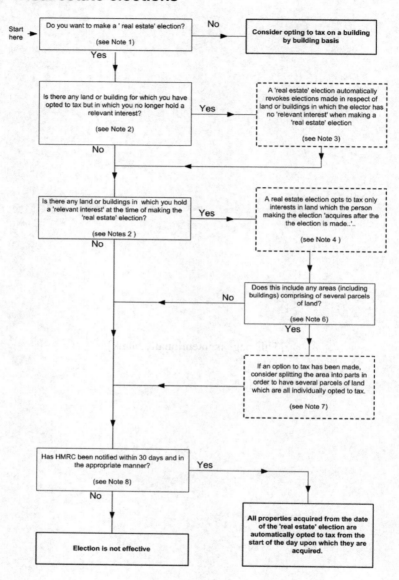

Start here → Do you want to make a ' real estate' election?

(see Note 1)

No → **Consider opting to tax on a building by building basis**

Yes

Is there any land or building for which you have opted to tax but in which you no longer hold a relevant interest?

(see Note 2)

Yes → A 'real estate' election automatically revokes elections made in respect of land or buildings in which the elector has no 'relevant interest' when making a 'real estate' election

(see Note 3)

No

Is there any land or buildings in which you hold a 'relevant interest' at the time of making the 'real estate' election?

(see Notes 2)

Yes → A real estate election opts to tax only interests in land which the person making the election 'acquires after the the election is made..'..

(see Note 4)

No

Does this include any areas (including buildings) comprising of several parcels of land?

(see Note 6)

No

Yes

If an option to tax has been made, consider splitting the area into parts in order to have several parcels of land which are all individually opted to tax.

(see Note 7)

Has HMRC been notified within 30 days and in the appropriate manner?

(see Note 8)

Yes

No

Election is not effective

All properties acquired from the date of the 'real estate' election are automatically opted to tax from the start of the day upon which they are acquired.

Notes

(1)   Relevant interest

In respect of land or buildings, a 'relevant interest' is 'any interest in, right over or licence to occupy the building or land (or any part of it)'.

Legislation: VATA 1994, Sch. 10, para. 12

(2)   Options to tax which are automatically revoked

From 1 August 2009 an anti-avoidance measure denies automatic revocation in respect of land or buildings for which some supplies will arise after making the real estate election. See VAT Information Sheet 12/09.

> 'Although you cannot retain an option on a property in which you have no relevant interest at the time of making the REE (real estate election – author's insert), you may make a new option in respect of that property and notify it so that it has effect immediately ...'

(VAT Information Sheet 03/08, Annex 1, para. 4.4.3)

(3)   Land affected by a real estate election

> 'A person (E) may make ... (a 'real estate election') ... in relation to ... relevant interests in any land or buildings which E acquires after the elction is made ...'

Legislation: VATA 1994, Sch. 10, para. 21

(4)   Options to tax which continue

As real estate election neither revokes or nor supersedes an option to tax made in respect of land or building in which a 'relevant interest' is held when making the real estate election, the original option continues to take precedence.

(5)   An option to tax made in respect of areas of land

> 'An option to tax ... exercised in relation to any land (otherwise than by reference to any building or part of a building) ... may in circumstances specified in a public notice, be converted ... into separate options to tax ...'

Legislation: VATA 1994, Sch. 10, para. 22(6)

Land, Property and Construction

(6) Creating several parcels

'The choice is only available in relation to land or buildings in which you have a relevant interest at the time you make the REE. Each parcel of land must meet conditions … '

(VAT Information Sheet 03/08, Annex 1, para. 4.5.1)

(7) Notifying HMRC

HMRC must be notified on the correct form. They must also be advised of, and provided with certain information about, any relevant interests in land held at the time of making the real estate election.

(8) Further information

Notice 742A, Section 14 and VAT Information Sheet 03/08.

Land, Property and Construction

[This page is intentionally blank]

15-730 Option to tax – anti-avoidance measure

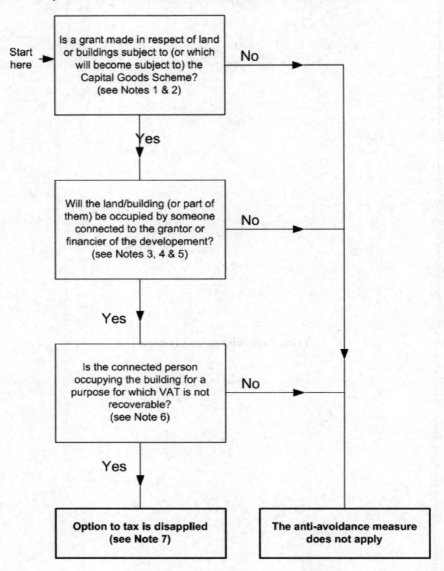

Notes

Land, Property and Construction

(1)   Capital Goods Scheme

The Capital Goods Scheme applies to land, buildings, refurbishments and civil engineering works costing more than £250,000. For more information, see 7-760.

(2)   Relevant transactions

'... "grant" refers to the act that transfers the land or building, such as a freehold sale ... the leasing or licensing of land or a building, or the assignment or surrender of that lease ...'

(3)   Meaning of occupied

'... "occupation" of land for the purposes of para. 3A(7) (the option to tax anti-avoidance measure) requires more than a right to use the land ...' The Principal and Fellows of *Newnham College Cambridge v R & C Commrs* [2006] BVC 483, [2008] BVC 452, where the House of Lords upheld the decision of the Court of Appeal.

(4)   Connected persons

Whether persons are connected is determined in accordance with s. 839 of ICTA 1988 (VATA 1994, Sch. 10, para. 34(2)). From August 2009, banks are not connected merely because of any government shareholding.

(5)   Financier

'... a person is only deemed to have been responsible for financing a development if two key conditions are met:

(a)   at the time the finance is provided, or the agreement to provide the finance is entered into, the person providing the finance must intend or expect that he or the grantor, or somebody connected to either of them, will occupy the particular development for other than eligible purposes; and

(b)   the funds must be for the purpose of financing the purchase, construction or refurbishment of that development.' (Notice 742A, para. 13.7)

(6)   Use of the land/buildings

Using the land or buildings in connection with the making of exempt supplies or for non-business activities will bring the development within the scope of this anti-avoidance measure.

(7)   Further information

For further information, see 15-300, Notice 742A and Revenue and Customs Brief 33/09 and VAT Information Sheet 12/09.

15-750 When construction services may be zero-rated

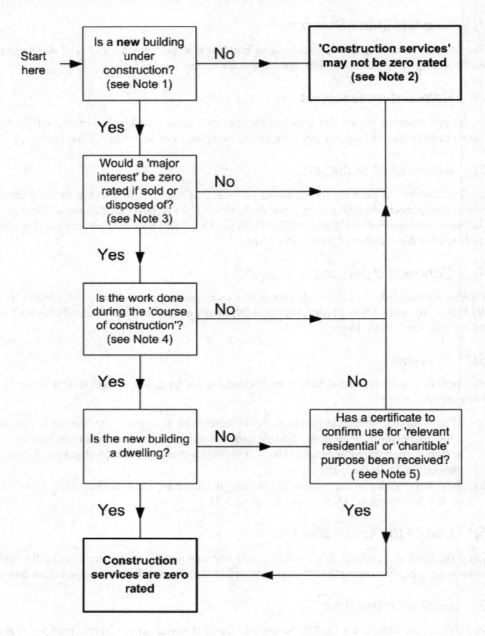

Notes

(1)   New buildings

For these purposes, a new building includes the following:

- the creation of an entire new building;
- the erection of a new building following the demolition, or almost complete demolition, of an existing building;
- an enlargement to an existing building to the extent that the enlargement creates an additional dwelling or dwellings;
- certain annexes to buildings used for charitable purposes.

(2)   Other zero-rated construction services

Certain 'construction services' carried out when converting certain buildings for housing associations or in respect of listed buildings may also be zero-rated.

(3)   Zero-rated sales or disposals

Subject to a number of conditions, the first grant of a 'major interest' in a new dwelling, a building used 'solely for a relevant residential purpose' or 'solely for a relevant charitable purpose' is a zero-rated supply. The grant of a 'major interest' may be the freehold or a lease of more than 21 years.

(4)   'Course of construction'

To qualify for zero-rating, the 'construction services' must be carried out during the 'course of construction'. HMRC interpret this to mean as follows:

- (a)   'work ... prior to the completion of the building'; or
- (b)   'any other service closely connected to the construction of the building'.

It is not always clear when a building is completed. It must be determined by considering, as appropriate, the date of issue of a 'Completion statement', the intention of the developer, the planning consent (including variations), the date of sale and the date of occupation.

(5)   Certificates, etc.

These supplies may not be zero-rated unless the supply is made to the person who will use the building for 'a relevant residential purpose' or 'relevant charitable purposes' and that person certifies in advance in writing that the building will be so used.

(6)   Further information

For more information, see 15-560 and Notice 708.

15-770 Protected buildings – when the zero-rate applies to construction services – until 1 October 2012

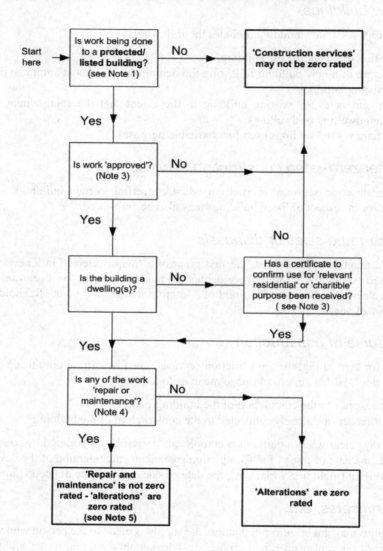

Start here → Is work being done to a **protected/ listed building**? (see Note 1)

— No → **'Construction services' may not be zero rated**

Yes ↓

Is work 'approved'? (Note 3)

— No →

Yes ↓

Is the building a dwelling(s)? — No → Has a certificate to confirm use for 'relevant residential' or 'charitible' purpose been received? (see Note 3)

— Yes →

Yes ↓

Is any of the work 'repair or maintenance'? (Note 4) — No →

Yes ↓

'Repair and maintenance' is not zero rated - 'alterations' are zero rated (see Note 5)

'Alterations' are zero rated

Notes

Warning: From 1 October 2012 the following zero-rating relief for alterations to listed buildings is removed, except for supplies to which the transitional arrangements apply (see 15-360).

(1) Listed buildings or monuments

To qualify for any work to be zero-rated, the building or monument must normally be Grade I, Grade II(*), Grade II or the equivalent in Scotland and Northern Ireland. Other listed buildings or monuments are excluded from the scope of this zero-rating.

(2) 'Approved'

The work must be 'approved' in advance. Work is 'approved' when:

(a) it required and received listed building consent from the appropriate local planning authority; or

(b) the 'ecclesiastical exemption' applies and listed building need not be obtained; or

(c) the work would normally require listed building consent but is disencumbered because the building is on Crown or Duchy land.

(3) Certificates, etc.

These supplies may not be zero-rated unless the supply is made to the person who will use the building for 'a relevant residential purpose' or 'relevant charitable purposes' and that person certifies in advance in writing that the building will be so used.

(4) Repair and maintenance

'Works of repair or maintenance are those tasks designed to minimise, for as long as possible, the need for, and future scale and cost of, further attention to the fabric of the building ...' (Notice 708, para. 9.3.1)

(5) Apportionment

'Works of repair or maintenance are standard-rated ... If you are supplying both zero-rated and standard-rated work you must apportion your supply on a fair and reasonable basis to reflect the differing liabilities' (Notice 708, para. 9.7.1).

(6) Further information

For more information, see 13-100 et seq and Notice 708.

15-775   When transitional rules apply to work to protected buildings

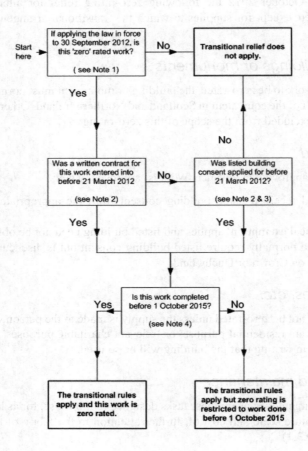

Start here → If applying the law in force to 30 September 2012, is this 'zero' rated work?

(see Note 1)

No → Transitional relief does not apply.

Yes

Was a written contract for this work entered into before 21 March 2012

(see Note 2)

No → Was listed building consent applied for before 21 March 2012?

(see Note 2 & 3)

No

Yes   **Yes**

Is this work completed before 1 October 2015?

(see Note 4)

Yes ← | → **No**

The transitional rules apply and this work is zero rated.

The transitional rules apply but zero rating is restricted to work done before 1 October 2015

Notes

(1) Work qualifying for transition relief

The only work qualifying for transitional relief is "approved alteration" which would have been zero-rated under the law as it was until 30 September 2012.

(2) Limitations on contracts entered into or listed building consent applied for before 21 March 2012

Transitional relief is restricted to these contracts and applications as they 'stood immediately before 21 March 2012'.

(3) Listed building consent

This means consent applied for in accordance with the following:

(a) in the case of an ecclesiastical building to which s. 60 of the *Planning (Listed Buildings and Conservation Areas) Act* 1990 applies, consent for the approved alterations by a competent body with the authority to approve alterations to such buildings, or

(b) in any other case, consent under any provision of:

(i) Part 1 of the *Planning (Listed Buildings and Conservation Areas) Act* 1990;

(ii) Part 1 of the *Planning (Listed Buildings and Conservation Areas) (Scotland) Act* 1997;

(iii) Part 5 of the *Planning (Northern Ireland) Order* 1991;

(iv) Part 1 of the *Ancient Monuments and Archaeological Areas Act* 1979; or

(v) Part 2 of the *Historic Monuments and Archaeological Objects (Northern Ireland) Order* 1995.

(4) Work spanning 1 October 2015

Any work performed after this date will be standard-rated.

Land, Property and Construction

Schemes

RETAIL SCHEMES

16-000   Introduction to retail schemes

An essential feature of VAT is the VAT invoice. The supplier of taxable supplies is obliged to issue such a document when making a supply to a taxable person, and the invoice usually forms the prime source record in accounting for the tax. The customer uses it as evidence for reclaiming the tax. In effect, the tax invoice serves as the bedrock of the whole VAT system until the chain reaches the stage of retail sales to final customers, where the tax is really collected.

It would be unreasonable to expect retailers to issue invoices for every tiny supply made and they are only obliged to issue invoices in respect of supplies made to taxable persons. As a result, they do not necessarily hold copy invoices or individual records of each transaction from which to arrive at their output tax liabilities. Instead, retailers are permitted, subject to the approval of HMRC, to estimate the tax due on their sales, using methods of estimation laid down by, or agreed with, HMRC. These methods of estimation are known as retail schemes.

The purpose of this section is to provide an overview of the retail schemes.

The first thing to understand about the retail schemes is that they are not trivial. Whatever the size of the retail business, the choice of the right scheme and the proper operation of it are crucial in arriving at the amount of tax due and, ultimately, the amount of profit made.

The second thing to realise is that in many parts the public Notices about retail schemes published by HMRC have the force of law.

Other material: Notice 727; Notices 727/2 to 727/5

Legislation: VATA 1994 Sch. 11, para. 2(6)

VAT Reporter: ¶45-000

16-020   Retailer

Although use of the retail schemes is available to retailers, the term 'retailer' is not defined in the legislation or in the notices. Notice 727, says that the schemes are intended for businesses who cannot reasonably be expected to account for VAT in the normal way, and that retail supplies are generally of low value and made to a large number of customers in small quantities.

The notice goes on, in a statement having the force of law, to exclude from the schemes supplies (including supplies by retailers) made to other VAT-registered businesses, except for occasional cash sales. In practice, therefore, use of the schemes is restricted to retail businesses as commonly understood.

Other material: Notice 727

VAT Reporter: ¶45-000

16-040   Outline of retail schemes

There are four main types of scheme available, plus normal VAT accounting. Which is preferable depends on the nature of the retail business and of the supplies which it makes. There are also restrictions on eligibility to use the schemes, depending on the size of the retail business.

Types of retail schemes

All of the retail schemes depend on an estimate of the VAT content of the 'daily gross takings' (DGT) of the business. Matters affecting the DGT, and so common to all of the schemes, are covered at 16-100.

The four main types of retail scheme are:

(1)   point-of-sale scheme – as the name implies, this depends on analysing takings between different categories of supply at the point of sale (for instance, by the use of a multi-rate till, or of separate tills for supplies made at different rates);

(2)   apportionment schemes – the DGT is split by reference to the respective amounts of purchases for resale liable to VAT at the different rates;

(3)   direct calculation schemes – the element of the DGT representing sales of goods at the minority rate for that business is taken to be the expected selling price of minority rate purchases for resale (possibly adjusted for stock movements), and the balance is taken to represent sales at the majority rate. Thus, a business selling mainly standard-rated goods would use purchases of zero-rated goods to work out the expected sales of zero-rated goods, and the balance of DGT would be taken to be standard-rated;

(4)   bespoke schemes – these are specially agreed schemes tailored for specific retailers and set out in considerable detail in the correspondence agreeing their terms. Retailers with turnover above £130m can only use a bespoke scheme, or normal VAT accounting.

A common feature of all of the schemes is that they are designed to provide a split of the DGT between supplies liable at different rates of VAT. Once this has been done, the output tax liability for the period concerned is calculated by applying the appropriate VAT fraction (16-060) to each category of supplies.

Eligibility for schemes

HMRC have power to refuse the use of a retail scheme if it appears to them that it does not produce a fair and reasonable result, or that the retailer could reasonably be expected to account for VAT normally, or that it is necessary for the protection of the revenue.

Although it seems unlikely that HMRC will engage in the wholesale refusal of the use of schemes on the ground that VAT can be accounted for normally (except, perhaps, in the case of businesses which already operate full sales ledgers itemising all sales), they are likely to be more sceptical than hitherto about claims of inability to account normally.

When the turnover of the retail business exceeds £130m the business must negotiate a bespoke scheme with HMRC. At the other end of the scale Apportionment Scheme 1 and Direct Calculation Scheme 1 are restricted to retailers with a turnover less than £1m.

There can also be restrictions on the availability of some schemes depending whether the supplies made include services, own-produced goods, exempt supplies, etc.

Subject to eligibility, it may be possible for a retailer to use a mixture of schemes to deal with different parts of the same business. This should always be agreed with HMRC.

VAT Reporter: ¶45-005

Other material: Notice 727

16-060   The VAT fraction

Under each scheme, once takings at a positive rate have been established, it is necessary to calculate the VAT content. This is done by applying the VAT fraction to the gross takings for the rate concerned.

For takings liable to the standard rate of 15 per cent, the VAT fraction is 3/23rds (equivalent to 15/115).

For takings liable at the standard rate of 17.5 per cent, the VAT fraction is 7/47ths (equivalent to 17.5/117.5). Applying this to the gross takings for that rate gives the same result as applying 17.5 per cent to the net of VAT amount.

For takings liable at the standard rate of 20 per cent the VAT fraction is 1/6th (equivalent to 20/120)

Similarly, the VAT fraction for takings liable at the lower rate of five per cent is 1/21st.

For further details see 1-000.

VAT Reporter: ¶18-018

16-080 Point-of-sale retail scheme

The point-of-sale scheme involves identifying the VAT liability of sales at the point of sale, so that an exact split can be made of the daily gross takings. This is not the same as making a separate permanent record of each supply made, as under the normal VAT scheme, but merely maintaining running totals in some way or another. Possible ways include the use of appropriate tills, which can identify individual sales and their VAT liability (although these would not normally capture details of the exact goods supplied, and of customers, as under the normal VAT system). Alternatives might include the use of separate tills for differently rated supplies, or of a manual record of one type of sale.

The point-of-sale scheme, operated correctly, clearly gives the most accurate calculation of the retailer's VAT liability. However, it also carries with it the danger of inaccurate operation if the system (including the capabilities of the staff operating it) is faulty in some way. HMRC indicate that a retailer wishing to use the point-of-sale scheme is responsible for ensuring that adequate systems to operate it are in place, including at the busiest periods.

Electronic point of sale

HMRC's views of how these systems should be operated are given in a VAT Information Sheet.

Other material: Notice 727/3; VAT Information Sheet 11/03, August 2003

VAT Reporter: ¶45-800

16-100 Apportionment retail schemes

The apportionment schemes work from records of goods purchased for resale at each applicable VAT rate, and use these to apportion the 'daily gross takings' (DGT) on the basis that the same proportions apply to them. There is no attempt to identify the liability of sales as and when they are made.

The principle is straightforward, but the mechanics of calculation are a little more complex, especially for the second apportionment scheme.

Apportionment Scheme 1

The first apportionment scheme is available only to retailers with turnover not exceeding £1 million per annum It is based strictly on the cost of goods for resale, and stocks on hand at commencement, or at VAT year-ends, are ignored.

Most of the time, it is simply necessary to identify the cost of goods purchased for resale for the VAT period concerned, convert this to arrive at ratios for each liability of goods, then apply these ratios to the DGT for the same period.

Once a year (for the period ending 31 March, 30 April or 31 May, depending on the applicable VAT quarters), the calculation must be done, not for that quarter, but for the whole VAT year, and the VAT paid to date then knocked off the resultant liability for the year as a whole. This annual calculation removes the temptation to manipulate the results artificially by, for example, ensuring that disproportionate amounts of zero-rated purchases take place in periods where sales are seasonally high.

This scheme clearly lacks accuracy, because it is based purely on the purchase price of differently rated goods and because there are no stock adjustments. The advantage which it possesses is simplicity.

One of the inaccuracies, the basing of the scheme on the cost of goods for resale, may be particularly significant for some businesses. As HMRC point out in their notice, a business which tends to have a higher mark-up on its zero-rated goods than on its standard-rated goods is likely to find itself paying more VAT than would be the case using another scheme. By the same token and for the same reason, a business with a lower mark-up on its zero-rated goods than on its standard-rated ones is likely to pay less.

Depending on the amounts involved, it may be worth using the scheme even at the price of a small VAT disadvantage simply on administrative grounds.

Apportionment Scheme 2

The second apportionment scheme is similar to the first in that it is based on an analysis of all purchases for resale, but it differs in that reduces the inaccuracies. It does this in two ways:

(1) the calculations are not based on the costs of goods for resale, but on their expected selling prices; and

(2) it takes account of stock when the scheme is first used, and operates a 'smoothing' scheme thereafter (presumably to thwart attempts at manipulation without going to the extent of having a full stock adjustment approach).

The calculation of expected selling prices is an added complication, and one which can give rise to disputes with HMRC. Ultimately, this must be a matter of informed opinion, backed up by evidence. HMRC point out that it should be a realistic estimate taking account of relevant factors such as price changes (such as sell-by-date reductions, special offers, wastage, breakages, etc.). No doubt the retailer prefers the expected selling price of standard-rated goods to be low, and that of zero-rated goods to be high, and HMRC prefer the opposite, so there is ample room for dispute here with equivalent arguments produced on each side depending on the rating of the goods concerned.

The smoothing scheme is a rolling one. Broadly speaking, the purchases used to arrive at a proportion for the current period's DGT are those of the current quarter plus the previous three (a year's worth in all). Clearly, there is not a full year's worth to take into account in the earliest period's of using the scheme, but the opening stock is brought into each of the first three quarters as being equivalent to a quarter in itself.

Other material: Notice 727/4

VAT Reporter: ¶45-850

16-120   Direct calculation retail schemes

The direct calculation schemes are similar to apportionment schemes in that they seek to estimate the VAT liability on sales from records held on purchases for resale. They differ in that they reduce administrative requirements by working from only a part of purchases, being the 'minority' goods sold.

This means that calculations are based on the purchases whose VAT rate constitutes the minority of total sales. A trader whose sales are 40 per cent zero-rated and 60 per cent standard-rated would work from the purchase records for zero-rated goods, while one whose sales ratios were the other way round would work from purchase records for standard-rated goods. Clearly, this scheme is inappropriate if the rates applicable to sales are more or less evenly balanced, as extra work could be needed each period to decide which were the minority goods.

In either case, the direct calculation schemes work from the expected selling prices of the goods, not from their purchase prices (in contrast to the first apportionment scheme).

Direct Calculation Scheme 1

The first direct calculation scheme is available only to retailers with turnover not exceeding £1 million per annum. It is based strictly on the expected selling price of 'minority' goods purchased for resale, and stocks-on-hand at commencement, or at VAT year-ends, are ignored. There is not even an annual adjustment.

For each VAT period, the retailer must identify the expected selling prices of 'minority' goods obtained for resale. This part of the 'daily gross takings' (DGT) is taken to be liable to VAT at the minority rate(s), and the remainder is taken to be liable at the rate applicable to the majority goods.

This is the end of the calculation. There is no annual adjustment.

Direct Calculation Scheme 2

The second direct calculation scheme is similar to the first. The only difference is that it requires an adjustment to take account of stocks on hand when use of the scheme starts, and at the end of each VAT year.

The basic calculation for each quarter (including the fourth quarter of a VAT year, ending on 31 March, 30 April or 31 May according to VAT periods applicable) is identical to the first direct calculation scheme. However, an annual adjustment must also be made for the fourth quarter. This is a calculation for the year as a whole, based on purchases for the year as a whole adjusted for opening and closing stocks, and applied to the DGT for the year as a whole. This gives rise to an output tax liability for the year as a whole, and the annual adjustment is the difference between that and the amounts calculated for the separate periods. Thus, there are two figures for output tax to include in the fourth quarter return:

(1)   the amount calculated for that period; and

(2)   the annual adjustment.

Other material: Notice 727/5

VAT Reporter: ¶45-870

16-150   Bespoke retail schemes

The bespoke retail schemes are schemes specifically agreed between the retailer and HMRC, and the terms of them should be laid down in detail. They are intended to be based on the precise circumstances of the retailer concerned. Bespoke schemes are available, in principle, to all retailers (other than those who HMRC consider can reasonably be expected to account for VAT under the normal VAT system, and so refuse to allow the use of a retail scheme). They are of most interest to retailers with turnover in excess of £130 million per annum (until 1 April 2009, the figure is £100 million), who are not permitted to use the published schemes and must agree a bespoke scheme if they are to use a retail scheme at all.

Bespoke schemes are often based on published schemes, but may differ considerably. HMRC emphasise that their agreement to bespoke schemes must be based on full disclosure by the retailer. It can therefore be expected that HMRC will seek retrospective revocation of a bespoke scheme agreed by them which appears to provide an undue tax advantage based on facts not disclosed to them when the scheme was agreed. Furthermore, an agreement of a bespoke scheme generally includes a date by which its operation and continued applicability is to be reviewed, and a requirement for the retailer to notify HMRC of any changes to the business which may mean that the scheme no longer produces a fair and reasonable result.

Anyone wishing to agree a bespoke retail scheme with HMRC needs to proceed on a basis of openness if they are to be able to rely upon it. Experience with special partial exemption methods, and litigation resulting from them, shows that it is wise also to pay close attention to the precise terms of the scheme and likely effects, rather than taking a broad brush approach, before agreement is finalised. Once the scheme is agreed, it is similar in effect to legislation or to a private, legally, binding contract.

Other material: Notice 727/2

VAT Reporter: ¶45-330

16-180   Special retail schemes for particular businesses

There are some published special adaptations to the published retail schemes to deal with the position of businesses which commonly buy in goods for resale at one VAT rate, but which have a different liability when sold, or to deal with special relationships which arise in the retail process (as with retail florists dealing with long distance sales, where one florist receives the cash from the customer but another supplies the flowers at a distant location).

These adaptations cover:

(1)   caterers;

(2)   retail chemists; and

(3)   florists.

Other material: Notice 727

VAT Reporter: ¶46-190

16-210   Changing retail schemes

Once a retail scheme has been adopted, it must normally be used for at least a year, and any change of scheme should normally take place from a scheme anniversary. However, if a retailer becomes ineligible to use an existing scheme, then a change must be made to a different scheme or to normal VAT accounting from the start of the next VAT period.

On a change of scheme, there may be a final adjustment to be made for the previous retail scheme, similar to an annual adjustment.

Other material: Notice 727, Section 4

VAT Reporter: ¶46-170

16-250   Ceasing to use a scheme

An adjustment may be necessary on ceasing to use a retail scheme at all. This is similar to the annual adjustment, and applies to the first apportionment scheme and the second direct calculation scheme, and may apply to a bespoke scheme.

Other material: Notice 727, Section 6

VAT Reporter: ¶46-170

16-280   Change of VAT rate

There are special rules to deal with changes in VAT rates, and these are contained in the relevant scheme notices.

Other material: Notice 727, Section 7

16-310   Retail schemes and daily gross takings

The key figure for all of the retail schemes is the amount of daily gross takings (DGT). It is a requirement for each scheme that the retailer keeps a record of DGT.

The DGT includes all receipts from customers, such as cash, cheques, debit or credit card vouchers, and amounts receivable under electronic transactions. To these must be added the full value of credit sales as they occur, payments in kind, the face value of gift tokens, etc. redeemed, and any other payments received. Payments received for credit sales are not included (or, if initially included, can then be deducted). Deductions can also be made for various matters listed in the notices, such as dishonoured cheques from cash customers, counterfeit notes, etc.

Other material: Notice 727, Section 4

Cases: *R v C & E Commrs, ex parte Littlewoods Home Shopping Group Plc* [1998] BVC 161

VAT Reporter: ¶45-380

16-350   Business promotion schemes

Retailers inevitably become involved in the operation of business promotion schemes, both their own and those operated by manufacturers. The current treatment of some of these is given in the notices, and there is a brief discussion at 18-830. The VAT treatment of many business promotion schemes is currently uncertain, and the possible variations of schemes are endless.

Other material: Notice 700/7

VAT Reporter: ¶45-380

16-400   Conclusion to retail schemes

This section has given an overview of the retail schemes. Those involved with them should make a detailed study of the relevant notices.

It should always be borne in mind that the schemes are designed to produce an estimate of output tax, not an exact result, working from global figures. Because there is not a detailed record of each transaction, it is easy to make errors in operating the schemes. Visiting officers seek to verify both the total amount of the 'daily gross takings' (DGT) recorded and the split between rates.

In order to minimise the risk of error, the retailer should operate his own credibility checks, comparing the scheme figures with the annual accounts, management accounts, etc. and generally ensuring that the figures used for VAT return purposes tie up with the actual performance of the business.

Particular care should be taken to keep a record of any factors which give rise to a drop in DGT compared with expectations, in order to prove that the takings have been fully recorded. Examples are special discounts, stock losses, etc. It is also well worth keeping old price lists, as a form of evidence of the margins actually being achieved.

VAT Reporter: ¶102

SECOND-HAND GOODS SCHEME

16-430 Introduction

VAT is intended ultimately to be collected at the retail stage of the supply chain. When a taxable supply is made by a trader to a final consumer, tax is accountable on the supply but cannot be recovered by the consumer. This works well for goods and services which are fully consumed by the consumer, but difficulties arise in the case of certain more durable goods which may pass back into the business system.

Under the ordinary scheme of VAT, if goods which have borne tax are sold by the consumer back into the business sector, then supplied again to another consumer, tax will arise on this new transfer into the non-business sector. As a result, the same article will be subjected to VAT twice.

> ### *Example: double taxation*
>
> Trader Alf sells an article to a consumer for £100 plus VAT. Some time later, the consumer sells the article to trader Barry, for £40, and trader Barry subsequently sells it to another consumer for £55 plus VAT of £11. The article has now borne VAT of £20 on the first sale to a consumer and £11 on the second, totalling £31.

In order to mitigate this double taxation, dealers in second-hand goods may operate a margin scheme. The aim of this is to tax the dealer's margin (i.e. the difference between the selling price of the goods and their purchase price), rather than the full selling price.

VAT Reporter: ¶48-625

16-460   Outline of scheme

The basic idea of the second-hand goods scheme is to restrict the amount of tax due on goods sold under them to tax on the trader's margin, rather than on the entire amount charged on reselling the goods.

The trader must calculate the difference between the price at which he buys the goods and that at which he sells them, and account for tax at $^1/_6$ of the gross profit.

Example: sale under scheme

A trader buys goods under the second-hand goods scheme for £40, and re-sells them for £60. VAT is due at $^1/_6$ of £20 (£60 − £40), giving a liability of £3.33.

The position is the same as if he had made a supply not covered by such a scheme for a VAT-inclusive price of £20.

Where goods are sold under the second-hand goods scheme, the trader must not issue a tax invoice showing the amount of VAT due. This prevents the trader from having to reveal his margin to his customer. It also means that, if the customer is a taxable person, the customer will be unable to reclaim the tax charged as input tax. However, the trader in second-hand goods is not obliged to sell the goods under the scheme and can, instead, sell them under the ordinary VAT system, charging tax on the full price (see 6-360).

VAT Reporter: ¶48-625

16-490   Eligible goods

The second-hand goods scheme is available for:

(1)   tangible movable property suitable for further use as it is or after repair;

(2)   works of art;

(3)   collectors' items; and

(4)   antiques.

However, it is not available for supplies of precious metals or precious stones. Goods made of precious metals are regarded as being excluded from the scheme if the price for which they are sold does not exceed the market value of the raw materials. Precious stones are excluded only when not mounted, set or strung.

The goods must not have been purchased on a tax invoice, and a tax invoice must not be issued when they are sold.

The margin scheme cannot be used for the sale of otherwise eligible goods obtained under a transfer of a going concern unless they were also eligible for sale under the scheme in the hands of the transferor.

Legislation: *Value Added Tax (Special Provisions) Order* 1995 (SI 1995/1268), art. 2; VATA 1994, s. 21

Other material: Notice 718, Section 20

VAT Reporter: ¶48-630

16-520   Records

In order to apply the second-hand goods scheme, the trader must keep certain records specified by HMRC. The principal records required are a stock book and purchase and sale invoices.

The stock book must identify the goods concerned, and keep track of buying and selling prices. In the case of second-hand horses and ponies, a special three-part form is used for each animal, instead of a stock book.

Full details of the records and procedures can be found in the various scheme notices published by HMRC. It is important to comply fully with the conditions in the notices, as these have the force of law.

If these records are not kept, the goods cannot be sold under the scheme and tax must be accounted for on the full selling price. However, some relief may be allowed in the case of second-hand car sales for which full scheme records have not been kept. If HMRC are satisfied that the dealer's mark-up does not exceed 100 per cent, the tax due will be restricted to:

(1)   tax on the purchase price, if records of the purchase are held; or

(2)   tax on half the sale price, if records of the sale are held.

Other material: Notice 718, Section 5;

VAT Reporter: ¶48-730

16-550   Dealer's margin

The dealer's margin on which the charge to tax is based when goods are sold under the scheme is the full selling price (before deducting any auctioneers' commissions, etc.) less the price which the dealer paid for the goods. If the dealer has carried out work on the goods, the cost of such work cannot be included in the cost of the goods to the dealer. However, any VAT incurred on such costs will be recoverable as input tax.

Where goods have been obtained under a transfer of a going concern, the cost of them for margin-scheme purposes is the cost to the transferor, not the cost allocated under the business transfer. Where there has been a series of transfers of going concerns affecting the same goods, the cost is the cost to the original transferor.

The transferee is not entitled to sell the goods under the margin scheme unless the transferor would have been entitled to do so. Similar rules apply to goods obtained by way of an assignment of rights under a conditional sale or HP agreement.

It should be noted that the scheme must be applied separately to each article sold under it (unless global accounting applies – see below). If some items are sold at a profit, and others at a loss, the losses cannot be set against the profits. VAT is due on the full amount of the profits, with no reduction for losses made on other items.

Legislation: *Value Added Tax (Special Provisions) Order* 1995 (SI 1995/1268), art. 12

Other material: Notice 718, Section 3;

VAT Reporter: ¶48-625

16-580   Used motor cars

Car dealer

When a car dealer re-sells a second-hand motor car, he cannot make use of the second-hand goods scheme unless he keeps the full records required under the scheme.

Non-dealers

However, a taxable person who is not a car dealer can re-sell a motor car used in the business, and account for tax only on any excess of proceeds over costs, without having any special records.

It should be noted that the second-hand goods scheme does not apply to used motor cars where the dealer pays VAT on the purchase of the car (generally, cars purchased for wholly business use on or after 1 August 1995, on which the original business purchaser could recover VAT: see 6-300). In practice, it will usually be ex-leasing cars which are excluded from the scheme because of this, and dealers need to keep separate records of 'qualifying' cars (on which VAT has been charged) and cars eligible for the scheme.

Cars acquired under transfer of a going concern

The second-hand goods scheme cannot be used for the sale of a car acquired under a transfer of a going concern unless the transferor would also have been eligible to use the second-hand goods scheme. Where a car has been obtained under a transfer of a going concern, the cost of it for margin-scheme purposes is the cost to the transferor, not the cost allocated under the business transfer. Where there has been a series of transfers of going concerns affecting the same vehicle, the cost is the cost to the original transferor.

Similar rules apply to vehicles obtained by way of an assignment of rights under a conditional sale or HP agreement.

Legislation *Value Added Tax (Cars) Order* 1992 (SI 1992/3122), art. 8

Other material: Notice 718/1

VAT Reporter: ¶48-740

16-610   Trade-ins and part-exchange

The way in which a business dealing in second-hand goods deals with trade-ins can affect its VAT liabilities, because no relief is given for losses on second-hand goods. This is particularly common in the case of second-hand cars accepted as trade-ins against new cars. A cash purchaser of a new car would frequently be able to obtain a considerable discount from the list price. If a customer trading in an old car is charged the list price for the new one, but given an inflated trade-in price on the old, this increases the likelihood that the dealer will have an unrelieved loss on the subsequent sale of the old car.

It will generally pay the dealer, therefore, to allow the maximum discount on the new car and reduce the amount allowed on the trade-in accordingly.

Even if there would be no loss on the sale of the old car, this approach more closely reflects the commercial position, and also produces a cashflow benefit unless the old car is sold in the same prescribed accounting period as the new car (in which case the cash flow effect is neutral).

Other material: Notice 718, para. 13.6 and Notice 718/1, para. 10.4

16-640   Global accounting

It is not always easy to apply the second-hand goods scheme to individual items. To cater for dealers in low value bulk volume goods, it is possible to utilise a global accounting margin scheme. Under this scheme, the trader must account for VAT in each period on the difference between the total selling and purchase price of eligible goods for the period concerned.

Global accounting is not available for:

(1)   motor vehicles, aircraft, boats, outboard motors, caravans, motorcycles, horses and ponies; and

(2)   items bought for more than £500.

If a bulk purchase includes items costing more than £500, these must be separated out and dealt with under the 'strict' second-hand goods scheme.

If the margin for a period is negative (because eligible purchases have exceeded sales), this is carried forward and set against the margin for a future period.

An adjustment is required on ceasing to use global accounting for any reason (including on de-registration, transfer of the business, etc.).

Legislation: *Value Added Tax (Special Provisions) Order* 1995 (SI 1995/1268), art. 13

Other material: Notice 718, para. 14 and Notice 718/1, para. 10

VAT Reporter: ¶48-745

16-670   Intra-EC supplies

Goods supplied under the second-hand goods scheme to a person in another EC State are dealt with in the same way as supplies to UK customers. The distance selling rules do not apply to goods supplied under the scheme.

Other material: Notice 718, Section 7

16-700   Auctioneers and agents acting in own name

Sales by auctioneers and agents acting in their own name are treated as supplies both to and by them.

There is a special accounting scheme for auctioneers and agents selling second-hand goods. Where margin scheme goods are sold by an agent acting in his own name, the selling price of the goods is deemed to be increased by the amount of any commission charged to the purchaser. Where goods are sold by an auctioneer acting in his own name, he may calculate the selling price for margin scheme purposes by deducting from the successful bid the value of his services to the seller and adding to it the value of his services to the buyer. Where an agent's or auctioneer's commission, etc. is taken into account in arriving at the selling price of the goods, as above, then it is treated as outside the scope of VAT in his hands.

Auctioneers may, by concession, apply it to sales of new goods grown, made or produced (including bloodstock or livestock reared from birth) by unregistered persons. The auctioneer must obtain from the unregistered person a certificate giving his name and address, and confirming that he is neither registered nor required to be registered for VAT.

Other material: Notice 718/2

VAT Reporter: ¶48-755

Schemes

16-730   Imports of works of art, etc.

Goods imported from outside the EU may not be sold on using the margin schemes. The CJEU has ruled that:

> 'the margin scheme was not applicable to supplies of goods … which the taxable dealer himself had imported into the European Union under the normal VAT scheme.'

Subject to conditions, HMRC accept the margin scheme may be used for imports of works of art, antiques and collectors' items to which an effective VAT rate of five per cent is applied at importation – see 5-180.

Legislation: *VAT (Special Provisions) Order* 1995 (SI 1995/1268), art. 12(3)

Case: *Direktsia 'Obzhalvane I upravlenie na izpalneneito' – Varna v Auto Nokolovi OOD* (Case C-203/10) Judgment delivered 3 March 2011

Other material: Notice 718, paras 8.1 and 10.1

VAT Reporter: ¶48-630

SMALL BUSINESSES

16-750   Special schemes for small businesses

Three special schemes are available to businesses with relatively low turnover. These are the cash accounting scheme, the annual accounting scheme and the flat rate scheme. There are also some matters affecting registration which, by their nature, are only of relevance to smaller businesses or to businesses starting up.

16-770   Cash accounting

The cash accounting scheme is intended to permit small businesses to account for VAT by reference to payments made and received, rather than the time when supplies are made and received.

(1) Eligibility

This scheme is available to traders whose taxable turnover for the next 12 months is expected to be below £1.35 million. Taxable turnover includes zero-rated supplies, but excludes supplies of capital assets used in the business. Turnover for this purpose excludes VAT.

In order to be eligible to use the scheme, the trader must be up to date with returns and payments of VAT, must not have lost entitlement to use the scheme within the previous year, and must have a clean record in respect of honesty, etc. However, a trader who is in debt to

HMRC, and has reached agreement with them on settling that debt, can apply to join the scheme.

A trader wishing to use the scheme must use it for the whole of his business, keep proper records, and generally abide by the scheme rules as set out in Notice 731.

However, the scheme cannot be used for the following supplies:

(1)   supplies under hire-purchase agreements, lease purchase agreements, etc.;

(2)   supplies where a VAT invoice is issued and full payment of the amount shown on it is not due for a period in excess of six months from the invoice date; and

(3)   supplies in respect of which a VAT invoice is issued in advance of performance (although an invoice can be issued, before complete performance of a supply, for goods and services actually provided up to the date of the invoice).

Legislation: *Value Added Tax Regulations* 1995 (SI 1995/2518), reg. 59

Other material: Notice 731, para. 2.1

VAT Reporter: ¶55-460

(2) Effect of scheme

A trader using the scheme must account for tax on supplies made when payment is received for them, and reclaim input tax on supplies obtained when they are paid for. Tax on the importation of goods must be accounted for and reclaimed outside of the scheme, in accordance with the ordinary rules.

The general effect of the scheme is to defer the date when output tax is accounted for and at the same time to defer the date when input tax may be reclaimed. It will also provide automatic bad debt relief. While many traders may obtain a cash flow advantage by using the scheme, it may be disadvantageous to the following:

(1)   retailers, as they already account for tax when cash is received and will lose the benefit of being able to deduct input tax before supplies are paid for;

(2)   businesses which can achieve the same effect for output tax by the use of special time of supply rules while continuing to reclaim input tax on an invoice basis; and

(3)   businesses whose supplies are predominantly zero-rated.

New businesses will often prefer to use the ordinary VAT scheme at first, while start-up expenditure is being incurred, and switch to cash accounting later.

VAT Reporter: ¶55-450

Legislation: *Value Added Tax Regulations* 1995 (SI 1995/2518), reg. 57

(3) Date of receipt and payment

Type of receipt	When to account for the VAT on the receipt
Cash	When received
Giro, standing order, direct debit	The date the bank credits the account.
*Credit or debit card	The date the sales voucher is made out.
*Cheque	The date the cheque is received or the date on the cheque, whichever is the later.
*Payment collected by agent	The period in which the agent collects the money on your behalf. The value is the amount of the taxable debt, not the amount of credit given you by the agent.
*Factoring	Where you remain responsible for any loss, the VAT period in which the factor collects the money.

Where the factor bears any loss, the VAT period in which the factor pays you. The amount is the amount that the factor collects in relation to the debt, not any lesser amount paid to you by the factor. If the factor writes off the debt, then account for any VAT on any advance in the period the advance was paid. If the debt is subsequently re-assigned to you, then use bad debt relief. |
| *Selling bad debts | Account for payment in the VAT period in which the debt is sold.

Account for the whole amount of VAT on the debt, not any lesser amount received when the debt is sold. |

*   indicates the instruction has the force of law

Type of receipt	When to reclaim the VAT on the purchase
Cash	The date paid.
Giro, standing order, direct debit	The date the bank debits the account.
*Credit or debit card	The date a sales voucher is made out.
*Cheque	The date you send the cheque or the date on the cheque whichever is the later.

*   indicates the instruction has the force of law

In all cases, if a cheque, debit or credit card payment is later dishonoured, then the VAT account must be amended according to the instructions in Notice 700/45 How to correct errors and make adjustments or claims.

Other material: Notice 731, Section 4

(4) Input tax evidence

In order to reclaim input tax in respect of a cash payment (notes and coins, etc.), the trader must obtain a receipted tax invoice. This is in contrast with the normal scheme of VAT, where there is never any need for a VAT invoice to be receipted.

VAT Reporter: ¶55-465

(5) Net payments

Payments which are reduced by, say, an auctioneer's commission must be grossed up to the full amount due. Payments covering more than one invoice or supply must be apportioned in a 'fair and reasonable' manner.

Other material: Notice 731, Section 5 and 8

VAT Reporter: ¶55-480

(6) Duration of use

A trader who joins the scheme can continue to use it until such time as his turnover renders him ineligible for it. This arises if at the end of a prescribed accounting period his turnover for 12 months then ending has exceeded £1.6 million.

In such a case, the trader must leave the scheme at the end of the prescribed accounting period concerned.

Other material: Notice 731, para. 6.2

Legislation: *Value Added Tax Regulations* 1995 (SI 1995/2518), reg. 60

VAT Reporter: ¶55-455

(7) Joining the scheme

A trader joining the scheme must keep careful records to analyse receipts and payments between those relating to supplies made and received before and after joining. VAT will already have been accounted for, or reclaimed, in respect of the supplies which occurred before entry into the scheme. Consequently, no further VAT is due, or deductible, at the time of payment.

VAT Reporter: ¶55-455

Other material: Notice 731, Section 3

(8) Leaving the scheme

A trader who remains eligible for the scheme, but wishes to leave it, may do so at the end of any VAT period, if he either derives no benefit from it or cannot meet the accounting requirements.

On leaving the scheme, the trader must revert to normal VAT accounting. VAT must also be accounted for in respect of supplies made under the scheme and not yet paid for. From 1 April 2004, when a person using the cash accounting scheme brings outstanding VAT into account when he voluntarily changes to the standard, invoice-based system or when he reaches the maximum turnover limit, he will have six months in which to apply transitional arrangements. A new regulation was introduced in to the *Value Added Tax Regulation* 1995 (SI 1995/2518) to deal with this situation.

People leaving the cash accounting scheme are to be given some help in the transition period by being able to claim bad debt relief at the end of the prescribed accounting period in which he leaves the scheme provided that other conditions are met. A new regulation made this change.

When a trader voluntarily leaves the cash accounting scheme or when he reaches the upper turnover limit, there are to be transitional arrangements. These are very welcome because the spectre of having a huge VAT bill when leaving the scheme has caused many problems.

The scheme may be withdrawn from a trader who is guilty of dishonest conduct while using it, or if HMRC consider it necessary for the protection of the revenue. These traders are not to be able to benefit from the lenient transitional way in to the standard system. They will therefore still immediately have to account for VAT on invoices raised and repay VAT claimed on unpaid purchases if they have the scheme withdrawn. They will apparently not be barred from benefiting from the bad debt relief provision introduced by Regulation 64A.

Legislation: *Value Added Tax Regulations* 1995 (SI 1995/2518), reg. 60

Other material: Notice 731, Section 6

VAT Reporter: ¶55-485

(9) Deregistration

A trader, using the cash accounting scheme, who de-registers must pay VAT on supplies made under the scheme and the VAT on which has not already been accounted for under the cash accounting scheme.

Legislation: *Value Added Tax Regulations* 1995 (SI 1995/2518), reg. 63

Other material: Notice 731, Section 7

VAT Reporter: ¶55-485

16-800   Annual accounting

The annual accounting scheme is available only to businesses which regularly pay tax to HMRC, not to repayment traders. Its use is optional, so businesses which prefer to account for tax quarterly (or monthly) can continue to do this.

Businesses opting for annual accounting make VAT returns only once a year. However, they are obliged to make payments on account of the ultimate liability. An estimate is made (by HMRC) of the likely annual liability. This is based on the past performance of the business and any further information which the trader provides about likely future prospects. The trader then makes either nine interim payments on account or three (larger) interim payments on account.

At the end of the year, the trader makes a return for the whole year, and this is due (with any final balancing payment) two months after the end of the year.

The following apply:

- Businesses with an annual taxable turnover of up to £1,350,000 can join the scheme.
- The turnover limit above which businesses must leave the scheme is £1,600,000.

If at any time it seems likely that turnover for the current year will exceed £1,600,000, the trader must notify HMRC of this, in which case it is open to them to withdraw authorisation to use the scheme.

The trader can opt in or out of the scheme each year. A trader who is late submitting the annual VAT return will be compulsorily removed from the scheme.

Legislation: *Value Added Tax Regulations* 1995 (SI 1995/2518), reg. 50

Other material: Notice 732

VAT Reporter: ¶55-300

16-820   Flat rate scheme

An optional flat rate scheme is available as a simplification to ease the VAT accounting burden on small businesses with a taxable turnover of £150,000 (excluding VAT) or less. The second test that total turnover had to be of £187,500 or less including taxable and exempt supplies together with any non-taxable income was abolished with effect from 1 April 2009.

VAT-registered businesses or those applying for VAT registration who wish to use the scheme can make an application by using the application form (Form VAT 600) in VAT Notice 733 (Flat rate scheme for small businesses) available on the HMRC website at *www.hmrc.gov.uk* or via the National Advice Service. Applications may be submitted online by downloading the application form and emailing it to frsapplications@hmrc.gov.uk or sending a paper copy to the relevant registration unit (see Hardman's Tax Rates and Tables 19-805 or Key Data 1-710).

The scheme is meant to assist small businesses in reducing the need to keep detailed records of purchases and sales, requiring them only to retain a VAT account, a record of the flat rate calculation including the flat rate percentage used, the flatrate turnover for the period, the tax payable and copies of invoices issued. However, please note the following:

- a person using the flat rate scheme must continue to issue VAT invoices to VAT-registered customers;
- a person using the flat rate scheme must maintain sufficient records for direct tax purposes;
- all business records must be retained for a period of six years.

Legislation: *Value Added Tax Regulations* 1995 (SI 1995/2518), reg. 55A–55V, 57A and 69A

Other material: Notice 733 Flat Rate Scheme for Small Businesses

VAT Reporter: ¶55-350

How the scheme works

The VAT payable is calculated using a flat rate percentage applied to the turnover depending on the trade sector or main trade sector in which the business is conducted. It is necessary to decide upon the 'main business activity' of the business and apply the relevant percentage. In case of difficulty, the National Advice Service will give help. For a table of the relevant percentages, see Hardman's Tax Rates and Tables 19-040 or Key Data 1-100.

Flat Rate scheme users can choose whether to account for VAT on a quarterly basis and whether to combine the scheme with the annual accounting scheme.

The record of turnover is based on:

(a)   cash receipts (that is similar to the cash accounting scheme);
(b)   daily gross takings (that is similar to a retail scheme);
(c)   invoices issued (see also reg. 55G).

It is a simple and reasonably painless process to calculate the net VAT payable each quarter from the gross takings recorded as daily gross takings, sales listings or cashbook entries.

Interest on bank deposits

The Tax Tribunal has held that interest on bank deposits does not form part of the 'relevant turnover' for the purposes of the flat rate scheme calculations.

One per cent reduction for newly VAT-registered businesses

During the first year of VAT registration, a business opting for the flat rate scheme benefits from a one per cent reduction in the relevant trade percentage. The reduction may be applied until the day before the first anniversary of the business becoming VAT-registered.

Input tax

Input tax is not claimed on any purchase invoices included in the scheme (see below for items of capital expenditure exceeding £2,000). The scheme is not therefore suitable for repayment businesses.

A business is entitled to reclaim input tax on capital expenditure goods exceeding £2,000 outside the scheme. If the input tax is reclaimed, VAT on the eventual sale of the asset must also be accounted for outside the scheme.

A claim to recover input tax on the construction of a new riding arena costing more than £60,000 was denied to Sally March who used the flat rate scheme. The Tribunal ruled that the firm which constructed the arena supplied services (not goods) to Sally March. This prevented Sally March from recovering the input tax. The relief for capital purchases costing more than £2,000 applied to 'capital expenditure goods'. It does not apply to purchases of services.

Legislation: *Value Added Tax Regulations* 1995 (SI 1995/2518), reg. 55D, 55E, 55G, 55H, 55JB and 55K

Cases: *March* [2009] TC 00062; *Thexton Training Ltd* [2011] TC 00919

Other material: Notice 733 Flat Rate Scheme for Small Businesses; Notice 732 para. 9.1

VAT Reporter: ¶55-355

Eligibility

The flat rate scheme is available to all businesses except:

- those who are or have been in the previous 24 months closely 'associated' with another business (HMRC take 'associated' to mean that one business is under the dominant influence of another or the two businesses are closely bound by financial, economic or organisational links);
- or are or have been in the past 24 months in a VAT group;
- or in the previous 12 months been assessed for a VAT civil fraud offence, made a payment to compound proceedings in respect of VAT under CEMA 1979, s. 152, or convicted of a VAT offence;
- or are using a margin scheme for second-hand goods; or
- trading as tour operators.

If the business is required to operate the capital goods scheme, then it will not be eligible for the flat rate scheme.

Retrospective entry into the scheme

Normally applications will not be accepted for periods for which liability has already been calculated on the normal (or any other) basis. There have to be special circumstances for such an application to be successful. The Tribunal and subsequently the High Court was asked to consider this where an officer had failed to alert a taxpayer to the flat rate scheme during an assurance visit leading to an application for retrospective admission to the scheme.

A tribunal is only permitted to consider whether the decision of HMRC is unreasonable. The High Court overturned the decision of the Tribunal and decided that the taxpayer was given every opportunity to 'advance the facts and arguments upon which he wanted to rely and the question was carefully considered on at least three occasions by different officers'. The decision fell within the wide discretion that HMRC are given and within the normal policy published in Notice 733.

Withdrawal from the scheme

Once in the scheme, a business will be able to operate it until its income exceeds £230,000 in its accounting year or where there are reasonable grounds to expect the income to exceed £230,000 in the next 30 days. If HMRC are satisfied that during the next year the turnover will not exceed £190,000, the business will be allowed to remain in the scheme.

The above thresholds are *VAT inclusive*.

In addition, if the business:

- becomes closely associated with another business;
- becomes eligible to be registered in a VAT group;
- becomes registered for VAT in the name of a division;
- becomes a tour operator;
- opts to use one of the margin schemes for second-hand goods;
- intends to acquire, construct or otherwise obtain a capital item to which the capital goods scheme applies,

then the business must withdraw from the scheme.

HMRC may withdraw permission to use the scheme if they consider it is necessary for the protection of the revenue or if any false statement was made in the application for authorisation to use the scheme.

A business may voluntarily choose to leave the scheme at any time by notifying HMRC in writing, but will be unable to rejoin the flat rate scheme for at least another year.

Businesses may withdraw from the scheme from a current date. Applications to withdraw from the scheme from an earlier date are only allowed in 'exceptional circumstances'. The First Tier Tribunal agreed with HMRC that paying too much VAT because of using FRS is not an 'exceptional circumstance' for these purposes.

Legislation: *Value Added Tax Regulations* 1995 (SI 1995/2518), reg. 55L, 55M, 55P, and 55Q

Cases: *R & C Commrs v Burke* [2010] BVC 563; *Northern Renovations Ltd* [2012] TC 02086; [2012] UKFTT 409 (TC)

Other material: Notice 733 Flat Rate Scheme for Small Businesses

VAT Reporter: ¶55-355 and ¶55-360

Stock and assets

Stock and assets for newly registered businesses

A business newly registering for VAT and starting to use the flat rate scheme can reclaim the input tax incurred on stock and assets on hand at the time of registration in the normal way (6-640).

When input tax is reclaimed on capital assets, any subsequent disposal of those assets has to be accounted for under normal VAT accounting rules. Any relevant output tax should be added to the flat rate calculation of VAT due.

Stock on leaving the scheme

If the value of stock on hand has increased during the period of using the scheme, then input tax may be recovered on this increase.

This additional input tax must be calculated according to the method in Notice 733.

Assets on leaving the scheme

If the business recovers the VAT on a capital asset (for example as a pre-registration expense or under the facility to recover input tax on assets costing more than £2,000) on leaving the scheme, there is a deemed self-supply on those assets.

The self supply must be accounted for in the first normal accounting period following ending use of the scheme. A fully taxable business is normally able to recover the self-supply in full whereas a partly exempt business may be limited by the partial exemption method in use.

Legislation: *Value Added Tax Regulations* 1995 (SI 1995/2518), reg. 55F, 55R and 55S

Other material: Notice 733 Flat Rate Scheme for Small Business

VAT Reporter: ¶55-355

Motoring scale charge

Users of the flat rate scheme do not pay the motoring scale charge.

Bad debt relief

Bad debt relief is available. There are special arrangements for those using the cash turnover method. These arrangements are set out in Notice 733.

Legislation: *Value Added Tax Regulations* 1995 (SI 1995/2518), reg. 55V

Other material: Notice 733 Flat Rate Scheme for Small Business

VAT Reporter: ¶18-994

Intra-Community trade

Income received from the sale of goods to customers in other EU States form part of the VAT inclusive turnover of the business.

Selling services in other EU States depends on the place of supply of those services. Services outside the scope of UK VAT do not form part of the flat rate turnover.

The purchase of goods from other EU States must be accounted for in Box 2 of the VAT return as with a business using the normal VAT system. This acquisition tax is treated as ordinary input tax and is not normally recoverable under the flat rate scheme.

There is no adjustment to the flat rate turnover for reverse charges on purchases.

Legislation: *Value Added Tax Regulations* 1995 (SI 1995/2518), reg. 55C and 55T

Cases: *West (t/a West One) v R & C Commrs* No. 19,677; [2007] BVC 4,006

Other material: Notice 725 The Single Market; Notice 741 Place of supply of Services

VAT Reporter: ¶140 and ¶55-350

Preparing accounts for Direct Tax purposes

HMRC have confirmed that for businesses who are using the scheme, it is expected that accounts will be prepared using gross receipts less flat rate VAT percentage for turnover and that expenses will include the irrecoverable input VAT. For those businesses using the scheme for only part of a year, accounts figures for the time on the scheme should be added to those for the time not on the scheme to arrive at the total for the year. For both indirect tax and direct tax purposes, there is a requirement to keep a record of sales and purchases. But, for businesses using the scheme, that record does not have to analyse gross, VAT and net separately. The records (whether normal system or flat rate scheme) need only be complete, orderly and easy to follow.

Other material: Notice 733 Flat Rate Scheme for Small Business

VAT Reporter: ¶55-350

Appeals

It is possible to appeal against HMRC's refusal to authorise use of the scheme or withdrawal of authorisation to use the scheme.

Legislation: VATA 1995, s. 83(1)(fza)

Other material: Notice 733 Flat Rate Scheme for Small Business

VAT Reporter: ¶55-350

OTHER SCHEMES

16-850   Farmers' flat rate scheme

A farmer who chooses to use the scheme ceases to be registered for VAT in respect of his farming activities, and so ceases to be able to recover input tax. However, he is able to charge a 'flat rate addition' (FRA) at a special rate of four per cent on supplies to taxable persons. These customers can recover the FRA as input tax, but the flat rate scheme farmer is allowed to retain the money instead of paying it over to HMRC.

Eligibility

The scheme is available to farmers who carry on 'designated activities'. These include crop production, stock farming, forestry, fish farming, the processing of own produce and the provision of such agricultural services as contracting, and hiring out agricultural equipment. Activities such as dealing in agricultural produce are not covered.

A person who carries on designated activities and also other taxable activities cannot join the scheme unless turnover from the other activities falls below the VAT registration limit.

Certification

A farmer who wishes to join the scheme must apply to HMRC for certification as a flat rate farmer. They will issue a certificate only if they are satisfied that the applicant has not been convicted of a VAT offence, or been liable to a civil fraud penalty, etc. in the previous three years and that the FRA in the first year is not likely to exceed the input tax, which would otherwise have been reclaimed, by more than £3,000.

It is not clear what will happen if the financial benefits of being a flat rate farmer exceed £3,000 in later years. There is no specific provision dealing with this. The regulations provide a general power by which HMRC can cancel a certificate if they consider it necessary to do so for the protection of the revenue. However, it is considered that they could not use this power to cancel a certificate merely because the flat rate farmer had succeeded in expanding the activity so that FRA exceeded potential input tax by a considerable sum.

Effect of certification

Once a certificate has been issued, the flat rate farmer ceases to be a taxable person and, from that time, supplies under the scheme are disregarded in calculating turnover for VAT registration purposes. There is no requirement to account for VAT on goods on hand at the time of deregistration, the normal deemed supply rules being disapplied in this instance.

Apart from disregarding designated activities, the farmer continues to be liable to the normal rules on registration both in respect of turnover and in respect of acquisitions from other EC States.

Operation of the scheme

While certified under the scheme, the flat rate farmer can charge FRA at four per cent on supplies made to taxable persons in the course of a designated activity. This applies even where the supplies would normally be zero-rated.

The taxable customer can recover the FRA as if it were input tax. To facilitate this, the farmer must provide the customer with an invoice showing:

(1)   an identifying number;

(2)   the farmer's name, address and certificate number;

(3)   the customer's name and address;

(4)   the date of the supply;

(5)   a description of the goods or services supplied;

(6)   the amount of the consideration for the supply (net of FRA); and

(7)   the amount of the FRA.

Records

The flat rate farmer has the usual requirements to retain business records for six years. In particular, he must keep copies of invoices issued under the scheme.

Termination

If the flat rate farmer becomes compulsorily registrable in respect of his non-farming activities, ceases to make qualifying supplies or becomes insolvent or incapacitated, HMRC may terminate the agreement. In addition, HMRC have the power to terminate the agreement if the flat rate farmer is recovering substantially more under the scheme than would otherwise be the case. Also, the farmer may apply for his certification to be cancelled after he has been in the scheme for at least a year. He may wish to do this if he is about to incur large amounts of input tax which he wishes to reclaim.

Re-certification will not normally be granted for at least three years.

General

The £3,000 limit on first year benefits makes the flat rate scheme less attractive than it might otherwise be. However, there seems to be nothing to prevent a farmer from joining the scheme, then expanding his designated activities to increase the financial benefit.

The scheme remains attractive to some businesses, such as nurseries, which make standard-rated supplies in the course of designated activities to members of the general public, and it is understood that these account for most of the early entries to the scheme.

Legislation: *Value Added Tax Regulations* 1995 (SI 1995/2518), reg. 202; VATA 1994, s. 54

Other material: Notice 700/46

VAT Reporter: ¶53-500 and ¶3-130

16-890   Tour operators

Any business based in the EU which buys in travel facilities, such as holiday accommodation and passenger transport, and sells them on to a traveller without material change must account for VAT using the tour operators margin scheme (TOMS). The business does not have to be a tour operator in the traditional sense to be bound by these regulations; they apply to any business that buys and resells the relevant services.

The sale of admission tickets and similar are not within TOMS unless sold as part of a package of 'travel services' to which TOMS applies. This follows from a CJEU ruling that TOMS did not apply to 'sales of opera tickets in isolation, without the provision of travel services'.

Under the scheme, the tour operator:

- accounts for output tax on the difference between the price paid for the travel facilities and the price charged to the traveller, and
- is unable to claim input tax incurred in respect of such travel facilities; this bars claims whether the VAT is incurred in the UK or elsewhere, although input tax may still be reclaimed in respect of overheads.

The purpose of the scheme is to enable tour operators based in the EU to register and account for VAT in just one EU Member State. The scheme does not apply to travel agents acting wholly on a commission basis.

TOMS does not apply to wholesale supplies of travel and accommodation sold to business customers. It does apply to business customers who are buying the travel or accommodation for their own consumption.

Legislation: VATA 1994, s. 53; *Value Added Tax (Tour Operators) Order* 1987 (SI 1987/1806)

Cases: *Van Ginkel Waddinxveen BV v Inspecteur der Omzetbelasting, Utrecht* (Case C-163/91) [1996] BVC 398; *Minerva Kulturreisen GmbH v Finanzamt Freital* (Case C-31/10) Judgment delivered 9 December 2010

Other material: Notice 709/5; VAT Information Sheet 03/96, July 1996 and VAT Information Sheet 04/96, July 1996; HM Revenue and Customs Brief 27/09, HM Revenue and Customs Brief 74/09 and HM Revenue and Customs Brief 21/10

VAT Reporter: ¶54-450

Special Persons, Special Circumstances

SPECIAL PERSONS, SPECIAL CIRCUMSTANCES

17-000   Introduction to special persons, special circumstances

As has been seen earlier, VAT is accounted for by taxable persons and all business activities of any one person are covered by a single VAT registration.

Although the tax is, in principle, collected by reference to the individual supplies made by businesses, some aspects have to be dealt with and understood by reference to the person rather than the separate supplies. For instance, the amount of input tax recoverable by a partially exempt person is, in some respects, the subject of such a global calculation.

In principle, VAT applies to all taxable persons in the same way. However, there are some types of entity whose treatment is special in some way or another. The purpose of this section is to provide a brief summary of such persons and their treatment.

17-020   Limited liability partnerships

The *Limited Liability Partnership Act* 2000 permits the formation of limited liability partnerships (LLPs) .

An LLP has its own legal identity, separate from that of its members, and has a certificate of incorporation.

An LLP is therefore regarded for VAT purposes as a separate entity, with its own liability to be registered, ability to be registered voluntarily, etc.

As with 'ordinary' partnerships, the partners of an LLP are not seen as making supplies to the LLP simply by acting as partners (but presumably, as with ordinary partnerships, there remains the possibility of supplies passing between the partners and the partnership where this follows from the surrounding circumstances, such as payments by way of consideration as opposed to a partnership profit share).

Where an existing 'ordinary' partnership changes to an LLP, the LLP will require a fresh registration (since it is a separate legal entity). If the existing partnership ceases to exist, it may be possible to transfer the registration number to the LLP under the transfer of a going concern rules.

As a corporate body (and unlike an 'ordinary' partnership), an LLP is eligible for group treatment where, for instance, it controls one or more limited companies. In addition, if the members of an LLP also control one or more limited companies, HMRC are prepared to see

Special Persons

them as doing so as partners with the consequence that the LLP and the companies may be grouped for VAT purposes.

Other material: Notice 700/2

VAT Reporter: ¶43-320

17-050   Joint ventures not involving partnership

Special problems can arise where two or more persons carry on a business venture jointly, but under terms not intended to create a formal partnership. Different aspects of the venture, in terms of obtaining supplies and making supplies, may be handled by the different parties, but a final settlement between them is then made.

Determining the true nature of the enterprise and the VAT treatment that flows from this can be tremendously tricky and varies depending upon the precise terms of agreement and the way in which it is implemented. Often, there is no formal agreement and the course of dealing which takes place may be open to a number of interpretations.

Partnership

If the terms are such that the parties share in any losses as well as profits, it may well be that a partnership exists, even though the parties did not intend this and may have sought to avoid it. In other cases, it may be that each party makes and receives supplies independently, and supplies also flow between the parties.

Joint venture and joint venture accounting

In practice, there are many cases where HMRC are prepared to accept that there is a joint venture not amounting to a partnership and, where each party is registered for VAT, to permit joint venture accounting for VAT whereby each venturer accounts for and reclaims output and input tax on supplies passing through his hands, and settlement payments between the venturers are ignored.

There does not seem to be any particular basis in law for this treatment but, pragmatically, it is often the most convenient approach and gives the right net answer. It is wise to obtain agreement from HMRC before using it.

Clarification

Frequently, it will have little effect on the venturers which treatment applies, provided that it is known from the outset. If an incorrect treatment (or one which is open to challenge) is followed at the start, then it may be costly to correct later. There may be penalties if a new registration is needed, but not implemented, there may be tax due on supplies not recognised at the time, and input tax may be lost because invoices are not made out in the right name. Such losses can be avoided if the uncertainties are recognised at the outset and a ruling sought from HMRC as to the VAT treatment.

Commercial considerations

In some cases, the true nature of the arrangements may be crucial. For instance, in share farming agreements it would often be disadvantageous to draw up the terms in such a way that the underlying transaction was the exempt grant of a right over land, or licence to occupy land, by the landowner in return for a share of the net proceeds of the farming activities carried on by the farmer who joins in the venture. Input tax on supplies attributable to the exempt supply would be exempt input tax in the landowner's hands. In such cases where a particular result is desired, great care is needed to ensure that result is in fact achieved, and an acceptable VAT treatment is negotiated with HMRC.

Other material: HMRC Guidance Manual Taxable Person Section VTAXPER 50000

VAT Reporter: ¶43-710

GROUPS OF COMPANIES

17-080   Group treatment

There are special rules for groups of companies which, in broad terms, enable a group to be treated as a single entity for VAT purposes. This helps to recognise the fact that, in many cases, the companies in a group are so inter-linked as to amount, in reality, to a single business entity. The same sort of economic and financial linkage can, of course, occur between entities which are not limited companies; however, there is no similar treatment available in such cases.

Group treatment of companies is not compulsory. It is an option which the companies concerned can choose to exercise, subject to the consent of HMRC.

Application for group treatment between some or all of the companies in a potential VAT group can have a significant effect on the overall VAT liability of the group. It is particularly important where partial exemption is concerned, and especially if there are taxable supplies passing between members of the group. The group treatment rules therefore provide a powerful tool of VAT planning. It should be noted, however, that the position is as with most VAT planning – the tools available can help to avoid unnecessary VAT costs without undue changes in the business structure, but are not usually suited to the creation of schemes to avoid tax which is properly due.

Legislation: VATA 1994, s. 43

VAT Reporter: ¶43-420

17-110   Eligibility for group treatment

Group treatment is available only between bodies corporate, and only if each company concerned is established, or has a fixed establishment, in the UK.

Furthermore, the companies must be under common control, meeting one of the following tests:

(1)   one of them controls each of the others; or

(2)   one person (either a body corporate or an individual) controls all of them; or

(3)   two or more individuals carrying on business in partnership control all of them.

A person controls a company if that person is empowered by statute to control its activities, or is its holding company (or, in the case of an individual or partnership, meets the criteria of a holding company) within the meaning of the *Companies Act* 1985. In broad terms, this means that the 'controlling' entity must:

(1)   hold a majority of the voting rights in that company; or

(2)   be a member of it and have the right to appoint or remove a majority of its board of directors; or

(3)   be a member of it and control alone under an agreement with other members, a majority of the voting rights in it.

Where the members of a limited liability partnership also control one or more limited companies, HMRC are prepared to see them as doing so as partners. Since the limited liability partnership is also regarded as a body corporate, this means that the partnership, as well as the companies concerned, is eligible for grouping.

Further eligibility rules

Additional eligibility rules apply to VAT groups with a turnover of more than £10 million or when there are 'reasonable grounds' for expecting the turnover to exceed £10 million during the forthcoming year. The turnover of companies wishing to join the group must be taken into account when considering the turnover for the forthcoming year.

These additional eligibility rules do not apply to all corporate bodies applying to join a VAT group. The additional rules do not apply when the corporate body wishing to join the group is one of the following:

* a body corporate that controls all the other group members;
* a body corporate whose activities another body corporate is empowered by statute to control;
* a body corporate whose only activity is acting as a trustee of an occupational pension scheme;
* a charity.

Further, the additional eligibility rules only apply in the following circumstances:

(a)   the body concerned supplies goods or services to the VAT group which, if it were not a member of the group, would be liable to the standard or reduced rate of tax; and

(b)   the group would not able to fully recover the tax due on those supplies.

When the addition eligibility rules apply the body wishing to join the VAT group is only eligible to do so if both the following conditions apply.

(a) Under 50 per cent of 'the benefits of the relevant business activity accrue, directly or indirectly, to one or more third parties'. This may be profits (whether or not distributed), charges for managing the business activity or goods or services supplied at above the open market value.

(b) Under generally accepted accounting practice, the accounts for the body applying to join the group will be consolidated into the controlling body's group accounts or would be so consolidated if person concerned prepared group accounts. Also, the accounts of the body joining the group would not be required to be the consolidated accounts prepared of a third party.

One group at a time

A company or body corporate cannot belong to two VAT groups at the same time.

Legislation: VATA 1994, s. 43(3) and (8) and s. 43D; *Value Added Tax (Groups: Eligibility) Order* 2004 (SI 2004/1931)

Other material: Notice 700/2

VAT Reporter: ¶43-420

17-130   Application for group treatment

An application for group treatment or changes to a group structure should normally be made using forms VAT 50 and VAT 51.

Date from which formation or change takes effect

The effective date for the formation, change or cessation of a VAT group is normally the date upon which the relevant application is received by HMRC. HMRC have 90 days from the receipt of the application in which to refuse it, in which case it is deemed never to have had effect.

HMRC may allow the change to be effective from an 'earlier or later' date. It is only in certain circumstances that HMRC allow an application to be backdated. An application may be backdated for up to 30 days to coincide with the commencement of a VAT period. The VAT period may be that of an already registered group or the VAT period of a body corporate forming, joining or leaving the group. Backdating more than 30 days is only allowed when HMRC are at fault – they may have lost the application or have been dilatory in processing it!

HMRC are more lax about moving the effective date to some time after they received the relevant application forms. Such requests are normally allowed.

HMRC have the power to refuse the following 'for the protection of the revenue':

• formation of a new VAT group;

- addition of a company to an existing VAT group;
- removal of a company from an existing VAT group;
- changing the nominated representative member; and
- disbanding a VAT group

HMRC also have the power to remove a member from a VAT group 'for the protection of the revenue'. In this case, they are able to issue a direction to terminate its inclusion in the VAT group concerned. The direction will specify the date from which the termination is effective. The date must be the date of the direction or a future date. Under this provision, it cannot be back-dated.

Measures for the 'protection of the revenue'

HMRC interpretation of their powers 'for the protection of the revenue' as it affects groups has been explained extensively in a Public Notice.

HMRC have stated that they will not normally use these powers when they consider that any perceived revenue loss flows naturally from the normal operation of grouping. It is only when the revenue loss goes beyond this that HMRC will invoke their powers to 'protect the revenue'.

In *National Westminster Bank Plc* [1998] BVC 2,264, the tribunal stated that "the phrase 'necessary for the protection of the revenue' must be considered as a totality and involves a balancing exercise in which the Commissioners must weigh the effect on the Appellants of refusal of grouping against the loss of revenue likely to result from grouping."

HMRC have said that they will follow this approach.

In the event that HMRC consider the refusal or alteration of a VAT group, they will normally ask for:

- information about the administrative savings likely to occur because of VAT grouping;
- estimates of the revenue impact of the formation of the group;
- anticipated adverse effects if the change to the group of the formation of the group were to be refused.

In the event that there seems to be an abnormal revenue loss which outweighs any anticipated administrative saving, it is likely that HMRC will use their powers.

Contrived structures

HMRC have stated that they will use their powers to change or refuse VAT grouping where they consider that the arrangement is a 'contrived structure'.

An example of this would be where a company is included in a VAT group in order to benefit from VAT grouping but in reality the company is a third party supplier. One scheme singled out as being not allowed is where the holding company of the VAT group holds dividend paying shares but another party takes the profit. Evidently, this scheme has been used to enable partially exempt groups to avoid paying tax on bought-in supplies.

Legislation: VATA 1994, s. 43B(3)

Cases: *National Westminster Bank Plc* [1998] BVC 2,264

Other material: Notice 700/2, Section 4

VAT Reporter: ¶43-470

17-150   Effect of group treatment

When application is made for group treatment, a company in the group must be nominated to act as the 'representative member' of the group. If the application is accepted, then the VAT treatment which follows is very much as if all of the activities carried on by companies within the group treatment were actually carried on by the representative member. In particular:

(1)   supplies between members of the group are disregarded (as would be supplies between different departments of a single entity);

(2)   all supplies by or to members of the group are treated as if they were made to or by the representative member; and

(3)   importations of goods by members of the group are treated as if done by the representative member.

In one case, it was held that, where a retailer supplied goods paid for by credit cards issued by a company in the same VAT group, the retail scheme should be applied as if the retailer was providing credit to its customers directly.

Special status companies

In some instances, the VAT liability of a supply depends upon the status of the person making the supply. For instance, supplies of insurance only qualify for exemption when made by an authorised insurer. In such cases, the liability is to be determined by reference to the status of the company actually making the supply, not by reference to the status of the representative member of the group (which is deemed to make the supply for VAT accounting purposes).

Joint and several liability

VAT returns are made by the representative member and cover supplies made by or to all members of the VAT group. Although the representative member is liable, in the first instance, to account for any tax due, all members of the group are in the end jointly and severally liable for such tax.

Legislation: VATA 1994, s. 43(1)

653

Other material: Notice 700/2, Section 5

Cases: *C & E Commrs v Kingfisher Plc* [1994] BVC 3

VAT Reporter: ¶43-450

17-180   Ceasing to be eligible

If a company within a group treatment ceases to be eligible for group treatment because it no longer meets the control requirements, HMRC may exclude it from the group treatment from a date specified by them in a notice excluding the company (which may be a date earlier than that of the notice, but not a date before eligibility ceased).

A court has held that, where a company ceases to be eligible for group treatment, HMRC are obliged to remove it from the group with effect from the date when eligibility ceased.

However, this judgment was overturned on appeal, with the court finding that an ineligible company must remain within the VAT group until the date specified by HMRC in a notice (Court of Appeal, judgment delivered 17 October 2001).

Following that judgment, HMRC have announced that it would be rare for them to set a later date for removal from group treatment than the date when eligibility ceases. In practice, they will normally agree the date requested, and will set a later date only if tax avoidance is involved or may arise.

Legislation: VATA 1994, s. 43(6)

Cases: *C & E Commrs v Barclays Bank Plc* [2000] BVC 332; *C & E Commrs v Barclays Bank Plc* [2001] BVC 606 Court of Appeal

Other material: Notice 700/2, para. 7.2

VAT Reporter: ¶43-450

17-210   Exclusion from group treatment

HMRC have power to issue a notice excluding a company from a group treatment, if they consider it necessary for the protection of the revenue (see 17-740). Such a notice has effect from the date when it is issued, or from a later date specified in the notice.

Other material: Notice 700/2, para. 7.5

VAT Reporter: ¶43-475

17-240   Uses of group treatment

The usefulness, or otherwise, of group treatment depends upon the precise facts of the particular case, and a detailed analysis of the circumstances is always necessary to determine the best treatment. Having said that, it is possible to summarise some of the main uses as follows:

(1) Administrative convenience

Where the activities of a group are closely inter-linked and centrally administered, it may be easier to deal with a central VAT return which excludes intra-group transactions.

(2) Internally generated input tax

A frequently occurring position is that in which a company making exempt supplies acquires resources from companies in the same group, by way of taxable supplies. Typically, this might involve management charges or recharges of staff costs. The tax on such supplies is irrecoverable and, if the resources concerned did not bear VAT when first acquired into the commercial group (e.g. labour costs), this is a completely unnecessary and artificial loss. If the companies are within the same VAT group, no charge to tax arises on the intra-group supplies, so that the artificial loss of internally generated tax is avoided.

(3) Exempt intra-group supplies

Another case where loss can arise without group treatment is that where functions are separated between companies in the commercial group, giving rise to exempt supplies within the group. A typical example is that of a group property holding company letting premises, by way of exempt supplies, to operating companies involved in making taxable supplies. Without group treatment, such a company will be exempt or partially exempt, and so unable to recover input tax on expenses relating to the properties. This is an unnecessary loss, as the tax ultimately relates to the taxable supplies made by the tenant. If the companies are included in a group treatment, then the intra-group supply will be ignored and the input tax relating to the property will be attributed to the onward taxable supplies by the tenant. In this way, the loss of input tax is avoided.

VAT Reporter: ¶43-452

17-280   Exempt supplies

Although a VAT group of companies is effectively treated as a single entity for most VAT purposes, an exception is made for some certain exempt supplies. For instance, in determining whether certain exempt supplies can be treated as taxable for these purposes, the businesses carried on by different companies in the VAT group are looked at separately.

Other material: Notice 706, Section 12

VAT Reporter: ¶43-450

17-310　Group acquisition of business

If a VAT group acquires a business as a going concern, and is partially exempt during the return period or longer period concerned, then a self supply of VAT arises on the acquisition. The group is deemed to have supplied those assets acquired which attract VAT at a positive rate, at market value, on the day of the transfer. The group is also deemed to have received a supply of these assets, so that the tax also qualifies for treatment as input tax. However, the fact that the group is partially exempt means that it may not be able to recover as input tax the whole of the tax which it must account for as output tax.

This provision does not apply if it can be shown that the transferor acquired the assets concerned more than three years before the day of the transfer. Also, HMRC have power to reduce the tax due if they are satisfied that the transferor did not obtain full input tax credit on the acquisition of them (e.g. because the transferor was partially exempt).

Legislation: VATA 1994, s. 44

Other material: Notice 700/2, para. 5.6

VAT Reporter: ¶43-450

17-350　Anti-avoidance – power to make directions

HMRC have powers to counter avoidance schemes involving the use of VAT groups,

Directions

HMRC can make various directions:

(1)　that an intra-group supply which would normally be disregarded under VATA 1994, s. 43(1)(a) is not to be disregarded; or

(2)　that a company which was (or is) a member of a group during a specified period is to be treated as if it were not a member of the group; or

(3)　that a company which was not (or is not) a member of a group during a specified period, but was (or is) eligible to be a member of it, is to be treated as if it were a member of the group.

A direction may also specify which company is to be assumed to be the representative member of the group in question. It appears, therefore, that HMRC can in effect 'direct' into existence a VAT group which would not otherwise exist at all.

A direction can vary an earlier direction. The power to make a direction is not affected by HMRC' earlier refusal or non-refusal of an application under VATA 1994, s. 43 (i.e. an application to form, vary or disband a group, etc.).

Conditions for making a direction

A direction may only be made if:

(1)   a 'relevant event' occurs; and

(2)   there is or may be a positive rated supply which falls to be taxed by reference to an amount less than its full value and in respect of which:

(a)   a person becomes entitled to credit for input tax allowable as attributable to the supply; or

(b)   a person becomes entitled to a repayment 'in respect of' the supply under the provisions relating to repayments to overseas traders.

The input tax at (2)(a) appears to be input tax in the hands of the person making the 'undervalue' supply. While that at (2)(b) appears to be tax on the supply itself, it seems more likely that it is intended once more to be input tax in the supplier's hands.

A 'relevant event' occurs when a company joins or leaves a VAT group, or 'enters into any transaction'.

However, HMRC cannot make a direction if they are satisfied, in respect of the relevant event concerned, that its main purpose (or, if there was more than one main purpose, each of them) was a genuine commercial purpose unconnected with bringing about the circumstances whereby the supply is taxed at an undervalue, etc.

There is specific provision that, if the relevant event is a company's departure from a group as a result of a direction by HMRC (either for the protection of the revenue or because eligibility for grouping has ceased), the 'genuine commercial purpose' defence against a direction cannot apply.

Directions – time-limits and notification

A direction must be made within six years after the later of:

(1)   the 'relevant event' which triggers the direction; or

(2)   the end of the prescribed accounting period at the end of which the entitlement to deduct input tax relating to the undervalue supply arose.

A direction in respect of a supply may be given to the person who made the supply or to any body corporate which is then the representative member of the group of which the supplier was a member at the time of the supply. It seems that if, by the time HMRC seek to make a direction, the supplier has ceased to exist and the group has disbanded, there will be no one left on whom a direction can be served under this head.

A direction relating to a company (i.e. a direction to treat it as grouped or de-grouped for a specified period) may be served on that company or on the person who is, or is treated as, the representative member of the group concerned at the time when the direction is made.

Effects and assessments

Although a direction can only be made by reference to a 'relevant event' occurring, it can have effect for periods before then, and for periods before the 'relevant event' concerned.

Once a direction has been made, those affected by it must account for VAT on the assumptions contained in the direction.

For earlier periods, HMRC may assess to the best of their judgment to collect any unpaid tax arising as a result of the assumptions as to grouping, etc. contained in the direction, being any output tax due as a result of it plus any input tax credit or repayment which has been obtained but would not have been due on the assumptions contained in the direction.

An assessment may be made on the person to whom the direction is given, or on any other relevant person (being the representative member of any group of which the person receiving the direction has been, or been treated as, a member, or which is treated under the direction as being the representative member of that group). An assessment must be made within one year of the making of the direction, and notification of it may be incorporated into the direction itself.

Amounts assessed can be recovered from the person assessed or, if that person is treated as a member of a VAT group, from the representative member of the group; where more than one person is liable to pay the tax, they are to be treated as jointly and severally liable.

Default interest may be due on amounts assessed under these provisions, but runs only from the date when the assessment is notified.

Appeals: against direction

There is to be a right of appeal against the making of a direction under these provisions, and against any resultant assessment.

However, a tribunal can only allow an appeal against a direction if it is satisfied that HMRC could not reasonably have been satisfied that the conditions for making a direction had been met or if it is itself satisfied, in respect of the relevant event concerned, that its main purpose (or, if there was more than one main purpose, each of them) was a genuine commercial purpose unconnected with bringing about the circumstances whereby the supply is taxed at an undervalue, etc.

Presumably, once it is established that the direction is properly made, an appeal against an assessment must come down to argument about the numbers or about who is liable.

Legislation: VATA 1994, s. 43; Sch. 9A

Other material: Notice 700/2 ,Section 8 Group and divisional registration

VAT Reporter: ¶43-425

17-400   Anti-avoidance – imported services

There are special provisions which apply where a member of a VAT group has an overseas branch, the overseas branch receives supplies of services falling within VATA 1994, Sch. 5 (i.e. services supplied where received; see ¶3-980(5)) which are then resupplied to another member of the group. Under these provisions, the intra-group supply is not disregarded. The representative member is treated as supplying the services to itself, and that supply is treated as made in the UK. There are additional provisions to prevent this measure being avoided by such devices as an intra-group transfer of a going concern.

AGENTS

17-440   Areas of difficulty

Two areas of difficulty arise in respect of agents, or persons describing themselves as such. The first is that of determining whether there is in fact an agent/principal relationship. If there is, the further difficulty arises of applying the special rules for agents.

A person who is an agent is one empowered to act on behalf of his principal in some matter. The concept does not extend, say, to a motor distributor who describes himself as an agent for a manufacturer, but in fact buys and sells as principal.

The views of HMRC are as follows:

> 'To act as an agent, you must have agreed with your principal to act on his behalf in relation to the particular transaction concerned. This may be a written or oral agreement, or merely inferred from the way you and your principal conduct your business affairs. Whatever form this relationship takes:
>
> - it must always be clearly established between you and your principal, and you must be able to show to HMRC and Excise that you are arranging the transactions for your principal, rather than trading on your own account;
> - you will not be the owner of any goods, or use any of the services which you buy or sell for your principal;
> - you will not alter the nature or value of any of the supplies made between your principal and third parties.'

The importance of the legal arrangements between the parties, and of recording these, is emphasised by *C & E Commrs v Music and Video Exchange Ltd* [1992] BVC 30.

The basic rule is that the supplies arranged by an agent for his principal are supplies to or by the principal, and do not affect the agent's VAT position in any way. The agent is making a separate supply of agency services to the principal, for a fee or commission, and this will normally be taxable at the standard rate (although it may sometimes be exempt or zero-rated).

Cases: *C & E Commrs v Music and Video Exchange Ltd* [1992] BVC 30

Special Persons

Other material: Notice 700, Section 22

VAT Reporter: ¶54-050

17-480   Agent acting in own name

In some cases, an agent may appear to act in his own name, so that the parties with whom he deals are not aware that they are really dealing with the principal. In the past it was generally possible to treat the main supply as made both to and by the agent (so that the entries for the main supply cancelled out in the agent's records), while recognising a separate supply of agency services to the principal. This treatment can still be used for domestic UK transactions (although the revised treatment described below can be adopted as an alternative).

A different treatment applies for a UK agent acting in a non-EC or intra-EC supply. The agent is treated as a principal participating in the main supply, and no separate supply of agency services is recognised. In effect, the agent's commission (or other remuneration) is treated as a mark-up. The policy was summarised in a Business Brief as follows:

'VAT TREATMENT OF SUPPLIES INVOLVING UK UNDISCLOSED AGENTS

This Business Brief outlines Customs' revised policy on the VAT treatment of supplies through UK undisclosed agents. The changes are to put the VAT treatment of UK undisclosed agents on the same footing as that for commissionaires elsewhere in the Community. They follow representations from the trade and their advisers, and have been agreed after consultation with members of the Joint VAT Consultative Committee and the VAT Practitioners Group.

Background

The revised policy is intended to ease problems faced by UK undisclosed agents which are caused by differences between UK common law on agency and Roman civil law concepts, briefly summarised below. The problems arise where undisclosed agents are involved in non-EC or intra-Community supplies.

Undisclosed agents take part in a supply of goods or services while acting in their own name – but they are supplying the goods or services on behalf of another. This means the third party to the transaction is unaware of the involvement of an agent.

Problems arising

Currently, there is potential distortion of competition between UK undisclosed agents and commissionaires, who are seen as principals under Roman law in other Member States. Commissionaires therefore take part in the supply, with their commission included as a mark-up in the price. However, in UK law, there is an underlying supply between the principal and the customer and a separate supply of agents' services to their principals. This means that, unlike commissionaires, UK agents have to charge VAT to their non-EC principals. If the non-EC principal is unwilling to register in the UK to recover this, the agent may have to bear the VAT cost.

There is potential for confusion as to the place of supply of services. For example, where undisclosed agents are involved in a supply taking place where the supplier is based, there may be uncertainty about the place of the onward supply by the agents. In the case of services subject to reverse charge, there may be uncertainty as to who should account for the reverse charge.

Different values of supplies through UK undisclosed agents and commissionaires result in difficulties and mismatches on EC Sales Lists and declarations made for the purposes of international trade statistics (Intrastat).

Basis for change

HMRC believe that the wording of section 47 of the 1994 VAT Act offers some flexibility. As far as goods are concerned, HMRC are prepared to take a relaxed view of the supply position under section 47(1) and, in relation to services, they are relying on their powers under section 47(3) 'to think fit' to treat the supplies in the way prescribed.

Revised VAT treatment

The revised treatment will only apply to supplies made on or after 1 July 2000. From then, agents who are involved in non-EC or intra-Community supplies, and bring themselves within the terms of section 47 VAT Act 1994 by acting in their own name, will be treated as principals for VAT purposes. They will be seen as taking a full part in the underlying supply of any goods or services. Consequently, as the agent will be taking part in the supply, HMRC will no longer recognise a separate supply of the agents' own services to their principal and the commission they retain will be seen as subsumed in the value of the onward underlying supply.

This revised treatment will be for VAT purposes only. It will have no impact on the legal status of agents or the way in which they are treated for the purposes of other taxes or legislation.

Impact of the changes

The following illustrates the impact of the revised treatment in relation to both imported/acquired goods and international services. For these purposes, the price paid by the final customer is £100; the commission retained by the agent is £20; and the money passed back to the principal is £80: all net of VAT.

Goods imported or acquired into the UK

The VAT value at importation will be decided by the HMRC rules as at present and will not change.

The VAT value at acquisition will be £80 by virtue of section 20(3) VAT Act 1994 based on the value of the invoice raised by the EC principal to the UK undisclosed agent. The agent will be responsible for Intrastat declarations and must account for acquisition tax.

Agents, being treated as a principal, will be entitled to recover import/acquisition VAT, subject to the normal rules.

They will then make an onward supply in their own name to the customer for £100, and account for output tax.

The commission of £20 will be seen as subsumed in the value of their onward supply of the goods, and they will no longer be treated as making a separate supply of their own services to the non-UK principal.

Costs incurred in the UK, such as warehousing and handling, may be seen as supplies to the agent and input tax recovery allowed, subject to the normal rules.

Special Persons

In most cases, under the new arrangements, the net VAT liability will be no different than under present rules.

International services

Agents who are involved in international services and act in their own name under section 47(3) VAT Act 94 will be treated as principals in the same way as elsewhere in the EC. The services will be seen as supplied to the UK agents as though they were a principal and supplied on by them. This means that the agents will be treated as taking a full part in the supply chain. As in the case of imported goods above, their commission will be seen as subsumed in the value of the onward supply. They will not be regarded as making a separate supply of their own services to the principal.

Where a service is supplied in the supplier's place of establishment, then, as the UK agents are treated as the supplier, the supply will take place in the UK and will be subject to UK VAT. For services listed in Schedule 5, VAT Act 94 (see Notice 741 for further details), which are treated as supplied in the customer's place of establishment, the agents will be treated as receiving these supplies and must therefore account for the reverse charge. They will then make an onward supply in the UK and account for output tax in the normal way.

Section 47(3) will apply in this way in all cases where agents act in their own name in relation to international services. It will apply to services being supplied both to and from the UK.

UK undisclosed agents involved in domestic supplies

As the difficulties outlined in the 'Problems arising' section above do not apply to UK undisclosed agents in their involvement with domestic supplies, HMRC do not want to disturb the current commercial arrangements where agents invoice their principals for a separate supply of their own services. However, if they want to, undisclosed agents can adopt the revised VAT treatment set out in this Business Brief for their domestic transactions also.

Further help

To assist businesses further, we are also issuing a VAT Information Sheet which we hope will answer most of the questions likely to arise. This will be available shortly on our website at *www. hmce.gov.uk* and from local VAT offices.'

Other material: Notice 700, Section 24; Business Brief 09/00, 30 June 2000

VAT Reporter: ¶54-100

17-520 Agent for non-resident importer

If goods are imported into the UK from outside the EC (or acquired from another EC State) by a taxable person, and supplied by him as agent for a person who is not a taxable person, he is treated as having imported (or acquired) the goods, and supplied them, as principal. Consequently, he is liable to account for any tax due on the supply, and can also recover the VAT on the importation (or acquisition).

In applying this provision, if the principal is non-resident and has his principal place of business outside the UK, he can be treated as not being a taxable person in respect of the transaction (even though he is really a taxable person) if he is not registrable by reference to some other activity.

Legislation: VATA 1994, s. 47(1) and (2)

OTHERS

17-570   Clubs and associations

The main thing to remember about clubs and associations is that they are, in principle, subject to the same VAT rules as other entities. Difficulties often arise because the people running them do not regard themselves as carrying on a business and so do not consider that VAT might be in point.

Furthermore, the very act of providing the benefits of membership in return for a subscription is specifically defined as amounting to the carrying on of a business for VAT purposes.

Compliance with the VAT legislation by a club, association or organisation, the affairs of which are managed by its members or by committees of members, is the joint and several responsibility of members holding office as president, chairman, treasurer, secretary or similar offices. If there are none of these, then it is the joint and several responsibility of those members holding office as committee members, and if there are none such, it is the joint and several responsibility of all of the members.

The registration of a club, etc. is carried out in the name of the club and changes in membership are ignored in determining whether goods and services are supplied to or by it.

Legislation: VATA 1994, s. 46(3) and 94(2)(a); *Value Added Tax Regulations* 1995 (SI 1995/2518), reg. 8

Other material: Notice 701/5

VAT Reporter: ¶43-881

17-630   Charities: liabilities and reliefs

As with clubs, etc. the prime fact about charities which is not generally understood is that they are, in principle, subject to exactly the same VAT regime as any other entity. As a general rule, supplies made by charities are taxed in the same way as supplies by other entities. There is no general relief from VAT for supplies made by commercial organisations to charities.

Having said that, there are some specific and tightly drawn reliefs for certain supplies to or by charities, provided that all relevant conditions are met. These apply particularly in the fields of health and welfare, and fund raising, and are covered in the Zero-rating, Reduced rate, Exemption division at 12-000ff. There are also important reliefs in connection with property nd construction, for buildings used for a relevant charitable purpose.

r **material:** Notice 701/1

Reporter: ¶50-000

17-680   The Crown: government departments

Taxable supplies by government departments are subject to VAT in the ordinary way if done in the course of a business. Furthermore, where government departments make supplies, not in the course of business, but similar to supplies made by taxable persons in the course of business, the Treasury may direct that they be treated as if made in the course of a business, and so are taxable. This avoids distortions of competition between government departments and commercial enterprises. The directions by the Treasury are published in the *London Gazette*. The internet address for the *London Gazette* is: *www.london-gazette.co.uk*.

There are further provisions enabling the Treasury to allow refunds of tax on certain supplies obtained by government departments, and to treat as supplies transactions between government departments and between them and the Crown Estate Commissioners.

Government departments include Northern Ireland departments, bodies exercising functions on behalf of Ministers, and parts of government departments if designated by the Treasury.

Legislation: VATA 1994, s. 41(1) and (2)

VAT Reporter: ¶54-000

17-730   Local authorities, etc.

Local authorities are liable to be registered in respect of taxable business activities, whatever their level of turnover. Business activities of local authorities are taxed in the ordinary way, and input tax blocked in respect of exempt business activities.

As far as non-business activities of local authorities, and certain similar entities, are concerned, no output tax is chargeable, but the local authority, etc. is entitled to reclaim VAT incurred on its related costs. Technically, this is not a recovery of input tax, but the provision of central government funding for local authorities. Four-year capping applies to these refunds.

Local authorities also have a more generous partial exemption regime available to them than is available to businesses generally. Broadly speaking, if their total input tax relating wholly or partly to exempt activities (i.e. directly attributable exempt input tax plus residual input tax) is below five per cent of total input tax, they can be treated as fully taxable. If the five per cent limit is exceeded, they must then apportion the residual input tax and apply the usual de minimis rules.

The bodies to which this relief applies include such entities as local authorities, water authorities, port health authorities, police authorities, the BBC, etc. and any body specified in a suitable Treasury order. Local authorities include the council of a city, district, London borough, parish or group of parishes, etc.

Childcare and certain welfare services

The amount of input tax which some local authorities may recover increased with effect from 1 April 2005 when certain services were re-classified as non-business activities. Input tax recovery was blocked because the affected services are exempt supplies.

According to available information, it is services 'of a social nature where local authorities have a special duty to ensure provision' which will be reclassified. Two examples of this are childcare and welfare.

Voluntary aided schools

HMRC have amended their policy regarding the rate of VAT recovery on expenditure on capital works by voluntary aided (VA) schools. With effect from 1 September 2009 local authorities will not be able to reclaim such input tax unless the local authority is statutorily responsible or where the local authority rather than the governing body procures the supply of works and also pays for the supply.

Academy schools

From 1 April 2011 academy schools are put on a level with local authority schools and are able to recover VAT on similar expenses. Section 33B has been inserted into VATA 1994.

Leisure facilities

Various consequences flow from the way in which the local authority organises the provision of the leisure facilities. The most common arrangements are set out in the flowchart at 18-945.

Complications arise in connection with payments between the local authority and third party organisations used to operate or provide the leisure facilities. Clearly, these problems do not occur when the facilities are operated and managed in-house by the local authority direct service organisation.

When management of the facilities is devolved to a commercial contractor, the contractor's charges to the local authority are taxable. The local authority accounts for VAT on the takings.

A local authority may continue to make payments to a profit or non-profit making organisation to which it has transferred its leisure facilities. Commonly, the payments are intended to

Special Persons

make good the shortfall between takings and operating costs. Such payments are usually consideration for the provision of services to the local authority by the organisation running the facilities. However, shortfall funding linked to prices charged to users can be additional takings for the profit or non-profit making organisation

Local authorities will often be able to recover any tax charged to it in these circumstances. However, it is necessary to consider the link with supplies which the local authority may make with the organisations concerned.

Legislation: VATA 1994, s. 33(1) and (3) and s. 42

Other material: Notice 749; Revenue and Customs Brief 53/09

Cases: *Edinburgh Leisure, South Lanarkshire Leisure and Renfrewshire Leisure* [2005] BVC 2,146

VAT Reporter: ¶51-100

17-780   Bodies covered by public law

Interpretation of art. 13 amended

Article 13(1) of the Principle VAT Directive states: 'regional and local government authorities and other bodies governed by public law' are not regarded as taxable persons when engaging in activities as 'public authorities'. Such public bodies act as public authorities when the carry out their activities under a special legal regime that applies to them and not to other bodies.

There have been three recent cases that have led HMRC to examine their interpretation of 'a body governed by public law' and revise its view.

These cases served to narrow the view of a 'public body' and remove private sector organisations which happen to undertake functions on behalf of the state from the parameters of a 'public body'.

Following these cases, HMRC have concluded that the term 'body governed by public law' should be narrow in its application. A body will only satisfy this criterion if it is a public sector body forming part of the UK's public administration.

Providers of further education and higher education have assumed that they are a 'public body' under art. 13(1). This has supported their argument for zero-rating under VATA 1994, Sch. 8, Grp. 5 and/or reduced-rating under VATA 1994, Sch. 7A. From now on, that will not be generally accepted. Each case will be reviewed on its merits. It is possible that where an organisation qualifies as a public body in respect of one area of activity, that would only mean that supplies in respect of that activity are outside the scope of VAT and will not affect the liability of supplies made to the organisation.

From 17 July 2012

Article 13 was transposed into UK legislation with effect from 17 July 2012. This affects states, regional and local government authorities and other bodies governed by public law in the following ways:

(1)   When these bodies make supplies listed in Annex 1 to Directive 2006/112, they do so 'in the course or furtherance of a business' unless these supplies are 'on such a small scale as to be negligible'.

(2)   Supplies not listed in Annex 1 shall be treated as supplied in the course or furtherance of a business 'if (and only if) not charging VAT…would lead to a significant distortion of competition'

Legislation: VATA 1994, s. 41J and EU Directive 2006/112, art. 13 and Annex 1

Other material: Revenue and Customs Brief 27/08 issued 19 May 2008; Notice 749

Cases: *Edinburgh's Telford College v R & C Commrs* [2006] BVC 583 Court of Session; *Riverside Housing Association* [2006] BVC 2,314 in the High Court; *The Chancellors, Masters and Scholars of the University of Cambridge* No. 20,610 [2008] BVC 2,274

17-820   Museums, etc.

Certain non-charging national museums and galleries can, subject to the usual rules, reclaim VAT which they incur.

The refund scheme allows certain non-charging national museums and galleries to recover VAT they incur on their purchases by adding it to input tax claimed on their VAT returns. A qualifying museum or gallery can recover the VAT attributable to free rights of admission from the date specified in a Treasury Order.

HM Treasury decide which national museums and galleries are to be eligible for the scheme. The relevant museums and galleries are specified in *Value Added Tax (Refund of Tax to Museums and Galleries) Order* 2001 (SI 2001/2879).

Legislation: VATA 1994, s. 33A

Other material: Notice 998, VAT refund scheme for National museums and galleries

VAT Reporter: ¶50-880

17-870   Shared staff: paymaster arrangements

Closely related businesses often share the same staff. If one business employs the staff and recharges others for their share of the costs, this gives rise to a standard-rated supply by the employing business. This does not give rise to any particular problem when the businesses are fully taxable, provided that the employing company remembers to charge and account for VAT. Indeed, if the employer business is partially exempt and the others are fully taxable, it can give rise to a marginal advantage by improving the employer's recovery of residual input tax.

The position is different if one or more of the businesses is unable to recover the whole of its input tax. Here, irrecoverable VAT is artificially generated by the arrangements. It is common for limited companies to avoid such a liability by entering into a group treatment (17-080ff.). However, grouping is not always suitable, and is unavailable to unincorporated businesses.

Another way of avoiding such an unnecessary liability is to enter into a paymaster arrangement. Under such an arrangement, the staff are formally employed under joint contracts of employment by all of the businesses concerned. One of the businesses (the paymaster) operates the payroll, paying the staff, dealing with PAYE, NIC, pension contributions, etc. The exact recharge by the paymaster to another employer of the other employer's share of the staff employment costs is not regarded as being consideration for a supply. However, any additional charge for operating the payroll is seen as consideration for a taxable supply.

It is essential when entering into a paymaster arrangement to ensure that all formalities are properly complied with.

In a case involving an outsourcing arrangement for IT services together with joint employment contracts for the staff, the Tribunal looked behind the contracts to ascertain what actually happened and decided that there was a single supply of services, not a supply of IT services plus a recharge of the salaries of jointly employed staff. This resulted in the whole amount being liable to VAT.

Cases: *CGI Group (Europe) Ltd* [2010] UKFTT 396 (TC); [2011] TC 00678

Other material: Notice 700/34

VAT Reporter: ¶18-520

E-COMMERCE

17-920   Introduction

The purpose of this section is to highlight the main VAT issues which arise with electronic commerce and the relevant rules and regulations that apply. While this section is not meant to be a comprehensive guide to VAT on its own, some explanation of VAT basics is given as well as references to other background material.

The basic precept is that VAT is a tax on the supply of goods and services. A supply of goods is fairly simple to recognise – the transfer of exclusive ownership usually accompanied by the physical delivery of the goods – whereas services can be more difficult to deal with. For

VAT purposes a supply of services is anything done for consideration which is not a supply of goods.

The VAT rules for services are different from those for goods and this is significant for electronic commerce. This is because items which are delivered electronically are treated as services for VAT purposes and can have a different treatment from similar items delivered physically and treated as goods.

An example of this, where the VAT treatment is different, is the area of electronically supplied publications. There is a zero rate available for printed matter such as magazines, newsletters, leaflets and brochures, etc. This does not apply to electronic media and any such publications supplied by these means are not eligible for zero-rating in the same way.

VAT rates and methods of collection depend upon four main factors:

(1) what is being supplied (goods or services and any applicable specific rules);

(2) where suppliers and customers are located (same country, another EU Member State or outside the EU);

(3) the VAT status (registered or not registered) of customers and suppliers in the EU;

(4) the place of effective use or enjoyment of the services.

The rules for determining the place of supply, particularly for services, can be quite complicated, and a supply cannot simply be treated as not subject to VAT if the customer is established in a country outside the United Kingdom.

17-980   Selling goods over the internet

Many businesses now advertise their products on the internet and customers are able to order goods, which are then delivered, usually with payment being made by credit card prior to delivery. In such cases the VAT treatment of these supplies is no different from that for mail or telephone orders. The following paragraphs cover issues such as the tax point and delivery charges and then examples relating to where the customer is located.

VAT Reporter: ¶13-550

Tax point for supplies ordered via the internet

The tax point (the time at which VAT must be accounted for by the supplier) is the earliest of the date of receipt of payment, the date of issue of a VAT invoice, or the date the goods are delivered/made available to the customer. Usually, with internet orders from consumers, payment is made by credit card and the date on which VAT must be accounted for is therefore the date payment is received from the credit card company. VAT accounting should not be delayed, however, if the credit card company delays payment pending satisfactory delivery of the goods, in which case the delivery date is the tax point. The value on which VAT must be accounted for is the gross amount received, without any credit for the credit card company's commission charges, etc.

669

Legislation: VATA 1994, s. 6

Other material: Notice 700, Section 14

Place of supply

The place of supply, important for determining under which regime VAT, if any, is chargeable, is the place where the goods are when they are dispatched to the customer's order. If the goods are in the United Kingdom at this point, the supply takes place in the United Kingdom; if the goods are in another Member State, the supply is subject to that country's VAT regime, and; if the goods are outside the EU, then the supply is outside the scope of VAT. In the examples listed below, it is assumed that the goods are held in the same country as the supplier belongs . If the supplier is established in the United Kingdom but the goods are in another Member State (for instance as is sometimes the case with consignment stock), then registration in that Member State would be required, and if the stock is held outside the EU, then the supply is outside the scope of VAT regardless of where the supplier is established.

In the case of goods that are assembled or built, these are treated as supplied where the assembly takes place, and the examples below do not apply. For example, sales of a greenhouse from a UK supplier to a German customer, where the supplier assembles the greenhouse in Germany, are treated as supplied in Germany.

The following examples assume the supplier is a UK business and that the goods are held at UK premises prior to dispatch to the customer:

- customers in the UK – a supply to a customer in the UK will be standard-rated, unless the goods qualify for zero-rating as books, children's clothing or food, for example;
- customers who are private individuals (and other non-VAT-registered persons) residing in another EU Member State – a supply to a non-registered person, such as private individuals, public bodies, charities and businesses which are too small to register or whose activities are totally exempt, is subject to UK VAT at the appropriate rate (e.g. zero rate for food, books, children's clothing, etc.). If the value of supplies to any one Member State exceeds certain monetary thresholds, when registration in that Member State is required. This is known as distance selling;
- customers in another Member State who are 'in business' – where a supply is made to a VAT-registered customer in another Member State it is known as a 'dispatch' (or 'dispatch') for VAT purposes;
- customers outside the EU – goods delivered to a destination outside the EU are zero-rated as exports, regardless of whether the customer is VAT registered or not, provided that the supplier holds the requisite proof of export.

Legislation: VATA 1994, s. 7A

Other material: Notice 741A

Delivery charges

Delivery charges are treated as having the same VAT liability as the goods which are being supplied. This is because the supply is of the goods delivered to the customer's address and the delivery charges are an additional payment for the supply of the goods at that address. If the goods are zero-rated, such as books, children's clothing or food, then the delivery charge will also be zero-rated. Otherwise delivery charges are standard rated. This applies even if the cost of delivery is purchase of postage stamps, which are exempt when purchased from the post office.

Other material: Notice 700/24

18-020   Buying goods over the internet

Goods purchased from a UK supplier

Where goods are purchased from a UK supplier they will be standard-rated, unless the goods qualify for zero-rating as books, children's clothing or food, for example.

Goods purchased from a supplier in another EU Member State

If the supplier is not VAT registered, there will be no VAT charged on the supply.

If the supplier is VAT registered in another Member State, and does not have a UK VAT registration because of distance selling provisions, then VAT will be charged in accordance with that country's VAT regime. If customers are VAT registered, then they will need to make their VAT registration number available to the supplier, who will quote it on his sales invoice and not charge the customer VAT. Instead, the customer is responsible for accounting for the VAT on taxable items (not zero-rated) as an 'acquisition', by entering the VAT due (20 per cent × the value (including cost of transport, insurance, packing, etc.)) in box 2 of the VAT return, and also claiming it as input tax (part of the box 4 figure) providing that the customer is entitled to do so (i.e. subject to the partial exemption rules or input tax blocking rules).

Where a business registered in another Member State is not yet making any distance sales to the UK but has either opted or intends to opt to make the place of supply the UK, there will be an entitlement to register on an intending trader basis. Applicants must provide written evidence to show that they have notified the fiscal authority in their home State that they have exercised an option to make the place of supply the UK.

Where a person registered in another Member State provides a distance-selling UK VAT invoice to a person in the UK, the invoice must contain the legend 'SECTION 14(2) VATA INVOICE' (*Value Added Tax Regulations* 1995 (SI 1995/2518), reg. 19)

Legislation: VATA 1994, s. 7

Other material: Notice 725

Special Persons

Goods purchased from a supplier outside the EU

Where goods are purchased from a supplier outside the EU, the purchaser is required to treat the goods as an import for VAT purposes, and will be liable to any VAT or Customs Duty payable on import. It should be noted that items with a value of under £18.00 (including post and packing) are free from VAT (except alcohol and tobacco products). This £18 limit reduces to £15 from November 2011. Duty rates vary from product to product. HMRC requires payment of VAT and any Customs Duty prior to allowing their removal from the port in most circumstances. Where the goods arrive by post, the Post Office collect the VAT and Customs Duty on behalf of HMRC.

Where goods are imported by a VAT registered business, VAT and any Customs Duty is generally payable at the port before removal of the goods, although deferment of VAT and duty is available. It is important that the import documentation, usually a form C88, Single Administrative Document (SAD), is completed with the purchaser as importer, otherwise the certificate of VAT paid on import, the evidence for recovery of VAT on imports, will not be correctly issued.

Legislation: VATA 1994, s. 7

Other material: Notice 702

18-070 Electronic products

What is an electronic product?

An electronic product is a product which is capable of being sold and transferred electronically over the internet, either by downloading or via email, etc. For VAT purposes electronic products are treated as services and typical examples include software, music, photographs, games, newspapers and magazines. As services, they are not liable to Customs Duties, but are liable to VAT. The correct VAT treatment depends upon the type of service being supplied.

In cases where free downloads of electronic products are provided, these are not subject to VAT as there is no supply for VAT purposes – there is a provision of services, but as there is no consideration, there is no supply.

Examples of these types of products are:

- photographs and other images;
- software – 'off the shelf' or customised, and updating thereof;
- provision of online information;
- digitised newspapers and other online publications;
- technical or educational material;
- website supply, web-hosting and distance maintenance of programs and equipment;
- making databases available, e.g. search engines and internet directories;
- music;
- film;

- broadcasts and events solely provided over the internet – not simultaneously broadcast by radio or television;
- games, including games of chance and gambling games;
- distance teaching and workbooks marked automatically without human intervention;
- online auction services and internet service packages (ISPs).

Legislation: Council Implementing Regulation (EU) 282/2011

Other material: Notice 741A, para. 15.12

VAT Reporter: ¶65-510

Place of supply

There are three variations to the normal place of supply rules which have to be considered when dealing with electronic products. These are:

(1) firms based outside the EC that supply electronic products to non-business customers belonging in the EC;

(2) supplies by businesses belonging in the EU to non-business customers belonging outside the EC;

(3) when supplying businesses, to take account of where the electronic services are 'used and enjoyed'.

See also 5-985.

Legislation: VATA 1994, s. 7A

Other material: Notice 741A, Section 2

VAT Reporter: ¶13-500

Place of 'belonging'

For all of the above services, therefore, it is vital to determine where the customer belongs for VAT purposes. A business 'belongs' in a country if they have a business establishment most closely connected with the supply in that country. An individual 'belongs' in a country if they are usually resident in that country.

It can sometimes be difficult to ascertain where your customer 'belongs' when the only contact you have is an email address. However, it is the supplier's responsibility to ensure that the customer belongs where they declare they do. HMRC may accept the customer's postal address providing it has been used to send catalogues, samples, goods, invoices, correspondence, etc. which have not been returned. Alternatively, a comparison of the customer's address with credit/debit card billing details, or the issuing bank's location; or the use of geo-location or proprietary software to verify where the customer belongs, or the

Special Persons

use of systems that are configured to identify where the service is used and enjoyed (e.g. telecommunications suppliers).

Legislation: VATA 1994, s. 9

Other material: Notice 741A, Section 3 and 19

Checking VAT registration numbers of customers

In cases where the VAT treatment depends upon quoting the customer's VAT registration number, the validity of the number should be checked in all cases where the value of any single transaction is over £500, or if the total of transactions to any one customer in a quarter exceeds £500. VAT registration numbers may be checked by making enquiries on the National Advice Helpline or by checking the format of the number at the Europa website. If a customer claims to be in business but cannot produce a VAT registration number, then alternative evidence should be obtained, such as contracts, business letterheads, commercial website address, publicity material, certificates from fiscal authorities, etc.

Other material: VAT Information Sheet 05/03

Effective use or enjoyment

For supplies of digitised products to business customers, there is also an overriding factor which may alter the place of supply, namely, if the effective use or enjoyment of the service is elsewhere than where the customer belongs. For example, if a UK business subscribes to an ISP service, but that service is used from Jersey (outside the EU) or if a US business subscribes to an online information service, but that service is used in the UK.

Where the effective use or enjoyment is different from where the customer belongs, as in the above examples, then the place of supply is changed to the place where the effective use or enjoyment takes place.

Other material: Notice 741A, Section 17

18-090 Electronic products

Summary table of VAT treatment for digitised products

Supplier status	Customer VAT status	VAT treatment
UK business	UK business	UK standard rate
UK business	EU business	Outside the scope with input tax recovery – EU customer accounts for reverse charge
UK business	EU individual	UK standard rate
UK business	Non-EU business or individual	Outside the scope with input tax recovery

Supplier status	Customer VAT status	VAT treatment
EU business	UK individual	Standard rated at rate applicable to supplier's member state
EU business	UK business	Reverse charge accounted for by UK customer
Non-EU business	UK individual	Registration required by non-EU business in at least one member state
Non-EU business	UK business	Reverse charge accounted for by UK customer

Note: When the customer is a business customer it is necessary to consider where 'use and enjoyment' of the product occurs – see below.

TRANSFER OF A BUSINESS AS A GOING CONCERN

18-120   Purchase or sale of a business

The transfer of a business (or of part of a business) as a going concern is treated as not being a supply for VAT purposes, provided that certain conditions are met. Although this is a relieving provision, it does give rise to special problems in practice. These generally concern the question of whether the going concern transfer provisions do, in fact, apply and, if so, recognition of the consequences of them. It should be noted in particular that the non-taxing of such a supply is not a voluntary matter, but mandatory.

If the provisions apply, then no VAT is chargeable by the transferor in connection with the sale of the business. It follows that, if the transferor incorrectly charges VAT in this case, the amount charged as tax is not recoverable in the hands of the transferee. The transferee must therefore be careful not to agree to pay VAT on a transaction unless convinced that the going concern transfer provisions do not apply.

By the same token, if assets of a business are sold, but the conditions for a going concern transfer are not met, then the vendor is at risk. If the vendor mistakenly thinks that non-supply treatment applies, then HMRC may seek VAT from the transferor, who is unable to recover the tax from the transferee (unless the relevant contracts have been carefully drawn up and the transferee can be located and also has the financial resources to pay).

Legislation: *Value Added Tax (Special Provisions) Order* 1995 (SI 1995/1268), art. 5

Other material: Notice 700/9

VAT Reporter: ¶54-155

18-160   Treatment of going concern transfers – general

Where a business is transferred as a going concern, a special VAT treatment applies. The transfer is treated as not amounting to a supply for VAT purposes. This means that:

- no VAT is chargeable on any sale of assets which would otherwise attract VAT;
- if the transfer involves assets covered by the capital goods scheme, the purchaser takes over responsibility for making appropriate adjustments for the remainder of the adjustment period (so the purchaser needs to be sure of getting all relevant information from the vendor);
- the transferee may not reclaim any VAT wrongly charged by the vendor; and
- if tax should have been charged but was not, the vendor is responsible for the payment of such tax.

It is important that both vendors and purchasers of a business under the TOGC provisions should understand the situation and proceed accordingly – with care.

Legislation: *Value Added Tax (Special Provisions) Order* 1995 (SI 1995/1268), art. 5; *Value Added Tax Regulations* 1995 (SI 1995/2518), reg. 114

Other material: Notice 700/9

VAT Reporter: ¶54-160

18-200   When the going concern transfer provisions apply

The following conditions apply.

(1)   If the transfer is of only part of a business, that part must be capable of separate operation.

(2)   The assets transferred must be intended to be used by the transferee in carrying on the same kind of business as that carried on by the transferor. In applying this test, regard must be had to the kind of business carried on by the transferor in respect of the assets transferred, where the transfer is of part of a business. Where the transferee is to incorporate the assets into an existing business of his, regard must be had to the business use to which the assets transferred are to be put rather than to the totality of the transferee's business activities.

(3)   If the transferor is a taxable person the treatment will not apply unless the transferee either is already a taxable person or becomes so immediately as a result of the transfer. See 8-350 and flowchart 18-950.

Legislation: *Value Added Tax (Special Provisions) Order* 1995 (SI 1995/1268), art. 5

Other material: Notice 700/9, para. 2.3

VAT Reporter: ¶54-160

18-240 Treatment compulsory not optional

It is important to note that the treatment is compulsory, not optional. If any of the conditions fails to be met then the assets are supplied, and VAT must be accounted for accordingly. In the latter case, the sale price agreed between the parties will be VAT inclusive unless the contract provides for the addition of VAT if applicable.

It follows that it is vital to both parties to determine correctly whether the going concern transfer provisions apply. Although any written evidence, such as contracts, will be helpful in ascertaining the position, it is necessary to look at all of the surrounding facts in arriving at the answer.

Other material: Notice 700/9, para. 2.2

VAT Reporter: ¶54-150

18-280 Existence of a going concern

A case much referred to by the tribunals in dealing with going concern transfers is *Kenmir Ltd* although this was not in fact a VAT case. Widgery J said:

'In deciding whether a transaction amounted to the transfer of a business, regard must be had to its substance rather than its form, and consideration must be given to the whole of the circumstances, weighing the factors which point in one direction against those which point in another. In the end, the vital consideration is whether the effect of the transaction was to put the transferee in possession of a going concern, the activities of which he could carry on without interruption. Many factors may be relevant to this decision though few will be conclusive in themselves. Thus, if the new employer carries on business in the same manner as before this will point to the existence of a transfer, but the converse is not necessarily true, because a transfer may be complete even though the transferee does not choose to avail himself of all rights which he acquires thereunder. Similarly, an express assignment of goodwill is strong evidence of a transfer of the business, but the absence of such an assignment is not conclusive if the transferee [note: it is believed that this should read "transferor"] has effectively deprived himself of the power to compete. The absence of the assignment of premises, stock-in-trade or outstanding contracts will likewise not be conclusive if the particular circumstances of the transferee nevertheless enable him to carry on substantially the same business as before.'

In *Spijkers*, the European Court of Justice stated at para. 13:

'... it is necessary to take account of all the factual circumstances of the transaction in question, including the type of undertaking or business in question, the transfer or otherwise of tangible assets such as buildings and stocks, the value of intangible assets at the date of transfer, whether the majority of the staff are taken over by the new employer, the transfer or otherwise of the circle of customers and the degree of similarity between activities before and after the transfer and the duration of any interruption in those activities. It should be made clear, however, that each of these factors is only a part of the overall assessment which is required and therefore they cannot be examined independently of each other.'

Special Persons

677

Continuing the business

This has been examined by the ECJ and the main points to be gained from *Zita Modes Sàrl*, are:

'• In order for there to be such a transfer, the assets transferred must form a sufficient whole to allow the pursuit of an economic activity and that activity must be pursued by the transferee.

• The transferee must, however, intend to operate the business or the part of the undertaking transferred and not simply to immediately liquidate the activity concerned and sell the stock, if any.'

In addition, it must be appreciated that the wording of any advertisements and announcements to actual or prospective customers may be relevant in deciding if there was a transfer of a going concern.

Cases: *Kenmir Ltd v Frizell* [1968] 1 WLR 329; *Spijkers v Gebroeders Benedik Abattoir CV* (Case 24/85) [1986] ECR 1119; *Zita Modes Sàrl v Administration de l'enregistrement et des domains* (Case C-497/01) [2005] BVC 772

Other material: Notice 700/9, para. 2.3 and para. 2.4

VAT Reporter: ¶54-158

Short gap in trading

A short gap in trading may not stop a going concern transfer, e.g. where the gap is for redecoration of the premises by the new owner.

In *Spijkers*, the Advocate General stated at p. 299:

'… the fact that at the date of transfer trading has ceased or has been substantially reduced does not prevent there being a transfer of a business if the wherewithal to carry on the business, such as plant, building and employees, are available and are transferred … That after the sale there is a gap before trading is resumed is a relevant fact but it is not conclusive …'

That after the sale there is a gap before trading is resumed is a relevant fact but it is not conclusive …'

Cases: *ECSG Ltd (formerly Spectrum Electrical Group Ltd)* [1990] 5 BVC 1,396; *Spijkers v Gebroeders Benedik Abattoir CV* (Case 24/85) [1986] ECR 1119

Other material: Notice 700/9, para. 2.3.6

VAT Reporter: ¶54-160

18-320 Assets used for same kind of business as that of transferor

There is also the question of whether the assets are to be used for the same kind of business as that carried on by the transferor. This is of particular relevance to the transferor, since he has no real control over the use to which the assets are put. It will also be a matter of concern to the transferee, where VAT is charged on the transfer (since he must validate his claim to deduct input tax), or where the contract is written so that VAT is to be added to the price if it is applicable.

Case	Seller's business	Purchaser's business	TOGC?
G Draper (Marlow)	Pub selling one sort of beer	Pub selling different type of beer to different clientele	Yes – it was still a pub
Housand Tahmassebi t/a Sale Pepe	Indian restaurant	Italian restaurant	Yes – it was still a restaurant business
ICB Ltd	Quarries selling stone.	Road building – quarries purchased as an in-house supply of stone.	No – the new owner did not continue to sell stone
Delta Newsagents	Acquiring newsagents shops and subsequently granting franchises	Running a newsagents under a franchise agreement	No – the business of Delta was to grant the franchises, not run the newsagent's shop

In practical terms, the answer must be to obtain a ruling from HMRC, based on disclosure of the full facts, in any case where the correct legal treatment is in doubt. In all cases, it will be necessary for the buyer and seller of a business (or of business assets) to satisfy themselves that the sale contract is worded in such a way as to protect their interests. Consideration could be given to paying amounts which may become due as VAT into some kind of holding arrangement (such as an escrow account, or into the hands of a lawyer acting as stakeholder) while the correct treatment is determined.

Cases: *G Draper (Marlow)* [1986] 2 BVC 208,096; *Houshang Tahmassebi (t/a Sale Pepe)* No. 13,177 [1996] BVC 4,088; *ICB Ltd* [1985] 2 BVC 205,177; *Delta Newsagents* [1986] 2 BVC 208,119

Legislation: *Value Added Tax (Special Provisions) Order* 1995 (SI 1995/1268), art. 5

Other material: Notice 700/9, para. 2.3.2

VAT Reporter: ¶54-163

Special Persons

18-370   Land and buildings included in a TOGC

Two further conditions apply to transfers of a going concern which include certain land and buildings. These conditions apply to land or buildings which are assets of a trading business or a property rental business. Examples that HMRC consider to be property rental businesses are given in Notice 700/9

The transfers of land or buildings to which the two additional conditions apply are as follows:

- freehold non-residential buildings which are under three years old. These are buildings which are liable to VAT when 'new' – see 15-200;
- any land or buildings where the transferor has elected to 'waive the exemption' – see 15-300.

Legislation: *Value Added Tax (Special Provisions) Order* 1995 (SI 1995/1268), art. 5(2)

Other material: Notice 742A, para. 11.2; Notice 700/9, para. 2.4

VAT Reporter: ¶54-166

Option for taxation by the transferee

The transferee must opt for taxation in respect of the property concerned, and give HMRC written notification of this, before the first tax point arises in respect of the supply.

Following litigation on the point, HMRC now accept that it is sufficient, in the case of a written notification by letter, that the buyer has properly addressed, prepaid, and posted the letter by the relevant date. It does not have to be received by them by that date. However, they warn that it will be prudent to retain evidence of posting.

Legislation: *Value Added Tax (Special Provisions) Order* 1995 (SI 1995/1268), art. 5(2)

Other material: Notice 742A, para. 11.2; Notice 700/9, para. 2.4

VAT Reporter: ¶54-170

Anti-avoidance

The transferee must notify the transferor that the transferee's election to 'waive the exemption' will not be nullified because of another anti-avoidance measure. The other anti-avoidance measure is in:

- the grant giving rise to the supply is made by a developer of the land; and
- at the time of the grant, it is the intention or expectation of the grantor or the person financing the development that the land will become exempt land.

If the transferee does not give such a notification, the transfer is a taxable transaction.

Legislation: *Value Added Tax (Special Provisions) Order* 1995 (SI 1995/1268), art. 5(2B)(b); VATA 1994, Sch. 10, para. 12(1)

Other material: Notice 742A; Notice 700/9, para 2.4

VAT Reporter: ¶54-170

18-410 Property rental business

The TOGC regulations also apply to transfers of 'property rental' businesses. Identifying a 'property rental' business for these purposes is not always straightforward. For example it is not always necessary to have a sitting tenant in the property or properties being transferred.

HMRC's examples of a 'property rental' businesses follows.

'If you:
- own the freehold of a property which you let to a tenant and sell the freehold with the benefit of the existing lease, a business of property rental is transferred to the purchaser. This is a business transferred as a TOGC even if the property is only partly tenanted. Similarly, if you own the lease of a property (which is subject to a sub-lease) and you assign your lease with the benefit of the sub-lease, this is a business transferred as a TOGC
- own a building where there is a contract to pay rent in the future but where the tenants are enjoying an initial rent free period, even if the building is sold during the rent free period, you are carrying on a business of property rental
- granted a lease in respect of a building but the tenants are not yet in occupation, you are carrying on a property rental business
- own a property and have found a tenant but not actually entered into a lease agreement when you transfer the freehold to a third party (with the benefit of a contractual agreement for a lease but before the lease has been signed), there is sufficient evidence of intended economic activity for there to be a property rental business capable of being transferred
- are a property developer selling a site as a package (to a single buyer) which is a mixture of let and unlet, finished or unfinished properties, and the sale of the site would otherwise have been standard rated, then subject to the purchaser opting to tax for the whole site, the whole site can be regarded as a business transferred as a going concern.
- own a number of let freehold properties, and you sell one of them, the sale of this single let or partly let property can be a TOGC of a property rental business
- have a partially-let building this is capable of being a property rental business, providing that the letting constitutes economic activity. This may include electricity sub-stations or space for advertising hoardings providing that there is a lease in place.
- purchase the freehold and leasehold of a property from separate sellers without the interests merging and the lease has not been extinguished, providing you continue to exploit the asset by receiving rent from the tenant, then such a transaction can be a TOGC.'

Other material: Notice 700/9, Section 6 and 8

VAT Reporter: ¶54-166

Special Persons

18-460   TOGC to VAT Group

If a business is acquired, as a going concern by a VAT group of companies, and that group is partially exempt at some time in the VAT accounting period, or longer period concerned, then tax may be due under a self supply procedure (17-310).

Particular attention should be given in cases where there is the transfer of a property letting business to (or from) a VAT Group.

HMRC clarify their policy concerning VAT groups and transfers of going concerns (TOGCs) in the particular context of property rental businesses in Notice 700/9/2002 para. 7.3.

HMRC give the following three examples of their policy.

(1)   If a member of a VAT group sells a property, let to another member of the VAT group, to a third party, this will not be seen as a TOGC.

(2)   If a landlord sells a let property to a new landlord in the same VAT group as the tenant, this will not be a TOGC.

(3)   However, if a landlord sells a property let to a number of tenants, one of which is a member of the same VAT group, this will be a TOGC (presumably the same applies where one of several tenants is a member of the purchaser's VAT group).

Legislation: VATA 1994, s. 44

Other material: Notice 700/9, Section 5

VAT Reporter: ¶54-155

18-510   Registration of transferee

Where a business is transferred as a going concern, the transferee is deemed to have made the transferor's supplies for the purpose of determining whether he must register.

If the transferor's taxable supplies in the year to the date of transfer of the going concern exceeded the registration threshold, the transferee is registered from the date of transfer and not one month later.

The transferee must notify HMRC of the transfer within 30 days of the date of transfer.

Legislation: VATA 1994, s. 49(1)(a) and Sch. 1

Other material: Notice 700/9, para. 3.5

VAT Reporter: ¶54-160

18-560   TOGC – retention of records

The following apply:

- the seller will keep the business records in all but a few specified cases;
- the seller must make available to the buyer all information necessary for the buyer to comply with his duties under the VAT Act; and
- HMRC may disclose to the buyer information held that is needed by the buyer to comply with his duties under the VAT Act.

Other material: Notice 700/9, para. 3.6; Notice 700/21, para. 2.9 Keeping VAT Records

VAT Reporter: ¶54-155

18-600   Transfer of registration number

Where a business is transferred as a going concern, the purchaser can take over the VAT registration number of the vendor. This only applies if the transferor has, at the time of the transfer, a valid VAT registration and this will be cancelled as a result of the transfer. In order to effect a transfer of a VAT registration number, both the transferor and the transferee must make an election to this effect using form VAT 68.

If a registration number is transferred, the transferee effectively takes over any liability of the transferor towards HMRC in terms of the submission of returns or the payment of tax, and also any rights to repayment of input tax. The precise extent to which liability carries over to the transferee is not absolutely clear, but appears to be restricted to paying outstanding tax (as at the date of the transfer) as shown on the returns submitted by the transferor, as well as submitting any outstanding returns which the transferor has failed to make, and the amounts of tax due in respect of these. A tribunal has held that the transferee's liability does not extend to the payment of amounts due because returns submitted by the transferor were incorrect. Even so, it must generally be considered unwise for the purchaser of a business to take over the vendor's registration number.

Cases: *Pets Place (UK) Ltd* [1997] BVC 2,164

Legislation: *Value Added Tax Regulations* 1995 (SI 1995/2518), reg. 6(2)

Other material: Notice 700/9, para. 3.4

VAT Reporter: ¶54-175

18-640   Costs – treatment of input tax

The treatment of input tax incurred by a vendor in connection with a transfer of a business, or part of a business, as a going concern has been clarified by the European Court of Justice's judgment in *Abbey National Plc* delivered on 22 February 2001, and HMRC's policy following this case is confirmed in Business Brief 8/01 (2 July 2001).

Input tax on costs relating to the transfer of an entire business is residual, so fully deductible if the business is fully taxable, non-deductible if it is wholly exempt, and partly deductible if it is partially exempt.

Input tax on costs relating to the transfer of an identifiable part of a business is linked with the supplies made by that part which is transferred. Its status is determined by reference to the supplies made by the part transferred, rather than by the status of the whole of the transferor's supplies. Thus, if a partly exempt trader transfers a fully taxable part of the business, the related input tax is wholly recoverable. Conversely, costs relating to a wholly exempt part of a business transferred as a going concern by a partly exempt trader will be non-deductible.

Cases: *Abbey National Plc v C & E Commrs* (Case C-408/98) [2001] BVC 581

Other material: Notice 700/9, para. 2.6

VAT Reporter: ¶54-150

18-680   Second-hand goods

When used second-hand goods are acquired as part of a transfer of a going concern (TOGC) that is not subject to tax (see 18-120), special rules apply. A transferee wishing to use the margin scheme for the goods acquired in this way must consider the following.

(a)   To establish who was the last person to acquire the goods other than by way of a TOGC. This may be the immediate transferee or a predecessor. It is then necessary to be satisfied that that person was entitled to sell the goods concerned under the margin scheme. If that person was ineligible to use the margin scheme the transferee may not use the scheme for the goods concerned.

(b)   The purchase price for the transferor is that paid by the person who was last acquired the goods other than by way of a TOGC.

Legislation: *Value Added Tax (Special Provisions) Order* 1995 (SI 1995/1268), art. 12

Other material: Notice 718 Margin Scheme

SHARE ISSUES, CREDIT NOTES AND BUSINESS PROMOTION SCHEMES

18-730   Raising capital by issuing shares, etc.

The consequences of issuing new shares and recovering input tax on the associated costs was considered by the European Court of Justice ('ECJ'). In *Kretztechnik AG v Finanzamt Linz* [2006] BVC 66, the ECJ ruled as follows:

(a)   a new share issue is outside the scope of VAT;

(b) the costs of making the new issue are a general business overhead.

Until this case, HMRC maintained that issuing new shares was a supply for VAT purposes. HRMC considered new share issues to be exempt supplies within the scope of VATA 1994, Sch. 9, Grp. 5. This was wrong. The ECJ concluded that 'a new share issue ... was not a supply for a consideration ... and did not fall within the scope ...' of VAT.

This supersedes the Court of Appeal decision in *Trinity Mirror Plc v C & E Commrs* [2001] BVC 167 when the Court of Appeal decided that the issue of shares was an exempt supply. The UK is bound by the *Kretztechnic* decision.

Raising capital

HMRC's accept that issuing securities to raise capital are not supplies for VAT purposes. This is almost immaterial of the type of security or the type company. It matters not whether the security is issued by a private or public company.

The liability of the sale of existing shares/securities is unaffected. These continue to be exempt supplies.

Examples given by HMRC of the types of new issues or occasions when *Kretztechnic* applies are as follows:

- 'preference shares, a special rights issue, a bonus issue or the issue of scrip dividends'
- 'other types of security, such as bonds, debentures or loan notes'
- 'shares or other securities ... issued in order to affect a company takeover or as part of a company restructuring ...'

Intermediary or underwriting services

HMRC advise there is no change to the liability of 'intermediary and underwriting services' relating to new issues which are not supplies. The relevant 'intermediary and underwriting services' continue to be exempt supplies

Shares issued to nominees

The case of *Water Hall Group Plc* [2003] BVC 4,085 concerned the issues of new shares to a UK nominee company. The actual purchasers belonged outside the EU. The Tribunal concluded that the shares were supplied to the UK nominee company. It was not possible to look through the nominee company to the actual purchaser.

HMRC have concluded that *Water Hall* is no longer relevant. It applied to the issue of new shares. These are no longer supplies because of *Kretztechnic*. It did not apply to the sale or transfer of existing shares.

When determining the place of belonging of the buyer or seller of existing shares, HMRC advise as follows:

Special Persons

'Supplies of existing shares are to be regarded as being made to or by the person who actually makes the purchase or sale of the shares. Where the actual purchaser is not known to the seller, the place of belonging of a nominee account for the purchaser, if known, may be used to determine the place of supply. If neither is known, you should treat the supply as made in the UK or refer to the special rules in paragraph 9.2 of Public Notice 701/49 "Finance and Securities"'

Shares and other securities issued to persons belonging outside EU

Input tax on costs relating to shares issued to persons belonging outside the EU was recoverable. It was recoverable because of a specific order – *Value Added Tax (Input Tax) (Specified Supplies) Order* 1999 (SI 1999/3121).

This specific order no longer applies to shares and relevant securities issued to persons belonging outside the EU. As these issues are no longer supplies, the input tax on the related costs must be dealt with in the normal way. It is residual tax for partially exempt businesses. It is fully recoverable by business which able to recover input tax in full.

The special for apportioning input tax on costs related to financial supplies (reg. 103B, *Value Added Tax Regulations* 1995 (SI 1995/2518)) no longer applies to issues of new share and other securities affected by the *Kretztechnic* ruling. It continues to apply to other incidental financial supplies which are exempt because they are within the scope of VATA 1994, Grp. 5, Sch. 9.

Intermediaries and shares/securities issued by or to persons belonging outside EU

Input tax incurred by intermediaries in connection with services that they provide when 'shares or other securities' are issued to someone belonging outside the EU or by a business belonging outside the EU was recoverable. This was because of the specific order referred to above. Again, this is changing.

There is no change for 'shares or other securities' issued by someone belonging outside the EU. However, input tax recovery in other circumstances will be blocked because the relevant intermediary services are an exempt supply. HMRC are implementing this change with effect from 1 January 2006.

Legislation: *Value Added Tax Regulations* 1995 (SI 1995/2518), reg. 103B

Cases: *Kretztechnik AG v Finanzamt Linz* [2006] BVC 66; *Trinity Mirror Plc v C & E Commrs* [2001] BVC 167; *RAP Group Plc v C & E Commrs* [2001] BVC 65; *Halladale Group Plc* [2003] BVC 4,140

Other material: Notice 706, para. 8.7

VAT Reporter: ¶11-012

18-790 Use of credit notes

Although the use of credit notes is normal commercial practice, it may give rise to VAT problems if not dealt with correctly. To be valid for VAT purposes, a credit note should meet the following conditions:

(a) reflect a genuine mistake or overcharge or an agreed reduction and be issued within one month of this being discovered or agreed;

(b) give genuine value to the customer to correct the overcharge or mistake.

A credit note should be headed 'credit note' and contain the following information:

(a) the date;
(b) a unique number;
(c) the name and address of the customer;
(d) the name, address and VAT registration number of the supplier;
(e) a reason for the adjustment;
(f) a description of the goods or services;
(g) quantities and amounts concerned;
(h) net amount refunded;
(i) VAT due on amount refunded;
(j) number and date of original invoice (If not possible there needs to be some means of satisfying HMRC that VAT was accounted for on the original supply.

The VAT accounts of the affected person should be adjusted accordingly (see 4-590).

Specific regulations concerning the contents of a credit note have been made in respect adjustments necessary due to a change in rate of VAT.

HMRC have been known to express a general view that they have absolute discretion in the issue of credit notes, so that no credit note is valid for VAT purposes unless authorised by them. In *British United Shoe Machinery Co Ltd v C & E Commrs* (1977) 1 BVC 1,062, this view was rejected, and the tribunal held that a credit note is valid if it has been 'issued bona fide in order to correct a genuine mistake or overcharge, or to give a proper credit'. HMRC seem also to accept that credit notes can properly be issued to give a customer a credit of some kind or to allow a contingent discount.

The circumstances in which a credit note may properly be issued are further defined in the Sixth Directive as follows:

> 'In the case of cancellation, refusal or total or partial non-payment, or where the price is reduced after the supply takes place, the taxable amount shall be reduced accordingly under conditions which shall be determined by the Member States. However, in the case of total or partial non-payment, Member States may derogate from this rule.'

Where the customer is unable or unwilling to pay the full amount due, this provision will not act to reduce the value of the supply for VAT purposes, because of the power of derogation. However, it seems that the remainder of art. 11(C)(1) has direct effect in the UK, in the absence of UK law which implements it.

Special Persons

In summary, the *British United Shoe Machinery* case gives authority for the issue of a credit note where there was a genuine mistake in the original invoice, thus allowing for the correction of mere error. The Sixth Directive goes further (as does the *British United Shoe Machinery* case to an extent) and allows for the issue of a credit note:

(1)   where the supply concerned does not, in fact, take place;

(2)   where the customer refuses to accept the supply (e.g. rejects faulty goods); or

(3)   where the terms of the contract are varied after the supply has taken place (and the invoice been issued), so that the amount payable is reduced.

It appears that, for (3) above to apply, there needs to be agreement between the supplier and the customer in order to bring about a genuine variation of the terms of the contract between them. Unilateral action by the supplier is not sufficient, nor is a price 'reduction' relating merely to the insolvency of the customer (i.e. the supplier issuing a credit note because the customer is insolvent and simply cannot pay).

In order to be valid, a credit note must actually be issued to the customer. Raising a credit note as an internal document, and processing it, but deliberately failing to send it to the customer would amount to a fraud on the revenue, and attract appropriate penalties.

HMRC allow the use of credit notes which relate to the net of VAT amounts only, and do not affect the VAT charged on the supply. In such cases, the credit note should be marked 'This is not a credit note for VAT', and the parties should make the appropriate adjustments to their taxable inputs and outputs even though the amount of tax is unaffected.

'Non-VAT' credit notes may be preferable where the customer is fully taxable, since their use saves having to justify a VAT adjustment to HMRC. It should be noted that both supplier and customer must agree to use such a credit note.

Where an invoice has been incorrectly issued, creating a possible liability although no supply has actually been intended or taken place, it may in effect be cancelled by the issue of a credit note, despite the lack of good faith by the person issuing the invoice, if this is done in sufficient time to eliminate the risk of any loss to the tax revenues (such as might arise if the purported customer was able to claim input tax recovery).

Legislation: Directive 2006/112, art. 90; *Value Added Tax Regulations* 1995 (SI 1995/2518), reg. 15

Cases: *British United Shoe Machinery Co Ltd v C & E Commrs* (1977) 1 BVC 1,062; *Mannesmann Demag Hamilton Ltd* (1983) 2 BVC 208,015; *Silvermere Golf and Equestrian Centre Ltd* (1981) 1 BVC 1,158; *Schmeink and Cofreth AG & Co KG v Finanzamt Borken; Strobel v Finanzamt Esslingen* (Case C-454/98) [2000] BVC 377

Other material: Notice 700, Section 18

VAT Reporter: ¶56-050

18-830   Business promotion schemes

Business promotion schemes, including the use of vouchers, free gifts, etc. can give rise to many VAT problems. The appropriate treatment depends on the detailed workings of each scheme. In addition, the meaning of the relevant law, and particularly the application of the EC law as to the taxable amount, is currently far from certain.

The most important point to make clear is that each business promotion scheme needs to be considered on its own facts and from first principles, and it is dangerous to generalise. The range of schemes operated is restricted only by the limits (if any) of human ingenuity.

The commercial nature of a scheme, in terms of its purpose, is ultimately determined and demonstrated by how it is presented to the customer. However, there can be many different mechanisms to achieve one commercial effect, and it is necessary to look at the underlying detail in order to determine the VAT position. Often, there will still be uncertainty, partly because there are many cases involving several parties, who may not have considered their exact legal position, and partly because promotion schemes tend to involve areas of law whose interpretation is in a state of flux.

The following descriptions of some typical schemes should therefore be read as providing some indications of how business promotions might be analysed, not as providing definitive answers for any particular case.

Coupons

Many promotions involve the use of coupons, and the forms of promotions change all the time.

The treatment of various coupons and vouchers is outlined at 4-770.

Linked goods

Linked goods schemes involve selling two items for a single price. The legal position is simple – the price paid is consideration for the supply of both items and must be apportioned between the two. If both items are liable at the same rate, then there is no difficulty at all. If they are liable at different rates, an apportionment must, in principle, be made, but there is a concession permitting tax to be paid according to the liability of the main goods where the value of the linked goods is very small. Of course, the concession would only be used if the main goods were zero-rated and the linked goods were standard-rated.

Incentive goods

There are schemes where special offers are made to encourage people to become customers for the first time. An example is that in *Empire Stores Ltd v C & E Commrs* where new customers could obtain a 'gift' as well as the goods ordered when paying for their first order of catalogue goods.

The European Court of Justice accepted that the introduction (or self-introduction) of a new customer was consideration for the supply of the gift goods, the taxable amount being the cost price of the gift goods. As this case was restricted to supplies to new customers, there is no implication from it that supplies of linked goods as above, with no conditions as to the nature of the customer, necessarily involve consideration over and above the price paid by the customer.

Cases: *Empire Stores Ltd v C & E Commrs* (Case C-33/93) [1994] BVC 253

Dealer loader schemes

Dealer loader schemes are business promotions whereby a customer is offered gift goods for ordering a target quantity of main goods.

If the gift goods are provided in return for a single order of goods, the main goods and the gift goods are treated as a combined supply, and the consideration must be apportioned. By concession, no apportionment is required if:

(1)   the gift goods are of a kind used in the recipient's business;

(2)   the gift goods are not intended for personal use by the recipient; and

(3)   both the main goods and the gift goods are standard-rated.

If the gift goods are provided in return for orders reaching a pre-determined target over time, HMRC see them as a separate supply by way of gift. VAT is therefore due on the cost of them (unless the cost to the donor is below £50), in which case no VAT is due. By concession, HMRC treat the gift goods and the main goods as a combined supply, with VAT due only on the consideration due from the customer, if:

(1)   the gift goods are of a kind used in the recipient's business;

(2)   the gift goods are not intended for personal use by the recipient; and

(3)   the gift goods are shown on the invoice on which the target is met.

Legislation: VATA 1994, Sch. 4, para. 5

VAT Reporter: ¶49-000

Joint promotions

Promotions are often organised by one or more traders jointly. In these cases, a degree of care is needed to establish who is supplying what, and to whom.

An example would be of a hobby magazine running a competition for readers, with prizes contributed by a manufacturer of goods relevant to the hobby concerned. In such a case, there may be a supply of the prize goods by the manufacturer to the magazine, with the magazine then making gifts of the prizes to competitors. Alternatively, the gifts to competitors may be directly from the manufacturer to the competitors, with the magazine merely acting as agent.

Organisation of schemes through marketing promotions companies

Promotion schemes are often handled for companies by marketing promotions companies. In these cases, it is essential to analyse the arrangements and find out who is making which supplies. It is all too easy on, say, a dealer loader promotion for the promotions company to fail to account for output tax on the promotional goods, considering this to be the responsibility of its client, while the client fails to account for the tax because it both lacks the detailed information (all the transactions having passed through the records of the promotions company) and believes that the promotions company is handling the whole project.

Other material: Notice 700/7

VAT Reporter: ¶49-000

FLOWCHARTS

18-945 Common arrangements for local authority leisure service

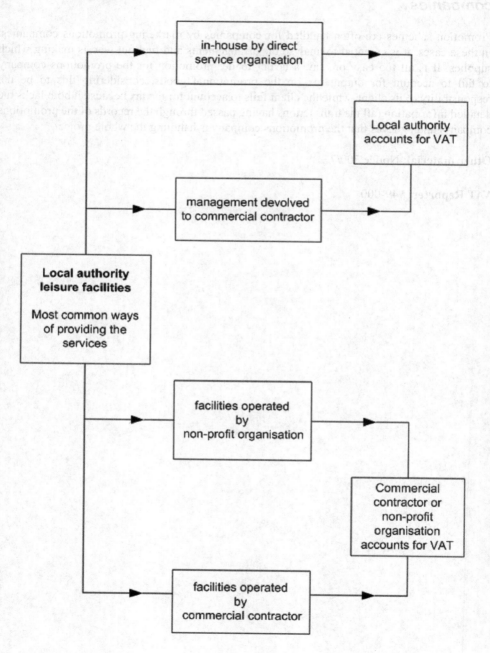

In-house by direct service organisation → Local authority accounts for VAT

management devolved to commercial contractor →

Local authority leisure facilities

Most common ways of providing the services

facilities operated by non-profit organisation → Commercial contractor or non-profit organisation accounts for VAT

facilities operated by commercial contractor →

[This page is intentionally blank]

18-950   TOGC – the right considerations

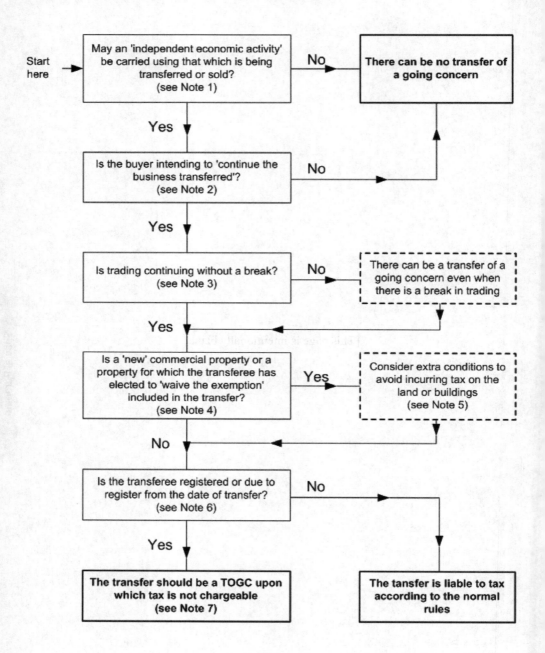

Notes

(1) 'Independent economic activity' and continuing the business

The assets transferred must be sufficient for a person to undertake an 'independent economic activity'. It must be more than the 'simple transfer of assets, such as the sale of stock'. Also the transferee must '… intend to operate the business or the part of the undertaking transferred and not simply to immediately liquidate the activity concerned …' – *Zita Modes Sàrl v Administration de l'enregistrement et des domains* [2005] BVC 772.

(2) Factors to be considered

'… it is necessary to take account of all the factual circumstances of the transaction in question …' – *Spijkers v Gebroeders Benedik Abattoir CV* (Case 24/85) [1986] ECR 1119.

'… an express assignment of goodwill is strong evidence of a transfer of the business, but the absence of such an assignment is not conclusive …' – *Kenmir v Frizzell* (QB [1968] 1 WLR 329).

(3) Break in trading

'… the fact that at the date of transfer trading has ceased … does not prevent there being a transfer of a business … a gap before trading is resumed is a relevant fact but it is not conclusive …' – *Spijkers v Gebroeders Benedik Abattoir CV* (Case 24/85) [1986] ECR 1119.

(4) 'New' commercial property

A 'new' commercial property is one which is under three years old. It is a commercial if not designed as dwelling, not used solely for relevant residential or charitable purposes.

(5) Extra conditions – transferee's obligations

The extra rules to be considered apply to the transferee who must elect to 'waive the exemption' from the 'relevant date' or before and warrant that the relevant anti-avoidance does not apply (15-120).

(6) Need for transferee to be registered

When the transferor is VAT-registered, the transferee must be, or on transfer immediately become, registered if the transfer of the assets is to be relieved from tax.

(7) Further information

For further information, see Notice 700/9 Transfer of a business as a going concern and Business Brief 12/04 21 April 2004.

Special Persons

695

Appeals and Disputes

HMRC REVIEW

19-000   Introduction

There are often matters about which Her Majesty's Revenue and Customs (HMRC) and the business person disagree. It is important to ensure that any dispute is taken through the correct route. Some matters come under the jurisdiction of the First-, or Second-tier Tribunal (Tax); others mean that a complaint may be made against a particular officer whilst certain disputes may only be resolved by the Adjudicator.

19-050   Introduction to HMRC Review

'Review' is the term used to describe the process whereby HMRC are asked to take a second look at an assessment or other decision.

There is currently no obligation to seek a review of a VAT decision before an appeal can be made to the Tribunal, although it is mandatory for HMRC to offer a review.

Once an appeal is made to the Tribunal, it is not possible to request – or accept the offer – of a review. If a review is being undertaken, it is not allowable to appeal to the Tribunal until completion of the review.

VAT Reporter: ¶61-020

19-080   When to accept a review

It is mandatory for HMRC to offer a review of any decision. The offer must be made when the decision is notified to the taxpayer. The taxpayer has 30 days in which to accept the offer.

If the taxpayer does not accept the offer of a review within the 30 days, then HMRC will still carry out a review if it is considered that the taxpayer has a 'reasonable excuse' for the delay. Their decision as to whether the taxpayer has a reasonable excuse is final although appeal may be made to the tribunal against the original decision.

A review is a much more informal procedure than an appeal to the First- or Second-tier Tribunal and can be requested in respect of any decision by HMRC, whether or not it is a decision of a kind to be found listed at 19-240.

VAT Reporter: ¶61-400

Appeals and Disputes

Other material: Appeals, reviews and tribunals guidance manual, Section 3000; *www.hmrc.gov.uk/dealingwith/appeals/indirecttax.htm*

Legislation: VATA 1994, s. 83A

19-100   Effect on time to lodge an appeal

An appeal must be lodged within 30 days of the conclusion of the review.

If the offer of a review is not accepted, then an appeal must be made within 30 days of the decision or, if later, the end of the period for the acceptance of the review.

Legislation: VATA 1994, s. 83G

VAT Reporter: ¶61-445

19-120   Who carries out the review?

A person who receives an assessment or other decision with which he or she cannot agree can first ask the officer who made the decision to reconsider. Alternatively, he or she can accept the offer of a review by another officer and, if so, it is reasonable that HRMC ensure that the reviewing officer is genuinely independent. HMRC promise that the review will be carried out by an officer who has not previously been involved with the decision.

The review must be completed within 45 days of the date of accepting the review offer (or later, by agreement between the taxpayer and the review team).

Other material: Appeals, reviews and tribunals guidance manual, Section 3400; *www.hmrc.gov.uk/dealingwith/appeals/indirecttax.htm*

VAT Reporter: ¶61-020

19-150   How do HMRC review the matter?

HMRC are normally prepared to carry out a review even if no new material is available. They will normally take into account the comments and findings of the original officer as well as ask this person to comment on the arguments put forward by the business. If new evidence or information comes to light they may ask the original officer to look at the matter afresh.

The review team will try to weed out poorly founded or incorrect decisions. A major role of the review team is to reach an agreement without recourse to the tribunal except where there is genuine disagreement. This may be through negotiation and compromise.

Other material: Appeals, reviews and tribunals guidance manual, Section 3400

VAT Reporter: ¶61-020

19-160   Should a person seek a review or appeal to a tribunal?

Local reconsiderations	*Tribunal*
Pros:	**Cons:**
There is a more flexible approach	This is a formal procedure and may be stressful and costly
The disputed matter is not restricted to one listed below at 19-240	The dispute is restricted to one listed below at 19-240
Discretionary decisions can be changed	An appeal against a discretionary decision can only be allowed if it is found to be unreasonable
VAT returns and payments need not be up to date	VAT returns and payments must be up to date
The tax in dispute does not need to be paid to or deposited with HMRC	As appropriate, the tax due must be paid or deposited with HMRC unless it would lead to hardship
Cons:	**Pros:**
This may be a waste of time if views are entrenched	HMRC's headquarters should review the matter before it goes to tribunal
It is not possible to claim costs	Costs may be payable if the appellant wins

ALTERNATIVE DISPUTE RESOLUTION

19-170   Introduction

HMRC have introduced a scheme of alternative dispute resolution (ADR) for small and medium-sized businesses (SMEs). This was started as a pilot scheme in North Wales/North West England but has been extended to South Wales, South West England and parts of London. It covers direct tax disputes as well as VAT.

ADR has proved to be valuable in resolving disputes in the commercial world.

19-180   The scheme

HMRC have trained 'facilitators' who are independent and have not been involved with the dispute before. The facilitators work with both sides in order to broker an agreement between them.

Once accepted for the process, the taxpayer will be asked by the facilitator to sign a Memorandum of Understanding indicating the taxpayer's understanding and agreement to the process. Taking part in ADR does not prevent the taxpayer from subsequently asking for an HMRC review or following through the matter by appealing to the Tax Tribunal.

During the trial period ADR will only be available to SMEs before an appealable tax decision or assessment has been made by HMRC.

Appeals and Disputes

Inclusion in the ADR process

If a taxpayer – or their representative – believes that the dispute may be eligible for the ADR process they should telephone 01492 523747 weekdays between 9am and 4pm. HMRC will respond within 30 days.

Other material:www.hmrc.gov.uk/adr/index.htm; www.hmrc.gov.uk/adr/intro-note.pdf

APPEALING TO THE FIRST- OR SECOND-TIER TRIBUNAL

19-200   Introduction

The First-and Upper-tier Tribunal introduced on 1 April 2009 by the *Tribunals, Courts and Enforcement Act* 2007 are the first levels of the system to which an appeal may be made. It tends to be a more informal occasion than an appearance in the High Court. Decisions made by a First-tier Tribunal are not binding on any other tribunal but are obviously persuasive. Those made by the Upper-tier Tribunal should be binding on those of the lower court.

VAT Reporter: ¶61-300

19-210   First-tier Tribunal

There are four types of hearing:
- Paper hearing.
- Basic hearing.
- Standard hearing.
- Complex hearing.

Paper hearing

The Appellant submits a statement of case and the Chairman makes a decision based on the available papers. There is no appearance before the Tribunal. It is possible for the Appellant to request a basic hearing in order to appear before the Tribunal and make verbal representations.

Basic hearing

There is an exchange of documents before a simple hearing held before a chairman.

Standard hearing

This concerns more detailed cases. It will involve a hearing and is likely to involve slightly more formal case management and exchange of documents, etc.

Complex hearing

These hearings involve either complex or important principles or points of law or have a large amount of money at stake.

It will involve a more lengthy hearing where complex evidence and arguments are presented.

Other material: Tribunal Notice – 'Making an Appeal' Sections 13 and 14

VAT Reporter: ¶61-320

19-220   Upper-tier Tribunal

This is the Upper Tribunal.

It will hear appeals on a point of law from the First-tier Tribunal if the Appellant is given permission from the First-tier Tribunal to appeal.

With the consent of both parties, the First-tier Tribunal has the power to refer a case to the President of the Tax Tribunal of the First-tier Tribunal and ask for it to be considered for transfer to the Upper Tier. With the agreement of the President of the Finance and Tax Chamber of the Upper Tribunal, this may be done. Cases selected for such treatment are those that involve complex legal points but where the facts are likely to be agreed.

There is a Judicial Review role given to the Upper Tribunal. Hence it will hear such matters as those where it is claimed that HMRC acted unreasonably.

Other material: Tribunal Notice, 'At your hearing', Section 7

VAT Reporter: ¶61-325

19-240   What is appealable to a tribunal?

The list below sets out the categories of assessment and ruling by HMRC that can form the subject of an appeal to the Tribunal.

It should be noted that this list of categories is not exhaustive: in particular, there is no appeal against any assessment in respect of interest on VAT recovered or recoverable by assessment. However, if you have a client who is in difficulties as a result of a decision by HMRC, and it does not appear that the decision falls within any of the categories listed below, then specialist advice may be required.

Those categories that are marked * are those types of appeal where the tribunal only has a supervisory jurisdiction. In these cases, the tribunal can only determine whether HMRC has acted reasonably. It cannot replace HMRC's decision with its own. There are also restrictions on the scope for appealing certain decisions or assessments in respect of the amount of input

Appeals and Disputes

tax credit available to a VAT-registered person. The decision or appeal must relate to a determination by HMRC that the input tax was wholly or partly attributable to expenditure in respect of something in the nature of 'a luxury, amusement or entertainment'. This restriction is highly contentious and, again, if you have a client for whom this is of relevance specialist advice may be required.

The categories of decision and assessment which can form the subject of an appeal to the Tribunal are as follows.

(1) The registration or cancellation of the registration of any person.

(2) The VAT chargeable on:

(a) the supply of any goods or services;

(b) an acquisition of goods from another Member State; or

(c) an importation of goods from a place outside the Member States;

an appeal can only be made in respect of a decision concerning the amount of VAT chargeable on an importation of goods from outside the EU if a departmental reconsideration has first been carried out – however, this does not apply and an appeal can be made in any event if:

(a) the appeal relates to a decision:

(i) as to whether the importation should be zero-rated; and

(ii) if it should not be zero-rated, which rate of VAT should be charged; and

(b) HMRC has not been given notice requiring it to review the decision.

(3) The amount of any input tax which may be credited to a VAT-registered person.

(4) A claim for a refund of tax paid on an acquisition in another Member State.

(5) A decision regarding approval (or withdrawal of approval) of a person as a fiscal warehouse keeper, or the conditions to which such approval is subject, or for the withdrawal of fiscal warehouse status from any premises.

(6) The proportion of input tax allowable to a partly exempt VAT-registered person.

(7) A claim by a VAT-registered person for repayment of VAT paid on goods imported for a partly private purpose.

(8) A decision in respect of the flat rate scheme concerning refusal to use the scheme or the percentage applicable.

(9) The amount of any refund claimed by a DIY builder.

(10) Any claim for a bad debt relief refund.

(11) Any claim for a refund of tax paid by a person who is not VAT-registered on the removal of goods consisting of a new means of transport to another Member State.

(12) Any refusal of group registration; * with limited powers in certain circumstances.

(13) A direction to terminate group treatment.

(14) Any requirement to give security as a condition of the right to make taxable supplies, or as a result of failing to appoint a VAT representative having been directed to do so.

(15) Any refusal or cancellation of certification of a person as a flat-rate farmer or any refusal to cancel such certification.

(16) Any liability to a penalty or surcharge.

(17) A decision regarding the assessment of a portion of a penalty for dishonesty on a director.

(18) Any assessment to VAT, or the amount of such an assessment (this includes an assessment on a person who is not registered for VAT who has acquired goods from another Member State without notifying HMRC or where HMRC consider that particulars or information supplied are incomplete).

(19) The amount of any penalty, interest or surcharge specified in an assessment.

(20) The making of an assessment because VAT has been lost:

    (a)   as a result of conduct involving dishonesty;

    (b)   as a result of conduct for which a person has been convicted of fraud; or

    (c)   where a penalty arises for failure to notify liability to register.

(21) Any liability of HMRC to pay interest as a consequence of official error, or the amount of such interest.

(22) An assessment, or the amount of such an assessment, in respect of interest paid because of official error where HMRC subsequently consider that the payee was not entitled to the interest.

(23) Any claim for recovery of overpaid VAT, including any assessment, or the amount of such an assessment, made to clawback a repayment of overpaid VAT.

(24) Any assessment, or the amount of such an assessment, made in respect of amounts a person may be obliged to repay to HMRC under arrangements to reimburse customers in respect of overpaid VAT.

(25) Any direction, or supplementary direction, that persons named in the direction be treated as a single person carrying on the business activities named in the direction and liable to be registered as a consequence.

(26) Any valuation direction regarding a supply to a connected person or regarding supplies through persons who are not liable to be registered.

(27) Any valuation direction regarding an acquisition from another Member State by a connected person.

(28) A direction or assessment under the anti-avoidance provisions regarding group registrations.

(29) Any refusal to permit a person to account for VAT under a retail scheme.

(30) Any refusal to permit the use, or continued use, of the cash accounting scheme.

(31) Any requirements imposed by HMRC, in a particular, case in respect of computer invoices and/or self-billed invoices.

(32) A direction to revert to making payments on account according to the prescribed formula rather than the preceding month basis.

(33) A direction made under the disclosure of anti-avoidance schemes legislation to treat one or more businesses as a single business for VAT purposes.

Appeals and Disputes

(34) Liability to any penalty imposed under the disclosure of anti-avoidance schemes legislation.

(35) A review made under the money-laundering regulations to consider the registration of a applicant, cancellation of registration or imposition of a penalty.

VAT Reporter: ¶62-200

Legislation: VATA 1994, s. 83

Other material: Tribunal notice, 'Making an Appeal', Annex A

19-260   Who may appeal to a tribunal?

There is no statutory guidance or limitation as to who may appeal. However, case law indicates that the following may appeal:
(a)   the supplier of goods or services; and
(b)   the recipient of a supply of goods or services if he or she can demonstrate that they have sufficient legal interest in the decision or assessment appealed against – a recipient of a supply who was not VAT-registered could only appeal on the ground that a supply should not be subject to VAT.

An appeal by a partnership (other than a Scottish partnership) need only be made by one or more of the partners. It is deemed, however, to have been made by all the partners.

An appeal made by a member of a group registration must be made by the representative member.

Where a VAT number has been transferred under the procedure utilising Form VAT 68 – following a transfer of a going concern – any appeal must be made by the purchaser, even if the decision relates to a period prior to the transfer.

Where an appellant dies, becomes insolvent or otherwise incapacitated, the appellant's successor, or HMRC, can apply to the tribunal for the successor to be substituted as the appellant. The successor must give consent.

VAT Reporter: ¶61-300

19-280   Time limit for appealing

An appeal must be made to the appropriate tribunal centre within 30 days of the disputed decision, assessment or the notification of a decision of a review, unless the circumstances outlined below apply.

The Tribunal has the discretion to extend the time limits for making the appeal. Therefore, an appellant can apply to have the above time limits extended by the tribunal, but it should be noted that:

(a)   HMRC may object to such an application; and

(b)   even if HMRC do not object, the tribunal may refuse such an application unless it considers there are good grounds for the application; therefore, it is essential to ensure that there is a good reason for applying for an extension.

Legislation: VATA 1994, s. 83G

Cases: *Corporate Synergy International (in Liquidation)* [2011] UKFTT 352 (TC); [2011] TC 01212; *Jem Leisure Ltd* [2011] UKFTT 778 (TC); [2011] TC 01612

Other material: Tribunal notice, 'Making an Appeal', Section 10

VAT Reporter: ¶61-440

19-290   Payment of tax before appeal

In many instances the disputed tax must be paid before the tribunal can accept the appeal. The categories of appeal to which this applies are numbers (2), (16), (18), (19), (20) and (34) 19-240.

Payment of the tax before the appeal can be heard may be waived in cases of 'hardship'. The principles to be followed when considering if an appellant will suffer 'hardship' if made to pay the tax before the appeal is heard have been described by the courts as follows:

(1)   '... Hardship should not operate as a fetter on the right of appeal...

(2)   The test is one of capacity to pay without financial hardship, and must be applied in a way which complies with the principle of proportionality...

(3)   The hardship enquiry should be directed to the ability of an appellant to pay from resources which are immediately or readily available. It should not involve a lengthy investigation of assets and liabilities, and an ability to pay in the future... This is a reflection of the broader principle that the issue of hardship ought to be capable of prompt resolution on readily available material.'

A 'hardship' application should be made when submitting the appeal.

Legislation: VATA 1994, s. 84(3B)

Other material: Tribunal notice, 'Making an Appeal', Section 7

Cases: *R (on the Application of ToTel Ltd) v R & C Commrs* [2011] EWHC 652 (Admin)

Appeals and Disputes

19-300   Notes on completing appeal notice

Notice of Appeal Ref TS-TaxAp1 (02.09) should be completed in respect of any VAT appeal made to the VAT and Duties Tribunal. This should be obtainable from the Tribunal Service or via the internet. The Notes and the Explanatory Leaflet are extensive and the following aide-mémoire merely highlights some of the key points.

(1)   The completed Form should be sent to the Tribunals Service, Tax, 2nd Floor, 54 Hagley Road, Birmingham, B16 8PE. It may be submitted by email and all documents scanned and sent with the application. The email address is taxappeals@tribunals.gsi.gov.uk.

(2)   Always remember to use black ink in completing the Form.

(3)   Do not forget to attach the disputed assessment or decision.

(4)   Remember in the case of a company or partnership to include any trading name used.

(5)   Do not forget to notify the tribunal centre of any address changes.

(6)   The 'nature of the business' refers to the business relevant to the appeal.

(7)   By including your details as representative, you ensure that all correspondence from the tribunal is sent to you. Any changes should again be notified. Your status means the function you perform (e.g. accountant or consultant).

(8)   Time limits/hardship – relevant documents including any refusal by HMRC to allow the hardship application should accompany the appeal notice.

(9)   Grounds – make sure these are given as fully and as clearly as possible.

(10)   Result – it is necessary to tell the Tribunal the result required.

VAT Reporter: ¶70-766

Other material: Tribunal notice, 'Making an Appeal', Section 12

19-340   Representation at an appeal

Any taxpayer may represent him or herself at both the First-tier and the Upper-tier Tribunal. They may choose to instruct their accountant or any other person to present their case. If the case goes to the Court of Appeal or the Supreme Court, then any person instructed to present the case must have the right to appear in that court.

It must be considered whether to seek the assistance of suitably qualified counsel for a hearing before a Tribunal. The following extract from an article by Stephen Oliver QC, President of the VAT and Duties Tribunals, discussing the need for representation at the VAT and Duties Tribunal (the system prior to 31 March 2009) outlines the reasons for seeking the assistance of suitably qualified counsel:

'If the appeal is about VAT, excise or customs duties, you have a right to represent your client, whatever your qualifications.

Is it going to be worth your time and effort doing the advocacy yourself? There is no point in bringing the case to the tribunal unless it is done properly. I have sat as a judge at every level of court with a fact-finding role. Finding facts and drawing conclusions from facts becomes more difficult as you move "down" the ladder. Advocacy in the High Court and the Crown Court is in most cases conducted by barristers who know the ropes and are constrained by a code of conduct in advocacy. In "tribunals" the fact-finding exercise can become acutely difficult. This is particularly the case where the taxpayer's representative is inexperienced and assumes that presenting the case is the straightforward business of telling the tribunal what he or she thinks to be the client's side of the story. It is not as easy as that. We see far too many promising cases ruined because the representative fails to produce the right evidence or completely misunderstands how to prove his or her client's case.

There are numerous instances where you can comfortably represent your client in appeals before the general commissioners, the special commissioners and the VAT and Duties Tribunals. Examples are "pre-trial" applications, appeals against the less serious "penalties" such as default surcharge assessments and appeals where the facts are not really in issue and where the legal questions are not complex. But where the success of the appeal depends on marshalling your own side's evidence to prove facts or on challenging the evidence adduced by the Revenue authority, you are entering an arena where advocacy is at a premium. The same goes for the situation where over a long period of time you have been acting for a client – and where you hope to continue to do so; there you should not act as advocate because your own working papers and your own advice may so easily be involved and required as primary evidence. In those circumstances there will almost certainly be a saving of worry and expense to client, practitioner and the tribunal alike if the conduct of the appeal is put in the hands of an independent advocate.'

Other material: Tribunal notice, 'At the hearing', Section 3

VAT Reporter: ¶61-810

19-360   Settling appeals by agreement with HMRC

Preferably, a dispute giving rise to an appeal should be settled by agreement. Where this happens, the consequences are the same as if the tribunal had determined the appeal. Such an agreement can, therefore, uphold, vary, discharge or cancel the disputed decision.

The agreement must be in writing or be confirmed by a notice from one party to the other (normally a letter from HMRC to the appellant). In those cases where agreement must be confirmed by notice in writing, the date of the agreement is taken as the date of that notice. This is important if the appellant wishes to withdraw from the agreement (see below).

The appellant has 30 days from the date of an agreement to repudiate or resile by notice in writing to HMRC. It is unusual for this right to be exercised as agreements often take so long to reach it is unlikely that there will be a reason for the appellant to change its mind shortly afterwards. However, it does give the opportunity for second thoughts.

If an appellant notifies HMRC that it wants to withdraw, and HMRC do not write to the appellant within 30 days to oppose the withdrawal of the appeal, the decision under appeal is treated as upheld without variation.

Appeals and Disputes

All references above to an appellant include references to an appellant's representative, where that representative has been named on a Form Ref TS-TaxAp1 (02.09).

VAT Reporter: ¶61-385

19-400   Costs

The practice is that costs are not awarded except for Complex Category appeals and appeals to the Upper-tier Tribunal. However, there is the facility for a 'Wasted Costs Order' to be made or for the Tribunal to order costs where the appellant has acted unreasonably.

The rules of the First- and Upper-tier Tribunal require that when costs are awarded against an individual (not a body corporate) the Tribunal must consider the ability of that individual to pay the costs.

Complex Category Costs

The normal costs regime (costs follow the result) applies in Complex Category cases in all Tiers.

However, the Appellant can opt out of this regime for the First-tier Tribunal if he requests exclusion from the costs regime within 28 days of the notice of allocation to the Complex Category. Thus, the Appellant will neither pay costs if he loses nor be awarded costs if the Tribunal decides in his favour.

This opt-out cannot be applied to instances where the Tribunal awards costs for wasting time or behaving unreasonably.

This opt-out does not apply in the Upper Tier.

Wasted Costs Order

This may be awarded against the legal or other representative if they have acted unreasonably. It is not an order that is used against the party themselves.

Acting unreasonably

The Tribunal can order the Appellant to pay costs when it is decided that the Appellant has behaved unreasonably.

Legislation: *The Tribunal Procedure (Upper Tribunal) Rules* 2008 (SI 2008/2698), r. 10; *The Tribunal Procedure (First-tier Tribunal) (Tax Chamber) Rules* 2009 (SI 2009/273), r. 10

Other material: Tribunal notice, 'Making an Appeal', Section 8

VAT Reporter: ¶61-805

19-440   Appealing to Higher Courts

Either party has the right to ask permission to appeal to the Court of Appeal or the Supreme Court (House of Lords).

European ruling

Any matter that involves a point of European Law (and VAT is the chosen turnover tax in Europe) may be referred by any of the courts to the European Court of Justice for a preliminary ruling under Article 234 EC of the EC Treaty. See flowchart 19-780.

Other material: Article 234 of the EC Treaty

VAT Reporter: ¶62-010

OTHER REMEDIES AND DISPUTES

19-480   Introduction

Where your client does not agree with an assessment or other decision made by HMRC, the usual response will be either to appeal to the Tribunal or to accept a review by HMRC. However, there are situations where those remedies are either not available or not appropriate. Set out below are some of the other remedies now available for resolving disputes with HMRC.

19-500   Complaints made directly to HMRC

A factsheet, 'Complaints and putting things right', on HMRC's website sets out the attitude of HMRC to complaints. It is helpful in making a complaint if your client can point to any breach of the undertakings given in the Taxpayer's Charter.

A complaint should be made wherever possible to the officer concerned. However, this is not always practicable and a complaint should then be made to the Complaints Manager at the relevant office. The addresses of these may be obtained from the National Advice Service or via HMRC website.

A complaint should be supported with as much relevant information as possible. HMRC have undertaken to try and respond to complaints within 10 working days.

Other material: Notice 700, para. 2.8; HMRC Factsheet May 2007 'Complaints and putting things right'

VAT Reporter: ¶59-560; ¶61-100

Appeals and Disputes

19-540   The Adjudicator

Where satisfaction is not forthcoming from HMRC in response to a complaint, the matter can be referred to the Adjudicator.

The Adjudicator only considers a case if a complaint has first been made to HMRC. Complaints should be referred to the Adjudicator within six months of review by HMRC.

The Adjudicator considers complaints regarding:
(a)   excessive delay;
(b)   mistakes;
(c)   discourtesy;
(d)   the exercise of discretionary powers; and
(e)   the manner in which a person or his property has been searched.

The Adjudicator does not consider:
(a)   matters that can be appealed to the VAT and Duties Tribunal;
(b)   matters that are the subject of current criminal proceedings; or
(c)   matters that have been, or are being, investigated by the Parliamentary Ombudsman.

Other material: Leaflet AO2 How to complain about HMRC

VAT Reporter: ¶61-105

19-560   Parliamentary Ombudsman

Your client can ask his MP to refer the complaint to the Parliamentary Ombudsman. This can be done after, or instead of, a reference to the Adjudicator. However, note that the Adjudicator will not consider a matter once it has been referred to the Parliamentary Ombudsman.

VAT Reporter: ¶61-110

19-580   Complaints to the European Commission

If you think that HMRC have failed to comply with any aspect of EC law, then you can complain to the European Commission. They will investigate the matter in complete confidence and will report the outcome to you.

The Commission has produced a form which sets out the information that is needed for a complaint to be investigated by it. All information may be found on the Europa website (*http://europa.eu*).

19-600 Judicial review

Judicial review describes the process whereby application is made to the Court (the Court of Session in Scotland) to review the exercise of an administrative power or discretion. For example, such an application can be made if HMRC refuse to apply a published extra-statutory concession without giving a satisfactory reason for not doing so.

The Upper Tribunal has the power to hear such judicial review matters.

Application for judicial review can be made if it is alleged that HMRC has acted:
(a) illegally;
(b) irrationally; or
(c) without procedural propriety.

Specialist advice should be sought before giving serious consideration to applying for judicial review.

VAT Reporter: ¶61-335

FLOWCHARTS

19-700   Criteria for appealing to the Tribunal

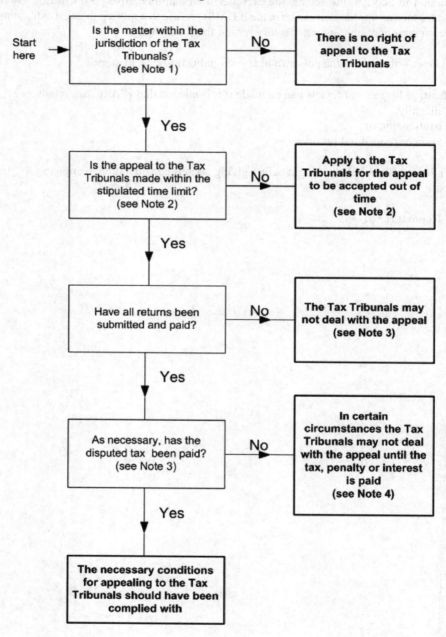

Start here → Is the matter within the jurisdiction of the Tax Tribunals? (see Note 1)

— No → There is no right of appeal to the Tax Tribunals

Yes ↓

Is the appeal to the Tax Tribunals made within the stipulated time limit? (see Note 2)

— No → Apply to the Tax Tribunals for the appeal to be accepted out of time (see Note 2)

Yes ↓

Have all returns been submitted and paid?

— No → The Tax Tribunals may not deal with the appeal (see Note 3)

Yes ↓

As necessary, has the disputed tax been paid? (see Note 3)

— No → In certain circumstances the Tax Tribunals may not deal with the appeal until the tax, penalty or interest is paid (see Note 4)

Yes ↓

The necessary conditions for appealing to the Tax Tribunals should have been complied with

Notes

(1) Jurisdiction of Tribunals

The Tribunals cannot deal with an appeal unless it is about a matter listed in VATA 1994, s. 83 or VATA 1994, s. 84(10) (see 19-240). Most decisions, rulings and assessments made by HMRC may be appealed.

(2) Time limit for lodging the appeal

An appeal to the Tribunals should be lodged within 30 days of the date of the disputed assessment or decision or notification of the result of a review. The Tribunals have discretion to accept appeals out of time (see 19-280).

(3) Returns and payment

The Tribunals may not deal with an appeal from a registered trader until the person concerned has submitted, and paid, all the returns that they are due to make. It is not always necessary to have paid all the tax due before submitting the appeal. An arrangement to pay the tax over a period of time is sometimes sufficient.

(4) Paying the disputed tax before the appeal

It is a requirement with some matters that the tax, penalty or interest is paid or deposited with HMRC before the Tribunals may hear the appeal. This applies when the intended appeal relates to any of the following:

- tax chargeable on any goods or services;
- tax chargeable on the importation of goods;
- an assessment to recover input tax; and
- the amount of tax assessed.

HMRC or the Tribunals may waive this condition if payment in advance would cause financial 'hardship' to the person wishing to appeal.

Appeals and Disputes

19-760   Appeal Structure

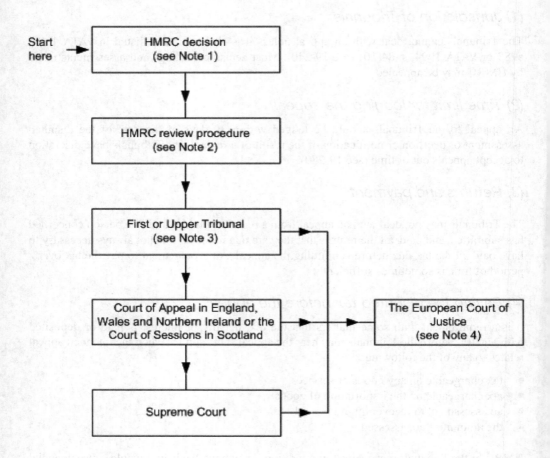

Notes

(1) HMRC decision

The appeal process begins when HMRC issue a decision which is disputed by those to whom it applies. It may be an oral or written decision.

(2) Internal review procedures

HMRC will offer a review of any decision prior to any possible further appeal. This review will be carried out by an officer who has not been involved with the case to date.

(3) Tribunals, Courts and Enforcement Act 2007

There is a First-tier Tribunal and a Second- or Upper-tier Tribunal. Some complex cases may go direct to the Upper-tier Tribunal and this Tribunal will also hear matters of Judicial Review. It is possible to appeal to the Upper-tier Tribunal from the First-tier Tribunal with permission on a point of law. See 19-440.

(4) European Court of Justice ('ECJ')

Any of the British courts may refer a question concerning European law to the ECJ for a preliminary ruling.

(5) Process when question referred to ECJ

For further information about the sequence of events when a question is referred to the ECJ, see the flowchart 19-780.

Appeals and Disputes

19-780   Reference to the ECJ

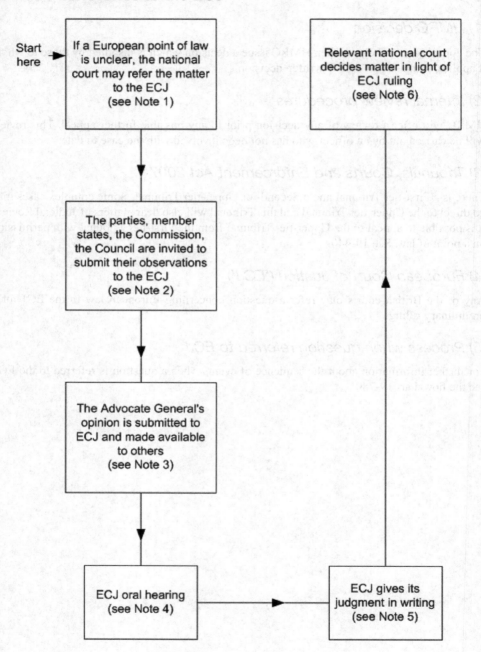

Start here → If a European point of law is unclear, the national court may refer the matter to the ECJ (see Note 1)

The parties, member states, the Commission, the Council are invited to submit their observations to the ECJ (see Note 2)

The Advocate General's opinion is submitted to ECJ and made available to others (see Note 3)

ECJ oral hearing (see Note 4)

ECJ gives its judgment in writing (see Note 5)

Relevant national court decides matter in light of ECJ ruling (see Note 6)

Notes

(1) A point involving European law may be referred to the European Court for a preliminary ruling under Article 234 EC. The First-tier Tribunal, the Upper-tier Tribunal, High Court, Court of Appeal, House of Lords or Supreme Court, Court of Session, etc. are all able to make such a reference.

(2) The Council is informed if the matter involves a Council measure.

(3) Although the Advocate General's opinion is often followed, there have been many occasions when the Court has chosen not to do so.

(4) The parties, the Commission, Member States and, if relevant, the Council, may chose to make oral and/or written observations.

(5) This is the final ruling of the European Court. The same matter may not be re-presented to them although the same case may subsequently give rise to a further reference on a different matter.

(6) The reference is regarded as a step in the main proceedings and each party is at liberty to apply for costs, as may be relevant after the national court has decided the case. Member States that submit observations and the Commission are not entitled to costs.

Case Table

(References are to paragraph numbers)

Legislation Finding List

(References are to paragraph numbers)

Value Added Tax Act 1994 – continued

Official Publications

(References are to paragraph numbers)

Provision	Paragraph
Budget Notices	
60/2007	8-420; 11-620
77/2008	13-990
78/2008	9-410
42/2010	6-200
Business Briefs	
15/92	6-340
1/95	13-750
9/96	13-750
18/98	14-650
9/00	17-480
23/02	9-520
27/02	9-410
27/03	9-520
29/03	14-500(1)
30/03	14-400(4)
12/04	18-950
25/04	9-620
28/04	9-800
5/05	14-500(3)
12/05	3-425; 15-100
14/05	10-680
18/05	10-470
1/06	8-420
15/06	4-820
22/06	2-650
23/06	7-830
Extra-Statutory Concessions	
3.3	13-750
3.17	13-350(4)
3.18	15-280
3.29	3-200(2); 4-900; 15-160
3.35	14-600
HMRC Briefs	
6/07	14-500(1)
14/07	9-520
23/07	7-310; 7-967
29/07	3-200(2); 4-900
31/07	7-110
48/07	13-990
20/08	9-760
27/08	17-780
36/08	14-750
38/08	9-410(3); 9-420
54/08	11-600
57/08	15-200
63/08	14-350
6/09	14-600
14/09	9-430

Provision	Paragraph
18/09	9-520
27/09	16-890
31/09	4-690
33/09	15-730
37/09	9-810
39/09	13-450; 15-160
46/09	5-610
52/09	10-230; 10-500
53/09	17-730
64/09	14-300
67/09	15-280
74/09	16-890
75/09	14-350
2/10	6-840; 7-943
8/10	15-300(4)
9/10	14-450
13/10	5-710; 13-400(4)
15/10	14-650
20/10	13-450
21/10	16-890
25/10	13-750
26/10	15-160
28/10	5-610
29/10	15-450
30/10	10-100
31/10	14-250
33/10	15-160; 15-300(4)
35/10	5-610
36/10	9-660
37/10	14-650
43/10	9-410
44/10	6-320
47/10	7-700
51/10	3-160(2)
52/10	11-640
53/10	6-200; 6-830; 7-943
54/10	14-400(4)
1/11	14-350
2/11	15-440
3/11	15-300(8)
4/11	3-200(2); 15-200
13/11	15-280
19/11	12-800
20/11	5-400(6)
24/11	9-800
27/11	14-400(4)
28/11	4-830
30/11	14-650
36/11	4-830; 14-400(4)
37/11	15-280
41/11	13-600

Index

(References are to paragraph numbers)

Pro